SECOND EDITION

CLIMATE
CHANGE

The Science, Impacts and Solutions

A. BARRIE PITTOCK

CSIRO
PUBLISHING

earthscan
publishing for a sustainable future

National Library of Australia Cataloguing-in-Publication entry

Pittock, A. Barrie, 1938–
Climate change : the science, impacts and solutions / A. Barrie Pittock.

2nd ed.
9780643094840 (pbk.)

Includes index.
Bibliography.

Climatic changes – Government policy.
Climatic changes – Risk assessment.
Global environmental change.
Greenhouse effect, Atmospheric.
Global warming.

551.6

Library of Congress Cataloging-in-Publication Data has been applied for.

Published exclusively in Australia, New Zealand and the Americas, and non-exclusively in other territories of the world (excluding Europe, the Middle East, Asia and Africa), by:

CSIRO PUBLISHING
150 Oxford Street (PO Box 1139)
Collingwood VIC 3066
Australia

Telephone: +61 3 9662 7666
Local call: 1300 788 000 (Australia only)
Fax: +61 3 9662 7555
Email: publishing.sales@csiro.au
Web site: www.publish.csiro.au

Published exclusively in Europe, the Middle East, Asia (including India, Japan, China and South-East Asia) and Africa, and non-exclusively in other territories of the world (excluding Australia, New Zealand and the Americas), by Earthscan, with ISBN 978-1-84407-648-2 (paperback) and ISBN 978-1-84407-786-1 (hardback).

Earthscan
Dunstan House
14a St Cross Street
London, EC1N 8XA, UK
Telephone: +44 (0)20 7841 1930
Fax: +44 (0)20 7242 1474
Email: earthinfo@earthscan.co.uk
Web site: www.earthscan.co.uk

22883 Quicksilver Drive, Sterling, VA 20166-2012, USA

Front cover photos by (left to right): iStockphoto, NASA, NASA, the Australian National University

Set in 10.5/14 Palatino
Edited by Susannah Burgess
Cover and text design by James Kelly
Typeset by Planman Technologies
Index by Wordsharper Publishing Services
Printed in Australia by Ligare

The book has been printed on paper certified by the Programme for the Endorsement of Forest Chain of Custody (PEFC). PEFC is committed to sustainable forest management through third party forest certification of responsibly managed forests.

CSIRO PUBLISHING publishes and distributes scientific, technical and health science books, magazines and journals from Australia to a worldwide audience and conducts these activities autonomously from the research activities of the Commonwealth Scientific and Industrial Research Organisation (CSIRO).

The views expressed in this publication are those of the author(s) and do not necessarily represent those of, and should not be attributed to, the publisher or CSIRO.

Earthscan
uses **Greenhouse Friendly**™
ENVI 50/50 Recycled

CONSUMER   ENVI is an Australian Government
certified Greenhouse Friendly™ Product.

PEFC™
PEFC/21-31-17

CONTENTS

FOREWORD

Barrie Pittock has been a leading researcher of considerable standing worldwide on various aspects of climate change. The quality and content of research carried out by him has established a benchmark that sets the standard for several of his peers and provides a model for young researchers.

In this book he has provided a comprehensive analysis of various aspects of climate change, which he begins by examining the physical and biological aspects of climate change and a detailed analysis of the science of the climate system. The book assumes great topical interest for the reader because of several questions that the author has posed and attempted to answer, such as the recent heatwave that took place in Paris in the summer of 2003, the frequency of closure of the Thames barrier, and the melting of glaciers which affects not only parts of Europe but even the high mountain glaciers in the Himalayas.

A study of paleoclimate is an important component of present-day climate change research, and the book goes through a lucid and useful assessment of the evidence that is available to us today in understanding and quantifying the nature and extent of climate change in the past. Also presented in considerable detail are projections of climate change in the future including a discussion of the emissions scenarios developed and used by the IPCC and projections obtained from it as well as from other sources.

An extremely eloquent statement is conveyed in the title of Chapter 4, which states 'Uncertainty is inevitable, but risk is certain'. This really is the key message in this book particularly as it goes on to describe the impacts of climate change, the seriousness with which these should be considered and the imperative need for adaptation. In Chapter 8 a comprehensive and detailed assessment is provided on several mitigation actions. The volume ends by making a logical transition into political issues that have national as well as international dimensions.

For sheer breadth and comprehensiveness of coverage, Barrie Pittock's book fills a unique void in the literature in this field. Coming as it does from an author who knows the scientific and technical complexities of the whole subject, this book should be seen as a valuable reference for scientists and policymakers alike.

In my view, which is shared by a growing body of concerned citizens worldwide, climate change is a challenge faced by the global community that will require unprecedented resolve and increasing ingenuity to tackle in the years ahead. Efforts to be made would need to be based on knowledge and informed assessment of the future. Barrie Pittock's book provides information and analysis that will greatly assist and guide decision makers on what needs to be done.

DR RAJENDRA K PACHAURI
Director-General, The Energy and Resources Institute, India *and*
Chairman, Intergovernmental Panel on Climate Change
2005

ACKNOWLEDGEMENTS

This book is the result of many years working on climate change, nearly all based in CSIRO Atmospheric Research (now part of CSIRO Marine and Atmospheric Research) in Australia and especially with the Intergovernmental Panel on Climate Change (IPCC). I therefore thank many colleagues in CSIRO and many others from numerous countries whom I met through IPCC or other forums. My views have been influenced by their collective research and arguments, as well as my own research, and I owe them all a debt of gratitude.

A book such as this inevitably draws from and builds on the work that has gone before it. Since subtle changes in wording can easily lead to misinterpretation in this field, some content in this book has been carefully paraphrased from, or closely follows the original sources to ensure accuracy. Some sections in the present book are drawn from the following: parts of the IPCC Reports, especially the Fourth Assessment Report in 2007; a book that I edited for the Australian Greenhouse Office (AGO) in 2003 *Climate Change: An Australian Guide to the Science and Potential Impacts*; and a paper I wrote for the journal *Climatic Change* in 2002 'What we know and don't know about climate change: reflections on the IPCC TAR' (*Climatic Change* vol. 53, pp. 393–411). This applies particularly to parts of Chapter 3 on projecting the future, Chapter 5 on projected climate changes, Chapter 6 on impacts and Chapter 7 on adaptation concepts. I thank the AGO, the IPCC and Springer (publishers of *Climatic Change*) for permission to use some common wording. I have endeavoured to acknowledge all sources in the text, captions or endnotes, however, if any have been overlooked I apologise to the original authors and/or publishers.

The following Figures come from other sources, who granted permission to use them, for which I am grateful. Some have been modified, and the original sources are not responsible for any changes.

These are: Figures 1, 7, 10, 15, 16, 17, and 28 (all unchanged) from IPCC; Figure 4 from UK Environment Agency; Figure 5 from INVS, France; Figure 9 from David Etheridge, CSIRO; Figures 13, 14, and 26 from Roger Jones, CSIRO; Figure 18 from US NASA; Figure 19, 20, and 21 from the US National Snow and Ice Data Center; Figure 23 from T. Coleman, Insurance Group Australia; Figure 28 from the Water Corporation, Western Australia; Figure 30 from Dr. Jim Hansen, NASA Goddard Institute for Space Science; Figure 31 from Martin Dix of CSIRO and courtesy of the modelling groups, the Programme for Climate Model Diagnosis and Intercomparison Project phase 3 (CMIP3) of the World Climate Research Programme; Figure 33 from CSIRO Climate Impacts Group and Government of New South Wales; Figure 34 from Greg Bourne, now at WWF Australia; Figure 35 from the Murray-Darling Basin Commission; and Figure 36 from Kathy McInnes, CSIRO and Chalapan Kaluwin, AMSAT, Fiji.

Particular people I want to thank are:

From CSIRO: Tom Beer, Willem Bouma, Peter K Campbell, John Church, Kevin Hennessy, Paul Holper, Roger Jones, Kathy McInnes, Simon Torok, Penny Whetton, and John Wright. Also Rachel Anning (UK Environment Agency), Martin Beniston (Universite de Fribourg, Switzerland), Andre Berger (Université Catholique de Louvain, Belgium), Greg Bourne (WWF, Australia), Mark Diesendorf (University of NSW), Pascal Empereur-Bissonnet (INVS, France), Andrew Glikson (ANU), James Hansen (NASA GISS), Dale Hess (BoM and CSIRO, Australia), William Howard (U. Tasmania), Murari Lal (Climate, Energy and Sustainable Development Analyis Centre, India), Keith Lovegrove (ANU); Mark Maslin (U. College London, UK), Mike MacCracken (Climate Institute, Washington), Tony McMichael (ANU, Australia), Bettina Menne

(WHO, Italy), Neville Nicholls (BoM, Australia), Martin Parry (Jackson Institute, UK), Jamie Pittock (WWF and ANU, Australia), Thomas W. Pogge (Columbia University, USA), Alan Robock (Rutgers University), Brian Sadler (IOCI, Australia), David Spratt (Carbon Equity, Australia), Philip Sutton (Greenleap Strategic Insitute, Australia), and Christopher Thomas (NSW GH Office, Australia). Probably I have omitted some people who helped, and apologise to them for my oversight.

Special thanks goes to Graeme Pearman and Greg Ayers, successive Chiefs of CSIRO Atmospheric Research and CMAR, for my position as a Post-Retirement Fellow, and more recently as an Honorary Fellow. Special thanks also to Paul Durack and Roger Jones for help with Figures, and to John Manger, Ann Crabb (first edition), Tracey Millen and colleagues at CSIRO Publishing. Their insightful and helpful editing comments and discussions have greatly improved the book.

The views expressed in this work are my own and do not necessarily represent the views of CSIRO, the AGO, the IPCC or other parties.

Finally, I want to thank my partner Diana Pittock, for her support and forbearance during the writing and extensive revision of this book.

INTRODUCTION

Human-induced climate change is a huge, highly topical and rapidly changing subject. New books, reports and scientific papers on the subject are appearing with amazing frequency. It is tempting to say that if they were all piled in a heap and buried underground the amount of carbon so sequestered would solve the problem. But seriously, there is a need to justify yet another book on the subject.

This book is a substantial update of my *Climate Change: Turning Up the Heat* (2005). That book was meant as a serious discussion of the science, implications and policy questions arising, addressed to an educated non-specialist audience. It presented both sides of many arguments, rather than adopting a racy and simplified advocacy position. It was, in the words of some friends, a 'solid read'. It found a niche as a tertiary textbook in many multi-disciplinary courses, where its objectivity and comprehensiveness were appreciated.

Developments since 2005, in the science, the observations and the politics of climate change are so substantial that they warrant major changes to both the content and tone of the book. Hence the new title *Climate Change: The Science, Impacts and Solutions*.

The urgency of the climate change challenge is now far more apparent than in 2005, with new observations showing that on many fronts climate change and its impacts are occurring faster than expected. There is a growing probability that we are approaching or have already passed one or more 'tipping points' that may lead to irreversible trends. This is now well documented, but there is a need for a concise and accurate summary of the evidence and its implications for individual and joint action. The message is not new, but a growing sense of urgency is needed, and clarity about the choices and opportunities is essential. It is also essential to convey the need for continual updating, and to provide the means to do so via relevant regular publications, learned journals and websites.

Back in 1972 I wrote a paper entitled 'How important are climatic changes?' It concluded that human dependence on a stable climate might be more critical than was generally believed. This dependence, I argued, is readily seen in the relationship between rainfall patterns and patterns of land and water use, including use for industrial and urban purposes. The paper argued that the severity of the economic adjustments required by a change in climate depend on the relation between the existing economy and its climatic environment, and the rapidity of climate change.

My first projections of possible future patterns of climate change were published in 1980, based on the early findings of relatively crude computer models of climate, combined with a look at the contrasts between individual warm and cold years, paleo-climatic reconstructions of earlier warm epochs, and some theoretical arguments.

In 1988 I founded the Climate Impact Group in CSIRO in Australia. This group sought to bridge the gap between climate modellers, with their projections of climate change and sea-level rise, and people interested in the potential effects on crops, water resources, coastal zones and other parts of the natural and social systems and environment. Despite reservations from some colleagues who wanted greater certainty before going public on scientific findings that identify risk, the Climate Impact Group approach of publicly quantifying risk won wide respect. This culminated in the award in 1999 of an Australian Public Service Medal, and in 2003 of the Sherman Eureka Prize for Environmental Research, one of Australia's most prestigious national awards for environmental science.

The object of the CSIRO Climate Impact Group's endeavours was never to make exact predictions of what will happen, because we recognised that there are inevitable uncertainties about both the science and socio-economic conditions resulting from human behaviour. Rather, we sought to provide the best possible advice as to what might happen, its impacts on society, and on the consequences of various policy choices, so that decision-makers could make informed risk assessments and choices that would influence future outcomes.

These days, writing, or even updating a book on a 'hot topic' like climate change is a bit of a wild ride. Lots of things keep happening during the process. This includes the US Presidential election of November 2008, the international economic crisis, and the wild fluctuations in the price of oil. The implications of such events remain to be played out, and are merely touched on in this book. Several other major developments have stood out in the case of this book and are dealt with more fully.

The Intergovernmental Panel on Climate Change (IPCC) report in 2007 strongly confirmed that climate change due to human activities is happening and that its consequences are likely to be serious. Further, it broadly confirmed the findings of the UK Stern Review that the consequences of climate change under business-as-usual scenarios are likely to be far more expensive than efforts to limit climate change by reducing greenhouse gas emissions. It also pointed out that stabilising concentrations of carbon dioxide equivalent (treating all greenhouse gases as if they were carbon dioxide) at 450 ppm still leaves a more than 50% chance of global warmings greater than 2°C relative to preindustrial conditions, and possibly as high as 3°C.

We are thus forced to consider whether in order to avoid dangerous climate change we must keep greenhouse gas concentrations well below 450 ppm carbon dioxide equivalent. This is a 'big ask', as concentrations of carbon dioxide alone are already in 2008 about 380 ppm and rising at an increasing rate, recently about 2 ppm each year. This highlights the urgency of reducing greenhouse gas emissions far below present levels in the next decade, rather than several decades down the track. Indeed, IPCC suggests that to stabilise greenhouse gas concentrations at less than 450 ppm may require us to take carbon dioxide out of the atmosphere after it has overshot this target.

Further pointers towards urgency have arisen from the well-documented observations in the last two years of more rapid climate change, and of the kicking in of positive feedback (amplifying) processes that lead to an acceleration of global warming and sea-level rise. Carbon dioxide concentrations, global warming and sea-level rise are all tracking near the upper end of the range of uncertainty in the 2007 IPCC report.

Arctic sea ice is melting more rapidly than projected in the IPCC report, and reached a startlingly low minimum extent in September 2007. Moreover, permafrost is melting, floating ice shelves have rapidly disintegrated by processes not previously considered, forests are burning more frequently, droughts in mid-latitudes are getting worse, and so it goes.

All this leads to the possibility of apocalyptic outcomes, with associated gloom and doom: multi-metre sea-level rise displacing millions of people, regional water shortages and mass starvation, conflict and economic disaster. Faced with such possibilities, three broad psychological reactions are likely: nihilism (it's all hopeless so let's enjoy ourselves while we can), fundamentalism (falling back on some rigid set of beliefs such as that God, or the free market, will save us), or activism in the belief that we can still deal with the problem if we apply ourselves with a sufficient sense of urgency.

I tend to favour the third approach, in the belief that human beings are intelligent creatures and that with ingenuity and commitment we can achieve the seemingly unachievable, as happened in the Second World War and the Space Race. There is also still a lot of uncertainty, and the situation may not be quite as bad as we may fear, so let's give it a good try.

A few contrarians continue to raise the same tired objections that some particular observations or details are in doubt. They continue to accuse climate modellers of neglecting well-recognised mechanisms like solar variability or water vapour effects, which have long been included in climate modelling. They refuse to look at the balance of evidence as presented in the IPCC reports, and prefer to seize on the odd observation that might not fit, or some alternative theory, without applying the same scepticism to their favoured 'fact' or theory. Others set out a false dichotomy between combating climate change and other global problems, or propagate scare stories about the cost of reducing emissions.

Responsible decision-makers must follow a risk management strategy, and look at the balance of evidence, the full range of uncertainty, and put climate change in the context of other global problems, which in general exacerbate each other. I favour the advice and examples of the social and technological optimists and entrepreneurs who argue and demonstrate that we can rapidly develop a prosperous future with low greenhouse gas emissions if we put our minds to it. That way we can improve living standards both in the industrialised and developing countries, while minimising the risks and costs of climate change damage. Necessity, as the saying goes, is the mother of invention. We are not short of inventions that might conserve energy and reduce greenhouse gas emissions. What is needed is a commitment to developing these into large-scale production and application, with the implicit opportunity for new more energy-efficient and sustainable technologies. Efficiency, that is, using less energy, can be profitable, and the large-scale application of renewable energy technologies can reduce their cost until they are competitive.

While acknowledged uncertainties mean we are dealing with risks rather than certainties, the risks will increase over coming decades if we do not act. If we sit back and say to ourselves that the risks are too small to worry about, or too costly to prevent, they are likely to catch up with us all too soon. We, as consumers, business people and members of the public can turn things around by our choices and especially by making our opinions known. We do not have to wait for national governments to act, or for laws and taxes to compel us. Individual and group choices, initiatives, ingenuity, innovation and action can achieve wonders.

However, our individual and corporate actions would be far more more effective if we could persuade governments to recognise the urgency and act now to really push for a reduction in greenhouse emissions this decade. Climate change, abrupt or not, is a real risk. It is also a challenge and an opportunity for innovative thinking and action. With a bit of luck and a lot of skill, we can transform the challenge of climate change into a positive opportunity. Reducing greenhouse gas emissions will also help avoid other environmental damages and promote sustainable development and greater equity between peoples and countries.

Public opinion and government attitudes are changing rapidly, even in countries whose governments have been slow to commit to urgent action on climate change. One of the stand-out reluctant countries, my very own Australia, has recently committed itself, after a change of government, to the Kyoto Protocol and the new negotiation process for more stringent emissions reductions in the future. New information is being absorbed and stronger advocacy is convincing people it is time to act. The 'former next President of the United States', Al Gore, has been influential with his film and book *An Inconvenient Truth*. Hurricane Katrina in August 2005 convinced people that even rich countries like the United States are vulnerable to climate disasters, and numerous books advocating action, such as those by George Monbiot, Mark Lynas and Tim Flannery have appeared and sold well.

Above all, IPCC has been forthright, if still guarded, in its statements. Along with Al Gore and many other activists, the IPCC 2007 report has stirred the world to action, as was recognised by the awarding of the Nobel Peace Prize to Al Gore and the IPCC in 2007.

However, even the IPCC is inevitably behind the times, as its 2007 report only assessed new material up to about May 2006. Much new information has become available since then, and I have attempted to summarise it in what follows. This book is meant to continue the process of developing and informing an intelligent approach to meeting the challenge of climate change and seizing the opportunity to help create a better and more sustainable world where other global problems can also be addressed. It is intended to answer, in readily understood terms, frequently asked questions about climate change, such as:

- What is the relationship between natural climate variations and human-induced climate change?

- What are the major concerns regarding climate change?

- Why are there arguments about the reality of climate change, and its policy implications?

- How does climate change relate to other problems like population growth, poverty, pollution and land degradation?

- How urgent is the problem? What can we do about it, and how much will it cost?

This book is meant, in a concise and understandable manner, to sort fact from fiction. It recognises that uncertainties are inevitable, and sets climate change in a framework of assessing climate risk alongside all the other human problems about which we have imperfect knowledge. It should help readers to choose a sensible course between the head-in-the-sand reaction of some contrarians and the doom-and-gloom view of some alarmists. It builds on the scientific base of the well-tested and accepted reports of the Intergovernmental Panel on Climate Change, putting the findings in the context of other human concerns.

We must look beyond the doom and gloom. Projections of rapid climate change with severe consequences are a prophecy, not in the sense that they are bound to come true, but in the sense of a prophetic warning that if we continue on our present course these are the logical consequences. Modern scientific 'prophets of doom' follow in the tradition of the Old Testament prophets. The Biblical prophets were not preaching damnation, but appealing for a change of direction, so that damnation could be avoided. Similarly, climate scientists who warn about potentially dangerous climate change hope that such forebodings will motivate people to act to avoid the danger.

Hope lies not only in science, but in going beyond the science to grapple with the policy questions and the moral imperatives that the scientific projections throw into stark relief. In this book I go some way down this road, making direct links between the science and the consequences, which are important for policy. If this encourages you to address the issues, to make your own assessment of the risk, and to act accordingly, this book will have achieved its purpose.

Now a few words to the serious student of climate change on how to use this book.

First, it covers a huge range of subjects and disciplines from physics, chemistry and the other 'hard' and social sciences, to politics and policy. My original expertise was in physics (with a side interest in anthropology), so I have been forced to learn about the other subjects from books, papers and especially from websites and talking to people. Climate change is an overarching topic, and the reality is that everything is connected to everything else (for example see Chapter 9), so policy-relevance requires an enquiring and open mind.

Second, there is a set of endnotes at the end of each chapter. These not only document what is said (often including opposing points of view), but supply pointers to more information, and especially to websites or ongoing publications where you can update what is in the book. Frankly, nobody can be expected to keep up to date in detail on every aspect of climate change science and policy. The number of scientific papers on the subject has grown exponentially over the last decade. One of my colleagues estimates that if every relevant scientific publication since the IPCC 2007 report is referenced in the next edition in three or four years' time, it would require about a thousand pages just to list all the references. I have selected websites and learned journals in my endnotes that will enable you to keep up where you can, but even that is not complete – I have obviously missed or selected from a larger number of relevant references. But web searches these days are amazingly efficient at finding what you need to know. Use them well and with good judgement as to the reliability and possible biases of the source.

Finally, I want to dedicate this book to my grandchildren, Jenny, Ella, Kyan and Gem, whose future is at stake, along with that of all future generations. It is for them that we must meet the challenge of climate change. If the urgency is as great as I fear it is, it is us and our children, alive today, who will have to deal with the consequences. We can have a positive influence on our children's future.

1

Climate change matters

Today, global climate change is a fact. The climate has changed visibly, tangibly, measurably. An additional increase in average temperatures is not only possible, but very probable, while human intervention in the natural climate system plays an important, if not decisive role.

BRUNO PORRO, CHIEF RISK OFFICER, SWISS REINSURANCE, 2002.[1]

Climate change is a major concern in relation to the minerals sector and sustainable development. It is, potentially, one of the greatest of all threats to the environment, to biodiversity and ultimately to our quality of life.

FACING THE FUTURE, MINING MINERALS AND SUSTAINABLE DEVELOPMENT AUSTRALIA, 2002.[2]

We, the human species, are confronting a planetary emergency – a threat to the survival of our civilization that is gathering ominous and destructive potential even as we gather here. But there is hopeful news as well: we have the ability to solve this crisis and avoid the worst – though not all – of its consequences, if we act boldly, decisively and quickly.

AL GORE, *NOBEL PEACE PRIZE LECTURE*, 10 DECEMBER 2007.[3]

Climate is critical to the world as we know it. The landscape, and the plants and animals in it, are all determined to a large extent by climate acting over long intervals of time. Over geological time, climate has helped to shape mountains, build up the soil, determine the nature of the rivers, and build flood plains and deltas. At least until the advent of irrigation and industrialisation, climate determined food supplies and where human beings could live.

Today, with modern technology, humans can live in places where it was impossible before. This is achieved by the provision of buildings and complex infrastructure tuned to the existing climate, such as urban and rural water supplies, drainage, bridges, roads and other communications. These involve huge investments of time and money. Trade, particularly of food and fibre for manufactured goods, has also been strongly influenced by climate. Roads, buildings and towns are designed taking local climate into consideration. Design rules, both formal and informal, zoning and safety standards are developed to cope not just with average climate but also with climatic extremes such as floods and droughts. If the climate changes, human society must adapt by changing its designs, rules and infrastructure – often at great expense, especially for retrofitting existing infrastructure.

In broad terms, 'climate' is the typical range of weather, including its variability, experienced at a particular place. It is often expressed statistically, in terms of averages over a season or number of years, of temperature or rainfall and sometimes in terms of other variables such as wind, humidity, and so on. Variability is an important factor. 'Climate variability' is variability in the average weather behaviour at a particular location from one year to another, or one decade to another. Changes in the behaviour of the weather over longer time scales, such as one century to another, are usually referred to as 'climate change'.

Conventionally, 30-year intervals have been used for calculating averages and estimating weather variability. However, natural climate varies on time scales from year-to-year, through decade-to-decade to longer-term fluctuations over centuries and millennia.

Extreme weather events are part of climate. Their impact is reflected in the design of human settlements and activities (such as farming) so as to be able to survive floods, droughts, severe storms and other weather-related stresses or catastrophes. Because climate can vary from decade to decade, reliable averages of the frequency and magnitudes of extreme events require weather observations over longer periods than the conventional 30 years. Engineers design infrastructure (buildings, bridges, dams, drains, etc.) to cope with extreme weather events that occur on average only once in every 50, 100 or 1000 years. The more serious the consequence of design failure under extreme weather conditions, the longer the time interval considered, for example for a large dam as opposed to a street drain.

Turning up the heat

Climate has changed greatly over geological timescales, as we shall see in Chapter 2. But what is of immediate concern is that climate has shown an almost unprecedented rapid global warming trend in the last few decades.

Since the start of reliable observations in the nineteenth century, scientists from weather services and research laboratories in many countries have examined local, regional and global average surface air and water temperatures, on land, from ships and more recently from orbiting satellites.

The World Meteorological Organization, which coordinates weather services around the globe, has declared that 2005 and 1998 were the two warmest years on record, since reliable weather records began in 1861, and just warmer than 2003. The decade of 1998–2007 was the warmest on record. Twelve of the last 13 years (1995–2007), with the exception of 1996, rank amongst the 12 warmest years since reliable records began in 1850. Since the start of the twentieth century the global average surface temperature has risen by $0.74 \pm 0.18°C$, and the linear warming trend over the last 50 years, around $0.13 \pm 0.3°C$ per decade, is nearly twice that for the last 100 years.[4]

Note that when scientists give such estimates they usually include a range of uncertainty, which in the former case above is $\pm0.18°C$. Thus the increase could be as low as $0.56°C$ or as high as $0.92°C$. In this case the uncertainties allow for possible inaccuracies in individual measurements, and how well the average from the limited number of individual measurement stations represents the average from all locations.

Indirect evidence from tree rings, ice cores, boreholes, and other climate-sensitive indicators (see Chapter 2) indicates that, despite a lesser warm interval round 1000 AD (the so-called 'Medieval Warm Period') the warmth of the last half century is unusual in at least the previous 1300 years. Moreover, the last time the polar regions were significantly warmer than the present for an extended period (some 125 000 years ago), reductions in polar ice volume led to global sea levels 4 to 6 m above the present. Variations of the Earth's surface temperature since 1850, along with global average sea level from 1870 and northern hemisphere snow cover since the 1920s, are shown in **Figure 1**.

Based on such observations, the Intergovernmental Panel on Climate Change (IPCC) in 2007 concluded that 'warming of the climate system is unequivocal, as is now evident from observations of increases in global average air and ocean temperatures, widespread melting of snow and ice, and rising global average sea level'.

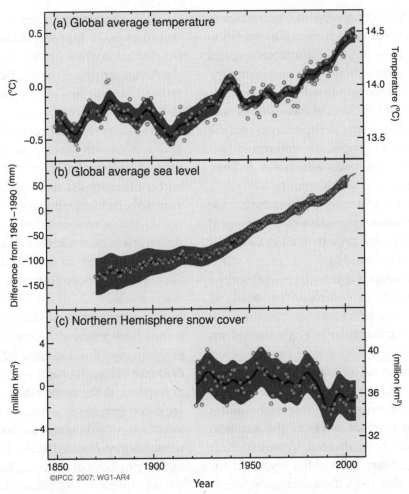

Figure 1: Observed changes in (a) global average surface temperature, (b) global average sea level and (c) northern hemisphere snow cover, from the start of good measurements. This is Figure SPM-3 from the IPCC 2007 Working Group I report (used with permission from IPCC).

Three things are notable about these IPCC conclusions. First, it shows that a warming of at least 0.56°C almost certainly occurred. Second, the most likely value of 0.74°C, while it may appear to be small, is already a sizeable fraction of the global warming of about 5°C that took place from the last glaciation around 20000 years ago to the present interglacial period (which commenced some 10000 years ago). Prehistoric global warming led to a complete transformation of the Earth's surface, with the disappearance of massive ice sheets, and continent-wide changes in vegetation cover, regional extinctions and a sea-level rise of about 120 metres.

Most importantly, the average rate of warming at the end of the last glaciation was about 5°C in some 10 000 years, or 0.05°C per century, while the observed rate of warming in the last 50 years is 1.3°C per century and the estimated rate over the next 100 years could be more than 5°C per century, which is 100 times as fast as during the last deglaciation. Such rapid rates of warming would make adaptation by natural and human systems extremely difficult or impossible (see Chapters 2 and 7).

Some critics have questioned the IPCC's estimated warming figures on the following main grounds. First, there are questions of uncertainties due to changes in instruments. Instrumental changes include changes in the housing of thermometers ('meteorological screens') which affect the ventilation and radiant heat reaching the thermometers, and changes in ships' observations from measuring the temperature of water obtained from buckets dropped over the side of ships to measurements of the temperature of sea water pumped in to cool the ships' engines. These changes are well recognised by scientists and have been allowed for. They contribute to the estimate of uncertainty.

Second, there are concerns that estimates are biased by observations from stations where local warming is caused by the growth of cities (an effect known as 'urban heat islands').

The heat island effect is due to the heat absorbed or given out by buildings and roads (especially at night). However, this effect works both ways on observed trends. In many large cities, observing sites, which were originally near city centres (and thus subject to warming as the cities grew) were replaced by observing sites at airports outside the cities. This led to a temporary observed cooling until urbanisation reached as far as the airports. Observations from sites affected by urban heat islands have, in general, been either corrected for this effect or excluded from the averages. A recent study of temperature trends on windy nights versus all nights shows similar warming trends, even though wind disperses locally generated heat and greatly reduces any heat island effect.[5]

One of the strengths of the surface observations is that those from land surface meteorological stations tend to agree well with nearby ship observations, despite different sources of possible errors. Average sea surface temperatures show similar trends to land-based observations for the same regions. Airborne observations from balloon-borne radio-sondes at near-ground levels also tend to support the land-based observational trends.

Another issue often raised is the apparent difference between the trends in temperature found in surface observations and those from satellites, which began in 1979. The satellite observations are not straightforward, as corrections are needed for instrumental changes and satellite orbital variations. Moreover, they record average air temperatures over the lowest several kilometres of the atmosphere (including the lower stratosphere at mid- to high-latitudes) rather than surface air temperatures, so they do not measure the same thing as surface observations. Recent corrections to the satellite and radiosonde estimates to take account of these problems have removed the discrepancies and confirm that surface and tropospheric (lower atmospheric) warming are occurring.

All the above criticisms of the temperature records have been addressed explicitly in successive IPCC reports and can now be dismissed.[6] Legitimate estimates of uncertainty are given in the IPCC assessments.

Supporting evidence for recent global warming comes from many different regions and types of phenomena. For example, there is now ample evidence of retreat of alpine and continental glaciers in response to the twentieth century warming (there are exceptions in some mid- to high-latitude coastal locations where snowfall has increased).[7] This retreat has accelerated in the last couple of decades as the rate of global warming has increased. **Figure 2** shows dramatic evidence of this for the Trient Glacier in the Valais region of southern Switzerland. The surviving glacier is in the upper centre, extending right to the skyline. Measured retreat of the terminus of the glacier since 1986–87 is roughly 500 metres by 2000 and another 200 metres by 2003. Early twentieth-century terminal and lateral moraines (where rock and earth are dumped at the end or sides of the glacier by the flowing and receding ice) are evident, free of trees, indicating recent ice retreat, and the present terminus of the glacier is slumped, indicating rapid melting.[8] Similar pictures, often paired with earlier ones, are available for many glaciers worldwide.[9]

Changes in other aspects of climate, broadly consistent with global warming, have also occurred over the last century. These include decreases of about 10% in snow cover as observed by satellites since the 1960s (see **Figure 1c**), and a large decrease in spring and summer sea-ice since the 1950s in the northern hemisphere. The latter reached a record low in 2007, and the melt rate is much faster than projected in the 2007 IPCC report. Warming has also been rapid near the Antarctic Peninsula, although not around most of mainland Antarctica.

Observed melting of permafrost is documented, especially for Alaska, by the US Arctic Research Commission in its *Permafrost Task Force Report* in 2003, and around the Arctic by the Arctic Climate Impact Assessment (ACIA) in 2004 and kept up to date by the annual National Oceanic Atmospheric Administration (NOAA) 'Report Card' on the state of the Arctic. Observed changes in the Arctic and their implications are summarised in **Box 1** from ACIA.[10]

According to the NOAA Arctic 'Report Card', a decrease in sea-ice extent in the Arctic summer of 40% since the 1980s is consistent with an increase in spring and, to a lesser extent, summer temperatures at high northern latitudes. Trends in summer (September) and winter (March) sea ice extent from 1979 to 2007 are 11.3 and 2.8% per decade, respectively.[11] Antarctic sea-ice extent has fluctuated in recent decades but remained fairly stable, apart from the area around the Antarctic Peninsula where rapid regional warming has led to sea-ice retreat and the disintegration of several large semi-permanent ice shelves attached to the mainland (see Chapter 5, **Figure 21** below).

Other changes include rapid recession of the ice cap on Mt Kilimanjaro in Kenya and other tropical glaciers in Africa, New Guinea and South America, as well as glaciers in Canada, the United States and China. Permafrost is melting in Siberia (where it has caused problems with roads, pipelines and buildings) and in the European Alps (where it has threatened the stability of some mountain peaks and cable car stations due to repeated melting and freezing of water in crevices in the rocks, forcing them apart). Catastrophic release of water dammed behind the terminal moraines of retreating glaciers in high valleys is of increasing concern in parts of the Himalayas, notably Bhutan and Nepal, according to a United Nations Environment Program report. All of these phenomena have accelerated in recent decades.[7, 12]

Measurements of the Southern Patagonian ice sheet in South America indicate rapid melting, with the rate of melting estimated from gravity measurements by satellite as 27.9 ± 11 cubic km per year from 2002 to 2006. This is equivalent to nearly 1 mm per decade rise in global average sea level.[13]

Global warming has led to thermal expansion of the ocean waters as well as melting of mountain glaciers. John Church, from CSIRO in Australia, and colleagues recently compared model calculations of regional sea-level rise with observations from tide gauge and satellite altimeter records. They concluded that the best estimate of average sea-level rise globally for the period 1950 to 2000 is about 1.8 to 1.9 ± 0.2 mm per year (that is just under 10 cm), and that sea-level rise is greatest (about 3 mm per year or 30 cm per century) in the eastern equatorial Pacific and western equatorial Indian Ocean. Observed rates of rise are smallest (about 1 mm per year) in the western equatorial Pacific and eastern Indian Ocean, particularly the north-west coast of Australia. Regional variations are weaker for much of the rest of the global oceans, and are due to different rates of warming in different parts of the oceans, and changes in winds, currents and atmospheric pressure.[14]

Recent observations indicate that the global rate of sea-level rise increased to about 3 mm per year in the period 1993 to 2008. This could be in part a natural fluctuation, including effects of major volcanic dust clouds reducing surface warming in some years. However, it could also be a result of an increasing contribution from the melting of the Greenland and Antarctic ice sheets, as has been observed locally. The total twentieth-century rise is estimated to be 17 ± 5 cm. This has no doubt contributed to coastal erosion in many regions, but in most cases the sea-level rise impact was not enough to be identified as such, due to other more localised factors such as variations in storminess and the construction of sea walls and other structures. James Hansen argues that the acceleration will increase rapidly due to increasing contributions from the major ice sheets, leading to up to several metres sea-level rise by 2100.[15]

BOX 1: KEY FINDINGS OF THE ARCTIC CLIMATE IMPACT ASSESSMENT

1. The Arctic climate is now warming rapidly and much larger changes are expected.

2. Arctic warming and its consequences have worldwide implications.

3. Arctic vegetation zones are projected to shift, bringing wide-ranging impacts.

4. Animal species' diversity, ranges and distribution will change.

5. Many coastal communities and facilities face increasing exposure to storms.

6. Reduced sea ice is very likely to increase marine transport and access to resources.

7. Thawing ground will disrupt transportation, buildings, and other infrastructure.

8. Indigenous communities are facing major economic and cultural impacts.

9. Elevated ultraviolet radiation levels [a combined effect of global warming and stratospheric ozone depletion] will affect people, plants, and animals.

10. Multiple influences interact to cause impacts to people and ecosystems.

Figure 2: The Trient Glacier near Forclaz in the Valais region of southern Switzerland in 2000. Rapid retreat has occurred during the latter part of the twentieth century. (Photograph by AB Pittock.)

Evidence for a strengthening of the global hydrological cycle, in which more rapid evaporation takes place in low latitudes, and more rain and snowfall occurs at high latitudes, comes from observations of salinity increases in the tropical and sub-tropical surface waters of the Atlantic Ocean over the last 50 years. This is accompanied by a freshening of surface waters in the high latitudes of the North and South Atlantic. Estimates indicate that net evaporation rates over the tropical Atlantic must have increased by 5–10% over the past four decades, with an accelerated trend since 1990.[16]

Other regional changes are also evident in rainfall, cloud cover and extreme temperature events, but due to large natural variability these are not yet quite so well established. Migration polewards of the mid-latitude storms tracks associated with the so-called 'annular modes' is leading to greater aridity in some mid-latitude regions and increased precipitation at high latitudes.[17] However, regional climate properties often vary on timescales of several decades. These are difficult to distinguish from longer-term changes without records longer than those presently available in some regions.

Why is the present rapid warming happening?

Scientists believe the rapid warming in the last several decades is due mostly to human-induced changes to the atmosphere, on top of some natural variations. Climate change induced by human activity may occur due to changes in the composition of the Earth's atmosphere from waste gases due to industry, farm animals and land clearing, or changes in the land surface reflectivity caused by land clearing, cropping and irrigation. These gases include several, such as carbon dioxide, methane and oxides of nitrogen, that can absorb heat radiation (long-wave or infra-red radiation) from the Sun or the Earth. When warmed by the Sun or the Earth they give off heat radiation both upwards into space and downwards to the Earth. These gases are called greenhouse gases and act like a thick blanket surrounding the Earth. In effect, the Earth's surface has to warm up to give off as much energy as heat radiation as is being absorbed from the incident sunlight (which includes visible, ultraviolet and infra-red radiation). Soot particles from fires can also lead to local surface warming by absorbing sunlight, but reflective particles, such as those formed from sulfurous fumes (sulfate aerosols) can lead to local cooling by preventing sunlight reaching the Earth's surface.

Natural greenhouse gases include carbon dioxide, methane and water vapour. These help to keep Earth some 33°C warmer than if there were no greenhouse gases and clouds in the atmosphere.

Human activities have increased the concentrations of several greenhouse gases in the atmosphere, leading to what is termed the 'enhanced greenhouse effect'. These gases include carbon dioxide, methane and several other artificial chemicals. The Kyoto Protocol, set up to begin the task of reducing greenhouse gas emissions (see Chapter 11), includes a package or 'basket' of six main gases to be regulated. Besides carbon dioxide (CO_2) and methane (CH_4), these are nitrous oxide (N_2O), hydrofluorocarbons (HFCs), perfluorocarbons (PFCs) and sulfur hexafluoride (SF_6).

Anthropogenic, or human-caused increases in carbon dioxide, come mainly from the burning of fossil fuels such as coal, oil and natural gas, the destruction of forests and carbon-rich soil and the manufacture of cement from limestone. The concentration of carbon dioxide before major land clearing and industrialisation in the eighteenth century was about 265 parts per million (ppm). Methane comes from decaying vegetable matter in rice paddies, digestive processes in sheep and cattle, burning and decay of biological matter and from fossil fuel production. HFCs are manufactured gases once widely used in refrigerants and other industries, but which are largely being phased out of use because of their potential to destroy atmospheric ozone. PFCs and SF_6 are industrial gases used in the electronic and electrical industries, fire fighting, solvents and other industries.

Water vapour concentrations in the atmosphere are closely controlled by the surface temperature. These can act as an amplifier of warming due to increases in other greenhouse gases or indeed warming due to Earth's orbital variations. Similarly clouds can act as an amplifier by absorbing heat radiation, or as a reducer of warming by reflecting incoming sunlight. The net result of clouds on the Earth's temperature depends on their height, latitude and droplet size.

Amplifying effects are called positive feedbacks (as in electronic circuitry). Loss of snow cover due to warming is another positive feedback, as it leads to greater absorption of sunlight at the Earth's surface and thus more warming. On the time-scale of the glacial-interglacial cycles of thousands of years, carbon dioxide concentrations in the atmosphere also act as a positive feedback, with the initial warming effect coming from variations in the Earth's orbit around the Sun. The amplification comes from warmer oceans giving off dissolved carbon dioxide, and thus increasing the natural warming via the greenhouse effect (see Chapter 2).

As early as the nineteenth century some scientists noted that increased emissions of carbon dioxide might lead to global warming (see Chapter 11). Present estimates of future climate change are based on projections of future emissions of greenhouse gases and resulting concentrations of these gases in the atmosphere. These estimates also depend on factors such as the sensitivity of global climate to increases in greenhouse gas concentrations; the simultaneous warming or cooling effects of natural climate fluctuations; and changes in dust and other particles in the atmosphere from volcanoes, dust storms and industry. Such projections are discussed in more detail in Chapter 3 and Chapter 5.

Given that climate has changed during the twentieth century, the key question is how much of this is due to human-induced increased greenhouse gas emissions, and how much to other more natural causes. This has great relevance to policy because, if the changes are due to human activity, they are likely to continue and even accelerate unless we change human behaviour and reduce our emissions of greenhouse gases.[18]

The IPCC Fourth Assessment Report in 2007 concluded:

- Global atmospheric concentrations of carbon dioxide, methane and nitrous oxide have increased markedly as a result of human activities since 1750 … The global increases in carbon dioxide concentration are due primarily to fossil fuel use and land use change, while those of methane and nitrous oxide are primarily due to agriculture.

- The understanding of anthropogenic warming and cooling influences on climate has improved since the [Third Assessment Report in 2001], leading to very high confidence [at least 90%] that the global average net effect of human activities since 1750 has been one of warming with a radiative forcing of +1.6 [+0.6 to +2.4] W m^{-2}.

An important verification of expected impacts of increased greenhouse gases on climate comes from a study by James Hansen and colleagues. They calculated the energy imbalance at the surface due to increased greenhouse gas concentrations in the atmosphere and compared this with precise measurements of increasing heat content of the oceans over the past decade. This study highlighted the importance of the delay in ocean warming, which implies future warming, sea-level rise and ice sheet disintegration.[18]

A paper by William Ruddiman of the University of Virginia, in 2003, raises the possibility that human influence on the climate has been significant since well before the Industrial Revolution due to the cutting down of primeval forests to make way for agriculture, and irrigated rice farming in Asia. Ruddiman claims that the Earth's orbital changes should have led to a decline in carbon dioxide and methane concentrations in the atmosphere from 8000 years ago. Instead there was a rise of 100 parts per billion in methane concentrations, and of 20 to 25 ppm in carbon dioxide by the start of the industrial era. He calculates that this has led to the

Earth being 0.8°C warmer than if humans had not been active, an effect hidden because it has cancelled out a natural cooling due to orbital variations.[19]

Simulations of the response to natural forcings alone (that is, natural changes causing the climate to change), such as variability in energy from the Sun and the effects of volcanic dust, do not explain the warming experienced in the second half of the twentieth century. However, they may have contributed to the observed warming in the previous 50 years (see Chapter 2). The sulfate aerosol effect would have caused cooling over the last half century, although by how much is uncertain. This cooling effect has become less since the 1980s as sulfur emissions have been reduced in North America and Europe in order to reduce urban pollution and acid rain.

The best agreement between model simulations of climate and observations over the last 140 years has been found when all the above human-induced and natural forcing factors are combined. These results show that the factors included are sufficient to explain the observed changes, but do not exclude the possibility of other minor factors contributing.[20]

Furthermore, it is very likely that the twentieth century warming has contributed significantly to the observed sea-level rise of some 10 to 20 cm, through the expansion of sea water as it gets warmer, and widespread melting of land-based ice. Observed sea-level rise and model estimates are in agreement, within the uncertainties, with a lack of significant acceleration of sea-level rise detected during most of the twentieth century. The lack of an observed acceleration up to the 1990s is due to long time lags in warming the deep oceans, but there is evidence of an acceleration in the last decade probably due to rapidly increasing contributions from melting of land-based ice in Alaska, Patagonia and Greenland.[14]

Studies by US scientists of twentieth century drying trends in the Mediterranean and African monsoon regions suggest that the observed warming trend in the Indian Ocean, which is related to the enhanced greenhouse effect, is the most important feature driving these dryings, through its dynamic effects on atmospheric circulation. Another study shows a tendency for more severe droughts in Australia, related to higher temperatures and increased surface evaporation. Both studies see tentative attribution of drying trends to the enhanced greenhouse effect, and are pointers to future regional climate changes.[21]

A deepening and polewards shift of the belts of low atmospheric pressure surrounding each pole, known technically as an increase in the northern and southern 'annular modes' of the atmospheric circulation, has been observed in the last several decades. It is also found in model simulations of climate with increasing greenhouse gas concentrations. However, the observed shift is greater than the simulated projections. Model simulations have now at least partially resolved this difference by including the effect of reductions in ozone in the upper atmosphere, which have occurred especially in the high latitude winter, since the 1970s (see Chapter 9). Both enhanced greenhouse gases and ozone reductions in the upper atmosphere increase the equator-to-pole temperature difference, leading to a strengthening of the westerly winds at high latitudes. These changes help explain decreasing rainfall in southern Australia, and a stronger North Atlantic Oscillation, which affects storm tracks and climate in Europe.[17]

Climate models suggest a possible slowdown of the overturning circulation in the North Atlantic that is driven by vertical differences in temperature and salinity (known as the 'thermo-haline circulation'). Such a change could result from surface warming, increased rainfall and runoff at high latitudes, and reduced sea-ice formation.[22] The reality of a slowdown of the thermo-haline circulation is supported by some recent observations from several areas, as well as paleo-climatic evidence that it has occurred before (see Chapter 2).[23] This could lead to rapid climate changes in the North Atlantic region, and has prompted the setting up of a monitoring and research program called the Rapid Climate Change Programme (RAPID) by the UK Natural Environment Research Council and the US National Science Foundation. The aim is to improve the ability to quantify the chances and magnitude of future rapid climate change.[24] Its main focus is the Atlantic Ocean's circulation, including the possibility of a slow-down in the Gulf Stream, relative cooling in Western Europe and a reduction in the Atlantic Ocean's ability to absorb carbon dioxide from the atmosphere.

The importance of delayed climate responses

Delayed climate responses to greenhouse gas emissions require early action. At present there is a large imbalance between present and past emissions of carbon dioxide into the atmosphere and their slow removal into the deep ocean. Even if we stopped emitting greenhouse gases tomorrow, the increase in atmospheric concentration of carbon dioxide as a result of the burning of fossil fuels and destruction of forests since the industrial revolution would persist for centuries. This is due to the slow rate at which carbon dioxide already in the atmosphere, surface ocean waters and the biosphere (plants, animals and soil biota) can be reabsorbed into the large reservoirs (called 'sinks') on the ocean floor and in the solid earth. It is as if we are pouring

a large amount of water into three connected bowls, from which there is only one small outlet drain.

This is illustrated schematically in **Figure 3**. The relative magnitude and rapidity of carbon dioxide flows are indicated approximately by the width of the arrows. Fossil fuel emissions of carbon dioxide into the atmosphere (large upwards arrow) reach equilibrium with carbon in the land and soil biota and in the shallow oceans ('CO_2 exchange' arrows) in only one to ten years. Carbon dioxide is only slowly removed into the deep ocean, taking hundreds to thousands of years ('natural CO_2 removal').

Rapid exchanges take place between the biosphere (plants, animals and soil) and the atmosphere, but due to limitations of climate and soil fertility, the biosphere cannot expand enough to take up the huge increase in carbon dioxide from fossil carbon. Most of the former fossil carbon stays as carbon dioxide in the atmosphere, where it changes the climate, or is absorbed into the surface layers of the oceans, where it changes the chemistry of the oceans. The portion that stays in the atmosphere is known as the 'airborne fraction' and is currently about 50% of all emitted carbon dioxide. The fraction dissolved in the ocean is limited by the

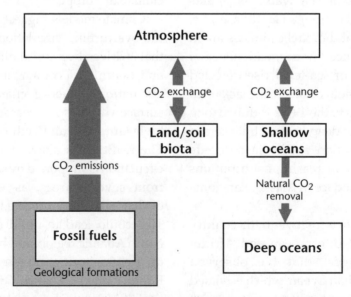

Figure 3: Flows between carbon reservoirs. This schematic diagram illustrates the present imbalance between emissions of carbon dioxide into the atmosphere, soil and land biota and shallow oceans, and its eventual removal into the deep oceans.

solubility of carbon dioxide in the surface waters of the oceans and the rate of downward penetration of the carbon dioxide. Thus, the airborne fraction will increase, as the upper oceans get warmer, because warmer water can hold less dissolved carbon dioxide, and there will also be less mixing of the warmer water into the relatively cold deep oceans. The resulting atmospheric carbon dioxide concentration will remain for centuries near the highest levels reached, since natural processes can only return carbon to its natural sinks in the deep oceans over many centuries.

More or less permanent natural sinks for carbon include carbon-rich detritus from marine organisms, mainly microscopic algae and plankton, but also from larger creatures, which fall to the ocean floor. Carbon is also transported to the oceans by rivers and wind-borne organic particles, and some of this also ends up on the ocean floor in sediment layers. Carbon is also stored in plants and the soil on land, but this can be returned to the atmosphere rapidly by fire or decomposition. The possibility of increasing sinks artificially is discussed in Chapter 8, which deals with mitigation.

Emissions of carbon dioxide from the burning of fossil fuels (oil, coal and natural gas) and deforestation will have to be reduced eventually by more than 80% globally relative to present emissions to stop concentrations increasing in the atmosphere (Chapter 8). This will take several decades to achieve without disrupting human society. The more we delay reducing greenhouse gas emissions, the larger the inevitable magnitude of climate change will be, and the more drastic will be the reductions in emissions needed later to avoid dangerous levels of climate change. To use the water-into-bowls analogy again, it is as if we wanted to stop the water rising above a certain level, but were slow to reduce the rate at which we kept adding water – the slower we are to reduce the input, the more drastically we will need to reduce it later.

Carbon dioxide concentrations in the atmosphere will stabilise only when the rate of emissions is reduced to the rate of deposition or sequestration into the deep oceans (or, as represented in **Figure 3**,

not until the left-hand emissions arrow and the lower-right removal arrow become the same size). Alternatively, there is the possibility of artificially increasing the rate of sequestration of carbon or carbon dioxide into the deep ocean or into subterranean storages (artificially widening the downwards arrow) or even of long-lasting charcoal ('biochar') into the soil. Artificial sequestration into the oceans is controversial, while subterranean sequestration is less controversial and is already happening in some cases (Chapter 8). Balancing the inflows and outflows of carbon dioxide into the atmosphere will take many decades or even centuries.

Furthermore, because of the slow mixing and overturning of the oceans, surface temperatures will continue to rise slowly for centuries, even after concentrations of carbon dioxide in the atmosphere have stabilised, and the deep oceans will continue to warm. This will lead to continuing thermal expansion, and thus rising sea levels, for centuries after stabilisation of greenhouse gas concentrations. Our children and grandchildren will be seeing the inevitable results of our continuing greenhouse gas emissions long after we have gone.

Recent developments suggesting that Greenland and even the West Antarctic Ice Sheet may be destabilised by even 2°C global warming (see Chapter 3) makes matters even worse, with multimetre rises in sea level possible. This suggests that stabilised concentrations of greenhouse gases may in fact have to be reduced, that is, that we may go through a peak concentration of greenhouse gases in the atmosphere and then have to reduce them. This is termed an 'overshoot scenario' and would require that emissions be reduced to zero or even become negative later this century. That is, carbon dioxide and other greenhouse gases may have to be removed from the atmosphere.[25]

The 2007 IPCC report discusses the possibility of such overshoot emissions scenarios. They would require that carbon dioxide be removed through some process that naturally or artificially takes carbon dioxide out of the atmosphere, most likely via growing plants or algae, which may or may not

BOX 2: DELAYED CLIMATE SYSTEM RESPONSES MATTER

Slow or delayed responses are widespread (but not universal) characteristics of the interacting climate, ecological, and socio-economic systems. This means that some impacts of human-induced climate change may be slow to become apparent, and some could be irreversible if climate change is not limited in both rate and magnitude before crossing thresholds at which critical changes may occur. The positions of such thresholds are poorly known.

Several important policy-relevant considerations follow from these delayed response effects:

• Stabilisation of the climate and climate-impacted systems will only be achieved long after human-induced emissions of greenhouse gases have been reduced.

• Stabilisation at any level of greenhouse gas concentrations requires ultimate reduction of global net emissions to a small fraction of current emissions. It will likely take centuries to reduce carbon dioxide concentrations much below the highest levels reached unless active steps are taken to remove carbon dioxide from the atmosphere (see Chapter 8).

• Social and economic time scales for change are not fixed. They can be changed by policies, and by choices made by individuals, or by reaching critical thresholds where change may become rapid and traumatic (for example, emergency programs, policy revolutions, technological breakthroughs, famine or war).

• Higher rates of warming and multiple stresses increase the likelihood of crossing critical thresholds of change in climatic, ecological, and socio-economic systems (see Chapter 6).

• Delays and uncertainty in the climate, ecological, and socio-economic systems mean that safety margins should be considered in setting strategies, targets and timetables for avoiding dangerous levels of climate change.

• Inevitable delays in slowing down climate change make some adaptation essential, and affect the optimal mix of adaptation and mitigation strategies.

• Slow responses in the climate system, and the possibility of reaching critical thresholds in the interacting climate, ecological and socio-economic systems, make anticipatory adaptation and mitigation actions desirable. Delayed reductions in emissions in the near-term will likely lead to an 'overshoot' scenario, with a need for faster reductions and removal of greenhouse gases from the atmosphere at a later time, probably at greater cost.

Source: Mainly updated from IPCC 2001 Synthesis Report, pp. 87–96.

be used for fuel and the carbon or carbon dioxide somehow removed from the climate system by storage or sequestration. Pyrolysis of biomass and the sequestration of the resulting biochar is one possibility.[26] These possibilities are discussed in Chapter 8.

Observed impacts[27]

While the 0.74°C increase in global average surface temperature since the beginning of the twentieth century may seem small, observational evidence indicates that climate changes have already affected a variety of physical and biological systems. As well as shrinkage of glaciers and thawing of permafrost mentioned above, examples of observed changes linked to climate include: shifts in ice freeze and break-up dates on rivers and lakes; increases in rainfall and rainfall intensity in most mid- and high latitudes of the northern hemisphere; lengthening of growing seasons; and earlier dates of flowering of trees, emergence of insects, and egg-laying in birds. Statistically significant associations between changes in regional climate and observed changes in physical and biological systems have been documented in freshwater, terrestrial and marine environments on all continents.

The 2007 IPCC report from Working Group II found that of more than 29 000 sets of observations of physical and biological systems, reported in 75 studies, more than 89% showed significant change consistent with the direction of change expected as a response to warming. Further, it found that the spatial agreement between regions of significant warming across the globe and the location of observed changes in systems was consistent with global warming rather than local variability.

In general, warming effects on biological systems include average range shifts polewards of around 5 to 10 km per decade, and events in spring occurring two or three days earlier per decade. Plants and animals will also move to higher elevations. Such movements are limited in many places by coastlines, limited height of mountains or alienation of land due to clearing or other human interference. This particularly affects many biological reserves set up to protect rare and endangered species.

Several modelling studies that linked responses in some physical and biological systems with climate changes found that the best fit with the observations occurred when both natural and enhanced greenhouse forcings were included.

The IPCC also reported that warming has already affected agricultural and forestry management (earlier spring plantings and changes to forest fire and pest occurrences). There are also early indications of impacts on mountain settlements from melting glaciers, and on drier conditions in

Sahelian and southern Africa. Sea-level rise and human development are also affecting coastal wetlands and mangroves.

IPCC Working Group I has also reported that increasing carbon dioxide concentrations in the atmosphere has led the oceans to become more acidic, with an average decrease in pH of 0.1 units since 1750.[28] Continuation of this trend is expected to adversely affect many oceanic species that grow shells including coral and many shellfish.[28]

Satellite observations point to longer growing seasons, with earlier 'greening' of vegetation in spring. This may increase total growth if water and nutrients are not limiting, but could also lead to problems with differences in seasonal timing between some species and others on which they rely for food or other services like pollination. Hotter and drier summers may also cause losses of vegetation due to heat stress and fire.[29]

Attribution of changes in crop production is complex, with climate change being only one factor along with changes in crop varieties, application of fertilisers, effects of pollutants such as ozone and nitrogen fallout, and direct effects of increasing carbon dioxide concentrations affecting water use efficiency and photosynthesis. Nevertheless, at least two papers claim to have detected yield trends due to climate change in Australia and the United States.[30]

Attributing observed changes to climate change is complicated by possible multiple causes. This is strikingly illustrated by the increasing use of the Thames Barrier in the UK, a moveable gate-like structure designed to control flooding in the lower Thames River, which became operational in 1983. The number of times the Thames Barrier has been closed each year since 1983 is shown in **Figure 4** by the black columns; theoretical closures from 1930 based on tidal and river flow data are denoted by the grey columns. The increase in the frequency of closure since 1983 could readily be taken as evidence of rising sea level or storminess. However, these closures could be occurring due to a combination of several effects, including relative sea-level rise

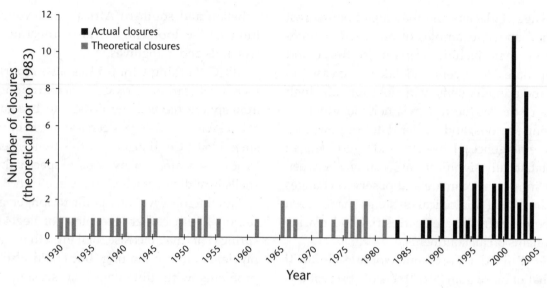

Figure 4: Has climate change increased the frequency of closure of the Thames Barrier? (Figure courtesy of Environment Agency, UK.)

(part of which may be due to land subsidence), increased storminess and changing operational procedures.[31]

According to a review of this data in 2003, the barrier is now sometimes used to retain water in the Thames River at low tide during drought, as well as to reduce the risk of flooding from the sea at high tide. Increased relative sea-level rise and increased storminess are both likely, at least in part, to be due to the enhanced greenhouse effect, and increased drought may also be related to climate change, but sorting out the relative importance of these possible causes requires a more detailed analysis.

Another recent example of a climate impact that is at least a forerunner of what may be expected with continued global warming is the series of extreme high temperatures experienced in Europe during the northern summer of 2003. Maximum temperatures were up to 5°C above the long-term averages for the same dates between 1961 and 1990, and the French Health Ministry reported 14 802 more deaths in August than would be expected on the basis of recent summers. Thousands more excess deaths were reported in Germany, Spain and the UK. Drought conditions, low river flows and wild fires were widespread across Europe during this period. The World Monitoring Glaciers

Service in Zurich reported an average loss of ice in Alpine glaciers in Europe equivalent to a 5 to 10% reduction of the total volume of all Alpine glaciers.[32]

Daily maximum and minimum temperatures in Paris at the height of the heatwave, with the corresponding deaths recorded in major Parisian hospitals are shown in **Figure 5**. The line with triangles shows daily maximum temperatures, and the line with squares shows daily minimum temperatures (scale on right). Vertical bars are the daily number of deaths recorded in Paris (scale on left). Maximum deaths occur near the end of the heatwave on 13 August. The excess death rate was due largely to the aged and infirm in non airconditioned apartments. A longer-term warming might lead to adaptations such as the installation of airconditioners, but this would be costly and energy-intensive. This European heatwave was chosen as a case study by the 2007 IPCC in its Working Group II report.

Martin Beniston and Henry Diaz cite the 2003 heatwave in Europe as an example of what to expect in future warmer summers, while Gerry Meehl of NCAR (USA) and colleague show that more frequent and intense heatwaves are to be expected, especially in Europe and North America, in the second half of

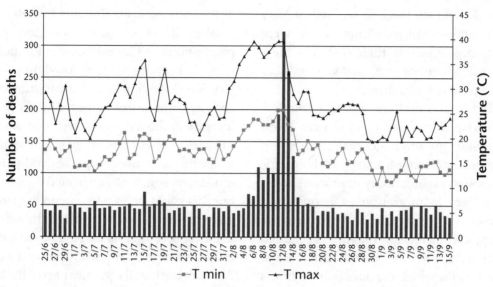

Figure 5: Deaths during the heatwave in Paris, July–August 2003. (Figure courtesy of Institut de Veille Sanitaire, InVS, France, per Pascal Empereur-Bissonnet.)

the twenty-first century. Peter Stott of the UK Meteorological Office and others estimate that human influence has at least doubled the risk of a heatwave in Europe exceeding the magnitude of that in 2003 and that the likelihood of such events may increase 100-fold over the next 40 years.[33]

Such changes will also likely affect the global carbon balance, with more frequent heat stress and fires reducing carbon uptake in forests, and even leading to net inputs of carbon dioxide into the atmosphere, as has been observed during the hot summer of 2003 in Europe.[29]

Trends in human vulnerability

It is often argued that as human societies become richer and more technologically advanced, they become less dependent on nature and more able to adapt to climatic change. Poorer societies are likely to be more adversely affected by climate change than richer ones, so the capacity of a society to adapt, it is said, will inevitably increase with economic development. In terms of the number of deaths from weather and climatic disasters, such as storms, floods and droughts, this appears to be borne out by common observations and statistics. However, the same statistics show that monetary damages from

such disasters are greater in many richer developed countries, and that, irrespective of climate change, there is a rising trend in such damages.

Even in rich countries, there are trends towards greater exposure to weather and climatic hazards, such as flooding by rivers and along low-lying coasts, drought, hail and windstorms. Examples include the increasing population and investments along the hurricane-prone Atlantic Coast of the United States, and the cyclone-prone coasts of northern Australia. These developments lead to greater potential economic losses. Reductions in loss of life are only achieved through large expenditures, for example on cyclone-proof buildings, early warning systems, evacuation, and rescue services.

Evidence that human societies are becoming more vulnerable to climate-related disasters comes from the observed rapid increase in damages from climatic hazards in the last several decades of the twentieth century.[34]

Some vulnerable cities, even in developed countries such as the United States and Australia, are at present unprepared for direct hits by major tropical storms, even without climate change. This is despite warnings of possible disaster, as in the case of New Orleans with hurricane Katrina in

August 2005. Several studies had warned of New Orleans' vulnerability, but recommendations were not acted on, largely due to their cost. The New Orleans losses illustrate the particular vulnerability of the poor, even in rich countries.[35]

Trends that make matters worse ('counter-adaptive' trends) are widely in evidence. These include population growth in general, increases in per capita consumption of water and energy, preferential growth in climatically hazardous areas, increased barriers to migration of people and natural ecosystems, the spread of new monoculture crop cultivars, and increasing reliance on limited technological fixes. The last include flood levee banks and sea walls, which encourage investment in hazard zones as they provide protection from small hazards, but fail when larger hazards occur. This was evident in the case of the major floods in the upper Mississippi Valley in the United States in 1993, when major levees were breached causing millions of dollars damage. Reversing such counter-adaptive trends is not easy.[36]

Evidence of increasing vulnerability comes from the observed rapid increase in damages from climatic hazards in the last several decades of the twentieth century.[34] **Table 1** summarises some of the evidence up to the late 1990s. Data up to 2006, from the *World Disasters Report 2007*, shows that the number of reported disasters increased by a further 60% from 1987–96 to 1997–2006.

While part of this increase in the number of weather-related disasters and damages may have been due to an increase in the frequency of climatic hazards, this has not been clearly established. Most of the increase is attributable to better reporting of smaller disasters and increased exposure of populations and investments in locations subject to climatic hazards, such as low-lying coastal zones, riverine floodplains, and areas subject to tropical cyclones and storm surges. The much more rapid increase in the number of reported weather-related disasters as opposed to non-weather-related disasters, such as earthquakes and tsunamis, hints at an increase in weather-related disaster occurrence, but this could be in part due to the smaller spatial scale of some weather-related disasters. The 2007 IPCC report suggests that the actual increase due to climate change is around 2% per year (some 22% per decade), but that the greater part of the total increase is due to increasing vulnerability.

The Mississippi flood example suggests societal changes may in some cases have more influence on vulnerability and resilience to climatic variability and extremes than climate change, and that they either compound or reduce the effects of climate change. Much more attention needs to be paid to such questions, which have strong policy implications through the identification of developmental trends that may make exposure, adaptive capacity and mitigation potential better or worse.

Climate change adds to the impact of these counter-adaptive societal trends.

Projections of future climate change

In 2001 the IPCC developed a set of climate change projections, based on plausible scenarios for future greenhouse gas emissions (the so-called SRES

TABLE 1: Increase in disasters since 1960. Comparison, decade by decade, of the number and costs (US$ billion) of catastrophic weather-related and non-weather-related events since the 1960s. Note the marked increase in weather-related disasters and their costs, but only a small increase in non-weather related disasters. Data comes from the International Federation of Red Cross and Red Crescent Societies annual *World Disasters Report 2004*.

	1960–69	1970–79	1980–89	1990–99	Ratio 90s/60s
Number of weather-related disasters	16	29	44	72	4.5
Number of non weather-related disasters	11	18	19	17	1.5
Economic losses	50.8	74.5	118.4	399.0	7.9
Insured losses	6.7	10.8	21.6	91.9	13.6

scenarios developed in 2000). These were based on 'story lines' about future development affecting greenhouse gas emissions, as an update on earlier scenarios used in 1992 and 1996 (see Chapter 3 for details). Using models of the carbon cycle, that is, of how carbon is moved around between the atmosphere, the biosphere, the soil and the oceans, the IPCC estimated that by the year 2100, atmospheric carbon dioxide concentrations would range in total anywhere from 490 to 1260 ppm. Such concentrations are 75 to 350% higher than the pre-industrial estimate of 280 ppm in 1750. Carbon dioxide concentrations in late 2007 were already about 382 ppm, or 36% above the pre-industrial value and continue to increase at 2 to 3% per annum.

These projected concentrations of carbon dioxide in the 2001 IPCC report led to estimates that by 2100 average global surface temperatures are likely to be between 1.4 and 5.8°C warmer than in the IPCC baseline year of 1990 (see Chapter 5). The IPCC did not say what the probabilities of the various increases were within this range because estimates of probability are difficult and depend on how society changes its use of fossil fuels in the future. The IPCC also estimated sea-level rise by 2100 to be in the range of 9 to 88 cm, mostly from thermal expansion of the oceans as they warm up and melting of mountain glaciers.

For the 2007 report IPCC chose not to use the whole set of SRES scenarios in detailed model calculations, due to the demand on computing resources, but instead used three of the five main scenarios, not including the A1FI or fossil fuel intensive scenario. This was omitted arguably because of criticism that the A1FI scenario was too high. In fact, emissions have since 1990 been following at or above the A1FI levels. Fortunately IPCC did also calculate, using simplified models, the climatic effect of this higher scenario (see Chapter 5).

The 2007 IPCC report found, for the full range of SRES emissions scenarios, that global warming by 2100 would be in the range 1.1 to 6.4°C, relative to 1980–99 averages. Estimates of sea-level rise were given as 18 to 59 cm, but with the caveat that this omitted uncertainties in climate-carbon cycle

feedbacks and in 'the full effects of changes in ice sheet flow'. The report suggests that an additional 10–20 cm of sea-level rise could occur due to increases in ice sheet flow, and that 'larger values cannot be excluded'. Accelerations in outflow from Greenland and parts of Antarctica since the IPCC report was drafted suggest that indeed sea-level rise could be well above the upper estimates in the IPCC report by 2100.

The projected warming in the twenty-first century is likely to be between two and 10 times as large as the observed warming in the twentieth century, and larger than any since the large and abrupt Younger Dryas event 11 000 years ago (see Chapter 2). Projected temperatures would be much warmer than during the so-called Medieval Warm Period, which was most evident in the North Atlantic region around 800 to 1300 AD. Warming as large and rapid as that projected for the twenty-first century might be expected to create severe problems for natural ecosystems and human societies. Indeed evidence from past climate changes of similar magnitude point to major impacts, which, if humans had been present in numbers like today, would have been disastrous.

Potential increases in sea level remain very uncertain, but could well be above the upper end of the 2007 IPCC estimates. An increasing number of scientists now agree with James Hansen in arguing that sea-level rise could be well in excess of a metre by 2100 (see Chapter 5), with potentially disastrous consequences for many coastal communities and resources.[15]

Facing the challenge

Scientific research in the latter half of the twentieth century led many climate scientists to alert governments to the issue of climate change. This was done individually and through conferences and policy statements. This led to the setting up of the Intergovernmental Panel on Climate Change to provide policy-relevant scientific advice, and it led to discussion in the United Nations General Assembly (see chapter 11).

The General Assembly called for a United Nations Framework Convention on Climate Change (UNFCCC) in 1990. The Convention was finally adopted in New York in May 1992, and was opened for signatures at the Intergovernmental Conference on Sustainable Development, held in Rio de Janeiro in 1992. Framework conventions are general agreements that leave the details of implementation to be worked out later via a series of protocols, legal devices or agreements to be adopted by the countries that signed the Convention. Up to late 2007, 193 countries have ratified the UNFCCC.

The objective of the UNFCCC is stated in Article 2 to be:

> ... the stabilisation of greenhouse gas concentrations in the atmosphere at a level that would prevent dangerous anthropogenic interference with the climate system. Such a level should be achieved within a timeframe sufficient to allow ecosystems to adapt naturally to climate change, to ensure that food production is not threatened, and to enable economic development to proceed in a sustainable manner.[37]

The UNFCCC contains no binding commitments on emissions levels, but it does lay down some general principles and objectives to shape future negotiations on these commitments. These include that:

- Developed countries (most members of the Organisation for Economic Cooperation and Development (OECD)) plus former communist states undergoing transition to a market economy, collectively known as 'Annex I' countries, should take the lead with abatement measures.

- The climatic and economic vulnerabilities of developing countries should be recognised.

- Abatement, or emissions reductions, should be consistent with sustainable development and not infringe the goals of an open and supportive international economy.

These provisions, and negotiations towards their implementation, have led to much argument between the countries that are parties to the Convention (and who meet as the 'Conference of Parties', or COP), especially over the contents and implementation of the Kyoto Protocol adopted in 1997. The Kyoto Protocol is a first agreement to start the process of reducing greenhouse gas emissions, with very modest targets set for reductions in Annex I countries averaging 5.2% relative to 1990 emissions, to be achieved by 2008–12. These arguments have been compounded by uncertainties as to the actual risk from climate change, and the costs of impacts and abatement measures. There has also been a clash of various national and corporate interests, ideological positions, and economic advantages. As at 12 December 2007, 176 countries had ratified the Protocol, with those agreeing to an emissions reduction target accounting for some 63.7% of world emissions. Australia agreed to ratify the Protocol following a change of government in November 2007. The one major country refusing to ratify the Protocol as of late 2008 is the United States.[38] These political matters are discussed more fully in Chapters 10 and 11.

Conclusion

This discussion strongly suggests that climate change is happening, and is projected to increase due to the ongoing and increasing release of greenhouse gases into the atmosphere. The main greenhouse gas (other than water vapour) is carbon dioxide, and its concentration in the atmosphere has increased from the pre-industrial value of about 280 ppm to some 382 ppm in 2008. It will take centuries to reduce this concentration, and possibly more than a century even to stop it increasing. Meanwhile this increase in greenhouse gases has already had impacts on the climate, and on natural ecosystems and human societies, and has committed us to further climate change due to the lags in the climate system.

The impacts of climate change will become more serious as global warming continues over the coming decades, with an increasing risk of drastic changes to the climate system. Whether this is disastrous will depend on how rapidly greenhouse gas emissions can be reduced and at what level greenhouse gas concentrations can be stabilised. As we shall see in Chapters 6 and 8, greenhouse gas concentrations may in fact need to be reduced below some potentially dangerous level reached in the next decade or two if we are to avoid highly damaging impacts. Our capacity to adapt is limited and adaptation is costly, so it is imperative that humans reduce their emissions of greenhouse gases as soon as possible to limit the rate and magnitude of climate change. Globally, practically all countries have already agreed that there is a problem and, despite differences, through the UNFCCC and other channels they are trying to work towards a solution.

In the following chapters we look in more detail at the complexities of climate change and its potential impacts. We will also examine potential policy responses, namely adaptation and mitigation, in the context of other environmental and developmental problems and the varying interests of different countries. My own position is that, despite some costs, there are realistic and mutually beneficial solutions, which can be reached with some effort and cooperation. Our task is to see that this happens, and that it starts now.

ENDNOTES

1. Preface to *Opportunities and Risks of Climate Change* (2002) Swiss Reinsurance, p. 4, available at http://www.swissre.com.

2. From 'Facing the future' (2002), a report to the International Institute for Environment and Development, p. 52, available at http://www.iied.org/mmsd.

3. Full texts of the speeches at the 2007 Nobel Peace Prize ceremony awarded to Al Gore and the IPCC for work related to climate change can be found at http://www.nobelprize.org.

4. Latest information on recent global temperatures is available from the World Meteorological Organization at http://www.wmo.int/pages/mediacentre/press_releases/. See for example press release no. 805 re 2007. See also http://www.nasa.gov/topics/earth/features/earth_temp_prt.htm, and http://www.ncdc.noaa.gov/gcag/index.jsp, where data can be accessed and plotted. A full discussion of observational evidence is in the IPCC Climate Change 2007, Working Group I report, Summary for Policymakers and Chapter 3, at http://www.ipcc.ch.

5. See 'Large-scale warming is not urban', by David Parker, *Nature*, **432**, pp. 290 (18 November 2004). A detailed discussion of many of the sceptics' arguments is found in the IPCC report as above. For corrections to satellite observations see Fu and colleagues, *Nature*, **429**, pp. 55–8 (2004), and *Science*, **304**, pp. 805–6 (2004). See also http://www.realclimate.com/ and http://royalsociety.org/page.asp?id=4761.

6. See IPCC 2007 report, Working Group I, Chapter 3.

7. See http://www.geo.unizh.ch/wgms/. Recession of mountain glaciers is discussed in Chapter 4.5 of the IPCC 2007 report, WGI. Maps of decreasing glacier extent on Mt Kilimanjaro can be found in Hastenrath and Greischar, *Journal of Glaciology*, **43**, pp. 455–9 (1997). See also George Woodwell in *Ambio* Special Report 13, (November 2004), pp. 35–8. Further documentation of glacier and ice sheet retreat is found in papers such as Mark and Seltzer in *Journal of Glaciology*, **49**, p. 271 (2003) for Peru; Shiyini and colleagues, same journal, p.117 (2003) for north-west China. He and colleagues, *Journal of Geophysical Research*, **108** (D17), doi:10.1029/2002JD003365, p. 4530 (2003) for south-west China; and Chuca and colleagues in *Journal of Glaciology*, **49**, pp. 449–55 for Spain. See also the report by Mark Dyurgerov 'Glacier mass balance and regime: data of measurements and analysis', Occasional Paper no. 55 (2002), Institute of Arctic and Alpine Research, University of Colorado; and 'The status of research on glaciers and global glacier recession: a review', by RG Barry, *Progress in Physical Geography* **30**, pp. 285–306 (2006).

8. Other pictures of the Trient Glacier can be found at http://www.dpeck.info/mts/trient2.htm and relevant data at http://commons.wikimedia.org/wiki/Image:Trient_glacier_stats.svg.

9. See for example http://www.worldviewofglobal warming.org/.

10. Earlier spring snowmelt in Alaska is reported in Stone and others, *Journal of Geophysical Research*, **107**, no. D10, 10.1029/2000JD000286 (2002). Melting of permafrost in the high Arctic is described in Goldman, *Science*, **297**, pp. 1493–4 (2002). Other articles on recent changes in the Arctic are also in this issue of *Science*. See also Sturm and others in *Scientific American*, **289** (4) pp. 42–9 (October 2003) and further reading listed there, and 'Climate change, permafrost, and impacts on civil infrastructure', US Arctic Research Commission, Permafrost Task Force Report, (December 2003), Special Report 01–03. The Arctic Climate Impact Assessment (ACIA) report (2004) can be found at http://www.acia.uaf.edu/.

11. The NOAA 'Report Card' (2007) is at http://www.arctic.noaa.gov/reportcard/. See also: Thierry Fichefet and colleagues, *EOS*, **85**, p. 39 (20 April 2004); W Meier, J Stroeve, F Fetterer, K Knowles, 'Reductions in arctic sea ice cover no longer limited to summer', *EOS* **86**, p. 326 (2005); Serreze and others, in *Geophysical Research Letters*, **30** (3), doi:10.1029/2002GL016406 (2002); and Stroeve and others, 'Arctic sea ice decline: faster than forecast', in *Geophysical Research Letters*, **34**, L09501, doi:10.1029/2007GL029703 (2007). A Sea Ice Index is available at http://nsidc.org/data/seaice_index/. See also *Vanishing Ice*, NASA Earth Observatory (May 2003) at http://earthobservatory.nasa.gov/Features/vanishing; http://cires.colorado.edu/steffen/melt/index.html, and Comiso and Parkinson, 'Satellite-observed changes in the Arctic', in *Physics Today* (August 2004), pp. 38–44. Regular updates are available at the US National Snow and Ice Data Center, for example, http://nsidc.org/news/press/2007_seaiceminimum/20070810_index.html. See also NASA website at http://nasa.gov/centers/goddard/news and http://earthobservatory.nasa.gov/.

12. Problems arising from the thawing of permafrost in the European Alps are discussed in *Nature*, **14**, p. 712 (August 2003). The problem of glacier lake outbursts is dealt with in a special report from the United Nations Environment Programme, and in Kattelmann, *Natural Hazards*, **28**, pp. 145–54 (2003), who recommends draining the lakes. A number of studies document an increase in the number of days of ice-free flow in rivers, including a recent paper by Hodgkins, Dudley and Huntington in *Climatic Change*, **71**, pp. 319–40 (2005).

13. Satellite data on the melting of the Patagonian Ice Sheet is by JL Chen and others, in *Geophysical Research Letters*, **34**, L22501 doi:10.1029/2007GL031871 (2007). See also Eric Rignot and collaborators in *Science*, **302**, pp. 434–7 (17 October 2003), and S Harrison, and others, *The Holocene* **16**, pp. 611–20 (2006).

14. Relevant papers include: Church and White, 'A 20th century acceleration in global sea-level rise, *Geophysical Research Letters*, **33**, doi:10.1029/2005GL024826 (2006); Shepherd and Wingham, 'Recent sea-level contributions of the Antarctic and Greenland ice sheets', *Science*, **315**, pp. 1529–32 (2007); Gehrels and others, 'A 20th century acceleration of sea-level rise in New Zealand', *Geophysical Research Letters*, **35**, doi:10.1029/2007GL032632 (2008); and Domingues and others, 'Improved estimates of upper-ocean warming and multi-dimensional sea-level rise', *Nature*, **453**, pp. 1090–93 (19 June 2008). See also a regional map of local sea-level rise, 1993–2008 from NASA at http://photojournal.jpl.nasa.gov/catalog/PIA11002.

15. Hansen's argument was first put in *Climatic Change*, **68**, pp. 269–79 (2005), and again in 'Scientific reticence and sea level rise', *Environmental Research Letters*, **2**, doi: 10.1088/1748-9326/2/2/024002 (2007).

16. See Curry and others, *Nature*, **426**, pp. 826–9 (2003) and *Bulletin of the American Meteorological Society* (March 2004) pp. 328–30.

17. A recent paper on the well-known poleward movement of the atmospheric circulation systems is by DJ Seidel and others in *Nature Geoscience*, **1**, pp. 21–4 (2008). See also Chapter 5. Observed changes in the annular mode, and their simulation in climate models, are discussed in papers by Hartmann and others, *Proceedings National Academy of Sciences of the US*, **97**, pp. 1312–417 (2000); Thompson and Wallace, *Journal of Climate*, **13**, pp. 1000–16 (2000); Gillett and others, *Nature*, **422**, pp. 292–4 (2003); Marshall, *Journal of Climate*, **16**, pp. 4134–43 (2003); and Ostermeier and Wallace, *Journal of Climate*, **16**, pp. 336–41 (2003).

18. James Hansen and colleagues, 'Earth's energy imbalance: confirmation and implications', *Science*, **308**, pp. 1431–5 (2005).

19. William Ruddiman, 'The anthropogenic greenhouse era began thousands of years ago', *Climatic Change*, **61**, pp. 261–93 (December 2003).

20. Attribution studies are comprehensively reviewed in Chapter 9 of IPCC 2007 report, WGI. Another review of attribution is 'Detecting and attributing external influences on the climate system: A review of recent advances', by The International Ad Hoc Detection and Attribution Group, in *Journal of Climate*, **18**, pp. 1291–314 (2005).

21. The study of Mediterranean and African monsoon drying is by Hoerling and colleagues, paper presented at CLIVAR/PAGES/IPCC Drought Workshop, November 16–21 (2003). The Australian study is by Nicholls, in *Climatic Change*, **63**, pp. 323–36 (2004).

22. Modelling of the slowdown in the thermo-haline circulation is reviewed in Stocker, *International Journal of Earth Sciences*, **88**, pp. 365–74 (2000) and Lockwood, *International Journal of Climatology*, **21**, pp. 1153–79 (2001). Observational evidence suggesting a possible slowdown in the thermo-haline circulation comes from Delworth and Dixon, *Journal of Climate*, **13**, pp. 3721–7 (2000); Matear and others, *Geochemistry, Geophysics, Geosystems*, **1**, Paper no. 20000GC000086 (21 November 2000); Kim and others, *Geophysical Research Letters*, **28**, pp. 3293–6 (2001); Dickson and others, *Nature*, **416**, pp. 832–7 (2002); Gille, *Science*, **295**, pp. 1275–7 (2002); Fukasawa and others, *Nature*, **427**, pp. 825–7 (2004), and Peterson and colleagues in *Science*, **298**, pp. 2171–3 (2002). The RAPID project has a website http://www.soc.soton.ac.uk/rapid/rapid.php. See also Vellinga and Wood, *Climatic Change*, **91**, pp. 43–63 (2008).

23. Observational evidence, supporting the possibility that a slowdown of the thermo-haline circulation in the oceans is already under way, includes Delworth and Dixon, *Journal of Climate*, **13**, pp. 3721–7 (2000); Dickson and others, *Nature*, **416**, pp. 832–7 (2002); Gille, *Science*, **295**, pp. 1275–7 (2002); Hansen and others, *Nature*, **411**, pp. 927–30 (2001); Kim and colleagues, *Geophysical Research Letters*, **28**, pp. 3293–6 (2001); Matear and colleagues, *Geochemistry, Geophysics, Geosystems*, **1** (11), 1050, doi:10.1029/2000GC000086 (2000), and Fukasawa and others, *Nature*, **427**, pp. 825–7 (2004). See also Baehr and others, *Climatic Change*, **91**, pp. 11–27 (2008).

24. The RAPID project is reported briefly in *Nature*, **427**, p. 769 (26 February 2004) and more fully by M Srokosz in *EOS* (Transactions of the American Geophysical Society) (24 February 2004), pp. 78, 83. See also http://www.noc.soton.ac.uk/rapid/.

25. See IPCC 2007 report, WGIII, Fig. SPM-6 and related text.

26. See http://www.biochar-international.org.

27. The IPCC 2007 report, WGII, has two chapters on observations, Chapter 3 on atmospheric and surface climate change, and Chapter 4 on observed changes in snow, ice and frozen ground. Projected ecological impacts are found in the WGII report, in chapters by sector and region. See also the paper 'Attributing physical and biological impacts to anthropogenic climate change', *Nature*, **453**, pp. 353–7 (15 May 2008). And see Pew Centre, *Observed Impacts of Global Climate Change in the U.S.* (2004); and Reale and others, *Proceedings of the Royal Society of London*, **B270**, pp. 586–91 (2003); and an Australian review by Hughes, *Austral Ecology*, **28**, pp. 423–43 (2003).

28. See the IPCC 2007 report, WGI, Chapter 5.4 and Box 7.3. Projections of future changes and their impacts are in Chapter 10.4. See also WGII, Chapter 4 for more on impacts.

29. For effects of heat stress on the carbon balance see A Angert and others in *Proceedings National Academy of Sciences* (US), **102**, pp. 10 823–7 (2005). For effects of the 2003 summer in Europe see P Ciais and others, *Nature*, **437**, pp. 529–33 (2005).

30. The Australian crop yield study is Nicholls, *Nature*, **387**, pp. 484–5 (1997). The US study is Lobell and Asner, *Science*, **299**, p. 1032 (2003), with a comment in the same issue, p. 997. A critical view is presented by Godden and others, *Nature*, **391**, pp. 447–8 (1998).

31. The frequency of closures of the Thames Barrier was used as an indicator of climate change in *Science*, **303**, p. 176 (2004). For changes in the operating rules for closure see *Review of UK Climate Change Indicators* (June 2003, revised January 2004) at http://www.nbu.ac.uk/iccuk/.

32. See *ECMWF Newsletter*, no. 99 (Autumn/winter 2003) pp. 2–8. See also *Weatherwise* (March/April 2004), pp. 24, 27.

33. See Beniston and Diaz in *Global and Planetary Change*, **44**, pp. 73–81 (2004); Meehl and Tebaldi in *Science*, **305**, pp. 994–7 (2004), and Stott and others in *Nature*, **432**, pp. 610–13 (2004). See also IPCC 2007 WGII report, cross-chapter case study, available at http://www.ipcc.ch.

34. Changnon and Changnon, *Natural Hazards*, **18**, pp. 287–300 (1999); Pielke and Landsea, *Weather and Forecasting*, **13**, pp. 351–61 (1998); Changnon and others, *Bulletin American Meteorological Society*, **81**, pp. 437–42 (2000); and Vellinger and Mills, in McCarthy and others, Chapter 8. The decadal average data in Table 1 is from *World Disasters Report 2004*. Updated data, although not strictly comparable, can be found in *World Disasters Report 2007* (at http://www.ifrc.org) and in *Natural and human-induced environmental hazards* (2005) on the ICSU website at http://www.icsu.or. See also the *Report of the Workshop on Climate Change and Disaster Losses* (2006) at http://sciencepolicy.colorado.edu/sparc/research/projects/extreme_events/munich_workshop/index.html, and *Annual Review: Natural Catastrophes 2004* from Munich Reinsurance at http://www.munichre.com.

35. For a remarkably accurate forecast of what would happen if a major hurricane struck New Orleans see Mark Fischetti, 'Drowning New Orleans', *Scientific American* (October 2001) pp. 68–77. See also, 'Washing Away', Special report, *New Orleans Times-Picayune*, (23–27 June 2002) at http://www.nola.com/hurricane/content.ssf?/washingaway/index.html. Also see: SB Goldenberg and others, *Science*, **293**, pp. 474–9 (20 July 2001), 'The recent increase in Atlantic hurricane activity: causes and implications'; and JB Elsner and others, 'Estimated return periods for Hurricane Katrina' in *Geophysical Research Letters*, **33**, L08704 (2006).

36. See accounts by Nan Walker and others in *EOS*, **75**, p. 409 (6 September 1994); and the article by Lee Larson at http://www.nwrfc.noaa.gov/floods/papers/oh_2/great.htm; and Sheaffer, Mullan and Hinch in *Environment*, **44** (1), pp. 33–43 (2002).

37. The text of the UNFCCC can be found at http://unfccc.int/2860.php.

38. Several histories exist of the climate change negotiations and expositions of the UNFCCC and the Kyoto Protocol: Grubb, Vrolijk and Brack (1999), *The Kyoto Protocol: A Guide and Assessment*, Royal Institute of International Affairs and Earthscan Publications, London; and Oberthur and Ott (1999), *The Kyoto Protocol: International Climate Policy for the 21st Century*, Springer-Verlag, Berlin. See also Chapter 11 and related endnotes, and http://www.iisd.ca/.

2

Learning from the past[1]

Given all the fuss about climate change, it is important that we understand the Earth's climate and how it works. We base this knowledge on two things:

- knowledge of how the climate has behaved in the past, and

- our ability to explain past climate changes.

If we can explain the past, we can build conceptual and then detailed computer models. These will enable us to make predictions about future climate changes, given the likelihood of future changes in those factors which drive the climate system. As a general rule, if something happened once, the system is such that it could happen again, given similar preconditions. But we only truly understand the system if we can explain what happened before. If we have that understanding, we have some ability to predict what may happen from now on, especially if we see similar preconditions occurring.

Life has existed on the Earth for 3.5 thousand million years, so potentially we have a very long record to examine for climatic behaviour, although it is only since the start of the Cenozoic period, about 65 million years ago, that we have a useful climatic record. This record plus theories based on the laws of physics, chemistry and mathematics can tell us what sort of things influence climate. Ideally this helps us to develop a 'model' of the climate system, that is, how the solid earth, water, atmosphere and biosphere interact with the energy from the Sun to produce climate. Such a model may be merely a set of qualitative ideas, or a set of quantitative mathematical representations of those ideas, which can be used to make calculations on a computer.

Once we have such a model of the climate system, detailed knowledge of past conditions and climatic behaviour enables us to test how well the model works. Such testing can be done by looking at episodes of climatic change in the distant past, or by looking at what has happened over the last century or so, for which we have much more detailed observations.

Accordingly, we can use two main types of climatic data for analysing past climatic variations:

- Direct or instrumental measurements. These generally started up to about 200 years ago with the advent of modern instruments such as thermometers, rain gauges and anemometers, and were discussed in Chapter 1. They provide a fairly accurate record, but the record is too short to sample the whole range of climate changes that have occurred before and may occur again.

- 'Proxy' or indirect data. Such data can provide a much longer time perspective, and are obtained from natural or human archives that in some way record past climate variations. Proxy data includes written records of harvests, or properties of artefacts or substances that have been influenced by climate in the past. Notable examples are

geological formations such as glacial moraines (soil and rocks left behind by retreating glaciers), the annual growth rings in trees, layers of sediment deposited on the beds of lakes or oceans, or the radioactive isotopes of various chemical elements deposited in ice cores, tree rings or sediments. Proxy data is vitally important to our understanding of past climatic variations and changes, so it merits further explanation.

Proxy data: clues from the past

Dramatic evidence of past climates comes from landscape features such as U-shaped valleys (see **Figure 6**) and large and small lakes dammed behind glacial moraines. These are evidence that glaciers and ice caps once covered far more of the Earth's surface than today. The Great Lakes in North America are a striking example: they were formed at the southern edge of huge ice caps covering Canada and the northern parts of what is now the United States. When we map such features and

Figure 6: The glacial valley above Lautenbrunnen, Switzerland, in 1999. This characteristically U-shaped valley was carved out by a large glacier during the last glacial period some 20 000 years ago. The glacier, visible in the distance, has now receded many kilometres up the valley in response to a global average warming of only some 4 or 5°C in the last 20 000 to 10 000 years. The glacier is retreating further now due to warming in the twentieth century. This is dramatic evidence of past natural climatic change and of the potential impacts of future climate changes that may be due to human influence. (Photograph by AB Pittock.)

make inferences about climate from them, we are using 'proxy' evidence or data to make scientific deductions about past or paleo-climates ('paleo-' means old or ancient).

There are many types of proxy data used by climatologists (**Table 2**), and they are often used in combination to build up a reliable picture of the past.[2] Each has its merits and limitations. The interpretations made from them depend on sometimes complex models or understandings of what caused the proxy data and under what conditions. For example, glaciers result from snow that has accumulated in higher elevations compacting into ice and gradually flowing downwards along valleys, until it reaches lower elevations where it melts or evaporates. Relationships between the length of a glacier and the temperature and snowfall can be deduced from observations, or from first principles from the mathematical relationships between snowfall, depth of ice or snow, volume, evaporation, melting,

bottom friction, elasticity of the ice, and so on. This can all be put in a mathematical model and the changes with time calculated on a computer.

Proxy data must be calibrated against instrumental data for a meaningful climate interpretation to be made, and they vary in usefulness according to how closely related they are to climate, and how well the dates can be determined. The dating and time resolution (the ability to separate adjacent time intervals) is especially important where attempts are made to look at spatial patterns of change, or to see whether one event preceded another, as may be necessary to help establish cause and effect.

Dating of glaciers can be done from fragments of plant material in the terminal moraines, or found under where the glacier was after it has receded again. Such dates can come from radioactive carbon concentrations, since short-lived isotopes such as ^{14}C (formed in the atmosphere by cosmic rays striking air molecules) gradually disappear after

TABLE 2: Proxy indicators of climate-related variables[2]

Indicator	Property measured	Time resolution	Time span	Climate-related information obtained
Tree rings	Width, density, isotopic ratios, trace elements	Annual	Centuries to millennia	Temperature, rainfall, fire
Lake and bog sediments	Deposition rates, species assemblages from shells and pollen, macrofossils, charcoal	Annual	Millennia	Rainfall, atmospheric water balance, vegetation type, fire
Coral growth rings	Density, isotope ratios, fluorescence	Annual	Centuries	Temperature, salinity, river outflows
Ice cores	Isotopes, fractional melting, annual layer thickness, dust grain size, gas bubbles	Annual	Millennia	Temperature, snow accumulation rate, windiness, gas concentrations
Ocean sediment cores	Species assemblages from shells and pollens, deposition rates, isotopic ratios, air-borne dust, pollen	Usually multi-decadal or centuries	Millennia	Sea temperatures, salinity, acidity, ice volumes and sea level, river outflows, aridity, land vegetation
Boreholes	Temperature profile	Decades	Centuries	Surface air temperature
Old groundwater	Isotopes, noble gases	Centuries	Millennia	Temperature
Glacial moraines	Maximum glacier length	Decades	Centuries to millennia	Temperature and precipitation
Sand dunes	Orientation, grain size	Centuries	Millennia	Wind direction and speed, aridity
Coastal landforms	Ledges, former beach lines, debris lines	Decades to centuries	Decades to millennia	Former sea-level, tropical cyclones
Documentary evidence	Reports of extremes, harvests, dates of break-up of river or lake ice	Annual	Centuries to millennia	Temperature, precipitation

the plant material dies. Dates from radiocarbon are useful for material up to about 50000 years old, but only accurate to within a few per cent of the age from the present. Dating for much older material comes from other isotopes with longer decay times. An example is Uranium isotope 238, which decays to Uranium 234, and which in turn decays to Thorium 230. Ratios of ^{230}Th to ^{234}U can be used for dating back millions of years. Time resolution with these methods is coarse.

Estimates of spatial patterns of decadal, annual or seasonal climate variations in past centuries, however, must rely on proxy evidence having finer time resolution. That is, it needs to resolve annual or seasonal variations. This evidence includes the width or density of annual growth rings in trees; layer thickness and particle size in annual layers in sediment cores from the bottom of lakes or oceans; the isotopic composition, chemistry and thickness of annual layers in ice cores; isotopes from coral growth layers; and scattered historical information from human documentation of things like crop yields, floods, frosts and the break-up of frozen rivers.

Annual growth rings in trees are a good example. These can often be counted back from the present using samples from many different trees of overlapping age. In some cases, for example, with Oak in Western Europe, Kauri in New Zealand, and Bristlecone Pine in the western United States, this record can be taken back thousands of years. Similar dating is possible from annual layers of silt in lakes, although in longer time series from the floor of the ocean where sediment layers may be disturbed by burrowing creatures, radioactive dating is necessary. Sediment records may go back many thousands or millions of years using much longer-lived isotopes than ^{14}C.

The record of the ice ages

By studying many different proxy data records from places around the globe scientists have found evidence of global-scale climate changes. Climate has varied from times known loosely as 'ice ages' or 'glacial periods', when huge ice sheets covered large areas that are now ice-free, to periods like now when ice sheets are largely confined to Antarctica, Greenland and the floating Arctic sea ice. Records indicate that climate changes occurred over the last two million years in a rather regular cyclic manner, with glacial periods lasting roughly 100000 years, and warmer interglacial periods occurring in between. The latter lasted much shorter time intervals of around 10000 years (see **Figure 7**). These climatic fluctuations were accompanied by large variations in global average sea level, of up to about 120 metres, and resulted in dramatic changes in vegetation cover, lakes, rivers and wetlands, and the distribution of plants and animals.

Huge areas of the continental shelves were exposed during the glacial periods, joining Alaska to Siberia, the Australian mainland to New Guinea and Tasmania, Britain and Ireland to Western Europe, and many South-East Asian islands to the Asian mainland. At the end of the last glaciation some 18000 years ago, the ice sheets melted over Canada, northern Europe and elsewhere, and the Greenland and Antarctic ice sheets contracted. This again flooded the above areas of the continental shelves, taking thousands of years to do so.

Smaller changes in relative sea levels are still occurring regionally due to the continental plates slowly rebounding and flexing. This happens because of the removal of the weight of the ice sheets from the continental interiors and the increased weight of sea water along the continental margins. Thus much of Scandinavia is still rising relative to the sea, while parts of the east coast of the United States are gradually subsiding. Sea-level changes are thus not uniform, and estimates of actual global average sea-level rise must come from combining measurements from many parts of the world.

Life survived, and indeed flourished, despite these huge climatically forced variations in the environment, but many individual species of plants and animals became extinct, and others had to migrate large distances to more congenial

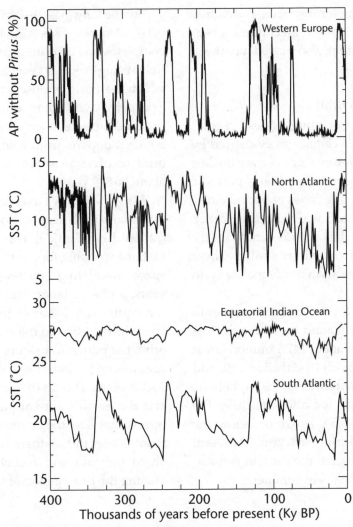

Figure 7: Climate variations over the last 400 thousand years. The top graph shows percentage variations in tree pollen amount, excluding pine tree species. High percentages correspond to warm climates. The lower three curves show estimated sea surface temperatures in the North Atlantic, equatorial Indian Ocean and the South Atlantic, based on deep-sea cores. Variations between glacial and interglacial periods were large in high latitude regions, but much less in low latitudes. Variability was much greater in the North Atlantic region. (Graphs are from Figure 2.23 in the IPCC 2001 WGI report.)

regions. The latter included our human ancestors, who skirted around ice sheets to migrate from Asia to North America, and crossed small straits to migrate from South-East Asia to Australia. Rising sea levels between 20 000 and 10 000 years ago forced people to move from land that is now under the Black Sea, and many to move inland from coastal plains in North America, Europe and Australasia. Such mass migrations would be much more difficult now, with six billion people and rigid national boundaries, than at the end of the last ice age when the Earth was only sparsely populated by humans.[3]

The causes of past climate change

There are many contributory causes of past climate change, including continental drift, variations in the Earth's orbit around the Sun, changes in solar output, volcanic emissions, cosmic collisions and particulate matter in the atmosphere, commonly referred to as 'aerosols'. Natural greenhouse gases, which absorb heat radiation, also played a part.

Variations in the Earth's orbit[4]

The remarkable history of more or less regular fluctuations in the Earth's climate, as evidenced by the sea-level and temperature records over the last two million years, suggests a strong periodic influence on the climate. The series of periodicities, or regular variations, associated with the Earth's orbit around the Sun is the obvious candidate for this, since the periods involved are similar. These orbital characteristics are shown schematically in **Figure 8**.

During the course of a year, the Earth moves in a slightly elliptical orbit around the Sun, which is at present at a distance of about 147.1 million km at its point of closest approach ('perihelion', P), and 152.1 million km at its furthest distance ('aphelion', A). This causes the solar radiation reaching the Earth to vary by about 3.5% above or below the average 'solar constant' during each year. At present the strongest radiation reaches the earth in January, during the southern hemisphere summer.

But the long axis (A–P in Figure 8) of the elliptical orbit also revolves slowly around the Sun. It completes one revolution after an irregular interval that averages 96 600 years and so the time of year at which the Earth is closest to the Sun changes very gradually with that timescale. To complicate matters, the eccentricity of the orbit (the degree to which it departs from being circular) varies as the orbit revolves in space, with the same period of about 96 000 years.

Also, the Earth's axis of rotation is not upright ('normal') with respect to the plane of its orbit (called the 'ecliptic'). This spin axis wobbles like that of a spinning top, so that it marks out a cone in space completing one revolution in about 26 000 years, a phenomenon known as the precession of the equinoxes. Because the precession is in the opposite direction to the rotation of the Earth in its orbit, the perihelion recurs at the same time of the year after a period of less than 26 000 years, about 20 600 years. The tilt of the Earth's axis of rotation, and the Earth's annual journey around the Sun, means that first the northern hemisphere, and six months later the southern hemisphere, is more full-on to the Sun and receives more solar energy, causing the progression of the seasons.

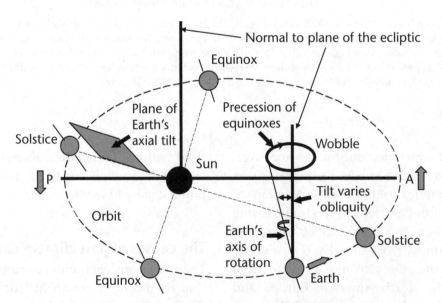

Figure 8: Geometry of the Sun–Earth system. This figure illustrates the origin of changes in solar radiation reaching the Earth at particular latitudes and seasons associated with variations in the Earth's orbit around the Sun. (P = perihelion, A = aphelion.)

Finally, the tilt of the Earth's axis of rotation from the normal to the ecliptic (known as the obliquity of the ecliptic) itself varies, undergoing a slow oscillation, with a period of about 40 000 years, between 24°36' and 21°59'. At present the angle is 23°27' and decreasing. This is why the Tropics of Cancer and Capricorn (where the Sun is overhead in mid-summer) are at about 23°27' north and south, respectively.

How do these astronomical periodicities help to explain the glacial–interglacial record? That question occurred to the Serbian climatologist Milutin Milankovitch in the 1930s. Milankovitch theorised that variations in solar energy received over the northern continents at about 65°N due to these orbital variations, particularly in the northern summer, would have driven the growth and decay of the continental ice sheets. He argued that a span of cool summers, caused by relatively large Earth–Sun distances, would result in winter snow accumulating from year to year as it failed to completely melt, whereas warm summers would cause winter snow to melt and glaciers and ice sheets to recede. In 1938 Milankovitch published tables of how solar radiation varied with time at key latitudes, notably 65°N. These tables have been recalculated more accurately since, and the original theory seems to hold true.

On the much longer time scales (hundreds of millions of years) associated with large tectonic changes like continental drift and uplift, changes in the distribution of land and sea and in elevation of the continents play a large part in climate, and vary the effect of the astronomical cycles. Milankovitch's focus on 65°N was reasonable because during the Pleistocene and Holocene epochs (the last two million years) large continental areas where snow could accumulate existed at these latitudes.

With the advent of more powerful computers and mathematical techniques, the association between the astronomical cycles and the climatic record has been refined. Hays and others in 1976 demonstrated excellent time correspondence between the cycle of the eccentricity of the orbit at about 96 000 years and the main observed glacial–interglacial cycle. About half the total variation in the climatic record is contained in the periodicity due to eccentricity, with some 25% due to the obliquity cycle (about 40 000 years) and 10% due to precession.

Role of greenhouse gases in amplifying climate changes

Computer models of climate can now be used to calculate quantitatively the effects of the various drivers of climatic change. Use of climate models shows that variations in solar energy at the Earth associated with the astronomical cycles cannot by themselves explain the relative strength of the observed periodicities in the climatic record. According to these models the effects of the orbital eccentricity cycle must have been amplified or enhanced by some other factor. That additional factor has now been identified as variations in the greenhouse gas concentrations present in the atmosphere. Most notable are the concentrations of carbon dioxide and methane, both of which are stored in large quantities in peat, tundra and ocean sediments during colder climates, and are released into the atmosphere in warmer climates. Any warming due to orbital changes results in more carbon dioxide and methane being released into the atmosphere, leading to greater warming.

This explanation is supported by paleo-evidence for varying concentrations of these gases in the atmosphere, notably from measured concentrations in gas bubbles stored in ice cores from Antarctica and Greenland (see **Figure 9**). Recent work by William Ruddiman at the University of Virginia confirms the Milankovitch theory and the crucial role of amplification by methane and carbon dioxide variations.[5]

Comparing modelled changes over the astronomical cycles with observed paleo-climatic changes enables an independent estimate to be made of the sensitivity of the climate to changes in greenhouse gas concentrations. This suggests a climate sensitivity (global warming for a stabilised doubling of carbon dioxide concentrations) in the upper part of the range adopted by the Intergovernmental Panel on Climate Change (IPCC)

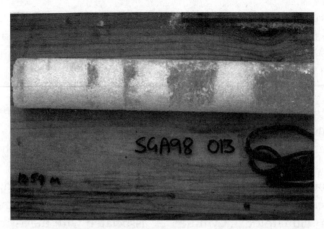

Figure 9: Ice core drilled from Antarctica. This core from Law Dome in East Antarctica is shallow and only about 50 years old. Ice layers formed from refrozen melt water during summer months alternate with winter snow layers. Water isotopes are measured and used as proxies of temperature. Incorporated impurities from marine emissions, volcanic eruptions, atmospheric chemistry and so on provide information on conditions in the past. When the ice becomes deeper and denser, the air inclusions are sealed off and represent samples of the past atmosphere from which past concentrations of carbon dioxide and methane can be measured. (Photo courtesy of David Etheridge, CSIRO Atmospheric Research.)

in its 2007 report, which remains 1.5 to 4.5°C (with some qualifications).[6]

The results relating to the Milankovitch cycles provide strong support for the role of greenhouse gases in changing past climate, and confirm that any changes to greenhouse gas concentrations in this century are very likely to affect future climate.

However, some sceptics have claimed that because in parts of some paleo-climatic records temperature variations precede changes in greenhouse gas concentrations, this means that greenhouse gases merely respond to climate change. In fact, orbital variations initiated some past global warming and this led to the release of more greenhouse gases, which caused more global warming.

Variations in solar output

The basic source of all energy for driving the climate system on Earth is radiation from the Sun. Thus any variations in solar output would drive changes in the climate. There is a long history of claims to have detected effects of solar variations on surface weather and climate, but many of these claims have been based on poor statistics (as I demonstrated in critical reviews of the scientific literature some

30 years ago). It is only in recent decades that accurate measurements of solar variations have been made. These have been used to extrapolate estimates of variations in solar radiation back in time using correlations with sunspot numbers, which have been observed since the 1700s.[7]

The IPCC in its *Fourth Assessment Report* in 2007 discusses recent estimates of the increase in solar radiation since the 'Maunder Minimum' in the sixteenth century of about 1 Watt per square metre, or approximately 0.1% of the total irradiance (or solar constant). Various suggestions have been made as to how such a small change may be amplified in the atmosphere, for example by effects on ozone or clouds. The effect on ozone has been modelled, and is taken into account, while the other mechanisms remain highly speculative.[8]

Climate models have been run with various types of forcing including changes in greenhouse gases, volcanic particles, ozone, solar variations and the effects of air pollution particles. When used to simulate the observed temperature variations over the twentieth century, the climate models tend to give a better reproduction of the observations if they do include solar variations. This is especially so for the first half of the twentieth century, when solar radiation was increasing and increases in greenhouse gases were relatively small. However, solar radiation did not increase much during the second half of the twentieth century, but both temperature and greenhouse gases did.

All reconstructions of solar radiation changes over the twentieth century due to solar variability indicate that it was only about 20 to 25% of the total change in radiation at the Earth's surface. The bulk of the changes in radiation were due to increased greenhouse gases. Changes in solar radiation cannot explain the rapid global warming in the 1980s and 1990s, and future warming is likely to be increasingly dominated by increases in greenhouse gases, unless substantial greenhouse gas emission reductions are achieved in the next few decades.

Volcanoes, cosmic collisions and aerosols

After Mt Tambora in Indonesia exploded in 1815, the northern hemisphere experienced what became known as the 'year without a summer' in 1816. This inspired Lord Byron to write his poem *Darkness*, which included the lines:

I had a dream, which was not all a dream.
The bright sun was extinguish'd, and the stars
Did wander darkling in the eternal space,
Rayless, and pathless, and the icy earth
Swung blind and blackening in the moonless air …

While Byron's poem rather exaggerated the situation, there were many crop failures in the summer of 1816.

A recent major explosive volcanic eruption was Mt Pinatubo in the Philippines in 1991. Such eruptions inject large quantities of dust particles and reactive gases (mainly sulfur dioxide and hydrogen sulfide) into the lower and upper atmosphere. If the particles and sulfurous gases remain in the troposphere (the well-mixed lower atmosphere where clouds and rain occur), they can be washed out in a matter of days to weeks, and so have little climatic effect. However, if the dust and reactive gases enter the more stable region of the stratosphere, which is free from water clouds and precipitation, the dust and gases can remain for longer periods. The heavier large particles still fall out due to gravity, but finer particles, mostly formed in the atmosphere by chemical reactions between gases, may stay in the stratosphere for many years.

The most long-lasting effects come from small sulfate particles that form in the stratosphere due to reactions between the sulfurous gases and ozone. These generally remain in the stratosphere until the lower stratospheric air is exchanged with the troposphere, when they can be washed out. This can take several years for the larger ones, and the finest particles can remain in the middle and upper stratosphere for decades.

Observations suggest that for the few years following a major explosive volcanic eruption regional effects on climate occur, with warming in the stratosphere and cooling at the surface, due to the particles absorbing some sunlight and reflecting more back into space. Regional surface cooling of about 1°C has been observed, along with warming in the stratosphere by a few degrees. Both these effects are well reproduced by recent climate models. Effects are greatly reduced by the second year after such eruptions, and are quite minor after several years. So unless there are a series of major eruptions in quick succession, no major climatic effects are to be expected. Projections of future climate changes usually have an implicit reservation that volcanic eruptions may provide a temporary interruption to any warming trend.

Collisions of Earth with a major meteor or asteroid could be far more disastrous, and there is geological evidence for such events in the past. None having major effects has been recorded in human history. However in the 1980s, they did provide some inspiration and an analogy in considerations of the possible climatic effects of a nuclear war (via the release of large clouds of smoke from burning cities) – an effect known as 'nuclear winter'.[9] Major cosmic collisions are far less likely than major volcanic eruptions in the next few centuries, and are ignored in current climatic projections.

More relevant to current projections are the presence of large quantities of small particles in the lower atmosphere commonly referred to as 'aerosols'. These arise mainly from the emission of sulfurous gases and soot particles, from the burning of fossil fuels, as well as more natural dust particles from arid windy surfaces. All of these particles have only short lifetimes in the lower atmosphere before they fall out or are washed out. However, they are quickly replaced as more fossil fuels are burnt, or by wind erosion in arid areas.[10]

Measurements from the ground and satellites indicate the large presence of such particles regionally, and that they have significant effects on regional climate. Aerosols directly absorb or reflect incoming solar energy, and also absorb some outgoing heat radiation. Absorption of solar energy will cause local heating in the lower atmosphere, which may in turn heat the surface. Thus soot particles add to global warming. Absorption by particles of heat radiation from the surface also tends to heat the surface. However, reflection of incoming solar radiation has a cooling effect at the surface. This is thought to have dominated in recent decades, leading to some polluted regions downwind of major industrial areas experiencing less warming than would have otherwise occurred.

A recent dramatic example of how aerosols affect the daily temperature cycle was observed in the United States when commercial aircraft were grounded following the terrorist attack on 11 September 2001. As reported in *Nature* on 8 August 2002, this led to fewer vapour trails from aircraft, with a statistically significant increase in the difference between daily maximum and minimum temperatures.

There are also indirect effects of aerosols on clouds, first suggested by Sean Twomey of the University of Arizona in 1977, that is, a reduction in cloud droplet size due to the particles acting as condensation nuclei. This increases the reflectivity of the clouds, and decreases precipitation efficiency, which increases cloud water content and cloud lifetime, leading to further surface cooling.[11]

Recent excitement about so-called 'global dimming' (for example a paper by G Stanhill in *Weather*, January 2005, and various media reports) is in fact a rediscovery and measurement of these effects of aerosols, which have long been held responsible in part for the cooling experienced in the northern hemisphere in the 1950s and 1960s.[12] The direct effects of aerosols have been included in most recent global climate model simulations, and some simulations have also included estimates of the indirect effects.

Aerosol amounts due to industrial activity are now decreasing in some regions, especially in Europe and North America, due to efforts to clean up emissions of sulfurous gases because of acid rain and urban pollution effects. Thus, while greenhouse gas emissions continue to increase, the particles that were having a cooling effect are decreasing, leading to a greater dominance of increased greenhouse warming on the observed climate. This is part of the explanation for the increased rate of global average warming in the last two decades. When aerosol effects are added to global climate model simulations, they better account for the temperature variations observed over the twentieth century. They also seem to have had effects on atmospheric circulation and rainfall, largely due to their effects on the monsoons.[13]

Past records from sedimentary layers offshore of the continents (notably China, north Africa and Australia), and in ice cores from Greenland and Antarctica, indicate that increases in wind-blown dust have occurred in previous more arid climates. Depending on the size and radiation absorptive qualities of these particles, they may have locally contributed to warming or cooling. They certainly testify to the ability of climate change to alter the frequency and severity of dust storms and soil erosion through changes in land cover and windiness.

Rapid climate changes in the past[14]

Despite the slowly varying nature of the astronomical variations, the paleo-climatic record is replete with examples of surprisingly rapid climatic changes. The extreme rapidity of some of these changes has only become apparent in recent decades as improved analysis, sampling and dating techniques have enabled changes to be observed on time scales of years to decades rather than centuries and millennia. Older analyses had smoothed out very rapid changes that can now be seen clearly.

Richard Alley, Chair of the Committee on Abrupt Climate Change of the US National Research Council (NRC), wrote in the preface to its 2002 report:

Large, abrupt climate changes have repeatedly affected much or all of the earth, locally reaching as much as 10°C change in 10 years. Available evidence suggests that abrupt climate changes are not only possible but likely in the future, potentially with large impacts on ecosystems and societies.

Alley is not talking about abrupt external causes of change such as large meteor impacts or nuclear war, but rather abrupt climate changes that can occur when variables that are gradually changing push the Earth system across some threshold of instability. He likens this to how the slowly increasing pressure of a finger can flip a light switch from off to on. Gradual changes in the Earth's orbit, or drifting of the continents, can switch the Earth to a new and very different climatic state. When orbital changes and rising greenhouse gas concentrations warmed the Earth after the last glaciation, paleo-records show that the smooth changes were punctuated by abrupt global or regional coolings and warmings, wettings and dryings.

It should be added that such a switch cannot readily be turned off again, due to large delays or inertia in the climate system: it is more like one of those sensor switches used for lighting, which can be turned on by some sudden movement but only turn themselves off in their own good time.

The best known of these large and abrupt past changes was the Younger Dryas event, indicated, along with two other lesser events, by the shading in **Figure 10**. The Younger Dryas was a sudden interruption of a gradual global warming after the end of the last glaciation, and began about 12800 years ago. This sudden return to a cold global climate lasted for 1200 years, and was followed by a very rapid warming of about 8°C in 10 years, taking the climate to interglacial conditions not much different from today. Proxy data for the Younger Dryas event is especially prominent in the ice core records from Greenland (top curve), where there is evidence of cooling, reduced snow accumulation, and changes in windiness and dust accumulation. Within about 30 years of the final warming, atmospheric methane concentration rose about 50%, reflecting changes in wetlands in both the tropics and high latitudes.

Evidence for a similar late-glacial reversal comes from ice cores on Baffin Island in Canada, and glaciers in Peru and Bolivia, and this is probably also the Younger Dryas. However in Antarctica the evidence is mixed, with records from Byrd showing relative warmth at the time of the cold conditions in Greenland.

Pollen evidence for changes in vegetation, however, provides a wider geographical coverage. During the Younger Dryas cooling occurred throughout Europe, from Norway to Spain and Italy, with the strongest effects near the western coast. Average July temperatures in Norway were 7–9°C lower than today, and as much as 8°C lower than today in Spain. Evidence also comes from North America that the Younger Dryas had significant effects there. Fossil pollens show that in the southern New England region of the United States July temperatures were 3–4°C cooler and in the eastern maritime provinces of Canada they were 6–7°C cooler. Evidence of somewhat weaker effects is also found in the US Midwest, coastal British Columbia and Alaska, Costa Rica and Guatemala. In the southern hemisphere evidence is more confusing, with some cooling, but some areas where warming may have occurred, and others where no effects are found in the records. Glaciers advanced during the Younger Dryas in many European regions, notably in Norway, Finland and Scotland, and also in Canada, Wyoming in the US and Ecuador. Ice retreated in Peru, probably due to reduced precipitation, but the Franz Joseph Glacier advanced in New Zealand.

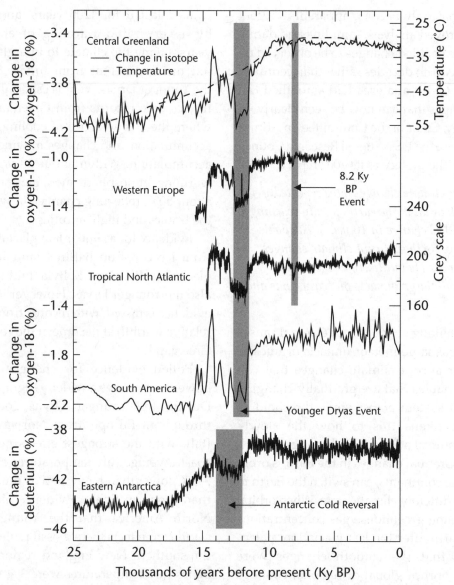

Figure 10: Records of climatic variations from the height of the last glaciation until the present. This includes three rapid climate change events (shaded), namely the Younger Dryas, the Antarctic Cold Reversal and the 8.2 thousand years before present event. (Source: IPCC 2001a, Figure 2.24, used with permission.)

Marine sediment cores from the North Atlantic during the Younger Dryas show an increased abundance of polar planktonic species, which suggests that the formation of deep water, by the sinking of surface water, was reduced in the region. Other oceanic evidence supports this and provides evidence for the origin of the Younger Dryas event in the waters of the North Atlantic. Marine records from many other parts of the world, including the Caribbean, the North Pacific, the Indian Ocean and the Arabian Sea point to a global scale phenomenon, although some regions show little effect.

Despite the need for more data, the picture emerges of the Younger Dryas as cold, dry and windy in many regions at least of the northern hemisphere. However, there are locally wetter regions, possibly associated with changes in the tracks of storms. At the same time, the far South

Atlantic, the southern Indian Ocean and Antarctica were relatively warm. Changes were largest around the North Atlantic, and appear to have been associated with reduced deep water formation and related changes in ocean circulation. Deep water formation results from the sinking of cold, high salinity and thus more dense surface waters. Slowing or cessation of deep water formation was due to warming or freshening of the surface waters.

Events similar in size, rate and extent to the Younger Dryas event occurred some 24 times during the 110 000 year record derived from the ice cores of central Greenland. They all show gradual cooling from a warm interval, then more abrupt cooling, a cold interval, and finally an abrupt warming. The warm times have been termed Dansgaard/Oeschger events, and the sequences Dansgaard/Oeschger oscillations. The colder phases were marked by increased rafting by icebergs of glacial debris (rocks and dirt scraped up by glaciers) into colder, fresher surface water, and by a reduction in the strength of North Atlantic deep water formation. Changes in material such as dust and methane from outside Greenland, trapped in the ice cores, demonstrate that these events affected large areas of the Earth simultaneously.

Despite only gradual changes in driving forces, these observed rapid climate changes appear to have occurred because the drivers reached some sort of tipping point or threshold at which climate flips into a new state. Such mechanisms suggest that similar rapid climate changes could happen again, even when driven by only gradual increases in greenhouse gases. We will return to the significance of these past events for climate change risk in the twenty-first century and beyond in Chapter 5, which deals with what climate changes are likely, and in Chapter 6, on climate change impacts.

The last 10 000 years

Climatic changes since the Younger Dryas event more than 10 000 years ago have generally been much smaller in amplitude, but nevertheless sometimes rapid, with sudden increases in the frequency and severity of extreme events such as droughts and floods. Even these relatively small changes evidently had large impacts on ecosystems and human societies, although usually at a regional rather than global scale.

In relation to human impacts, it is sometimes difficult to pin down exactly what was cause and what was effect, due to variations in factors other than climate. Population pressures, diseases, wars, economic forces, technological changes and resource substitutions can all affect human societies in ways that may or may not be related to climate. However, in some cases the climatic influence is clear and well documented. A case in point is the settlement of Greenland by the Vikings in the twelfth century during what is known as the Medieval Warm Period, and the abandonment of these settlements during the fifteenth century as conditions in the North Atlantic region became cooler, agriculture became more marginal, sea ice extended and the settlements became more isolated.

The extent to which human history has been influenced by climate has been long debated by historians and climatologists.[15] The US historian-geographer Huntington in 1915 famously advocated a form of climatic determinism, that is, that climate determined human racial differences and levels of civilisation.[16] Carpenter and Lamb in the 1960s argue for the influence of climate on Greek civilisation, and Le Roy Ladurie, in his seminal book in 1971, for a wider influence especially on European history.[17] Dansgaard and colleagues in 1975 argued for a strong influence on Norse culture, especially in regard to the settlement of Iceland and Greenland, and Singh in 1971 for a determining climatic impact on the civilisation of the Indus valley in north-west India, which collapsed following droughts in the eighteenth century BC.[18] Climatic fluctuations are also argued to have influenced the migrations of peoples in the South Pacific, including the settlement of New Zealand by the Maori peoples around 800 AD.[19] The Zhou Dynasty in China was affected by increasing aridity around 1150 AD.[20]

Climatic fluctuations such as extended drought are thought to have played a major part in the abandonment of American Indian settlements in the south-western United States around 1090 AD, and again in the thirteenth century AD,[21] and the fall of the Mayan civilisation in Central America around 850 AD.[22] Extensive analysis of tree ring data, lake levels and sand dunes in the Great Plains of the United States indicates that over the last 2000 years extended drought conditions comparable with, or more severe than, that of the 1930s dust bowl occurred on several occasions. It was concluded that if such large-scale droughts were to occur in future they would have a significant impact on North American society, with a reduction in water supply, crop failure, rangeland stress, suspension of recreational and tourist activity and heat-related deaths.[23]

Large areas of the African and European continents underwent massive changes in their vegetation cover and ecosystems in the early and mid-Holocene periods, some ten to five thousand years ago. This must have had enormous impacts on the lives of the scattered human inhabitants at those times, forcing large-scale population movements or population losses.

In Africa, the Sahara went from a largely grassy area, populated by hunter–gathering peoples who left artefacts and records of the animals they hunted in rock paintings, to desert rather suddenly around 6000 years ago. Evidence for this is found in lake sediments and estimated levels, and in marine and land pollen records. This change is thought to be related to the Earth's orbital variations and an amplification of the effect of changing solar radiation by the interaction of the vegetation with climate, possibly passing some critical threshold. This sudden drying may have spurred migration into the Nile Valley and the start of the Egyptian civilisation. Climate models have partly simulated these rapid climate changes, although results differ from one model to another.[24]

And in East Africa, lake levels and salinity fluctuations in Lake Naivasha (Kenya) indicate that the era from 1000 to 1270 AD (during the Medieval Warm Period in Europe) was significantly drier than today, while the era 1270–1850 AD was relatively wet (corresponding at least in part to the cool period in Europe known as the Little Ice Age). Moreover, three shorter periods of drought, in 1390–1420, 1560–1625 and 1760–1840 correspond to periods of political unrest and large-scale migration, according to oral traditions, with periods of prosperity in between.

Evidence for a Little Ice Age and a Medieval Warm Period is fairly widespread across Europe and parts of North America, to a lesser extent elsewhere in the northern hemisphere, and much less evident in the southern hemisphere. Pollen and charcoal analyses from sediments in parts of the north-western United States, and from Yellowstone National Park and central Idaho point to greater fire frequency during the Medieval Warm Period, and lesser fire frequency during the Little Ice Age. However, in Alberta, Canada, the same sort of analyses point to the opposite tendency. This local effect has been related to declining groundwater levels at one site in Alberta, leading to a change from fire-prone shrub Birch trees to less fire-prone Aspen.[25]

Records of prehistoric tropical cyclones occur in the form of ridges of coral rubble, sand, shell and pumice; erosional terraces in raised gravel beaches; barrier washover deposits; and various other sediments. Such records for a number of sites around the world suggest that the frequency and possibly the intensity of tropical cyclones have varied in the past. However, the number of events analysed is small and statistical significance is therefore not great.

Changes in sea level since the end of the last glaciation are dominated by the slow but massive rise of some 120 metres due to the melting of the huge continental ice sheets in the northern hemisphere between about 20000 and 8000 years ago. This was not entirely regular, but was punctuated by pauses and sudden rises of a few metres due to temporary glacial re-advances and sudden outbursts of melt-water stored by huge glacial dams or surges in glacial motion and iceberg formation.

Sea-level changes in the last 8000 years[26] or so has tended to be small and regional, with rises in some regions and relative falls in others, mainly due to earth movements and rebound of the continental plates. The majority of the Earth's coastlines are at present subject to relative sea-level rise and erosion. Local consolidation of sediments, either due to slow natural adjustments, earthquakes, or withdrawal of groundwater, oil or natural gas, has contributed to coastal problems.[27] Notable is the loss of some ancient cities around the Mediterranean coast, such as ancient Alexandria, Menouthis and Heraklion in Egypt, and others around Greece, Italy and Turkey. Growing subsidence problems also exist in other cities such as Bangkok, London and Venice, and in the Chesapeake Bay region in the United States. These problems would be accentuated by any systematic sea-level rise due to the enhanced greenhouse effect, especially if sea-level rise accelerates, as now seems likely.

There is also clear evidence that melting of ice caps has led to the underlying land slowly rising as the weight of ice was removed. This is called 'glacial rebound', and as well as causing local sea-level falls (with compensating rises elsewhere as the water is displaced), it adds stress to tectonic faultlines, leading to local increases in earthquake activity.[28]

As regards proxy evidence for temperature variations, we saw in Chapter 1 that the proxy record over the last 1300 years suggests that the twentieth century saw the largest temperature rise, at least in the northern hemisphere, with the sharpest rise occurring since the 1970s. The original claim for a 'hockey stick' like temperature record over the last 1000 years, implicit in the results of Michael Mann and others was challenged by Soon and Baliunas in a paper in 2003 claiming that: 'Across the world, many records reveal that the twentieth century is probably not the warmest nor a uniquely extreme climatic period of the last millennium.' However, this is very misleading, since the paper does not compare estimates of past *global* or *hemispheric* average temperatures with those of the twentieth century, but merely *non-synchronous* (that is, not occurring region by region at the same time) and unquantified temperature (and rainfall) 'anomalies' in each local record. Local

anomalies can occur for many reasons, and often cancel out across larger regions, so the number of occurrences of short warm periods in long records from many different regions is not comparable to hemispheric average warming such as has occurred in the twentieth century.[29]

More recent re-analyses of the temperature record show more variability over the last 1300 years, but continued to find an unprecedented warming in the second half of the twentieth century. This warming has continued into the twenty-first century, with the last decade being the warmest on record. Moreover, as pointed out by Tim Osborn and Keith Briffa of the Climatic Research Unit in the UK, the larger estimated temperature variations in the 1000-year record suggest a greater climate sensitivity to small changes in forcing factors and this would also apply to greenhouse gases.[30] This is consistent with the claims for human influences over this period, via changes in land cover, made by William Ruddiman.[5]

Ruddiman suggests that the cool period before the Medieval Warm Period, and the Little Ice Age after it, may both have been due to bubonic plague-induced depopulation in western Asia and Europe, which led to regrowth of forest on abandoned farmlands. This theory has caused wide discussion in the scientific community. If true, it suggests high climate sensitivity to relatively small changes in greenhouse gas concentrations and that humans are capable of achieving these changes. Moreover, it means that while past human activity may have helped to avoid prolonged conditions like the Little Ice Age by widespread land clearing, projected increases in greenhouse gas concentrations at a rate at least ten times faster than our ancestors achieved means that we will see much larger warmings in the twenty-first century and beyond.

Conclusions from the past record

Past climatic changes are relevant because they demonstrate what is possible in the natural climate system when forces occur such as volcanic eruptions or variations in the Earth's orbit around the Sun.

Orbital variations act slowly, on time scales of thousands of years, while volcanic eruptions act in a matter of days or weeks. Now we are forcing changes on the climate system due to large greenhouse gas emissions on a time scale of decades to a century. These are equivalent to changes which occurred previously over thousands of years. Therefore we might well expect similar impacts on natural systems to those which occurred in the past over thousands of years, but telescoped into a much faster time frame, leading to rapid and possibly catastrophic changes.

Climate change has occurred naturally in the past due to internal fluctuations in the climate system consisting of the atmosphere (air, water vapour, constituent gases, clouds and particles), the hydrosphere (oceans, lakes, rivers and groundwater), and the cryosphere (continental ice sheets, mountain glaciers, sea ice and surface snow cover). External changes such as volcanic eruptions, variations in the Sun's output and the Earth's orbital variations, and changes in the solid Earth (continental drift, mountain building, erosion and siltation) have also driven changes in climate.

At the end of the last glaciation, average global warming occurred at a rate of about 1°C or less per thousand years, although there were short periods during which warming was much faster. The last of these was at the end of the so-called Younger Dryas reversal, about 11 500 years ago. Since then, and certainly since the dawn of civilisation, rates of warming have never exceeded about 0.5°C per century (0.05°C per decade) for periods of more than a few decades.

Our interest in the past is not only in what sorts of climate changes can happen, but also in what sort of impacts they had on natural systems such as plants, animals and landscapes. However, in interpreting paleo-climate induced changes we must think carefully about rates of change rates of adaptation, and changed circumstances as regards human populations and societies.

Pollen records show that in response to warming after the end of the last glaciation around 15 000 to 10 000 years ago, forests migrated at rates of, at most, tens of metres per century. Over the next century we can expect climate to change so rapidly that forests would need to migrate at rates of hundreds of kilometres per century to remain in their optimal climatic zones. This is clearly unlikely. What is far more likely is that forests that no longer are located in their correct climatic zones will die from heat stress, drought, disease and fire. Similarly, many crops will no longer yield well in their present locations, and will have to be re-located hundreds of kilometres away to provide equivalent climate conditions. But most often the crops will be on different soils, on land owned by other people, and even in different countries. Dislocations to society will therefore be large, far larger than was the case for the small numbers of hunter–gatherers who existed tens of thousands of years ago.

Paleo-climatic analogies to our present predicament confuse many people. They argue that if large climate changes occurred before, and humans and other species survived, then life, and even humans, can survive today, so there is not much to be concerned about. This fails to consider the different time scales, the very different place of humanity in the ecosystems then compared to now, and the many restrictions that exist today which limit our ability to adapt to such large and rapid changes. These include national boundaries, mass reliance on relatively few crops for food, and other environmental stresses caused by some six billion people. Human beings and their societies may well be threatened, not with extinction, but with severe disruption, and possibly catastrophic economic and social effects. This is especially so if we happen to cross a threshold which leads to rapid climate change of a magnitude and speed unparalleled since the Younger Dryas event, and one which cannot be quickly reversed.

The upshot of all these studies is that climate change of the magnitude we are expecting in the next 100 years and beyond has happened before, although usually at a much slower rate and from a cooler starting point. Projected changes in climate by 2100 are comparable to those from the last glaciation (20 000 years ago) to the present, which led to large rises in sea level, massive changes in plant and animal numbers and distribution, and changes in the land–sea borders. Some places changed from tundra to temperate forests, and others from forests to desert. Today we face similar change, but much faster, and from a base climate which is already as warm as any experienced since human societies began.

ENDNOTES

1. Much of the information on past climatic variations in this chapter is drawn from IPCC 2001 report, WG1, Chapter 2 'Observed Climate Variability and Change' and IPCC 2007, WG1, Chapters 2, 4, 6 and 9. Recommended references on paleo-climatology include RS Bradley, *Paleoclimatology: Reconstructing Climate of the Quaternary*, 2nd edn, International Geophysics Series, vol. 68, Harcourt Academic Press, San Diego (1999) and Thomas Crowley, *Paleoclimatology*, Oxford University Press, New York (1991). See also Fritts, *Tree Rings and Climate*, Blackburn Press, Caldwell, New Jersey (reprint 1991) regarding the use of tree rings, and the *Tree Ring Newsletter* at http://www.treeringsociety.org. The text *Quaternary Environments* by MAJ Williams and others, Edward Arnold, London, 2nd edn, (1998), is another excellent resource, with a detailed Appendix describing various methods for dating paleo-climatic records.

2. A more extensive table and discussion of proxy climate indicators is found in the NRC (2002) book on *Abrupt Climate Change* (see endnote 14).

3. Migration of ancient peoples across land bridges, and their subsequent isolation by sea-level rise, is discussed for the Australian region in Mulvaney and Kamminga, *Prehistory of Australia*, Allen & Unwin, Sydney (1999) and Mulvaney and Golson, *Aboriginal Man and Environment in Australia*, Australian National University Press, Canberra (1971). See also Bird and others, *Quaternary International*, **118–119**, pp. 145–63 (2004). Migration across the Bering Strait land bridge was once the favoured theory for North America, but it may have been by small boats along the then coast, see *Scientific American* (September 2000) pp. 62–7. The dispersal of people from the flooding of the Black Sea is discussed in Ryan and Pitman, *Marine Geology*, **138**, pp. 119–26 (1997), and in *Nature*, **430**, pp. 718–19 (12 August 2004).

4. The astronomical theory of the glacial–interglacial cycles is discussed in Frakes, *Climates Throughout Geological Time*, Elsevier, Amsterdam (1979), with key papers by Hays and others, *Science*, **194**, pp. 1121–32 (1976), Imbrie and others, *Paleoceanography*, **7**, pp. 701–38 (1992) and **8**, pp. 699–735 (1993), Shackleton, *Science*, **289**, pp. 1897–902 (2000), Ruddiman, *Quaternary Science Reviews*, **22**, pp. 1597–629 (2003) and *EOS*, **85** (6 January 2004). See also MAJ Williams and others, *Quaternary Environments*, Edward Arnold, London (1993).

5. Ruddiman's work on the role of greenhouse gases in the Milankovitch theory is reported in *EOS* (6 January 2004) and references therein. See also WE Ruddiman, *Plows, Plagues and Petroleum*, Princeton University Press, Princeton (2006).

6. The IPCC 2007 estimates of climate sensitivity to doubling of carbon dioxide concentrations are slightly higher than in the 2001 report. Instead of the bald statement that the range is likely between 1.5 and 4.5°C, it now qualifies this by saying that it is very unlikely to be less than 1.5°C but could be substantially higher than 4.5°C.

7. See Pittock in *Reviews of Geophysics and Space Physics*, **16**, pp. 400–20 (1978) and in *Quarterly Journal of the Royal Meteorological Society*, **109**, pp. 23–55 (1983). More recent studies include Thomas Crowley in *Science*, **289**, pp. 270–77 (2000); Judith Lean in *Geophysical Research Letters*, **19**, p. 1591 (1992); and Meehl and others, in *Journal of Climate*, **16**, pp. 426–44 (2003). Solar and volcanic influences are discussed in the IPCC 2007 report, WGI, Chapters 1.4.3 and 2.7.1.

8. The role of solar variability in climate is also discussed in Lean and Rind, *Science*, **292**, pp. 234–6 (2001), Philipona and Durr, *Geophysical Research Letters*, doi: 10.1029/2004GL020937, 2004) and Lockwood and Frohlich, 'Recent oppositely directed trends in solar climate forcing and the global mean surface temperature', *Proceedings Royal Society A*,

doi:10.1098/rspa.2007.1880 (2007). See also Damon and Lault in *EOS*, **85**, p. 370, (28 September 2004) for a discussion of how errors have been repeated in a series of papers claiming a strong role for solar forcing.

9. Possible climatic effects of a major nuclear war ('nuclear winter') are described in a special issue of *Ambio* (Royal Swedish Academy of Science), **18** (7) (1989), and in the SCOPE Report no. 28, *Environmental Consequences of Nuclear War*, John Wiley and Sons, Chichester (1986). Alvarez and others in *Science*, **208**, pp. 1095–108 (1980) discuss climatic effects of cosmic collisions with the Earth.

10. Possible effects of human emissions leading to increased particulates in the atmosphere and surface cooling were discussed by Reid Bryson and Wayne Wendland in *Global Effects of Environmental Pollution*, Fred Singer (ed.), pp. 130–38, D Reidel Publishers, Dordrecht (1970) and in the *Report of the Study of Man's Impact on Climate (SMIC)*, MIT Press, Cambridge, Massachusetts (1971).

11. Indirect aerosol effects were first discussed by Sean Twomey in 1977 in the *Journal of Atmospheric Sciences*, **34**, pp. 1149–52. Effects of volcanic emissions are discussed in a chapter by Alan Robock in *The State of the Planet: Frontiers and Challenges in Geophysics*, Geophysical Monograph 150, American Geophysical Union, Washington DC, pp. 125–34 (2004). See also: Robock and Oppenheimer (eds), *Volcanism and the Earth's Atmosphere*, Geophysical Monograph 139, American Geophysical Union, Washington DC (2003).

12. 'Global dimming' is in fact regional, not global, as documented by Pinhas Alpert and colleagues in *Geophysical Research Letters*, **32**, L17802 (2005).

13. Aerosol effects on climate are discussed extensively in the IPCC 2007 report, WGI, Chapters 2.4 and 7.5. More recently, possible effects of aerosols, primarily in the northern hemisphere, on the southern hemisphere climate have been documented in a series of papers by: Cai and others, *Geophysical Research Letters*, **33**, L21707, doi:10.1029/2006GL027513 (2006); Rotstayn and others, *Journal of Geophysical Research*, **112**, D09202, doi:10.1029/2006JD007712 (2007); and Cai and Cowan, *Geophysical Research Letters*, **34**, L23709, doi:10.1029/2007GL031706 (2007).

14. Rapid climate change events, including the Younger Dryas event, are discussed more fully in sections 6.4.2 and 6.5.2 of the IPCC 2007 report; a review by R Alley and others in *Science*, **299**, pp. 2005–10 (2003); and in the US National Research Council report *Abrupt Climate Change: Inevitable Surprises* (2002). See also MC MacCracken, F Moore and JC Topping Jr, *Sudden and Disruptive Climate Change*, Earthscan, London (2008). See also 'The physics of climate modelling', by GA Schmidt, in *Physics Today* (January 2007) pp. 72–3.

15. A discussion on the effect of climate change on human history, with numerous references, is found in Chapter 7 of Pittock and others (eds), *Climatic Change and Variability: A Southern Perspective*, Cambridge University Press (1978). See also: Reid Bryson and Thomas Murray, *Climates of Hunger*, University of Wisconsin Press (1977); Wigley, Ingram and Farmer (eds), *Climate and History*, Cambridge University Press (1981); Lamb, *Climate, History and the Modern World*, Methuen (1982); and Jones, Ogilvie, Davies and Briffa, *History and Climate: Memories of the Future?*, Kluwer Academic/Plenum Publishing (2001).

16. Huntington's book is *Civilization and Climate*, Yale University Press (1915).

17. See Carpenter, *Discontinuity in Greek Civilization* Cambridge University Press (1966), and Lamb, 'Climatic changes during the course of early Greek history', in *Antiquity*, **42**, pp. 231–3 (1968). Le Roy Ladurie's book is *Times of Feast, Times of Famine*, George Allen & Unwin (1971), and Doubleday (1972).

18. Dansgaard and colleagues 'Climatic changes, Norsemen and modern man', *Nature*, **255**, pp. 24–8 (1975). Singh's paper is in *Archaeology and Physical Anthropology in Oceania*, **6**, pp. 177–89 (1971).

19. Pacific Islander and Maori migrations are discussed by Finney in *Science*, **196**, pp. 1277–85 (1977); Wilson and Hendy in *Nature*, **234**, pp. 344–5 (1971); Bridgman in *Palaeogeography, Palaeoclimatology, Paleoecology*, **41**, pp. 193–206 (1983); and Patrick Nunn in *Geoarchaeology: An International Journal*, **15**, pp. 714–40 (2000), *Geografiska Annaler*, **85B**, pp. 219–29 (2003) and *Asia Pacific Viewpoint*, **44**, pp. 63–72 (2003).

20. See Chun Chang Huang and colleagues in *Climatic Change*, **61**, pp. 361–78 (2003).

21. The Anasazi, ancestors of the modern Pueblo Indians of the American South-west, were forced to migrate by drought. See *Anasazi America: Seventeen Centuries on the Road from Center Place* by David Stuart, University of New Mexico Press (2000), and review in *Science*, **290**, pp. 941–3 (3 November 2000).

22. See Haug and colleagues, *Science*, **299**, pp. 1731–5 (2003).

23. See de Menocal's review 'Cultural responses to climate change during the late Holocene' in *Science*, **292**, pp. 667–73 (2001); Rosenmeier and others, *Quaternary Reviews*, **57**, pp. 183–90 (2002), and references therein; and Foreman, Oglesby and Webb in *Global and Planetary Change*, **29**, pp. 1–29 (2001). Woodhouse and Overpeck, in *Bulletin American Meteorological Society*, **79**, pp. 2693–714 (1998), review drought in the same region over the last 2000 years. See also Trenberth and others, *EOS*, **85**, p. 20 (January 2004), and references therein.

24. Causes of the Saharan drying are examined in Claussen and colleagues, 'Simulation of an abrupt change in Saharan vegetation in the mid-Holocene', *Geophysical Research Letters*, **26**, pp. 2037–40 (1999) and Noblet-Ducoudre, Claussen and Prentice, in *Climate Dynamics*, **16**, pp. 643–59 (2000).

25. See Whitlock and colleagues in *Forest Ecology and Management*, **178**, pp. 5–21 (2003); Meyer and Pierce in *Forest Ecology and Management*, **178**, pp. 89–104 (2003); and Campbell and Campbell in *Palaeogeography, Palaeoclimatology, Palaeoecology*, **164**, pp. 263–80 (2003).

26. Sea-level change during the present interglacial is well covered in the IPCC 2007 report, WGI, Chapter 5.5. For more recent information see endnote 14 in Chapter 1.

27. For variations in regional sea level and its potential impacts on types of coasts see IPCC 2007 report, WGI, Chapters 5.5.4 and WGII, Chapter 6.4.1.1 and references therein.

28. A number of papers have connected deglaciation with the onset of earthquakes in close proximity to former ice masses. See R Arvidsson, 'Fennoscandian earthquakes: whole crustal rupturing related to postglacial rebound', *Science*, **274**, pp. 744–6 (1996); Muir-Wood, 'Deglaciation seismotectonics: a principal influence on intraplate seismogenesis at high latitudes', *Quaternary Science Reviews*, **19**, pp. 1399–411 (2000); Stewart and others 'Glacio-seismotectonics: ice sheets, crustal deformation and seismicity', *Quarternary Science Reviews*, **19**, pp. 1367–91 (2000); and P Wu, P Johnston and K Lambeck, 'Postglacial rebound and fault instability in Fennoscandia', *Geophysical Journal International*, **139**, pp. 657–70 (1999).

29. See Soon and Baliunas, *Climate Research*, **23**, pp. 89–110 (2003), and rebuttal by Mann and others in *EOS*, **84** (27) pp. 256–57. There is a further attack on the temperature reconstructions in Figure 1 by McIntyre and McKitrick in *Energy and Environment*, **14**, pp. 751–71 (2003). This centres on the different selection and correction of data. Mann and co-authors are the recognised experts in this field, and thus best qualified to make the expert judgements on data quality and representativeness needed. Mann and Jones in *Geophysical Research Letters*, **30** (15) pp. 1820–3 (2003) have extended the temperature reconstruction back to 2000 years. See other discussions in IPCC 2007 report, WGI, Chapters 3.2 and 6.6, and on various commentary websites such as that of the UK Royal Society at http://royalsociety.org/page.asp?id=6229, Real Climate at http://www.realclimate.org/ and the Australian Climate Change Department's 'Frequently Asked Questions' at http://www.climatechange.gov.au/science/faq/index.html.

30. See Hans von Storch and others, *Science*, **306**, pp. 679–82 and comment pp. 621–2 (22 October 2004); and Osborn and Briffa, *Science*, **306**, pp. 621–2 (2004). See also the discussion in IPCC 2007 report, WGI, Chapter 6.6.

3

Projecting the future

Foresight provides the ability to influence the future rather than to predict it.

RICHARD FREEMAN.

*As we know, there are known knowns. There are things we know we know. We also know
there are known unknowns. That is to say we know there are some things we do not know.
But there are also unknown unknowns, the ones we don't know we don't know.*

DONALD RUMSFELD, US SECRETARY OF DEFENSE, NEWS BRIEFING 12 FEBRUARY 2002.

*The scenarios point to both risks and opportunities in the future. Of particular significance
are the risks of crossing thresholds, the potential of reaching turning points in the
relationship between people and the environment, and the need to account for interlinkages
in pursuing a more sustainable path.*

GLOBAL ENVIRONMENTAL OUTLOOK 4, UNEP 2007.

The need for, and nature of, foresight

While I am not a fan of Donald Rumsfeld, I think the quote above from one of his news briefings drew some rather unfair lambasting. It summarises, if one concentrates on its meaning and applies it to climate change, some important aspects of the science of climate change as well as defence policy questions. That is, there is a whole range of aspects of climate change, with some much more certain than others. There are also uncertainties and possibilities we are aware of, and may even be able to quantify in terms of risk. But, there is also a possibility that there are things about climate that we simply do not know, and which may totally surprise us.

The Intergovernmental Panel on Climate Change (IPCC) was formed to provide foresight in relation to the possible human impacts on climate, with a view to helping governments formulate wiser policy options and decisions in relation to climate change. Foresight is the act or power of seeing into the future, a perception gained by looking forward, and care or provision for the future. It is an everyday occurrence. Prudent people use foresight to decide or plan their actions so as to improve their future prospects. In this spirit governments around the world have recognised that human societies, through their use of resources and waste products are capable of changing the environment, including the climate.

Foresight requires some estimate of future conditions. In the case of climate change this includes projections of future emissions of greenhouse gases and particulates into the atmosphere, consequent concentrations of these pollutants in the atmosphere, and their effects on the climate. In addition, so as to understand how serious this might be, estimates are also needed of the consequences for society in terms of potential impacts on areas such as agriculture, water supply, health and building safety and comfort. This is complicated by the fact that impacts depend not just on the stresses applied by climate, but also on the strength and adaptability of society. This requires an understanding of how changes in society will affect its capacity to absorb or adapt to climatic stress.

There are other complicating factors in any attempt to project the future, namely non-linearities and thresholds. Non-linearities are when steady inputs to a system cause unsteady outputs. For example, steady effort to push a bicycle up a steady hill gives easily predictable progress, but if the slope changes, and especially if the top of the hill is reached, rapid changes in the bicycle's progress can occur. Similarly, if a flood is rising results are predictable until it reaches the top of a levee bank, when overtopping may erode the levee, causing it to collapse, and a consequent disaster. Simple extrapolation is not good enough. Predictions of what will happen must take such irregularities and thresholds in the system into account. We will discuss this further in the context of climate change in Chapter 5.

There are, as viewed from the present, many possible futures. How we foresee the future possibilities, and the conscious or unconscious choices we make that will influence development of society, will help determine which of the possible futures will actually occur. The purpose, from a policy perspective, is not to predict which of the possible futures will occur, but rather to inform us so that we might choose which one we would prefer and attempt to bring to reality.

Predictions, scenarios and projections

People are often confused by various terms used to characterise future climate changes, namely 'predictions', 'scenarios' and 'projections'. A prediction is a statement that something *will* happen in the future, based on known conditions at the time the prediction is made, and assumptions as to the physical or other processes that will lead to change. Such predictions are seldom certain because present conditions are often not known precisely, and the processes affecting the future are not perfectly understood. Predictions are thus best expressed with probabilities attached. Daily weather forecasts are 'predictions' in this sense – they are predictions of what the weather will be like, but have uncertainties due to inexact observations and weather models. They are often expressed in probabilistic terms, such as 'There is a 60% chance of rain tomorrow'.

A scenario is a plausible description of some future state, with no statement of probability. It is used to enable people to explore the question 'What if such and such were to happen?' Scenarios are often used in literature to stretch the imagination, and increasingly in businesses and government to help to develop a range of strategies or contingency plans to cope with possible changes in business or other conditions. Scenarios are alternative pictures of how the future might develop. They are used to assess consequences, and thus to provide a basis for policies that might influence future developments, or enable businesses or governments to cope with the future situation if and when it occurs. Examples might include businesses planning for various possible future developments like a new competitor, a fire, or a failure of the electricity supply. No one knows when or if these contingencies or scenarios may happen, but the business needs plans in place to ensure survival if they do happen.

Projections are sets of future conditions, or consequences, based on explicit assumptions, such as scenarios. For example, in the case of a business faced with loss of production due to a fire, how much production would be lost, how soon can it be recovered, and how will it affect contracts and the solvency of the company? Even for a given scenario or set of assumptions, projections introduce further uncertainties due to the use of inexact rules or 'models' connecting the scenario conditions to the projected outcomes. Thus, a climate model can project the future climate based on a given scenario for future greenhouse gas emissions, and a crop model may project how this would affect yield. Such projections are conditional on the scenario and the models used.

A key issue in projecting the future on the basis of a scenario is the plausibility of the scenario. If a scenario is not plausible it is not worth worrying about in setting policy, but if it is plausible we may need to take its possibility into account. Scenario plausibility has several elements: that the scenario must be logically, physically, biologically, and historically possible.[1]

Plausible scenarios are useful for asking 'What if ...' questions, and thus for helping to make policy choices that may influence which of the 'what ifs' actually comes to pass. In the climate change context they are useful for influencing policy regarding the need to reduce greenhouse gas emissions. If reducing greenhouse gas emissions is costly, the urgency and extent of such reductions depends not just on the possibility of a scenario, but also on its probability. The probability of projections based on given scenarios is therefore a legitimate issue.[2]

Even in the absence of estimated probabilities, scenarios are also of use in relation to adaptation policy (that is, how to cope with unavoidable climate change) in that they suggest what conditions we might need to adapt to in future. Scenarios help us to anticipate what sort of adaptations might be needed, and to identify the need for increased resilience (capacity to bounce back) and adaptive capacity (capacity to adapt to change). However, in order to answer specific planning questions like 'How large should the spillway of a new dam at location x be in order to cope with the maximum possible flood at that location in 2070?' it is necessary to know more than that a given change in rainfall is *possible*. Rather, the *probability* of such a change needs to be known, since expensive engineering design needs to be based on cost-effective risk minimisation.

Climate change projections based on high-emission scenarios for greenhouse gases may, hopefully, be seen in retrospect as self-denying prophecies: if high emissions demonstrably lead to disastrous impacts, they may well be avoided through policy settings aimed at lowering emissions. This would be the logical outcome of a proper and well-informed risk-management strategy.

The emissions scenarios used by the IPCC

In order to provide policy-relevant advice on the consequences of human-induced climate change in the twenty-first century, the IPCC commissioned a range of scenarios of greenhouse gas and sulfate aerosol emissions up to the year 2100. These emission scenarios were developed by a panel of authors, with wide consultation, and an open process of review and comment by experts and governments, followed by subsequent revisions. The scenarios were reported in the 'Special report on emissions scenarios' (SRES), published in 2000. They were intended to feed into projections of climate change in the *Third Assessment Report* in 2001, and to enable a discussion of the potential impacts, adaptations and vulnerability of sectors, regions and countries.[3]

Future emissions are the product of complex interacting systems driven by population change, socio-economic development, and technological change. All of which are highly uncertain, especially when extended as far as the year 2100.

The original 40 SRES scenarios were based on four different 'storylines' of internally consistent developments across different driving forces (see **Box 3**), and multiple modelling approaches. This led to a reduced total of 35 scenarios containing data on all gases required to force climate models. Resulting accumulated emissions by 2100, expressed in units of thousands of millions of tonnes of carbon equivalent (Gtc) range from a low of 770 Gtc to approximately 2540 Gtc. This range compares with previous IPCC projections from 1992 and 1995 (based on what is known as the IS92 scenarios), which range from 770 to 2140 Gtc, so the upper end of the SRES projected range was greater than before. Accumulated emissions are an important indicator of eventual climatic effects because the effective

BOX 3: THE SRES EMISSIONS SCENARIOS

A1. The A1 storyline and group of related scenarios describe a future world of very rapid economic growth, global population that peaks in mid-century and declines thereafter, and the rapid introduction of new and more efficient technologies. Major underlying themes are convergence among regions, capacity building and increased cultural and social interactions, with a substantial reduction in regional differences in per capita income. The A1 group scenario is split into three groups that describe alternative directions of technological change in the energy system. The three A1 groups are distinguished by their technological emphasis: fossil intensive (A1FI), non-fossil energy sources (A1T), or a balance across all sources (A1B) (where balanced is defined as not relying too heavily on one particular energy source, on the assumption that similar improvement rates apply to all energy supply and end-use technologies).

A2. The A2 storyline and group of scenarios describe a very heterogeneous world. The underlying theme is self-reliance and preservation of local identities. Fertility patterns across regions converge very slowly, which results in continuously increasing population. Economic development is primarily oriented to particular regions and per capita economic growth and technological change more fragmented and slower than other storylines.

B1. The B1 storyline and group of scenarios describe a convergent world with the same global population that peaks in mid-century and declines thereafter, as in the A1 storyline but with rapid change in economic structures toward a service and information economy, with reductions in material intensity and the introduction of clean and resource-efficient technologies. The emphasis is on global solutions to economic, social and environmental sustainability, including improved equity, but without additional climate initiatives.

B2. The B2 storyline and group of scenarios describe a world in which the emphasis is on local solutions to economic, social and environmental sustainability. It is a world with continuously increasing global population, at a rate lower than A2, intermediate levels of economic development, and less rapid and more diverse technological change than in the A1 and B1 storylines. While the scenario is also oriented toward environmental protection and social equity, it focuses on local and regional levels.

Source: IPCC 2001 Working Group I, Box 4 of Technical Summary.

lifetime of carbon dioxide in the atmosphere is so long that this figure largely determines eventual carbon dioxide concentrations and the resulting global warming.

Corresponding projected carbon dioxide concentrations for the illustrative scenarios in the year 2100 range from 540 to 970 ppm, that is, roughly 2 to 3.5 times pre-industrial levels. As the scenarios only went to 2100 and concentrations had not stabilised by then, stabilised concentrations are likely to be well in excess of these numbers.

The SRES scenarios include estimated emissions of carbon dioxide, methane, nitrous oxide and sulfur dioxide. Generally, the SRES emission scenarios contain higher upper limits on carbon dioxide emissions, but lower emissions of sulfur dioxide than the previous IS92 scenarios. The higher upper limit carbon dioxide emissions would increase the upper limits of global warming due to increased infra-red absorption, but a large part of the increase in warming relative to earlier scenarios comes from the lower sulfur dioxide emissions, which lead to reduced regional cooling by sulfate aerosols in highly industrialised regions such as Europe, the United States and southern and eastern Asia.

Explicit policy options to reduce greenhouse emissions, such as might be adopted under the United Nations Framework Convention on Climate Change (UNFCCC), were excluded from the SRES scenarios. However, other socio-economic and technological trends considered by the SRES lead in some cases to considerable reductions in greenhouse gas and/or sulfur emissions. These scenarios were all characterised by the SRES as 'plausible', but no further estimates of probability were attached, and indeed estimates of probability would be difficult to derive with any confidence. They are clearly not predictions, and do not have equal probability of occurrence in the real world.

Some critics, mainly statistical economists, argued on technical grounds, related to how currency exchange rates between countries are calculated, that the high emissions scenarios were unrealistic. However, carbon dioxide emissions are related, in the final analysis, simply to population, energy use per capita and carbon dioxide emissions per unit energy. Thus the use of different exchange rates in measuring gross domestic product makes no difference to calculated emissions in each individual country. Whether or not it makes any difference globally depends on how the national figures are combined to get global ones, that is, whether the addition is done before or after emissions are calculated. National emissions depend on national energy use and the carbon per unit energy, not on how the national economy is measured.[4]

In any case, the critics miss the real point, which is that the SRES scenarios are not predictions, but merely a plausible range of emissions, used to bound discussion of climate change impacts. Moreover, the climate models used to produce the projections of climate change that underlie the IPCC assessment are developed and validated separately from the emissions scenarios. Any re-assessment of the range of the SRES scenarios may affect the upper and/or lower bounds of the projected climate change over the next 100 years, but are most unlikely to alter the main conclusions that significant climate change is likely to occur, with significant impacts. The SRES emissions projections were drawn from the published literature, and consistent with it, including several more recent studies that used more sophisticated models than were available at the time the SRES scenarios were developed.

The IPCC 2007 report adopts the SRES scenarios (see Chapter 10.2 of WGI) but does not model in detail the outcomes of the A1FI or fossil fuel intensive scenarios. Although no explanation is given for this omission, it is evidently in part a response to the criticism of A1FI as an 'extreme' or unrealistic scenario.

However, estimates and measurements of greenhouse gas emissions and carbon dioxide concentrations in the atmosphere, documented by Stefan Rahmstorf and others in 2007, show that since 1990 (the starting date for the SRES scenarios) emissions and concentrations have been at or above the highest of the SRES scenarios, the A1FI or fossil fuel intensive scenario. Indeed, global average temperatures and sea-level rise have also risen faster since 1990 than that calculated on the basis of all but the highest of the SRES senarios.[5] Mike Raupach of CSIRO, Australia, notes (personal communication) that the 50-year average growth rate for carbon dioxide emissions to 2050 under the A1FI scenario is 2.4% per annum, whereas the observed growth rate from 2000 to 2006 was 3.3% per annum.

As a number of papers have shown, the reasons for this are several. They include faster rates of growth of the economies of developing countries, especially China and India, than many economists thought possible. There has also been a reversal in the downward trend in emissions per unit economic growth ('carbon intensity') since 2000, and an increase in the fraction of emissions that stay in the atmosphere (the 'airborne fraction') due to decreases in the natural carbon sinks. Peter Sheehan of Victoria University in Melbourne, Australia, estimates that, with unchanged policies, global coal use will rise by nearly 60% over the decade to 2010 and that global emissions of carbon dioxide from fossil fuel combustion are likely to nearly double their 2000 level by 2020. This exceeds the IPCC fossil fuel intensive scenario.[5] The global economic crisis of 2008 may change this picture.

Emissions of chemicals, mainly sulfur dioxide and hydrogen sulfide from the burning of fossil fuels, lead to the formation of sulfate aerosols, which have a localised cooling effect and also cause urban air pollution and acid rain. Historically, such emissions have been concentrated in the large industrial regions of the United States, Europe and southern and eastern Asia. The resulting localised cooling has counteracted or masked some of the warming due to increasing greenhouse gas concentrations in and immediately downwind of these regions. However, it has been relatively easy to reduce these aerosol-forming emissions by the use of low-sulfur fuels and scrubbing of the combustion fumes. This is well under way in the United States and Europe, but not to the same extent in southern and eastern Asia. SRES scenarios project continuing reductions in aerosols in North America and Europe, and also in Asia in coming decades.

The result of these changes in sulfur emissions and aerosol levels is that the masking effect on enhanced greenhouse warming is rapidly disappearing over North America and Europe, as seen in recent record warmth in these regions. A similar effect is expected to occur later over Asia, and is one reason for a projected increase in the rate of global warming. This is one reason why the resulting projected global warming in the IPCC 2001 and 2007 reports are larger than in the *Second Assessment Report* in 1995, when a less rapid reduction in sulfur emissions was expected.

Several other factors that may impact on projections have not been taken into account in the SRES scenarios, as is evident from the discussion above regarding the A1FI scenario, which must now be considered moderate rather than extreme unless emissions reduction policies are implemented. Other factors include the emission of carbon black particles, largely from open fires such as wildfires,

land clearing and burning of stubble. Such emissions have short lifetimes in the atmosphere, but seasonally they can be large and may have significant regional surface warming effects. Any increase in wildfires may increase this effect.

Another factor is the effect of land clearing, farming and irrigation on absorption or reflection of sunlight at the land surface. Again, this varies regionally, but is in general only important in limited areas of the continents. Its main effect is on local surface heating and the effect of this on cumulus convection, although this can have downwind effects on the weather if the area concerned is large. Climate model calculations have found that this effect may be important where large forest areas are being cleared, such as in the Amazon Basin, and ideally it should be included in climate change simulations. Land clearing can in general be reversed in most areas, and indeed some farmlands in developed countries have recently reverted to forests. Scenarios of land-use change are being developed in consultation with the IPCC.

Irrigation also affects surface climate via the cooling effect of evaporation, and also by injecting moisture into the atmosphere. But again, the areas are relatively small, especially in comparison with the area of the oceans, so they have little effect on large area and global water budgets. Climatic effects of irrigation are essentially local. Moreover, while evaporation has a local cooling effect, it results in latent heat being transported elsewhere in the atmosphere, and it is released as sensible heat (that is, heat felt as a higher temperature) where condensation occurs.

The IPCC 2007 report considers the effects of climate change on the global carbon cycle that lead to the land biosphere and the oceans both taking up less carbon dioxide than if these effects are ignored. For the A2 emissions scenario in the middle of the SRES range the feedback of climate change on the carbon cycle leads to an additional 20 to 220 parts per million of carbon dioxide in the atmosphere by 2100 depending on the model. This means that global warming will be greater than with the standard simulations for a given emissions scenario, and that greater emissions reduction are required to achieve the same stabilisation level of carbon dioxide in the atmosphere.

It also discusses the effect of acidification of the oceans by increasing carbon dioxide and that this will probably reduce the capacity of the oceans to absorb carbon dioxide, as will a slowdown in vertical mixing in the oceans as the surface warms faster than the deep water. These latter effects have not yet been fully quantified.[6]

Projections of socio-economic futures

An important consideration in estimating potential impacts of climate change is the future exposure of populations, human systems and ecosystems to climatically induced stresses, and the capacity of those so exposed to adapt to the stresses. With the notable exception of the UK Fast Track project, this has been largely neglected, with only the most general comments on likely changes in exposure and the capacity of societies to absorb or adapt to climate changes.[7] For example, sea-level rise and storm surges are likely to cause more damage in particular low-lying coastal zones where populations and investments are tending to increase most rapidly. Wealth versus poverty also affects adaptive capacity, for example, the capacity to pay for adequate protective sea walls or levees for protection against floods, as in New Orleans in 2005.

As stated by Edward Parsons and colleagues in reference to the 2001 US National Assessment of Potential Consequences of Climate Variability and Change, constructing socio-economic scenarios for impact assessment is more complex and challenging than constructing scenarios of future emissions.[8] Emissions scenarios require only a few national-level characteristics such as population, economic growth, total energy use, and carbon emissions per unit economic output. However, socio-economic determinants of vulnerability and adaptation to climate change can be very localised, may not be obvious, and interact strongly with other factors such as social organisation and technological progress. Local vulnerability may be linked with international competition and commodity prices, which in turn may be affected by changes elsewhere.

Ideally, socio-economic scenarios used to estimate future emissions of greenhouse gases should be used at the local or regional scale as the basis for consistent estimates of exposure and adaptive capacity. The SRES scenarios contain such data at a broad regional level, for example in 13 world regions for scenarios A1, B1 and A2 and 11 regions for scenario B2, although these data have not been widely used in impact studies. It is complicated, however, by the fact that different global socio-economic scenarios may lead to similar magnitudes of climate change globally and regionally but with different regional exposures and adaptive capacities.

The global SRES socio-economic scenarios have been reduced to a national scale by Stuart Gaffin for the United States and Wolfgang Lutz for Austria. Additionally, the UK Fast Track project went on to produce finer resolution data at a sub-national scale in order to estimate and map global impacts of climate change on a number of industrial and societal sectors. However, downscaling was often based on assumed uniform behaviour across each nation. Generally, the socio-economic data have not been provided at the space scales appropriate to specific regions that may be at risk, for example, estimates of vulnerability and adaptability to sea-level rise on rapidly developing coastal strips in the south-eastern US, south-eastern China or north-eastern Australia.

In the case of coastal exposure to sea-level rise and storm surges, existing trends make it reasonable to assume greater growth rates in population and investment in coastal areas than in national averages. This affects not only the exposure, but also the rate of localised sea-level rise, since greater coastal populations tend to withdraw more ground water, leading to greater local subsidence.

Scenarios of future population changes are well documented by both the United Nations and the International Institute of Applied Systems Analysis

(IIASA), although the UN studies tend to be broad scale. They were downscaled to the national level by IIASA. There is a convenient discussion entitled 'The end of world population growth' by Wolfgang Lutz of IIASA, which suggests that global population is likely to peak in the twenty-first century, with early declines in many developed countries, but continued growth mainly in the poorest countries of Africa and southern Asia until later in the century. Joel Cohen of Rockefeller University also projects population trends until 2050, and emphasises the importance of migration from the poorer to the richer countries.[9] Migration is discussed again in Chapters 6 and 10, where we consider the potential impacts of climate change, and especially sea-level rise, on migration for economic and environmental reasons.

The United Nations Environment Programme has published a series of Global Environment Outlooks. The latest, published in 2007, looks at environmental change and related policies and provides an outlook up to 2050. It takes four contrasting socio-economic scenarios:

- markets first, in which most of the world adopts the values and expectations prevailing in today's industrialised countries,

- policy first, where decisive initiatives are taken by governments trying to reach specific social and environmental goals,

- security first, in which there is a world of striking disparities, where inequality and conflict prevail, and

- sustainability first, in which a new environment and development paradigm emerges in response to the challenge of sustainability.[10]

As might be expected, the effect in relation to greenhouse gas emissions is that the first and third scenarios, lacking effective environmental policies, lead to significant increases in greenhouse gases by 2050. The policy first scenario leads to actual reductions in emissions starting around 2030, while the sustainability first scenario leads to a decline by the mid-2020s. Different environmental outcomes in other areas will also clearly affect societal capacity to adapt. But in all four scenarios atmospheric carbon dioxide concentrations are still increasing and sea-level rise is still accelerating in 2050. Thus one of the most significant lessons drawn from the scenario exercise by the authors is that much of the environmental change that will occur over the next several decades has already been set in motion by past and current actions. Nevertheless, the authors conclude that: 'the scenarios clearly illustrate that the future that will unfold in the long-term will be very dependent on the decisions individuals and society make today'.

Some idea of future exposure and adaptive capacity could be based on various scenarios of regional population growth and socio-economic conditions contained in various foresighting studies already undertaken. Nevertheless, the broad storylines of the global SRES scenarios need to be borne in mind when assessing likely exposure and adaptive capacity at the local level.

It may be more relevant for many local or national studies, to use local scenarios for socio-economic development in that country. These may capture some of the relevant detail about internal shifts in growth patterns, and community dependence on local industries, which may be affected by technological change or global commodity prices. Some of these local scenarios also have policy relevance, although their consistency with global scenarios is problematic. This may not be critical, however, since any global scenario, such as the SRES scenarios, will not apply uniformly in regard to socio-economic changes, so that local departures from the broad-scale scenarios may not greatly affect global emissions and resulting climate changes.

For example, two closely related reports for the Australian Business Foundation aimed 'to identify alternative, plausible scenarios for the future of business in Australia' and explored four alternative scenarios styled 'Sound the Retreat', 'Brave Old World', 'First Global Nation' and 'Green is Gold'. The last dealt explicitly with global environmental concerns.[11]

Another study, commissioned by the Business Council of Australia, was called 'Population Futures', Australian Academy of Technological Sciences and Engineering (2001). This aimed to assess the environmental constraints to population growth in Australia, out to 2050, and to assess technological, behavioural, pricing and settlement planning interventions that might be used to manage population-related environmental issues. Its focus was more on what impact an increased population might have on the environment, rather than on what influence environmental problems, such as climate change, might have on the human population.

An ongoing Australian study by the Resources Futures Program of CSIRO Sustainable Ecosystems has an integrated approach where interactions between the environment and population are simulated. This study aims essentially at providing insight into options for Australia's population, technology, resources and environment to 2050 with an emphasis on sustainability. It looks at the consequences of low, medium and high population growth rates, and explores the consequences for people, urban infrastructure, the natural environment, energy, water and a range of other issues.[12] Amongst the conclusions of their 2002 report 'Future dilemmas' was a need to recognise that:

- Australia's social, economic and physical systems are linked over very long time scales,

- short-term decisions have long-term consequences, and

- there is inbuilt inertia in our institutional systems, requiring time for change to take effect.

These conclusions apply in many places besides Australia, and are themes reflected in the various IPCC Assessment Reports. They suggest that any realistic assessment of the overall impacts of climate change on any local or national community, and of its capacity to cope with or adapt to climate change, will need to integrate studies of socio-economic futures with climate change studies. They are all part of an interconnected future.

To date very few international climate impacts studies have taken different possible socio-economic futures into account although alternative socio-economic scenarios are central to the IPCC SRES emissions scenarios. These and other issues are discussed in the 2007 IPCC report, WGII, Chapter 2.4.6 and are a key to realistic impacts and adaptation studies.

Forecasting the weather

Foresight is routinely used in regard to the weather, and affects many of our day-to-day decisions. It is therefore useful to compare the basis for weather forecasting with that for climate projections, in order to understand both what they have in common and what the differences are.

Weather forecasting used to be based on experience with past situations, which developed into changed weather patterns that experts could either remember or look up from past records. This was called 'analogue forecasting', that is using the past as an analogue for the future. During and after the Second World War, things started to change with the use of growing theoretical understanding of how weather disturbances grow, move and decay. Quantitative calculations of how the atmosphere changes were pioneered by Lewis Fry Richardson, an English Quaker schoolteacher and scientist who, by hand, calculated solutions to the governing equations of motion and continuity of matter to produce the first numerical weather forecast. His work, done in the trenches as an ambulance worker in the First World War, was published in 1922.[13]

However, Richardson's calculation was not very accurate, and application of his methods had to wait for the development of large electronic computers. John von Neumann and Jules Charney took up the challenge at Princeton University just after the Second World War, using one of the first electronic computers. The first computer-based weather forecasts were issued in 1955.

It quickly became apparent that the skill of numerical weather forecasting decreases rapidly with time into the future. Mathematical theory, developed by Edward Lorenz of Massachusetts Institute of Technology demonstrated that the accuracy of forecasts declines due to the growth of errors present in the initial input data. Known as 'chaos theory', this shows that small differences in initial conditions, such as those that arise from imperfect observations of the present weather, lead to larger and larger errors with time. Lorenz used the analogy of a pinball machine to explain what happens.[14]

In a pinball machine, a rolling ball hits a post (or pin) and bounces off in a straight line until it strikes a second pin, then a third and so on. Lorenz considered that if the ball, in its initial motion, ran over a small piece of dust it would be slightly deflected, striking the pin at a slightly different angle. After several such strikes the ball would be travelling in a sufficiently different direction to miss a pin that it would have hit in the no-dust case, so that the predictability of which pins it would strike later on would rapidly decrease. The predictability is critically dependent on knowing exactly what path the ball takes in its first encounter, and the more accurately that is known the more strikes could be accurately predicted. However, if the experiment were repeated many times, an average path could be found, and it would be possible to say how probable it was that the ball would strike a particular pin. Thus it would not be possible to predict with complete confidence which pin would be hit, but from repeated observations the probabilities of striking various pins could be determined.

Weather forecasting is a similar type of initial value problem, that is, one in which the eventual outcome depends on how accurately the initial conditions are known. Any error in specifying the initial conditions is amplified (that is, made larger) and eventually leads to a breakdown in predictability of the exact outcome, although it may result in the ability to predict the probability of various outcomes, that is, to predict the statistics of the weather. Lorenz and others showed that the limit of predictability of particular weather is about three weeks.

Progress towards improved weather forecasts is partly due to better observations of initial conditions, and more accurate calculations that minimise any rounding-off errors. Thus numerical weather models calculate properties of the atmosphere to many decimal places to slow down the propagation of errors. Repeated model calculations of the same situation with imperceptibly different initial conditions can also provide multiple forecasts, with the average usually being more reliable than a single forecast. This is known as 'ensemble forecasting'.

Other improvements in weather forecasting have come from the incorporation of heat and moisture exchange between the atmosphere and the oceans, assisted by satellite observations of sea-surface temperatures. The fact that the skill of numerical weather prediction has improved over the years is testimony to improved observations of initial conditions (including satellite observations), the growing understanding of how the atmosphere and oceans combine to produce weather, and to how this is incorporated into computer models.[15]

Why climate projections are different

Numerical prediction of climate is a different problem, even though it starts with the same equations governing atmospheric motion and continuity of matter (the amount of air and water in the atmosphere). There are two main differences:

- First, climate projections are not about predicting the exact weather at any time in the future, but rather about projecting the statistics (average behaviour and variability) of the future weather. This reduces the relevance of short-term chaotic behaviour in the atmosphere.

- Second, because climate projections are about the statistics of weather many months, years or even centuries into the future, much slower influences on the weather or climate must be taken into account, and indeed tend to dominate the picture.

Thus the propagation of errors in initial conditions is not important, but rather the knowledge of slower internal variations in the climate system, and so-called 'boundary conditions' and how they may change. Slower internal variations include exchanges of heat, salt and chemicals such as carbon dioxide with the deep ocean, and the growth and decay of ice sheets and glaciers. **Figure 11** shows some of the components that are included in the internal part of a climate model. Others, not shown, include interactive soil and vegetation, atmospheric chemistry, and cloud interactions with particles (aerosols).[16]

External factors include changes in atmospheric and land surface properties, variations in the orbit of the Earth around the Sun, solar variability and volcanic eruptions (which put gases and particles into the atmosphere). Some of these external factors can be specified as inputs or boundary conditions to the climate models, rather than calculated. However, they can be calculated internally in an enlarged climate system, if they can be predicted and the equations can be added to the model. As computers become bigger, faster and cheaper, more and more that used to be external to the climate models can now be incorporated into the models and thus predicted rather than given as external boundary conditions.

How good are climate models?

Two or three decades ago most climate models considered the oceans to be external and used prescribed sea-surface temperatures at the bottom of the atmosphere. Results were conditional on the assumed sea-surface temperatures. Today, faster computers enable nearly all climate models to have an interactive ocean, and indeed ocean currents and deep water temperatures are calculated. Historically, the scientific literature is full of papers describing simulations of climate using models of varying complexity and detail, and it is important in reading these papers to understand just what is calculated and what is given as assumed input. It is also important not to rely on outdated assessments of the skill of climate models, which tends to occur in the critiques of climate modelling by some who question climate change. Citing out-of-date assessments of climate models ignores recent improvements in modelling and shows a lack of appreciation of how much work has gone into improving their accuracy.

A range of different types of climate models are available, and various names or abbreviations are used to indicate differences in their complexity. For example, there are very simple 'energy balance

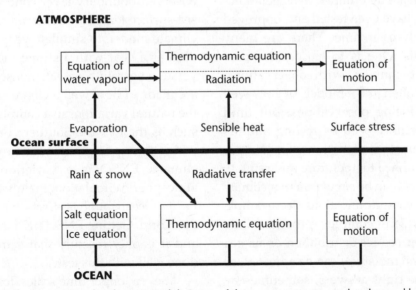

Figure 11: Some internal components of a climate model. Some of these components can be changed by external forces (such as variations in the Earth's orbit around the Sun or in solar radiation) or changes in the composition and radiative properties of the atmosphere (such as the addition of more greenhouse gases or particles of dust). (After John Mitchell, UK Meteorological Office, 2003.)[17]

models' which calculate only the incoming and outgoing energy into the climate system to determine the Earth's global average surface temperature, or that in latitude bands. These ignore lots of internal processes and do not give outputs useful at particular locations on Earth, but they are quick and cheap to use and are often used to study a wide range of conditions.

Next there are 'atmospheric general circulation models' or AGCMs. These calculate what goes on in the atmosphere, including changes to cloud cover and properties, but have prescribed or given sea-surface temperatures. Thus, they do not allow for changes in the ocean climate (currents, and temperature and salinity with location and depth).

Today nearly all climate models used for climate projections have fully interactive oceans. These are called 'coupled atmosphere–ocean general circulation models' or AOGCMs, and usually include calculations of sea-ice cover. Even so, there are still many external components of the climate system that are only gradually being internalised into climate models, even where these components act on and are changed by the climate. These components include glaciers, continental ice sheets, and surface properties, such as surface roughness and reflectivity that are determined by vegetation.

Climate models have been tested and improved quite systematically over time. There are many ways of doing this. One is to closely compare simulated present climates with observations. Climate modellers often judge models by how well they do in reproducing observations, but until recently this has mainly been by testing outputs from models against observations for simple variables such as surface temperature and rainfall. However, this process can be circular in that climate models, with all their simplifications (for example in how they represent complex processes like cumulus convection, sea-ice distribution or air–sea exchange of heat and moisture) can be adjusted, or 'tuned', to give the right answers, sometimes by making compensating errors. Such errors might then lead to serious differences from reality in some other variable not included in the tests. Comparing simulated outputs for many more variables, some of which were not used to tune the models, now checks this.

Other tests used include how well the climate models simulate variations in climate over the daily cycle, for example daily maximum and minimum temperatures, or depth of the well-mixed surface layer of the atmosphere. Changes in average cloud cover and rainfall with time of day are other more sophisticated variables that are sometimes tested.

Related tests involve calculating in the models variables that can be compared with satellite observations, such as cloud cover and energy radiated back to space from the top of the atmosphere. Until recently many climate models have not done very well on some of these tests, but they are improving.[18]

To test longer time-scale variations, tests are made of how well climate models simulate the annual cycle of the seasons. Different test locations from those the model builders may have looked at when building their models are often used. For example, how well does an Australian climate model perform over Europe, or a European model perform over Africa?

A popular test is to use a climate model with observed boundary layer conditions, for example sea-surface temperatures in an atmospheric global climate model, to simulate year-to-year variations such as a year with a strong monsoon over India versus a year with a weak monsoon. Similarly, tests are made of how well a climate model reproduces the natural variations in a complex weather pattern such as the El Niño-Southern Oscillation (ENSO), which is important in year-to-year variations in climate. ENSO is a variation in oceanic and atmospheric circulation, mainly across the tropical Pacific Ocean, but has effects in many other parts of the world. Getting ENSO right is an important test, and it is only recently that some AOGCMs have done well with this test.

At even longer time scales, tests can be made as to how well climate models can reproduce paleo-climatic variations. This is only possible where changes in external conditions can be well specified, such as changes in solar energy input, atmospheric composition, land–sea distribution and surface properties. It is also necessary to have lots of paleo-evidence for climate patterns at the time being simulated to see if the climate models reproduce it well. This is a tall order, but nevertheless paleo-modelling is useful as a test of climate models, and also helps us to understand and test theories of what causes climate fluctuations and what is possible.

In order to provide climate change projections relevant to many local and regional climate change impacts, climate models need to provide output at finer and finer spatial scales. That is, where global climate models a decade back only gave output data on climate changes at distances several hundred kilometres apart, for many purposes the need is for data at locations only a few tens of kilometres apart. The limitation was essentially computer capacity, since the number of calculations increases roughly by a factor of eight for every halving of the distance between data points.

There are three ways in which this finer spatial resolution can be achieved:

- running global climate models at finer and finer spatial scales,

- statistical downscaling, which uses observed relationships between large-scale weather variables and local weather, and

- running local or regional climate models driven by output from global models.

Rapid improvements in computer speed and capacity have enabled global climate models to be run at *finer and finer spatial resolutions*. Some models now routinely produce output at spatial scales as fine as 100 or even 50 kilometres, although this still cannot be done for many different scenarios. There has also been a technical development using variable spatial resolution in global models, whereby it is possible to run a global model with coarse resolution over most of the globe, but fine resolution over an area of interest. This latter option is fine if you only want detailed information about

one region, for example if you are in a national laboratory modelling for information relevant to one region, such as the UK or Japan. However, while it is important to get detailed information for your own region, many countries will also want to know what may happen in detail in other parts of the world, at least for broad policy reasons, and maybe even for telling what the impacts of climate change may be on trade partners and competitors.

The need for truly global simulations at fine spatial scales thus remains important. Japan has recognised this and has built the Earth Simulator supercomputer capable of modelling the climate at fine scales for the whole globe. It contains the equivalent of many hundreds of ordinary supercomputers (circa 2004), and currently is running a climate model with 100 levels and a horizontal resolution of 10 kilometres, compared to most AOGCMs that have a resolution of around 100 or more kilometres.[19]

The second way of getting finer spatial detail for particular locations is to use statistical relationships between the observed large-scale climate patterns and local climate to derive estimates of local changes from model-simulated large-scale changes. This is called *statistical downscaling*, and requires a lot of detailed climate observations for the region of interest. It is also important that the statistical relationships between the large-scale changes and local change will be valid under conditions of climate change as opposed to present observed climate variability. That is not the case with all large-scale variables and must be tested.

The third method for obtaining detailed local output is to use a *local or regional fine-scale climate model* driven by the output of a global coarse-resolution model. The easy way to do this is to use output from the global model at the boundaries of the regional model domain to determine the model values at the boundaries of the regional model, and force the regional model to adjust its values inside the boundaries to be consistent with this. This is termed 'one-way nesting'.

However, local changes within the region may in reality force changes at a larger scale, for example if the region includes a large lake from which the atmosphere may pick up additional moisture. To account for this possibility, ideally the output from the regional model should be fed back into the global model and thus modify the large-scale climate. This is termed 'two-way nesting'. Many climate-modelling groups have performed one-way nesting, but two-way nesting is less common, and has revealed sometimes-significant differences in results for the same region.

The performance of fine spatial resolution modelling has also been carefully tested by comparing different models over the same regions, and by trying to reproduce particular historical situations using regional models forced at their boundaries by observations. Results have been mixed, and in general it is conceded that regional detail is not as reliable as the large-scale output. This applies particularly to rainfall patterns, although regional detail is necessary especially for rainfall because it can vary greatly over small distances due to topography and land–sea boundaries.[20]

Overall, model performance and verification is complex, but is being actively tested and improved. Climate models provide projections that are far more sophisticated and reliable than simple extrapolations from observed climate trends. They are far more reliable than handwaving arguments about future climate made by some sceptics that are often made on the basis of simple extrapolations or correlations. Moreover, the IPCC and other bodies studying climate change have taken the uncertainties into account. These uncertainties are being progressively decreased to provide more reliable and policy-relevant information.

The IPCC 2001 report summarises its conclusions regarding the state of coupled atmosphere–ocean climate models as follows:

Coupled models have evolved and improved significantly since [1995]. In general, they provide credible simulations of climate, at least down to sub-continental scales and over temporal scales from seasonal to decadal. The varying sets of strengths and weaknesses that models display lead us to conclude that no single model can be considered 'best' and it is important to utilise results from a range of coupled models. We consider coupled models, as a class, to be suitable tools to provide useful projections of future climates.

A whole chapter of the 2007 IPCC report (WGII, Chapter 8) is devoted to climate models and their evaluation and expounds on their strengths and weaknesses.

The state of climate projections

Projecting the future is an everyday procedure for providing insight into what may happen. It forms the basis of many decisions about what to do. In relation to climate it is made more difficult by the complexity of the climate system, the long time scales and the possible human influences on climate through future human behaviour.

Projecting future climate is not just a matter of extrapolating from recent trends, but of using computer models that take many different processes into account. While climate models are based on weather prediction models, they involve longer time scales and include slower processes. They are not dependent on getting the detailed initial conditions correct. The performance of modern climate models is tested in many ways and they are rapidly becoming more reliable.

Prediction of human behaviour, and thus of future greenhouse gas emissions, is probably less reliable than predicting climate on the basis of a particular scenario of human behaviour. Therefore any climate projections based on climate models is conditional on scenarios of human behaviour. The SRES scenarios for future greenhouse gas emissions, used by the IPCC in its 2001 and 2007 reports, cover a wide range of possibilities, which was not influenced by climate policy. What is more relevant for climate policy are projections for a range of policy-driven scenarios. These will be discussed later in this book.

ENDNOTES

1. I am indebted to Roger H Bradbury, 'Can the Future be Known?' *Greenhouse Beyond Kyoto: Issues, Opportunities and Challenges*, Conference Proceedings, Bureau of Rural Resources, Canberra (1998) for ideas on what is plausible. See http://affashop.gov.au/product.asp?prodid=13231

2. Whether probabilities are needed for climate change scenarios is debated in Lempert and Schlesinger, *Climatic Change*, **45**, pp. 387–401 (2000); Barnett, *World Development*, **29**, pp. 977–93 (2001); Pittock and others, *Nature*, **413**, p. 249 (2001); and Schneider, *Nature*, **411**, pp. 17–19 (2002).

3. The IPCC SRES scenarios are fully documented in Nakicenovic, *Technological Forecasting and Social Change*, **63**, pp. 105–385 (2000) and **65**, pp. 149–66 (2000); and Nakicenovic and Swart, *Special Report on Emissions Scenarios*, IPCC (2000) available at http://www.ipcc.ch. The possibility that emissions may follow either a low-carbon or a high-carbon development pathway, rather than an intermediate one, is discussed in Gritsevskyi and Nakicenovic, *Energy Policy*, **28**, pp. 907–21 (2000).

4. The argument over the use of different exchange rates (market exchange rates, MER, or purchasing power parity, PPP) in calculating future global carbon dioxide emissions is reviewed in part by McKibben and colleagues in *Long Run Projections for Climate Change Scenarios*, Lowry Institute for International Policy, Working Papers in International Economics, no. 1.04 (May 2004). Key papers appeared in the journal *Energy and Environment*, **14**, pp. 159–85 (2003) by Castles and Henderson; **14**, pp. 187–214, by Nakinovic and others; **14**, pp. 415–35, by Castles and Henderson; and **15**, pp. 11–24 (2004), by Grubler and others. Pant and Fisher, from the Australian Bureau of Agricultural and Resource Economics, conclude in a 2004 paper *PPP versus MER: Comparison of real incomes across nations* that: 'The use of MER by IPCC … remains valid and the critique by Castles and Henderson cannot be sustained.' See http://www.abare.gov.au.

5. Papers documenting global emissions tracking at or above the A1FI scenario include: JG Canadell and others, 'Contributions to accelerating atmospheric CO_2 growth from economic activity, carbon intensity, and efficiency of natural sinks', *Proceedings of the National Academy of Sciences* (USA), **104**, pp. 18 866–70 (2007). S Rahmstorf and others, 'Recent climate change: Observations compared to projections', *Science*, **316**, p. 709 (2007). MR Raupach and others, 'Global and regional drivers of accelerating CO_2 emissions', *Proceedings of the National Academy of Sciences* (USA), **104**, pp. 10 288–93 (2007). P Sheehan and F Sun 'Energy use in China: interpreting changing trends and future directions', Victoria University, CSES Climate Change Working Paper no. 13, available at http://www.cfses.com. (2007). P Sheehan, 'The new growth path: implications for climate change analysis and policy', Victoria University, CSES Climate Change Working Paper no. 14 (2007), available at http://www.cfses.com.

6. These feedback effects are discussed in IPCC 2007 report, WGI, Chapter 10.4.

7. The use of the SRES socio-economic scenarios in the UK Fast Tracks project is described by Nigel Arnell and others in *Global Environmental Change*, **14**, pp. 3–20. See also the discussion in the IPCC 2007 report, WGII, Chapter 2.4.6.

8. See Edward Parsons and others, *Climatic Change*, **57**, pp. 9–42 (2004).

9. Population scenarios are discussed in Arnell and others, op.cit., and in Lutz and others, *Nature*, **412**, pp. 543–5 (2001). See also W Lutz (ed.) *The Future Population of the World: What Can We Assume Today?* 2nd edn, Earthscan, London (1996). Nico Keilman discusses probabilistic population forecasts in *Nature*, **412**, pp. 490–1 (2001). See also Joel Cohen in *Science*, **302**, pp. 1172–5 (2003).

10. See *Global Environment Outlook 4* (GEO4) report available at http://www.unep.org/GEO/. The scenarios are discussed in Chapter 9 of GEO4. Key conclusions can be found on p. 451 of the report.

11. See *Alternative Futures: Scenarios for Business in Australia to the Year 2015*, GBN Australia (1999), and *Alternative Futures for Business in Australia to the Year 2015: Towards Strategies*, GBN Australia (2000).

12. See *Future Dilemmas: Options to 2050 for Australia's Population, Technology, Resources and Environment*, CSIRO (2002). It can be found at http://www.cse.csiro.au/research/futuredilemmas/. Later studies focus on particular sectors and regions.

13. There is a short account of Richardson's work on numerical weather forecasting in *The Meteorological Magazine*, **122**, pp. 69–70 (March 1993) by Peter Lynch. See also: Oliver M Ashford, *Prophet or Professor? The Life and Work of Lewis Fry Richardson*. Adam Hilger, Bristol and Boston (1985); and Lewis F Richardson (1922) *Weather Prediction by Numerical Process*, Cambridge University Press reprinted by Dover Publications, New York (1965) with a new Introduction by Sydney Chapman.

14. See Edward Lorenz, *The Essence of Chaos*, University of Washington Press (1996) and James Gleick, *Chaos: Making a New Science*, Penguin, New York (1988).

15. Skill in weather forecasting is discussed in IT Jolliffe and DB Stephenson *Forecast Verification. A Practitioner's Guide in Atmospheric Science*, Wiley and Sons (2003) and RW Katz and AH Murphy (eds), *Economic Value of Weather and Climate Forecasts*, Cambridge University Press, Cambridge (1997). See also the journal *Weather Forecasting* for up-to-date information. National Weather Bureaus usually discuss progress in improving forecasting skill in their annual reports.

16. Detailed descriptions of global climate models and their performance can be found in the IPCC Fourth Assessment Report, WGI, Chapter 8, while that for Regional Climate Models and downscaling is in chapter 11.10. Standard texts on climate modelling include K McGuffie and A Henderson-Sellers, *A Climate Modelling Primer*, Wiley, New York (2005), and WM Washington and CL Parkinson, *An Introduction to Three-Dimensional Climate Modelling*, Oxford University Press, Oxford, and University Science Books (2005). See also Haltiner and Martin, *Climate System Modelling*, Cambridge University Press, Cambridge (1992).

17. Figure 11 is based on one by John Mitchell in *Handbook of Weather, Climate, and Water: Dynamics, Climate, Physical Meteorology, Weather Systems, and Measurements*, Thomas Potter and Bradley Colman (eds), John Wiley and Sons (2003).

18. Improvements in the skill of weather prediction models is documented by Hollingsworth and others in *Bulletin of the World Meteorological Organization*, **52** (1), pp. 33–9 (2003).

19. The Earth Simulator Center in Japan is at http://www.es.jamstec.go.jp. Their computer in 2007 consisted of 640 processor nodes running in parallel, with a total peak performance of 40 Teraflops (40 10^{12} floating-point operations per second) and a total main memory of 10 Terabytes.

20. The performance and techniques of regional climate models and statistical downscaling are reviewed in Chapter 11.10 of the IPCC 2007 report, WGI, and in Wang and others, 'Regional climate modelling, progress: challenges and prospects', *Journal of the Meteorological Society of Japan*, **82**, pp. 1599–628 (2004). See also *Climate Change Prediction: A Challenging Scientific Problem*, by Alan Thorpe (UK Institute of Physics), at http://www.iop.org; and Ronald Prinn, 'Complexities in the Climate System and Uncertainties in Forecasts' in *The State of the Planet: Frontiers and Challenges in Geophysics*, Geophysical Monograph 150, American Geophysical Union, Washington, DC (2004).

4

Uncertainty is inevitable, but risk is certain

… it would be wrong to completely ignore possible developments simply because they are regarded as not very probable – or not sufficiently probable to justify an examination of their possible consequences. Probability itself should not be the criterion for deciding whether or not to prepare ourselves for an event, but only for how we prepare ourselves.

Swiss Reinsurance Company, *Opportunities and Risks of Climate Change*, 2002.

Where there are threats of serious or irreversible damage, lack of full scientific certainty shall not be used as a reason for postponing cost-effective measures to prevent environmental degradation.

The Precautionary Principle, as stated in the Rio Declaration at the Earth Summit, June 1992.

Despite uncertainties, decisions have to be made

Many years ago, when I supervised first year physics students at Melbourne University, we used to give them a steel ball and a micrometer to measure its diameter. We asked them to measure it ten times and see what values they got. Many of them were surprised to find that the answers were not all the same, for example, 53.1, 52.8, 53.2, 52.9, 53.1, 53.5, 53.0, 52.9, 53.2, and 53.3 mm. Why did they get such a range of answers to a simple measurement of a clear physical quantity? And what then was the actual diameter? Well there are several reasons for a range of answers, for example, no ball is exactly spherical, it changes its diameter as it expands or contracts due to changes in temperature, and the measurement depends on how hard the micrometer is tightened. The 'actual diameter' cannot be known exactly: the

measurements range from 52.8 to 53.5, the average is 53.1, and the 'standard error' (root mean square deviation from the average) is about 0.14. The exact numbers will depend on who did the measurements, under what conditions they did them, and on the number of measurements made.

As this example illustrates, contrary to a widely held belief, no measurement of a continuous quantity is absolutely exact.

Moreover, nothing is absolutely certain in science. It is common in the physical sciences to say that something is 'true', 'certain' or 'well-established' if the evidence suggests that there is less than a 5% chance (1 in 20) of it being wrong. If you want to be even more cautious, you might insist on less than a 1% chance (1 in 100), or even a 0.1% chance (1 in 1000). Such a low probability of being wrong applies to such common expectations as the Sun rising tomorrow morning, something that would only fail if something extreme like a cosmic collision were to happen. It also applies to many practical engineering matters, that is, matters of applied science, like the design of a bridge or dam to ensure that it will not collapse. Here the design standard is set to ensure that there is only a very small chance of failure, because failure would be catastrophic.

However, even in the case of engineering design there is a choice of safety level or risk level, which may depend on expected frequency and duration of use, expense and urgency – for example lesser safety levels may be legitimately applied to a temporary bridge built in wartime than for a permanent structure in peacetime. Such choices are a matter of circumstance, purpose and values.

There are many circumstances where a less exacting standard of certainty is sufficient to find a proposition, prediction or theory useful. For example, we find weather forecasts useful even if the chances of their being wrong are ten per cent (1 in 10) or even 33% (1 in 3). This is because, in most cases, the consequences of being wrong are not disastrous, for example if we would only get wet if we did not take an umbrella. Given that we know that weather forecasts are not entirely accurate, we might hedge our bets and take an umbrella anyway.

Even where losses may be incurred if a forecast is wrong, we will gain on average by acting repeatedly on imperfect forecasts, if they have some skill, than by ignoring them. For instance, if forecasts are wrong one time in three, we may still gain on average by acting many times on them, because we will have acted correctly two times in every three. This might apply, for instance, to a farmer acting on seasonal rainfall forecasts as he or she decides how much to plant: good harvests two years in three may well make up for a crop failure one year in three.

How we react to uncertainty depends on what is hanging on the results. For example, forecasts of tropical cyclone landings on the coast are serious – if we are prudent we take precautions even if we are only near the possible path of a tropical cyclone, because we know that there is a margin for error in the predictions. In such cases, we take precautions *because* we know that, even if the exact prediction

is that it will miss us, the exact prediction is uncertain. Even a small chance of a disaster makes it worthwhile to take precautions.

In a more extreme case, most of us prudently insure our house against loss by fire, even though we believe that it is very unlikely that our house will burn down. We know that the total loss of our house would be disastrous, and the premium we pay the insurance company is relatively small, so we insure against the low probability of a fire. Whether we insure depends on the relative size of the premium versus the size of the potential loss, as well as on the probability of a fire.

When it comes to so-called 'laws' about, or predictions of human behaviour (as opposed to the behaviour of the physical world), uncertainty is usually much greater. This applies in many of the social sciences, for example economics. Economic forecasts are made based on various theories (often just simple extrapolations) of human behaviour and various assumptions. These assumptions may not hold in the future as human behaviour may change or be influenced by factors not considered.

As the case of insurance demonstrates, uncertainty does not prevent decisions being made. Indeed, in any practical situation passive or active decisions are inevitably made all the time, despite uncertainty. We either decide to take out insurance, or we decide (perhaps unconsciously) not to do so. Investors and policy-makers make decisions every day despite uncertainties – they assess probabilities and risks and then make decisions, because without these decisions nothing would be done.

Uncertainty in climate change projections

In any estimates of future climate change there are a number of sources of uncertainty. Some of these arise from the science itself, and some from uncertainty about future human behaviour – especially future emissions of greenhouse gases. As it happens, these two major sources of uncertainty each account for about half the total uncertainty. This is fortunate, since it means that, despite the total uncertainty, different assumptions about future human behaviour can be used to test the effect of such behaviour on climate. This can give us useful information about what sort of human behaviour is desirable to avoid the worst possible climate changes. In other words, it is useful for developing policy.

In the case of future climate impacts, there are a number of different assumptions, and a number of models of different parts of the climate system. These range from models of human society leading to future greenhouse gas emissions (socio-economic models), through models of how much of the emitted greenhouse gases stay in the atmosphere (carbon cycle models), to their effects on global climate (climate models), local or regional climatic changes (downscaling models), and eventually to the effects of climate change on biological and human systems (sectoral impact models). Sectoral impact models must also consider the adaptive capacity of society, which will change with time and also lead to uncertainty. Uncertainties at each stage in this chain of reasoning lead to what some authors have called a 'cascade of uncertainty', as shown in **Figure 12**.[1]

There is a long list of uncertainties relating to possible future climate change and its impacts. To start

with the causes of climate change, we need to know future greenhouse gas emissions, and any other effects such as emissions leading to more particles in the atmosphere, or natural climatic variability and change. Human emissions will depend on world population growth, the rate of growth in energy use per person, the mix of energy sources (for example coal and oil versus sun and wind) and energy efficiency (that is, emissions per unit energy produced, and economic production per unit energy used), rates of deforestation or reforestation, and industrial emissions such as the manufacture of steel or fertiliser. Most of these factors are a product of human behaviour, which may change with attitudes to quality of life and wealth. Many depend on rates of technological change, including research and development, and rates of penetration or adoption of new technologies. Nearly all of these factors can be influenced by policy, which may depend on the understanding policy-makers have of the consequences of alternative policies.

Other uncertainties relating to the causes of climate change include natural climate fluctuations due to internal processes in the climate system (for example changes in vegetation or deep ocean

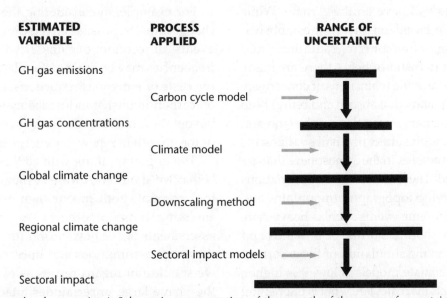

ESTIMATED VARIABLE	PROCESS APPLIED	RANGE OF UNCERTAINTY
GH gas emissions		
	Carbon cycle model	
GH gas concentrations		
	Climate model	
Global climate change		
	Downscaling method	
Regional climate change		
	Sectoral impact models	
Sectoral impact		

Figure 12: The 'cascade of uncertainty'. Schematic representation of the growth of the range of uncertainties in the chain of reasoning associated with climate change and its potential impacts. New uncertainties at each step expand the total range of uncertainty at the previous step. However, the individual ranges are not additive since the extremes will become progressively less likely as different ranges of uncertainty are combined. (After Henderson-Sellers, 1993; Jones, 2000.)

circulation), or natural external forces operating on the climate system (including periodic variations in the Earth's orbit around the Sun, variations in solar energy output, and volcanic eruptions). There are possible further effects on climate due to human activities such as land clearing, irrigation, and atmospheric pollution (for example, carbon black from fires or increased dust from desertification).

There are also uncertainties about how much of the emissions into the atmosphere stay there. This requires modelling of the chemical processes in the atmosphere for methane and nitrous oxide, and modelling of removal processes for particulates such as washout or gravitational settling over the oceans and land surfaces. Removal processes for the main greenhouse gas, carbon dioxide, largely depend on biological interactions, the temperature-dependent solubility of carbon dioxide in water (it is more soluble in colder water) and rates of overturning of the surface waters of the ocean. Growth rates of vegetation and plankton, the effects of forest fires, and interactions between climate itself and the rates of all these processes are all factors.

Given the emissions and how much stays in the atmosphere, climate models are needed to calculate what effect the changed concentrations of greenhouse gases will have on the climate. While these models are based on the well-established laws of motion, atmospheric radiation, and thermodynamics (transfer of heat), there are many uncertainties. Some of the main areas of concern are the behaviour of clouds that absorb and reflect both heat and light radiation, interactions at the land and ocean surfaces, and the effect of small spatial scale and very rapid processes in the atmosphere that are not well modelled. These include rainfall variations in regions of varying topography (mountains and coastlines), and extreme events such as heavy rain, tropical cyclones, thunderstorms, peak winds and hail. Confidence in the simulation of these sorts of events in global climate models is low. It is higher, however, in models that calculate what is happening on finer spatial scales, especially in finer scale regional models, which can be driven by the global models at their boundaries.

Then there are the uncertainties in models that calculate the impacts of climate change, for example on crop production, river flow, flooding, coastal storm surges, and damage costs. How well do crop models treat the effects of different soils, of increasing atmospheric concentrations of carbon dioxide on plant growth, and of pests and diseases? Costing is a vexed question (discussed in Chapters 6, 7 and 8), that includes assessment of the costs and benefits of various adaptations to climate change and of measures to reduce emissions.

The first rule in assessing uncertainty, and particularly arguments based on results of assessments, is that we should understand what uncertainties have been taken into account and what assumptions have been made. This applies especially in areas where ranges of uncertainty are often not given, such as estimates of the costs of climate change impacts or of mitigation or adaptation measures. Too often results of such assessments seem to be biased, intentionally or not, towards the outcomes wanted by special interests that commission or fund the studies. This often takes the form of choices as to what is included, what scenarios are used, what values are assumed, and what alternatives are considered.

For example, in considering the cost of climate change impacts, possible adverse impacts of extreme events or economic gains from reduced frost frequencies may be ignored. Similarly, in estimating the costs of emissions reductions, adverse impacts on carbon intensive industries may be considered but not the economic benefits from energy efficiency or the growth in renewable energy industries.

The important thing with all these uncertainties is that we should be aware of them and take them into account, both in our own estimates and in assessing those of others. We should examine assessments to see how clearly (or 'transparently') they state assumptions and uncertainties. Further, we should not regard results as of no use at all if they have large uncertainties attached to them – after all, admitted uncertainty implies a degree of understanding and honesty, and such results still limit the possibilities. Moreover, the most likely results are probably somewhere near the middle of the range of uncertainty, unless the study is biased by its assumptions. Some knowledge is better than none, provided we use it wisely in full awareness of its limitations. Obviously, where uncertainties are large we should try to reduce them, but in the mean time we need to make the best of what we have to guide both adaptation and mitigation policy.

When it comes to estimating how uncertain projections of future climate change and climate change impacts may be, we need to distinguish between two types of uncertainty. One is the uncertainty about something that can be measured repeatedly. This can in principle be reduced by taking more measurements: the best answer is likely to be the average derived from the most measurements and is in most cases the most frequent answer. Statisticians call this a 'frequentist' problem. The example at the start of this chapter, of measuring the diameter of a steel ball, illustrates this.

The other sort of uncertainty arises when there cannot be repeated measurements. This is usually because we are dealing with some prediction of the future based on a theory or model, often with assumptions about future behaviour or influences. Future climate cannot be measured now, and there will only be one future climate. Here uncertainty can be estimated by calculating the effects of different assumptions in the input data, the theory and the models. In this case we need to use additional knowledge about the assumptions and models, such as how uncertain they are, and then explore the range of results arising from the range of plausible assumptions or models. Estimation of uncertainty of future climate or its impacts requires us to look at the results of all the possible combinations of assumptions, which may number in the thousands. This sort of uncertainty estimate requires complex computations. It is known as 'Bayesian statistics' after the eighteenth century Reverend Thomas Bayes, who first suggested the method, but did not have a computer to carry out the calculations.[2]

People working on climate impacts, including the scientists and policy advisors associated with the Intergovernmental Panel on Climate Change (IPCC), have only recently started to come to grips with this complex problem, and there was a new emphasis on quantifying uncertainty in the IPCC's *Third Assessment Report* in 2001 and the *Fourth* report in 2007. Thus, many of the estimates of uncertainty given in this book are preliminary, and may not cover the full range of uncertainty in some cases. In particular, there may be unexpected developments and 'surprises', which may well lead to larger, or to smaller, climate changes and impacts.

Indeed, new observations, especially in the last few years, suggest that some key uncertainties may be larger than previously thought, especially in the direction of more rapid climate change and sea-level rise. These are discussed in Chapter 5.

Genuine scepticism about over-confident predictions is to be applauded. A good example is a book that at first glance might be thought to rubbish climate models – *Useless Arithmetic: Why Environmental Scientists Can't Predict the Future*, (Columbia University Press, 2007). However, as Fred Pearce notes in a review in *New Scientist*, the book in fact commends the authors of the IPCC for 'painfully long discussions about errors, uncertainties and missing data'. Pearce notes that the book trashes more models for complacency than for predicting disaster. In my view, this book advocates just what I am advocating: the use of models well-informed by observations and updated as new information comes in – and with a full recognition of uncertainty.[3]

From polarisation to probability and risk

People respond in different ways to uncertainty. Sometimes they get confused and see it as a reason for concluding that they know nothing useful on the subject, and therefore see no reason to act. This is especially the case if action to deal with a potential risk would have up front costs. This is the position taken by many who challenge the reality or seriousness of human-induced climate change. These people in denial tend to focus on the uncertainties, particularly at the low end of the range of possibilities, rather than on what is known. Some (but not all) may have a vested interest (financial or ideological) in doing nothing, and use the uncertainty as an excuse for delaying meaningful action.

In other situations, however, people may conclude that although there is uncertainty, it is worth taking a gamble and doing something even if the odds are only marginally favourable. We all do this to a certain extent. Farmers do this as part of their everyday coping with the uncertainties of the weather. Some people even gamble when the odds are stacked against them, as in gambling casinos or lotteries. In other cases, people may decide that even a small chance of a damaging outcome makes it worthwhile to take some form of insurance, even at some expense.

How we react to uncertainty depends in large part on how well we understand the odds, and on what is at stake. Consider a weather forecast of a 30% chance of rain in a rather large district (typically 100 km by 100 km). What that usually means is a 30% chance that it will rain somewhere in the district (but not necessarily at our particular location) some time in the next 24 hours. If all that is at issue is whether we should walk the dog we may accept the risk and go anyway. But if we were thinking of pouring a large slab of concrete that might be ruined by heavy rain and cost us thousands of dollars, we may well hesitate to do it. We would want to know what sort of rain was expected, and certainly look into providing covers to go over the slab.

So we need to understand what the uncertainty means for our particular situation, and to weigh the possible consequences of either taking the risk or avoiding it. It is not only the probability that matters, but also the consequences.

Consider a simple example of a climate change prediction, such as that which arose from a study of future climate change impacts on the Macquarie River in New South Wales, Australia. Here the projected rainfall changes in all four seasons spanned a range from increase to decrease, with slightly more chance of an increase in summer and a stronger chance of a decrease in winter. To the uninformed or the sceptic this might well signal that the change could be zero, so there is nothing to worry about. Two things argue against this

superficial conclusion, first the real probability of negative changes in rainfall, and second the combined effects of rainfall changes and warming on water supply and demand. In this case the projected rainfall change by 2070 in winter (which is the wettest season, with most runoff into the rivers) ranged from a decrease of 25% to an increase of 8%. While this still spans zero, it means that the most likely change is a decrease of around 8%, with about a 50% chance that the decrease will be more than 8% (the middle of the range of uncertainty). Moreover, the warming was projected to be between 1.0 and 6.0°C by 2070, which would increase evaporative losses of water, thereby reducing runoff and increasing water consumption by crops and towns in the valley. Using runoff models, the projected change in runoff into the main water storage dam was in fact between no change (zero) and a decrease of 35% by 2070, which means a 50% chance of water supply decreasing by more than 17%. It is this figure that needs to be considered in calculating what is at stake in the Macquarie River basin for irrigation farmers, town water supply, and the economy of the region. So an apparently very uncertain projection of rainfall change translates, when all things are considered, into a result that has important implications for planning and policy.[4]

To put this in more general terms, what matters is not the probability of a particular numerical outcome coming to pass, which is usually quite small, but the cumulative probability of getting a range of outcomes that is of practical importance. It is not a matter of the accuracy of a particular prediction, but of the probability of a range of outcomes with serious consequences. This is usually expressed as a risk assessment, where risk is understood as the probability of an outcome multiplied by its consequences. Thus a likely outcome having large consequences is a large risk, while a small probability of a low-consequence outcome is a small risk. A high probability of a small but non-negligible effect may also be worth worrying about, as would be a low, but not-negligible probability of a very serious effect.

In the case of climate change, natural and human systems have been forced by past natural climate variability to evolve or adapt so that most of the time they operate within a 'comfortable' range in which they operate well. Sometimes systems exist outside that range in climatic conditions in which they survive, but not well. This is sometimes called the 'coping' range. Occasionally, natural and human systems experience extreme climatic events that are damaging, sometimes fatally. These events are called 'natural disasters' and include droughts, floods, storm surges and wildfires. Climate change moves the average climate so that comfortable conditions become less common, and extreme events, which can be defined as those falling outside the previous coping range, become more common or of greater severity. What is of concern in climate change is therefore the risk associated with changes that take us more frequently into more extreme conditions that are damaging or disastrous. What we are concerned about is the probability of changes that push us over the threshold into these extremes.

Figure 13 illustrates how normal climate variability, with no climate change, covers a range of values that may be favourable for a given activity, but sometimes goes outside that range to cause loss

or other problems. Even if we cannot say when exactly the threshold will be exceeded, we can estimate, from a long record of observations of the variable, how frequently on average the threshold is exceeded. This enables us to calculate the risk to our enterprise and what sort of precautions we need to take to survive that risk.

The case of climate change is shown in **Figure 14**. Here an unchanging climate is shown at the left, and a changing climate at the right. Again, the coping range and thresholds for vulnerability are shown by the horizontal lines. In the upper graph we see how climate change can cause the variable (such as rainfall) to rapidly increase the frequency with which it exceeds the threshold for vulnerability, and thus the risk to the enterprise. The lower graph includes an extension of the coping range due to improving our ability to cope (called 'adaptation'), which reduces the vulnerability to climate change and thus the risk.

Fortunately, the probability of exceeding a particular impact threshold of, say, temperature or rainfall at some time in the future can be determined more confidently than the probability that the temperature or rainfall will have a particular value at that time.

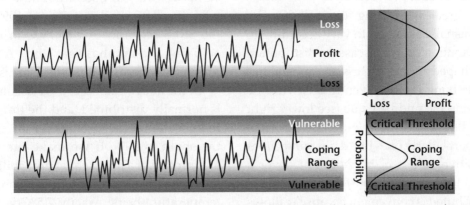

Figure 13: The concept of exceeding a threshold. This schematic illustrates at lower left a coping range under an unchanging but variable climate for a variable such as rainfall (with time increasing towards the right), and an output such as profit from a crop (upper right). Vulnerability is assumed not to change over time. The upper time series and chart shows a relationship between climate and profit and loss. The lower time series and chart shows the same time series divided into a coping range using critical thresholds to separate the coping range from a state of vulnerability. The bell-shaped curve in the lower right-hand side is the probability distribution for the variable having a particular value. The upper critical threshold might represent the onset of dangerous flooding, while the lower threshold might represent the onset of drought. Darker shading represents more severe consequences. (Figure courtesy of RN Jones, CSIRO.)

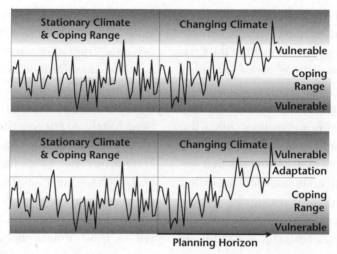

Figure 14: The effect of climate change on vulnerability. Illustrates the coping range for a variable such as rainfall, showing how climate change can rapidly lead to exceeding the threshold for vulnerability more frequently (upper curve), and how adaptation to change can reduce that vulnerability (lower curve). (Figure courtesy of RN Jones, CSIRO.)

To understand why this is so, we need to know what a *probability distribution* is, and what it looks like. This is the way in which the probability of a particular variable having a particular value varies with the value of the variable. For instance, the temperature at some place x at some time y could be anywhere between 5.0°C and 10.0°C, with a very small chance (say less than one in 20) of it being either less than 5.0°C or greater than 10.0°C, but a large chance of it being between those two values, and probably greatest of being about 7.5°C. The probability is usually assumed to vary according to a 'normal distribution', in which case the distribution graph is bell-shaped and we can assign probabilities of the variable lying in any given range, with the most likely being the middle value (see lower right of **Figure 13**). But not all variables follow a normal distribution (particularly ones like daily rainfall that can have positive values or be zero, but never a negative value). An assumption that a variable is normally distributed is convenient because it allows us to apply simple statistics to its behaviour, but it is not always appropriate.

Assigning a *normal distribution* to a variable is an assumption, and if we really have no idea what the probability distribution looks like, apart from its limiting values, a more conservative (that is,

cautious) assumption is to assume that any value within the range has an equal probability. Arguably that is what the IPCC report in 2001 did by failing to discuss different probabilities for different scenarios of future carbon dioxide emissions, and of resulting global warming estimates. An assumption of equal probability gives a much greater probability to the extremes of the range than in a normal distribution. (As it happens, the most extreme of the SRES scenarios, the A1FI scenario, now looks closest to what has happened so far since 1990 – the start of the SRES scenarios – but IPCC in its 2007 report actually de-emphasised the A1FI scenario, presumably because it thought it least likely.)

In the above example, if we assume the variable is normally distributed, and the threshold is 7.5°C, then we find the probability of exceeding this threshold is 50%. If we make the very different assumption of a flat or equal probability distribution over the range, then, although the probability of the temperature being exactly 7.5°C is much smaller, the probability of the temperature exceeding this value is still 50%. This is because the probability of exceeding a threshold integrates (or adds up) all the values below the threshold.

Such a result is even more robust when we consider the result of combining two or more ranges of uncertainty. This is because the probability of exceeding a particular threshold is the result of a number of different individual *probability distributions* for a number of different variables all of which contribute to the uncertainty. While any one of these probability distributions may be difficult to quantify, the probability distribution of the combination is often less uncertain, and in general more likely to be peaked, and for combinations of more variables becomes in general closer to being normally distributed. This is because when any two probability distributions are combined, the probability of combining extreme values of the two variables to produce a new extreme of the combination is less than the probability of multiple combinations of the two variables leading to the same intermediate value of the product.

What this means in practice is that the probability distribution of any variable influenced by multiple uncertainties is likely to be bell shaped, with the most likely value near the middle of the combined uncertainty range, and the cumulative probability of exceeding the mid-range value is likely to be around 50%. While this is a good rule of thumb, there are exceptions, especially where the combined variable (for example, runoff in a river) cannot be negative. In the latter case, the probability distribution is likely to be skewed, with more small values and a few large values.

Estimating risk

The IPCC, in its successive reports has been reluctant to attach probabilities to particular magnitudes of warmings within the large range of 1.4 to 5.8°C (in the 2001 report) and 1.1 to 6.4°C (in the 2007 report) that it estimated for the year 2100. This was due to the great difficulty of assigning probabilities to the relevant population, socio-economic and technological factors that would determine greenhouse gas emissions decades ahead. This difficulty was accentuated by the likely influence of future policies on these factors that determine emissions. Moreover, multiple scenarios of the future are useful to decision-makers, even

without likelihoods, if they help decision-makers choose between policies that may lead to desirable or undesirable outcomes.

Nevertheless, the lack of probability estimates presents problems in developing policy for reducing greenhouse gas emissions and in planning for adaptation to climate changes. Decision-makers need to base decisions on some risk assessment both in mitigation and adaptation policies, since such policies involve costs. Clearly, as the rapid rise in carbon dioxide emissions since 1990 has shown, estimates need to be re-assessed as new information comes to hand. What was once considered unlikely may become more likely as events or scientific understanding progress.

The United Nations Framework Convention on Climate Change (UNFCCC) states that the central objective must be to avoid concentrations of greenhouse gases that may lead to 'dangerous interference with the climate system'. Therefore, developing appropriate mitigation policy requires an understanding not only of the impacts of any given concentration of greenhouse gases in the atmosphere (which has a range of uncertainty), but also of the *likelihood* of reaching a critical level of greenhouse gas concentrations (a dangerous threshold) at some time in the future. The urgency and severity of any mitigation measures needed to avoid reaching a critical threshold depends on the *risk* (probability multiplied by consequence) of what may happen if such measures are not taken.

Similarly, appropriate adaptation policy is related to the rate and magnitude of climate change that affects design parameters or critical thresholds for particular infrastructure (buildings, dams, drains, sea walls, etc.) and activities (farming, water supply, etc.). For example, engineers designing a dam required to last 100 years or more need to know the likely maximum flood flows for which a spillway will need to cope to avoid possible collapse of the dam. Engineers and planners require similar estimates for the height of bridges, size of drains, or setbacks from rivers or coastlines subject to possible flooding or coastal storms. It is relatively easy to establish the sensitivity of systems to climate change, and to suggest measures for increasing adaptability and resilience, such as higher bridges, larger spillways and stronger buildings. But the extent and urgency of the measures that should be taken depends on the probability of a given change and its consequences. Such measures incur costs, so a risk assessment is needed.

Risk cannot be managed or treated efficiently unless it is properly assessed. This requires an estimate of both the probability of an event occurring and an assessment of its consequences. The risk of exceeding some critical level of consequences (defined by collective global value judgements in the case of the UNFCCC) is central to deciding the urgency and extent of reduction in global greenhouse gas emissions (that is, mitigation) that is needed. Once a global emissions reduction target is agreed, there will then be a need to decide on national or other local targets on an equitable basis. That involves negotiation, possible compromises and further uncertainty.

Some scientists have argued that it is too difficult to assign probabilities to future climate change. However, Steve Schneider of Stanford University has argued that, in the absence of better expert advice, decision-makers will make their own formal or informal estimates of probability, and that this is worse than using informed estimates provided by relevant experts.[5] That such probability estimates for global warming are possible is illustrated by a number of estimates in the scientific literature, although they get varying answers.[6] Most find single-peaked probability distributions (that is, a single most probable outcome), but a study by Gritsevskyi and Nakicenovik of the International Institute of Applied Systems Analysis found a double-peaked distribution (that is, two very different but more or less equally likely outcomes).[7] They attributed this to a split in technological development pathways towards either a low-carbon emissions technology or a high-carbon emissions technology, rather than some mixture of the two. This suggests that an early and deliberate choice of emissions technology pathways may be crucial to future outcomes.

Although probability estimates are needed, and in principle possible, methods for deriving probabilities require further development and cannot be said to be well-established at present. In fact, a risk management approach requires not an assessment of the probability of a particular emission amount or global warming at some future time, but rather, as Roger Jones of CSIRO (Australia) has pointed out, an estimate of the likelihood of exceeding an identified critical impact threshold. This integrates the probabilities from the greatest or upper limit warming down to some critical level, and is much less dependent on the underlying assumptions.[8]

However, the relatively low but not negligible probability of large or catastrophic changes, sometimes called 'surprises', must also be considered, since these may contribute appreciably to the overall risk. Indeed, even if such catastrophic changes occur many decades or even centuries into the future, they may dominate any risk assessment because of their very high costs (see discussion in Chapter 6). The importance of these potentially high-risk events means that high priority must be placed on better understanding them, especially their likelihood, potential impacts, and any precursors that may enable them to be detected in advance and avoided. Those who argue that the risk from climate change is small often ignore these uncertainties on the high-impact end of the range of possibilities. High impact outcomes may not be simply marginal, as is assumed in most cost-benefit analyses, but could result in the failure of the whole system, for example, not simply higher food prices, but mass starvation and community breakdown.

Instead of discounting future costs to negligible amounts in today's terms, future costs may increase due to growth in populations and investments at risk, and possible negative inflation. Future costs may also 'blow out' if catastrophic change occurs that causes system failure rather than just marginal losses.[9]

It is interesting to note that a joint US–European project called 'RAPID' is now focusing on one possibly catastrophic possibility, a slow-down of certain North Atlantic currents including the Gulf Stream, which could have large regional effects on climate in Europe and elsewhere. Early detection of any change is seen as a high priority.[10]

If probabilities are not attached to possible climate change impacts, the present wide range of IPCC projected warmings suggests that engineers and planners, as they adapt design standards and zoning to climate change, will need, for the time being, to foster resilience and adaptive capacity. They will need to hedge their bets, and delay investment decisions, or gamble on whether humanity will go down high or low emissions development pathways.[11]

However, probabilities would allow proper risk assessments and the costs and benefits of specific adaptation policies to be calculated. This is a high priority for further research to assist in policy development.[12] It implies a somewhat different approach, involving dealing with uncertainty by a strategy that emphasises flexibility and changes with the circumstances.[13] Probability estimates need to be updated as new observations of changes and processes come in, even if the processes have not yet been included in climate models. Thus observations pointing to processes leading to accelerated outflow from or melting of the Greenland and Antarctic ice sheets should lead to revised estimates of the probability of rapid sea-level rise.

Uncertainty and the role of sceptics

Genuine questioning and scepticism in science is good: it is one of the ways that science progresses, leading to the critical examination of assumptions and conclusions, and eventually the substitution of newer and more reliable theories for older ones that are less robust. This is the scientific method of hypothesis testing and development of new paradigms. However challengers need to do three things:

1. apply their critical faculties to both sides of an argument,

2. admit uncertainties that may work for or against any particular proposition,

3. accept that risk management may require appropriate policy responses despite uncertainty.

It is a safe generalisation that in a world of many uncertainties, one test of whether a scientist, or scientific challenger, is open to all the evidence and therefore unprejudiced is whether they say 'on the one hand this, and on the other hand that'. While such admissions of uncertainty are often used to put down scientists, genuine scientists seldom make statements without some qualification or caveat because there are usually at least two sides to any complex argument. People who admit to only one side are usually either biased or taking a 'devil's advocate' role.

Some genuine sceptics (often academic scientists) take the 'devil's advocate' position to stimulate debate and test propositions. This is bolstered by one traditional academic view of science as a process leading to a body of tested propositions or theories that can be regarded as 'truths' (at least until subsequently disproved). This view, in statistical terms, traditionally requires that a proposition be established at the 95 or 99% probability level (that is, 95 or 99 chances out of 100 that it is true, respectively) before it can be regarded as established. On this basis one or two pieces of contrary evidence is usually enough to discredit a proposition. Such a view protects the limited body of 'truth' from any falsehood, but may end up denying as unproven many propositions that might be true. For example, if a proposition has been shown to have an 80% chance of being true, this view would reject it as unproven, when in fact it may well be true and could have serious consequences.

This academic view of science takes little account of the relative consequences of whether a proposition is true or false, and fails to acknowledge that decisions on practical matters may require us to act despite uncertainty. If this view were adopted in daily life we would seldom insure against accidents because they are not certain to happen to us. It ignores the concept of risk, that is, that in making practical decisions we weigh the probability of an event against its consequences. Policy-relevant or applied scientific advice must take account of risk even when it is less than 95% certain.

Another problem with this view that 'it must be proven beyond reasonable doubt' is that in practical matters outside the laboratory it is often difficult to find counter-evidence of a proposition that is any more certain than each individual line of evidence for the proposition. We cannot then automatically use a single apparently inconsistent 'observation' or published paper to 'disprove' a proposition: we need to test the contrary line of evidence at least as rigorously as the supporting evidence, and decide on a balance of evidence, considering all the uncertainties. For example, if we have ten sets of observations pointing to global warming (land temperatures, ocean temperatures, sea ice, glaciers, snow cover, plant flowering dates, bird distributions, dates of river ice break-up, bore hole temperatures, melting permafrost), and one which does not (some satellite data), do we simply conclude that the 10 sets are wrong, or do we look critically at the reliability of all the evidence and decide which is more likely?

The devil's advocate position is legitimate in a purely scientific debate, where there is plenty of time for contending arguments to be put and an eventual decision reached by the scientific community as a whole. However, where critical policy issues or urgent decisions are at stake, responsible scientists will give balanced advice, admitting and taking into account uncertainties on both sides of any debate.

In the current debate about the reality, seriousness and urgency of climate change, governments, through the IPCC, requested a pro tem consensus position, based on the balance of evidence. The conclusions from the IPCC have always been subject to uncertainty, always subject to revision, and as the science has progressed the conclusions have been expressed more and more explicitly in terms of estimated ranges and probabilities.

A number of people have emerged who deny there is significant human-induced global warming and treat science like a debate in which they apparently see their job as to selectively use any possible argument against a proposition to which they are opposed for non-scientific reasons, instead of looking at the balance of evidence. In adversarial politics, where 'point-scoring' is common, and often accepted as legitimate, such selective use of evidence is often condoned, even if its source is dubious and its veracity in doubt. However, in a debate affecting world affairs, economies and human welfare, debate should be responsibly directed at finding the balance of evidence, the testing of all statements, and the free admittance of all doubts and uncertainties, whether they favour a particular proposition or not. In this context, one-sided challengers should more accurately be labelled 'contrarians' rather than sceptics, since they are sceptical of one position but do not also question the contrary.[14]

Examining the projection of global warming by 2100 in the range of 1.1 to 6.4°C, made by the IPCC in its *Fourth Assessment Report* in 2007, a genuine sceptic may well say that the range of uncertainty has been underestimated. But what some contrarians argue is that the warming may be (or is definitely) less than 1.1°C because of some selected uncertainty. How often do you hear these same contrarians argue that due to uncertainty it might equally well be greater than 6.4°C?

An Australian mathematician, Ian Enting, has described the common sceptics' arguments in a book called *Twisted: The Distorted Mathematics of Greenhouse Denial*.[15] Enting argues that the sceptics' arguments preclude them from being taken as a valid alternative view of the science because of distortion of the data, inconsistencies between arguments, and discrepancies between what individuals commonly tell the media and what the same individuals say when subject to greater scrutiny. He characterises much of the sceptics' behaviour as public relations, and quotes Richard Feynman, the American Nobel Prize winner, as saying '… reality must take precedence over public relations, for nature cannot be fooled'. Reality, in the form of recent observations, indeed tells us that climate change is happening, and doing so faster than even the IPCC has predicted.

It is invidious to ascribe motives to particular individuals, and in most cases I will not do that here. However, we can think of a number of possible underlying positions or interests, related to the enhanced greenhouse effect and its impacts, which may motivate or explain the positions held and arguments used by some contrarians.

One such prejudice comes from people, often scientists in disciplines other than climatology, who are not convinced of the value of predictive modelling in the physical and mathematical sciences. Sometimes such people think of a 'model' as merely a theoretical framework to explain a set of observations, rather than a set of well-tested mathematical non-linear equations that can be used to project behaviour of physical and chemical systems forward in time. Such people may be deeply suspicious of any claim to use a 'model' to predict future behaviour, even of a purely physical phenomenon, however simple or complex. The fact is, of course, that such predictive models do exist and are used routinely for many practical purposes such as daily weather forecasting, predicting the tides, and predicting the motions of the planets. Climate projections are just more complex, and admittedly more uncertain, than some of these examples. Climatologists are well aware and open about the uncertainties. If climatologists are doing their job well, they build their models carefully, test the model's components and overall performance, and carefully estimate their reliability and possible errors. This is part of a climatologist's job description.

Another question raised by some contrarians comes from those familiar with the geological and other paleo-evidence of past natural changes in climate, which clearly were large, and not the result of human influence. These contrarians say that if such changes happened naturally in the past, why should any changes occurring now be due to human influence? Or else they argue that, since life survived such changes in the past, it will survive similar changes in the future, so why worry about it? However, while natural climate change has happened before and can happen again, this does not rule out the simultaneous occurrence of human-induced climate change. Moreover, human-induced climate change may be more immediate and rapid than past changes, and it would happen at a time when there are an unprecedented six billion human beings alive on Earth. Considering the consequences to such a human population if it had existed during the last glacial cycle should dispel any equanimity about the consequences of imminent rapid climate change.

Another class of contrarian is those who are driven by economic and political judgements. A case in point is the best-selling book *The Skeptical Environmentalist* by the Danish statistician Bjørn Lomberg, whose reasoning is quite explicit. Lomberg takes the position that many environmental issues have been exaggerated and proceeds selectively to produce statistics pointing to environmental improvements in recent decades (many the result of agitation by the environmental movement). Considering the enhanced greenhouse effect, Lomberg, while tending to downplay the risks from climate change, concedes that it is a reality. His argument is not that human-induced climate change is not happening, but rather that it is manageable, and that reducing greenhouse gas emissions would be prohibitively expensive.[16]

Lomberg in his more recent book *Cool It*, aimed specifically at concern about climate change, again claims that the impacts of climate change will be negligible and easily dealt with, and that emissions reductions are not urgent and will be enormously costly.[17] These claims are not true, as is evident later in this book. His claims are value-judgements based on discounting the more severe possible impacts, technological optimism regarding our adaptive capacity, and technological pessimism regarding our ability to reduce greenhouse gas emissions at low cost. His arguments have been roundly debunked on the Grist website and elsewhere.

An open letter by a large group of sceptics (many without relevant expertise) addressed to the Secretary-General of the United Nations at the Bali Climate Change Conference in December 2007 made sweeping assertions that recent observed climate changes are entirely natural, cannot be stopped, and that the cost of measures to reduce emissions would be prohibitive. They advocated that money should instead be spent on building resilience to climate change. Once again, they clearly either did not read, or took little notice of and completely dismissed the detailed studies reported in the 2007 IPCC report. Many of their claims are confounded later in this book.[18]

Some of the more extreme contrarians have characterised 'environmentalism' as a new religion or ideology, or as some new form of totalitarianism. Variously, such contrarians may hold beliefs about 'environmentalists' whom they see as wishing to halt 'progress' or 'development' for ideological reasons. They tend to ascribe ulterior motives to proponents with a genuine concern about human-induced climate change, and do not accept the need to consider the supporting evidence on its merits. It is true that some environmental alarmists do highlight as fact extreme disaster scenarios that may be uncertain to occur (and thus these alarmists suffer from some of the same selective characteristics as contrarians). However, this does not excuse the selective denial by contrarians of more likely possibilities. Moreover, recent evidence suggests that some of the scenarios for climate change once thought 'extreme' (even by me) are not as unlikely as scientists thought just a few years ago (see Chapter 5). So-called 'extreme' environmentalism is often a matter of a low tolerance of even small probabilities of large adverse impacts. It is in such cases a value judgement about risk tolerance.

Other contrarians are deeply suspicious of the motives and integrity of climate scientists. Allied with this is often a deep suspicion of international climate science as too much influenced by funding and government (despite there being no consensus amongst governments on many matters related to climate change). They especially suspect the IPCC as deeply biased and flawed and accuse it of censoring or doctoring its reports. This is quite contrary to the rigorous open reviews and other procedures adopted by the IPCC to safeguard against bias, and the fact that its reports have to be approved by a whole range of governments with many different views and interests. This view also ignores the endorsement of the science by the independent academies of science of all the G8 countries (UK, France, Russia, Germany, US, Japan, Italy and Canada) along with those of Brazil, China and India. In a statement published in June 2005 these academies said 'The scientific understanding of climate change is now sufficiently clear to justify nations taking prompt action' (See http://www.royalsociety.org).

Beyond all these possible motivations for contrarian prejudice are those who have a real or perceived economic interest in denying that human-induced climate change is a reality. Some of these genuinely believe the enhanced greenhouse effect is not so, while others fail to see any urgency and seek to delay action for their own (and possibly others') economic benefit.[19]

Occasionally individual contrarians are accused of arguing the way they do purely for their own economic benefit, in order to receive payments from fossil fuel industries or other interests and lobbies such as politically conservative think tanks. In many individual cases I know, it seems to me that such contrarians do not seek out payments; rather, such economic or political lobby groups seek out contrarians and pay to promote their contrarian views through grants, paid tours, publications, testimonies and so forth. These sponsored contrarians may in a sense be hired guns, but they were often contrarians, or even genuine sceptics, first, and are usually genuine in their beliefs. This makes them more convincing through their sincerity, but no more correct.

The economic self-interest argument is often used against those scientists who believe there is a real problem of human-induced climate change, namely that scientists say these things because it gets them grants or pays their salaries. This is the charge of lack of integrity and ascribing of ulterior motives to do bad science that most offends the contrarians when applied to them. In the case of the climatologists engaged in the science it is an ironic argument for scientists in countries such as the United States and Australia, where governments in the recent past have not always welcomed explicit policy-related conclusions and recommendations that question government inaction.[20]

The public perception of the debate over climate change has been shaped by the media's common adherence to a doctrine of 'balanced reporting'. This tends to give equal space to the considered judgements of the scientific community, expressed in peer-reviewed publications such as the IPCC reports, and the often completely un-refereed opinions or advocacy of a contrarian minority. Although this is changing in some cases, there has been a media tendency for giving equal space to unequal scientific arguments, which often misrepresents the balance of evidence and plays into the hands of vested interests opposed to any real action to limit climate change.[21]

Peer review is the process in which scientists normally submit their research findings to a journal, which sends the draft paper out to be assessed for competence, significance and originality by independent experts in the relevant field. These experts do not necessarily agree with the conclusions, but if they agree that the arguments and conclusions are worthy of consideration, then the paper is published. The peer review system means that statements based on such papers tend to be more reliable than other kinds of statements or claims. Claims made by politicians, newspaper columnists, special interest think tanks and campaign groups are not normally subject to such independent quality review beforehand, but are often given equal weight in media reports.

Peer review is not perfect and does not guarantee correctness. It is just the first stage: a hypothesis or argument that survives this first test is still subject to further testing by other scientists. However, peer-reviewed papers and reports can be considered to be more than an opinion, and should not be lightly dismissed in favour of untested opinions. An awareness of the peer-review system and the sources of information can help the media, the public and decision-makers to distinguish between arguments derived from well-based scientific judgements and those arising from un-checked personal opinions.[22]

Application of the 'Precautionary Principle'

In summary, uncertainty in regard to the rate and magnitude of climate change, and in relation to its effects, operates in both directions: it can mean that effects may be less than the current best estimates, or more. This raises the problem, common to most human endeavours, of how to make decisions in the face of uncertainty. The problem is even more acute, in the case of climate change, because decisions made now may determine consequences many decades into the future.

Clearly there are a number of strategies, which are used consciously or unconsciously in everyday life. Essentially these amount to weighing the potential consequences in terms of the probabilities and what is at stake (that is, in formal terms, we do a risk assessment). If the consequences of a particular course of action may be disastrous, we tend to avoid that eventuality by cautious action, taking out some form of insurance, or working to prevent the worst potential consequences from occurring. And if we believe that we can reduce the uncertainty by seeking better information we tend to delay the decisions or take a bet each way until we become better informed. This is called hedging our bets.[23] We may make a tentative or pro tem decision, to avoid the worst happening, and then review the decision in the light of developments. This is called adaptive decision-making. The whole process is one of risk management.[12]

The *Precautionary Principle*, as included in the Rio Declaration at the Earth Summit in June 1992, and assented to by representatives of most of the nations of the world, states

Where there are threats of serious or irreversible damage, lack of full scientific certainty shall not be used as a reason for postponing cost-effective measures to prevent environmental degradation.

This principle has been incorporated into many environmental agreements and regulatory regimes, including Article 3 of the UNFCCC, where it is expressed as:

The parties should take precautionary measures to anticipate, prevent or minimize the causes of climate change and mitigate against its adverse affects. Where there are threats of serious or irreversible damage, lack of full certainty should not be used as a reason for postponing such measures, taking into account that policies and measures to deal with climate change should be cost-effective so as to ensure global benefits at the lowest possible cost.

This is the type of reasoning that, in a broader context, has long governed engineering design, safety regulations, the insurance industry, and indeed foreign policy and military planning. It is normal to consider worst case scenarios and to consider what action is appropriate either to avoid such scenarios coming to fruition, or to deal with them if they do occur.

Uncertainty should be seen, not as a reason for inaction on climate change, but as a reason for proceeding cautiously, with a readiness to adapt policies to changing insights and circumstances, as we continue to conduct what the Toronto Conference on climate change in 1988 called an uncontrolled global experiment.

This leads to two key questions: what counts as serious environmental damage that should be avoided, and what measures are justified as reasonable and cost-effective responses? The answers to these questions are really what successive IPCC reports, and the UNFCCC are all about: they are complex and multi-faceted, combining scientific information and human values.[24] Differing human values and different self-interests will inevitably lead to controversy, debate, and the exercise of political power in deciding what action is actually taken by governments, businesses and ordinary people.

In what follows, this book will explore the above questions, with a view to suggesting what a creative and adaptive policy response might entail, and how we might help it along.

ENDNOTES

1. See Henderson-Sellers, *Climatic Change*, **25**, pp. 203–24 (1993); and Jones, *Climatic Change*, **45**, pp. 403–19 (2000).

2. For frequentist versus Bayesian statistics see DR Cox, *Frequentist and Bayesian Statistics: A Critique*, Nuffield College, Oxford, UK, at http://www.physics.ox.ac.uk/phystat05/proceedings/files/papbayesrev.pdf, and standard texts, for example, VD Barnett, *Comparative Statistical Inference*, 3rd edn, Wiley, Chichester (1999); DR Cox, *Principles of Statistical Inference*, Cambridge University Press (2006).

3. See OH Pilkey and L Pilkey-Jarvis, *Useless Arithmetic: Why Environmental Scientists Can't Predict the Future*, Columbia University Press (2007), and a review in *New Scientist* (17 March 2007).

4. The Macquarie River study is by RN Jones and CM Page (2001) in *Modsim 2001*, *International Congress on Modelling and Simulation*, Ghassemi and others (eds), pp. 673–8.

5. See Schneider, *Nature*, **411**, pp. 17–19 (2001).

6. Estimates of the probability of various amounts of future global warming, based on various assumptions, have been made by Shlyakter and others, in *Chemosphere*, **30**, pp. 1585–618 (1995); Schneider, in *Nature*, **411**, pp. 17–19 (2001); Webster and others in *Atmospheric Environment*, **36**, pp. 3659–70 (2002); and Wigley and Raper in *Science*, **293**, pp. 451–4 (2001).

7. Gritsevskyi and Nakicenovik 'Modelling uncertainty of induced technological change' in *Energy Policy*, **28**, pp. 907–21 (2001).

8. See Jones, *Climatic Change*, **45**, pp. 403–19 (2000) and 'Managing Climate Change Risks', Chapter 8 in *The Benefits of Climate Change Policies*, Organisation for Economic Cooperation and Development, pp. 249–97 (2004), at http://www.oecd.org.

9. See for example Richard Tol, *Climatic Change*, **56**, pp. 265–89 (2003), and Newell and Pizer, *Discounting the Benefits of Climate Change Mitigation: How Much Do Uncertain Rates Increase Valuations?* Economics Technical Series, Pew Center on Global Change (2001). See http://www.pewclimate.org.

10. For Project 'RAPID' see *Nature*, **427**, p. 769 (26 February 2004) and http://www.noc.soton.ac.uk/rapid/rapid.php.

11. Barnett, in *World Development*, **29**, pp. 977–93 (2000); and Lempert and Schlesinger, *Climatic Change*, **45**, pp. 387–401 (2000) argue that, given uncertainty, increasing resilience is the best means of adapting to climate change. However, whatever information can be supplied about the likelihood of particular climate changes can minimise the cost of adaptation.

12. A recent summary of risk management approaches is provided by the IPCC 2007 report, WGII, Chapter 2. See also: Beer and Foran, in *Risk Management and the Future*, T Beer (ed.), AMEEF, Melbourne, pp. 39–67 (2000); Jones, *Natural Hazards*, **23**, pp. 197–230 (2001); New and Hulme, in *Integrated Assessment*, **1**, pp. 203–13 (2000); and T Beer 'Geophysical Risk, Vulnerability, and Sustainability' in *The State of the Planet: Frontiers and Challenges in Geophysics*, Geophysical Monograph 150, American Geophysical Union, Washington DC, pp. 375–85 (2004).

13. This approach is advocated by Popper, Lempert and Bankes, in *Scientific American* (April 2005) pp. 48–53.

14. A semantic discussion of the meaning of the word 'sceptic' can be found in an article by Michael Shermer, publisher of *Skeptic* magazine, http://www.skeptic.com, in *Scientific American* (April 2002) p. 23.

15. Ian Enting's book *Twisted: The Distorted Mathematics of Greenhouse Denial* is published by the Australian Mathematical Sciences Institute (2007), see http://www.amsi.org.au/twisted.

16. See: Bjørn Lomberg, *The Skeptical Environmentalist: Measuring the Real State of the World*, Cambridge University Press (2001). Two critical reviews are: Stuart Plimm and Jeff Harvey 'No need to worry about the future', *Nature*, **414**, pp. 149–50 (2001), and Michael Grubb, 'Relying on manna from heaven?' *Science*, **294**, pp. 1285–7 (2001). Other books sceptical of the enhanced greenhouse effect include John L Daly *The greenhouse trap: why the greenhouse effect will not end life on Earth*, Bantam Books, Sydney (1989), Patrick J Michaels and Robert C Balling Jr, *The Satanic Gases: Clearing the Air about Global Warming*, Cato Institute, Washington DC (2000).

17. Lomberg's more recent book is *Cool It: The Skeptical Environmentalists's Guide to Global Warming*, Knopf (2007). See interviews in *Scientific American* (26 November 2007) and *New Scientist* (27 October 2007) and article in the *Guardian* (17 October 2007) by Jessica Aldred. An extensive critique can be found on Gristmill at: Part 1: http://gristmill.grist.org.story/2007/9/13/105130/672; Part 2: http://gristmill.grist.org.story/2007/9/14/142514/357; Part 3: http://gristmill.grist.org.story/2007/9/17/151133/245.

See also http://gristmill.org.story/2007/9/17/21135/7701 for a review by Bill McKibben. Other websites for discussion of global warming scepticism include http://www.skepticalscience.com/, http://www.greenhouse.gov.au/science/hottopics and the website run by several climate scientists at http://www.realclimate.org. The UK Royal Society also has a website devoted to climate change controversies, at http://royalsociety.org/page.asp?id=6229. Fred Pearce presented a brief review of common contrarian arguments in 'Climate change: menace or myth?' *New Scientist* (12 February 2005) pp. 38–43.

18. The open letter to the UN Secretary-General and the list of signatories can be found at http://www.nationalpost.com/story-printer.html?id=164002. Comments on the individual arguments can be found on the websites listed in endnote 17 above.

19. Documentation of the fact that some leading contrarians have been funded by fossil fuel groups such as the US Western Fuels Association, Exxon and Mobil Oil will be found in Ross Gelbspan, 'The heat is on', *Harper Magazine* (December 1995) pp. 31–7; Ross Gelbspan, *The Heat is On: The High Stakes Battle over Earth's Threatened Climate*,

Reading, Massachussets (1997); and *Smoke, Mirrors and Hot Air*, Union of Concerned Scientists (2007) at http://www.ucsusa.org/assets/documents/global_warming/exxon_report.pdf. See also endnote 15.

20. For Australia, see for example Clive Hamilton, *Scorcher: the Dirty Politics of Climate Change*, Black Inc., Melbourne (2007); Guy Pearse, *High and Dry*, Viking (Penguin), Ringwood (2007); Clive Hamilton and Sarah Maddison (eds), *Silencing Dissent*, Allen & Unwin, Crows Nest, NSW (2007). For the USA, see Union of Concerned Scientists, *Agencies Control Scientists' Contacts with Media* (2007), at http://www.ucsusa.org/; James Hansen, *Political interference with government climate change science*, Testimony to Committee on Oversight and Government Reform, US House of Representatives (19 March 2007); 'US scientists fight political meddling', *Nature*, **439**, pp. 896–7 (23 February 2006).

21. The effect of media adherence to 'balance' in the US, in leading to bias, is documented in Boykoff and Boykoff, in *Global Environmental Change*, **14**, pp. 125–36 (2004). See also Demerritt in *Annals of the Association of American Geographers*, **91**, pp. 307–37 (2001); MT Boykroff in *Climatic Change*, **86**, pp. 1–11 (2008); and B Ward, *Climatic Change*, **86**, pp. 13–17 (2008).

22. The system of scientific peer review is discussed in *Peer Review and the Acceptance of New Scientific Ideas*, by the Working Party of Sense About Science, at http://www.senseaboutscience.org.uk/.

23. The need to hedge against an uncertain climate future is discussed in economic terms by Gary Yohe and colleagues in *Science*, **306**, pp. 416–17 (2002). They conclude that uncertainty is the reason for acting in the near term, and it cannot be used as a justification for doing nothing.

24. For a further discussion see the IPCC Workshop Report (May 2004), *Describing Scientific Uncertainties in Climate Change to Support Analysis of Risk and of Options*, at http://ipcc-wg1.ucar.edu/meeting/URW/product/URW_Report_v2.pdf. See also a series of articles in *Global Environmental Change*, **17**, pp. 1–85, with some emphasis on uncertainty in relation to adaptation.

5

What climate changes are likely?

In terms of key environmental parameters, the Earth system has recently moved well outside the range of natural variability exhibited over at least the last half million years. The nature of changes now occurring simultaneously in the Earth System, their magnitude and rates of change are unprecedented and unsustainable.

PAUL CRUTZEN (NOBEL LAUREATE) AND WILL STEFFEN (INTERNATIONAL GEOSPHERE-BIOSPHERE PROGRAMME, EXECUTIVE DIRECTOR), 2003.[1]

The Earth's climate is now clearly out of balance and is warming ... Evidence from most oceans and all continents except Antarctica shows warming attributable to human activities. Recent changes in many physical and biological systems are linked with this regional climate change. A sustained effort, involving many AGU members and summarized in the 2007 assessments of the Intergovernmental Panel on Climate Change, continues to improve our scientific understanding of the climate.

AMERICAN GEOPHYSICAL UNION, REVISED POSITION STATEMENT, DECEMBER 2007.[2]

Although the consequences of global climate change may seem to be the stuff of Hollywood – some imagined, dystopian future – the melting ice of the Arctic, the spreading deserts of Africa, and the swamping of lowlying lands are all too real. We already live in an 'age of consequences', one that will increasingly be defined by the intersection of climate change and the security of nations.

THE AGE OF CONSEQUENCES, CENTER FOR A NEW AMERICAN SECURITY, 2007.[3]

Human-induced climate change is only an issue if it is large enough and rapid enough to create real problems for natural ecosystems and for human societies. In this and the following chapter we will look at the magnitude and rate of climate change, including sea-level rise and changes in extreme events, that are likely to result from human-induced emissions of greenhouse gases, and at what the effects might be on nature and society.

Given the acknowledged uncertainties, the Intergovernmental Panel on Climate Change (IPCC) has tried in successive reports to state what it was confident about, and what was more or less likely or possible, but still rather uncertain. The statement from the American Geophysical Union – the professional association of American geophysical scientists – does the same in a very summary form. The IPCC, in its reports in 2001 and 2007 extended this process to a treatment of possible sudden or irreversible changes in the climate system which might be catastrophic, but about which we know relatively little regarding likelihood, timing, magnitude and impacts.

Complete surprises are possible. A prime example is the sudden appearance of the 'ozone hole', which first occurred without warning over Antarctica during the 1970s in the southern hemisphere's spring. The ozone hole appeared far more rapidly and is far more long lasting than anyone anticipated in the early 1970s. At that time scientists like me were worrying about possible gradual destruction of ozone in the upper atmosphere. We were taken by surprise when it happened in a few years over Antarctica, far from the sources of the chemicals thought to be threatening the ozone layer. 'Repairing' the ozone hole is likely to take the best part of a century, despite strong international agreements on doing so (see Chapter 9 for a more detailed discussion of the ozone problem). And it could have been far worse. As Paul Crutzen stated, on receipt of the Nobel Prize for his work on ozone:

> ... if the chemical industry had developed
> organobromine compounds [which contain bromine]
> instead of the CFCs [which contain chlorine]
> ... then without any preparedness, we would have
> been faced with a catastrophic ozone hole
> everywhere and in all seasons during the 1970s ...
> Noting that nobody had given any thought to the
> atmospheric consequences of the release of Cl or
> Br [chlorine or bromine] before 1974, I can only
> conclude that mankind has been extremely lucky.[4]

As I write this in 2008 we are in a much stronger position in regard to climate change in that it has been anticipated in general terms, we have been warned, and we already have an international convention in place to deal with it. However, we are still being surprised by the unforeseen rapidity of some developments, such as the rapid retreat of Arctic sea ice in the last few years, and the necessary sense of urgency is still not universally accepted.

Projected climate changes

The magnitude of eventual climate change depends to a first approximation on the accumulated emissions. On the basis of the *Special Report on Emissions Scenarios* (SRES)[5] discussed in Chapter 3, the projected accumulated emissions by 2100, expressed in units of thousands of millions of tonnes of carbon equivalent (Gtc), range from a low of 770 Gtc with the B1 scenario to approximately 2540 Gtc with the A1FI (or fossil fuel intensive) scenario. This range compares with the earlier IPCC IS92 projections ranging from 770 to 2140 Gtc, so the upper end of the range is now greater than before. Corresponding projected carbon dioxide concentrations by 2100 range from 540 to 970 parts per million (ppm). While the A2 emissions scenario reaches the same high rate of emissions by 2100 as the A1FI (see **Figure 16**, left-hand panel), it does so more gradually and thus has lower accumulated emissions and results in less global warming by 2100. This is important in terms of the impression created by the 2007 IPCC report because the latter, in its Figure SPM-5 of WGI (right-hand panel of **Figure 16)** does not show a graph of the warming resulting from the A1FI scenario, although it was shown in the corresponding Figure in the IPCC 2001 report, which is reproduced here as **Figures 15**. As discussed in Chapter 3, the A1FI scenario is the closest to what has actually happened since 1990.

Note **Figure 16** (right-hand panel) shows only three of the SRES scenarios, A2, A1B and B1, as well as one where the concentrations of all greenhouse gases were held fixed at 2000 levels (to show the commitment to warming from past emissions). Although the choice of SRES scenarios to be modelled in detail was made ostensively merely to limit the number of simulations, it had the effect of eliminating the one with the greatest warming impact by 2100. However, ranges of warmings by 2100 for all SRES marker scenarios are given in the sidebars at the right of the Figure, and in the tabulated results which are summarised below in **Table 3**.

This chapter describes projected changes in climate based on both these SRES 'transient scenarios' (which are not driven by climate policies) and 'stabilisation scenarios' that assume policies leading to a levelling off of greenhouse gas

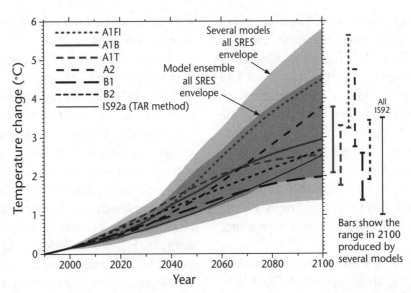

Figure 15: Global average temperature projections for six illustrative SRES scenarios, as depicted in the 2001 IPCC report. The darker shading represents the envelope of the full set of 35 SRES scenarios used as input to the climate models, using the then accepted average climate sensitivity of 2.8°C. The lighter shading is the envelope based on a range of climate sensitivities in the range 1.7 to 4.2°C. The bars show, for each of the six illustrative SRES scenarios, the range of model results in 2100. For comparison, the IPCC IS92 range of warmings in 2100 is also shown. (Adapted with permission from the IPCC 2001 WGI report, Figure 5 (d) of Summary for Policymakers.)

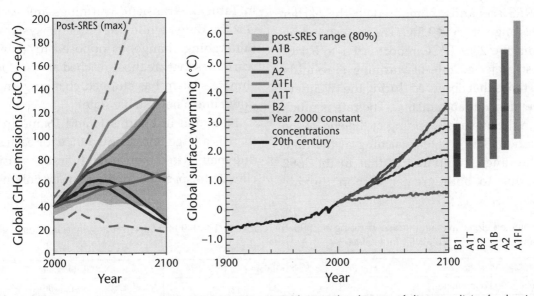

Figure 16: Left Panel: Global greenhouse gas emissions (in CO_2-equivalent) in the absence of climate policies for the six illustrative SRES marker scenarios (solid lines) and the 80th percentile range of recent scenarios published post-SRES (dark grey shaded area). Dashed lines show the full range of post-SRES scenarios. Right Panel: Solid lines are multi-model global averages of surface warming for scenarios A2, A1B and B1, shown as continuations of the twentieth century simulations. These projections also take into account emissions of short-lived GHGs and aerosols. The lowest curve is not a scenario, but is for AOGCM simulations where atmospheric concentrations are held constant at year 2000 values. The bars at the right indicate the best estimate (solid line within each bar) and the likely range assessed for the six SRES marker scenarios at 2090–2099. All temperatures are relative to the period 1980–1999. This is Figure SPM-5 of the IPCC 2007 Synthesis Report (reproduced with permission from IPCC).

concentrations at various values. Many different stabilisation scenarios have appeared in the literature since the 2001 IPCC report, and these are summarised in Working Group III, Chapter 3.3.5, of the 2007 IPCC report. Likely climate changes projected on the basis of all these scenarios include surface warming, changes to rain and snowfall, increased evaporation, changes to the magnitude and frequency of extreme events such as droughts and floods, rises in sea level, and the possibilities of abrupt changes and large-scale changes of the climate system such as ocean currents or the melting of ice sheets.

The policy-relevant questions are how rapidly such effects will occur, their magnitude, and how well we would be able to adapt to them. If we cannot adapt at reasonable cost we will need to avoid such scenarios by reducing greenhouse gas emissions.

Surface warming

The IPCC's 2001 report projects global average surface temperature increases ranging from 1.4 to 5.8°C by 2100 (see **Figure 15**) for non-climate-policy SRES scenarios, compared to the earlier IPCC IS92 range of 1.5 to 3.5°C. The corresponding range from the 2007 IPCC report is 1.1 to 6.4°C. This latest projected rate of warming is roughly two to 10 times that observed during the twentieth century, which was about 0.6°C. The rate is much faster than the average warming at the end of the last glaciation. The greater warming at the high end of the range, compared to that in the IS92 range is due to both greater carbon dioxide

emissions in the high emissions scenarios and less sulfur emissions.

About half the range of uncertainty in projected warming is due to the choice of scenarios, which in reality can be influenced by policy developments, and half to the uncertainty for a given scenario, which is due to scientific uncertainties. The latter essentially concerns the sensitivity of climate to a given increase in carbon dioxide concentrations. This scientific uncertainty is a high priority for further research and is greatly affected by various positive (amplifying) or negative (stabilising or damping) 'feedback' effects including cloud cover, possible reductions in oceanic and biospheric uptake of carbon, and changes in surface properties such as snow and ice cover, and vegetation. The rate and magnitude of such feedbacks is the subject of much current research and observation, with the IPCC stating in its 2007 report that the climate sensitivity is likely to be in the range 1.5 to 4.5°C, but that it could be considerably higher.

The estimated transient warmings for the SRES scenarios in the 2007 IPCC report are summarised in **Table 3**. 'Transient' warmings are reached at a certain date, while the climate system is still undergoing change, as opposed to 'equilibrium' warmings that are those reached at a time when the climate system has stopped changing and settled down into a new, stable state.

Note that in **Figures 15** and **16** and in **Table 3**, there is a large uncertainty range for each scenario, due mainly to the uncertainty in the sensitivity of climate to specified increases in greenhouse gases.

TABLE 3: Projected global average surface warming at 2090–99 relative to 1980–99 for various transient scenarios of greenhouse gas emissions. After IPCC 2007, WGI Table SPM-3

Scenario	Best estimate (°C)	Likely range (°C)
Constant year 2000 concentrations	0.6	0.3–0.9
SRES B1	1.8	1.1–2.9
SRES A1T	2.4	1.4–3.8
SRES B2	2.4	1.4–3.8
SRES A1B	2.8	1.7–4.4
SRES A2	3.4	2.0–5.4
SRES A1FI	4.0	2.4–6.4

Estimates are based on the IPCC 2007 hierarchy of climate models of varying degrees of complexity, with a range of different climate sensitivities.

It is significant that there is relatively little difference in transient warmings by 2050 for the various emissions scenarios, with warmings only diverging rapidly in the latter half of the century. This is due to the relatively small difference in cumulative emissions by 2050 implied by the different emissions pathways and the slow response of the climate system, which is still catching up to the effects of earlier emissions. The warming at 2050 is largely determined by changes already in the pipeline due to past emissions, but changes in emissions in the next few decades will make a big difference to warmings by 2100.

It is worth adding, for the sake of those who might be influenced by the occasional cooler year to doubt global warming, that in the next decade interannual variability of the climate system, such as that associated with El Niño, fluctuations in the ocean circulation, and anomalies in ocean heat content, can still lead to some years that are slightly cooler than the recent average. Indeed, some British climatologists have developed an improved method of predicting climate over the next decade that takes account of the internal variations as well as the long-term trend. They suggest that climate will continue to warm, with at least half of the years after 2009 predicted to exceed the warmest year currently on record.[6]

Natural interannual variability of global sea surface temperature is largely due to varying heat exchange between the atmosphere and the ocean. This is mainly due to the El Niño–La Niña cycle, with El Niño years tending to be warmer due to reduced upwelling of cold water in the eastern tropical Pacific. Atmospheric and oceanic circulation changes due to global warming also affect the heat exchange with the deep ocean, especially in the Southern Ocean around 50–60 degrees south. In addition, increased heat energy at the surface due to increasing greenhouse gases is being partially absorbed as latent heat, leading to the rapid melting of Arctic sea ice, mountain glaciers and parts of major ice sheets. This

must be slowing the increase in sensible heat (that reflected in temperature rises). Surface temperature is thus likely to rise faster once the ice is melted.[7]

Stabilisation emissions scenarios and their resultant global warmings are more relevant to policy than the SRES transient scenarios, since they describe outcomes based on various prescribed emissions reduction programs, such as may be introduced to reduce the magnitude of future climate change. Concern about climate change has already led to limited national and international policies that have reduced emissions slightly relative to what they might have been otherwise. And growing concern about climate change will likely lead to greater policy-induced reductions in emissions in the near future, even though recent emissions have in fact been at or above the rate in the SRES fossil fuel-intensive scenario A1FI. Comparison of outcomes under various equilibrium warming scenarios gives some idea of the effect on climate of various emissions reduction programs and targets.

The eventual stabilised global warmings from stabilised emissions are reported in the 2007 IPCC report and are summarised in **Table 4**.[8] They are given for various groupings or categories of scenarios, stabilising at carbon dioxide concentrations in ranges from 350–400 ppm (category I) to 660–790 ppm in category VI (column 2). These correspond to larger ranges of carbon dioxide-equivalent (column 3), where other greenhouse gases and aerosols are included as the equivalent amount of carbon dioxide. Column 4 shows the year at which CO_2 emissions must peak, or reach a maximum, if the scenario is to stabilise at the desired value, while column 5 shows the percentage change in carbon dioxide emissions necessary by 2050 if this is to be achieved. Column 6 shows the eventual global average warming above pre-industrial temperatures for each category of emission scenario. I have left out the eventual sea-level rise estimates, since those in the IPCC report leave out the effects of ice sheet melting and disintegration, which will clearly dominate over thermal expansion of the oceans on a time scale of centuries. (We will return to sea-level rise below, see **Table 6**.)

TABLE 4: Characteristics and results of various categories of greenhouse gas concentration stabilisation scenarios

Emissions scenario category	CO_2 concentration at stabilisation (ppm)	CO_2-equivalent concentration at stabilisation (ppm)	Peak year for emissions	Change in emissions needed by 2050 (%)	Eventual warming above pre-industrial (°C)
I	350 to 400	445 to 490	2000 to 2015	−85 to −50	2.0 to 2.4
II	400 to 440	490 to 535	2000 to 2020	−60 to −30	2.4 to 2.8
III	440 to 485	535 to 590	2010 to 2030	−30 to +5	2.8 to 3.2
IV	485 to 570	590 to 710	2020 to 2060	+10 to +60	3.2 to 4.0
V	570 to 660	710 to 855	2050 to 2080	+25 to +85	4.0 to 4.9
VI	660 to 790	855 to 1130	2060 to 2090	+90 to +140	4.9 to 6.1

In 2005 the CO_2 concentration was already 379 ppm, while the CO_2-equivalent concentration was slightly less at 375 ppm, due to the negative (cooling) effect of aerosols. (The importance of the aerosol effect is declining as greenhouse gases are long-lived and thus cumulative in the atmosphere, whereas aerosols are rapidly removed from the atmosphere and thus not cumulative.) Note that the warmings given in column 6 are for an assumed climate sensitivity of 3.0°C, whereas the full range of sensitivities is 1.5 to 4.5°C or greater (see **Figure 28**).[9] We will return to that in our discussion of stabilisation targets in Chapter 8.

Regional warmings[10]

While average global warming is of importance, most interest is in regional impacts, for which more detailed estimates of regional warming are required. Fortunately, there is broad agreement on the patterns of warming around the globe in various climate models. Warming in continental interiors and in the high latitudes of the northern hemisphere is expected to be greatest with less expected over the oceans and windward coastlines. Indeed high northern latitudes may warm at several times the rate of the global average, and continental interiors up to twice as fast as the surrounding oceans (see **Figure 17**, left side). The least warming is expected over the Southern Ocean due to its large capacity to transport surface heat into the deep ocean, and possibly in the North Atlantic region, depending on the behaviour of the ocean circulation (see later). Warming may be greater in the eastern tropical Pacific than in the west, which may lead to a more El-Niño-like

average condition (although year-to-year variability around that average may increase).

After stabilisation of greenhouse gas concentrations in the atmosphere, warming will continue for centuries, especially in the Southern Ocean region, leading to ongoing regional climate change in the vicinity, especially in Australia and New Zealand, and possibly in southern Africa, Argentina and Chile.

Precipitation and evaporation[11]

Global average precipitation (rain or snowfall) and evaporation are projected by climate models to increase by about 1 to 9% by 2100, depending on which scenario and climate model is used. However, projected precipitation changes vary more from region to region, with increases over mid- to high-latitudes in both hemispheres (see **Figure 17**, middle). Decreases are projected in subtropical and lower mid-latitudes, notably Central America, the Caribbean and the south-western United States, Southern Europe, North Africa and the Middle East, and in the western mid-latitude regions of the southern continents. This is generally associated with the polewards migration of the mid-latitude westerlies associated with a strengthening of the northern and southern 'annular modes' of circulation and the related changes in surface pressure patterns (**Figure 17**, right side).[12] Surface pressure tends to increase at mid-latitudes and decrease at high latitudes.

Decreases in annual average precipitation in the subtropical and mid-latitudes are up to 20% in the climate models by 2100 for the A1B scenario, which is mid-range. Even more rapid changes have been observed, and this is in part explained by the additional effect of decreases in stratospheric ozone,

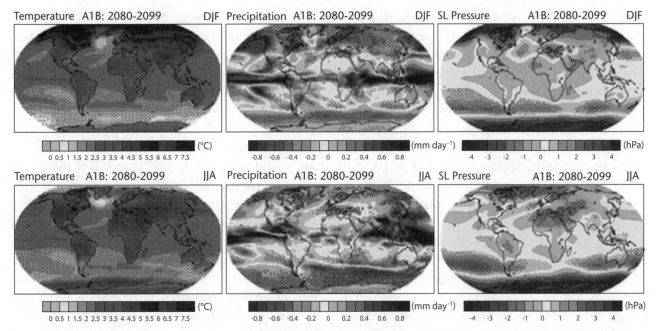

Figure 17: Changes projected for the period 2080–2099 relative to 1980–1999, averaged from several climate models for the mid-range SRES emissions scenario A1B. Changes are for the northern winter (top) and northern summer (bottom), for temperature (°C, at left), precipitation (mm per day, centre), and sea level pressure (hPa or mBar, right). This is IPCC 2007 WGI Figure 10.9 (used with permission). This and other IPCC-based figures can be seen in colour at http://www.ipcc.ch.

which adds to the polewards movement of the westerlies, especially in the southern hemisphere.

Precipitation increases are projected in the tropical regions, notably over the oceans and tropical East Africa, extreme Southern Asia, and at high northern latitudes including northern Europe, again of up to 20% for mid-range emissions scenarios by 2100.

However, Frank Wentz and colleagues point out that while climate models and satellite observations both indicate that total water content of the atmosphere will increase at around 7% for each °C rise in global surface temperature, the models predict a slower rate of increase in global precipitation and evaporation, that is, that the water cycle speeds up, but not as fast as total water content, possibly due to a slower increase in evaporation due to lower wind speeds. They report that recent satellite observations indicate that precipitation has in fact increased at the same rate as atmospheric water content. Xuebin Zhang and colleagues in a study to detect human influence on twentieth century precipitation trends also find that precipitation has changed faster than the climate models have predicted. If these two papers are

correct it has profound implications for potential impacts on agriculture and water supplies, the severity of droughts, and for flood frequencies and other extremes.[13]

One Australian sceptic has claimed that this accelerated evaporation would cool the surface and thus reduce global warming. This is nonsense. Increased evaporation means that increased latent heat is absorbed into the atmosphere, and transported, mainly polewards, to where the water vapour would condense, releasing the latent heat. Thus a stronger hydrologic cycle would accelerate heat transport polewards, causing greater warming at high latitudes. The climate models already capture this process. It would simply be stronger if Wentz and colleagues are correct.

In any case, a study by Pall and others found that extreme precipitation increases, both in observations of daily precipitation and in models, in proportion to the large increase in available atmospheric moisture, rather than at the slower rate indicated for increases in average rainfall in the same models.[14]

Precipitation changes will vary greatly on finer spatial scales due to topographic and coastal effects.

These changes are best simulated using regional climate models, but agreement is sometimes poor between models. Changes in rainfall intensity and seasonality are expected, but these changes are quite uncertain in many areas. Higher temperatures will mean that more precipitation will fall as rain rather than snow, changing the seasonality of river flows in many snow-fed catchments such as those in the western United States, northern Europe, and those fed by runoff from the Andes in South America, and the mountains of central Asia (notably India, Pakistan and China).

There has been an observed strengthening and polewards movement of the atmospheric low-pressure belts around the North and South Poles during the late twentieth century. This is simulated in climate models that include the effects of enhanced greenhouse gases and stratospheric ozone depletion (see **Figure 17**, right side). This effect is expected to continue through the twenty-first century, with any lessening of the ozone depletion effect being more than made up for by strengthening of the greenhouse effect. Storm belts will also shift, and the North Atlantic Oscillation may stay in a more positive mode, affecting climate over Europe. These circulation changes help explain the modelled and observed regional precipitation changes. In the southern hemisphere the increase in north–south temperature differences due to the lag in warming in the Southern Ocean will reverse after stabilisation of greenhouse gas concentrations as the Southern Ocean continues to warm. This may lead to a partial reversal of precipitation changes associated with the shift southward of the westerlies.

Extreme events

According to the IPCC 2007 report, it is likely that changes in some extreme events were observed during the twentieth century (**Table 5** below), however, there is some uncertainty due to limited data. More changes in extreme events are likely in the twenty-first century. Daily maximum and minimum temperatures, and the number of hot days are very likely to increase, with fewer cold and frosty days. In general there will be a reduced diurnal temperature range (the difference between daily maximum and minimum temperatures). The heat or discomfort index is very likely to increase in most tropical and mid-latitude areas. More intense precipitation events are very likely over many areas (causing more frequent flooding), and increased summer drying is likely over mid-latitude continental interiors, with an increased risk of drought. The intensity of tropical cyclone winds and peak rainfalls is likely to increase. Extra-tropical storms (low pressure systems) are also likely to be more intense, and follow higher latitude paths. Greater extremes of flood and

TABLE 5: Changes in extreme events. IPCC 2007 report estimates of confidence in observed changes during the twentieth century, and projected changes in the twenty-first century, for extreme weather and climate events

Changes in phenomenon	Confidence in observed changes (post-1960)	Confidence in projected changes (during the twenty-first century)
Higher maximum temperatures and more hot days over nearly all land areas	Very likely	Virtually certain
Higher minimum temperatures, fewer cold days and frost days over nearly all land areas	Very likely	Virtually certain
Reduced diurnal temperature range over most land areas	Very likely	Virtually certain
Intense precipitation events, (frequency or proportion of total rainfall)	Likely	Very likely
Increased risk of drought in mid-latitude continental areas	Likely	Likely
Increase in tropical cyclone peak wind intensities and rainfall, with lower central pressures	Likely in some regions	Likely
Extreme extra-tropical storms: increased frequency/intensity and polewards shift	Likely	Likely
Coastal storm surges and flooding more severe (due to both higher mean sea level and more intense storms)	Very likely due to sea-level rise last century	Virtually certain

drought are likely with the El Niño–Southern Oscillation cycle (El Niño and La Niña), which is expected to continue. An increased frequency of extreme high sea level due to storm surges is likely. These changes are summarised in **Table 5**.[15]

In general, any increase in the average of a climate variable such as temperature or rainfall tends to have an exaggerated effect on less frequent extremes associated with normal climate variability, such as very cold or hot days. The increase in average reduces the frequency of occurrence of extremes on the low side and increases their frequency on the high side. Changes in variability can also occur, which may strengthen or weaken the changes in extremes.

This is supported by a review of the paleo-records of natural floods, which found the magnitude and frequency of floods are highly sensitive to even modest changes of climate equivalent to or smaller than those expected from global warming in the twenty-first century. The review suggested that times of rapid climate change have a tendency to be associated with more frequent occurrences of large and extreme floods. Consistent with this, a study of great flood events in 29 river basins around the world shows an increase in frequency since 1953. Using climate models, the study found that the frequency of such large floods will increase further during the twenty-first century, by a factor of two to eight.[16]

Recent high spatial resolution climate modelling studies found that an increase in intense precipitation is very likely in many parts of Europe, despite a possible reduction in summer rainfall over a large part of the continent.[17] Along with increases in total rainfall in northern Europe, this means that severe flooding is likely to become more frequent, especially in winter, despite a general tendency towards drier summers. This will be exacerbated by more precipitation falling as rain rather than as snow. The proportion of total precipitation derived from extreme and heavy events will continue to increase relative to that from light to moderate events.

Some recent analyses of pan evaporation observations (that is, measurements of rates of evaporation from a water surface in an open pan) suggest that pan evaporation, and by inference solar radiation reaching the Earth's surface, decreased in many areas from the 1960s through to the 1980s. This may have been due to increasing aerosol pollution, particularly in the northern hemisphere, or to changes in cloud amounts. It has been suggested that these decreasing trends challenge climate change projections that indicate increases in potential evaporation in many areas.[18]

Against this, pan evaporation is not the same as actual evaporation, which can show an opposite trend. Moreover, pan evaporation has increased in some areas since the 1980s, and there is evidence that solar radiation in these areas is also increasing, most likely due to decreasing aerosols.[19] In any case, recent climate model calculations do take account of the direct effects on evaporation of atmospheric aerosols, and some models even include the indirect effects via aerosol-induced changes to cloud properties (see Chapter 2). The fact that total global rainfall has increased, especially at high latitudes, and that high latitude ocean surface waters have become fresher,[20] suggests that the global hydrological cycle has in fact sped up at least as fast, if not faster, than the climate models suggest.

A recent study by Cai and Cowan underlines the importance of warming in amplifying the effect of rainfall deficiencies. Drought is often defined in terms of cumulative rainfall deficits relative to the average in a given region. But drought is better defined in policy-relevant terms by soil moisture deficit or decreases in runoff, which are a combination of rainfall deficit and actual evaporative losses. Cai and Cowan show that for the extensive Murray-Darling Basin in Australia, the record from 1950 to 2006 shows that, after removing the effect of rainfall variations, a rise in average temperature of 1°C leads to an approximate 15% reduction in annual inflow. Thus actual warming makes droughts, even for the same rainfall deficiency, much more severe.[21]

Large floods and widespread droughts are commonly due to one or other extreme of naturally occurring variations in circulation patterns including the North Atlantic Oscillation (NAO) and the El Niño–Southern Oscillation (ENSO). The NAO consists of fluctuating pressure differences between the Icelandic low pressure region and the Azores high pressure region in the North Atlantic. ENSO is a coupled atmosphere–ocean phenomenon across the tropical Pacific involving sea-surface temperature and atmospheric pressure fluctuations. These phenomena also influence other important climatic events such as the favoured tracks of storms in the North Atlantic and the location of tropical cyclones in the Pacific. Both phenomena also have long-distance or teleconnections to weather and climate elsewhere. How global warming affects these circulation patterns is very important, as it will have strong implications for storm tracks and rainfall patterns in both hemispheres.[22]

A progressive shift in the NAO towards its more positive phase has been observed since 1950, and has been associated with a slow warming of the tropical oceans. This is supported by an analysis of observed and modelled trends in global sea-level pressure patterns, which points to a human influence, with a polewards shift in mid- to high-latitude pressure patterns.

Future behaviour of ENSO is of critical importance to many countries affected by ENSO-related rainfall variations and storm frequency. The relationship between ENSO and rainfall has varied with time over Australia, both in the historical record and in the longer record from coral cores in the Great Barrier Reef. However, paleo-climatic data suggest that ENSO has been a feature of global climate through past warm periods. Different global climate model simulations for a warmer world show differing results, with many showing a more El Niño-like average condition, but others showing little change. Observations and models tend to suggest that the east-west sea surface temperature and the pressure contrast across the tropical Pacific on average decreases with global warming, leading to a more El Niño-like average state, but that ENSO variability continues around that changed average condition. ENSO extremes may well be associated with more extreme floods and droughts due to the intensification of the hydrological cycle.

The situation with projections of tropical cyclone behaviour is mixed. Evidence to date suggests that that there will likely be more intense tropical cyclones with higher rainfall peak intensities. There could also be substantial changes in the region of formation if there are changes in ENSO. While the number of intense cyclones may increase, there is a suggestion that the total numbers globally may decrease. So far there is no evidence for a substantial increase in polewards movement of tropical cyclones, either in observations or model projections.[23]

A category of extratropical cyclones known as explosively developing cyclones, which includes some mid-latitude east coast low pressure systems, can cause severe flooding due to heavy rainfall, storm surges and high winds. Some modelling results suggest that east coast lows might intensify with higher sea surface temperatures. A statistically significant increase in explosively developing cyclones in the southern hemisphere has been detected from 1979 to 1999.

More generally, extratropical cyclones are expected to increase in intensity but decrease in number, and storm tracks are moving polewards with increased global warming. There is also a suggestion that peak wave heights will increase as a result of the more intense storms.[24]

Global warming could also influence another class of extreme event that was not considered by the IPCC in its 2007 report, namely earthquakes.[25] Of course earthquakes occur irrespective of climate change. They occur when one part of the Earth's crust moves against another, and can trigger tsunamis or tidal waves if they occur under the sea.

Shifts in weight on an area of the Earth's crust, due for example to the filling of large dams, can cause small local earthquakes. Such shifts in weight have occurred in the past due to the melting of glaciers and ice sheets. The weight of glaciers and ice sheets depresses the Earth's crust under them, and their removal leads to the underlying crust slowly rising. This glacial rebound is still occurring in many areas close to the former ice sheets that covered much of Fennoscandia and North America some 20000 years ago. There is good evidence that regional earthquake fault instability increased at the end of the last glaciation.

Further melting of mountain glaciers and remnant ice sheets due to global warming over parts of Canada, Patagonia, Alaska and of course Greenland and Antarctica could lead to further land movements, triggering localised earthquakes. There is a large element of random or chaotic behaviour in earthquake occurrence, and skill in forecasting them is very limited. Nevertheless, it is arguable that the frequency of at least small earthquakes might increase as glaciers and ice sheets melt, and also perhaps as a result of rising global sea level. Sea-level rise would increase the load on the continental shelves, even far from the melting ice. How significant this is, and the time scale on which seismic effects might occur, remains to be determined, but the consequences could be significant.

For many extreme events, fine-scale processes may also play a major role, which so far has not been fully explored. Diffenbaugh and others show for the United States that fine-scale topography including coastal effects and rain shadows, snow cover and surface moisture variations can feed back onto the intensity of extreme temperatures and rainfalls.[26]

The frequency and severity of other extreme climate-related events, some not discussed by the IPCC because of their small scale and a lack of studies, are also likely to be affected by climate change. These include the occurrence of flash flooding, severe thunderstorms and hail, landslides, extreme sea-level events and wildfires. Some of these will be discussed further in Chapter 6 on impacts. One recent study with a high-resolution model over the United States suggests up to 100% increases in severe thunderstorms in some regions by 2100.[27]

Sea-level rise[28]

Sea-level rise is obviously important, given that a rapidly increasing number of people live in low-lying coastal areas and there is massive investment in infrastructure, including cities, ports, refineries, power stations and tourist resorts.

Projections of global sea-level rise by the IPCC in 2001 ranged from 9 to 88 cm by 2100, but in the 2007 report the upfront 'model-based' estimate was 18 to 59 cm. This range includes thermal expansion of the oceans and meltwater from mountain glaciers and a contribution due to increased ice flow from Greenland and Antarctica 'at the rates observed for 1993–2003, but these flow rates could increase or decrease in the future'. The report expressly states that the estimates do not include uncertainties in the climate-carbon cycle feedback 'nor do they include the full effects of changes in ice sheet flow because a basis in published literature is lacking'. It goes on to suggest that 'if this contribution were to grow linearly with global average temperature, the upper ranges of sea-level rise for SRES scenarios ... would increase by 0.1 to 0.2 m'. It adds that 'larger values cannot be excluded, but understanding of these effects is too limited to assess their likelihood or to provide best estimates or an upper bound for sea-level rise'.

If greenhouse gas concentrations were stabilised (even at present levels), the 2007 IPCC report notes that sea-level rise would continue for hundreds of years, due to the slow but continuing warming of the deep oceans and the contraction of the Greenland ice sheet. It points out that future temperatures in Greenland may well reach levels comparable to those inferred for the last interglacial period 125 000 years ago, when polar land-based ice was much reduced and sea level was 4 to 6 metres above the present. While the report implies that this may take several centuries, it notes that processes suggested by recent observations but not at present included in ice sheet models 'could increase the vulnerability of the ice sheets to warming, increasing future sea-level rise'.

Since the cut-off date in 2006 for new work to be considered for the 2007 IPCC report many new observations and papers have appeared relevant to global sea-level rise estimates. The vast majority of these suggest that sea-level rise is likely to occur faster than projected in the IPCC report in 2007.

A new estimate by Rahmstorf in 2007, based on a constant relationship between observed decade-by-decade twentieth century rates of sea-level rise and global warming relative to pre-industrial times, shows that the sea-level rise by 2100 should be in the range of 50 to 140 cm,

TABLE 6: Various projections of global average sea-level rise (SLR) by 2001 from the 2001 and 2007 IPCC reports and some more recent estimates

Case	Warming to 2100 (°C)	Sea-level rise to 2100 (cm)
IPCC (2001) full range	1.4 to 5.8	**9 to 88** (allows for ice sheet dynamics)
IPCC (2007) B1 (low case)	1.1 to 2.9	**18** to 38 (dynamics caveat only)
IPCC (2007) A1FI (high case)	2.4 to 6.4	26 **to 59** (dynamics caveat only)
Rahmstorf (2007)	1.4 to 5.8	**50 to 140** (linear relation of SLR to warming)
Jim Hansen, NOAA (2007)		**Up to 5 m** (exponential relation of SLR to warming)

depending on the rate of global warming.[29] However, if the rate of sea-level rise were to increase faster than global warming due to positive feedback processes, as argued by Hansen in 2005, 2007 and Rignot in 2008, sea-level rise by 2100 could be several metres. Rignot states that: 'Depending on how fast global temperature rises, sea level may or may not be driven up by 1–3 m (about 3–10 ft) by 2100. So, there is no reason to panic at this point, but also no basis for providing reassurance.'[30] These more recent estimates are included in **Table 6**, which compares them with the IPCC projections.

The Greenland Ice Sheet is at a generally lower latitude than Antarctica and has widespread marginal surface melting in summer.[31] The area of surface melting has rapidly increased in recent years, notably since 2002, as is shown in **Figure 18**.

NASA researcher Scott Luthcke commented in 2007: 'In the 1990s, the ice was very close to balance, with gains at about the same level as losses. That situation has now changed significantly.' Penetration of this meltwater through moulins (crevasses and tunnels in the ice) to the lower boundary of the ice is thought to have lubricated the flow of ice over the bedrock and led to accelerated glacier flow rates. Melting of tidewater glaciers (glaciers the lower reaches of which float or are grounded below sea level) from the bottom, pushing back the grounding line, may also be contributing to acceleration of flow.[32]

Outlet glaciers have accelerated rapidly in recent years, with Rignot and Kanagaratnam reporting from satellite radar interferometry that widespread acceleration occurred south of 66°N between 1996 and 2000, expanding to 70°N in 2005. Accelerated

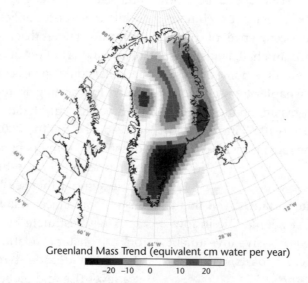

Greenland Mass Trend (equivalent cm water per year)

−20 −10   0   10   20

Figure 18: Trend in depth of ice over Greenland between 2003 and 2005, in cm of water equivalent per year. There are large areas of mass loss of up to 20 cm or more per year over much of southern Greenland, and also further north in lower elevation areas. There is a much smaller area of mass gain in the highest area of the ice plateau in the north-central region. (Image from the NASA Earth Observatory.)

discharge in the west and, particularly, in the east more than doubled the outflow from 90 to 220 cubic kilometres per year. Thomas and others in 2006, using laser altimeter measurements, report that net mass loss from Greenland more than doubled between 1993/4–1998/9 and 1998/9–2004.[33]

These observational results indicate mass losses considerably faster than were modelled by glaciologists using models that did not take account of the recently identified mechanisms of meltwater lubrication and tidewater glacier undercutting. Indeed, Hansen in 2005[30] suggests that various other positive feedbacks may come into play as the ice sheet slumps, most notably that more precipitation on the ice sheet interior will fall in summer as rain rather than snow, thereby accelerating the effect of surface melting and bottom lubrication. At present, as is shown in **Figure 18**, marginal areas are slumping, but the high plateau is still accumulating mass. The latter may change in the future.[34]

Simulations and paleo-climatic data indicate that Greenland and Antarctica together contributed several metres to sea-level rise 130 000 to 127 000 years ago, at a time when global temperatures were about the same as presently projected for 2100. Overpeck and others in 2006 conclude that peak rates of sea-level rise may well exceed 1 metre per century, and that this may be strongly related to warming of the upper 200 m of the ocean producing rapid thinning of ice shelves (and tidewater glacier outlets) from below. Glikson in a 2008 paper argues, on the basis of paleo-analogues from past rapid climate changes, including the Dansgaard-Oeschinger glacial cycles during the last glaciation, that sea level rose by around 5 m per 1°C global warming, and that this has occurred on century time scales in the past.[35]

Further evidence that positive feedbacks in the Arctic have commenced comes from satellite observations of rapid decreases in Arctic sea ice extent.[36] Data from the US National Snow and Ice Data Center (NSIDC, 2007) indicates that the sea ice extent on 10 September 2007 was at a record low of 4.24 million square kilometres (see **Figure 19**). This is more than a million square kilometres below the previous minimum in 2005. Thus the Arctic Ocean has lost a mirror roughly the size of Texas and New Mexico combined, meaning that much more solar energy is being absorbed by the ocean. This will lead to further decreases in sea ice, further undercutting of tidewater glaciers in Greenland, and possibly greater summer surface melting of the Greenland ice sheet, causing a further acceleration of sea-level rise. Indeed, precipitation over coastal Greenland in summer will increasingly fall as rain rather than snow, adding to the surface melting and acceleration of the outlet glaciers.

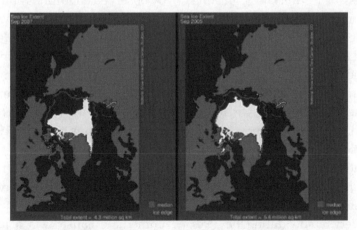

Figure 19: Arctic sea ice extent (white) in September 2007 (left) compared to the previous minimum in September 2005 (right). The thin line represents the median extent in the period 1979–2000. The area of the September 2007 ice minimum (for the whole of September) was 4.28 million square km, compared to the previous record low extent of 5.57 million square km in September 2005. This is equivalent to losing a reflector of sunlight of area approximately 1000 km 1300 km. (Credit: National Snow and Ice Data Center, press release 1 October 2007, see http://www.nsidc.org.)

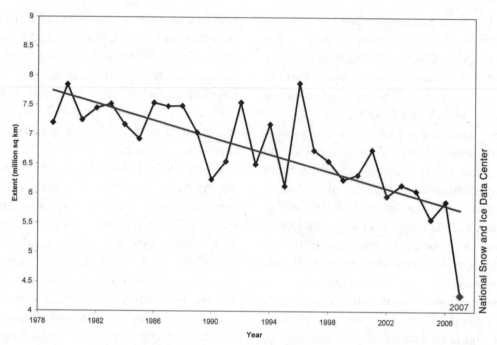

Figure 20: The September ice extent in the Arctic from 1979 to 2007. The rate of decline is now about 10% per decade, but appears to be accelerating. It is now much faster than was projected by climate models using the SRES scenarios. (Credit: National Snow and Ice Data Center press release, 1 October 2007. See http://www.nsidc.org.)

The trend in Arctic sea ice extent since 1979 is shown in **Figure 20**. The recent decreasing trend is much faster and outside the range of projections from the various climate models. IPCC 2007 estimates would see summer ice gone by late this century, but more recent extrapolations from the observed record suggest it could happen in the next one or two decades. Decrease in sea ice extent has been accompanied by more extensive percentage loss of ice thickness, making further losses in extent more likely. Extrapolation is tricky because there are clearly regional effects, notably, the rapid loss in 2007 had its immediate cause in rapid warming on the Pacific side and rapid transpolar drift of ice from the Siberian coast towards the North Atlantic. However, whatever the regional variations, the fact is that decreased sea ice extent means more absorption of solar radiation and greater warming.

Antarctica's contribution to sea-level changes is particularly uncertain, with the possibility of surprises.[37] Floating ice shelves, notably the Wordie and Larsen A and B shelves, broke up very rapidly during the 1990s and early 2000s following regional warming of about 2.5°C over the previous 50 years. The 1600 square kilometres of Larsen A suddenly disintegrated in 39

days during 1994–95, and the 3245 square kilometres of Larsen B in only 41 days in 2002 (**Figure 21**).

The rapid regional warming around the Antarctic Peninsula was not well predicted by older global climate models. However, modelling by Michiel van den Broeke and colleagues suggests an explanation.[38] They used a high-resolution (55 km spacing) regional atmospheric climate model driven by observed conditions at the boundary to compare years with a strong and a weak circumpolar vortex (upper atmospheric circulation around the pole). Results showed a change in the surface winds such that it was much warmer over the Weddell Sea and the adjacent Antarctic Peninsula when there was a stronger circumpolar vortex. The trend towards such conditions since the 1970s has been discussed earlier in this chapter.

The very rapid disintegration of the Wordie and Larsen ice shelves was unexpected. Their break-up was likely due in part to basal melting, but its immediate cause was a large extent of summer meltwater pools (visible in the top frame of **Figure 21**) penetrating into crevasses created by ice movement, causing major fractures in the shelves. Some of the

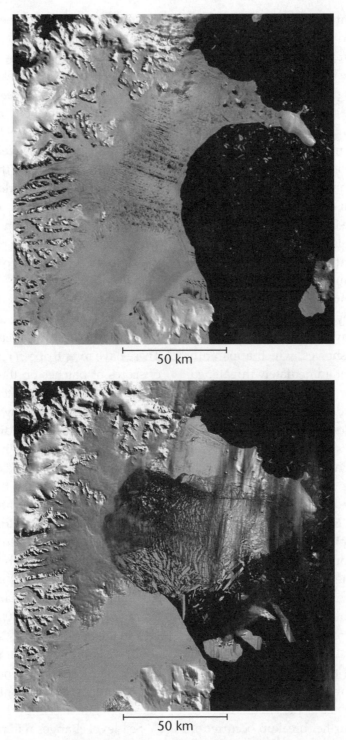

Figure 21: Satellite images of the break-up of the Larsen B ice shelf in 2002. The Larsen B ice shelf as it appeared on 31 January 2002 (top) and on 5 March 2002 (bottom). Dark areas on the ice shelf on 31 January are meltwater pools. These rapidly drained into crevasses that opened up causing disintegration of the ice shelf as seen on 5 March. Note the more chunky icebergs in the lower right of the frame that are the result of normal iceberg calving from the nearby Filchner-Ronne ice shelf. Some thin cloud also appears in the bottom image. (Images provided by the US National Snow and Ice Data Center, University of Colorado and NASA's MODIS sensors.)

narrow ice shelf fragments (often up to 200 metres thick) may have speeded the break-up by tipping over, releasing energy that sent shock waves through the ice shelf. These narrow shelf fragments are visible in the bottom frame of **Figure 21**.[39]

The break-up of the ice shelves has been followed, in the case of the Larsen Ice Shelves, by an acceleration and active surging of a number of former contributory glaciers which are already making a small but significant contribution to sea-level rise. This has led to the confirmation of an earlier theory in 1978 by John Mercer of Ohio State University that ice shelves tend to hold back outlet glaciers.[40]

The rapid disintegration of the Wordie and Larsen ice shelves is causing a rethink as to the stability of the West Antarctic Ice Sheet (WAIS), which, if it were to totally disintegrate, would add some 6 metres to global average sea level. The Ross and Filchner-Ronne ice shelves, which apparently stabilise the WAIS, are not immediately threatened, although Randy Showstack from *EOS* magazine reports that only a few degrees warming may be needed to threaten the Ross Ice Shelf, the largest in Antarctica. Widespread surface melting has been reported on the Ross Ice Shelf during warm summer episodes. MJM Williams of the Danish Center for Earth System Science and colleagues suggest that the Amery Ice Shelf off East Antarctica (the third largest embayed ice shelf in Antarctica) may be threatened by a 3°C regional warming. Increases in basal melt rates under the ice shelves due to ocean warming and changing circulation beneath the ice shelves may be responsible.

Satellite radar measurements show that, in the Amundsen Sea sector of West Antarctica the small fringing ice shelves have already thinned by up to 5.5 metres per year during the last decade or so. In this region, in late February 2008, the Wilkins Ice Shelf started to disintegrate. Further breakup occurred in May of 2008, during the winter half year, which is extraordinary. The thinning or breakup of the ice shelves, presumably due to warmer ocean currents, is accompanied by thinning and acceleration of their tributary glaciers, notably the Pine Island Glacier. These outlet glaciers drain a region thought to be the most vulnerable part of the West Antarctic Ice Sheet, because it is grounded below sea level. Recent aircraft and satellite observations show that local glaciers are discharging about 250 cubic kilometres of ice each year to the ocean, almost 60% more than is accumulating in their catchment areas, and at a faster rate than in the 1990s. Collapse of this region would raise global sea level by about 1 metre.[41]

Later this century, as the global warming trend continues, warming could affect the much larger Filchner-Ronne and Ross ice shelves, which could lead to the disintegration of the rest of the WAIS, with eventually several more metres of sea-level rise, although the speed of such a disintegration is highly uncertain.

Another potentially destabilising feature of Antarctica is the existence of an extensive network of freshwater lakes and streams under the ice sheet. These have recently been revealed by the rise and fall of scores of patches on the surface of the ice sheet. While the volumes of water are small in themselves they seem to affect the flow rates in the overlying ice streams that eventually discharge into the oceans. Also, Corr and Vaughan have reported evidence of volcanic activity in the West Antarctic region, but do not see this as explaining the general thinning of the ice shelves nor the acceleration of the outlet glaciers.[42]

The Patagonian icefields in South America have been observed to be losing volume in recent decades, with estimates based on the retreat of the largest 63 outlet glaciers increasing from a rate of 0.042 ± 0.002 mm per year in equivalent sea level, averaged from 1969 to 2000, to 0.105 ± 0.011 mm per year in the period 1995 to 2000. The latter is a rate of about 42 cubic km of ice per year, and 1 mm per decade rise in sea level. The Alaskan glaciers, which are five times larger, contribute about 3 mm per decade to global sea-level rise.[43]

Sea-level changes will not be uniform across the world. According to the 2007 IPCC report the models show qualitative agreement that the range of regional variation in sea-level change over the coming century is about ±30 to 40% of the global average. This is due to different rates of regional penetration of warming into the deep oceans (and thus of thermal expansion of the water column), changes in atmospheric pressure and surface winds, ocean currents and salinity. Despite differences in detail between models, there is agreement that sea-level rise will be greatest in the Arctic (due to freshening) and least south of 60°S (due to circulation changes and low thermal expansion). There is also a belt of higher sea-level rise around 40 to 50°S.[44]

Further, highly localised land movements, both isostatic (the slow flexing of continental plates as the weight of ice sheets, sediments and water changes) and tectonic (earthquakes and other plate movements) will continue through the twenty-first century, causing local variations about the global average sea-level rise. It can be expected that by 2100, many regions currently experiencing relative sea-level fall will instead have a rising relative sea level as the increasing volume of the oceans due to climate change begins to dominate over local effects. Additionally, extreme high water levels due to storm surges will occur with increasing frequency as a result of average sea-level rise. Their frequency may be further increased if storms become more frequent or severe as a result of climate change. Moreover, changes in wave energy and direction associated with changes in storm tracks and intensity, will change rates and locations of coastal erosion.[45] For all these reasons, projections of local sea-level rise related changes need to be quite location-specific.

Thresholds and abrupt or irreversible changes

Complex systems do not always vary in a smooth fashion that enables easy extrapolation. This is the case for climate, where sudden changes in regime can occur over wide areas, and are apparently associated with some shift in the circulation pattern. Abrupt changes in ecosystems have also been observed. The mathematical theory of such regime changes is still being developed.[46]

Past large-scale abrupt changes in the climate system have already been discussed in Chapter 2. Such abrupt changes also occur regionally, for example in rainfall. For example summer half-year rainfall increased over large parts of eastern Australia around 1945, largely reversing a decrease in the 1890s, while there was a sudden decrease in rainfall in the south-west of Western Australia around 1967–72, which has not reversed since. Such abrupt changes have also been found in climate model simulations. They arise due to the existence of multiple quasi-equilibrium states in complex systems and the transitions between them.[47]

For example Katrin Meissner and colleagues found in their climate model that on time scales of thousands of years it had two different responses depending on the assumed CO_2 concentrations. For concentrations less than 400 ppm they found a steady state, but for concentrations above 440 ppm they found the climate system oscillated between two very different states, ones with or without exchange of water with the deep Southern Ocean, with a rapid change between them.[48]

Such abrupt changes may or may not be predictable, as they occur as part of natural climate variability on a time scale of decades, often due to the accumulation of random or chaotic events (stochastic processes). It is a bit like the 'random walk' of an inebriated person that may or may not lead that person into walking over a cliff. Abrupt changes may also be brought on by some uniform but gradual changes that slowly move the climate to some critical point or threshold where it flips to another regime. Such thresholds may not be anticipated, or, even if they are anticipated, not fully understood. This problem is even more acute when we consider the possibility of rapid and irreversible changes to the climate system, which have been termed 'large-scale singular events'.

Large-scale singular events, or 'discontinuities' are an especially important category of abrupt or threshold events because of their large potential impacts. For the first time, the IPCC report in 2001 emphasised the potential importance of plausible abrupt or irreversible Earth system events. Although uncertain, and in some cases taking a century or more to come about, such events might have such large impacts globally that their possibility becomes an important part of any risk analysis.

In its 2007 report the IPCC explains that:

... if [a] system contains more than one equilibrium state, transitions to structurally different states are possible. Upon the crossing of a tipping point (bifurcation point), the evolution of the system is no longer controlled by the time scale of the forcing, but rather determined by its internal dynamics, which can be either faster than the forcing, or significantly slower. Only the former case would be termed 'abrupt climate change', but the latter is of equal importance. For the long-term evolution of a climate variable one must distinguish between reversible and irreversible changes. The notion of 'climate surprises' refers to abrupt transitions or temporary or permanent transitions to different states in parts of the climate system ...[49]

Examples of abrupt or irreversible climate change given by IPCC in 2007 include:

- the slowdown or cessation of the Atlantic Meridional Circulation or MOC (otherwise known as the Thermo-Haline Circulation or THC),

- the rapid disappearance of Arctic sea ice,

- rapid loss or disappearance of mountain glaciers or ice caps,

- increased melting or collapse of the Greenland or West Antarctic ice sheets,

- large-scale vegetation change such as desertification as in the Sahel or the Amazon, or vegetation and soils turning into sources rather than sinks of carbon, and

- abrupt changes or irreversible trends in large-scale atmosphere and ocean circulation patterns such as the El Niño–Southern Oscillation (ENSO), the North Atlantic Oscillation, and the Arctic and Antarctic oscillations (or Annular Modes).

In 2002 the US National Research Council issued a major report entitled *Abrupt Climate Change: Inevitable Surprises* that provides a comprehensive treatment of abrupt climate change. This has been summarised by Richard Alley and colleagues, who state that 'it is conceivable that human forcing of climate change is increasing the probability of large, abrupt events. Were such an event to recur, the economic and ecological impacts could be large and potentially serious.' They go on to say: 'Slowing the rate of human forcing of the climate system may delay or even avoid crossing the thresholds [that would lead to abrupt climate change].[50]

The timing and probability of occurrence of large-scale discontinuities is difficult to determine because these events are triggered by complex interactions between components of the climate system. Large or sudden impacts could lag behind the triggering mechanisms by decades or centuries. These triggers are sensitive to the magnitude and rate of climate change so that large global warmings have a greater potential to lead to large-scale discontinuities in the climate system.[51]

Timothy Lenton and others, drawing on an international workshop held in 2005, the pertinent literature and an expert elicitation, have identified and described a list of 'tipping elements' in the Earth's climate system. They define these as 'subsystems of the Earth system that are at least subcontinental in scale and can be switched – under certain circumstances – into a qualitatively different state by small perturbations'. They define the 'tipping point' as 'the corresponding critical point – in forcing and a feature of the system – at which the future state of the system is qualitatively altered'. **Table 7** is a much abridged and modified version of their table of policy-relevant tipping points (ones that people care about enough to affect policy), their properties and potential impacts.[52]

Surface waters in the North Atlantic Ocean presently become colder and more saline as they travel north-east in the Gulf Stream. This leads to convective overturning (sinking) of the surface waters, which helps drive the currents. The slowdown or complete cessation of convective overturning of the waters of the North Atlantic could arise due to several causes. These include surface warming due to the enhanced greenhouse effect, and lower salinity of surface waters due to

TABLE 7: Selected tipping points, their properties and impacts, based on TM Lenton and others, PNAS 105, pp. 1786–93 (2008).[52]

Tipping element and property	Controlling parameter(s)	Tipping point: global warming relative to 1980–1999 (°C)	Transition time scale	Key impacts
Arctic summer sea-ice area	Local warming, ocean heat transport	0.5 to 2	Rapid (decade)	Greater warming, changed ecosystems, navigable ocean
Greenland Ice Sheet volume	Local air temperature	1 to 2	Slow (centuries)	Sea-level rise 2–7 m
West Antarctic Ice Sheet volume	Local air and water temperatures	3 to 5	Slow (centuries)	Sea-level rise 5 m
Atlantic Thermo-haline Circulation, overturning rate	Freshwater input to Arctic/North Atlantic	3 to 5	Gradual (century)	Regional cooling, southward shift of Intertropical Convergence Zone (ITCZ)
El Niño–Southern Oscillation (ENSO), amplitude	Depth and sharpness of thermocline in East Tropical Pacific	3 to 6	Gradual (century)	More extreme droughts and floods in affected regions
Indian summer monsoon rainfall	Albedo over India	N/A	Rapid (1 year)	Drought, decreased carrying capacity
Sahara/Sahel and West Africa monsoon, vegetation increase	Precipitation	3 to 5	Rapid (decade)	Increased carrying capacity
Amazon rainforest, decrease	Precipitation and length of dry season	3 to 4	Gradual (50 years)	Decreased rainfall, biodiversity loss
Boreal forest, tree fraction	Local temperature	7	Gradual (50 years)	Biome switch
Antarctic bottom water formation	Precipitation and evaporation	Not clear	Gradual (century)	Ocean circulation, carbon storage
Tundra, tree fraction	Growing degree days	Not clear	Gradual (century)	More warming (via albedo), biome switch
Permafrost volume	Local temperature	Poorly determined, but low start	Gradual (<century)	Methane and CO_2 release, biome switch, increased warming
Marine methane hydrates volume	Temperature and pressure of sediment	Not known	Millennia	Increased global warming
Ocean anoxia	Phosphorus input, stagnation	Not clear	Many millennia	Mass extinction of marine life
Decrease in Arctic ozone	Stratospheric cloud formation	Not clear	Rapid (year)	Increased surface ultraviolet radiation

increased rainfall at high latitudes and influxes of freshwater from rivers, melting glaciers and partial melting of the Greenland Ice Sheet. Already, large-scale salinity changes have been observed in the world's oceans, especially the Atlantic. Over the last 50 years, there has been an increase in surface salinity in tropical and subtropical waters and a freshening of the high latitude North and South Atlantic surface waters. This is clear evidence of strengthening of the hydrological cycle, with increased evaporation at low latitudes and increased precipitation at high latitudes. A continuation of this trend could trigger a cessation of overturning.[53]

Also, around Antarctica the main cause of convective overturning of the surface ocean is the freezing of seawater, which leads to a rejection of salt, and thus to dense highly saline water that sinks. Global warming would lead to a reduction in sea-ice formation, and thus reduced overturning there as well. However, this might be counteracted to some extent by increased westerly winds as the sub-polar westerlies are pushed further south and the Antarctic Circumpolar Current strengthens.

Evidence for the plausibility and impacts of such events comes from past events recorded in the paleo-record of climate and sea level, and from computer modelling both of past and possible future events. There is also increasing observational evidence suggesting that such processes may already be under way. Besides direct impact on surface climate, reduced overturning of the oceans would reduce oceanic uptake of carbon dioxide, and thus further increase the carbon dioxide concentration in the atmosphere.

Melting of the Greenland Ice Sheet and/or disintegration of the WAIS, both of which could be triggered very soon (if not already) by global warming, would likely take centuries to complete, but are potentially irreversible. These events are inevitable if carbon dioxide concentrations are allowed to reach two to three times pre-industrial values and could result from much smaller increases in greenhouse gases. The process could only be reversed if carbon dioxide were to be taken out of the atmosphere in such large quantities as to substantially reduce the carbon dioxide concentration and thus reverse global warming. Failing this, the Greenland and West Antarctic ice sheets would each contribute several metres to global mean sea level over the next several centuries. As discussed above in relation to sea level, the time scales for disintegration of the WAIS and the Greenland Ice Sheet are still under debate and there is some chance that they may occur more rapidly. Rapid melting of the Greenland Ice Sheet could also affect ocean circulation by freshening the North Atlantic and Arctic oceans more rapidly than otherwise and thus helping to slow or stop convective overturning.

Several mechanisms exist which could lead to an acceleration of global warming via positive feedbacks (amplification mechanisms) associated with the carbon cycle, a process known as 'runaway carbon dynamics'. One is destabilisation of the huge methane reserves stored in crystalline structures (hydrates) on the seabed of the continental shelves and slopes, and in permafrost regions on land. Estimates of the amount of carbon stored in gas (mainly methane) hydrates vary widely from more than 10 000 Gt to more recent estimates of about 1000+ Gt. Even the lower estimates are comparable with other known carbon stores and with the amount in the atmosphere. This compares with the present annual release of greenhouse gases, mainly from the burning of fossil fuels, of some 8–9 Gt of carbon per year. Methane is some 21 times as effective as carbon dioxide as a greenhouse gas, so even a modest leakage into the atmosphere from gas hydrates could greatly accelerate global warming.[54]

Warming of permafrost, which is already widely observed across the Arctic region, could lead to local, but in total, massive releases of methane from gas hydrates on land. In Arctic coastal areas sea ice is receding and increased wave action is already accelerating erosion of erstwhile frozen shorelines. Melting of permafrost and loss of structural integrity of hydrate deposits will increase slope failures, landslides and avalanches and threaten human infrastructure such as buildings, roads and pipelines. The effect of the thawing of permafrost on greenhouse gas emissions in particular locations is unclear. It will likely depend on the moisture status of the organic matter after thawing. Dry organic-rich soils tend to release more carbon dioxide and less methane, whereas moist conditions favour methane-making microbes, but also peat accumulation, which stores carbon. Projected increasing rainfall in high latitudes would favour wet conditions. Some methane released from hydrates will be absorbed and broken down before it reaches the surface, both in permafrost regions on land and in ocean floor hydrate deposits. On land, since methane is much more effective as a greenhouse gas, and much of the thawed permafrost will be wet, the net effect is likely to increase global warming.[55]

On the continental shelves and slopes warming of seawater at intermediate depths may melt gas hydrate deposits and cause massive slumping of sediments, not only releasing lots of methane, but possibly creating tidal waves or tsunamis. There is evidence that such a process may have occurred some 7000 years ago off the coast of Norway, where the Storegga slide, which was the size of Wales, apparently produced a 20 metre tsunami that may have wiped out Neolithic communities in north-east Scotland. However, the hydrate deposits would tend to be stabilised by the increasing pressure caused by sea-level rise (depending on the local sea water temperature profile). Calculations suggest that at present rates of warming the pressure effect may win, but if warming accelerates and sea-level rise is dominated by thermal expansion, deposits may be destabilised. Regional differences in this balance between warming of bottom water and pressure at depth may lead to destabilisation in some areas. This may be particularly evident on time scales of centuries as ice melts from Greenland and parts of Antarctica, causing the adjacent continental slope to rise due to loss of the weight of ice ('isostatic rebound'). Isostatic rebound after the last glaciation is still occurring in parts of Scotland, Norway and Sweden, where relative sea-level fall is occurring, reducing bottom water pressure.[56]

In a 2002 review, Euan Nisbet of the University of London concluded that the case is open for a major methane release in the twenty-first century, possibly from a large pool of free methane gas trapped below a hydrate deposit. He points to the possibility of large riverine floods, brought about by a more intense hydrological cycle, depositing large amounts of sediment that could destabilise hydrates through slippage in sediment deposits on continental slopes.[57]

Other possible feedbacks on the carbon cycle include decreased efficiency of the oceanic and terrestrial biospheric sinks of carbon due to global warming. Oceanic feedbacks include increasing stability and reduced overturning of the surface layers of the oceans (leading to reduced uptake of carbon dioxide from the atmosphere), and reduced solubility of carbon dioxide in warmer waters. This is complicated by observed and anticipated circulation changes especially in the Southern Ocean and North Atlantic. In addition, increasing acidity of the oceans due to higher carbon dioxide concentrations would affect many oceanic organisms in complex ways, possibly also reducing the biological uptake of carbon dioxide in the oceans.[58]

The terrestrial biosphere, which presently acts as a sink of carbon dioxide, could become a source by 2050. Carbon dioxide sinks vary due to changes in ocean circulation associated with ENSO and

subduction of surface waters into the deep ocean, carbon dioxide fertilisation of terrestrial forests, and temperature and rainfall effects on terrestrial plant growth. The main reason for the expected change of the terrestrial biosphere from a sink to a source by 2050 is increased respiration and decay of the increased biomass and soil carbon at higher temperatures. Two different climate models with interacting carbon cycles indicate that global warmings could be increased by one or more degrees by 2100 due to these interactions. Increasing fire frequencies and intensities may also cause faster increases of atmospheric carbon dioxide. Widespread forest and peat fires were observed to contribute significantly to carbon dioxide increases in 1994/95 and 1997/98 when large biomass burning took place in tropical and boreal regions. These and other observations suggest that biomass feedbacks may be occurring earlier than in the climate models.[59]

Other, possibly lesser, but still widespread climate changes are possible. For example, the IPCC 2007 report discusses the possibilities of major changes in the behaviour of the continental monsoons, ENSO and other patterns of climate variability. These are complex, for example, the monsoons will be intensified in general by increased land–sea temperature contrasts as the land warms up faster than the oceans. Moreover warmer air can hold more moisture and this may cause greater rainfall intensities. On the other hand, atmospheric particulates (aerosols) may have a cooling effect over land.[60]

Several recent studies have identified the importance of large-scale singular events in global estimates of risk, and in cost/benefit analyses as to the optimal timing of mitigation action to reduce the risk of such events. The possibility of such events increases the overall risk of dangerous impacts of climate change, making early action to reduce climate change more pressing.[61]

Scenarios in a nutshell

In summary, the full range of IPCC SRES emissions scenarios would lead to a wide range of global warmings (1.1 to 6.4°C) and sea-level rise (18 to 59 cm according to IPCC 2007, but more likely 1 metre and up to several metres) by 2100. About half the range in global average warming is due to the range of emissions scenarios and half to uncertainties in the science, mainly in the climate sensitivity. This leaves a lot of room for choice of emission reduction policies leading to lower emissions, and thus less climate change. Emissions policies that aim at stabilising greenhouse gas concentrations in the atmosphere anywhere below 1000ppm of carbon dioxide-equivalent would lead to smaller warmings than those resulting from the higher SRES scenarios. However, to limit global warming to less than 2 or 3°C would require much lower greenhouse gas emissions. We will discuss desirable targets for emission reductions in Chapter 8.

Changed frequencies and intensities of extreme weather events are likely with global warming, including more hot days, fewer cold nights, greater heat stress, more droughts in mid-latitude continental areas, more intense rain events, and increased intensity and rainfall from tropical cyclones or hurricanes.

Increasing evidence from observations suggests that a number of positive feedback processes are possible and may already be in operation. These include:

- permafrost melting and related changes in albedo,

- biomass feedbacks due to heat stress on plants, fire and other phenomena,

- rapid decrease in Arctic sea ice, allowing much greater absorption of solar radiation,

- atmospheric and ocean circulation changes that may reinforce adverse changes in the carbon cycle and ice sheet stability,

- rapid changes in Antarctica including loss of marginal ice shelves and acceleration of outlet glaciers,

- rapid changes in Greenland, with increased surface melting and acceleration of outlet glaciers,

- freshening and warming of the Arctic Ocean and far North Atlantic, that could slow down or stop the Meridional Overturning Circulation, with widespread regional consequences.

These and related phenomena can all interact to accelerate and reinforce climate change, as is illustrated in **Figure 22**. 'Global dimming' is the term used to describe the effect of particulate pollution (aerosols) in decreasing solar radiation incident at the Earth's surface. Since the 1970s this dimming effect has tended to decrease, largely as a result of decreases in sulfur emissions in North America and Europe.

Possibilities thus exist for sudden rapid and long-term (possibly irreversible) changes in global-scale

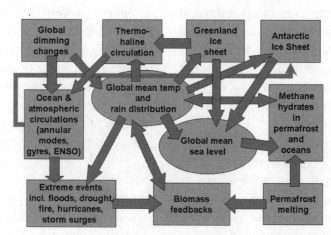

Figure 22: Links between various elements of the climate system, illustrating how changes in any one can interact with others to produce positive or negative feedback effects.

climate-related systems, including more rapid sea-level rise due to more rapid disintegration and melting of the Greenland and West Antarctic ice sheets, major changes to the circulation of the oceans with regional climate impacts (especially in regions bordering the North Atlantic), and accelerated release of methane and carbon dioxide into the atmosphere which would lead to greater global warming for the same greenhouse gas emissions.[62]

The IPCC in 2007 stated that the climate sensitivity (equilibrium warming for a doubling of CO_2 concentration) could be 'substantially higher' than the upper limit of the range it has adopted, which is 2.0 to 4.5°C. This raises the possibility of climate changes greater than those projected in the 2007 report, largely as a result of the processes shown in **Figure 22**. This implies a much greater chance of more severe climate changes and impacts, some of which could be catastrophic.

Even the projected global warmings reported by IPCC in 2007 lead to climate-related changes that would have major impacts on human and natural systems, as we shall see in the next chapter. This means that the stakes are high, and suggests there is a need for reducing greenhouse gas emissions so we can follow lower and safer emission pathways. How this might be achieved is a subject taken up later in this book.

ENDNOTES

1. From 'How long have we been in the Anthropocene era?' editorial comment, *Climatic Change*, **61**, pp. 251–7 (2003).

2. The American Geophysical Union is the largest professional body of all the Earth science disciplines, and has some 50 000 members, mostly from the United States and Canada, but with many members in other countries also. Most are researchers, or tertiary teachers and students. See http://www.agu.org.

3. The Center for a New American Security report is available at http://www.cnas.org.

4. Paul Crutzen's comments are in 'My life with O_y NO_x and other YZO_xs', *Les Prix Nobel* (The Nobel Prizes), Almqvist & Wiksell International, Stockholm, pp. 123–57 (1995).

5. See Nakicenovic and Swart, *Emissions Scenarios. A Special Report of the Working Group III of the Intergovernmental Panel on Climate Change*, Cambridge University Press, Cambridge, UK (2000).

6. See DM Smith and others, *Science*, **317**, pp. 796–9 (10 August 2007).

7. These year-to-year and regional effects can be seen on maps of sea-surface temperature anomalies (departures from previous long-term averages), which can be plotted easily at http://www.data.giss.nasa.gov.

8. The large number of different stabilisation scenarios now published are summarised in Chapter 3.3.5 of the IPCC 2007 report, WGIII. Table 4 is based on the IPCC 2007 Synthesis Report, Table SPM-6.

9. The equilibrium climate sensitivity is discussed in detail in the IPCC 2007 report, WGIII, Box 10.2, pp. 798–9.

10. Detailed regional warmings are described in the IPCC 2007 report, WGI, Chapter 10.3.2.1, pp. 764–7.

11. Results from the climate models are discussed in the IPCC 2007 report, WGI, Chapter 10.2.3.2. More detailed regional changes will be found in the relevant regional chapters of WGII.

12. Projected changes in the atmospheric circulation or modes of variability, including ENSO, the North Atlantic Oscillation and the annular modes are described in IPCC 2007, WGI, Chapter 10.3.5. However, there is little discussion of changes in wind speeds apart from tropical storms.

13. Changes in atmospheric water content, and its attribution to human influences, are discussed by KM Willett and others in *Nature*, **449**, pp. 710–13 (11 October 2007), and BD Santer and others, *Proceedings of the National Academy*

of Sciences, **104**, pp. 15 248–53 (25 September 2007). The paper by FJ Wentz and others is in *Science*, **317**, pp. 233–5 (13 July 2007) and that by X Zhang and others is in *Nature*, **448**, pp. 461–5 (26 July 2007).

14. See Pall and others in *Climate Dynamics*, **28**, pp. 351–63 (2007).

15. Table 5 is based in part on the relevant sections of the 2007 IPCC report, WGI: Chapter 3.8 for observed changes in extremes, and Chapter 10.3.6 and Table 11.2 for projected change in extremes.

16. The paleo flood record is reviewed by Knox in *Quaternary Science Reviews*, **19**, pp. 439–57 (2000), while modern flood records and model projections were studied by Milly and others, *Nature*, **415**, pp. 514–17 (2002). Other recent studies relevant to increased flooding and rainfall intensity, and to drought can be found in the IPCC 2007 report, WGII, Chapter 3.4.3.

17. An overview of the EU-funded project 'Modelling the impact of climate extremes' (MICE) can be found in *Climate Research*, **31**, pp. 121–33 (2006) by Hanson and others, as part of a special issue on the MICE results.

18. Observations of pan evaporation are discussed in the IPCC 2007 report, WGI, Chapter 3.3.3.

19. M Wild and others, *Science*, **308**, pp. 847–50 (2005).

20. See *Bulletin American Meteorological Society* (March 2004), pp. 328–30, and Curry and others, *Nature*, **426**, pp. 826–9 (2003).

21. See 'Evidence of impacts from rising temperature on inflows to the Murray-Darling Basin', *Geophysical Research Letters*, **35**, L07701, doi=10.1029/2008GLO33390 (2008). See also N Nicholls 'The changing nature of Australian droughts', *Climatic Change*, **63**, pp. 323–36 (2004).

22. See Glantz (ed.), *Once Burned, Twice Shy? Lessons Learned from the 1997–98 El Niño*, United Nations University Press, Tokyo (2001); Glantz, *La Niña and Its Impacts: Facts and Speculation*, United Nations University Press, Tokyo (2002); Ropelewski and Halpert, *Monthly Weather Review*, **115**, pp. 1606–26 (1987); Hoerling and Kumar, *Science*, **299**, pp. 691–4 (2003). Hoerling and others, *Science*, **292**, pp. 90–2 (2001) discuss the connection of the NAO with warming of the tropical ocean, and the human connection is made in Gillett and others, *Nature*, **422**, pp. 292–4 (2003). Future trends and possible changes in the character of the NAO are discussed in the IPCC 2007 report, WGII, Chapter 10.3.5.

23. See the IPCC 2007 report, WGI, Chapter 10.6.3.3; and 'Workshop on tropical cyclones and climate' in *Bulletin of the American Meteorological Society* (March 2007) pp. 389–91; Holland and Webster, 'Heightened tropical cyclone activity in the North Atlantic: natural variability of climate trend?', *Philosophical Transactions of the Royal Society A*, **365**, pp. 2695–716 (2007); and Judith Curry, 'Potential increased hurricane activity in a greenhouse warmed world', Chapter 2 in *Sudden and Disruptive Climate Change*, Michael C MacCracken, John C Topping Jr and Frances Moore (eds), Earthscan, London (2008).

24. Changes in extra-tropical storms and wave heights are reviewed in the IPCC 2007 report, WGI, Chapter 10.6.3.4.

25. The connections between melting glaciers, ice caps, and earthquakes are documented in Stewart and others, *Quaternary Science Reviews*, **19**, pp. 1367–91 (2000); Arvidsson, *Science*, **274**, pp. 744–6 (1986); Grollimund and others, *Geology*, **29** (2), pp. 175–8 (2001); Johnston, *Nature*, **330**, pp. 467–9 (1987); Johnston, *Science*, **274**, pp. 735–6 (1996); Wu and others, *Geophysical Journal International* **139**, pp. 657–70 (1999); and Sauber and Molnia, *Global and Planetary Change*, **42** (1–4), pp. 279–93 (2004). See also Bill McGuire 'Earth fire and fury', *New Scientist* (27 May 2006) pp. 32–6.

26. See NS Diffenbaugh and others, 'Fine-scale processes regulate the response of extreme events to global climate change', *Proceedings of the National Academy of Sciences*, **102**, pp. 15 774–8 (1 November 2005).

27. See Trapp and others 'Changes in severe thunderstorm frequency during the 21st century caused by anthropogenically enhanced global radiative forcing', in *Proceedings of the National Academy of Sciences*, **104**, pp. 19 719–23 (11 December 2007).

28. Sea-level rise is discussed in the IPCC 2007 report especially in the WGI Summary for Policymakers (SPM) and in WGI Chapter 10.6.

29. The Rahmstorf estimate is in *Science*, **315**, pp. 368–70 (2007). See also Horton and others *Geophysical Research Letters*, **35**, L02715, doi:10.1029/2007GL032486 (2008).

30. Hansen's theory for rapid disintegration of the Greenland ice cap is in *Scientific American* (March 2004) pp. 68–77, and in *Climatic Change*, **68**, pp. 269–79 (2005), and 'Scientific reticence and sea level rise', *Environmental Research Letters*, **2** (2007) 024002. It is based in part on correlations between surface melting and accelerated ice flow, reported by Zwally and others, *Science*, **297**, pp. 218–22 (2002). See also E Rignot in Chapter 5 of *Sudden and Disruptive Climate Change*, Michael C MacCracken, John C Topping Jr and Frances Moore (eds), Earthscan, London (2008).

31. Greenland ice melting is documented by the NASA Earth Observatory, see for example: NASA (2003): Vanishing ice, features, 7 May (available at: http://earthobservatory.nasa.gov/Features/vanishing/; NASA (2005): 'Satellites continue to see decline in Arctic sea ice in 2005', news release, 28 September (available at http://nasa.gov/centers/goddard/news); NASA (2006): 'Greenland ice loss doubles in past decade, raising sea level faster', news release, 16 February (available at http://earthobservatory.nasa.gov/Newsroom/NasaNews/2006/2006021621775.html); and 'Greenland ice sheet losing mass', at http://earthobservatory.nasa.gov/Newsroom/NewImages/images.php3?img_id=17434. See also 'State of the cryosphere' at http:/nsidc.org/sotc/iceshelves.html.

32. Melting of tidewater glaciers from below is discussed in R Bindschadler, 'Hitting the ice where it hurts', *Science*, **311**, pp. 1720–1 (2006).

33. The Rignot and Kanagaratnam paper is 'Changes in the velocity structure of the Greenland Ice Sheet', *Science*, **311**, pp. 986–90 (2006), and Thomas and others (2006) is 'Progressive increase in ice loss from Greenland', *Geophysical Research Letters*, **33**, L10503.

34. The ice modelling papers without recently identified mechanisms include R Greve,'On the response of the Greenland Ice Sheet to greenhouse climate change', *Climate Change*, **46**, pp. 289–303 (2000); P Huybrechts and J de Wolde, 'The dynamic response of the Greenland and Antarctic ice sheets to multiple-century climatic warming', *Journal of Climate*, **12**, pp. 2169–88 (1999), and Ridley and others, 'Elimination of the Greenland Ice Sheet in a high CO$_2$ climate', *Journal of Climate*, **18**, pp. 3409–27 (2005).

However, there are other recent papers on observations of, and the dynamics of, the melting of Greenland. These include RB Alley and others, 'Ice-sheet and sea-level changes', *Science*, **310**, pp. 456–60 (2005); JA Dowdeswell, *Science*, **311**, pp. 963–4 (2006); AG Fountain and others, *Nature*, **433**, pp. 618–21 (2005); and RA Kerr, 'A worrying trend of less ice, higher seas', *Science*, **311**, pp. 1698–1701 (2006).

Others include: Murray, *Nature*, **443**, pp. 277–8 (2006); Hanna and others, *Nature*, **443**, pp. 329–31 (2008); Velicogna and Wahr, *Journal of Climate*, **21**, pp. 331–41 (2006); Bamber and others, *Earth and Planetary Science Letters*, **257**, pp. 1–13 (2007); Fettweis and others, *Geophysical Research Letters*, **34**, L05502 (2007); Stearns and Hamilton, *Geophysical Research Letters*, **34**, L05503 (2007); Chylek and others, in *Journal of Geophysical Research*, **112**, D22S20 (2007); and Pritchard and others, *Geophysical Research Letters*, **35**, L01503 (2008). There is a good summary of the Arctic/Greenland situation on the American Meteorological Society's website for its Environmental Science Seminar Series, for the meeting on 25 November 2007, see: http://www.ametsoc.org/atmospolicy/ESSSSummaryPrint11262007.html.

35. The paleo-climatic papers are by: Otto-Bliesner and others, 'Simulating Arctic climate warmth and icefield retreat in the last interglacial', *Science*, **311**, pp. 1751–3 (2006); JT Overpeck and others, 'Paleoclimatic evidence for future ice-sheet instability and rapid sea-level rise', *Science*, **311**, pp. 1747–50 (2006); and AY Glikson, 'Milestones in the evolution of the atmosphere with reference to climate change', *Australian Journal of Earth Sciences*, **55**, pp. 125–39 (2008). See also Steffenson and others, 'High-resolution Greenland ice core data show abrupt climate change happens in a few years' *Sciencexpress* (19 June 2008) doi:10.1126/science.1157707, and Steig and Wolfe, 'Sprucing up Greenland', *Science*, **320**, pp. 1595–6 (20 June 2008).

36. The rapid loss of Arctic sea ice is documented by the National Snow and Ice Data Center in a science briefing by Mark Serreze and others at http://www.nsidc.org. See also: MM Holland and others, *Geophysical Research Letters*, **33**, L23503, doi:10.1029/2006GL028024 (2006); G Walker, *Nature*, **441**, p. 802 (15 June 2006); Q Schiermeier, *Nature*,

446 (8 March 2007); J Stroeve and others, *Geophysical Research Letters*, **34**, L09501, doi:10.1029/2007GL029703 (2007); JA Francis, , *Geophysical Research Letters*, **34**, L17503, doi:10.1029/2007GL030995 (2007); JE Overland and M Wang, *Geophysical Research Letters*, **34**, L17705, doi:10.1029/2007GL030808 (2007); MC Serreze and others, 'Perspectives on the Arctic's shrinking sea-ice cover', *Science*, **315**, pp. 1533–6; J-C Gascard and others, *EOS Transactions of the American Geophysical Union*, **89** (3), pp. 21–2 (15 January 2008); and CL Parkinson, 'Changes in polar sea ice coverage', Chapter 4 in *Sudden and Disruptive Climate Change*, Michael C MacCracken and others (eds), Earthscan, London (2008). For a more general coverage see 'Global Outlook for Ice and Snow', UNEP (2007) at http://www.unep.org/geo/geo_ice/.

37. The situation in Antarctica is well summarised in the UNEP report cited in endnote 36.

38. See M van den Broeke and others' study with a regional climate model in *Annals of Glaciology*, **39** (1), pp. 119–26 (2004), and M van den Broeke and others 'On Antarctic climate and change' in *Weather*, **59** (1), pp. 3–7 (2004). They discuss possible later effects on the Filchner-Ronne and Ross ice shelves. Vaughan and colleagues, *Science*, **293**, pp. 1777–9 (2001) discuss the warming around the Antarctic Peninsula. See also Carril and others, 'Climate response associated with the Southern Annular Mode in the surroundings of Antarctic Peninsula: A multimodel ensemble analysis', *Geophysical Research Letters*, **32**, L16713, (2005), and 'Eddy advective and diffusive transports of heat and salt in the Southern Ocean' by MM Lee and others in *Journal of Physical Oceanography* (2007).

39. The theory for the rapid disintegration of the Larsen A and B ice shelves comes from Rott and others, *Science*, **271**, pp. 788–92 (1996); Vaughan and Doake, *Nature*, **379**, pp. 328–31 (1996); Scambos and colleagues in *Journal of Glaciology*, **46**, pp. 516–30 (2000) and *Geophysical Research Letters*, doi:10.1029/2004GL020670 (2004); and Douglas MacAyeal and colleagues, *Journal of Glaciology*, **49**, p. 22 (2003). See also 'A structural glaciological analysis of the Larsen B ice shelf collapse' *Journal of Glaciology*, **54** (184), pp. 3–16 (2008).

40. De Angelis and Skvarca, *Science*, **299**, pp. 1560–2 (2003) and Rignot and others in *Geophysical Research Letters*, doi:10.1029/2004GL020697 (2004) report the accelerated flow of the contributory glaciers. See also Pritchard and Vaughan in *Journal of Geophysical Research*, **112**, F03S29 (2007). Mercer's paper 'West Antarctic Ice Sheet and CO_2 greenhouse effect: a threat of disaster' was in *Nature*, **271**, pp. 321–5 (1978).

41. The thinning of the ice shelves in the Amundsen Sea region is documented by Shepherd and others in *Geophysical Research Letters*, **31** (23) L23402 (2004), and its effect on the outlet glaciers by Payne and others, *Geophysical Research Letters*, **31**, L23401 (2004); Thomas and others in *Science*, **306**, pp. 255–8 (2004) and Joughin and others in *Geophysical Research Letters*, **30** (13), p. 1706 (2003). See also DG Vaughan and others 'West Antarctic links to sea level estimation' in *EOS*, **88**, pp. 485–6 (13 November 2007). The breakup of the Wilkins Ice Shelf was reported at earth.observatory. nasa.gov on 26 March 2008, and on http://www.sciencedaily.com on 14 June 2008.

42. The subglacial lakes and ice streams are documented by: Gray and others, *Geophysical Research Letters*, **32** (3), L03501 (2005); Wingham and others, *Nature*, **440**, pp. 1033–6 (2006); and Fricker and others, *Science*, **351**, pp. 1544–8 (2007). See also: Bell and others, *Nature*, **445**, pp. 904–7 (22 February 2007) and two popular accounts by RE Bell in *Scientific American* (February 2008) pp. 52–9, and J Kohler in *Nature*, **445**, pp. 830–1 (2007). The Corr and Vaughan paper is in *Nature Geoscience*, **1**, pp. 122–5 (2008).

43. The estimate of glacial loss leading to sea-level rise for the Patagonian icefields comes from Eric Rignot and colleagues in *Science*, **302**, pp. 434–7 (2003), while that from Alaska is quantified in *Science*, **297**, pp. 382–6 (2002).

44. Regional variations in sea-level rise are discussed in the IPCC 2007 report in section 5.5.2 for observed rise in the twentieth century, and in section 10.6 for projections for the twenty-first century.

45. Changes in wave climate are examined by Hemert and others, 'Waves and climate change on the Australian coast', *Journal of Coastal Research*, **SI 50**, pp. 432–7 (2007). Local subsidence due to extraction of groundwater, oil, and gas is another important factor.

46. The theory of sudden changes in climate regimes is discussed in Palmer, *Journal of Climate*, **12**, pp. 575–91 (1999); Crommelin, *Journal of the Atmospheric Sciences*, **59**, pp. 1533–49 (2002); and Stewart, *Nature*, **422**, pp. 571–3 (2003).

Abrupt changes in ecological systems are reported by Scheffer and colleagues, *Trends in Ecology and Evolution*, **8**, pp. 275–9 (1993) and *Nature*, **413**, pp. 591–6 (2001); Van de Koppel and others, *Trends in Ecology and Evolution*, **12**, pp. 352–6 (1997); and Nystrom and others, *Trends in Ecology and Evolution*, **15**, pp. 413–17 (2000).

47. A review of abrupt changes in various Earth systems is that by Steffen and others, *Environment*, **46**, pp. 8–20 (April 2004). Regional changes in Australian rainfall are discussed in for example, Kraus, *Quarterly Journal Royal Meteorological Society*, **80**, pp. 591–601 (1954); Gentilli, *World Survey of Climatology*, **13**, pp. 189–211 (1971); Pittock, *Search*, **6**, pp. 498–503 (1975); and Allan and Haylock, *Journal of Climate*, **7**, pp. 1356–67 (1993). Abrupt changes in climate model simulations are reported in Yonetani and Gordon, *Journal of Climate*, **14**, pp. 1765–79 (2001). Other references documenting past abrupt climate change and modelled future possibilities are Stocker, *International Journal of Earth Sciences*, **88**, pp. 365–73 (1999); Stocker, *Quaternary Science Reviews*, **19**, pp. 301–19 (2000); Stocker and Marchal, *Proceedings of the National Academy of Sciences US*, **97**, pp. 1362–5 (2000); Lockwood, *International Journal of Climatology*, **21**, pp. 1153–79 (2001); and Bard, *Physics Today*, **55** (12), pp. 32–8 (2002).

48. The example given is from KJ Missner and others, *Climate Dynamics*, **30**, pp. 161–74 (2008).

49. The IPCC 2007 report contains discussion of abrupt change in Chapter 8.7 and Box 10.1 of WGI.

50. The US National Research Council report on abrupt climate change is published by National Academy Press, Washington DC (2002). See also Richard Alley's summary in *Science*, **299**, pp. 2005–10 (2003) and Steffen and others in *Environment*, **46**, pp. 8–20 (April 2004).

51. The role of triggers and global warming are discussed in Schaeffer and others, *Geophysical Research Letters*, **29** (16), article 14 (2002), and Stocker, *International Journal of Earth Sciences*, **88**, pp. 365–74 (1999). See also Jose Rial and colleagues, in *Climatic Change*, **65**, pp. 11–38 (2004).

52. See Lenton and others, 'Tipping elements in the Earth's climate system', *Proceedings of the National Academy of Sciences*, **105**, pp. 1786–93 (12 February 2008). In my judgement, the time scale for the Arctic sea ice, Arctic permafrost, methane hydrates, Greenland and West Antarctic Ice Sheet tipping points may be shorter in the light of developments since the workshop in 2005 on which this paper is based. Another recent view on sudden climate change is that of D Shindell, 'Estimating the potential for twenty-first century sudden climate change', *Philosophical Transactions of the Royal Society A*, **365**, pp. 2675–94 (2007).

53. Observational evidence for changes possibly related to future abrupt change in the ocean circulation can be found in Delworth and Dixon, *Journal of Climate*, **13**, pp. 3721–7 (2000); Matear and colleagues, *Geochemistry, Geophysics, Geosystems*, **1**, paper no. 20000GC000086, (21 November 2000); Hansen and colleagues, *Nature*, **411**, pp. 927–30 (2001); Kim and others, *Geophysical Research Letters*, **28**, pp. 3293–6 (2001); Dickson and others, *Nature*, **416**, pp. 832–7 (2002); and Gille, *Science*, **295**, pp. 1275–7 (2002). See also Hansen and others in *Science*, **305**, pp. 953–4 (13 August 2004). Impacts on surface climate are discussed in for example, Vellinga and Wood, *Climatic Change*, **54**, pp. 251–67 (2002) and Matear and Hirst, *Tellus*, **51B**, pp. 722–33 (1999). The observed strengthening of the hydrological cycle with freshening of the North Atlantic surface waters is discussed in *Bulletin American Meteorological Society* (March 2004) pp. 328–30; and Curry and others, *Nature* , **426**, pp. 826–9 (2003). See also Chapters 8.7.2.1 and 10.3.4 in WGI of the IPCC 2007 report.

54. A summary of the gas hydrate hazard is *Issues in Risk Science, 03. Gas Hydrates: A Hazard for the 21st Century* by Mark Maslin, Benfield Hazard Research Centre. (Available at http://www.benfieldhrc.org.) However, the estimate of the amount of methane hydrate in the ocean sediments is revised downwards to about 1000 Gt by Milkov in *Earth-Science Reviews*, **66**, pp. 183–97 (2004), and Maslin seriously under-reports the amount of CO_2 in the atmosphere. See also 'Gas hydrates: relevance to world margin stability and climate change', *Geological Society Special Publication*, no. 137, London; Maslin and others, *Geology*, **26**, pp. 1107–10 (1998); and Maslin and others in *Geology*, **32**, pp. 53–6 (2004). See also: Maslin and others, *Geology*, **32**, pp. 53–6 (2004), and JE Beget, *The Holocene*, **17**, pp. 291–5 (2007). Recent reports (unpublished as of 2008) suggest methane emissions may already be increasing in the Arctic.

55. For observations of permafrost melting see: Arctic Climate Impact Assessment, 2004: *Impacts of a Warming Arctic*, Cambridge University Press, New York (available at http://www.acia.uaf.edu), and JE Overland, 'Arctic change: multiple observations and recent understanding, *Weather*, **61**, pp. 78–83 (2006). Projected increase in melting is given

in DM Lawrence and AG Slater, *Geophysical Research Letters*, **32**, L24401 (2005), while FS Chapin III and others, *Science*, **310**, pp. 657–60 (2005), and JA Foley, 'Tipping points in the tundra', *Science*, **310**, pp. 627–8 (2005) relate this to reflectivity or albedo changes.

Implications of the thawing of permafrost are discussed in *Science*, **304**, pp. 1618–20 (2004), and in *Climate Change, Permafrost, and Impacts on Civil Infrastructure*, US Arctic Research Commission, Special Report 01–03 (December 2003). Erosion of Arctic coasts after permafrost melting is discussed in *Land-Oceans Interactions in the Coastal Zone (LOICZ) Newsletter* (December 2003) see http://www.loicz.org.

56. The Storegga slide is described in Bouriak and colleagues, *Marine Geology*, **163**, pp. 125–48 (2000), with a more recent study by CK Paull and others in *Geophysical Research Letters*, **34**, L04601 (2007) suggesting that in fact not much methane may have been released locally during that event, but possibly earlier. Release of seabed methane is also discussed in Suess and others, *Scientific American* (November 1999) pp. 52–9; Wood and others, *Nature*, **420**, pp. 656–60 (2002); Lorenson and others, *EOS*, **83**, pp. 601 & 608–9 (2002); Hinrichs and others, *Science*, **299**, pp. 1214–17 (2003); Kennett and others, *Methane Hydrates in Quaternary Climate Change: The Clathrate Gun Hypothesis*, American Geophysical Union (2003) and Rind, *Bulletin American Meteorological Society*, **85**, pp. 279–81 (2004). Both D Archer in *Biogeosciences*, **4**, pp. 521–44 (2007) and Fyfe and Weaver in *Journal of Climate*, **19**, pp. 5903–17 assess the potential future effect of methane hydrate release and conclude that while the total effect could be large, it is likely to occur over centuries to millennia. Hill and others in *Proceedings of the National Academy of Sciences*, **103**, pp. 13 570–4 look at evidence of past seepages of hydrocarbons from the seafloor and implicate methane hydrates in a positive feedback effect that results in greater warming during deglaciation events. Best and others in *EOS* **87** (22) (30 May 2006) consider another process in which organic sediment buried in shallow coastal seabeds is further buried by sediments, when it goes on to decay, giving off methane gas that adds to global warming. They suggest this could be significant within the next century.

Natural gas hydrates are discussed extensively in *Natural Gas Hydrate in Oceanic and Permafrost Environments*, Michael D Max (ed.), Kluwer Academic Publishers, Dordrecht (2003), with the climate connection in Chapter 11, pp. 137–48. Paleo-climatic evidence suggesting a major global warming triggered by a methane hydrate release is reported in *Science*, **308**, pp. 1894–8 (24 June 2005).

57. The Nisbet review is in *Proceedings of the Royal Society London*, **A360**, pp. 581–607 (2002).

58. The carbon cycle is discussed in the 2007 IPCC report, WGI, Chapter 5.4.2 (observations) and Chapter 7.3.3 (terrestrial feedbacks) and Chapter 10.4.1 (projections). A general discussion of carbon cycle vulnerability is: JG Canadell and others (2007) 'Saturation of the terrestrial carbon sink' in JG Canadell, D Pataki and L Pitelka (eds) *Terrestrial Ecosystems in a Changing World*, Springer-Verlag, Berlin. A recent review on C-cycle feedbacks is by M Heimann and M Reichstein, *Nature*, **451**, pp. 289–92 (2008).

59. Observed variations are described in PH Bellamy and others, 'Carbon losses from all soils across England and Wales 1978–2003', *Nature*, **437**, pp. 245–8 (2005); and M Raupach and others, 'Impacts of decadal climate trends on Australian vegetation', paper presented at the Earth Observation Symposium, CSIRO, Canberra (15–16 February 2006). Past positive feedbacks are discussed in M Scheffer and others, 'Positive feedback between global warming and atmospheric CO_2 concentration inferred from past climate change', *Geophysical Research Letters*, **33**, L10702 (2006). See also A Angert and others, 'Drier summers cancel out the CO_2 uptake enhancement induced by warmer springs', *Proceedings of the National Academy of Science*, **102**, pp. 10 823–7 (2005).

The two interactive climate-carbon cycle simulations are: Cox and others, *Nature*, **408**, pp. 184–97 (2000); and Freidlingstein and colleagues, *Geophysical Research Letters*, **28**, pp. 1543–6 (2001). These are reconciled in Friedlingstein and co-authors, *Tellus*, **55B**, pp. 692–700 (2003). See also Francey and colleagues, *Nature*, **373**, pp. 326–30 (1995) and Bousquet and others, *Science*, **290**, pp. 1342–6 (2000). Another simulation by Matthews and colleagues using a Canadian Earth System Climate Model suggests a decrease in terrestrial carbon uptake during this century, but not a reversal from sink to source (see *Journal of Climate*, **18**, pp. 1609–28, 2005). For increased fire risk and its effects on atmospheric carbon dioxide see Stocks and colleagues, *Climatic Change*, **38**, pp. 1–13 (1998); Flannigan and others, *The Science of the Total Environment*, **262**, pp. 221–9 (2000); Cary, in Bradstock and others (eds) *Flammable Australia: Fire*

Regimes and Biodiversity of a Continent, Cambridge University Press (2002); Lavorel, *Global Change Newsletter*, no. 53, pp. 2–6 (2003); Page and others, *Nature*, **420**, pp. 61–5 (2002); Langenfelds and others, *Global Geochemical Cycles*, **16** (3), p. 1048 (2002); B Langmann, and A Heil, 'Release and dispersion of vegetation and peat fire emissions in the atmosphere over Indonesia 1997–1998', *Atmospheric Chemistry and Physics*, **4**, pp. 2145–60 (2004); and AL Westerling and others, 'Warming and earlier spring increases western U.S. forest wildfire activity', *Science*, **313**, pp. 940–3 (2006).

60. The IPCC 2007 report discussions of changes in monsoons, ENSO, etc. can be found in WGI, Chapter 10.3.5, and in the relevant chapters of WGII, including Chapter 19.

61. Risk and cost/benefit analyses in relation to large-scale singular events are discussed by Keller and others, *Climatic Change*, **47**, pp. 17–43 (2000); Baranzini and colleagues, *Energy Policy*, **31**, pp. 691–701 (2002); Vellinga and Wood, *Climatic Change*, **54**, pp. 251–67 (2002); Azar and Lindgren, *Climatic Change*, **56**, pp. 245–55 (2003); Howarth, *Climatic Change*, **56**, pp. 257–63 (2003); and Tol, *Climatic Change*, **56**, pp. 265–89 (2003). IPCC 2007 discusses this in WGII, Chapters 7 and 19 and in WGIII, Chapters 2.2.3 and 2.2.4.

62. This summary discussion of reasons why climate change may be more severe than commonly projected is based on my Chapter 1 in *Sudden and Disruptive Climate Change: Its Likelihood, Character and Avoidance*, Michael C MacCracken, Frances Moore and John C Topping (eds), Earthscan, London (2008). See also *EOS* **87** (34) (22 August 2006).

6

Impacts: why be concerned?

Humanity is conducting an unintended, uncontrolled, globally pervasive experiment whose ultimate consequences could be second only to a global nuclear war. The Earth's atmosphere is being changed at an unprecedented rate by pollutants resulting from human activities, inefficient and wasteful fossil fuel use and the effects of rapid population growth in many regions. These changes represent a major threat to international security and are already having harmful consequences over many parts of the globe.

INTERNATIONAL CONFERENCE ON THE CHANGING ATMOSPHERE: IMPLICATIONS FOR GLOBAL SECURITY, TORONTO, JUNE 1988.

Developments in mainstream scientific opinion on the relationship between emissions accumulations and climate outcomes, and the Review's own work on future 'business as usual' global emissions, suggest that the world is moving towards high risks of dangerous climate change more rapidly than has generally been understood.

ROSS GARNAUT, INTERIM REPORT, *GARNAUT CLIMATE CHANGE REVIEW*, FEBRUARY 2008.[1]

The key question for policy-makers (including you the reader) is whether projected climate changes due to greenhouse gas emissions are likely to lead to unacceptable impacts on human and natural systems. The United Nations Framework Convention on Climate Change seeks to avoid 'dangerous interference to the climate system', so we should ask whether what is projected would be dangerous.[2] If so, we must try to avoid it by adopting appropriate policies.

In 1988, despite having rather primitive climate models at their disposal, scientists at a major conference in Toronto reached the rather startling conclusion (quoted above) that human-induced climate change is a major threat to

international security. Today we have much more advanced climate models and improved understanding of the effects of climate change on human and natural systems. Successive reports from the Intergovernmental Panel on Climate Change (IPCC) have largely confirmed the 1988 statement by providing much more detail and a better basis.

However, our understanding is still far from complete, and both climate and the systems that are affected are extremely complex. New observations and research findings add, almost weekly, to a growing sense of concern that impacts are already being felt above the background 'noise' of natural climate variability, and that far greater impacts lie in store. (Serious students of climate change will follow links and do web searches related to news stories to get the most reliable scientific and other analysis on these new developments.)[3]

Climate change impacts are complex in that they can be both direct and indirect. For example, more rain may lead directly to either greater or smaller crop yields, depending on factors such as the type of crop, the soil and the present climate. Indirect effects could include changes in supply and demand as a result of these larger or smaller yields, both regionally and globally, and the resulting changes in commodity prices, the profitability of farming, and the affordability of food and effects on human health. Moreover, impacts can often be made more favourable by changing strategies so as to minimise losses and maximise gains. This is called adaptation, and is the subject of Chapter 7. In the present chapter we will mainly consider direct impacts of climate change, with some allowance for the more likely adaptations and some comments on indirect effects. But it is difficult to anticipate all potential adaptations, since many will derive from research and development yet to be done and will largely be inspired by the perceived needs as climate changes.

Direct impacts, adaptation and indirect effects are largely conditioned by the nature of the relevant human society, including its institutions, how well informed people are, and how readily they can adapt. These characteristics of society will change with time through population and economic growth or decline, new technologies and changing institutional arrangements. Another important factor, which has not been adequately studied, is the *rate* of change of climate, not just the magnitude of change. This is particularly important because rapid change requires rapid adaptation, and a subsequent need to change capital investments (for example in irrigation or flood control systems, building design, or port facilities), which will tend to be more expensive and not always possible.

Studies of specific local impacts of climate changes have been conducted by hundreds of research groups, many from organisations concerned with such matters as seasonal crop forecasts, water supply and coastal protection.[4] These groups have found that climate change and sea-level rise of the magnitude and rates suggested would greatly affect many natural systems like forests, rivers and wildlife, as well as human activities and society.

Examples include:

- changes in natural productivity and biodiversity, with an increased rate of extinctions,

- decreases in cereal crop yields in most tropical and sub-tropical countries, and in temperate countries for large warmings,

- increased water shortages in many water-scarce regions due to regional decreases in precipitation, increased evaporation and loss of glaciers and seasonal snow storages,

- adverse economic effects in many developing countries for even small warmings, and for developed countries for larger warmings,

- tens of millions of people on small islands and low-lying coastal areas at severe risk of flooding from sea-level rise and storm surges,

- increased threats to human health,

- increased inequities between poor and richer countries,

- increased risk of abrupt and irreversible climate changes.

Studies have been based in part on observations of past variations in climate and their effects on crop yields, river flow, flood and drought frequency and so on. Some projections of future effects have thus been based on extrapolations from past experience, while others have used mathematical models of known behaviour of systems to estimate future effects. For example, crop productivity models that simulate how plants grow and develop fruit or grain, and that take into account soil moisture, temperature, soil nutrients and carbon dioxide in the air, are used to predict crop yields. These are the same models used for seasonal forecasts, but with climate change inputs. Similarly, simple causal models can predict river flows by calculating how much rain falls in a river catchment, how much evaporates, how much penetrates into the soil and how much runs off.

When such models are used to calculate the present yields or river flows we say they are used to perform 'control simulations'. We can check how good such models are by comparing the control results with observations, especially for seasonal or year-to-year variability and observed variations. The models are then run with changes in climate according to some possible future, and a new climate change simulation result is produced. The difference between this and the control is the estimated effect of the assumed climate change.

Climate change impacts – reasons for concern

Many studies of impacts for various regions, industrial sectors, times in the future, and scenarios were summarised in the IPCC reports in 2001 and 2007. However, it was difficult to compare and summarise these quantitatively, especially for the full range of climate changes due to various emissions scenarios, since most studies were based on a limited number of scenarios, and nearly all were based on transient warming rather than stabilised conditions. The IPCC, however, in its 2001 report did summarise the impacts qualitatively under five categories or 'reasons for concern', which may be considered separately.[5] They are not all expressed in economic terms, since many impacts involve factors such as species loss or poor health that cannot readily be expressed in monetary terms.

The selected reasons for concern were:

- *Risks to unique and threatened systems*: natural systems are vulnerable to climate change, especially where migration to higher elevations or higher latitudes is not possible or too slow,

and increasing numbers will be irreversibly damaged as global warming increases. Ecosystems on mountains, small islands and polewards-facing coasts are especially vulnerable.

- *Risks from extreme climate events:* changes in the frequency and severity of extreme events are expected, and will likely be a major cause of damages to ecosystems, crops, and society. This is demonstrated by the observed rise in damages from extreme climatic events in recent decades both in terms of monetary losses and of lives lost. Whether or not the rise in damages to date is due to changes in extremes or to increased populations or assets in dangerous locations, the increase in damages shows increasing vulnerability. Clearly damages will increase further with greater climate change.

- *Distribution of impacts*: impacts of climate change will not be distributed equally over the globe. Adverse impacts are likely to be greater and to occur earlier in low-latitude developing countries than in mid- and high-latitude developed countries. This is mainly because low-latitude countries are near or above optimum temperatures for many crops and activities already. Such countries are also less able to adapt both because more heat-tolerant species and cultivars are less available and these countries tend to have less adaptive capacity. As warming increases with time even the more developed countries will experience adverse effects, but the poorer countries will remain more seriously affected. Thus inequality between countries will be made worse. Inequalities in impacts will also apply within countries between the poor and the rich, and between vulnerable and less vulnerable regions.

- *Aggregate impacts*: the consensus is that globally the total of all the market impacts (those that can be quantified in terms of money) may be small positive or negative (1 or 2% of GDP) at small global warmings (less than 2 or 3°C), but will become increasingly negative at greater warmings. The majority of people are expected to be worse off even at small warmings. Such impacts are poorly quantified and additional measures are necessary as many impacts cannot be expressed objectively in monetary terms.

• *Risks from future large-scale discontinuities*: While not well understood, there is a strong possibility that large-scale and possibly irreversible changes in Earth systems will result in large impacts at regional and global scales. Changes to the global-scale ocean circulation and the El Niño–Southern Oscillation (ENSO) are possible in the twenty-first century, and other changes may occur, possibly made inevitable by climate change this century. For example, rapid melting of the Greenland and West Antarctic ice sheets could occur (and may have started already), leading to several metres rise in sea level over one or more centuries.

The 2007 IPCC Working Group II report also discussed impacts in terms of the reasons for concern and 'key vulnerabilities' (Chapter 19), as well as by sector (Chapters 3 to 8) and region (Chapters 9 to 16). Joel B Smith and other IPCC authors argue in a forthcoming paper that these concerns are more serious than was believed in 2001.[5]

Thresholds and abrupt changes

Before we discuss the reasons for concern in more detail, it is worth looking at a group of phenomena that cuts across them – the pervasive influence of what are termed 'non-linear effects', thresholds and abrupt changes. We discussed them briefly in the previous chapter on what climate changes to expect, but they apply even more to impacts. They are effects that cannot be anticipated by simple extrapolation from recent experience.

For example if we are pushing a cart up a slope, then we expect that a further push will lead to a similar movement as the last push. This is true if the slope is steady, but if we reach the top of a hill, all of a sudden the next push may lead to the cart

taking off down the hill. This is a non-linear effect. We have reached a point or threshold, in this case the top of the hill, where conditions (properties of the system) change rapidly. An even more abrupt and irreversible change would occur if our cart reached a cliff top and went over. Climate change confronts us with many potential thresholds and possibly some rather large cliffs.[6]

Threshold events signal a distinct change in conditions. These may be due to direct physical limits or barriers, or to exceeding a level or benchmark nominated by society or economics. Climatic thresholds include frost, snow or monsoon onset. Biophysical thresholds represent a distinct change in conditions, such as the drying of a wetland, the cessation of flow in a river, flood, or breeding events. Behavioural thresholds are set by benchmarking a level of performance such as crop yield per hectare or net income. Operational thresholds might include sustainable herd size for grazing grasslands, design standards for buildings or drain sizes, heights of levee banks, the size of dam spillways or simply the difference between a profit and a loss. Movements of variables across thresholds can have much larger consequences than similar magnitude movements that stay below the thresholds. They may take us into a region where drastic, unacceptable or dangerous change occurs in the functioning of a system.

An interesting example is set by the damage to buildings caused by wind gusts. Australian insurance figures indicate damage rises dramatically for peak wind gusts in excess of 50 knots, or 25 metres per second (**Figure 23**). This is a very important threshold, since wind damage is one of the major economic impacts of climatic extremes, which may change in frequency or intensity with global warming according to how frequently and by how much the threshold is exceeded. In the period 1995–2002, the average cost of windstorm damage in the US from hurricanes, tornados and severe thunderstorms was about US$5 billion annually.[7]

Abrupt changes also occur in ecological systems.[8] Studies of lakes, coral reefs, oceans, forests and arid

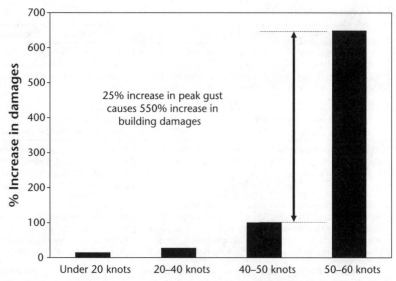

Figure 23: Wind speed threshold for damages. Insurance Australia Group building claims costs versus peak wind gust speeds show a disproportionate increase in costs when wind speeds exceed 50 knots (about 25 metres per second). A 25% increase in gust wind speed above this threshold causes a 550% increase in building damages. This is partly due to the 'snowballing' effect of flying debris. (Diagram after T Coleman, IAG, 2002, with permission.) (1 knot _0.5 metres per second.)

lands have all shown that smooth change can be interrupted by sudden shifts to some contrasting state. Such sudden changes in system behaviour often arise from an element of the system reaching a limit or threshold at which instability sets in, and the system moves into a new stable state. One frequently observed example is the change of a lake from a well-mixed system to one that is stably stratified, with the subsequent development of surface algal blooms and anoxic conditions at depth. When a system is close to such a threshold, even quite small random events or trends can force the system into a different state. In more mathematical terms, it may take the form of a switch from a negative to a positive feedback. According to Scheffer and colleagues, distance from a threshold of this sort is a measure of system resilience or ability to cope with small variations in conditions.

Abrupt changes, and exceeding thresholds, can occur in many climate change impact situations, ranging from water stress in an individual plant, through the topping of flood levee banks, to economic crises or forced migration due to rapid sea-level rise. The potential for such events lies behind many of the impacts within each category of

reasons for concern identified in the IPCC 2001 report. These categories are discussed below.

Risks to unique and threatened systems

Some of these impacts have already been observed over the last several decades, for example changes in the ranges for some already threatened species of plants, animals and birds, retreat of glaciers, shorter duration of river-, lake- and sea-ice and melting of permafrost. However, as we saw in Chapter 1, attribution of such observed changes to the rather minor global warming of the last century is often difficult in individual cases because of other possible causes, but made more convincing by their widespread and varied nature. The IPCC in its 2007 report concluded that there is now good evidence that recent warming is already strongly affecting natural biological systems, both on land and in the seas. This includes changes in abundance of species, with some local disappearances, polewards shifts in species, stress on coral reefs, and growing acidity of the oceans, which is expected to have adverse effects on many key species.[9]

TABLE 8: Some threatened and unique entities

Category	Entities	Comments
Water bodies	Closed lakes, especially small ones, but including Caspian and Aral Seas, and Lakes Balkash (Kazakhstan), Chad (Africa), Titicaca (South America) and Great Salt Lake (USA). Other lakes also affected, especially the African and American Great Lakes	Fine balance between inflow and evaporation in closed lakes, and in some others with large areas and small outflows. Impacts on fisheries, local climate, etc.
Glaciers	Tropical glaciers most sensitive, but many small glaciers will disappear	Impacts on related ecosystems, tourism, seasonal water supply and hydropower
Ecosystems	Alpine ecosystems, coastal wetlands, Cape Floral Kingdom and succulent Karoo (Africa), coral reefs, mangroves, fire-prone species	Ecosystems bound by altitude, coasts or land use change most vulnerable. Increased fire risk widespread. Many coastal wetlands and mangroves cannot retreat inland due to topography or development
Coastal settlements and communities	North Sea coast (Europe); US east and Gulf Coast; many low-lying islands and populous coasts of higher islands; mega-deltas including Bangladesh; coastal cities of China, Indonesia, Africa, Nile delta.	Sea-level rise and changed wave climates, storm surges and erosion will greatly alter coasts. Adaptations expensive and problematic (sea access, drainage, etc.). Could displace many people
Indigenous communities	Inuit/Arctic settlements and lifestyle. American Indian and Australian Aboriginal communities in arid or coastal areas	Traditional hunting and food gathering threatened. Reduced water supplies, coastal flooding and erosion

The real question is how projected climate changes, which are much larger than those of the twentieth century, will impact on physical and biological systems. **Table 8** lists some of the threatened and unique entities identified in the IPCC 2001 and 2007 reports.

Closed lakes are particularly vulnerable to increased evaporation from higher temperatures, as are lakes with outlets that are small compared with total evaporation from their surfaces. Many of these lakes have shown large fluctuations in the past, and some (most notably the Aral Sea, Lake Chad and the Great Salt Lake) have been affected greatly by withdrawal of water from tributary rivers for irrigation. Only large increases in precipitation in their catchments, and/or reduced withdrawals or river diversions will save them from shrinking further in a globally warming world.[10]

Tropical glaciers in Asia, Africa and Latin America, as well as New Guinea (where they mostly disappeared during the twentieth century) are most sensitive to global warming because they tend to be marginal and suffer little year-to-year variation in temperature. Their loss will mean a loss of cold-loving species of plants and animals, as well as changes to melt-fed rivers affecting riverine species.

Accelerated melting will cause floods in many upper reaches of rivers especially in spring and summer, until the glaciers have disappeared, when lack of meltwater will cause serious water shortages especially in summer and autumn. Similar effects are expected in temperate glaciers and glacier-fed rivers, which are important for irrigation and water supply in many countries including the western United States, parts of China, India, Pakistan, Europe and Latin America.[11]

Vulnerable ecosystems are those unable to migrate due to altitude limits, coasts on the colder boundaries (for example, coastal South Africa and the south-west of Australia), or where natural ecosystems are no longer possible beyond present boundaries due to land clearing or other development. Others at risk include species that cannot migrate fast enough to keep up with climate change, or species that cannot adapt when they lose the combination of temperature and precipitation necessary for their survival. Many species that rely on each other for food or shelter will be lost as some species die out due to climate changes, leaving dependent species bereft of support. Increased summer aridity will increase fire risk and severity in many locations, leading to repeated fires that will change ecosystems.

Freshwater and mangrove coastal areas will be threatened by sea-level rise, erosion and saline intrusion, often with little opportunity to retreat inland due to steeper topography or human imposed boundaries such as farms, roads or embankments.

Coral reefs are at particular risk. They are widespread in warm tropical waters and provide large economic benefits from tourism, fisheries and coastal protection. They are already subject to damage from non-climatic problems such as over-fishing, mining and pollution. Increasingly they are also threatened by coral bleaching and death from warmer water, slower growth rates due to increased ocean acidity from higher carbon dioxide concentrations, and in some cases by rapid sea-level rise.

Coral bleaching is a threshold phenomenon, with onset of bleaching at a critical temperature that varies from one location to another, due to different species composition and adaptation. Adaptation is thought to be slow compared to projected rates of warming, and repeated bleaching may lead to widespread death of particular types of corals, with more affected as temperatures increase. Bleaching episodes have already occurred with increasing frequency worldwide, associated with peaks in the ENSO cycle superimposed on a slow background warming. Increased coral calcification rates at higher temperatures are likely to be outweighed by deaths due to bleaching and reductions in calcification due to increasing acidification from higher dissolved CO_2 concentrations. **Box 4** summarises issues relating to coral reefs.[12]

The Australian Great Barrier Reef is the world's largest continuous reef system, a storehouse of marine biodiversity and breeding ground for seabirds and marine vertebrates. A 2005 report by Access Economics estimated the tourism associated with the Reef generated more than US$4 billion in 2004/5 and provided over 60000 equivalent full-time jobs.

Coastal settlements will also be threatened by sea-level rise, often exacerbated by subsidence due to groundwater or oil and gas withdrawal from underlying strata. Where this occurs in heavily built-up areas in rich countries protection by building sea walls is possible, but often at great financial and amenity costs. In poorer countries, or for small settlements, such defences may be uneconomic or impossible. Many millions of people will be involved in developing countries, leading to their displacement within countries and pressure for cross-border migration in some cases. Populations of low-lying countries and islands will be particularly seriously affected, losing not only their homes but in many cases traditional ways of life, ancestral connections, and even community and national identity or sovereignty.[13]

Sea-level rise is associated with a range of effects that are far more complex and threatening than simply retreat to the corresponding higher altitude contour line. Changed wave climates (direction and wave energy) and extreme events (storm surges and sometimes simultaneous high riverine runoff) will cause temporary or permanent flooding, and coastal erosion. Erosion will occur preferentially on sandy beaches and barrier dunes, or soft rock cliffs, with changes in along-shore sediment drift leading to accelerated erosion where sediment supply is cut off, such as in the lee of headlands, breakwaters and groynes, and preferential deposition in inlets, and against groynes, breakwaters and headlands. Effects will be particularly marked where there are coastal wetlands and estuaries.[14]

Many of the world's sandy shorelines have retreated in the last century, from a combination of factors of which mean sea-level rise was one. In vulnerable locations erosion rates have been metres per year. Anecdotal evidence abounds of missing house blocks and collapsed soft rock cliffs. The highly simplified Brunn rule suggests a rate of recession on long sandy beaches of some 50 to 200 times the rate of local relative sea-level rise. In less idealised situations this can be much larger, with erosion of protective dunes and infilling of inlets. This means that, with projected sea-level rise of the order of a metre by 2100, many coastlines will change substantially and a great deal of costly infrastructure, and coastal ecosystems, threatened.

Adaptation to sea-level rise will be expensive, and in many situations difficult due to poverty or

BOX 4: THREATS TO CORAL REEFS

Recent reports[12] indicate that coral reefs are valuable resources that are severely threatened by global warming and other stresses. Key points are:

- Coral reefs are unique and valuable ecosystems, and provide major services to humanity including fisheries, gene pools, coastal protection and a tourism industry worth billions of US dollars.

- Coral reefs are already declining due to over-fishing, mining and pollution.

- Outbreaks of coral bleaching have increased in frequency and magnitude over the last 30 years and are tightly linked to increasing water temperatures.

- Projected increase in temperatures will cause more frequent and intense coral bleaching unless adaptation is rapid.

- Increasingly frequent bleaching will mean more and more coral reefs will die.

- Increases in atmospheric carbon dioxide concentrations will increase acidity of oceans, slow calcification rates (growth) and make coral more fragile.

- Sea-level rise may invigorate growth of some shallow reef species, but drown others.

- Adaptation to global warming will be slow, incomplete and leave different devalued reefs.

- Migration to higher latitudes is unlikely due to lack of suitable substrata and the rapidity of warming.

- Coral reefs are global canaries warning of major changes to ecosystems.

- Management policies including protected areas, no-take zones and reduced pollution can prolong reef survival, but early and major reduction in emissions of greenhouse gases is necessary to prevent ongoing major damage to reefs.

administrative and other obstacles. Further, some protective measures such as rock walls or levees may fail during extreme events, exposing whole communities to flooding as in New Orleans in 2005. With progressive sea-level rise at rates presently uncertain, planning such protective structures or zoning new coastal development is problematic.[15]

Small indigenous communities will also be threatened, not only from sea-level rise in coastal communities, but in some cases from loss of water supplies due to increased aridity, or loss of food supplies as native species are lost due to climate change. Indigenous Arctic peoples will have to cope with loss of sea ice for hunting and fishing, changed migration routes of animals, coastal erosion due to wave action on ice-free coasts, loss of permafrost, and changes in the abundance of traditional food sources on land and in the water. Australian Aboriginal communities are also threatened by sea-level rise, changing indigenous food supplies and health impacts.[16] Generally, there will be risks from pests and diseases, especially vector-borne, respiratory or other infectious diseases, as traditional food supplies are threatened, lifestyles change, and water supplies for hygienic purposes are in some cases reduced.

Risks from extreme climate events

Extreme climatic events occur naturally in an unchanging but variable climate, virtually by definition. It is difficult to predict their individual occurrences more than a few days ahead, and to a first approximation their occurrence can be considered to be random. Nevertheless, we can develop statistics for their occurrence from observations of the recent past, and use these to state probabilities and risk of occurrence of a particular type and magnitude of extreme.

As discussed in Chapter 5, especially in **Table 5**, it is now widely accepted that many extreme events such as heatwaves, heavy rain events, floods and droughts will increase in frequency and magnitude in many regions with global warming, while others, notably cold days and frosts, will decrease. Tropical cyclones, and likely other large storms, will increase in severity, and perhaps change in frequency and preferred locations. Other types of extremes, such as thunderstorms, hail, and high winds may also change, although present knowledge is limited. As certain circulation systems such as ENSO and the North Atlantic Oscillation (NAO) may also change, regional climatic events associated with them, such as preferred tropical cyclone locations and mid-latitude storm tracks may change as well.

Such changes will have widespread impacts. Most climatic impacts arise from extreme weather events or climatic variables that exceed some critical level or threshold and thus affect the performance or behaviour of some physical or biological system. Physical, biological and indeed human systems in general have evolved, or are designed, to cope with a certain range of variations in the weather, based on past variability. However, when weather variables fall outside those limits, the affected system under-performs or fails.

In human systems we implicitly or explicitly plan and design systems and infrastructure to cope with the established range of climate variability, based on past experience. To help in developing design criteria, engineers routinely estimate the average time between floods or high winds of a particular magnitude (the 'return period') at particular locations. This applies, for example, to the design capacities of spillways, drains and bridges, the heights of levee banks and the strength of buildings. Similarly planners consider return periods of floods or coastal storm surges, in zoning and locating urban developments, and in setbacks from rivers or coasts. Return period estimates are normally based on recent instrumental records, where necessary augmented by statistical or physical modelling or data from neighbouring locations. Typically drains are designed to cope with a 25-year return period flood, small bridges maybe 100-year and large dams maybe a 10 000-year flood. The safety margin allowed for in design is related to the cost of a failure. However, climate change means that these statistics will change. Thus a central problem in planning for climate change, and estimating possible impacts, is how the statistics of extreme events are likely to change.

Similar problems arise in non-engineering applications such as the future effectiveness, economic performance or viability of activities or investments affected by the weather, such as farming, ski resorts, or health services.

William Easterling of Pennsylvania State University and colleagues in a review in 2000 point out that some apparently gradual biological changes are linked to responses to extreme weather and climate events. Sequences of extreme events, such as repeated floods or droughts, can compound damage and lead to irreversible change. For example, drought-affected forests are particularly prone to wildfire, and then to soil erosion arising from heavy drought-breaking rain. This in turn can cause siltation in rivers, sometimes filling deep waterholes that are refuges for aquatic life during low flow in rivers.[17]

A number of studies have found that a large part of the observed increase in deaths and financial losses from extreme events in recent decades is due to population growth and demographic shifts into hazardous locations. This means that many societies are becoming more vulnerable to extreme events – in other words, societies often display counter-adaptive behaviour.[18]

Nevertheless, small changes in average climate have a disproportionately large effect on the frequency of extreme events. This is because of the nature of frequency distributions (how frequency changes with magnitude). Extremes occur at the low frequency 'tails' of these frequency distributions. Frequencies in these tails change very rapidly as the frequency distribution moves up or down with the average. Moreover, variability can change, and this also rapidly changes the frequency of extremes. This is particularly important for high rainfall events, as global warming increases the moisture holding capacity of the atmosphere, and thus preferentially increases the likelihood of high intensity rainfall. Thus in many regions what was a 1-in-100 year flood in the twentieth century may well become a 1-in-25 year flood by late in the twenty-first century.

The impact of extremes often increases very rapidly with the magnitude of the extreme, as seen with wind speed in **Figure 23**. This is particularly true for flood damages, because the force of flowing water increases rapidly with velocity and depth, and damages increase very rapidly once flood depth exceeds zoning levels and thus the floods reach buildings not designed to withstand floods. Moreover, once a flood is large enough to damage a single building, debris washed downstream can act as a battering ram to damage other buildings. Wind damage has a similar 'snowballing' effect. Again, once floods breach levee banks a great increase in damages results. **Box 5** summarises a UK Government report on future flooding in England and Wales.[19]

Similar non-linear or disproportional increases in damages follow from coastal storm surges that exceed planning levels. This can occur due to average sea-level rise, and also from increases in the intensity of storms. In the case of tropical cyclones, the projected decrease in central pressure and increased wind speeds will both add to the increase in storm surge height, with additional stress from wind-driven waves and riverine flooding. The latter will be exacerbated by increased rainfall rates.

An example from calculations of the 1-in-100 year storm surge heights at Cairns, Australia, illustrates the problem. Under present conditions the 1-in-100 year flood height is 2.3 metres, but allowing for a small (10 hectopascal or mbar) decrease in average central pressure, possible by mid-century, the 1-in-100 year event becomes 2.6 metres, and with a 10 to 40 centimetre average sea-level rise becomes 2.7 to 3.0 metres. This leads to a potential area of inundation of 71 square kilometres, compared to about 32 square kilometres at present. The area presently liable to flooding is mainly wetlands, but the additional nearly 40 square kilometres would be mainly in the built-up urban area, including downtown Cairns. This makes no allowance for increased storm runoff that would make matters worse.[20]

Another problem with extreme events is that the impacts are often compounded by repeated events. Thus many systems may survive a single extreme flood or drought, but not repeated floods or droughts in quick succession. A long interval between extremes may allow time for recovery, both of natural systems and of human systems. But if an economy is set back by large damages and disruption by one extreme event, for example a tropical cyclone, a second one shortly after might well overwhelm the capacity of the society to recover, causing far more economic disruption and suffering than the first. Even in rich countries, two or more successive extreme events may force losses or complete failure on a farming enterprise. Farmers can be bankrupted and have to abandon their farms, unless they have disaster insurance. In poorer countries successions of disasters can set back

BOX 5: FUTURE FLOODING IN ENGLAND AND WALES[19]

In 2004 the UK Government released a report on future flooding in England and Wales. It addressed the question: how might the risks of flooding and coastal erosion change in the UK over the next 100 years? Over 200 billion pounds worth of assets are at risk, along with disruptions to transport and power. The report emphasised the long lead times involved to influence future risk since:

- Large engineering works have long gestation times and long lifetimes.

- It could take decades for changes in planning policies to take effect.

- The time delay inherent in the atmosphere and oceans means that action to reduce risk from climate change must be taken now.

- Four different socio-economic scenarios were used, termed:

  - World Markets (global interdependence and high emissions),

  - Global Sustainability (global interdependence with low emissions),

  - National Enterprise (national autonomy and medium to high emissions), and

  - Local Stewardship (national/local autonomy with medium to low emissions).

- Some key findings are:

  - If flood-management and expenditures were unchanged, annual losses would increase under all scenarios by 2080, by less than 1 billion pounds under the Local Stewardship scenario to around 27 billion pounds under the World Markets scenario.

  - Besides flooding from rivers and coasts, towns and cities would be subject to localised flooding caused by sewer and drainage systems overwhelmed by local downpours. Damages could be huge but are not yet quantified.

  - The number of people at risk would more than double by 2080.

  - Drivers of future flood risk include climate change, urbanisation, environmental regulations, rural land management, increasing national wealth and social impacts. Climate change has a high impact in all scenarios, with sea-level rise increasing the risk of coastal flooding four to 10 times, and precipitation changes increasing risk two to four times.

  - An integrated portfolio of responses could reduce the risk of river and coastal flooding from the worst scenario of 20 billion pounds annual damage down to around 2 billion pounds (still double the present damages).

economic development, for example in Bangladesh and Mozambique.

Disaster insurance often comes in the form of government-funded relief, but increasingly governments are designing relief schemes to only cope with 'exceptional circumstances', sometimes defined as a 1-in-20 year event. If climate change means that these events start to occur more frequently, governments will need to rethink the definition of exceptional circumstances, and ask whether restructuring the industry is better than continuing aid.

In other cases, private insurance companies provide disaster insurance. Many of these companies are already considering whether they need to increase their premiums, reduce their cover in the face of an increasing frequency of insurance claims, or to adopt more stringent rules as to what is insurable. Major insurance and reinsurance companies have been amongst business leaders in advocating policies to mitigate climate change.[21]

The role of extremes in agriculture and natural systems is complex. Ecosystem type, and even crop productivity, is often related in studies to average climate conditions. However, often this is a proxy for the effects of extremes, since in an unchanging climate the magnitude and frequency of extremes is related to that of the averages. In fact, the causal relationship is usually with the magnitude and frequency of such extremes as frost season, aridity and extreme high temperatures at particular stages in plant growth. Many crops, for instance, do badly in waterlogged soils (very wet conditions) and also under severe water stress (very dry conditions). Moreover, crop yields are often dependent on temperatures and soil moisture at flowering or grain filling times in the growth cycle, with extremely high temperatures reducing fertility and thus grain yield.[22] See **Box 6**.

Fire occurrence is the product of several variables, and of background conditions as well as extremes. It is a function of precipitation and temperature over a long interval of time, usually in excess of a single season, which determines both fuel density and its dryness. But fire outbreak also requires ignition (usually from lightning or human agency), high temperatures and winds, and low humidity on the day, if the fire is to spread. Proxy evidence of fire occurrences under past climates (see Chapter 2) and projected fire indices for future climate scenarios suggest that fire frequency and severity will likely increase in many regions under enhanced greenhouse conditions. Occasional fires can be beneficial in many ecosystems, thinning undergrowth and allowing regeneration. But too frequent fires can destroy seedlings and prevent regeneration, leading to the replacement of one species by another more fire-resistant one. This process can change mature forests to savannah or grassland.

Increased fire frequency and intensity will have a number of effects including, the changing of ecosystems, damage to buildings and infrastructure, loss of human lives, and threatening the survival of long-term carbon storage in the biosphere (forests and soil carbon). The latter means that increased fire may contribute to a magnification of the enhanced greenhouse effect by undoing the sequestering of carbon in plants and the soil that presently occurs in well-managed land ecosystems. If the huge boreal forests of the northern hemisphere continents and the vast peat deposits in the present tundra and some tropical areas (for example, Kalimantan in Indonesia) are burnt, fire may have a disastrous effect by accelerating climate change.[23]

Distribution of impacts[24]

The impact of global warming will not be distributed evenly amongst people, countries and regions. Some individuals, sectors, systems and regions will be less adversely affected, and might even gain in the short run. Others will suffer losses even with small levels of global warming. This pattern of gains and losses will vary with time. Increasing losses are projected as warming increases, but the incentive for early action may be less in countries that see early gains.

The regional chapters in the 2007 IPCC WGII report document in detail the very different ranges of impacts in different parts of the globe, with people in Africa, the Arctic, small islands and low-lying coastal areas most obviously the worst affected by rapid climate change and sea-level rise. Some of these regional or national impacts are discussed in Chapter 11 below.

In the broadest of general terms, there are two main reasons for the uneven distribution of impacts. One is present climate or location, and the other is relative wealth and level of economic and technological development.

Countries such as the Philippines, Guyana and Nigeria, which are at low latitudes with high average surface temperatures are more likely to be early losers, along with low-lying countries such as Bangladesh and Kiribati, which are subject to flooding by sea-level rise. Warm tropical countries have less opportunity to gain by temperature increases because they are already warm enough at all times of the year, and are less able to import plant and animal genetic resources from other regions to replace existing plants and animals which cannot adjust to even higher temperatures. The main issues for these countries are human survival and economic development.

On the other hand, mid- and high-latitude countries such as the United States and Russia may gain in the early stages of global warming from longer growing seasons, the opportunity to grow more heat-tolerant plants and crops, shorter shipping routes via the Arctic Ocean, and potential exploitation of Arctic oil and gas. This advantage, however, may be negated by water supply problems in mid-latitudes, the spread of tropical pests and diseases, heat stress in summer, and other problems. And as warming continues, even mid-latitude countries may run out of options for heat-tolerance. High-latitude countries may also find that, despite some early gains with greater warming, that gains turn to losses, due to the melting of permafrost, the death of many boreal forests, which may be burnt by wildfires along with peatlands, and increased flooding. There is also the possibility of sudden and irreversible effects causing marked regional climate changes and accelerated warming or sea-level rise. Key issues for these countries are equity and morality in the short

term and guarding against harm to themselves in the long term (see discussion in Chapter 10 below).

The second reason commonly advanced for an uneven distribution of impacts is the greater capacity of richer and more technologically advanced countries to adapt to climate change. This is because these countries can more readily afford the expense of investment in emergency preparedness, adaptations such as sea walls, plant breeding, and other research and development. Rich countries can also better afford to compensate losers within their own countries, with rehousing of displaced people, retraining and disaster relief.

In general, in today's climate, extreme climatic events such as floods, droughts and storm surges cause far more deaths in poor countries than in rich ones. This is because in rich countries the affected population is more likely to be warned of disasters, can be evacuated, fed and clothed, and has access to better health services. This ability to avoid casualties in rich countries is likely to continue as climate change hits home, although it may cost more.

Nevertheless, contrary to the emphasis on lives lost, damages in monetary terms from climatic disasters tend to be much higher, and to be increasing more rapidly, in rich countries than in poor ones. This is because there is much more financial investment in development, especially in disaster-prone coastal areas, in the rich countries, with a marked trend for populations to increase more rapidly in exposed areas. This is often exacerbated by protective measures against climatic disasters that are adequate for moderate but not for large extreme events (for example, New Orleans in 2005). Such measures encourage development and thus increase exposure to major disasters in disaster-prone areas.

Overall, however, there is little doubt that global warming will increase the inequity between the rich developed countries and the poorer developing ones. Economic studies that have attempted to quantify the cost of climate change impacts by region have come up with estimates of percentage change in present GDP for modest warmings (1 to 2.5°C).

BOX 6: IMPACTS ON FOOD PRODUCTION AND SECURITY[25]

The impacts of climate change on food production, prices and numbers at risk of hunger depend on a number of factors. These include regional climate change, biological effects of increasing atmospheric carbon dioxide, changes in floods, droughts and other extreme events, existing agricultural systems, adaptive capacity, changes in population, economic growth and technological innovation. A number of studies cited in the IPCC 2007 WGII report used the SRES family of scenarios of greenhouse gas emissions and socio-economic change.

Key studies used a linked system of climate scenarios, agricultural models, and national, regional and global economic models. Adaptation was generally at the farm level, such as changes in planting dates, fertiliser applications and irrigation, and at the regional level via new cultivars and irrigation systems. Economic adjustments included changes in national and regional investment in agriculture, crop switching, and price responses.

Results reported by Martin Parry and others in 2004 for four illustrative SRES scenarios (A1FI, A2, B1 and B2) showed small percentage gains (3 to 8%) in average crop yields in developed countries by 2080, but decreases in developing countries of 1 to 7%. This increased the inequity, measured by changes in yield, by between 7 and 10%. The authors state that: 'While global production appears stable, regional differences in crop production are likely to grow stronger through time, leading to significant polarisation of effects, with substantial increases in prices and risk of hunger among the poorer nations, especially under scenarios of greater inequality (A1FI and A2)'. Cereal price increases by 2080 under most scenarios were between 8 and 20%. Clearly, as the developed countries have a far smaller population than the developing countries, the majority of people will be worse off.

Parry and others state that their results are highly dependent on the benefits from increased CO_2 concentrations as measured in experiments, which are uncertain in the real world, and on effects of pests and diseases, which have not been estimated. Their results are for climate change scenarios simulated with only one climate model, that from the Hadley Centre in the UK. Other climate models would give different results, especially because of differing projected rainfall changes in particular decades.

Several more recent studies as reported by IPCC in 2007 do not show results for the A1FI scenario and therefore have a lower range of impacts (even though the A1FI scenario is closest to recent trends).

New conclusions reported by IPCC in 2007 include that:

- increases in frequency of extremes may lower crop yields beyond the impacts of average climate change,

- impacts of climate change on irrigation water requirements may be large [as also are changes in irrigation water supply],

- stabilisation of CO_2 concentrations through reduced emissions reduces damage to crop production in the long term, despite loss of the physiological benefits of higher CO_2 concentrations,

- the effects of trade lowers regional and global impacts, and

- the magnitude of climate impacts will be small compared to that from different socio-economic development paths; sub-Saharan Africa is likely to surpass Asia as the most food-insecure region.

None of these studies seem to have considered the potentially adverse effects on food supplies and prices of using croplands for biofuel production.[26]

They found around zero to a few per cent gains in Europe and North America, and losses of around four per cent in Africa. While these estimates have many shortcomings (see below), they do suggest increasing inequity. As warmings by 2100 are projected by the IPCC in 2007 to be in the range of 1.8 to 6.4°C, and damages are expected to increase rapidly with warmings greater than about 2°C, these estimates of uneven damages are a cause for concern.

Uppermost in many people's minds is the moral concern over increased inequity. This is given strong emphasis in international bodies. However, inequity between countries is clearly not of great practical concern in many rich countries, if the evidence of small and declining aid programs from some rich countries is anything to go by. There are, however, other more practical reasons why growing inequity between nations should be of concern to the rich, and which might lead to a genuine commitment to reduce inequity, rather than lip service to the ideal (see Chapter 10).

Aggregate impacts[27]

A number of studies have attempted to estimate the overall global cost of climate change impacts. These are beset by a number of problems that have only been partly overcome. Difficulties include:

- choosing appropriate measures of impacts, since many costs such as loss of species or lives cannot be put objectively in monetary terms,

- the need to overcome knowledge gaps and uncertainties to provide a complete picture, for instance in the understanding of the effects of changes in extreme events,

- forecasting changes in exposure to climate change, which is affected by economic growth and population change,

- anticipating adaptive capacity given its dependence on wealth and technology,

- problems in aggregating across different countries with different standards of living, and

- allowing for the passage of time in monetary costing (the so-called 'discount rate' or value of future consumption relative to today's value).

Agricultural and coastal impacts have been fairly well quantified (although with large remaining uncertainties), as has health to some extent (although it is controversial). Estimates of the cost of the loss of species and ecosystems are very uncertain. More generally, different studies get different results. This is partly due to whether they factor in the effects of extreme events and possible disasters, and how optimistically they estimate technological innovation and the capacity to adapt. Cross-links between water resources and agriculture, and the costs of learning and delays in adaptation, have not been adequately taken into account. Costs associated with exceeding critical impact thresholds, which may cause rapid increases, are usually neglected, but may dominate costs at larger warmings. Effects of rates of climate change have not been included in most studies, although it is clear that costs will be greater for rapid rates of change because adaptation will be more difficult and costly. Costs of non-market impacts such as health or species loss are subjective and perhaps best expressed in non-monetary terms.

Results to date suggest that the majority of people may be negatively affected at average global warmings of 1 to 2°C, although the net aggregate monetary impact may be slightly positive due to the dominance of rich countries in monetary terms. At higher levels of warming, estimated monetary impacts generally become negative, and studies allowing for disastrous possibilities can reach high negative outcomes, such as about 10% or more loss of world GDP for 6°C warming, as cited in the review by British government economist Sir Nicholas Stern.

The Stern Review has been widely influential but has also been attacked by sceptics as poorly based and value-laden. This is in part due to his choice of estimates of damages, which were at the large end of the range of published estimates because he favoured those that took account of extreme events. Stern also took seriously impacts out to 2100 that many economists discount as if they were marginal costs that could be ignored as too far into the future, or because they do not believe that 'business-as-usual' economic growth could produce such large emission scenarios and thus large impacts. The Stern Review estimates are not inconsistent with those in the IPCC 2007 report, which were largely arrived at independently and by different methods.[28]

Estimates of aggregate costs will only be realistic when more is known about the potential for future large-scale discontinuities in the climate system (see below) and full account is taken of potential changes in extreme events and consequent risk.

Waking the sleeping giants[29]

As discussed in Chapter 5, projected climate changes during the present century and beyond have the potential to initiate future large-scale and possibly irreversible changes in various Earth systems, resulting in impacts at continental or global scales. Fred Pearce in *New Scientist* (12 February 2005) aptly referred to these possibilities as 'waking the sleeping giants'. They are suggested by some model simulations, by past historical and paleo-records and by some recent observations (see Chapters 2 and 5). Their likelihood within the next 100 years is in most cases considered to be low, although more scientists are now arguing that more rapid changes are possible. Gradual but ongoing climatic changes set in train in the next several decades may make some of these large-scale discontinuities inevitable in the following centuries as thresholds for discontinuities are reached, with possibly huge impacts on natural and human systems.

Some of these possibilities have been identified in the previous chapter (see **Table 7**). The risk of such events is at present poorly quantified, both as to their likelihood in this or later centuries and the magnitude of their impacts on natural and human systems. In view of the plausibility of very large impacts, the mechanisms and preconditions for

such events should be intensively studied, both via computer modelling, and by close study of analogous past historical and paleo-events. Modelling and paleo-analysis must extend not only to the basic physical events but also to their global and regional impacts including changes in rainfall, aridity, flooding, and impacts on ecosystems and cropping potential.

Studies of past episodes of rapid climate change such as the Younger Dryas event deserve special attention, with a focus not only on mechanisms but also on regional impacts. Attention should also be paid to records and modelling of more regional non-linearities and discontinuities. There is much evidence to suggest that past climatic fluctuations have not been smooth, but rather have often involved rapid changes from one circulation regime to another.

Some scientists who are familiar with these past large variations in climate react by saying that if such changes happened before due to natural causes and life survived, what is there to worry about now? However, human populations at the time of the last deglaciation were relatively small, and people could migrate more or less freely to more suitable regions. That would be very difficult now, with more than six billion people, national borders and immigration restrictions.

Thus, despite the fact that the potential human consequences of each of these possible large-scale discontinuities have not been fully explored, it is worth looking briefly at the scope of the possible impacts.

Effects of a breakdown in the ocean circulation

Slow-down or cessation of the convective overturning in the North Atlantic (see Chapter 5) and around Antarctica would cause regional cooling, as well as connected changes elsewhere in the world. This overturning powers what has been described as the oceanic 'conveyor belt', which redistributes heat around the globe. North of 24°N the Gulf Stream presently conveys roughly a million gigawatts of energy northwards from the tropics, warming much of Europe by 5 to 10°C. Without deep-water formation, the Gulf Stream runs further south without releasing so much heat.

Partial or slow reductions in the North Atlantic overturning would lead to only small relative cooling in the Western European region, and this is likely also in parts of North America, as polewards heat transport is reduced. Such slow changes could be outweighed by general global warming, such that temperatures in Western Europe and parts of North America would not fall below the present. However, altered temperature differences with neighbouring regions would lead to changes in storm tracks, variability and severe weather events. The impacts of such events have not yet been quantified.

A study by Michael Vellinga and Richard Wood with the UK Hadley Centre climate model[30] suggests that weakening of the overturning in the North Atlantic may also lead to large shifts in precipitation in the tropics due to shifts in the thermal equator. Using an ecosystem model, they find that weakening of the oceanic circulation causes worldwide changes in ecosystem structure and function, including expansions of desert in the north of South America, West Africa and Australia, but reductions in desert in North America. These changes far from the North Atlantic are mainly due to precipitation changes, and have strong implications for food production. They are still quite uncertain, but point to wide implications, well beyond Western Europe.

If complete cessation of overturning were to happen this century, which is unlikely but not completely impossible, it might lead to colder temperatures in the North Atlantic region than at present, with greater warming elsewhere. A return to regionally cooler conditions in Europe and North America would have disastrous impacts on food production, health, economics and ecosystems. This could be worse than at the time of the Little Ice Age because of far larger human populations, and the greater inter-connectedness of global economies. Even if there were no direct climate change impacts elsewhere, if the economies of Europe and North America were to catch a cold, others would sneeze.

Most global climate models that have been run for such scenarios have only projected complete cessation of overturning for carbon dioxide concentrations exceeding twice pre-industrial levels, and at a point in time well beyond 2100, when the whole world would be considerably warmer than now. However, these computer simulations have not in general taken account of simultaneous forcing from decreased overturning around Antarctica, nor of accelerated melting of the Greenland ice sheet, as discussed in Chapter 5. The recent dramatic loss of Arctic sea ice and acceleration of melting and outflow from Greenland, both far faster than modelled, means that further surprises could be in store.

Modelling suggests that any such shutdown of the ocean circulation may be long-lasting relative to human lifetimes. Moreover, the paleo-climatic analogy of the Younger Dryas and similar events near the end of the last glaciation is only partial. At that time the Earth's orbital changes favoured a 'quick' recovery (which occurred after 1200 years), whereas there is no such force for recovery operating this time. We are thus not just talking about a short-term disaster from which the world might recover, but one that might last for millennia.

In a paper entitled 'Abrupt climate change: should we be worried?' (2003) Robert B Gagosian, President and Director of the illustrious Woods Hole Oceanographic Institute in Massachusetts, USA, states that two scenarios are useful to contemplate:[31]

Scenario 1: Conveyor slows down within next two decades. This could quickly and markedly cool the North Atlantic region, causing disruptions in global economic activity. These disruptions may be exacerbated because the climate changes occur in a direction opposite to what is commonly expected, and they occur at a pace that makes adaptation difficult.

Scenario 2: Conveyor slows down a century from now. In this case, cooling in the North Atlantic region may partially or totally offset the major effects of global warming in this region. Thus, the climate of the North Atlantic region may rapidly return to one that more resembles today's – even as other parts of the world, particularly less-developed regions, experience the unmitigated brunt of global warming. If the Conveyor subsequently turns up again, the 'deferred' warming may be delivered in a decade.

Clearly the consequences of either of Gagosian's scenarios are serious, although the first is the more alarming because of its rapid onset. The report to the US Pentagon by Peter Schwart and Doug Randall, widely reported in the media in 2004, seems to have taken the first scenario as its starting point, 'as an alternative to the scenarios of gradual climate warming that are so common'. While the resulting geo-political scenario has been widely criticised as sensationalist and even irresponsible, it seems to me that as a worst-case scenario it fulfils a purpose for the Pentagon, whose business is to plan for unlikely but not impossible scenarios. Schwart and Randall suggest that such an abrupt climate change scenario would lead to food shortages, decreased water supplies in key regions, and disruption to energy supplies, with likely downstream risks for US national security, including border management, global conflict and economic malaise.[32] Such topics are taken up under 'Security implications' below.

A paper presented by Michael Schlesinger of the University of Illinois, and colleagues at a conference on 'Avoiding Dangerous Climate Change' in England in 2005, states, on the basis of their simplified climate and economic modelling, that in the absence of an emissions reduction policy, there is a 50% chance of a collapse of the North Atlantic circulation by 2205. Even with the implementation of an immediate carbon tax of US$100 per tonne of carbon to reduce emissions, they calculate that the chance may still exceed 25%.[33]

The effects of a slowdown or cessation of Antarctic deep-water formation have been investigated by Australian oceanographers Richard Matear and Tony Hirst.[34] Using a simulation up to 2100, and later multi-century climate change simulations from the CSIRO climate model, they projected the impact on marine biogeochemical cycles. The key results were:

- reductions in the global oceanic uptake of carbon dioxide by about 14% by 2100,

- reductions in dissolved oxygen levels in the ocean interior over several centuries, causing expansion of an anoxic region in the mid-water of the eastern equatorial Pacific, and

- reductions in nutrient concentrations in the upper ocean, causing an expansion of regions that are nutrient limited and reducing biological production in the upper ocean, thus affecting fisheries.

Rapid sea-level rise from melting ice sheets

The ideas discussed in Chapter 5 regarding possible rapid melting of the Greenland and West Antarctic ice sheets suggest that sea-level rise may be more rapid than suggested by the IPCC 2007 range of 18 to 59 cm by 2100.

While the time scale for complete disintegration of the Greenland and West Antarctic ice sheets under these faster scenarios is still uncertain, the above ideas suggest that sea-level rises of the order of one or more metres in the twenty-first century, and more in the following centuries are possible. Only the broadest of estimates have been made of what impacts such large sea-level rises would have economically and on the numbers of people displaced. Martin Parry of the Jackson Environmental Institute, University of East Anglia, and others estimate that for the more modest sea-level rises expected by 2100 under the IPCC 2001 report scenarios, 50 to 100 million people may be subject to coastal flooding.[35] Greater sea-level rises could vastly inflate that figure. Such estimates depend greatly on what assumptions are made about population growth in the coastal zone, and the affordability and effectiveness of adaptation measures such as sea walls.

Apart from the huge economic costs of such coastal flooding, accommodating the huge numbers of people forced to leave the present coastal zones would be a major social and political issue. The internal disruption in many populous developing countries such as China, Indonesia, Bangladesh, Egypt and Nigeria would be enormous, with the likelihood of internal conflicts, poverty and disease. A number of low-lying island countries may be made uninhabitable, forcing migration, loss of national sovereignty and cultural identity and bringing demands for compensation. Cross-border migrations would be an issue in many regions.

The 2007 IPCC report has a cross-chapter case study on megadeltas.[36] A sample of 40 deltas globally, including all the large megadeltas, are inhabited by nearly 300 million people, with an average population density of 500 people per square km, notably in the Nile delta and Bangladesh. Many large and expanding cities are located in these deltas. One study indicates that more than one million people would be directly affected by 2050 in four megadeltas, in Bangladesh, Egypt, Nigeria and Vietnam. Much of the expected damage is due to sediment loss from dams and coastal erosion, but sea-level rise would greatly exacerbate the problems.

Even in developed countries, the cost and loss of amenity from sea walls and other defences, and accommodating and compensating people displaced from the coastal zones and cities would cause enormous economic and social strain. Large regions that are low-lying and in some cases already subsiding will be threatened, for example parts of eastern England, the Low Countries of Western Europe, Venice and other parts of the Adriatic coast, Florida, parts of the Gulf Coast, the Chesapeake Bay region and much of the Atlantic coast in the US, and parts of coastal cities in Australia. Loss of coastal wetland habitats would be sweeping, and many coastal coral reefs such as the Great Barrier Reef off Australia would be effectively drowned, exposing coasts to full wave energy, enhanced erosion and storm surges. Many local thresholds for impacts would be exceeded, as natural barriers and sea walls would be progressively overtopped. Erosion and re-alignment of coasts would be far greater and more complex than is suggested by simply translating the coast inland according to the existing contours. The threat of sea-level rise is already impacting on coastal development in many parts of the world, from Bangladesh, England and the US to Australia. In Australia the Insurance

Australia Group has urged the federal government to adopt various adaptation measures including coastal land value insurance, while a state planning authority has rejected proposed development plans because of 'foreseeable risk of inundation'.[37]

At what level of global warming rapid melting and ice sheet disintegration processes will get under way is not clear, but once started they are likely to be unstoppable. Recent observations suggest it could be quite soon, if not already with us. Rapid sea-level rise could continue until both Greenland and the WAIS are more or less completely melted, leaving the world with a sea-level rise of up to 10 to 12 metres lasting for millennia. This would be quite a legacy for our descendants.

Runaway carbon dynamics[38]

As discussed in Chapter 5, runaway carbon dynamics (rapid increases in carbon dioxide concentrations in the atmosphere due to positive feedbacks) would lead to an acceleration in global warming. It includes the likely reversal of the land-based carbon sinks in plants and soil, which today absorb carbon from the atmosphere, especially due to increasing plant growth caused by the fertilising effect of higher concentrations of carbon dioxide in the atmosphere. The role of the oceans in taking up carbon is complex. With warmer water dissolving less CO_2, warmer surface water tends to make for less overturning and thus less downwards transport of CO_2. However, stronger winds especially in the Southern Ocean may bring to the surface colder water that has higher CO_2 concentrations due to biochemistry, and which then outgasses.[39]

Other contributors to an acceleration in global warming include more frequent forest fires, the thawing of permafrost (which allows the decay of peat stored in the Arctic tundra), and the release of methane stored in ice-like hydrate crystals on the ocean floor (see Chapter 5).

These effects add up to a more rapid increase in greenhouse gas concentration in the atmosphere, adding to the enhanced greenhouse effect, accelerating global warming and leading to a greater and more rapid onset of all climate impacts. Exactly how rapid this process will be, and how far it will go is not yet understood, but once it gets under way it may be difficult to stop. Such an acceleration of global warming is equivalent to a greater climate sensitivity, and means that to stabilise greenhouse gas concentrations and global warming at any particular 'safe' level will require greater reductions in greenhouse gas emissions.

Security implications

The Pentagon report referred to above, by Schwart and Randall was greeted with some scepticism as an extreme and sensational document. However, several other studies of potential climate change impacts on national and international security have appeared since 2004. These include an Australian study *Heating Up the Planet: Climate Change and Security* that recommended that government agencies should 'examine the policy connections between climate change and national security [including] food, water, energy, health and environmental vulnerabilities, disaster planning and unregulated population movements' and 'factor climate wild cards into their security calculations and alternative futures planning and "think the unthinkable"'.[40]

In an even stronger and more detailed report, the US Center for Strategic and International Studies concluded that 'climate change will aggravate existing international crises and problems', including large-scale migrations of people due to rising temperatures and sea level. It went on to state that: 'The scale of the potential consequences associated with climate change – particularly in more dire and distant scenarios – made it difficult to grasp the extent and magnitude of the possible changes ahead'.[41]

The Chief Scientific Advisor to the UK Minister of Defence stated in 2007 that: 'The MoD regards climate change as a key strategic factor affecting societal stresses and the responses of communities and nations to those stresses. Consequently we have a pressing need for the best available advice on future climate change and, based on these predictions, assessments of the impacts of those changes on human societies at the regional and local scale'.[42]

The awarding of the Nobel Peace Prize to Al Gore and the IPCC in 2007 indicated some recognition that there are indeed international security issues involved, although most conflicts are the result of multiple stresses of which climate change may be only one.[43] Recent developments such as the territorial claims by Russia in the Arctic, presumably in anticipation of easier access to resources on the Arctic seafloor as sea ice cover is reduced, and the incipient dispute over international navigation rights in the North-West Passage, which Canada regards as within its territorial waters, are current examples of climate-related issues.[44]

Stabilisation of greenhouse gas concentrations[45]

All the five 'reasons for concern' about global warming increase in severity with the amount of warming. The big question for climate change policy is at what degree of warming does this become unacceptable or 'dangerous', and therefore what concentration of greenhouse gases in the atmosphere should be considered the upper limit? This will determine what emissions reduction strategies must be put into place.

Clearly, the projected rate and magnitude of warming and sea-level rise can be lessened by reducing greenhouse gas emissions, and the earlier and greater the emissions reductions, the smaller and slower the projected warming and sea-level rise would be. There remains a range of uncertainty, however, in the amount of warming that would result from any particular stabilised greenhouse gas concentration.

As stated above, the 2007 IPCC report gives the best estimate of climate sensitivity as 3.0°C, with a likely range from 2.0 to 4.5°C. Based on this range of sensitivities, the eventual warming due to various stabilised equivalent CO_2 concentrations are given in **Table 9**.

TABLE 9: Eventual warming (°C) above pre-industrial for various equilibrium concentrations of greenhouse gases in ppm CO_2-equivalent, for the best guess and likely range of climate sensitivities. Based on Table 10.8 in the 2007 IPCC report WGI. Note that concentration of CO_2 (only) is above 384 ppm and rising on average by about 2 ppm each year

Equilibrium concentration in ppm CO_2-equivalent	Warming for best guess climate sensitivity of 3.0°C	Warming range for likely sensitivity range of 2.0–4.5°C
350	1.0	0.6 to 1.4
450	2.1	1.4 to 3.1
550	2.9	1.9 to 4.4
650	3.6	2.4 to 5.5
750	4.3	2.8 to 6.4
1000	5.5	3.7 to 8.3
1200	6.3	4.2 to 9.4

Such warmings need to be considered in the light of the tipping points for the onset of massive changes in the climate system, listed in **Table 7**, and the uncertainties related to those. Note that the tipping points are given relative to 1980–1999, so they should be increased by about 0.7°C to be relative to pre-industrial temperatures as in **Table 9**. Comparison of possible warmings with estimates of tipping points suggests a real possibility that even for 450 ppm CO_2-equivalent the first few tipping points in **Table 7** may be exceeded. This is even more likely if recent observations in fact point to faster global warming and sea ice melt, and more accelerated outlet glaciers, than were considered likely in the 2007 IPCC report (which was based on earlier literature). We will return to this result in Chapter 8 on mitigation.

Commenting on this possibility, the 2007 IPCC report states that: 'Risk analyses given in some recent studies suggest that there is no longer high confidence that certain large-scale events (for example, deglaciation of major ice sheets) can be avoided, given historical climate change and the inertia of the climate system'.

Clearly, reducing emissions of greenhouse gases to stabilise their concentrations would delay and reduce damages caused by climate change. But if this is to include keeping below critical thresholds for various biophysical systems and possible major changes to the climate system the reduction targets may have to be very strict. Indeed, if the tipping points that may occur at lower warmings are to be avoided it may be necessary to follow a so-called 'overshoot' scenario where concentrations rise to a peak in excess of the long-term stabilisation value and are then reduced. This could only be achieved by taking greenhouse gases out of the atmosphere, for example by creating biomass energy and sequestering the CO_2 produced, or generating 'biochar' (see Chapter 8). Such overshoot scenarios, for a given stabilisation level, would result in some increase in medium-term impacts and especially in greater sea-level rise on a time-scale of several centuries.

Stabilisation of concentrations of greenhouse gases could take a century or more, and stabilisation of warming, and especially of sea-level rise and ice sheet melting, will take many centuries. Any policy on reducing greenhouse gas emissions needs to take account of potential impacts and the benefits of avoiding them centuries into the future. This is especially the case since potential impacts at high warmings could well be catastrophic rather than marginal, and therefore should not be discounted as is commonly done for marginal costs.

Apart from the question of avoiding potentially disastrous large-scale discontinuities in the climate system (the fifth of the five 'reasons for concern' originally spelt out in the 2001 IPCC report), stabilisation scenarios if followed would certainly reduce the seriousness of the first four reasons for concern. Thus risks to unique and threatened systems, and from extreme climate events, the unequal distribution of impacts, and aggregate impacts would all be reduced by reducing emissions by some mitigation policy.

The Fourth Assessment Report of the IPCC in 2007 illustrates this with a number of detailed charts and tables that show the increasing onset of impacts and damages for each additional degree of warming. Interpretation in relation to impacts after stabilisation is complicated by questions of the rates of change and of adaptive capacity a century or more into the future, but the conclusions are more straightforward for the twenty-first century transient path prior to stabilisation.[46]

Despite some early attempts to quantify these effects, for example, in the UK study of global effects, published in 2004, results must remain qualitative since there are so many complications and uncertainties.[47] Perhaps the most important of these is the effect of different socio-economic development scenarios on adaptive capacity and exposure, and thus on the realised impacts.

Socio-economic scenarios are of course interactive with the scenarios for emissions which depend on population and economic growth, and technological development and lifestyles. Any adoption of policies to reduce emissions will naturally also influence these other factors, and indeed may only be achievable by adopting policies on them, for example limiting population growth, changing lifestyles and favouring new low-carbon emitting technologies. Indeed, economic development in lesser-developed countries, using low emission technologies, is vital to increasing future adaptive capacity in these countries. Some of these links will be explored in Chapter 8 on mitigation, Chapter 9 on climate change in context, and in the later chapters related to policy options.

It should be added that, due to the inertia in the climate system, emissions reductions now would have little effect on impacts until several decades hence, after which they would make significant differences. This time lag effect is critical. It means that reducing impacts later in the century, or in following centuries, requires early emission reductions, unless far greater reliance is to be placed on negative emission technologies later to pull back from a dangerous level of greenhouse gas concentrations. The latter option would place a huge burden on future generations.

Growing reasons for concern

Despite acknowledged uncertainties, it is clear from this review of the potential impacts of climate change that there are substantial reasons for concern, which increase with global warming. Risks to unique and threatened systems and from extreme climate events are expected to increase. Global aggregate impacts measured in monetary terms are expected to turn negative at around 2 to 3°C warming relative to pre-industrial levels, although most people will be negatively affected at lesser warmings. Impacts will hit hardest at poorer countries, thereby increasing international inequity.

Moreover, there is growing concern that the risk of substantial and potentially catastrophic changes in the climate system, which may be unstoppable once they commence, will rise greatly for larger warmings. This may well dominate any risk assessment, and set low limits for increased concentrations of greenhouse gases if such potentially dangerous changes are to be avoided. Warmings of only about 2 to 3°C above pre-industrial levels may set largely irreversible changes to the climate system in motion, and this may not become apparent until it is too late to avoid the consequences. There is a chance of such warmings even for quite low concentrations of greenhouse gases, less than 450 ppm CO_2-equivalent, if climate sensitivity is in the upper part of the likely range of uncertainty.

We may be able to adapt to small changes in climate, but in some cases even this may be costly or have unwelcome side effects. We examine the capacity to adapt in Chapter 7, and the costs, benefits and means of reducing the rate and magnitude of climate change in Chapter 8. The message for now is that the projected climate changes are large enough and rapid enough to cause some pretty big problems which we need to take very seriously indeed.

ENDNOTES

1. The Garnaut Review in Australia has been called the Australian version of the Stern Review. It was set up by the various Australian state governments before the November 2007 federal election and will report to the Rudd Federal Government on what policy options should be adopted to deal with climate change, nationally and internationally. This quote is from its interim report in February 2008. See http://www.garnautreview.org.au.

2. The objective of the UNFCCC can be found in Article 2 of the Convention at http://www.unfccc.int.

3. For relevant web links to new developments try the ongoing organisational websites given in the relevant endnotes, or current issues of relevant learned journals. Many news services such as the BBC or specialised websites of relevant organisations enable you to register to be alerted to new material relevant to your interest.

4. The myriad local and regional studies have been referenced in the voluminous reports from the Intergovernmental Panel on Climate Change in successive reviews. See http://www.ipcc.ch.

5. The best explanation of the five IPCC reasons for concern will be found in Chapter 19 of the IPCC 2001 report, WGII, pp. 913–67, especially p. 917. See also IPCC 2007, WGII, pp. 73–6 and 795–7, and a paper by JB Smith and others, 'Dangerous climate change: an update on the IPCC reasons for concern', *Proceeding of the National Academy of Sciences*, accepted 2008.

6. One example is observed sudden changes in Australian rainfall and flood frequencies. These are documented by Franks and Kuczera in *Water Resources Research*, **38**, article no. 1062 (2002), and in climate model output by Yonetani and Gordon in *Journal of Climate*, **14**, pp. 1765–79 (2001). See also Vives and Jones, CSIRO Technical Paper no. 73, CSIRO Marine and Atmospheric Research (2005).

7. Figure 23, showing a threshold for wind damage, is from T Coleman, 'The impact of climate change on insurance against catastrophes', *Proceedings of the Living with Climate Change Conference*, Canberra, 19 December (2002). See: http://www.iag.com.au/pub/iag/results/presentations.shtml.

8. In ecosystems see Scheffer and others in *Nature*, **413**, pp. 591–6 (2001), and in lakes see *Trends in Ecology and Evolution*, **8**, pp. 275–9 (1993). For behavioural or operational thresholds see Jones in *Climate Research*, **13**, pp. 89–100 (2000).

9. For risks to unique and threatened species, see IPCC 2007 report, WGII, Chapter 19.3.7, pp. 795–6.

10. Past and projected future changes in lake levels are discussed in the IPCC 2007 report, WGII, Chapters 1.3.2 and 3.4.1 as well as in the regional chapters. The Caspian Sea is variously projected to drop between 0.5 and 9 m by 2100.

11. An extensive review of the literature on glacial melt in the Himalaya region of Nepal, India and China identifies many natural systems at risk as well as human systems including hydropower, agriculture and water supply. See: *An Overview of Glaciers, Glacier Retreat, and Subsequent Impacts in Nepal, India and China*, WWF Nepal Program (2005) available at http://www.panda.org/downloads/climate_change/himalyaglaciersreport2005pdf.

12. Box 4 is largely based on Buddemeier, Kleypas and Aranson 'Coral Reefs and Global Climate Change', Pew Center on Global Climate Change (2004) available at http://www.pewclimate.org, and 'The Townsville Declaration on Coral Reef Research and Management' (18 October 2002) quoted in *Australasian Science* (Jan/Feb 2003) pp. 29–32. See also Dennis in *Nature*, **415**, p. 947 (28 February 2002); UNEP *Synergies*, no. 7, (January 2003); and Roberts and others, *Science*, **295**, pp. 1280–4 (2002). For valuation of coral reefs see Carr and Mendelsohn, *Ambio*, **32**, pp. 353–7 (2003). A periodic report, *Status of Coral Reefs of the World*, produced under international auspices by the Australian Institute of Marine Sciences, and the latest briefing paper *Coral Reefs and climate change 2007* are available at http://www.aims.gov.au. Papers arguing for rapid adaptation of coral to bleaching are in *Nature*, **430**, pp. 741–2 (2004). Increased calcification rates with higher temperatures are reported in *Geophysical Research Letters* doi:10.1029/2004GL021541 (2004) by McNeil and others. See also the cross-chapter case study on the impacts of climate change on coral reefs in IPCC 2007 report, WGII, C2, pp. 850–7. Two recent papers by MP Lesser, and by

SD Donner and others, are in the *Proceedings of the National Academy of Sciences*, **104**, pp. 5259–60 and pp. 5483–8 (27 March 2007).

Acidification of the oceans is dealt with extensively in a report from the Royal Society of the UK, *Ocean Acidification due to Increasing Atmospheric Carbon Dioxide*, Policy Document 12/05, June 2005, see http://www.royalsoc.ac.uk. See also *Scientific American* (March 2006) pp. 38–45; *Nature*, **442**, pp. 978–80 (31 August 2006); *New Scientist* (5 August 2006) pp. 28–33; Gazeau and others, *Geophysical Research Letters*, **34**, L07603 (2007); and IPCC 2007 report, WGII, Box 4.4 and p. 236.

13. The effects of sea-level rise on coastal erosion and damages is discussed by Stive in *Climatic Change*, **64**, pp. 27–39 (2004) and in the same issue by Zhang, Douglas and Leatherman, pp. 41–58. The IPCC 2007 report provides a brief summary in WGII, Chapter 6.4.1.1.

14. Changes in wave climates will occur due to changes in storm tracks and intensities, and in prevailing winds, see Hemer and others, 'Waves and climate change on the Australian coast', *Journal of Coastal Research*, **SI50**, pp. 432–7 (2007). See also Cowell and others, 'Managing uncertainty in predicting climate-change impacts on beaches', *Journal of Coastal Research*, **22**, pp. 232–45 (2006).

15. Relevant publications include: Nicholls and Tol, 'Impacts and responses to sea-level rise: a global analysis of the SRES scenarios over the twenty-first century', *Philosophical Transactions of the Royal Society*, **A364**, pp. 1073–95 (2006). This study looks at costs and benefits from adaptation to the SRES scenarios with maximum sea-level rise of 35 cm by 2100. See also: 'Living with Coastal Erosion in Europe: Sediment and Space for Sustainability', Directorate General Environment, European Commission (30 May 2004); and Part 3 'The Potential for Dramatic Changes in Coastal Regions', in *Sudden and Disruptive Climate Change*, Michael C MacCracken and others (eds), Earthscan, London (2008). The last includes studies of impacts on Chesapeake Bay, the Gulf of Mexico and metropolitan New York in the US.

16. IPCC 2007 discusses impacts on Arctic indigenous communities in WGII, Chapter 17, while Australian Aboriginal and New Zealand Maori groups are mentioned in Chapter 11.4.8. Adaptation by such groups is discussed in Chapter 17.

17. Easterling and colleagues, *Science*, **289**, pp. 2068–74 (2000); Changnon and colleagues, *Bulletin of the American Meteorological Society*, **81**, pp. 427–42 (2000).

18. See discussion and references in IPCC 2007 report, WGI, Chapter 1.3.8.4, p. 110.

19. Box 5 on future flooding in England and Wales is based on a UK Office of Science and Technology report, see: http://www.environment-agency.gov.uk/subjects/flood/763964/?lang=_e/. A review of the major floods in the UK in 2007 can be found at the same website.

20. See McInnes and colleagues, in *Natural Hazards*, **30**, pp. 187–207 (2003). See also Pittock (ed.) *Climate Change: An Australian Guide to the Science and Potential Impacts*, pp. 133–4, Australian Greenhouse Office, at http://www. greenhouse.gov.au. See also IPCC 2007 report, WGII, Box 6.2.

21. See for example: Munich Re Group, *Weather Catastrophes and Climate Change: Is There Still Hope for Us*? (2005) at http://www.munichre.com; Dixon and others, RAND Institute for Civil Justice, Occasional Paper *Commercial Wind Insurance in the Gulf States* (2007), at http://www.rand.org; Association of British Insurers *Financial Risks of Climate Change* (2005) at http://www.abi.org.uk/climatechange; Evan Mills, 'Insurance in a climate of change', *Science*, **309**, pp. 1040–4, (12 August 2005); McAneney and others, 'A century of damage – property losses due to natural perils', in *Australian and New Zealand Institute of Insurance and Finance Journal*, **30** (3) (June/July 2007), available at http:// www.riskfrontiers.com/publications.html. See also IPCC 2007 report, WGII, Chapter 7.4.2.2.4.

22. See IPCC 2007 report, WGII, Chapter 5.2 for the present climate and Chapters 5.4.1 and 5.4.2 for future climate. There is also a special case study on the impacts of the European heatwave of 2003 (Box 5.1 and cross-chapter study C1).

23. Impacts of fire are discussed in IPCC 2007 report, Chapter 4 on ecosystems, especially pp. 217–18 and 229, and in various regional chapters. Effects on boreal forests and on Siberian and Indonesian peatlands are discussed in Chapter 10.2.4.4.

24. See IPCC 2007 report, WGII, Chapter 19.3.7, p. 796, and in the context of mitigation in WGIII, Chapter 2.6. See also the discussion of equity in Chapter 10 of this book.

25. Box 6 is largely based on Parry and colleagues' study of impacts on global food production in *Global Environmental Change*, **14**, pp. 53–67 (2004) and the updated material in the IPCC 2007 report, WGII. A number of more recent reports include: a special feature on 'Climate Change and Food Security' in the *Proceedings of the National Academy of Sciences* (11 December 2007) with several papers by authors of the IPCC 2007 chapter on 'Food, fibre and forest products'; an article on 'Food security under climate change' in *Science*, **319**, pp. 580–1 (February 2008) introducing a paper by Lobell and others on p. 607. Elsewhere, Lobel and Field estimate that warming since 1981 has already reduced yields of wheat, maize and barley globally, see *Environmental Research Letters*, **2**, 014002 (2007). See also David Schmel, 'Climate change and crop yields: beyond Cassandra' in *Science*, **312**, pp. 1889–90 (30 June 2006), which suggests that the positive effects of higher CO_2 concentrations may have been overestimated; and William R Cline, *Global Warming and Agriculture: Impact Estimates by Country*, Center for Global Development at http://www.cgdev.org/, which suggests large declines in yield in developing countries by 2080.

26. Effects of biofuel production on food supplies and prices are contentious, see for example, The Royal Society, *Sustainable Biofuels: Prospects and Challenges* (2008), available at http://www.royalsociety.org/ and Intelligent Energy Europe, *Biofuels: 13 Innovative Projects for an Energy-intelligent Europe* (2007), available from http://www.ec.europa.eu/energy/intelligent/library/publications_en.htm; see also RL Naylor and others, 'The Ripple Effect: Biofuels, Food Security and the Environment', *Environment* magazine (US) (November 2007) pp. 30–43. See also discussion in Chapter 8.

27. Aggregate impacts are discussed in the IPCC 2007 report, WGII, section 19.3.7, pp. 796–7.

28. See the Stern Review at http://www.hm-treasury.gov.uk/independent_reviews/stern_review_economics_climate_change/. A highly critical review of Stern by well-known climate change sceptics is 'The Stern Review: A dual critique' in *World Economics*, **7**, pp. 165–232. An Australian critique came from some staff members of the Productivity Commission at http://www.pc.gov.au/research/staffworking paper/sternreview. A large part of the argument over the Stern Review conclusions is based on different levels of risk aversion, with Stern actually taking a moderate view that targets should aim at a less than 50% chance of exceeding 2°C global warming. Many people would argue that even 2°C warming is too great a risk. See also a special issue of *Climatic Change*, 'The Stern Debate', **89** (3–4) (August 2008), and discussion in Chapter 10. A risk assessment approach can be found in the Energy Futures Forum report *The Heat is On: The Future of Energy in Australia* at http://www.csiro.au/resources/pfnd.html.

29. Many of the most relevant references are in the endnotes for Chapter 5 in the 'Thresholds and abrupt or irreversible changes' section, although they focus on the mechanisms rather than the impacts.

30. See *Climatic Change*, **54**, pp. 251–67 (2002).

31. Robert Gagosian's paper (2003) is available on the website http://www.whoi.edu/page.do?pid=12455.

32. The Schwart and Randall report for the Pentagon is *An Abrupt Climate Change Scenario and Its Implications for United States National Security*, available at http://www.gbn.org/ArticleDisplayServlet.srv?aid=26231.

33. See ME Schlesinger and others, 'Towards a risk assessment for the shutdown of the Atlantic thermo-haline circulation', Chapter 5 in *Avoiding Dangerous Climate Change*, HJ Schellnhuber (ed.) Cambridge University Press, Cambridge, UK (2006) available at http://www.defra.gov.uk.

34. See Matear and Hirst, *Global Biogeochemical Cycles*, **17**, p. 1125 (2003).

35. Estimates of sea-level rise effects by Parry and colleagues are in *Global Environmental Change*, **11**, pp. 181–3 (2001), and **14**, pp. 69–86 (2004).

36. The cross-chapter study on megadeltas is study C3 on pp. 858–63 of the 2007 IPCC report, WGII.

37. The complexities of coastal erosion and realignment are discussed in WGII, Chapter 6.4.1.1. The Insurance Australia Group submission dated 28 May 2008 is at http://www.iag.com.au/gov.submissions. The planning decision is from the Victorian Civil and Administrative Tribunal at http://www.vcat.vic.gov.au, '*Gippsland Coastal Board v South Gippsland Shire Council*'.

38. Many references relating to the carbon cycle can be found near the end of Chapter 5. See also the IPCC 2007 report, WGI, Chapters 5.4.2 (observations), 7.3.3 (terrestrial feedbacks) and 10.4.1 (projections).

39. See Le Quere and others, *Science*, **316**, pp. 1735–8 (22 June 2007) and Lenton and Matear in *Global Biogeochemical Cycles*, **21**, GB2016 (2007). Latest on the global carbon cycle can be found at http://www.globalcarbonproject.org.

40. See Alan Dupont and Graeme Pearman, at http://www.lowyinstitute.org, Lowy Institute Paper 12 (2006).

41. See *The Age of Consequences: The Foreign Policy and National Security Implications of Global Climate Change* (2007), available at http://www.csis.org.

42. The UK MoD statement is at http://www.mod.uk/news article 11 September 2007. There is also a report from International Alert titled *A Climate of Conflict* (2007) at http://www.international-alert.org/press/. Also see 'Ecology and political upheaval' by Jeffrey Sachs in *Scientific American* (July 2006) p. 21.

43. See the presentation speech for the 2007 Nobel Peace Prize at http://www.nobelprize.org, but also the article by Curtis Abraham in *New Scientist* (20 October 2007) p. 24.

44. Issues relating to the melting of Arctic sea ice were reported in *New Scientist* (21 January 2006), p. 24 and (18 August 2007) p. 4.

45. Effects of stabilisation are discussed in the IPCC 2007 report, WGII, Chapters 2.4.6.8 and 19.4.2.2. Overshoot scenarios are discussed on pp. 801–2 and 804 of WGII. Chapter 3 of the WGIII report has an extensive discussion of stabilisation scenarios and of the need for negative emissions to achieve the lower stabilisation targets.

46. See the IPCC 2007 report, for example, in the Synthesis Report Table SPM-3, WGII, Figure SPM-2, and in WGII Chapter 19, Table 19.1.

47. The UK study results are in a special issue of *Global Environmental Change*, **14**, pp. 1–99 (2004).

7

Adaptation: living with climate change

One thing we must be aware of is that even if the Kyoto Protocol is implemented in full, the emission of greenhouse gases will result in our having to contend with the effects of climate change for decades to come in the form of more frequent and more intensive natural catastrophes.

MUNICH REINSURANCE GROUP, *ANNUAL REVIEW: NATURAL CATASTROPHES 2001*, 2002.

To a nation such as Bangladesh, adaptation is an option not by choice, but by compulsion, as insurance to its efforts in achieving sustainable development. Even with the envisaged mitigation as under the Kyoto Protocol, adaptation would be necessary because of the impending effects of the already accumulated greenhouse gases in the atmosphere.

SALEEMUL HUQ, CHAIRMAN OF THE BANGLADESH CENTRE FOR ADVANCED STUDIES AND MIZAN KHAN, NORTH SOUTH UNIVERSITY, DHAKA, BANGLADESH.[1]

A wide array of adaptation options is available, but more extensive adaptation than is currently occurring is required to reduce vulnerability to climate change. There are barriers, limits and costs, which are not fully understood.

INTERGOVERNMENTAL PANEL ON CLIMATE CHANGE, SYNTHESIS REPORT, 2007.

Adaptation concepts and strategies[2]

Adaptation is an automatic or planned response to change that minimises the adverse effects and maximises any benefits. It is one of the two possible means of coping with human-induced climate change and sea-level rise. The other option is to reduce the magnitude of human-induced climate change by reducing greenhouse gas emissions. This is called mitigation and is discussed in the next chapter. Adaptation is essential to cope with the climate change and sea-level rise that we cannot avoid now and in the near future, while mitigation would limit the extent of future climate change.

Adaptation is essentially a local challenge, while mitigation is essentially a global process that will only be achieved by international cooperation and a common commitment.

Adaptation is necessary because climate change is already happening, and the long lag times in the climate system make further climate change, and especially sea-level rise, inevitable. Further climate change is already built into the system by past greenhouse gas emissions, that is, we are already committed to it. The effect happens decades to centuries after the cause and cannot readily be stopped. Additional to the existing commitment to climate change, even more climate change is made inevitable by the long time, at least several decades, between *deciding* to reduce emissions, and the socio-economic system changing enough to *actually* reduce greenhouse gas emissions sufficiently to stop making the situation worse. Very substantial reductions in greenhouse gas emissions will be necessary before greenhouse gas concentrations stop going up. In fact, for centuries to come, atmospheric carbon dioxide concentrations will not fall much below whatever maximum levels are reached, even after major reductions in emissions unless we actively withdraw greenhouse gases out of the atmosphere. This is due to the large reservoirs of carbon dioxide in the ocean, soil and biosphere, which are in equilibrium with the atmosphere on a time-scale of decades. The permanent sinks are much slower to act. In short, we cannot simply turn off climate change, so we must learn to live with it. That is why adaptation is essential.

Because there are uncertainties about future amounts and effects of climate change and sea-level rise, adaptation must be a risk management strategy, which takes account of the probabilities as well as of the costs and benefits. Moreover, adaptation has limits, beyond which it is too expensive or even unacceptable in terms of the changes it requires. For example, one adaptation to increasing flooding due to sea-level rise in low-lying island countries would be to emigrate, but that may be unacceptable for the people who would have to leave their homelands, and may not be welcomed as a solution by potential host countries.

If our ability to adapt reaches its limits we have an unacceptable or damaging situation that, at least at the local level, could be considered 'dangerous' and could lead to dire socio-economic consequences. That can only be avoided if we can reduce the level of climate change so as to stay within the limits of adaptability. In the broadest global terms, our ability to adapt is what must determine the targets we set for reducing greenhouse gas emissions, that is, mitigation policies should aim to avoid situations where we exceed the limits of adaptability. For this reason,

understanding adaptability is vital, not only so that people can adapt where possible, but also to determine how urgently, and by how much we must reduce global greenhouse gas emissions.

Methods of adaptation will vary with the activity or industry, with location, and on different scales in time and space. Generally local farmers, for instance, will adapt on a year-to-year basis to drier or warmer conditions by varying planting dates, crop varieties or irrigation use. But at the district, state or national level longer-term planning may be necessary to breed better-adapted crop varieties, conserve water, or develop more irrigation supplies. If the worst happens, governments may have to aid farmers, or even assist them to leave the industry if it is becoming unsupportable. This is already the case in Australia, where there is disagreement as to whether the current lack of water in some areas is merely a 'drought' from which recovery is possible with short-term aid, or whether it is more permanent, requiring farmers to change their livelihood.

It is argued by some that the best way to ensure adaptability is to increase resilience or the capacity to cope with natural year-to-year climate variability such as flood or drought years. This is true up to a point, but as climate change increases it will lead to extremes that are outside the limits of natural variability. In such cases ordinary resilience based on past climate variability may not be enough. Moreover, increasing resilience to cope with greater extremes will be uneconomic, or at least inefficient, unless guided by an understanding of the direction and magnitude of climate change. Increasing the capacity to cope with more tropical cyclones or hurricanes, for instance, does not make much sense if climate change is likely to lead to fewer tropical cyclones at that location. Thus, efficient adaptation strategies must be guided by an understanding of what to expect, that is, by informed foresight.

Foresight is also needed for adaptation because most adaptations cost money and thus require investment, and because they take time to put in place. For example, adaptation to more severe storms may require changes to building design or drainage systems, and these are best made in the design and construction phase of buildings or other investments, not as retrofits later when the need is urgent and the cost is greater. Strengthening flood levees *after* the old ones have failed is too late.

A handbook on methods for climate change impacts assessment and adaptation strategies has been developed by the United Nations Environment Program.[3] The handbook discusses the principles and strategies for adaptation. These can be summarised in eight alternative but not exclusive strategies:

1. *Bear losses*. This is the baseline response of 'doing nothing'. Bearing loss occurs when those affected have failed to act until it is too late, or have no capacity to respond in any other way (for example, in extremely poor communities) or where the costs of adaptation measures are considered to be high in relation to the risk or the expected damages. The big problem with this solution is that losses may become unbearable.

2. *Share losses*. This involves a wider community in sharing the losses. Sharing takes place in traditional societies and in the most complex, high-tech societies. In traditional societies, mechanisms include sharing losses with extended families, villages or similar small-scale communities. In societies organised on a larger-scale, losses are shared through emergency relief, rehabilitation, and reconstruction paid for by government funds or public appeals, or through private insurance. However, insurance usually applies only when the risk is considered random and uncertain for the individual insured, not when it is predictable. Even with shared losses, the accumulated loss to society may eventually become unacceptable, at which point other actions must be taken.

3. *Modify the threat*. For some risks, it is possible to exercise a degree of control over the specific environmental threat. For 'natural' events such as a flood or drought, possible measures include flood control works (dams, dikes, levees) or water storages. For climate change, attempts to modify the threat through such measures may quickly become too expensive, and the more sensible modification to reduce the threat is to slow the rate of climate change by reducing global greenhouse gas emissions and eventually stabilising greenhouse concentrations in the atmosphere. (Note, however, that in Intergovernmental Panel on Climate Change (IPCC) terminology, measures that reduce climate change are referred to as 'mitigation' of climate change, in distinction to 'adaptation', which is reserved for an optimal response to a given climate change.)

4. *Prevent effects*. A frequently used set of adaptation measures involves steps to prevent the effects of climate change and variability. Examples for agriculture would be changes in crop management practices such as increased irrigation, additional fertiliser, and pest and disease control.

5. *Change use*. Where the threat or reality of climate change makes the continuation of an economic activity impossible or extremely risky, consideration can be given to changing the use. For example, a farmer may choose to switch to crop varieties more adapted to lower soil moisture. Similarly, agricultural land may be returned to pasture or forest, or other uses may be found such as recreation, tourism, wildlife refuges, or national parks.

6. *Change location*. A more extreme response is to change the location of economic activities. For example, major crops and farming regions could be relocated away from areas of increased aridity and heat to areas that are currently cooler and which may become more attractive for some crops in the future. This may be possible in some countries, but not in others where migration to cities or other countries may be the only alternatives.

7. *Research.* Possibilities for adaptation can also be opened up by research into new technologies and methods of adaptation, such as greater water use efficiency, cheap water desalinisation, or new crop cultivars.

8. *Educate, inform, and encourage behavioural change.* Dissemination of knowledge through education and public information campaigns can lead to adaptive behavioural change. Such activities have been little recognised and given little priority in the past, but are likely to assume increased importance as the need to involve more communities, sectors, and regions in adaptation becomes apparent. Water conservation and fire prevention campaigns and regulations are already major adaptive trends in countries such as Australia. Discouragement of maladaptive trends such as development in low-lying coastal areas is another useful strategy. This may involve planning rules or other 'carrots and sticks'.

There are many examples of adaptation strategies and choices. Some examples are given below. **Figure 24**, adapted from a study of the threat of climate change to tourism in the European Alps, illustrates many of the above points.[4] A similar schematic diagram could be drawn up for most sectors and activities.

Costs and benefits of adaptation

Let there be no mistake about it: adaptation to climate change will cost money, time, effort and changes to how and why we do things. Adaptation will usually require planning and investment in new techniques, new infrastructure and/or new habits and lifestyles. These responses will have their advantages, or else we would not do them, but these advantages must be weighed against the costs of adaptation. Adaptation can have side benefits. It may also cause problems that lead to negative effects on other people or activities.

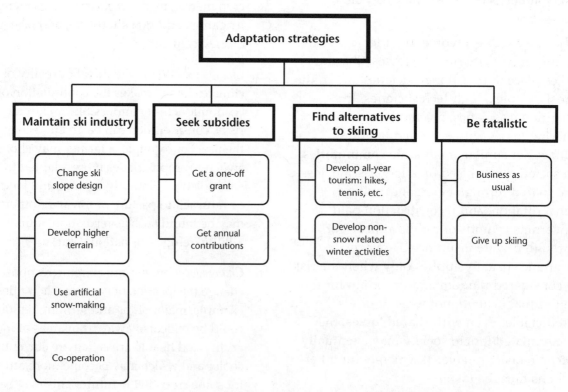

Figure 24: Adaptation options for the ski industry. Schematic showing the choice of adaptive strategies for a ski industry faced with the threat of global warming. The choice actually made will depend on the resort location and features, nature of competing tourist resorts, rate of warming and the views and preferences of stakeholders, including skiers, staff and resort owners. Cost and return on investments will be a major factor, and environmental considerations such as water supplies for artificial snow-making, power usage and visual impact will also be important.

Examples are not hard to find. Take adaptation to sea-level rise and coastal flooding from increased storm surges. The IPCC 2007 report's upfront projections for global average sea-level rise are 18 to 59 centimetres by 2100 but with a strong possibility that larger rises may occur (see Chapters 5 and 6). However, even if greenhouse gas emissions are stabilised, sea-level rise will continue at about the same rate for hundreds of years due to the large lag in the warming of the oceans. And we expect that the intensity of tropical cyclones will increase by about 10% for doubled carbon dioxide concentrations, likely in the latter half of the twenty-first century unless there are major policies to reduce greenhouse gas emissions.

So suppose you want to build a sea wall to protect a low-lying coastal city which is occasionally affected by storm surges from tropical cyclones. What height would you build it to, where would you build it, and who or what would you protect? What level of risk of overtopping is acceptable? Would you allow for protection only until 2050, or would you think it best to build it to last longer, say to provide protection until 2100? The latter would be cheaper in the long run, but more expensive now. Obviously this would cost millions of dollars, so who is to pay for it?

Perhaps more importantly, would a sea wall have undesirable side effects? Well, probably. First, it would have to go along the beach, so it would stop the view of the ocean from the city streets. (You can see this now, for example in Mali, the capital of the Maldives, and Apia, Samoa.) It might also lead to the disappearance of the beach, since as sea-level rises the beach line on a sandy beach would normally retreat inland. This would lead to destruction of the attractiveness of the beach to residents and tourists alike. In that case costly beach 'nourishment' would be needed (that is, dumping of more sand from somewhere else), or groynes built to maintain the beach. Moreover sea walls or groynes interrupt the lateral drift of sand or sediment along the coast, and this usually leads to erosion of nearby beaches beyond the ends of the wall. So there would most likely be ongoing costs, and disputes with neighbouring residents about loss of sand from their beaches.

Take another example. Climate change will likely increase the incidence of heavy rain events, interspersed with possibly more arid conditions reducing vegetation cover on land. This in turn may lead to increased soil erosion by wind and water. An obvious adaptation is planting more trees to hold the soil, reduce surface wind speeds, prevent erosion and provide shade for the animals. This could be done as extensive forestry plantations, or by more modest 'farm forestry' that is, rows or blocks of trees breaking up the wide-open landscape, but not completely replacing farming activities. Forest plantations have the added advantage of storing more carbon in the trees and soil, which would lead to financial gain in countries that engage in carbon emissions trading (where financial credit is gained for storing or reducing carbon emissions) under mitigation schemes such as those being implemented in Europe and elsewhere under the Kyoto Protocol.

In some situations planting more trees will also reduce dryland salinisation, which occurs in some countries due to rising water tables that bring salty groundwater near the surface, where the water evaporates and leaves the salt. However, there may be costly side effects as well, not the least of which is that trees use more water than grass so they may reduce runoff to the rivers, and thus water supply downstream.

Implementation

Adaptation can be purely reactive, autonomous or automatic in response to some perceived change in the climate. In natural systems this is the only type of adaptation, although humans can intervene to facilitate adaptation, in which case the systems become managed. For example, as climate changes natural species will die out in areas that become unsuitable, and may spread to other areas that become suitable. This is often a slow process, taking decades for seed to spread, germinate and grow into mature plants. Where there are obstacles, such as unsuitable soils or developed land, spread may be halted. Human intervention can facilitate and speed up such species migration by creating vegetation and wildlife corridors, planting seeds or seedlings in new areas, or by eliminating competition from other species.

However, in the case of natural ecosystems, which consist of a mix of interdependent species of plants and animals, whole ecosystems may not be able to move due to different mixes of changed climatic conditions. Changed climates may become more suitable for some species from the existing ecosystem but not for others. For example, increasing temperature may favour some species moving in one direction, but decreasing rainfall may favour movement in another direction. In this case species will migrate in different directions, breaking up the former ecosystem, and perhaps losing some species altogether as species formerly dependent on each other become separated.

In many situations farmers already adapt to variations in seasons on a year-to-year basis, for instance by planting later in the season if it is unusually cold or dry, or applying irrigation in dry years. In particularly bad years farmers may plant smaller areas, or even not at all, thus saving on the cost of seed, labour and fuel. Such adaptations to natural variability reduce losses, but often mean that income is less than in a good year, and is only made up to a living in the long term by gains in good years or by supplementary off-farm income. These forms of adaptation can be carried over into a situation of climate change without any conscious recognition that the climate is changing, but merely as a reaction to the current or recent past seasons.

However, where climate is changing, other longer-term adaptive strategies will be more appropriate, such as changes in crop cultivars or varieties, diversification, or even changing crops or activities altogether. To make these sorts of adaptations requires recognition of the problem, and foresight. It becomes crucial to look at alternative strategies for their cost and effectiveness, make choices, and make the necessary investments. This becomes active or planned adaptation.

Optimal adaptation strategies will only be adopted if there is a degree of foresight as to what is likely to happen and how it will affect people. Confidence is needed that the projected climate changes will occur,

with understanding of possibilities and alternatives. Uncertainty can never be totally eliminated, so any strategy must contain an element of hedging one's bets, by doing something that will be beneficial even if climate change does not happen quite as expected. Diversification is such a strategy. Agreement will also be necessary that the cost/benefit ratio for action is favourable, and the necessary human, economic and technical capacity to act must exist. If these conditions are not met, adaptation will be less than optimal. The first task in seeking optimal adaptation strategies is to become better informed.

One example of successful adaptation, in the face of sudden climate change and great uncertainty, is that of the water supply authority for Perth in Western Australia (see **Box 7**).[5] The best current explanation for the decrease in rainfall that occurred in the Perth catchments in the 1970s is that it was a combination of natural climate variability, the enhanced greenhouse effect and the effects of the depletion of ozone in the upper atmosphere. The circumpolar westerly winds have strengthened but moved further south, and the rain-bearing, low-pressure systems have moved with them (see discussion in Chapters 1 and 5).

A key problem in assessing the likely success of an adaptation strategy is judging how well the process is likely to be put into practice. This requires an understanding of the problem, and a conviction that adaptation is necessary and worthwhile. As in the Western Australian rainfall case, early acceptance that there may be a long-term problem rather than a short-term fluctuation is critical if large investments are needed. This requires good scientific understanding, and is not helped by unfounded scepticism or contrarian advocacy that confuses decision-makers and delays action.

The degree and success of adaptation is a key factor in assessing likely climate change impacts. Early climate impact assessments often assumed that no adaptation occurred, thus exaggerating likely impacts. In the literature this is sometimes referred to as the 'dumb farmer' assumption. In some later impacts assessments the contrary assumption was made, that of perfect adaptation,

BOX 7: ADAPTATION OF WATER SUPPLY IN WESTERN AUSTRALIA[5]

The south-west of Western Australia has already experienced the effects of climate change: in the 1970s a decrease in rainfall of roughly 10 to 20% resulted in a 40 to 50% reduction in inflow to the city of Perth's water supply; and this has not returned to previous levels in the last three decades (see **Figure 25**). As early as 1987, projections of climate change due to the enhanced greenhouse effect suggested that rainfall in the region would decline, although not appreciably until well into the twenty-first century.

Following the recommendations of a review paper by Brian Sadler (now Chair of the Indian Ocean Climate Initiative) and others in 1987, the Water Authority of Western Australia adopted a strategy that effectively assumed that the rainfall and yield would continue its decline. In an initial adjustment, the water system yield was written down by some 13%. This led to earlier development of work on alternative future water sources and promotion of water conservation. Research was encouraged into the causes of the rainfall decline and decisions were to be reviewed periodically based on experience and advances in climate science.

As Brian Sadler stated in 2003: '[The 1987] decision by water managers was controversial at the time and remained so for many years. However, against what has transpired, a decline of some 50% in streamflow by 2002, not 2040, the decision was far from extreme'. It is a good example of what Sadler calls 'informed adaptation', which is subject to adjustment as new information comes to light.

Consistent with this approach, the Indian Ocean Climate Initiative (see: http://www.ioci.org.au/) was set up by the Western Australia government in 1998 to investigate the reasons for the decline, methods of seasonal forecasting in the region, and the possible future implications of the enhanced greenhouse effect. More recently, the Western Australia government has adopted a greenhouse strategy to both mitigate and adapt to climate change and, in response to a further decline in water supply, a water desalinisation plant, powered by renewable energy, has been built.

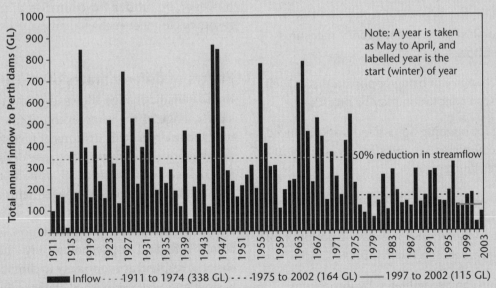

Figure 25: Annual streamflow into the water supply dams for Perth (Western Australia). Averages before and after the rainfall decrease of about 10–20% (depending on location) that occurred in 1974–75 are shown. Even lower averages occurred from 1997 to 2002 (shown) and from 2001–06 (not shown). The decrease in water supply was about 50% in the 1970s and even more since 1997. (Figure courtesy of the Water Corporation, WA, at http://www.watercorporation.com.au/.)

or the 'prescient farmer' assumption. Obviously, the most likely situation lies somewhere in between, and will depend on effective provision of reliable information to the farmer, planner, industry or government agency. Well-targeted research, to address all relevant questions for the decision-maker in the local situation, is essential. Series of consultations or representation of interested parties on research and implementation panels is advisable, so that adaptation options are understood, relevant and supported by all parties.

Key points regarding early adaptation[6] include:

- Adaptation can increase the robustness of infrastructure and capital investments to cope with climatic stresses such as floods, storm surges, extreme temperatures and high winds.

- Immediate benefits can often be gained by stopping present maladaptive policies and practices (such as building on flood plains or too close to sandy beaches).

- Climate change cannot be totally avoided and may occur more rapidly than anticipated.

- Early adaptation is more effective and less costly than last minute, emergency measures and retrofitting.

- Climate change can bring opportunities as well as threats, so adaptation may be profitable.

- Planning for ongoing adjustments and reduced economic lifetimes for investments is prudent as climate changes.

- Resilience of natural systems can be enhanced by reducing other non-climatic stresses and barriers to adaptation (for example pollution of coral reefs, creating eco-corridors).

- Adaptation can be facilitated by improving societal awareness and preparedness, for example through education and setting up early warning systems and evacuation plans.

Another good example of the adoption of an adaptation strategy is that of the Greater London Authority in the UK.[7] In the foreword to its 2008 report, Mayor Boris Johnson says:

Our climate is changing. This strategy starts the process of planning in detail for how our great city must adapt to these changes. If we don't make the necessary changes then many Londoners' quality of life will gradually deteriorate, we may fail to capitalise on some of the benefits that the changing climate will bring and we will be poorly prepared for the more extreme and damaging weather that science says we must expect in future.

… Urban areas are inherently vulnerable to the impact of climate change – the density of people and assets means that there is automatically more at stake. London's position astride a tidal river, in a region of the UK where relatively little rainfall has to be shared by more people and where London's microclimate can aggravate the impact of heatwaves, intensifies these challenges.

In Perth, Australia, and London, UK, these adaptation challenges can and are being met because both countries are relatively rich. It will, however, be harder for countries that have fewer resources to meet such challenges.

Effects of different rates of climatic change

Rapid climatic change allows less time to adapt than slow change of the same eventual magnitude, and may incur larger costs in terms of investment in new farming practices, rezoning and new design standards for engineered structures such as buildings, bridges, drains, dams and levees. Moreover, natural ecosystems have not only limited absolute ranges of adaptability, but also limited rates of adaptation. And human beings will find it psychologically and politically easier to respond appropriately to climatic change if it is slow and well established statistically, than if it is rapid but less clearly a part of some long-term change. For example, a short drying trend may be interpreted as a decadal-scale drought, for which normal drought assistance is appropriate, rather than part of a long-term trend requiring structural adjustments.

The situation as of September 2008 in Australia's Murray-Darling Basin is a sombre example. Advice from a number of key Australian scientists is that climate change is at least partly responsible for the 'record low river inflows', but many in the wider community and governments involved are reluctant to accept that it is not just another long drought. Depending on which is the case, radically different responses, affecting the lives of many residents, may be more appropriate.[8]

Nevertheless, few impact assessments have quantified the effects of rates of change as compared to the magnitude of change. Most have assumed that adaptation is to some new steady condition or else occurs instantaneously. Time lags and transitional costs have seldom been considered. This is one major reason why the IPCC in its 2001 and 2007 reports, in considering its five reasons for concern, used an essentially qualitative approach: there is simply not a sufficient body of evidence to assess the effects of different rates of change. What the IPCC 2001 report had to consider was whether rates of change within the projected range of 1.1 to 6.4°C per century, based on the 'Special report on emissions scenarios' (SRES), would substantially vary its conclusions. Clearly the more rapid rates would have greater effects, but the IPCC 2001 report considered that even the lowest estimated rate of change during this century would have serious effects increasing with time. This is still the case in the 2007 report.

Rates of change of climate after stabilisation of greenhouse gas concentrations will in general be much slower, and may therefore be easier to adapt to (apart from the higher base temperature by then), although such a slowing is not expected to occur for sea-level rise for centuries to come, so coastal adaptation will remain a serious ongoing problem. Indeed, sea-level rise will present horrendous ongoing challenges for adaptation if it occurs at a rate of a metre or more per century, as many scientists now believe is possible (see Chapters 5 and 6).

Studies concerning the effects of rates of change on natural and human systems are essential to understand what faces us in the twenty-first century and beyond, especially if rapid changes occur beyond some threshold warming. Questions arising include: How quickly can societies adapt and change, and at what social and financial costs? What is necessary to motivate behavioural change, and how can this motivation be increased? How dependent is it on reducing uncertainties and on learning from recent experience? To what extent will people respond to theoretical projections rather than past experience? How can humans facilitate desirable adaptive change in erstwhile natural systems? So far, we cannot answer these questions.

Equity issues in adaptation

Adaptation raises serious questions about equity between countries and even within countries. This is mainly because adaptation is necessary for people and countries that are adversely affected by climate change, many of whom are not the people or countries that historically caused the problem. This is a major source of contention between some rich developed countries, whose historical emissions are the main cause of climate change up to now, and the poorer developing countries that will experience some major impacts in the twenty-first century. This issue is developed further in Chapter 10.

Equity is already an issue in some Pacific Island countries that are moving roads and buildings further inland to avoid damaging storm surges, which they attribute to sea-level rise and climate change. They say they are not responsible for climate change, but the rich countries are, so the rich countries should be paying the costs of adaptation. Indeed, the government of Tuvalu in 2001 asked Australia to consider taking migrants from their very low-lying atolls, where people are already feeling threatened by sea-level rise. Up to the change of government in 2007, Australia refused to give such an undertaking, instead asking for more proof that climate change is responsible. This is expected to change with the new government.

Rich developed countries in general have more capacity to adapt. This is because they can afford the expense of new systems to counter adverse impacts, they can replace old systems and infrastructure made unworkable by climate change, and they can compensate losers through disaster relief, internal migration, employment programs, retraining and so forth. Many poorer countries cannot afford such adaptive measures. They will need international assistance to do so.

Indeed there is a strong connection between adaptive capacity and development issues. This is covered at length in the IPCC 2007 report, WGII, Chapter 18 'Inter-relationships between adaptation and mitigation'. A briefing paper from The Climate Group puts it well in their executive summary:

- *The success of adaptation relies on the success of development, and vice versa. Poverty reduction, good governance, education, environmental protection, health and gender equality all contribute to adaptive capacity.*

- *Substantially more money is needed to support adaptation in developing countries. Current levels of funding will soon have to be scaled up by two orders of magnitude (from US$ hundreds of million to US$ tens of billion per year).*

- *An agreement on adaptation ... will need to include concrete steps towards a strengthened knowledge base for adaptation, substantially more funding for developing countries, and enhanced adaptation planning and implementation at the national level.*[9]

An anecdote from my experience at meetings of the IPCC may clarify the point about adaptative capacity and resources. At one IPCC meeting the scientific authors were listening to the concerns with their draft report from government representatives. A delegate from Saudi Arabia questioned the statement that global warming would cause heat stress in dairy cattle, reducing milk production. He argued, with undoubted sincerity, that this is no problem since dairy cattle can be kept cool in air-conditioned sheds. Again,

when mention was made of potential water shortages from increasing aridity in some countries, he argued that desalinisation plants could easily solve this problem. In both cases, this was true in his experience in Saudi Arabia, but such adaptations are too expensive for most countries in the developing world. Both points were retained in the report.

It is only when all countries are as rich as Saudi Arabia that such expensive and energy-intensive adaptations would be possible for all, and at the cost of a huge increase in energy demand and probably more greenhouse gas emissions.

The IPCC has identified a number of barriers to adaptation in many developing countries and some of the poorer members of the former Soviet Union (referred to as 'countries in transition'):

- uncertain prices, lack of capital and credit,

- weak institutional structures and institutional instability,

- rigidity in land-use practices, and social conflicts,

- poor access to modern technology,

- lack of information and trained people.[10]

Ironically, development in many poor countries has tended to reduce resilience to climate change. There has been an erosion of ancient principles of mutual support in local communities, and in some cases replacement of complex, multi-species mixed farms with more vulnerable monocultures. Population growth, deforestation and increasing use of marginal land also adds to vulnerability. There are also examples where replacement of traditional structures by modern ones has increased vulnerability. For example, traditional houses in Samoa were elliptical in shape with thatched roofs. These have been replaced by rectangular structures roofed with imported sheet iron. While thatched roofs were liable to blow away in tropical cyclones, they were easily replaced at little cost. Moreover, flying roofing iron is highly lethal and destructive of neighbouring structures. In addition, traditional house frames were stronger.

Poor developing countries tend to be located at low latitudes, where crops and natural ecosystems are already near the highest temperatures on Earth. There is therefore little prospect of importing, or even breeding, crops that can tolerate even higher temperatures, because the genetic material does not exist and would be difficult to engineer. Many of these countries are also subject to tropical cyclone and flood damage to a greater extent than temperate countries.

Benito Muller of the Oxford Institute for Energy Studies has summarised the problem clearly. (Note that he uses the common diplomatic language where 'North' refers to developed countries and 'South' to developing countries, which is inappropriate for countries such as China, Australia and New Zealand.)

A surprisingly clear North–South Divide exists in the views on what is the paramount climate change equity problem. In the northern hemisphere, where the relevant discussion is spearheaded by non-government stakeholders (academic, NGO), it is regarded to be the issue of allocating emission mitigation targets; in the South, the concern – backed by many governments – is above all about the discrepancy between the responsibility for, and the sharing of climate impact burdens.

… One of the root causes of this divide is a fundamental difference in the perception of climate change itself. In the industrialised North there is a widely held 'ecological view' of the problem. Climate change is perceived as a problem of polluting the environment, of degrading the eco-system. As such, its essence is seen to be that of a wrongful act against 'Nature.' Accordingly, environmental effectiveness – the capacity to 'make good' the human-inflicted harm on Nature – becomes a key criterion in assessments of climate change measures. The chief victim from this perspective is Nature, mankind's role is primarily

that of culprit. And while climate impacts on human welfare are regarded as potentially life-style-threatening, they are taken to be self-inflicted and hence largely 'deserved'. Environmental integrity ('to do justice to Nature'), is the overriding moral objective. Issues of distributive justice are only of concern insofar as they could become obstacles in the pursuit of this paramount objective.

The reality in the South is quite different: climate change has primarily come to be seen as a human welfare problem – not least because of the assessment work carried out by the Intergovernmental Panel on Climate Change (IPCC). The harm is against humans, it is largely other-inflicted, and it is not life-style, but life-threatening. In short, the chief victim of climate change is not 'Nature', but people and the paramount inequity is one between human victims and human culprits. Climate change is a development problem, no doubt! But for the developing world it is not a problem of sustainable development – in the technical sense of 'learning to live within one's environmental means' – it is a problem of unsustainable development, in the non-technical sense of failing to survive.[11]

This is not to say that developing countries are not concerned about limiting greenhouse gas emissions, which they agree is necessary. It is merely to point out that their first priority is the welfare of their people in the face of increasing climatic disasters and the need for ongoing economic development. What these poorer countries ask for, in return for limiting their greenhouse gas emissions, is help in disaster management and relief, development aid, assistance with adaptation to climate change and access to new less carbon-intensive technology. At the Earth Summit in 1992, the developed countries committed themselves to devoting 0.7% of GDP to international development assistance, as first proposed by the United Nations back in 1970. However, only a handful of western

European countries have achieved this goal. Almost all rich nations have failed to reach their agreed obligations. Instead the amount of development aid has averaged around 0.2 to 0.4%.[12]

Enhancing adaptive capacity

Ability to adapt depends on the state of development. Under-development limits adaptive capacity because of a lack of resources to hedge against extreme but expected events. Thus enhancing adaptive capacity requires similar actions as promotion of sustainable development, including:

- improved access to resources,

- reduction of poverty,

- reducing inequities in wealth and resources between groups,

- improved information and education,

- improved infrastructure (roads, railways, power supplies, etc.),

- assurance that responses are comprehensive and inclusive of the people, not just technical,

- active involvement of all parties to ensure that actions are related to local needs and resources,

- improved institutional capacity and efficiency.

Adaptive capacity needs to be a major consideration in development, both in the lesser-developed countries and also in the developed countries, which are still subject to growth and change. This applies particularly to poor and remote communities within developed countries, such as indigenous peoples, and others particularly exposed to the impacts of climate change. All investments in growth and development need to take account of possible climate change and sea-level rise impacts and factor in ways to optimise the situation. Special attention needs to be paid to counter-adaptive trends such as population growth and building in flood plains, on low-lying coastal areas, on marginal lands, and on steep hillsides or regions potentially exposed to tropical cyclones.

Most capital investments in buildings and infrastructure have return periods or lifetimes of several decades or more. Therefore they must be designed and located to take account of future changes in climate. If not, they will need to be written off and replaced before their design life is complete, with great economic cost.

There are many hundreds of specific potential adaptation actions for particular sectors and communities. **Table 10** summarises some of these in general terms,[13] and there is a comprehensive guide published by the United Nations Development Programme in 2005. See also 'Climate Change and Adaptation' (Earthscan, 2008), which provides detailed studies from many developing countries.[14]

We have seen above that there are good reasons for adaptation to climate change, and many possibilities for improving adaptive capacity. There are some who argue that human inventiveness and increasing wealth means that we can adapt to almost any climate change, and therefore do not need to reduce emissions. This is the same argument discussed in Chapter 4, put by Bjorn Lomberg. Indur Goklany makes it in 'What to do about climate change' in a Cato Institute publication in 2008. Here Goklany ignores potentially catastrophic climate change and sea-level rise, under-estimates the costs of adaptation or failure to adapt to less severe climate change and extremes (for example, New Orleans in 2005), and is unduly pessimistic about technological change and innovation that might reduce emissions. Lomberg and Goklany pose a false antipathy between adaptation and mitigation. Both are necessary and indeed complementary strategies.[15]

The fact is that both adaptation and mitigation are needed, and both require a good measure of technological innovation and resourcefulness. Indeed, it is interesting to reflect on the role of technology, and the common tendency to look for 'either/or' solutions to problems. The problem of coping with climate change is so complex, especially as it interacts with other environmental and socio-economic problems, that no single solution is sufficient.

TABLE 10: Generalised examples of impacts and adaptations by sector

Sector	Potential impact	Potential adaptation	Comments
Hydrology and water resources	Increased floods and droughts, loss of snowpack and glaciers; regional and seasonal water deficits; saline intrusion in some island and coastal aquifers	Flood plain zoning, review levees and dam safety;[16] management, pricing, conservation, recycling; desalinisation plants	Major dams, water diversions, irrigation projects possible, but expensive and controversial with further climate changes creating design problems
Land-based ecosystems	Biodiversity loss in bounded areas including mountains; increased fire risk; weed invasion; salinisation	Landscape management, eco-corridors; fire protection; weed control; management	Increased management of 'natural' ecosystems, with increasing species and system losses
Aquatic ecosystems	Salinisation of coastal aquifers and wetlands; low river flows; eutrophication	Barriers to saltwater intrusion (where possible); increase environmental flows, reduce nutrients	Impacts will compound problems from increased population and water demand
Coastal ecosystems	Coral bleaching; more toxic algal blooms, acidification	Reduce other stresses, seed coral; reduce nutrient inflows	Population growth and pollution are other vital factors
Agriculture, grazing and forestry	Increased drought and fire risk; effects on global markets; spread of pests and diseases; increased soil erosion; initial benefit from increased CO_2 offset by climate change	Management and policy changes, fire prevention, seasonal forecasts; market planning, niche crops, carbon trading; exclusion spraying; land management; plant breeding, changed farm practices, change crop or industry	Sustainability in question in many regions
Horticulture	Reduced winter chill for fruiting, pests and diseases, drought	Change management, relocate, chemical sprays	Opportunities for tropical fruits at higher latitudes
Fisheries	Changes recruitment, nutrient supplies	Research, monitoring, management	Not well understood
Settlements and industry[17]	Increased extreme event hazards, coastal erosion, flooding and retreat	Zoning, design standards, disaster planning, insurance, coastal defences, retreat	Coastal settlements worst hit, coastal realignments much more than simple rise up existing contours
Electricity industry	Need increased peak capacity for air conditioning, drought threatens cooling water	Building design, shade, solar-powered air conditioning, renewable power with storage	Efficiency also affected, trend to renewables creates opportunities, changing price structure
Tourism	Increased heat index; loss of some attractions e.g., snow resorts, coral reefs, coastal wetlands	Cool tropical resorts, expand cooler resorts; alternative industries or relocate people	Losses and gains
Insurance	Increased exposure to 'natural hazards'	Revised building codes, rate incentives, zoning, reduced cover	This is happening now; may deter unwise developments
Human health	Expansion of range of vector-borne diseases, water supply issues, injuries from extreme events	Quarantine, eradication, control, window screens, medication, repellents, improve medical services, evacuation, refuges	Wealthy countries can cope, others may suffer

ENDNOTES

1. See 'Mainstreaming national adaptation plans' in *Tiempo* (September 2003) pp. 11–14.

2. See Chapter 17 in the IPCC 2007 report, WGII. There are many other publications regarding adaptation. See especially the journal *Mitigation and Adaptation Strategies for Global Change*, of which **4** (3 & 4) (1999) contains papers from an IPCC conference on adaptation. The Tyndall Centre for Climate Change Research has several *Working Papers* related to adaptation, including nos. 23, 26 and 27 (see http://www.tyndall.ac.uk). The Climate Change Knowledge Network at http://www.cckn.net gives access to other papers, including *Vulnerability and Adaptation to Climate Change: Concepts, Issues, Assessment Methods* by Santiago Olmos (July 2001). There is also a UNDP-GEF publication *Adaptation Policy Frameworks for Climate Change: Developing Strategies, Policies and Measures*, Cambridge

University Press, Cambridge, UK (2005). See http://www.undp.org/cc/apf.htm. The *Journal of International Development* also covers the links between development and adaptive capacity, for example, the paper by Neil Adger in **13**, pp. 921–31 (2001).

3. The UNEP handbook on adaptation is by Feenstra and others, *Handbook on Methods for Climate Change Impacts Assessment and Adaptation Strategies*, United Nations Environment Program, Nairobi (1998). Other useful documents include: Hansen and others, *Buying Time: A User's Manual for Building Resistance and Resilience to Climate Change in Natural Systems*, WWF (2003) at http://www.panda.org/climate/pa_manual; Asian Development Bank, Manila, *Climate Proofing: A Risk-based Approach* (2005); N Brooks, WN Adger and PM Kelly 'The determinants of vulnerability and adaptive capacity at the national level and the implications for adaptation' in *Global Environmental Change*, **15**, pp. 151–63 (2005); B Lim, E Spanger-Siegfried, I Burton, E Malone and S Huq (eds) *Adaptation Policy Frameworks for Climate Change: Developing Strategies, Policies and Measures*. Cambridge University Press, New York (2005).

4. The adaptation options in Figure 24 are based on those in Elsasser and Burki, *Climate Research*, **20**, pp. 253–7 (2002).

5. For the reaction to the decrease in rainfall in the south-west of Western Australia see Sadler *Informed Adaptation to a Changed Climate: Is South Western Australia a National Canary?* (2003), at http://www.ioci.org.au; and Pittock, *Climate Change: An Australian Guide to the Science and Potential Impacts* (2003) – see http://greenhouse.gov.au/science/guide/index.html. For earlier studies see Pittock, pp. 35–51, and Sadler and others, pp. 296–301 in *Greenhouse: Planning for Climate Change*, GI Pearman (ed.) CSIRO, Australia (1988). For ongoing reports see the Indian Ocean Climate Initiative at http://www.ioci.org.au.

6. Reasons for early adaptation are discussed in IPCC 2001 report, WGII, p. 890 and by Ian Burton in *Adapting to Climate Change: An International Perspective*, Joel Smith and others (eds), Springer-Verlag, New York, pp. 55–67 (1996). Generic approaches to adaptation by public bodies are also discussed in the IPCC 2001 report, WGII, p. 891.

7. See *The London Climate Change Adaptation Strategy*, Greater London Authority, August 2008, at http://www.london.gov.uk/mayor/publications/2008/docs/climate-change-adapt-strat.pdf.

8. See *Murray System Drought Update*, issue 15 (September 2008) at http://www.mdbc.gov.au/__data/page/1366/Drought_Update_Issue_15_-_September_2008.pdf

9. See the briefing paper from The Climate Group, *Adaptation: Needs, Financing and Institutions*, by RJT Klein and others (2008) at http://www.theclimategroup.org/special_projects/breaking_the_climate_deadlock/briefing_papers. Equity issues are also covered in the book *Fairness in Adaptation to Climate Change*, WN Adger, J Paavola, S Huq and MJ Mace (eds) MIT Press, Cambridge, Massachusetts, pp. 131–153 (2006). For more discussion of adaptation in developing countries see *Tiempo*, especially the article by Kalipada Chatterjee, no. 48, pp. 11–14 (June 2003) at http://www.cru.uea.ac.uk/tiempo, and the website for Development Alternatives at http://www.devalt.org. See also the discussion on equity in Chapter 10.

10. Barriers to adaptation are discussed in the IPCC 2001 report, WGII, p. 897, and enhancing adaptive capacity on p. 899.

11. The quote from Benito Muller comes from *Equity in Climate Change: The Great Divide*, Oxford Institute for Energy Studies, (September 2002) available from http://www.OxfordClimatePolicy.org, and 'A New Delhi Mandate', *Climate Policy*, **79**, pp. 1–3 (2002).

12. The aid figures come from Mick Kelly and Sarah Granich *The Point Seven Percent Solution*, at *Tiempo Climate Newswatch* at http://www.tiempocyberclimate.org/newswatch/comment040615.htm.

13. Table 10 is largely drawn from the Executive Summary of the IPCC 2001 report, WGII.

14. *Climate Change and Adaptation*, Neil Leary and others (eds), Earthscan, London (2008). See http://www.earthscan.co.uk.

15. I Goklany 'What to do about climate change' in *Policy Analysis*, no. 609 (February 2008) at http://www.cato.org.

16. Adaptation to floods is discussed in a paper in *Ambio* (August 2005) **6**, pp. 478–80 by Olli Varis. See also: Frans Klijn and colleagues in *Ambio*, **33**, pp. 141–7 (2004) for Europe, and John Scheaffer and colleagues in *Environment*, **44** (1), pp. 33–43 (2002) for the US.

17. Adaptation in the built environment is discussed by Auld and MacIver of the Adaptation and Impacts Research Group, Environment Canada, in *Cities and Communities: The Changing Climate and Increasing Vulnerability of Infrastructure*, Occasional paper 3 (January 2005).

8

Mitigation: limiting climate change

There is no substitute for energy: the whole edifice of modern life is built upon it. Although energy can be bought and sold like any other commodity, it is not 'just another commodity', but the precondition of all commodities, a basic factor equally with air, water and earth.

EF Schumacher, *Energy International*, September 1964.[1]

… if energy is used in a way that saves money, the rate of burning fossil fuels will not increase but decrease. This is because identical, and even greatly increased, energy services can still be provided using less total energy – but using it more productively – and also by replacing most or all of the remaining fossil fuel supplies with renewable sources.

Amory Lovins and others, *Least-Cost Energy: Solving the CO_2 Problem*, 1981.[2]

Many would argue that the uncertainty requires a conservative rather than ambitious approach to mitigation. But what is conservative in a context where the possible outcomes include some that most humans today would consider catastrophic? Conservatism may in fact require erring on the side of ambitious mitigation. After all, prudent risk management would suggest that it is worth the sacrifice of a significant amount of current income to avoid a small chance of a catastrophic outcome …

Ross Garnaut, Interim Report, *Garnaut Climate Change Review*, February 2008.[3]

Why mitigation is necessary[4]

The projected climate changes in the twenty-first century are so large that, even at the low end of the range of possibilities, impacts will require costly adaptations, and in some cases our capacity to adapt will not be enough to avoid serious damage to individuals and society. It will therefore be necessary to reduce climate change by reducing nett greenhouse gas emissions to the atmosphere. In the language used by the Intergovernmental Panel on Climate Change (IPCC) and the United Nations Framework Convention on Climate Change (UNFCCC), this is called 'mitigation'. The big questions are how much should emissions be reduced, how can this be done, and what will it cost?

The interplay of adaptation and mitigation as policy responses to increasing global warming is illustrated in **Figure 26**.[5] The black curves are the upper and lower bounds of the potential warming up until 2100, according to the IPCC Third Assessment in 2001, using the 'Special report on emission scenarios' (SRES) highest and lowest plausible scenarios, respectively.

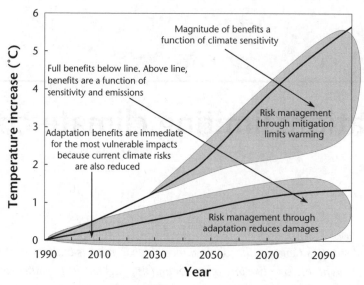

Figure 26: Regions of effectiveness of adaptation and mitigation strategies as responses to projected climate change in the twenty-first century. (Figure courtesy of R. Jones, CSIRO, Australia.)

The figure indicates, in the lower shaded area, that adaptation is effective where climate change is small enough for adaptation strategies to significantly reduce damages and take advantage of any opportunities posed by global warming, without unacceptable monetary or other costs. Adaptation can produce immediate gains over inaction, particularly because it can improve societal responses to climatic extremes occurring now. It is also necessary to cope with global warming that is already inevitable due to past emissions, and which will become inevitable due to future emissions until they are reduced to levels leading to stabilisation of climate.

Mitigation, in contrast to adaptation, needs time to take effect due to the lags in the climate system and the time necessary to reduce emissions sufficiently to stabilise climate. The figure shows how mitigation (upper shaded area) acts to reduce the upper bounds of projected warming, and thus to avoid the most extreme and damaging possibilities. Mitigation action taken now will have its most significant effects decades into the future, but is necessary now to limit future climate change to that which can be adapted to.

If, as some recent evidence suggests, global warming to date has already led to positive feedback or amplification effects, we may already be committed to larger global warming and sea-level rise than has been projected by the IPCC. In that case we may already be in danger of exceeding the limits of economic adaptation, effectively with a shorter time scale than indicated in the Figure. We do know that emissions are already tracking along the high end of the range of uncertainty, that is, along the upper curve in Figure 26. This means that adaptation is becoming increasingly difficult and mitigation more urgent.

If we take as our working definition of 'dangerous climate change' a change that exceeds the limits of acceptable adaptation strategies, and thus incurs unacceptable costs and damages, what we see in the diagram is that this will occur if the two regions of effectiveness of climate response strategies (the shaded areas) do not overlap. That is to say, a dangerous situation will arise if mitigation is too small or too slow to avoid global warming exceeding that for which adaptation strategies can work. If the two areas of policy response overlap we will be okay, but if they do not, we are in trouble.

Targets: how much mitigation is needed?

The percentage reduction needed in greenhouse gas emissions to avoid dangerous changes to the Earth's climate is large but uncertain. Stabilising the concentration of greenhouse gases in the

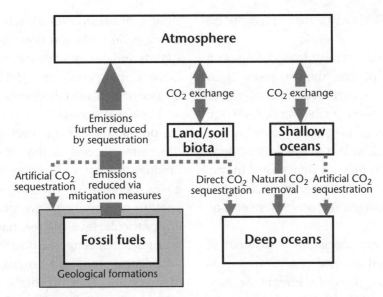

Figure 27: Broad types of mitigation options. In this figure, mitigation options include: reducing fossil fuel emissions (left upwards arrow) through energy conservation and efficiency and use of renewable energy; artificial sequestration of carbon into geological structures (left dotted arrow), or into the deep oceans (right dotted arrow) via fertilisation of plankton; and direct sequestration by pumping of carbon dioxide into the deep ocean (centre dotted arrow).

atmosphere requires total emissions per annum at some time in the future to be less than or equal to the total removal of greenhouse gases per annum from the combined atmosphere–shallow oceans–land/soil biota system. Removal can occur by natural processes or it can be artificially accelerated, as illustrated in **Figure 27**.

Here the broad upward arrow represents emissions from the burning of fossil fuels while the solid downward arrow denotes the natural long-term removal of carbon from the combined carbon reservoirs of the atmosphere–shallow ocean–land/soil biota, which are in equilibrium over a matter of a year or so (indicated by the double-headed arrows). To stabilise greenhouse gas concentrations in the atmosphere the alternatives are either to reduce emissions by limiting the consumption of fossil fuels by such measures as energy efficiency or substitution of renewable energy, or to remove and sequester the carbon dioxide from the use of fossil fuels in additional biomass and soil storage (increased 'carbon sinks'), in geological formations or into the deep ocean (dotted arrows). The last might be accomplished in one of two ways, either directly by pumping carbon dioxide into the deep ocean,

or via increased biological activity stimulated artificially in shallow oceans. The feasibility, risks and costs of these methods of sequestration are being debated (see below).

The precise reduction in emissions needed depends on what is the upper limit to concentrations of greenhouse gases that will avoid dangerous climate change, taking account not only of gradual climate change, but also of the global warming levels that might trigger abrupt and irreversible changes in the climate system. The longer emission reductions are delayed the faster they will need to be reduced later to reach the same stabilised atmospheric concentration of greenhouse gases, and the greater the commitment to further warming and sea-level rise due to the timelags in the climate system.

However, there are two major uncertainties in deciding what concentration of greenhouse gases is a suitable target to aim for. The first is uncertainty regarding how sensitive the global climate is to various increases in greenhouse gases. According to the IPCC in 2007, this uncertainty is large – a doubling of atmospheric carbon dioxide could cause an eventual increase in global average temperature in a likely range anywhere from 2.0

to 4.5°C, but the IPCC adds that it could be substantially larger.

The second major uncertainty in deciding on a target concentration of greenhouse gases is in determining what is a 'dangerous' level of global warming. As we have seen in Chapter 6, there are many different impacts of global warming on different sectors of society, and in different regions of the globe. Thus what may be 'dangerous' in one locality or to one entity (industry, group, activity or species) may not be dangerous somewhere else or to another entity.

In a global sense any decision as to what is a dangerous level will require consideration of a range of likely or possible effects at any particular concentration, and competing interests and claims for relief or justice. Since different groups or countries will experience different impacts of climate change, defining a dangerous level of climate change becomes a value-laden moral and political process, not a scientific one. This is especially so when one considers the possibility of catastrophic effects such as are included in the IPCC's fifth reason for concern (see Chapter 6), that is, sudden or irreversible effects having large regional or global impacts, such as rapid sea-level rise or major changes in the ocean circulations. Whether these risks, given their uncertainty, are considered 'dangerous' depends on one's level of risk tolerance.

Further, economic assessments are not enough since climate change will have value-laden impacts not readily expressed in monetary terms, such as species extinctions or loss of cultural property and values (for example, loss of homelands and independence in the case of some low-lying island nations).

Despite these difficulties, there seems to be wide agreement, at least among the non-governmental environmental organisations, and some governments, especially those in the European Union, that global average warmings in excess of 2°C above pre-industrial may be considered 'dangerous' in the terms of the UNFCCC. Such a level of warming is likely to lead, amongst other

things, to mass coral bleaching and the death of many coral reefs, the flooding of many low-lying islands and coasts, widespread crop failures at least in developing countries, and to the non-negligible chance of catastrophic changes.

Even if it becomes a firm political consensus, the problem with using such a level of warming to determine targets is that it still does not relate uniquely to a particular concentration of greenhouse gases because of the large uncertainty about climate sensitivity to greenhouse gases. Instead, any particular level of greenhouse gas concentration will lead to a range of possible global warmings, with a most probable warming but also a probability of warmings that are higher or lower than this central estimate. Indeed, we have already seen this to be the case in Chapter 5, where **Table 3** gives estimated ranges of warmings by 2100 for each of the SRES illustrative emissions scenarios, and **Table 4** gives warmings for various groups of scenarios for stabilisation of greenhouse gas concentrations.

Referring to **Table 3**, we see that if dangerous climate change is thought to occur for warmings of 2°C, then each of the SRES illustrative scenarios leads to a range of warmings at 2100 that has at least a moderate chance of exceeding the 2°C limit by 2100, ranging from around 30 to 40% for the lowest B1 scenario, to a certainty of exceeding the danger limit by 2100 for the higher emission A2 and A1FI scenarios. For the stabilisation scenarios, **Table 4** indicates that even the Group I set of scenarios, with actual CO_2 concentrations in the range of 350 to 400 ppm, and CO_2-equivalent concentrations (that is, including the other greenhouse gases plus particulates) of 445 to 490 ppm give rise to eventual warmings in the range 2.0 to 2.4°C, assuming a climate sensitivity of 3.0°C for a doubling of CO_2.

When we consider the full range of uncertainty in the climate sensitivity, as shown in **Figure 28**, the situation is much worse, since for high climate sensitivity even the lowest range of stabilisation scenarios (445–490 ppm CO_2-equivalent, Group I) leads to a significant chance of stabilised (or eventual)

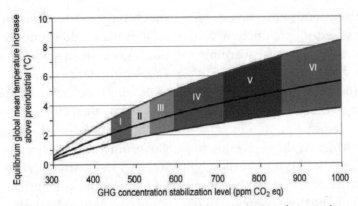

Figure 28: Eventual global warming range for various sets of stabilisation scenarios for greenhouse gas concentrations, in ppm CO_2-equivalent. The central curve is for a climate sensitivity of 3.0°C, the bottom curve for 1.5°C and the top curve for 4.5°C. This shows that for even the lowest group of emission scenarios, the chance of exceeding the 2.0°C 'danger' limit is greater than 50% and stabilised warmings could exceed 3°C. From IPCC 2007, Figure SPM-II of Synthesis Report (used with permission).

warmings greater than 2°C. Even more worrying, in **Table 4**, taken from IPCC 2007, it is noted that for the Group I scenarios, the peak year for concentrations is 2000 to 2015 and the change in emissions needed by 2050 is a decrease of 50 to 85%. Depending on one's degree of risk aversion, this suggests that urgent emissions reductions, with very stringent targets, are needed. Moreover, WGIII of the 2007 IPCC report notes, in the caption to its Figure SPM 7 that: 'To reach the lower stabilization levels some scenarios deploy removal of CO_2 from the atmosphere (negative emissions) using technologies such as biomass energy production utilizing carbon capture and storage'. This is accomplished after the concentration of greenhouse gases peaks at some value larger than the eventual stabilisation concentration. Such scenarios are termed 'overshoot' scenarios.

The reason drastic reductions in emissions are needed to achieve the more stringent stabilisation levels is that for greenhouse gases such as carbon dioxide that have long effective residence times in the atmosphere, reducing emissions below present levels has only a very slow impact on future concentrations. As stated by the IPCC 2007 report in WGI, p. 824, 'Because of slow removal processes, atmospheric CO_2 will continue to increase in the long term even if its emission is substantially reduced from present levels.'

It states that about 20% of CO_2 emissions will remain in the atmosphere for 'many millennia'. The report goes on to say that: 'In fact, only in the case of essentially complete elimination of emissions can the atmospheric concentration of CO_2 ultimately be stabilised at a constant level'. This is because stabilisation can only be achieved when continuing emissions are reduced to match the rate of natural (or artificially enhanced) removal of CO_2 from the combined atmosphere, active biosphere and upper ocean reservoirs into some reservoir, such as geological formations or deep ocean sediments, that cannot leak CO_2 back into the atmosphere.

The corresponding graph (2007 IPCC, WGI, p. 824) indicates that stabilising emissions at present levels would lead to more than a 60% increase in the present concentration of CO_2 by the year 2200, a 50% reduction in emissions from now would lead to about a 25% increase in concentrations by 2200, and only a 100% reduction in emissions would reduce concentrations by 2200, and then by only about 11%.

Shorter lived greenhouse gases will respond faster to reduced emissions, for example nitrous oxide, with a lifetime of about a century in the atmosphere needs only a 50% reduction in emissions to stabilise its concentration, while short lifetime gases such as methane (12 years) can stabilise concentrations at current emission levels. A complication arises in that aerosol pollution, which presently masks some of the greenhouse warming, is likely to be reduced by efforts to reduce CO_2 emissions, and this will rapidly reduce aerosol concentrations, making the equivalent CO_2 concentrations somewhat larger.

The commitment to further sea-level rise due to thermal expansion will respond even more slowly to reductions in CO_2 emissions, due to the slow processes that mix heat into the deep oceans, while the effect on sea-level rise from Greenland and Antarctica is highly uncertain because many of the recently observed accelerating processes are poorly represented in the models. The latter contributions may be more subject to the probability of exceeding thresholds for instability than thermal expansion, although the poorly determined threshold for a cessation of overturning of the ocean circulations could affect thermal expansion also.

Working group III of the 2007 IPCC report notes (p. 200) that 'while such "overshoot" scenarios might be inevitable for very low targets (given the climate system and socio-economic inertia), they might also provide important economic benefits. At the same time, however, studies note that the associated rate of warming from large overshoots might significantly increase the risk of exceeding critical climate thresholds.' Overshoots will also increase sea-level rise for centuries after stabilisation of concentrations due to the inertia in thermal expansion of the deep oceans, even if they do not trigger disintegration of the Greenland or Antarctic ice sheets.

The UK Stern Review on the economics of climate change in 2006 considered targets of 450 and 550 ppm CO_2-equivalent. It found that if emissions continued at the then rate, doubled pre-industrial concentrations would be reached by 2050 and would continue to grow thereafter, and that 550 ppm CO_2-equivalent would result in a 77 to 99% chance of a global average warming in excess of 2°C. Stern states that to stabilise at or below 550 ppm CO_2-equivalent would require emissions to peak in the next 10 to 20 years, and then fall at a rate of at least 1–3% per year, with

much larger reductions in emissions per unit of GDP if the world economy is to continue to grow. Stern goes on to say that to stabilise at 450 ppm CO_2-equivalent without overshooting, global emissions would need to peak by 2016, and reach 70% below then current levels by 2050.[6]

In a more recent enquiry for the Australian Government, an interim report by the Garnaut Review in February 2008 examines a 450 ppm CO_2-equivalent stabilisation scenario, which involves concentrations peaking at 500 ppm CO_2-equivalent before declining to the target concentration. The report states that this would require a peaking of global emissions by 2010 followed by a very rapid fall. It notes that recent acceleration of global emissions growth has made this task even harder than anticipated by Stern. Garnaut states that: 'Peaking of global emissions in the near future, followed by very rapid falls, is clearly not feasible, given long lead-times and lifetimes of energy sector investments, and the huge momentum of emissions growth especially but not only in developing countries'.[3]

This is clearly difficult, and it is made even more difficult by the prospect that stabilisation at 450 ppm CO_2-equivalent still leads to the possibility of exceeding 2°C global warming, and so a target of 400 ppm CO_2-equivalent or less may be necessary if one has a low risk tolerance. Indeed Spratt and Sutton in the book *Climate Code Red* (2008) go further and argue, on the grounds that anything more might lead to a climatic tipping point and global catastrophe, for a temperature cap of only 0.5°C above pre-industrial and an equilibrium greenhouse gas concentration of not more than 320 ppm CO_2-equivalent. They style this as a sustainability crisis:

Our conventional mode of politics is short-term, adversarial and incremental, fearful of deep, quick change and simply incapable of managing the transition at the necessary speed. The climate crisis will not respond to incremental modification of the business-as-usual model. There is an urgent need to reconceive the issue we face as a sustainability emergency, that takes us beyond the politics of failure-inducing compromise. The feasibility of rapid transitions is well established historically. We now need to 'think the unthinkable', because the sustainability emergency is now not so much a radical idea as simply an indispensable course of action if we are to return to a safe-climate planet.[7]

Similarly, US scientist James Hansen and others argue in a draft paper 'Target Atmospheric CO_2: Where should humanity aim?', that: 'If humanity wishes to preserve a planet similar to that on which civilization developed, paleo-climatic evidence and ongoing climate change suggest that CO_2 will need to be reduced from its current 385 ppm [CO_2 only] to at most 350 ppm [CO_2 only].'[8]

Garnaut comments on other such stringent proposals:

The Australian Conservation Foundation and other non-government organisations have asked the Review to focus as well on a 400 ppm objective. They argue that the risks of immense damage to aspects of the Australian environment, including the Great Barrier Reef and Kakadu National Park, are unacceptably high at 450 ppm.

We appreciate their concern, and note only that the prospects of achieving the global mitigation effort that would be necessary to achieve this outcome appear to be remote in early 2008. Changes in ambition would require radical changes in the global approach to mitigation, and also major technological progress in the development of low-emissions technologies. To keep the possibility of eventual attainment of a 400 ppm objective (with overshooting) alive, the 450 ppm objective could be pursued with a view to tightening emissions targets if at some future time the political and technological conditions for far reaching mitigation had improved.[3]

Garnaut goes on to say that there are several complications in considering targets, including:

First, there are considerable uncertainties attached to both climate change impacts and mitigation.

Many would argue that the uncertainty requires a conservative rather than ambitious approach to mitigation. But what is conservative in a context where the possible outcomes include some that most humans today would consider catastrophic? Conservatism may in fact require erring on the side of ambitious mitigation. After all, prudent risk management would suggest that it is worth the sacrifice of a significant amount of current income to avoid a small chance of a catastrophic outcome ...

A second complication is that the costs of mitigation come much earlier than the avoided costs of climate change. A dollar of cost now is worth less than a dollar of avoided cost later, for two good reasons. The first is that humans value the present somewhat more highly than the future – they discount future income to some extent, though the extent and even the need for discounting when it comes to inter-generational equity is a matter of debate. The second is that people in future are likely to be more prosperous than people today, suggesting higher valuation of a dollar today for this income distribution reason. Of course, the second of these reasons goes into reverse if and to the extent that climate change has the capacity to reduce the welfare of future generations below the welfare of the current generation.

Garnaut goes on to discuss international equity as another key complication (discussed in Chapter 11 of this book). But perhaps the key complication is exactly how it will be possible to remove large quantities of CO_2 out of the atmosphere, as is necessary in any overshoot scenario. This necessity will be a rapidly growing hidden cost of less stringent emission reductions in the next decade. It is discussed below when we come to ways of reducing emissions.

These arguments leave the decision of a target open to disagreement and tension between what seems politically realistic now and what may seem to be necessary to avoid disastrous climate change. My inclination is that we need to set as low a target as is politically feasible, with the important proviso that the target may have to be changed at short notice as new information comes to hand about rates of climate change, where the tipping points might be, and how easy it is in fact to reduce emissions once we set up the carrots and sticks to encourage innovation and investment in low-carbon technologies and to change lifestyles and behaviour. I remain optimistic that with suitable incentives such as an appropriately high price on carbon emissions, and ingenuity and entrepreneurship we can in fact reduce emissions surprisingly fast and at far less cost than many people imagine. But you the reader may well disagree about this tactic and it is certainly open to discussion.

Figure 29 is my attempt to show schematically how mitigation targets might be set. The figure indicates where scientific information is needed, and where value judgements (including risk tolerance levels) and politics take over. Mitigation targets result from a scientific understanding of the climate, natural and human systems, combined with value judgements as to what thresholds of change are to be avoided, and socio-political negotiation as to processes to achieve emissions reductions. The uncertainties regarding tipping

points for the climate system and thus the appropriate target for maximum global warming and related emission reduction targets must lead to the setting of pro tem targets. These should be subject to frequent reassessment as uncertainties are reduced due to better science, observed changes, and progress on mitigation. The success of legislative and market mechanisms in achieving emissions reductions must also be assessed.

The 2007 IPCC report, Working Group III, comments that:

Decision-making about the appropriate level of global mitigation over time involves an iterative risk management process that includes mitigation and adaptation, taking into account actual and avoided climate change damages, co-benefits, sustainability, equity, and attitudes to risk. Choices about the scale and timing of GHG mitigation involve balancing the economic costs of more rapid emission reductions now against the corresponding medium-term and long-term climate risks of delay.[9]

The important question, to my mind, is not what the exact target should be, but how such a large emission reduction might best be accomplished as

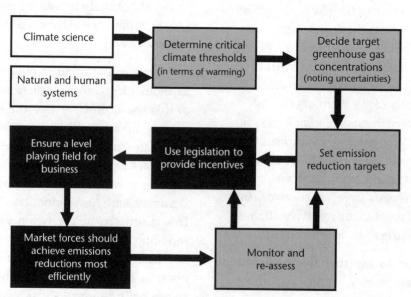

Figure 29: How mitigation targets might be set. In this figure, white boxes indicate where scientific input is dominant, grey boxes indicate where both scientific input and value judgements are needed, and black boxes where socio-economic and political processes take over.

quickly as possible. Highly demanding technological targets are not unprecedented. Previous tall technological targets that were achieved through strong national commitments include the US/UK Manhattan Project to produce nuclear weapons during the Second World War and the US race for a landing on the moon in the 1960s. However, achieving any large greenhouse emissions reduction target requires a truly global commitment and much more societal participation, perhaps more akin to the war-time mobilisation of whole societies during the Second World War. It is a matter of motivation, incentives and technological innovation. Its feasibility will be resolved by action. The importance of the UNFCCC and the Kyoto Protocol (the present target of which is clearly inadequate) is not the actual targets set, but the setting of a framework and tone within governments, businesses and society that drives action for emissions reduction. Setting a long-term target, even if subject to periodic revision, provides a degree of certainty in planning and expectations that facilitates action and commitment. It establishes a mindset necessary for success.

What is certain is that the longer the delay in reducing emissions the more disastrous will be the potential outcome. So early commitment to a process that gets rapid emission reductions under way globally is vital. For this, demanding short-term interim targets may be most appropriate. These could be several per cent global reductions per annum relative to present emissions, and greater reductions relative to 'business-as-usual' if present rates of growth in emissions (3% per annum in 2000 to 2004) are anything to go by. There would then need to be an ongoing review to set further targets, driven by new information and reduced uncertainties, and learning what works and what is possible by actually doing it.

Where we are now

Mitigation, or emissions reductions, must start from where we are now. For this, some facts are necessary. In the year 2004 (the latest I could find with reliable

numbers), global greenhouse gas emissions, measured as the equivalent amount of carbon dioxide, were 56.6% from fossil fuel carbon dioxide, 17.3% from carbon dioxide from land-use change (deforestation, decay of biomass, etc.), 14.3% from methane, 7.9% from nitrous oxide, and 1.1% from several other highly active greenhouse gases.[10]

Methane (CH_4) comes from biomass decomposition, coal mining, natural gas and oil system leakages, livestock, wastewater treatment, cultivation of rice, burning of savannah and some from burning of fossil fuels. Nitrous oxide (N_2O) comes from agricultural soils (especially where too much nitrogen fertiliser has been applied), industrial processes, automobiles and other fossil fuel burning, human sewage and animal manure. Other highly active greenhouse gases are mostly substitutes for ozone-depleting substances, and from various industrial processes including semiconductor manufacture, production of aluminium and magnesium, and electrical equipment.

While carbon dioxide from fossil fuels dominates total emissions of greenhouse gases, emissions from land-use change are important, particularly in some developing countries with large rates of forest clearing. Generally, developed countries currently contribute very little directly to carbon dioxide emissions from land-use change (although they buy rainforest timber and plantation palm oil[11]), but some 35% of emissions from developing countries is from land-use change, and more than 60% in the least developed countries. This largely reflects much higher proportions of the economy related to agriculture and forestry. Emissions from land-use change have figured in international negotiations because some countries believe they can reduce these emissions, or develop sinks (that is, remove carbon dioxide from the atmosphere) by reforestation and better retention of carbon in soils through minimum tillage and other measures. However, there is substantial uncertainty in estimating sources and sinks of carbon dioxide from land-use change, and also about definitions and permanence of carbon storage in forests and soils. Hence most of the following statistics do not include land-use change effects. Black carbon particles (soot) also contribute to surface warming but are usually not counted, and are quite local and short-lived, as are the reflecting particles (aerosols) which have a cooling effect.

By sectors, energy supply is the largest emitter, accounting for 25.9% of GHG emissions, with industry at 19.4%, forestry 17.4%, agriculture 13.5%, transport 13.1%, residential and commercial buildings at 7.9% and waste and wastewater at 2.8%. Thus emission reductions should involve reductions in emissions across a wide range of activities. Transportation has the fastest growing share of emissions in most countries, and is greater in industrialised countries. Land-use change and forestry is the largest emitter in Brazil and Indonesia, although such data is uncertain.[10]

Figure 30 summarises some useful information regarding annual emissions, cumulative emissions and emissions per person up to the year 2005 for various countries or regions. These statistics demonstrate a wide variety of national situations, and help to explain various perceived national interests and negotiation stances on mitigation policies.[12]

It is apparent from the figure that a relatively small number of countries contribute most of the greenhouse gas emissions. These countries in general have either large populations or high gross domestic product (GDP), or both. These are the two main drivers of high emissions, although carbon intensity (carbon emissions per unit GDP) is also important. Carbon intensity varies between countries, depending on economic structure, the mix of fuels used, and energy efficiency.

There is a marked contrast between the United States, which in 2005 was still the largest emitter with some 20.5% of global emissions and 27.8% of accumulated emissions since 1750, and China, which has recently increased its annual emissions rapidly to be the second largest emitter with 18.0% in 2005, but with only some 7.8% of cumulative emissions.

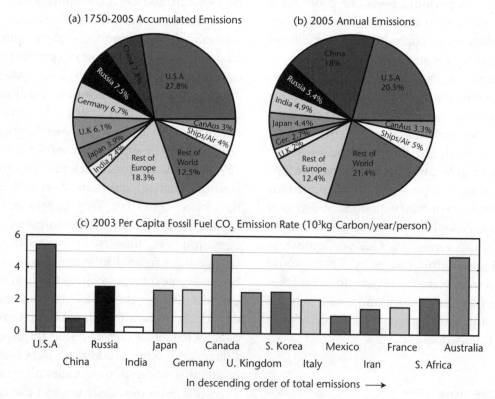

Figure 30: Fossil fuel emissions: (a) cumulative emissions 1750–2005, (b) 2005 annual emissions by source country or region, and (c) per capita emissions of the 15 largest sources in 2003. (Data sources: Carbon Dioxide Information Analysis Center, Oak Ridge National Laboratory for 1750–2003 and British Petroleum (2006) for 2004–2005. Data for Russia are 60% of USSR for 1850–1991 and Russian Federation thereafter. Diagrams courtesy of James Hansen, GISS.)

Emissions per person are also in great contrast, with the United States at about 5.4 tonnes of carbon per annum per person (to get CO_2 emissions multiply by 3.7), but China on only about 1 tonne per person. India, which is the next largest developing country, ranked number four in emissions in 2005, but contributed only 2.4% to accumulated emissions and less than half a tonne of carbon per person in 2005. But the growth rate of emissions from 1992 to 2004 was only 24% in the United States, compared to 109% in China and 97% in India.

These numbers raise in stark relief the issues of international equity and the vital need for cooperation if global emissions are to be reduced. They help to account for the developing countries' argument that the primary responsibility for early emissions reductions lies with the developed countries, but also highlight the necessity for the major developing countries to limit their emissions as well. Unless total global emissions are strongly reduced we will not be able to avoid reaching 'dangerous' levels of climate change.

Several recent papers have documented a large acceleration in CO_2 emissions in the last decade, due to rapid economic growth, especially in some developing countries, a cessation or decline of the former improvements in energy efficiency of gross domestic product and in carbon emissions per unit energy. There has also been a decline in the efficiency of natural sinks of CO_2, reflected in a greater percentage of emissions remaining in the atmosphere (an increase in the 'airborne fraction'). In the words of Josef Canadell and colleagues, 'All these changes characterize a carbon cycle that is generating stronger-than-expected and sooner-than-expected climate forcing'.[13]

Such results also highlight the conservative nature of the IPCC SRES scenarios, with present trends in emissions above that of the largest of the SRES illustrative scenarios (the A1FI scenario). This is due to the much more rapid and sustained economic growth of countries such as India and China than was thought possible when the SRES scenarios were created. This presents both a challenge to get this increase under control, and

opportunity since at least some major developing countries are rapidly becoming rich enough to tackle the problem through switching to less carbon-intensive industry and lifestyles and to better adapt to what cannot be avoided.

Against this, the economic crisis of 2008 has led to a temporary decline in economic growth. While this will cause a short-term slowdown in CO_2 emissions it will also likely reduce the cooling effect of aerosol pollution. The large expenditures in combating this economic crisis point to the capacity of governments to respond to the climate change challenge also.

We will discuss the politics of setting mitigation targets further, as it relates to the UNFCCC, in Chapters 10 and 11, and to possible future mitigation measures in the final chapter. Here we will discuss the suite of mitigation options.

How difficult is mitigation?

Reducing emissions of greenhouse gases is characterised by some economists, business people and politicians as severely limiting economic growth and likely to lead to reductions in future standards of living. They allege that it is opposed to progress, to the interests of the poor, and is overall too costly. As EF Schumacher put it in 1964, 'there is no substitute for energy' and energy is 'the precondition of all commodities'.[1] They point out that greenhouse gas emissions have been closely tied to fossil fuel energy use for a century or more. Such people argue that expenditure on mitigation now will slow economic growth and thus reduce the ability to cope with climate change in the future.

An alternative view is that of Sir David King, then UK Chief Science Adviser, in an article in *Science* magazine in 2004: '... it's a myth that reducing carbon emissions necessarily makes us poorer. Taking action to tackle climate change can create economic opportunities and higher living standards'.[14]

King cited the British experience, where between 1990 and 2000 the economy grew by some 30%, and employment by 4.8%, yet greenhouse gas emissions intensity (GHG emissions per unit GDP) fell markedly. He also noted that over the same period the Chinese economy grew very rapidly, yet their emissions intensity also fell (although this has not been the case in the last decade). Developing countries in particular have the opportunity, as they grow new industries, to use the most energy- and carbon-efficient technologies, with less of other pollutants also, thus avoiding the mistakes made by the developed countries.

Whether or not emissions reduction is a burden or an opportunity depends in part on a societal state of mind. In an old economy with high-carbon, emission-based industries, much economic and emotional capital is tied up in industries and infrastructure (such as factories, roads and power stations) that rely on burning fossil fuels and which are expensive to replace. A new low carbon-emissions society relying on energy-efficient and renewable energy technologies will be structured to make the most of the new technologies, with trained workers, the necessary infrastructure, and a positive market value placed on the new technologies and skills. The problem is the transition from one to the other.

The forward-looking low-carbon emissions technologies and skills will have a growing market edge as these become the wave of the future. Hence the recent motto of British Petroleum of 'Beyond Petroleum' and the recent Royal Dutch Shell focus on solar power, hydrogen as a carrier of energy, and other renewable technologies. While both BP and Shell (and many other energy companies) are still having an each-way bet (for example, Shell is in the business of mining oil sands in Canada, and has recently pulled out of a large wind energy project in the UK) those countries, businesses and individuals who anticipate coming changes are more likely to grow and profit from opportunities in the new low-carbon economy.[15]

Many technological solutions are being offered, and we will look at some of these below. They are the grounds for optimism that large emissions reductions can be achieved at moderate cost, for example as embodied in the now famous 'stabilization wedges' concept of Stephen Pacala and Robert Socolow, first published in *Science*, in 2004 (and updated in *Scientific American* in September 2006). Sir David King, cited above, is quoted as saying, 'What I'm looking for is technological solutions to a technologically driven problem, so the last thing we must do is eschew technology'. However, technological solutions all have their pros and cons, as we shall see below. They must be developed with great care and discrimination.[16]

Technological optimists argue for a multi-faceted approach using energy efficiencies, renewables, carbon capture and sequestration, and nuclear power. Some urge individual actions like changing light bulbs, driving less, recycling, planting trees, turning off electrical devices, etc., while others argue that only strong government actions to remove market failures and provide financial incentives will work. Andrew Szasz argues, 'To achieve real protection and security we must give up the illusion of individual responses and together seek substantive reform.'[17]

Some technological pessimists and social radicals argue that sufficient reductions cannot be achieved via technology but only by major changes in life-style and in the whole economic structure to remove the drive for economic, population and consumer growth. For example, Ted Trainer states that: 'A sustainable world order is not possible unless we move to much less affluent lifestyles within a steady-state economic system'.[18] We may well need a mix of all of these approaches.

Amongst the technological optimists are numerous solar energy entrepreneurial companies such as Nanosolar, which is building large factories to manufacture competitively priced printed thin solar cells; Solana which is building a 280-megawatt solar thermal power station in Arizona; and Ausra, which is proposing replacement of the US grid supply by solar thermal power with storage, and with energy left over to power transportation with lithium ion batteries and supercapacitors (more details below). Numerous articles and websites present and advocate such technological solutions (discussed below).[19]

Some economists and businesses have argued that there is no such thing as a 'free lunch' in relation to mitigation: if businesses could save money by being more energy efficient they would have done so already. However, emissions savings are possible at no cost, as has been shown many times by businesses that have accepted the challenge to look at what savings could be made. In businesses where energy costs have traditionally been only a small fraction of capital or labour costs, many have simply not bothered to look for savings in the 10% or so of their expenses that are related to energy. However, when they do take up the challenge they find that substantial savings can be made, thus increasing their overall profits. These are called 'no regrets' emissions reductions and are far more pervasive than was once thought.

Amory Lovins at the Rocky Mountain Institute in the US and colleagues have published several studies suggesting that people can transform industrial production so as to use less natural resources to produce higher standards of living in ways that are profitable. They give many examples, and more can be found at http://www.natcap.org. They point out that following the oil crises in the United States in the 1970s, most new US energy-using devices such as cars, buildings and domestic appliances, doubled in energy efficiency. In the period 1973–1986 there was a 35% increase in the economy with roughly zero growth in energy use.[20]

Lovins and colleagues maintain that energy efficiency can be improved by raising energy prices as in the oil crisis, *or* by paying attention to the issue. They argue that creating an informed, effective, and efficient market in energy-saving devices and practices can be more powerful than a bare price signal. Saving energy is profitable and benefits the national economy by increasing productivity.

The whole question of mitigation options, methods and costs is discussed at great length in the IPCC *Fourth Assessment Report*, Working Group III. Economic studies give widely different estimates of the costs of reducing emissions. Differences between estimates depend on assumptions about economic growth, the costs and availability of existing and new technologies, the availability of resources, the extent of 'no regrets' options and the choice of policy instruments or ways of achieving reductions.

Conclusions regarding the costs of emissions reductions also depend on:

- the timing and rate of emissions reductions,

- economic assumptions regarding discounting the future,

- the mix of economic measures such as trading in emissions permits (the buying and selling of emissions allowances) and the removal of institutional barriers to new technologies,

- transfer of technologies to developing countries, and

- assumptions regarding technical and social innovation.[21]

Emissions reductions will be less expensive if any associated tax revenues, or revenues from the sale of emissions permits, are used to reduce existing taxes which add to the costs of economic production, such as payroll taxes or taxes on capital. Cost estimates for emissions reduction are lowest when there is full trading globally in emissions permits, since then emissions reductions can be made where it is cheapest both geographically and by industrial sector. Appropriately regulated, trading can minimise inequities and hedge against uncertainties regarding costs and targets, which may change with time. Where reductions take place is then less dependent on who pays for the reductions, although equity issues must also be considered.

Emissions reductions can have both co-benefits and ancillary costs. Co-benefits occur, for example, with reductions in the burning of coal in power stations, as this reduces greenhouse gas emissions and also emissions of other pollutants that have detrimental health effects and cause acid rain. This saves on health and other costs, and could lead to an overall 'no-regrets' situation across the community. Similarly, present estimated health costs of pollution from fossil-fuelled road transport are large (around A\$3 billion annually in Australia alone).[22] This could be greatly reduced with present petrol–electric hybrid technology, and completely eliminated by a future change to hydrogen- or compressed air-fuelled vehicles. Another example is that of carbon dioxide removal from the atmosphere by growing trees, which can provide employment and income in rural areas and also has the co-benefits of providing windbreaks, reducing erosion, and eventually providing timber. However, ancillary costs might occur also, for example, growing forests increases water use, and thus reduces runoff and downstream water supplies.

The 2007 IPCC report, Working Group III, in summarising results from numerous studies, concluded that:

- *In 2030 macro-economic costs for multi-gas mitigation, consistent with emissions trajectories towards stabilization between 445 and 710 ppm CO_2-eq, are estimated at between a 3% decrease of global GDP and a small increase, compared to the baseline. However, regional costs may differ significantly from global averages.*

- *In 2050 global average macro-economic costs for multi-gas mitigation towards stabilization between 710 and 445 ppm CO_2-eq, are between a 1% gain to a 5.5% decrease of global GDP. For specific countries and sectors, costs vary considerably from the global average.*[21]

Note that these costs are estimated relative to the SRES range of emissions scenarios, which were considered by the IPCC to not be driven by climate change policy considerations (see **Box 3**). Thus for each stabilisation target, cost estimates vary according to which SRES scenario is taken as the reference. If we take the high emissions A1FI scenario as the reference, for example, costs of stabilisation are relatively large, whereas if we take a low emissions scenario such as B1 as the reference, costs are relatively small. The SRES authors did not assign probabilities to the SRES scenarios, but, as we have already noted, emissions over the last decade seem to be following at or above the A1FI

scenario. Whether this would continue if there was no climate policy intervention is not known, but it is arguable that with rising prosperity in some major developing countries, growth in emissions might begin to taper off and the affordability of reducing emissions would be greater.[23]

James Hansen argues that initially it may be easier and less costly to reduce emissions of greenhouse gases other than carbon dioxide, for example methane and nitrous oxide, and also carbon black. This would lessen the urgency of reducing carbon dioxide emissions in order to stabilise equivalent carbon dioxide concentrations in the 450 to 550 ppm range; however, substantial reductions in carbon dioxide emissions would still be necessary. (It is astounding to me that such a simple measure as stopping the flaring or waste emission to the atmosphere of unwanted natural gas, largely methane, from many oil wells is still not accomplished, despite a Global Gas Flaring Reduction program run by the World Bank.)[24]

Interestingly, some opponents of early mitigation measures have tended to contest the reality of the A1FI high emissions scenario and give more credence to the B1 low emissions scenarios. They argue that this justifies less policy intervention to reduce emissions. It would indeed be nice if this were true, but in reality it seems unlikely that the B1 scenarios would be followed without some motivation from climate change concerns. The B1 type future is indeed possible, at relatively little cost, but only by deliberate choice and policy decisions by both governments and private enterprise, and even the B1 scenario does not have low enough emissions to avoid the possibility of dangerous climate change.[23]

The costs of emissions reductions need to be weighed against the potential costs of climate change impacts in both developed and developing countries if emissions are not reduced. Costs of impacts that would be avoided by reducing emissions are discussed in Chapter 6. Such avoided costs increase with the amount of global warming, and thus with time and rate of emissions. In general, costs of emissions reductions are more immediate, and the avoided costs of impacts are greatest later.

Thus, how near-term costs are compared with long-term costs is important in any cost-benefits analysis. This is usually done using what is called a 'discount rate'. Normally, for short-term cost-benefit analysis, delayed costs are discounted to take account of a preference to have goods now rather than later, or of what benefit could be gained from money spent now on mitigation if it were instead invested in something else. Discount rates are usually roughly equal to interest rates or rates of inflation, but can vary from one activity to another.

The trouble with using conventional discount rates for comparing emission reduction costs with later avoided costs of climate change is that over periods of decades or centuries, avoided costs of millions of dollars would be discounted by factors of tens to hundreds. A number of economists have argued that this is inappropriate, in part because avoided costs cannot just be expressed in monetary terms (for example, species or heritage losses), but more importantly because future climate change costs could be disastrous and irreversible. These economists argue that future discount rates are very uncertain, and could be zero or even negative in the case of negative economic growth due to socio-economic disasters including climate change itself. Not only are future discount rates uncertain, but so too are future climate change impacts. This means that simple cost-benefit analysis is inappropriate to the issue of what is an appropriate rate of emissions reductions. Given large uncertainties, policies should rather be risk-averse, that is, they should aim to reduce the risk of potentially dangerous climate change impacts as rapidly as is economically possible. This is especially the case now that we have observations showing that changes are occurring faster than the climate models have predicted.

Importantly, the estimated costs of emissions reductions should be compared with the rates of economic growth. Given expected growth rates of several per cent per annum in GDP, a total decrease in GDP of anything from zero up to a few per cent by 2050, due to emissions reductions, is in reality only a delay in reaching the same much higher GDP figure (two or more times the present GDP) by a year at the most. Any loss of a few per cent would be made up for by the next year's growth in GDP.

It is also pertinent to note that many favourable technological developments have occurred in recent years that demonstrate large potential for mitigation if they are scaled up and commercialised as might happen if suitable financial incentives and investments are provided. These developments include:

- rapid deployment of wind turbines, and solar photovoltaics especially in Europe and parts of the United States and Asia,

- large-scale solar thermal power installations with energy storage,

- rapid elimination of industrial by-product gases,

- efficient hybrid gasoline/electric, low-pollution diesel and compressed air automobiles,

- advances in fuel cell technology,

- limited demonstration of underground storage or sequestration of carbon dioxide, and

- efficient public transport, bicycle- and pedestrian-friendly cities in parts of Europe and elsewhere.

While few of these technologies are as yet making large reductions in greenhouse gas emissions, their potential to do so within the next decade is large. In particular it should be noted that the often-repeated claim that renewable energy, especially wind and solar, cannot provide baseload power is clearly false. With widely distributed sources and energy storage via sensible or latent heat storage, hydrogen or other fuel generation, pumped water storages, or even compressed air, uneven primary energy sources can be evened out over the daily cycle and even for longer intervals during local fluctuations in winds or cloud cover. All these technologies are proven, as discussed later in this Chapter.

Indeed, decentralised energy generation networks are arguably more reliable for baseload power, and far more efficient than highly centralised systems that can be destabilised by failure in large power stations, labour disputes, or interruptions to grids. Decentralised generation facilitates co-generation, using otherwise wasted heat, and substantially reduces transmission losses. An ancilliary benefit of smaller decentralised power generation is that less water is needed for cooling large centralised generators. Lack of cooling water has become a serious problem for coal-fired power stations in drought stricken locations such as eastern Australia in the last decade.[25]

Another important development is the growing use of high voltage direct current transmission cables, which are far more efficient over long distances than alternating current cables, with typical transmission losses of only about 3% per 1000 km. Such cables can connect large renewable energy sources to distant consumers, for example, solar energy in North Africa to European markets, or remote solar, geothermal and tidal energy in Australia to its coastal cities or to South-East Asia.[26]

There is great optimism in the renewable energy industry, with rapid growth in global installed capacity in recent years (admittedly from a small base), and projections of even more rapid growth in the coming decade. Clean Edge, a US-based company that provides information for the investment market in clean energy technology, estimates rapid growth in solar, wind and biofuel installations, as summarised in **Table 11**.

The 2007 IPCC report (Working Group III Summary for Policymakers) summarises the potential for mitigation sector-by-sector as follows:

- Changes in lifestyle and behaviour patterns can contribute to climate change mitigation across all sectors. Management practices can also have a positive role.

- While studies use different methodologies, in all analysed world regions near-term health co-benefits from reduced air pollution as a result of actions to reduce GHG emissions can be substantial and may offset a substantial fraction of mitigation costs.

- New energy infrastructure investments in developing countries, upgrades of energy infrastructure in industrialized countries, and policies that promote energy security, can, in many cases, create opportunities to achieve GHG emission reductions compared to baseline scenarios. Additional co-benefits are country-specific but often include air pollution abatement, balance of trade improvement, provision of modern energy services to rural areas and employment.

- There are multiple mitigation options in the transport sector, but their effect may be counteracted by growth in the sector. Mitigation options are faced with many barriers, such as consumer preferences and lack of policy frameworks.

- Energy efficiency options for new and existing buildings could considerably reduce CO_2 emissions with net economic benefit. Many barriers exist against tapping this potential, but there are also large co-benefits.

- The economic potential in the industrial sector is predominantly located in energy intensive industries. Full use of available mitigation options is not being made in either industrialized or developing nations.

TABLE 11: Growth in global installation/production for solar photovoltaic power, wind power and biofuels. Estimates are by Clean Edge Inc. 2008[27]

	2003	2007	2017 estimate
Solar photovoltaic	620 MW	2821 MW	23 000 MW
Wind power	8000 MW	20 060 MW	76 000 MW
biofuels	7 billion gallons	15.6 billion gallons	46 billion gallons

- Agricultural practices collectively can make a significant contribution at low cost to increasing soil carbon sinks, to GHG emission reductions, and by contributing biomass feedstocks for energy use.

- Forest-related mitigation activities can considerably reduce emissions from sources and increase CO_2 removals by sinks at low costs, and can be designed to create synergies with adaptation and sustainable development.

- Post-consumer waste is a small contributor to global GHG emissions [mainly from land-fill methane and the burning of solid waste], but the waste sector can positively contribute to GHG mitigation at low cost and promote sustainable development.

- Geo-engineering options, such as ocean fertilisation to remove CO_2 directly from the atmosphere, or blocking sunlight by bringing material into the upper atmosphere, remain largely speculative and unproven, and with the risk of unknown side-effects. Reliable cost estimates for these options have not been published.

- [To this we should add carbon capture and sequestration associated with natural or artificial biofuel production as a means of taking carbon out of the atmosphere as will be needed in the case of overshoot scenarios.][28]

We will now look at some of these issues in more detail, starting with the cross-cutting issue of rising prices and shortages of oil.

The looming peak in oil production[29]

The coming peak in global oil production is a potentially important issue that may well influence the ease with which mitigation policies can be carried out, their costs, and indeed their urgency. When the peak in production will occur has been controversial since 1956 when M King Hubbert predicted that US oil production would peak in the early 1970s and then begin to decline (which it did). Nevertheless repeated global oil shortages in recent decades have caused sharp, if temporary, rises in the market price for oil, with downstream impacts on national and global economies. These fluctuations have been in part due to speculation and other transitory factors such as breakdowns, conflicts and weather extremes, but an underlying trend seems to be present. Moreover, many proponents of the idea that peak oil is already here argue that stated oil reserves are in many cases overstated and that this will be confirmed when oil production starts to decline over several more years. Whatever the true situation, security of oil supply (irrespective of price) has emerged as a major concern in many oil-consuming countries, particularly in relation to the unstable Middle East.

Some groups, such as the Energy Watch Group, have suggested that global oil production has already peaked, possibly with dire economic and other consequences[30], but that is not a view overtly stated by the International Energy Agency, although it has warned of shortages within the next few years and a possible peak or plateau about 2020.[31]

The US National Petroleum Council in 2007 issued a report 'Facing the hard truths about energy', that stated: 'The world is not running our of energy resources, but there are accumulating risks to continuing expansion of oil and natural gas production from the conventional sources relied upon historically. These risks create significant challenges to meeting projected energy demand.' It urged integrated energy policy, moderating demand and developing other sources of energy including use of coal with carbon capture and sequestration.[32]

Greater awareness of the imminence of a peak in global oil production by governments and industry could lead to several alternative responses, which could have quite different consequences:

- Higher priority in foreign policy to security of oil supplies, leading to oil-driven power politics, and a greater commitment to securing oil supplies at home through oil exploration and the opening up of presently closed areas such as designated wilderness areas.

- Research, development and investment in alternative fossil fuel sources of oil or other transport fuels, such as shale oil and tar sands, seabed methane, and gasification of coal.

- Emphasis on research and development of carbon capture and sequestration, or nuclear power to enable large increases in coal-based or nuclear-generated electricity and hydrogen for fuel cells.

- Strong support for renewable energy sources such as solar, wind, biomass, etc.

- Demand limitation through energy efficiency and less energy-demanding lifestyles. Uppermost here is less reliance on petroleum-powered automobiles and trucks for transport, in favour of more energy efficient and low-carbon public transport, railways and non-petroleum driven vehicles such as electric, hydrogen fuel cells or compressed air cars.

Securing dwindling oil supplies comes at a political, economic and environmental price, but is already evident to a degree in the foreign and domestic policies of a number of major countries. The second and third alternatives have their advocates in countries such as the US, Australia, Canada, China and Japan, but will likely lead to more expensive fuel with higher carbon dioxide emissions unless carbon dioxide capture and sequestration is made mandatory in all new fossil-fuel energy enterprises. Greene, Hobson and Li (2004) argue that conventional oil supplies will peak outside the Middle East between 2010 and 2030, and that a rapid transition will be needed to unconventional oil from oil sands and heavy oil if world consumption of petroleum fuels is to continue to increase. They ask if this transition is desirable, but explicitly do not discuss the possible transition to hydrogen from coal or renewable energy sources. Canada is already moving to exploit large oil sand deposits, with plans for carbon capture and

sequestration to be mandatory from 2018 onwards. The Canadian Prime Minister stated that: 'I see the oil sands continuing to grow in a way consistent with the government's desire to see a reduction of GHGs. We think both are achievable'.[33]

Renewable energy is the solution favoured by most environmentalists, and may in fact become more economically competitive due to increased fuel prices resulting from the other alternatives. Demand limitation is arguably the most cost-effective, but faces an acceptability hurdle related to personal perceptions of welfare and a good life. With better urban design it could in fact be quite attractive, as is already evident in many European cities.[34]

The faster the oil peak looms on the horizon the more urgent these responses become. From the climate change mitigation point of view this makes it critical that the focus should be on the third, fourth and fifth alternatives, which ensure that greenhouse gas emissions do not rise even faster. Some combination of these last three approaches would seem most likely to succeed in coping with the climate change issue, but traditional 'business-as-usual' attitudes would tend to favour the first two. Alternatives 1 and 2 are in line with the SRES A1FI scenarios, while alternatives 3, 4 and 5 are more consistent with the storyline behind the SRES B1 or low-emissions scenario.

The opening up of the Arctic Ocean by the melting of Arctic sea-ice may somewhat delay the oil crisis. It will save fuel on freight traffic between the Atlantic and Pacific oceans and allow exploitation of oil and gas deposits in the region. However there could be compensating negative effects, for example damage to pipelines and land transport due to melting of permafrost, and it also raises issues about territorial claims and rights of passage.[35]

Already some major oil companies and the Canadian government are moving to exploit tar sands and other unconventional oil sources[33], and several countries are moving to claim territorial rights in the Arctic region. The former is clearly counter-productive in relation to climate change and probably doomed to failure in the medium-term on economic grounds.

Clearly, achieving a low-emissions scenario is only likely to happen through conscious choice by governments, industry and consumers, and speedy investment in renewable alternatives. As far as oil is concerned, trends towards increased fuel efficiency, hybrid and efficient diesel vehicles, electric and compressed air cars, and better public transport need encouragement through measures such as congestion and fossil fuel taxes, fuel efficiency standards, carbon pricing and other measures. If the oil crisis deepens, as is likely, freeways may need to be turned into urban rail networks.[36]

All this sounds like a tall order. But Amory Lovins and colleagues claim in their US-oriented book *Winning the Oil Endgame* that:

Our strategy integrates four technological ways to displace oil: using oil twice as efficiently, then substituting biofuels, saved natural gas, and, optionally, hydrogen. Fully applying today's best efficiency technologies in a doubled-GDP 2025 economy would save half the projected U.S. oil use at half its forecast cost per barrel. Non-oil substitutes for the remaining consumption would also cost less than oil. These comparisons conservatively assign zero value to avoiding oil's many 'externalized' costs, including the costs incurred by military insecurity, rivalry with developing countries, pollution, and depletion. The vehicle improvements and other savings required needn't be as fast as those achieved after the 1979 oil shock.

The route we suggest for the transition beyond oil will expand customer choice and wealth, and will be led by business for profit. We propose novel public policies to accelerate this transition that are market-oriented without taxes and innovation driven without mandates. A$180-billion investment over the next decade will yield $130-billion annual savings by 2025; revitalize the automotive, truck, aviation, and hydrocarbon industries; create a million jobs in both industrial and rural areas; rebalance trade; make the United

States more secure, prosperous, equitable, and environmentally healthy; encourage other countries to get off oil too; and make the world more developed, fair, and peaceful.[37]

That may sound optimistic, but it is costed at 2005 oil prices, not the far higher oil prices of early 2008, and it ignores compressed air fuelled cars, which may be on the market in the US by 2010 according to Zero Pollution Motors.[38] Maybe we should have a go.

Mitigation options

Mitigation, or greenhouse gas emissions reductions, can be achieved in several general ways: through increased energy efficiency, fuel substitution, use of non-fossil-carbon fuels (including nuclear power and renewables), carbon sequestration (or removal from the climate system), and infrastructure and lifestyle changes. The challenge, if we are going to reduce the risk of dangerous climate change, is, as we have seen, how best to achieve a future like (but more policy-driven than) that described in the SRES B1 scenario (see **Box 3**) which relies less on high materials use and more on clean and resource-efficient technologies.

Increased energy efficiency[39]

Historically, carbon dioxide emissions were closely related to the gross domestic product (GDP) of individual countries during the early part of the twentieth century, but at the time of the oil crisis in 1973, when the real price of oil rose sharply, emissions fell away relative to GDP, which continued to rise. This was especially so in the United States, and was due to a sudden decrease in energy intensity (energy use per unit GDP, which is the inverse of energy efficiency), including more fuel-efficient automobiles, turning down the thermostats in buildings, and other emergency measures. In the United States, carbon intensity, measured in terms of carbon dioxide emissions per unit GDP, and indeed total emissions, continued to fall until about 1983, after which total emissions started to increase again, but more slowly than GDP. Globally energy efficiency has levelled off and carbon intensity slightly increased in the early 2000s.

Japan also showed a fall off in the rate of increase in emissions of carbon dioxide relative to continued rapid growth in GDP, beginning about 1978. China showed an even more dramatic increase in energy efficiency, with rapid economic growth but much slower growth in emissions, although energy efficiency started to decrease as economic growth accelerated in the early 2000s. Russia and other former Soviet Bloc countries have shown decreases in both GDP and in emissions, although that is changing as their economies have grown since the mid-1990s.

These experiences show that, given enough incentive (as in the oil crises), reductions in emissions per unit GDP can be achieved. Lessons learnt from these experiences can continue to influence future emissions. As Amory Lovins has long argued, focusing on energy efficiency will do more than protect the Earth's climate – it will make businesses and consumers richer. Lovins documents this argument in an article in the September 2005 *Scientific American* where he states that 'if properly done, climate protection would actually reduce costs, not raise them'. It is debateable whether this is the whole answer to reducing emissions, but at least it is a promising start and will defray some of the costs of emissions reduction.

An Australian Productivity Commission report in 2005 summarised some key issues in improving energy efficiency, some of which were:

- *Firms and households generally do not deliberately waste energy. But energy has been cheap and is only a small percentage of total outlays ... Energy efficiency has not been a high priority for them.*

- *The most important barriers to the adoption of privately cost-effective energy efficiency improvements appear to be:*

  – *a failure in the provision of information*

  – *the different incentives facing those who take decisions about installing energy-efficient products* [for example, building owners]

and those who might benefit from using them [for example, tenants].

- *The various educative, suasive and regulatory approaches to encourage or mandate greater energy efficiency continue to conflict with the signals given to energy users by Australia's relatively low energy prices.*

- *Some energy efficiency measures may not be privately cost effective, and yet may generate net public benefits because of their environmental outcomes. These measures may prove to be sound public policy, but they should be considered against other measures of achieving those environmental objectives.*[40]

In the then political climate of lack of real concern regarding climate change in Australia, the enquiry merely recommended mandatory labelling of products as 'a sufficient case had not been made' for national energy efficiency targets and obligations. Hopefully a different outcome will be forthcoming in 2009.

Growth in emissions from the building sector has been about 2–3% per annum in most developed countries, but much more in some rapidly developing countries such as China. This is largely due to increased dwelling sizes and numbers, increase in the commercial sector, and increased use of appliances, particularly heating in winter and cooling in summer. Key areas for improvement include better building design to reduce the need for artificial heating and cooling, by insulation, coatings on windows to reduce heat loss and reflect summer solar radiation, shading in summer, and passive solar heating in winter.[41]

Demonstration energy-efficient buildings show that large savings in running costs can be achieved at little or no additional capital expense. Even large office blocks can in many climates become almost independent of external energy supplies. The headquarters building of the World Meteorological Organization, in Geneva, is one such building. Many other energy efficient buildings are now in operation. According to an article in the September 2006 *Scientific American*, thousands of buildings in central

Europe and Scandinavia now have energy budgets typically one-sixth of the requirements of conventional buildings. Indeed, many people around the world are retrofitting their houses to save energy and costs with payback periods of a few years.

Combined heat and power systems for large buildings and compact neighbourhoods result in large gains in efficiency. Isolated power stations achieve about 30% efficiency, but if their waste heat is used they can achieve efficiencies nearer 85%. This may be best achieved through the use of natural gas powered fuel cells, with versions becoming commercially available which can supply individual houses or buildings, generating electricity, and at the same time providing hot water and central heating.

According to US industrialist Thomas Casten, 84 per cent of all new demand for energy services in the United States since 1996 has been met through improvements in efficiency.[42] He argues that local co-generation power plants can use the same technologies and fuels that are used by centralised electricity plants, but can be sized to meet the industrial host's needs for heat and waste energy, thus doing two jobs with the one fire. However, despite large energy savings, where fossil fuels are used, carbon capture and sequestration may be more difficult in decentralised plants.

Energy-efficient lighting is now achievable through a range of technical innovations including energy-saving light bulbs, fibre optics, and movement and light sensors to turn off lighting in empty or naturally lit rooms. Developing and choosing more energy efficient individual appliances is another major potential saving, as is getting into the habit of setting heating in winter to lower temperatures (along with putting on a sweater), and cooling in summer to higher temperature settings (and dispensing with jackets and ties).

Simple and acceptable lifestyle changes or habits can save both energy and money. It is estimated for example, that in a typical office building, cooling the interior to 25°C rather than 18°C, when the outside temperature is 32°C, would make energy savings of 25 to 50%, depending on the amount of waste heat

generated inside the building. All that is needed is more appropriate clothing. Similar considerations apply to air-conditioning in automobiles. Adherence to inappropriate sartorial fashion (for example, suits and neckties) can be a great waster of energy, as well as a source of discomfort.

Globally, about 20% of carbon dioxide emissions come from the transport sector. These emissions are growing at around 2–3% per annum. There are large potential improvements in fuel efficiency in road transport, with hybrid petrol-electric vehicles already on the market, with great gains from regenerative braking and gasoline engines running at their most efficient speeds, and fuel cell powered vehicles reaching feasibility.[43] Motor car manufacturers adopting hybrid petrol-electric or modern clean diesel engines (which are about as carbon efficient), are increasing sales at the expense of old-fashioned 'gas-guzzlers'. This was especially so in early 2008 when gasoline prices hovered at or above US$100 per barrel, whether or not this was due to the real impact of long-forecast peak oil, or to speculation.

Lightweight materials such as light metal alloys, fibre glass and ceramics are also reducing fuel needs. However, more economical vehicles may encourage greater usage, so that other incentives such as carbon emission pricing, congestion taxes, improved public transport, car pooling and reduced travel needs through better urban design and work arrangements are also needed.

Robert Jackson and William Schlesinger of Duke University estimate that for the United States a total reduction of 10% in carbon emissions could be achieved by a complete conversion to hybrid car technology, which would double fuel efficiency from about 10 km/L to over 20 km/L.[44] Hybrid car technology is already taking off. With appropriate incentives, including higher oil prices, it could be a major contributor to greenhouse gas emissions reductions within the next decade.

Hydrogen as a carrier of energy for driving cars is discussed below in the hydrogen economy section. It is dependent on efficient mobile storage and economical fuel cells. It is generally thought to be some decades away from commercial application to motor vehicles. However, Amory Lovins of the Rocky Mountain Institute argues that the early introduction of more efficient light-weight cars requiring less energy would lead to early reduction of emissions that would be enhanced by using hydrogen generated from natural gas, and more so by hydrogen generated using renewable sources. Local generation by wind or solar power would eliminate the need for expensive distribution networks.[45]

Other major innovations may be closer, including a compressed air car, with a strong carbon fibre storage tank, fuelled by air compressed at a filling station or an onboard plug-in compressor. A small air car is being commercialised in Europe by MDI of France, under contract in India by Tata Motors, and a six-seater version is expected to be available in the US in 2010 from Zero Pollution Motors.[46]

Several studies have examined the lifecycle costs and energy efficiency of various alternative motor vehicle fuels and engines, but continuing innovations complicate any comparison. A key issue is how the fuel or energy carrier is produced. It is possible to generate and store compressed air or hydrogen for fuel cells locally by processes that accumulate energy from variable sources such as solar or wind power.

Another lifestyle issue is one's diet. According to a Food and Agriculture Organization report in 2006, the livestock sector accounts for some 40% of total agricultural gross domestic product and some 18% of greenhouse gas emissions in carbon dioxide-equivalent. A significant part of that is from land-use change, and with increasing population and per capita consumption of meat, that may continue. The FAO suggests this can be reduced by more intense farming, reduced land clearing, restoration of soil carbon through conservation tillage, cover crops and agroforestry. Another important step is to reduce per capita consumption of red meat, which is the most emissions-intense food, in favour of white meat, or even better, grains, nuts and vegetables.[47]

A further consideration regarding food is how it is produced and how much it has travelled to get to your table. Local seasonal food will in general have to travel less and is more likely to have been produced under natural sunlight, whereas food that is not in season has usually been carried long distances or been produced in energy-intensive conditions such as in fossil-fuel-heated hot-houses.

Changes in infrastructure and behaviour

The Worldwatch Institute, in their 'State of the world 2007: our urban future' report points out that some time in 2008 more than half the world's population will be living in cities. In 2008 there are 20 cities with over 10 million people in each and by 2015 it is predicted that there will be 59 cities with between 1 million and 5 million people in Africa, 65 in Latin America and the Caribbean, and 253 in Asia. Clearly they will dominate global emissions as well as present other problems and opportunities.[48]

Evolutionary or adaptive structural changes to society are inevitable, and implicit in most forms of mitigation. How to reverse the increasing reliance on private automobile transport for commuting, shopping and other activities in modern cities is a critical example.

Clearly a more compact city, or one designed so as to minimise the necessity for travel would help, along with better public transport services. This would have co-benefits including fewer traffic accidents, less urban pollution, and closer proximity to the countryside for recreation. Other benefits include less urban sprawl that takes over agricultural land needed for future food supplies and greater economy for lower income families who cannot afford to run one or more cars, especially if oil prices continue to rise. Newman and Kenworthy estimate that urban car travel uses on average about twice as much energy as urban bus travel, 2.7 times as much as light rail and 6.6 times as much as electric train travel.[49]

Mitigation measures would encourage walking and bicycle use instead of cars for short trips, and car-pooling or public transport for longer trips. Measures include provision of bicycle lanes or separate bicycle paths, walking paths and pedestrian malls, more pedestrian friendly urban design, traffic lanes reserved for buses, and suburban parking areas and computerised linkup schemes for car-pooling and buses on demand, or parking facilities at suburban transport hubs. Such hubs would be designated high density growth areas.

There are many examples where such strategies have worked, such as in Toronto (Canada), Curitiba (Brazil), Bogota (Colombia) and Perth (Western Australia). In Curitiba, starting in 1974, priority was given to public buses with exclusive traffic lanes, carrying some 25 000 passengers each day. In 2007 a growing network of buses carried two million passengers throughout the metropolitan area. Jaime Lerner, former mayor of Curitiba, says '… cities are not problems, they are solutions' and 'To innovate is to start! … The present belongs to us and it is our responsibility to open paths.'

In Perth, a deliberate strategy to encourage use of public transport included full electrification of three existing rail lines in 1991, the opening of a new line in 1993 and of another in 2007. Rail patronage in Perth rose as a result from about 8000 daily in 1991 to nearly 30 000 in 1997 and more than 40 000 in 2008. This contrasts with Adelaide, South Australia, a similar sized city where rail patronage has remained almost unchanged since 1991. Peter Newman and Jeff Kenworthy, who helped inspire the changes in Perth, write: 'Cities need visions for how they can be transformed from car dependence and car saturation to greener modes of transport. And they need political leaders who can overcome the various barriers that prevent these visions from coming true'.[50] Today many organisations exist to link cities and local governments worldwide in their efforts to become more sustainable.[51]

The impending oil peak and rapidly rising oil prices is a powerful additional incentive and argument for better public transport and greenhouse-friendly urban design. New automobile freeways are no longer a sensible option, and any that are built should include rapid transit lines, or at least be designed so that they could be converted when the need for public transport dawns.

Another priority is to rapidly introduce less polluting cars. Hybrid petrol-electric cars have already made a mark, but expensive batteries with limited life have slowed demand. This could be overcome by a range of innovations and economic incentives. In the case of hydrogen fuel cell cars, an obstacle is the chicken and the egg problem of which comes first, more hydrogen powered cars or more hydrogen filling stations. Ways to break this vicious circle are needed. One would be for car manufacturers to build cars that can generate hydrogen for their fuel cells on board from a hydrocarbon fuel. Another would be for a planned program with incentives or subsidies to make hydrogen fuel cell cars cheaper and more attractive, coupled with incentives for refuelling stations to carry hydrogen. The structure of the market place may decide which fuel becomes the fuel of choice. A similar situation with the introduction of unleaded petrol and suitable car engines was managed successfully in many countries.[52]

An alternative might be to develop compressed air powered cars that could be supplied with air at filling stations or use plug-in, on-board air compressors.[38] Local generation of compressed air or hydrogen at filling stations from renewable energy such as wind or solar is also possible, thus saving on delivery of fuel.

Much of the inefficiency in supplying electric power is in the wasted heat generated at the power stations, and losses in the transmissions lines. Both these inefficiencies can be greatly reduced by encouraging decentralised power generation, where heat can be used for industrial or domestic purposes and there are no transmission losses. Fully electric cars could also be refuelled with plug-in batteries or from the electricity network supplied by renewable energy. Such arrangements could be made more attractive by reduced capital cost for fuel-efficient vehicles tied to energy supply contracts like the present contracts for mobile phones.[53]

Incentives including vehicle and building standards, a price on emissions and financial help (for example, tax deductions or low-interest loans) to build energy efficient buildings, or to retrofit old ones, would save on heating and cooling. Renewable energy or co-generation of heat and power could be incorporated in building designs with more appropriate planning guidelines, for example encouraging the generation of electricity and heat in buildings from natural gas fuelled fuel cells. An Australian comparison of embodied energy in various building materials finds that wood is about 1–3 MJ/kg, compared to mild steel at 34.0 MJ/kg and aluminium at 170 MJ/kg. Growing plants on building roofs and walls is another way to energy efficiency. Education as to what is desirable, what is available, and that it saves money in the long run, would facilitate change.[54]

Personal behaviour aimed at lowering greenhouse emissions is not only about big choices like lower-emissions transport and energy-efficient buildings. It is also about small personal things like turning off unused lights or electrical goods that are on standby mode, replacing incandescent lights with more efficient ones, and minimising travel. These seem like small actions, but if done by millions of people they can make a big difference.

Choosing low-emissions alternatives is made difficult if the right infrastructure (like convenient public transport) is not there, or is too expensive to use. Therefore campaigns to change individual behaviour must be accompanied by urgent government actions to facilitate such changes. As discussed above, other important personal behaviour items include food and dietary choices. Many sources of relevant information are available on the web.[55]

Where necessity requires activities that produce emissions, like for necessary travel or using electricity that is generated using fossil fuels, carbon-offsets may be appropriate. These are complex in that they may not be genuine or the best use of the money involved, and could have undesirable side-effects (for example, plantation forests that deprive others of river flow or that might not stay standing for long). Good local advice is therefore needed regarding different carbon-offset programs, with standards and accreditation desirable. There are websites that provide this advice in most places.[56]

Recycling and waste management to minimise emissions is another priority, along with means to reduce water demand in areas where water supplies are threatened by evaporative losses or reduced precipitation.

Good information is needed on all these matters, and as with many measures, it may be easier for the affluent to afford the low-emissions choice than for the poor. Therefore some form of financial help may be needed to engage the poor and ensure equitable arrangements, particularly if a price is put on emissions through carbon trading or carbon taxes. One possibility is for an individual emissions quota, with extra allowances for the needy, possibly via some credit card-like system.[57]

Fuel substitution

This is generally regarded as the substitution of one readily available fuel for another, as distinct from development of new alternative fuels or energy sources. As long as fossil fuels continue to dominate energy production, switching from coal to oil or gas can reduce greenhouse gas emissions. If energy efficiencies remain unchanged, shifting from coal to oil leads to a reduction in carbon emissions of about 26%, oil to gas about 23.5% and from coal to gas about 43%. Leakage of methane in the case of coal and gas, however, slightly increases the gap between coal and oil, but reduces the gap between oil and gas.

The opportunity and likelihood of making substantial reductions in carbon emissions by such substitution varies from country to country, with some major developing countries, notably China and India, being richly endowed with coal but poorly endowed with oil and gas. They can only make large substitutions by increasing imports, which they can ill afford. Nevertheless, China is partly switching to natural gas, largely because of regional pollution problems, with the development of international pipelines and gas terminals. Richer countries, such as the United States, Japan, Australia and western European countries can afford fuel substitution, and in some cases have their own gas supplies. However, some 70% of gas reserves are in the former Soviet Union and the Middle East. This raises energy security problems for potential importing countries.

In countries in Africa and South America, substitution of gas will also be hampered by lack of pipelines, requiring large investments in infrastructure.

Exploitation of coal-bed methane has the double advantage that it reduces leakage of methane from coal mines as well as being less carbon intensive as a fuel. This is a potentially substantial source of methane in some countries. For example in the coal-rich Australian state of Queensland, coal-bed methane in 2006 accounted for 63% of the high-growth Queensland gas market.[58] However, some gas sources contain a large fraction of carbon dioxide, sulfur and other pollutants that would require large amounts of energy to remove, thus increasing the effective carbon intensity of these sources.

Unconventional oil reserves such as shale oil are generally more carbon-intensive to exploit than conventional sources, and may also become less competitive with renewable energy sources as costs for the latter are reduced.

In some countries, the phasing out of nuclear power is leading to an increased reliance on fossil fuels, and in Brazil constraints on its former reliance on hydro-power, as its economy expands, is increasing reliance on fossil energy. In southern Australia large hydro-power generators are suffering from a decrease in available water supplies due to prolonged drought due at least in part to climate change. Hydro-electric supplies in Tasmania have been particularly badly affected by lower rainfall, with a high voltage direct current cable meant to supply hydro-electricity to Victoria in times of peak demand instead supplying coal-fired power to Tasmania.[59]

Disappearance of mountain glaciers and reductions in winter snow storage may also threaten hydropower supplies in many other locations.

Over several decades, limited availability of established reserves of natural gas and costs may limit switching to gas supplies for power generation in some countries, although large reserves of methane exist as methane hydrates on the ocean floor and in permafrost. Methane hydrates are cage-like molecular lattices of ice, inside which molecules of methane are trapped. They exist in permafrost regions, and beneath the ocean floor at depths exceeding 500 metres,

where high pressures occur. While both forms are susceptible to catastrophic release due to climate change and sea-level rise (see Chapter 5), they constitute a huge source of methane, which could be used, if they can be accessed safely, to substitute for coal and oil. According to the US Federal Methane Hydrate Advisory Committee, in its 2007 report to Congress, current estimates of natural gas trapped in hydrates within the US are of the order of 200 000 trillion cubic feet (TCF) compared to current US consumption of 22 TCF per annum. Moreover, methane hydrates exist in many different localities around the world and energy-hungry countries such as Japan, India, China and South Korea are all engaged in research in this area.[60]

The US committee notes that methane hydrates may have played an important part in past climatic change: 'Verifying the role of methane hydrates in global climate change is critical because of the fact that methane has a greenhouse warming potential 21 times that of CO_2. A better understanding of the pivotal role that hydrates might play in the global climate could influence U.S. policy choices related to global warming mitigation decisions'.

However, if a target greenhouse gas concentration as low as 450 ppm CO_2-equivalent is desired, substitution of natural gas or methane for coal and oil would, by itself, still not enable such a target to be reached.

Synthetic liquid fuels can be produced by a variety of processes including gas to liquid, coal to liquid and biomass to liquid. Emissions and economic analysis suggest that gas to liquid and biomass to liquid may be attractive alternatives to oil, but coal to liquid may be less so.[61]

All-electric cars potentially provide a major opportunity to replace oil supplies for motor transport. However, the benefits in terms of reducing greenhouse gas emissions depend on low-carbon sources for the electricity. This could be nuclear, coal-fired with carbon capture and sequestration, or large-scale renewables. Renewable electricity generated at off-peak times could be stored in batteries or as electrolytes. Electric cars that are recharged from mains electricity are already in use in parts of Europe, and General Motors and Nissan are reported to be planning to release commercially available cars in the US by 2010. In the UK a range of fully electric cars is being marketed by the MyCar company. Compressed air cars are another alternative, coming into production in the US in 2010.[62]

Nuclear power

In 2005 nuclear power globally accounted for about 6.4% of total energy supplies, although this varies greatly between countries. France gets the vast majority of its electricity from nuclear power, but many other countries have none. Some countries are phasing out nuclear power stations on environmental grounds. Growth has stalled in recent decades because of public concern heightened by the Chernobyl accident in 1986. Moreover, lower fossil-fuel prices (coal, and oil until recently) and high costs of licensing and safety precautions have made nuclear power uncompetitive. This is especially so in countries where power stations are run by the private sector, which expects high returns on capital investment. Many existing nuclear power stations are reaching their design lifetimes and are to be phased out in coming decades.[63]

Nuclear power advocates around the world have seized on global warming as an opportunity to promote nuclear power as the key business-as-usual (that is, increasing energy consumption) solution to reducing greenhouse gas emissions. However, nuclear power is not totally free of carbon dioxide emissions if embedded emissions in building and later dismantling the power stations, and in mining and refining the fuel, are taken into account. Averaged over their lifetime, emissions from nuclear reactors are thus highly dependent on their lifespan, with a typical payoff period to reduce total emissions of a decade or more.

The cost of nuclear power is not yet competitive with fossil fuels once capital costs, insurance, and waste disposal are taken into account, although it may be competitive if a price is put on carbon dioxide

emissions.[64] Moreover, high grade Uranium 235 supplies are in fact limited to a few decades at current rates of usage, meaning that breeder reactors may be required later this century, or lower grade ore will need to be mined and processed at greater economic and environmental cost. Nuclear fission power is thus not a major long-term solution, although it may contribute significantly to a medium-term suite of measures to maintain energy supplies if safety and other criteria can be met. Nuclear fusion, when it is proven safe and practical, may be a longer-term contributor to future energy supplies because it does not generate dangerous and costly waste and will not run out of economical fuel.

The European Commission in January 2007 stated that:

> It is for each Member State to decide whether or not to rely on nuclear power for the generation of electricity. Decisions to expand nuclear energy were recently taken in Finland and in France. Other EU countries ... have re-launched a debate on their nuclear energy policy. With 152 reactors spread over the EU 27, nuclear power contributes 30% of Europe's electricity today – however, if the planned phase-out policy within some EU Member States continues, this share will be significantly reduced. To meet the expected energy demand and to reduce European dependency on imports, decisions could be made on new investments or on the life extension of some plants.

> Reinforcing nuclear power generation could also represent one option for reducing CO_2 emissions and play a major role in addressing global climate change. Nuclear power is essentially carbon emissions-free and forms part of the Commission's carbon reduction scenario including the objective of reducing CO_2 emissions. This could also feature as an important consideration when discussing future emissions trading schemes.

> The most crucial factor affecting the prospect of growth of nuclear power is its underlying economics as a nuclear plant involves an up front

investment ranging from ⬄2 to ⬄3 billion. Nuclear energy generation incurs higher construction costs in comparison to fossil fuels, yet operating costs are significantly lower following the initial investments.[65]

The Director General of the International Atomic Energy Agency (IAEA) in June 2004 stated that: 'Nuclear power is not in competition with renewable energy sources, but has the advantage of supplying reliable baseload electricity needed to replace fossil fuel plants' [renewable power can do this also, see below]. He also pointed to its potential to supply hydrogen for fuel cells used in transport. In a 2007 statement he also referred to new reactors connected to the grid in China, India and Romania, with seven more under construction.[66]

A report by the European Greens in 2008 on the status of the world nuclear industry indicates that the average age of the 439 reactors then in operation was 23 years, and of the 117 reactors permanently shut down, the average age was about 22 years.[67]

According to the 2007 IPCC report, nuclear power suffers from several major barriers to wider use: long-term fuel resource constraints without recycling; economics; safety; waste management; security; proliferation; and adverse public opinion. Each of these points remains, at best, controversial at present, with heightened fears of terrorism adding to the safety and proliferation concerns. Sir David King in the UK is reported to have said that nuclear power 'is not necessarily the ideal way to make energy, [but] the dangers of climate change are certainly worse'[68], while James Lovelock in his book *The Revenge of Gaia* argues that it is the only short-term option because he has no faith in renewable energy filling the gap if we close down coal and oil.[69] (I will argue that renewables can meet the challenge if the right policies are put in place.)

According to an IAEA report, public opinion on nuclear power is ambivalent with most supporting existing nuclear power stations, but opposing new ones to combat climate change and many worried about the risk of terrorists acts involving radioactive materials and nuclear facilities. Another report by

Nick Pidgeon and others in 2008 finds that in the UK, 'People see both climate change and nuclear power as problematic in terms of risk and express only a "reluctant acceptance" of nuclear power as a "solution" to climate change'.[70] In Australia, the conservative government in 2007 was tending to encourage nuclear power for Australia, but after an election the new Labor government declared it not on, and the now opposition parties, in clear deference to public opinion, agreed. Nevertheless Australia is a major exporter of uranium and its government is determined for this to continue.

Regarding nuclear weapons proliferation, a study by the American Physical Society in 2005 points out that 'the technologies used in peaceful nuclear power programs overlap with those used in the production of fissionable material for nuclear weapons'.[71] It therefore urges, after special reference to the current problems with Iran, that 'technological advances and institutional changes are required to avoid proliferation by countries taking advantage of a global spread of nuclear power plants'. A recent opinion article in *Physics Today* by Alisa Carrigan argues that most weapons proliferation in the past has come with the help of scientists and engineers from the aspiring weapons states gaining first-hand experience in countries with a nuclear industry, rather than from the physical transfer of materials.[72]

It is salutary that nuclear power programs in the United States, France, UK, China and elsewhere have historically been associated with nuclear weapons programs, and in most cases have been subsidised. Privatisation of nuclear power programs in the US and UK have been associated with a drop in investment in new nuclear power plants.

A consortium of ten nations, the Generation IV International Forum, is pooling its research expertise to choose designs for a new generation of fail-safe nuclear reactors.[73] These would operate at higher temperatures, allowing more efficient electricity generation and the possibility of generating hydrogen from the thermochemical splitting of water. The latter could be used to fuel transport. However, to generate enough hydrogen to replace gasoline in the US would require hundreds of new nuclear power plants. Moreover, the need for new coolants and more corrosion-proof materials will be huge challenges. New demonstration reactors are unlikely to be delivered before the 2020s. A recent study by the Massachusetts Institute of Technology (MIT) looked at the potential for the power generated by nuclear reactors to triple by 2050, which would avoid nearly two billion tonnes of carbon emissions. However, the MIT report suggested this would not be economically competitive with fossil fuels, while the cost of renewable energy could fall dramatically over this time. It estimated the cost of nuclear electricity at US 6.7 cents per kWh, compared to wind power in the US currently around 4–5 cents per kWh.[74]

There is also a major international project, the International Thermonuclear Experimental Reactor (ITER), to build an experimental reactor to see whether fusion can fulfill its theoretical promise as a power source.[75] Planning is proceeding for a five million Euro facility in the south of France, but it may not deliver workable nuclear fusion for decades to come. The total price tag is currently estimated at about US$12 billion.

These considerations suggest that nuclear fission reactors are unlikely to play a major role in further replacing fossil fuels and reducing total emissions globally by 2050. However, nuclear fusion could be an option in the latter part of the twenty-first century, with far less radioactive waste, if feasibility can be demonstrated in the next few decades. The Bush Administration in the US placed considerable emphasis on cooperative international research programs such as GEN-4 and ITER to develop safe nuclear power and nuclear fusion, but these will not lead to significant reductions in greenhouse gas emissions over the next several decades. Whether or not the European Community will back nuclear power more strongly is highly contested at present, with a major effort in baseload renewable power seen by many as a viable alternative.[76]

Hydropower[77]

Globally, hydropower provided some 5.3% of energy supplied in 2005, although in some countries such as New Zealand, Norway and Brazil the proportion is much higher. While there is considerable potential for increases, for example in China and India, there are major concerns about the environmental and social impacts of large dams on fisheries, displacement of populations, riverine ecosystems, and other issues. Water storages can absorb CO_2 but many give off methane from decaying vegetable matter, so they may not be entirely emissions-free. Another major concern is the loss of stored carbon if forests are cleared to make way for water storages. This means that new dams may take years to decades to cause a net decrease in carbon emissions. Another significant obstacle is the distance between potential users and the potential sites for hydropower generation, leading in some cases to large costs and losses of power in transmission, although use of high voltage direct current cables may reduce the losses.

A classic report on the role of large dams, used for irrigation, flood control and hydro-electric generation is that by the World Commission on Dams in 2000. The report stated that:

> *Dams fundamentally alter rivers and the use of a natural resource, frequently entailing a reallocation of benefits from local riparian users to new groups of beneficiaries at a regional or national level. At the heart of the dams debate are issues of equity, governance, justice and power – issues that underlie the many intractable problems faced by humanity.*

The report went on to outline seven guiding principles for consideration of new dams, which basically called for recognition of many competing interests and the need for public acceptance and social justice. Climate change clearly complicates this picture even further.[78]

Global warming will increase the rate of evaporation and globally averaged precipitation (rain and snowfall), but this will be uneven in space and time, with changes in seasonality of rainfall, loss of storage in snow-pack and glaciers, increased aridity in many subtropical regions, more frequent droughts and intense rain events. These changes will impact on planning for hydropower dams, their operational requirements and security of supply, as plans will have to take into account changes in flood control and water supply measures needed for irrigation and other industrial and human uses.

Small scale (<10 MW) and micro (<1 MW) hydropower systems will be particularly badly affected by climate change. Hydropower is particularly well suited to providing peak load supplies (often at premium prices), including that generated by growing air conditioning loads, but is of course adversely affected by drought. It can also be used for pumped storage when other intermittent renewable power such as tidal, solar or wind power is available.

Regional or small-scale combined solar, wind or tidal generators with pumped hydro-storage may provide the best options for secure baseload power in many communities, obviating the need for centralised coal-fired generation. In coastal locations where freshwater is scarce or unreliable, pumped seawater may be a viable energy storage medium. Indeed, the role of large, small and pumped

hydropower in decentralised energy systems is important in the general push for decentralised power generation, which utilises waste heat, has smaller distribution losses and utilises renewable energy more efficiently.[79]

Solar energy

The solar radiation that reaches the Earth's surface is more than 10 000 times the current annual global energy consumption by humans (excluding food). Thus all the world's energy consumption could be generated from solar power from an area of desert only a few hundred kilometres on each side, depending on the efficiency of the energy harvesting method. Solar energy power generation in 2005, however, is less than 0.2% of total global energy production. Annual surface insolation varies with latitude, ranging between some 1000 w/m² in mid-latitude regions to 1200 w/m² in low-latitude dry desert regions. This is shown graphically in **Figure 31**, based on data obtained from the World Climate Research Programme's (WCRP's) Coupled Model Intercomparison Project phase 3 (CMIP3) multi-model dataset.[80]

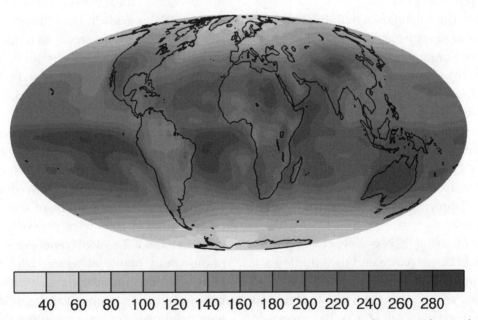

40 60 80 100 120 140 160 180 200 220 240 260 280

Figure 31: Incident solar energy on the Earth's surface. It is clear that maximum solar radiation incident on land areas is over subtropical to mid-latitude desert regions in both hemispheres. (Figure courtesy of the Program for Climate Model Diagnosis and Intercomparison, and Martin Dix of CSIRO, Australia.)[80]

There is thus a huge potential for harnessing solar energy, although not in the most populated regions. The problem with most forms of renewable energy is the remoteness of many good generation sites from consumer markets. Historically this has been a major objection to their widespread utilisation. Remoteness has implied the need for large investment in electrical transmission grids at great capital costs and with large transmission losses. However this is no longer the case with the advent of high voltage direct current (HVDC) cables.

HVDC technology is now widely available and in use in many countries. It requires converter stations at the transmission and receiving ends, but the cable in between can be cheaper and less damaging to the environment, and can be put underground, with less maintenance costs, or under the sea. The cost for the converter stations is higher than for alternating current, but that for the cables and right-of-way is lower for HVDC. Most importantly, the energy loss in transmission for HVDC is only some 3% for each thousand kilometres, making them much more economical for long distance transmission than HVAC. This makes widely dispersed renewable energy networks both feasible and economically attractive on a continental scale.

Inspired by the visionary Dr R Buckminster Fuller, the Global Energy Network Institute has for many years been urging such networks to decrease pollution, reduce hunger and poverty in developing countries and to increase trade.[81] HVDC transmission makes this possible. Indeed, there is a proposal, 'Clean Power from the Deserts' from the Trans-Mediterranean Renewable Energy Cooperation (TREC) for such a network linking renewable energy stations in Europe, the Middle East and North Africa, supplying local energy needs in the energy-rich source regions, all the electricity needs of Europe, and using excess energy for water desalinisation in North Africa and the Middle East. Groups exist in the UK, Germany and elsewhere to push this idea, with collaborators in Jordan and elsewhere. In Australia, Neil Howes has proposed a national electricity grid for Australia, the engineering company Worley Parsons is proposing

a network of 34 solar thermal power stations similarly linked and the Garnaut Climate Change Review discussed such a grid in its draft report.[82]

A German study looks at using concentrated solar power for seawater desalinisation as part of the TREC proposal (see above). This would be a bonus for the Middle Eastern and North African countries that may host concentrated solar power stations to supply electricity to Europe.[83]

A report for the Renewable Energy Policy Network for the 21st Century finds that grid-connected solar photovoltaics (PV) increased by 50% in both 2006 and 2007, to an estimated 7.7 GW. It found that solar heat collectors provided hot water and some space heating for about 50 million households worldwide, and increased in capacity by 19% in 2006 to reach 105 GW thermal capacity. The American Solar Energy Society in 2007 estimated that by 2030 solar photovoltaics could save the emission of 63 MT of carbon per annum in the US alone.[84]

Photovoltaics can be incorporated in window coatings and roofs of buildings, and could help to make many office buildings energy self-sufficient in lighting, heating and cooling. These and photovoltaic devices in individual houses are already incorporated into electricity grids in many locations so that any electricity generated surplus to requirements is fed into the grid. Feed-in tariffs (that is, guaranteed payments for excess electricity fed into the grid) in some European countries are fostering rapid growth in solar power in those countries.

The key problem with solar energy is not its availability and baseload capacity with storage and large grids, but its cost. However, costs of photovoltaic electricity is rapidly coming down due to improved technologies and economies of scale. Typical cost comparisons in 2005 were conventional coal-fired power at about 2 to 4 US cents per kWh, and large photovoltaic plants at nearer 20 cents per kWh. However, the Nanosolar company, founded in 2002, is now producing commercial quantities of solar cells with printing-press-style machines that set down a layer of solar-absorbing nano-ink onto thin metal sheets. They do not use silicon and cost about a tenth of earlier solar panels and are thus competitive with fossil fuel electricity. The company claims that by 2009 it will be producing several hundred MW worth of solar cells a year at a cost less than 1 cent per Watt for initial use in California and Germany.[85]

Another highly efficient and potentially cheap photovoltaic technology is the Australia SLIVER technology, developed at the Australian National University (ANU) and about to be manufactured in Adelaide by Origin Energy.[86]

A variant on solar cell technology is to use sun-tracking mirrors to focus sunlight on photovoltaic receivers consisting of arrays of high-efficiency solar cells that generate electricity. A 154 MW station of this sort is being built near Mildura in Victoria, Australia, providing regional employment and is connected to the national grid.[87]

Approximately 1.5 billion people are at present without access to electricity in developing countries and are a huge potential market for locally produced solar electricity as cheaper photovoltaic systems become available.

Concentrating solar-thermal power (CSP) plants have been overlooked in many assessments of renewable energy potential. However, they generally have lower costs than conventional photovoltaic cells (but not perhaps the Nanosolar thin films) and the great advantage of proven and economical energy storage to ensure baseload supplies of electricity. CSP plants focus solar energy at high temperatures onto boilers or other generators of electricity that can be fed into power grids, or even generate hydrogen for fuel cells. Nine plants in the Mohave Desert near Los Angeles, USA, have been supplying more than 350 MWe of power since 1989.

A Californian company, Ausra, has developed efficient solar concentrator systems that generate electricity by heating water that feeds steam into turbines. Heat is stored as needed as steam in large insulated tanks. In a series of peer-reviewed papers Ausra scientists claim that such plants could supply over 90% of the present US electricity grid, electricity for plug-in electric vehicles and for heating and cooling buildings. They have studied correlations between available power and consumption and

point out that most human electricity consumption occurs in daylight, especially for heating and cooling buildings, and that with up to 16 hours heat storage CSP can provide nearly all electricity and transport fuel needs.[88]

Similar electricity plants are being built by Solana for the Arizona Public Service company using as heat storage devices thermos-like buildings containing salt.[89] Other means of energy storage are in use elsewhere including generation of electrolytes that can be run through large batteries (vanadium redox batteries) to generate electricity as needed.[90] The US Department of Energy ran a Basic Energy Sciences workshop in 2005 on solar energy utilisation that also discussed using high temperature solar concentrators to generate hydrogen or other chemicals as fuel, and to store energy via the dissociation and synthesis of ammonia.[91]

Overall, the prospects for rapid growth in electricity generation and other energy generation from solar thermal technology looks at least as good as from photovoltaic, and it is relatively easy to supply energy on demand. This is contrary to the views often expressed by advocates of carbon capture and storage and of nuclear power.

Solar hot water systems are already in use in many private dwellings around the world, especially in locations where sunshine is plentiful. Here, as with photovoltaics, a key problem is the relatively high initial capital cost for individual households, which takes some years to recover through decreased charges for use of fossil fuel energy. Schemes to finance this initial cost via low-interest loans, and to write it off over time can facilitate such investments.[92]

A novel solar tower was planned for a site near Mildura, Australia, in 2002, with a capacity of 200 MWe. The concept relied on what is in effect a giant circular glasshouse of diameter 5 km, which warms air that rises through a 1 km high chimney at its centre. As the air is drawn into the tower it passes through air turbines that generate electricity. It also heats thermal storages (rocks or water tanks), enabling it to continue operation during the night. A 50 kW pilot system operated for seven years in

Spain in the 1980s, but no progress has been reported on the larger proposal as of August 2008.[93]

Photosynthesis is the most successful natural solar converting system on Earth, enabling crop production for food, fibre and energy. Artificial photosynthesis using algae would make it possible to use sunlight and carbon dioxide to produce large quantities of biomass and hydrogen from water, cleanly and cheaply. Research currently under way in several laboratories may eventually lead to artificial photosynthesis, hopefully competitive with other energy sources.[94]

In summary the two main central problems with solar energy – remoteness from markets and the need for storage to counter its intermittent nature – have now been largely solved. As low-loss transmission and various methods of energy storage have developed, solar energy has become more attractive. In any case, solar energy in a warmer world will be at its maximum just when it is needed to provide power for summer daytime air conditioning, in what will increasingly become a peak load situation. It is also capable of providing power for vehicles via batteries, hydrogen, compressed air or other storage devices, thus reducing emissions and dependence on oil. For these reasons, and with a price on carbon pollution, solar energy is set for rapid growth in the market place.

Wind power

According to the IPCC 2007 report, wind power has been one of the fastest growing renewable energy sources, with an average 28% per annum growth since 2000, and a record 40% growth in 2005.[95] Globally, over 20 GW (1 GW is one thousand million watts) was added in 2007. Current installed capacity worldwide at the end of 2006 was more than 94 GW, compared to 2.3 GW in 1991. Denmark and some regions of Spain and Germany already have 10% to 25% of their electricity generated from wind power. President George W Bush stated (28 September 2007) that: 'Wind power is becoming cost-effective in many parts of America. We've increased wind energy production by more than 300 percent'. In Australia, Pacific Hydro has five wind farms currently in operation, with a total capacity of more than 100 MW, and another five projects in development. Pacific Hydro also has renewable energy projects in the Philippines, Fiji and Chile.

The Global Wind Energy Council, in its 2007 report, found that 2007 saw a 27% increase in installed capacity, bringing the global total to more than 94 GW. The Council reports that the wind industry now exists in more than 70 countries, with the largest being (in descending order) Germany, US, Spain, India and China. It predicts that the wind market will grow by over 155% by 2012 to reach 240 GW installed capacity, with the fastest growth in the US and China. The International Energy Agency also released a major report 'Energy technology perspectives' in June 2008. This suggests that wind power, along with energy efficiency and fuel-switching, will play a major role in reducing emissions in the power sector in the next two decades. The IEA's 'BLUE scenario' predicts that wind energy will produce over 5000 TWh of electricity by 2050, accounting for up to 17% of global power production, with one-third of the resulting savings in emissions being in China and India. The IEA report calls for global revolution in ways that energy is supplied and used, with a transformation of the global energy economy.[96]

The potential for wind energy is very large, with the American Wind Energy Association citing a study by the Pacific Northwest Laboratory in 1991 that estimates the total wind energy potential in the contiguous United States at over 10 billion kWh annually, or more than twice the present total electricity generated in the US. The average size of wind turbines has increased dramatically in the last 25 years, with the largest now generating up to 5 MW, with a rotor diameter of more than 120 m. They have also become quieter and more efficient, and on good sites they can generate electricity at around US 3–5 cents per kWh, which is competitive with coal-fired power stations.

With new best-practice guidelines regarding noise, electromagnetic interference, aircraft flight paths, land use, protection of areas with high landscape value, bird and bat strike and consultation with local people, wind farms are becoming more acceptable. According to the British Wind Energy Association, extensive surveys of public opinion in the UK have shown 'a consistently high level of support for the development of wind farms, on average 70–80%, both in principle, as a good thing, and also in practice, among residents living near wind farms'. One local Scottish councillor is quoted as saying: 'The Ardrossan wind farm has been overwhelmingly accepted by local people – instead of spoiling the landscape we believe it has been enhanced. The turbines are impressive looking, bring a calming effect to the town and contrary to the belief that they would be noisy, we have found them to be silent workhorses'.[97] This is totally at odds with the 'not-in-my-backyard' (NIMBY) protests by a minority of ill-informed people in some proposed locations (ironically, many of these objectors live on exposed coasts that will be liable to erosion and flooding from rising sea levels).

Wind farms occupy less land than any other energy conversion system, with roads and tower bases less than 2% of a typical farm, and continued cropping and grazing possible on the rest of the land. Objections have centred on claims of unsightliness, noise and danger to birds, and there have been some clumsy public relations and installations. Noise is a rapidly vanishing problem with better, almost silent designs. Unsightliness is partly due to some unfortunate installations in special locations, but mainly in the eyes of some beholders, who apparently happily tolerate the sight of ugly power stations, smoke plumes, freeways, pollution and high-voltage transmission lines, which are features of industrialised societies. Clive Hamilton, an Australian environmental economist, argues that such 'environmentalists' need to take account of the greater good:

When some people look at a wind farm they see a symbol of industrialism despoiling a beautiful headland. Others see majestic and elegant machines that power our cities with zero pollution, proving with every rotation that humans can live in the world without destroying it. The latter vision must prevail.[98]

Martin Pasqualetti, an American expert on wind power, suggests that potential sites for wind power should be ranked not only by wind speeds but also by compatibility with local communities. He suggests two general strategies: work to change public opinion in favour of wind power, or install the turbines out of view, preferably on lonely farms which need rental income.[99]

Studies in Australia and the United States suggest that the danger to birds has been grossly exaggerated. Rotation speeds of modern wind turbines are slow enough for birds to avoid the rotor blades, and in one US study it was found that for every 10 000 birds killed by human activities, less than one death is caused by a wind turbine. Most human-caused bird deaths are from collisions with windows and buildings, motor vehicles and high tension wires, or from house cats, loss of habitat and pesticides. Nevertheless, careful siting in relation to nesting areas and flight paths, especially in relation to rare and endangered species, and with respect to scenic areas, is advisable, if only to minimise objections from the public.

Sites for wind farms depend critically on annual average wind speeds, with power generated varying as the cube of the wind speed, so that an 'excellent' site with an average annual wind speed of 8 m/s generates over 40% more power than a 'good' site with 7 m/s. If costs can be lowered to make 'good' sites economically viable, many more sites become available, enabling a greater choice of sites that have minimal visual impact.[100]

As with solar energy (see above), the intermittent nature of wind power requires either storage devices or integration into a widespread grid that would enable power generation to be averaged out over large areas experiencing different wind regimes.[101] Increasing links between solar-, wind- and pumped storage hydropower is likely, with implications for optimal siting, efficiency and river conservation. Backup for occasions of low output across the whole grid can be from hydropower or relatively cheap gas turbines that need to be operated only rarely. Wind forecasting can be used to schedule backup generators. Such backup is needed with coal-fired power stations anyway, in case of break down, so the problem is not new. Indeed, many coal-fired power stations will become increasingly affected by cooling water shortages in inland locations due to climate change, as has already happened in Australia. Moreover, coal-fired power stations that use sea-water for cooling will suffer increasing problems from tidal surges and coastal erosion as sea level rises.

The advent of high voltage direct current power lines also makes it possible to economically link remote wind farms and other renewable energy sources to distant markets (see discussion under solar power above). This may be especially useful for off-shore wind farms, which are becoming common in Europe because of higher wind speeds and distance from densely populated areas.

Another potentially useful application of wind power in the future may be to locally manufacture hydrogen for fuel cells in cars by electrolysis, or even to generate compressed air for air-powered motor vehicles (see above). This could be especially useful in association with remote vehicle refilling stations.

Biomass energy[102]

Historically, biomass, that is, the accumulation of organic material from plants and animals, has been a major energy source, especially in less developed areas, where it is used for fuel for stoves and heating, usually in the form of wood or cattle dung. With population growth, and for reasons of health, local and indoor air pollution, land degradation and exhaustion of supplies, use of traditional biomass burning is now often being phased out in favour of fossil-fuel generated electricity from urban and rural grids. Development of household scale biogas and of cleaner and more efficient stoves is helping at the local village level, but biomass energy at the larger regional scale may be more appropriate in more developed countries.

The simple view is that sustainable biomass energy effectively reduces greenhouse gas emissions because, even if renewable biomass is burned and the resulting carbon dioxide is released into the atmosphere, the fuel results from plants that take a similar amount of carbon dioxide out of the atmosphere. Biomass burning effectively harvests solar energy and recycles the carbon.

Accepting this view for the moment, if carbon dioxide from biomass burning were to be removed and more permanently sequestered underground or elsewhere, it would result in actual reductions in atmospheric concentrations of carbon dioxide. This may prove necessary in the future to reduce greenhouse gas concentrations to a safe level, below the maximum concentrations reached in the next century or so, thereby eventually slowing or stopping sea-level rise and bringing global warming down to acceptable levels.

The situation is in fact more complicated in that growing, fertilising, harvesting and transport of biomass uses energy that results in carbon emissions which must be subtracted from any potential savings, and nitrous oxide, a potent greenhouse gas, can be given off from nitrogenous fertilisers. Even more importantly, if land has to be cleared of forests or other vegetation in order to grow biomass for harvesting, then carbon stored in the original vegetation and soil will be released to the atmosphere. This may be far larger than any short-term savings from using biomass energy.[103]

Greenhouse gas emissions can be reduced in four ways using biomass:

- biofuels can be substituted for fossil fuels to generate heat and electricity,

- gaseous or liquid biofuels such as ethanol can substitute for oil in transportation,

- biomass, in the form of timber or compressed fibrous sheeting, can replace greenhouse intensive construction materials (that is materials formed using lots of fossil fuel energy) such as concrete, steel or aluminium, and

- carbon can be sequestered in the ground by suitable cultivation techniques, or by burying charcoal ('biochar') generated in pyrolysis.

The first use is dependent on access to large quantities of biomass, either agricultural or forestry waste or purpose-grown material. In some cases this can be combined with incineration of urban garbage. However, a key consideration must be the elimination of potentially hazardous or unhealthy pollution. Another problem is the need to transport the fuel from dispersed sources to the power plant. This costs money and uses energy. So the resulting emissions and economics dictate an optimal size for an exclusively biomass power station, although co-firing biomass in an existing coal-fired power station may be attractive.

Biomass can be gasified by heating it with steam and air, or via bioreactor cells and anaerobic digesters. Liquid fuels – methanol, ethanol and bio-diesel – can be produced from biomass, the last by pyrolysis (heating without oxygen). These can all be used in transport vehicles. Methanol burns more cleanly and efficiently than petroleum in internal combustion engines. It can also be used in fuel cells to generate electricity, including those in electric vehicles. Ethanol is also used in car engines, in varying proportions mixed with gasoline.[104]

The sequestering of carbon in the soil after pyrolysis of biomass effectively reduces CO_2 concentration in the atmosphere and thus provides a way of bringing CO_2 concentrations down from some peak level to reach a safer level at some later date. We will discuss this further in the section on carbon capture and sequestration.

An integrated pilot plant was set up in Western Australia to use native 'mallee' eucalyptus trees to reduce soil salinity, crush their leaves to produce eucalyptus oil, burn them for electric power production, and produce activated charcoal for use in water filters. As of 2006 Verve Energy pronounced it a success and was planning to build a commercial scale plant.[105]

First generation biomass plants utilise the sugars and starches in grains such as corn, but not the cellulosic material, which can still be fed to stock. Second generation plants will digest the cellulosic material and can therefore use much more plentiful biomass that may not compete with food supplies, especially if it uses more marginal land. Use of indigenous plant species may provide or preserve native habitat for conservation purposes and avoid the introduction of potentially invasive weed species, although some non-indigenous species may be more economically efficient if the native ecology is not valued.

The increased use of water and fertilisers for economically efficient biomass production may present problems. In an increasingly water-scarce world (at least in many low- and mid-latitude countries) biomass production may compete with increasing population and water demand for scarce supplies, while fertiliser use will reduce the energy gains from biomass production and risk pollution. These are further arguments for the utilisation primarily of marginal land with native vegetation better adapted to the local conditions.[106]

A much discussed problem with biomass for fuel is that it may force up the price of food such as corn if there is a large demand for it as feedstock for biomass energy. This is however a complex argument. There has been strong criticism, particularly of the current rapidly expanding biomass industry in the US, and of EU plans to set a quota for biomass energy in Europe, on the grounds that it is taking over agricultural land and forcing up the price of corn and thus of corn-fed chicken and beef. This objection has been equally strongly denied by others on the grounds that the price of corn makes very little difference to the price of processed foods, less than the rapidly increasing price of oil that biomass fuel replaces. Some even argue that a higher price for first world grain would make it more economically attractive for developing country farmers to grow grain locally, thus empowering the poor.[107]

The Rabobank, in a 2008 report 'Grains and oilseeds – is it a new era for prices?' says rising prices are likely due to a combination of record low global inventories, weather-induced supply side shocks, surging outside investor interest, record oil prices and demand for oilseeds and corn for feedstock for biofuel. However, Jacques Diouf, Director-General of the Food and Agricultural Organization (FAO) of the United Nations, blamed the reported food shortages and high prices in 2007–2008 on steady migration of rural populations in developing countries into the cities (adversely affecting food production), adverse weather conditions (such as droughts in Australia and Kazakhstan and floods in India and Bangladesh), and increasing demand for milk and meat in India and China (increasing demand for stock feed). FAO data show faster price rises for rice and wheat that are not used for biomass energy, than for maize that is. The futures trade and the falling US dollar may also have had an influence.[108]

Marland and Obersteiner comment that scenarios of biomass energy production often confine production to excess agricultural lands but early experience suggests it will often compete for the most productive lands and thus will tend to increase food prices and scarcity. This implies that biomass energy production must be seen as part of a wider picture and policy devised to ensure that food production is not harmed.[109]

Brazil pioneered the use of ethanol from sugar-cane waste for automobiles in the 1970s. The industry has grown strongly in recent years in the United States, Europe, Africa and Asia, with total consumption, according to the International Energy Agency, of about 29 billion litres in 2003. However, this is still only about 1% of global transport fuel usage. In Brazil, gasoline supplies contain up to 25% ethanol, while India and China are both aiming at 10% blends. Ethanol is seen as the preferred substitute for the octane enhancer methyl-tertiary-butyl-ether (MTBE), and as a means of increasing the viability of many agricultural enterprises otherwise in need of subsidies. It also reduces reliance on imported oil. Tax breaks and other subsidies are being used to enhance use of ethanol. In 2001, the European Union established a goal of 20% biofuels for transport by 2020, but there are ongoing debates about its achievability and environmental concerns.[110]

The large-scale use of biomass ethanol in the United States has been mandated by Congress and President Bush, not only to reduce greenhouse gas emissions, but also to reduce American reliance on Middle Eastern oil. The current requirement is for the use of 9 billion gallons (1 US gallon equals 3.78 litres) of renewable fuel in the US in 2008, which is about 3%, with a doubling by 2012.

Projections made by Khosla Ventures, a major investor in renewable energy technology, is that total ethanol production in the US could increase to 16.5 billion gallons by 2012, 39.4 billion by 2017 and 139 billion by 2027, mainly from cellulosic stock rather than corn. This would be at a price estimated at around US$1.25 per gallon.[107]

Global estimates of land available for biomass production span a very wide range. Peter Read, an enthusiast for biomass energy and sequestration, quotes estimates of potential rain-fed arable land not yet used for reportable economic activity, net of protected land and urban settlement, of some 3.82 Gha (38.2 million square km) – some 1.99 Gha is in tropical countries and 0.38 Gha in temperate areas. This 'available' land is occupied by people with hunting and gathering, slash-and-burn agriculture or other subsistence lifestyles. He argues that they could lead better lives tending to biomass production while preserving their habitat. A key question is whether these people could be persuaded to adopt such a new lifestyle.[109]

A study by the US Natural Resources Defense Council finds that ethanol from corn in 2008 reduces global warming pollution on average by 18% for every gallon of gasoline displaced, although the best processing plants can achieve a 35% saving.[111] Ethanol from corn uses only the starch from the kernel, leaving the rest of the corn (largely protein) as stock feed. Ethanol produced from cellulosic material, on the other hand, can reduce carbon emissions by over 75%, but the process is not yet as commercially developed. Corn-based ethanol is thus seen by Read as creating the market which cellulosic ethanol will eventually fill with greater efficiency and at less environmental risk. Cellulosic stock comes from wood waste, grasses, and unused parts of grain crops. Other feedstock for ethanol and related liquid fuels include algae, industrial waste and even municipal waste. Third generation biofuels will likely be based on cultivated micro-organisms and may use less land.

An Australian study assessed the total life-cycle greenhouse gas emissions associated with 100% biodiesel from various feedstocks, compared with conventional low-sulfur diesel. It found that when the feedstock is canola the saving was 49%, from tallow it was 76%, used cooking oil 87%, palm oil from existing plantations 80%. However GHG emissions from palm oil sourced from cleared rain- or peat swamp forests are 8 to 21 times respectively greater than from fossil-fuel diesel, and of course have serious ecosystem implications also.[112]

The economics of biomass energy can be assisted by its generation and consumption in isolated communities where transmission costs would be high, and by any credits for its contribution to reducing climate change, and in some cases to reducing groundwater salinity. Large areas of degraded land, particularly from over-grazing, could be stabilised by biomass plantations, preferably with native plants suited to the region. Multi-purpose facilities such as installations producing activated carbon, vegetable oils and electricity are also possible. Many species of deep-rooted trees can be coppiced for fuel, that is, the above ground growth is harvested for fuel while the roots survive and grow new shoots. This can reduce waterlogging in wet areas, reduce dryland salinity, provide shelter for stock, reduce wind and water erosion, and increase biodiversity and aesthetic values.

Various other technologies are also promising, including gasification and pyrolysis of biomass including municipal waste, plasma technology and microbial production. A device has recently been demonstrated which produces electricity from human waste sewage, which could mean that sewage treatment will pay for itself.[113]

In summary, constraints on the use of biomass include the necessary balance between the production of food, fodder and energy, especially in a world with growing population and demand. Land availability is thus an issue, especially if further land clearing is to be avoided because of its effect on biodiversity and stored carbon. In dry areas the additional water used may also be an issue, especially in a warming climate that will place a premium on water supplies. Increased potential for wildfires, discussed in Chapter 6, may also be a problem, especially for large-scale biomass plantations. Maintaining biodiversity and an ability to resist widespread attack by diseases and pests may argue against large monoculture plantations. Diverse on-farm plantations, which provide shelter for crops and animals and protect watercourses, may be preferable. Sustainability may also require a return of trace nutrients to the soil, either from the residue from biomass consumption or from fertilisers.

Various studies and reports from the US Natural Resources Defense Council, the British Royal Society and a British House of Commons committee all welcome the use of biomass fuels but warn of the need for careful evaluation of any given process for its effect in saving greenhouse gas emissions over its full life-cycle, other environmental effects such as other pollutants and health issues, and its effect on land-use change and food supply, all at a global and regional scale.

Substitution of biomass products for energy-intensive material such as steel and aluminium may be achieved by the use of products such as laminated wood, bamboo and agricultural waste. At present the trend is rather the opposite, with greater use of steel and aluminium due to diminishing resources from old growth forests and the huge demand for wood pulp for making paper. Reduced usage of paper, perhaps through electronic communications (although this is not current experience), and increased recycling of paper would contribute greatly to freeing up wood products for other uses such as building, which would reduce carbon dioxide emissions.

Tidal and wave energy

Richard Carew in his *Survey of Cornwall* in 1602 wrote:

> *Amongst other commodities afforded by the sea, the inhabitants make use of divers his creekes for grist mills, by thwarting a banke from side to side, in which a floodgate is placed, with two leaves; these the flowing tide openeth, and, after full sea, the waight of the ebb closeth fast, which no other force can doe: and so the imprisoned water payeth the ransome of driving an under sheete [undershot] wheel for his enlargement.*[114]

The tide mill at Looe, Cornwall, was built between 1614 and 1621, possibly at the suggestion of Carew, and was still in practical use in the early twentieth century, when it was replaced by electricity.

As is the case today, such tide power installations required a large tidal range, but today tidal dams or barrages need to be built across much larger inlets or estuaries. A 240 MW tidal power station has been operating at La Rance in France since 1967. However, such installations can greatly affect the tidal ecosystems and there are not many suitable sites. Other sites under consideration are on the Severn Estuary in the UK, where a proposed barrage could provide 4.4% of the UK electricity supply (some 17 TW) at a capital cost of some UK£15 billion, but with a lifetime of over 120 years. In some cases co-benefits include road links and flood control, but capital costs are very large. Turbines would generate power on both the ebb and flow of the tides.[115]

Another refinement is a 'double basin' type where incoming tides top up a high basin and outgoing tides drain a low basin. With a channel connecting the two, there can be a constant flow of water from the high to low basins. It is also possible to use a tidal-powered pump to lift water to a high basin, allowing for constant power to be generated from the latter irrespective of the tidal cycle.

The major ecosystem effects of barrages can be avoided using turbines installed on the sea floor to capture power from the currents rather like windmills do on land. Although the speed of tidal or other ocean currents is generally less than that of the wind, the much higher density of water means that ocean currents can provide the same power with smaller turbines than the wind. A 300 kW experimental tidal current turbine is being installed off the coast of Devon in the UK, and others are operating experimentally at Hammerfest in Norway and in Shetland's Yell Sound.

In summarising the prospects for tidal power, a report from the World Energy Council in 2007 states that:

> *The high capital costs associated with tidal barrage systems are likely to restrict development of this resource in the near future. The developments that do proceed in the early 21st century will most likely be associated with road and rail crossings to maximise the economic benefit. There is, however, more interest in entrainment systems now than at any time in the past 20 years and it is increasingly likely that new barrage and lagoon developments will be seen, especially in those locations which offer combination with transport infrastructure ... tidal barrage schemes could prove to be a major provider of strategic energy in the late 21st century and beyond. The technology for tidal barrage systems is already available and there is no doubt, given the experience at La Rance, that the resource is substantial and available.*

The report went on to say:

> *Full-scale prototype tidal-current systems are now being deployed. If these schemes continue to prove successful, then the first truly commercial developments will appear in the first decade of the 21st century. Tidal-current systems may not yet have the strategic potential of barrage systems but, in the short term at least, they do offer opportunities for supplying energy in rural, coastal and island communities. In the longer term, massive sites such as the Pentland Firth could become strategically important.*[116]

Harnessing wave power is also possible, using oscillating air columns, or buoys to drive turbines, but is generally expensive and subject to damage by extreme wave conditions. Annual average wave-power density is between 20 kW per linear metre in many inshore areas to 60–70 kW per metre in the deep ocean. Capturing the latter would require expensive transmission of power generated to shore.

An Australian company has successfully tested a baseload wave power technology called CETO. It uses submerged floats that in response to below surface wave action operate pistons that pressurise seawater. This is then piped ashore to drive turbines or to produce desalinated water. It is estimated that with a 500-buoy system it can generate 100 MW of 24-hour baseload power. Other wave and tidal technologies are under consideration.[117]

Geothermal power[118]

Three forms of geothermal power are in use in many countries around the world:

- shallow mild temperature rocks or soil used for direct heat extraction in winter and for cooling in summer – more than two million ground-source heat pumps are in use in some 30 countries for building heating and cooling,

- high temperature rocks containing super-heated steam, usually in geodynamically active regions (volcanic regions or thermal springs and geysers) at depths less than 2 km, with temperature above about 250°C, used for direct electricity generation, and

- hot dry rocks, often at depths of one or more kilometres, where heat is extracted by pumping water through the rock layers (which may be naturally porous or have to be artificially fractured), turned into steam and used in electrical generators.

This heat comes from solar radiation near the surface, by conduction from the hot interior of the Earth or from decay of radioactivity in the rocks. It is a huge resource, for example it is estimated that in the United States the geothermal energy in the top 2 km of the Earth's crust could supply America's

power demands (at present rates) for the next 30 000 years.

According to the International Geothermal Association, total installed generating capacity in 25 countries in 2005 is estimated at 9.1 GWe in 2005, up from 5.8 GWe in 1990. President Olafur Grimsson of Iceland, in testimony to a US Senate committee in 2007 gave the total geothermal electrical production in 2005 as 56.8 thousand GWh, mostly from 10 countries: USA, the Philippines, Mexico, Indonesia, Italy, Japan, New Zealand, Iceland, Costa Rica and Kenya (in descending order). He also noted that direct thermal energy used from geothermal sources was in total greater than for electricity generation, being some 76 thousand GWh thermal, with China the largest user of thermal power. Grimsson believes that geothermal power is a great potential resource in many developing countries and that much more could be developed in the United States. Iceland is helping to fund a United Nations University Geothermal Training Program in Iceland.[119]

In Australia, some 32 geothermal energy companies have formed since 2002. Geodynamics Ltd is developing a large hot rocks resource in the Cooper Basin on the border of South Australia and Queensland. It is aiming at a 50 MW hot fractured rock (HFR) plant connected to the grid by 2012, more than 500 MW by 2016, and an eventual 10 000 MW – the equivalent of 10 to 15 coal-fired power stations. Initial costs are large, and a major new transmission system will be needed from the remote site, with possible HVDC links to Adelaide and Brisbane.[120]

Further south in the Flinders Ranges at Paralana, another company, Petratherm is also planning to have power online by 2010, initially to a nearby mine, but later to Port Augusta to supply 260 to 520 MW to the 'on-grid' market. Petratherm is also developing geothermal power in Spain.[121]

Australia's total hot rocks resources are likely to be comparable to its demonstrated reserves of coal and natural gas. The economic consultancy ACIL Tasman estimates the cost of HFR electricity at around AUS$45 per MWh, which is less than the cost of black coal electricity if there is a $30 per tonne price on carbon dioxide emissions (which seems likely under the proposed Australian carbon trading scheme). They mention projected work programs of AUS$851 million through 2011, and estimate installed geothermal capacity by 2020 of 1500 MW, generating some 10000 GWh of electricity.[122]

There is also an opportunity to develop complementary solar power stations connecting to the same new transmission lines through desert country with very high solar potential.

The hydrogen economy[123]

Hydrogen is not an energy source but an energy carrier like electricity. It can be generated by the use of fossil fuel, by renewable energy or by using nuclear power. It is of enormous interest because when it is burned to provide energy in a turbine or internal combustion engine, or used to produce electricity in a fuel cell, its only waste product is water. It is thus a clean fuel at its point of use, which is good if it means that mobile sources of carbon dioxide, such as internal combustion engines in cars and trucks can be eliminated. The crunch, though, is how hydrogen can be generated without the emission of carbon dioxide. If it is produced from fossil fuels it is not free from greenhouse gas emissions, or from local pollution at its point of production.

To achieve a reduction in greenhouse gas emissions, hydrogen must be generated without, or with significantly reduced, emission of carbon dioxide to the atmosphere. This means it must be generated by renewable energy, nuclear power, or from fossil fuels in a process in which the carbon dioxide is removed from the emissions and disposed of other than in the atmosphere. Production by 'reforming' methane in natural gas does release carbon dioxide, but less than burning coal. The process of the capture and long-term storage or 'sequestration' of carbon dioxide is discussed below. The most likely means of production of hydrogen are the reforming of natural gas, or the hydrolysis of water using electricity.

Hydrogen gas has a very low amount of energy per unit volume. Therefore, in order to store and transport hydrogen, it has to be compressed or otherwise contained at high density. This uses the equivalent of some 10% of its intrinsic energy. Pipelines exist in Europe and the US to transport hydrogen, but these use higher pressure than natural gas pipelines, which adds cost. However, at least in a transition phase to using mainly hydrogen, it can be mixed with natural gas and transported in natural gas pipelines. Also, the existence of natural gas pipelines means that easements already exist along which hydrogen pipelines could be built, so reducing costs. Alternatively, high-pressure linings could be inserted in natural gas pipelines.

Much effort is going into research on technologies to generate hydrogen and to use it as a fuel in automobiles either directly in an internal combustion engine or in a fuel cell.[124] United States' President Bush initiated a US$1.2 billion budget for a Hydrogen Fuel Initiative and the 'FreedomCAR Partnership' to foster an industry decision by 2015 to commercialise hydrogen-powered fuel cell vehicles.[125] Several car manufacturers, including General Motors, BMW and DaimlerChrysler are working on hydrogen-powered fuel cell car technology.[126]

The main focus in the US government program is on generating hydrogen from natural gas and coal to 'provide the transition to a hydrogen economy' with carbon sequestration to avoid 'adding to concerns over the build-up of carbon gases in the atmosphere'. A principal aim is to reduce the US's dependence on foreign oil.

In Australia, a team in the Commonwealth Scientific and Industrial Research Organisation (CSIRO) is also investigating technologies for a hydrogen economy.[127]

It has been argued, however, by Demirdoven and Deutch of the Massachusetts Institute of Technology that hybrid petrol-electric or natural gas-electric vehicles are as energy efficient as hydrogen-fuelled fuel cell cars, and are available now. If the hydrogen comes from fossil fuels without carbon capture and sequestration, then there is no carbon dioxide emissions advantage. They argue that more effort should go into improving, and developing the market for hybrid vehicles, perhaps with tax credits, with hydrogen-fuelled fuel cells later. This is supported by a 2003 American Physical Society report, and a book by Joseph Romm *Hype About Hydrogen*. Romm states: 'If your concern is global warming, hydrogen cars are not what you'll be doing for the next 30 years'.[128]

In Europe, the European Union and nine European cities joined together to carry out a practical trial of hydrogen fuel cell buses in the Clean Urban Transport For Europe project (CUTE). The cities of Amsterdam (Netherlands), Barcelona and Madrid (Spain), Hamburg and Stuttgart (Germany), London (UK), Porto (Portugal) and Stockholm (Sweden) each trialled three Mercedes-Benz Citaro fuel cell buses, with hydrogen production in each city via electrolysis of water or natural gas reformers, and high pressure refuelling stations. The trials were reported a success in 2006.[129]

Further demonstration projects are putting 200 hydrogen powered vehicles into daily operation throughout Europe, another 50 buses on three continents, 8 fuel cell cars in Frankfurt and Mantova, and 158 small transport vehicles (mini vans and buses, scooters, cargo bicycles and wheelchairs) in several European countries. The last are seen as a possible entry point into a market of millions of mini vehicles. If these technologies are made competitive they will reduce European dependence on imported oil, clean the air in the cities, and, depending on the source of the hydrogen, substantially reduce greenhouse gas emissions.

Shell Hydrogen, with various partners, is working on projects in Iceland, Washington DC and California (USA), and Tokyo (Japan) as well as the CUTE project. Shell states that it aims to move to green (or fully renewable) hydrogen as soon as possible.[130] The Icelandic government has announced its intention to transform Iceland into the world's first hydrogen-based economy by 2050, and is trialling hydrogen-powered buses made by DaimlerChrysler.[131] Another hydrogen-fuel cell bus experiment is under way in Perth, Western Australia, in collaboration with CUTE and BP.[132]

BP is now in partnership with Rio Tinto in a group called 'Hydrogen Energy'.

Hydrogen may be produced in future from biomass, including a small device that converts liquid ethanol into hydrogen, which is then used in a fuel cell. This device may be suitable for safe portable power supplies, including drives for automobiles.[133] The use of micro-algae or solar furnaces to split water into hydrogen and oxygen is being developed at the French laboratories CNRS.[134]

Two reviews list many other initiatives on the way to a hydrogen economy,[135] and another in *Scientific American* by a group in the US Department of Energy discusses methods for storing hydrogen.[136]

There are some potential concerns about the widespread use of hydrogen. One is safety, hydrogen being an odourless gas that burns with an invisible flame, although it must be in a higher concentration with air (more than 13%) than methane before it can cause an explosion. Another is the leakage of hydrogen into the atmosphere. If it gets into the upper atmosphere it could react with hydroxyl (OH) radicals to form water vapour, adversely affecting the climate and the ozone layer, while even in the lower atmosphere its reaction with hydroxyl radicals may allow methane to last longer, thus adding to the greenhouse effect. The result will depend on how large the leakage of hydrogen is, and on natural sinks for hydrogen in the soil. The sinks are not well known, and estimates of possible leakage vary from 10 to 20% down to about 0.1%. Knowledge of these problems may lead to ways of avoiding them. Such concerns are dismissed as exaggerated in several publications of the Rocky Mountain Institute.[137]

Estimates of potential progress in moving to a hydrogen economy by mid-century vary wildly, but it is possible, according to the Rocky Mountain Institute, that it may account for 25–50% of transport fuel use in the United States by 2050. However, a 2004 review in *Science* entitled 'The hydrogen backlash' states: 'By focusing research on technologies that aren't likely to have a measurable impact until the second half of the century, the current hydrogen push fails to address the growing threat from greenhouse gas emissions from fossil fuels'.[138]

This reflects the views of some notable critics of the focus on a hydrogen economy, such as Ulf Bossel, a prominent consultant on fuel cell technology. They base their concern mainly on the physical nature of hydrogen as the lightest gas, which requires the use of significant amounts of energy for its packaging, storage, delivery and transfer as an energy carrier. They compare this unfavourably with the use of electricity or methane as carriers of energy. For example, they cite volumetric heating values for hydrogen at one atmosphere pressure and 25°C of about 11 kJ/litre, compared to methane at about 35 kJ/litre. This means that hydrogen must be highly compressed, liquefied or stored in hydrates, or transported in high-pressure pipelines. All of which consumes energy. They therefore oppose a 'pure-hydrogen-only-economy', preferring either electricity as a carrier of energy, or else a hydrocarbon such as methane. Where hydrogen is generated by renewable energy, they favour its use at source, either for local heating or to generate electricity. Elliasson, Bossel and Taylor state:

> ... *hydrogen generated by electrolysis may be the best link between – mostly physical – energy from renewable sources and chemical energy. It is also the ideal fuel for modern clean energy conversion devices like fuel cells and can be used in modified IC* [internal combustion] *engines. But hydrogen is far from ideal for carrying energy between primary sources to distant or mobile end users.*[139]

Bossel and colleagues prefer a 'synthetic liquid hydrocarbon economy' based on biomass distillation or fermentation.

Provided, however, hydrogen is generated from renewable sources, such as solar powered electrolysis, and is also used for powering its compression at source, loss of overall energy efficiency may be acceptable to avoid carbon dioxide emissions. This is especially so if, as Amory Lovins argues, priority is given to developing light

weight and highly efficient vehicles and hydrogen is generated locally in a highly distributed system.

An alternative to using hydrogen or methane is to use ammonia in fuel cells. While ammonia is hazardous, this is not an insuperable obstacle, and it liquefies at room temperatures and only eight atmospheres pressure so it is readily transported in vehicles. Use in a fuel cell generates electricity with only nitrogen and water as waste products, and industrial production of ammonia is a well established process.[140]

Hydrogen fuel cells can of course be used in a stationary situation, and indeed may be part of a distributed power system where hydrogen is generated by electrolysis from intermittent renewable sources such as wind, solar or tidal power and stored for later use. This could be part of a distributed power system as advocated by WWF.[141]

Carbon capture and sequestration[142]

While increased energy efficiency and more non-fossil fuel energy both have the potential to decrease carbon dioxide emissions significantly over the next several decades, these are widely believed in government and conventional business (but not by many advocating renewables) to be insufficient to avoid likely damaging climate change, especially with rapid economic growth in major developing countries such as India and China. An additional means to reduce emissions is to capture carbon dioxide at large point sources such as coal-, oil- or gas-fired power stations, and cement plants, and keep it out of the atmosphere. This is called carbon capture and sequestration (CCS). The goal is to produce energy from fossil fuels free of carbon dioxide emissions, at an affordable cost.[143]

The International Energy Agency has established a Greenhouse Gas R&D Programme to 'identify and evaluate technologies for reducing emissions of greenhouse gases arising from the use of fossil fuels' and issues reports and a newsletter.[144] Australia, as a leading coal exporter, has a strong interest in CO_2 sequestration.[145]

Storage of carbon in the subsurface involves introduction of CO_2, at sufficiently high pressure that it becomes liquid, into porous rock formations beneath the surface of the Earth, typically at depths of 1000 to 4000 metres (where it will stay in liquid form and take up much less volume). Although CO_2 is a relatively benign substance, the volume being considered is large. If developed to its envisaged potential, geologic sequestration will entail the pumping of CO_2 into the ground at roughly the rate we are extracting petroleum today. To have the desired impact on the atmospheric carbon budget, CO_2 must be efficiently retained underground for hundreds of years.

When foreign materials are emplaced in subsurface rock formations they change the chemical and physical environment. Understanding and predicting these changes are essential for determining how the subsurface will perform as a storage container. For example, some depleted oil and gas reservoirs in the United States and the Middle East which might be candidates for storage were originally found because of seepages at the surface. Also particular sequestration sites may have hundreds of oil or gas wells drilled in them which have been plugged with cement. These may be corroded over time, especially by acidified groundwater due to dissolved carbon dioxide.

Only proven extremely secure sites can be used for long-term storage. It is estimated that average leakage rates of less than 0.1 to 1% per annum might be attainable and acceptable, although any leakage is undesirable and would need careful monitoring.[146]

Another option for storage of carbon dioxide may be in deep sea sediments, which accumulate in presently stable low-current areas. These sediments are cold and at high pressure ensuring that the carbon dioxide would remain liquid. Such stores may be additionally protected by the formation of crystalline carbon dioxide hydrates.[147] However, with climate change deep ocean currents might change, disturbing such sediments.

The specific scientific issues that underlie sequestration technology involve the effects of fluid flow combined with chemical, thermal, mechanical, and biological interactions between fluids and surrounding geologic formations. Complex and coupled interactions occur both *rapidly* as the stored material is emplaced underground, and *gradually* over hundreds to thousands of years. The long sequestration times needed for effective storage and the intrinsic spatial variability of subsurface formations provide challenges to both geoscientists and engineers. A fundamental understanding of mineralogical and geochemical processes is integral to this success.

The possibility of carbon capture and sequestration from biomass fuels is of great interest, and is discussed separately in the next section, on land-based carbon sinks. This would not merely result in zero emissions, but would actually remove carbon dioxide from the atmosphere. This will be necessary to return atmospheric concentrations of carbon dioxide to values less than the maximum at stabilisation, as represented in **Figure 27**. As we have seen, the risk of dangerous interference in the climate system remains appreciable even at stabilisation levels of 450 ppm, especially if the global climate sensitivity is not at the low end of the IPCC estimated range (as the latest results suggest) and ice sheets become dynamically unstable at global warmings of 1–3°C as occurred in the geological past and seems to be occurring now. Efforts will therefore be needed to reduce carbon dioxide emissions to near zero or even below zero, in order to bring the carbon dioxide concentration down in as short a time as possible.

Another possibility is to cause captured CO_2 to react with minerals, by a carbonation process, to produce a stable solid (for example, magnesium or calcium carbonate) that can be safely stored. This would be leakage free and have large capacity, but according to a 2008 review it would cost about US$50 per tonne of CO_2.[148]

The need for carbon removal and sequestration is recognised in the IPCC *Special Report on Carbon Capture and Storage* in 2005 and in the 2007 IPCC report, although only as part of a portfolio of measures. After discussing other measures including advanced nuclear, advanced coal and gas and renewables, the 2007 report states

(WGIII, p. 254): 'Other technologies such as CCS, second-generation biofuels, concentrated solar power, ocean energy and biomass gasification, may make additional contributions in due course'. However, it makes clear that if you want to continue to use fossil fuels in a big way, carbon dioxide removal and storage is essential.

In general, carbon sequestration possibilities include underground or geological storage, injection into the deep ocean, mineralisation, biological sequestration in the oceans spurred on by iron fertilisation, and biological sequestration on land. Options for underground or geological disposal include:

- use of carbon dioxide in enhanced oil recovery,

- use of carbon dioxide in enhanced coal-bed methane recovery,

- depleted oil and gas reservoirs,

- deep un-mineable coal beds,

- large cavities or voids, and

- deep saline water-saturated reservoirs.

Removal of carbon dioxide from post-combustion fumes uses either a membrane that allows only the carbon dioxide to pass through it, or amine solvents to scrub flue gases (although other methods may be possible in future). Amine is heated to release the pure carbon dioxide and is then re-used. However, low concentrations of carbon dioxide in the power station flue gases means that large volumes have to be treated, requiring large equipment and large amounts of energy to generate the solvent, all of which is expensive. Pre-combustion capture avoids some of these problems, but requires the use of hydrogen as the carrier of energy. Steam reforming of natural gas produces carbon dioxide and hydrogen. The carbon dioxide is then separated from the hydrogen. Hydrogen can also be produced from oil, coal or biomass and the carbon dioxide removed similarly. Only in the case of biomass does this result in a net removal of carbon dioxide from the air.

Importantly, IPCC 2007 points out that available carbon capture technology captures only some 85–95% of the CO_2 generated in power plants, and the CCS process requires roughly 10–40% more energy than a non-CCS plant, mostly for capture and compression of the CO_2. Taking middle estimates of 90% capture requiring 25% more energy, a power plant equipped with CCS would produce about 12.5% of the emissions of a non-CCS plant. Thus every eight new CCS-equipped plants would be equivalent in terms of non-captured emissions to one new non-CCS plant. So an increase in electricity generating capacity using CCS would not be totally 'clean' and would still add significantly to global emissions. Long distance transport of captured CO_2 to sequestration sites, and the possibility of leakage along the way, would further add to these emissions.

Retro-fitting old coal-fired power stations with CCS would be the only way to actually reduce total CO_2 emissions, but this is generally more expensive and less effective than new power stations purpose-built for maximum efficiency. Retro-fitting is unlikely to happen without strong incentives such as a high price on carbon emissions and no 'grand-fathering' (that is, no free emissions permits to industries based on past emissions). The IPCC Special Report states that: 'Industrial sources of CO_2 can be more easily retrofitted with CO_2 sequestration, while integrated power plant systems would need profound adjustment. In order to reduce future retrofit costs, new plant designs could take future CCS application into account'. It is arguable that this should be the minimum requirement for any new coal-fired power station not only in the public interest, but in the future interest of the investor.

According to the IPCC WGIII report (Chapter 4.3.5) global storage capacities in geological formations are uncertain, but could be up to several thousand $GtCO_2$. This compares with present global emissions of about 8 GtC per annum and IPCC SRES projections of total emissions by 2100 in the range 770 to 2540 Gt of carbon (with extrapolations from the present rate of increase in emissions following the highest estimates). So storage capacity per se is not likely to be a limit on carbon sequestration provided the storages have long-term security from leakage, and it is economical to use them.

However the IPCC 2005 *Special Report on Carbon Capture and Storage* says (SPM, p. 9) that 'by 2050, given expected technical limitations, around 20–40% of global fossil fuel CO_2 emissions could be technically suitable for capture, including 30–60% of the CO_2 emissions from electricity generation and 30–40% of those from industry'. This is not so optimistic. It is also notable that if there were a 0.5% leakage rate from these storages, it could by 2100 amount to 10 $GtCO_2$ per annum under a fossil-fuel dependent scenario, or more than the present rate of emissions. Add to that the 5–15% of CO_2 not captured, and there is a real problem that underlines the IPCC view that CCS is only a small part of the solution to reducing emissions.

This view is widely supported. For example, John Marburger, President Bush's science advisor, told a meeting of the American Geophysical Union in December 2007, that the world's 'stunningly large fossil-fuel consumption numbers' and roughly 27 billion tons of carbon dioxide released annually 'create barriers for any carbon extraction and sequestration scheme'. He pointed out that even if geological storage is an unqualified success, it will be expensive to adopt.[149]

Deborah Adams, states that: 'Technology aside, CCS will stand or fall on the price of carbon ... In the absence of a regulatory reward for geologically storing CO_2, the incentive to invest in such projects is far from obvious. Even if such a reward is granted, it relies on a positive carbon price to provide a positive rate of return'. Stefan Bakker and colleagues, in their report for The Climate Group, state that: 'Modelling studies suggest that a carbon price in the order of US$30 per tonne of CO_2 would be required before CCS becomes a viable option ... However, in the short and intermediate term the CO_2 market price may need to be as high as $60–$100 per tonne of CO_2 in view of the financial and technological risks still related to CCS, and the volatility of the CO_2 price'.[150]

Costs of CCS from fossil fuels will make them less competitive with other low emissions technologies including renewables such as wind and solar, especially as the costs of the latter are falling rapidly with new developments and increasing scale.

Estimates of additional costs for CCS vary with techniques and distance from source to storage area. They range, according to the 2005 IPCC Special Report, from 1 to 5 US cents per kWh. This cost may be reduced with improved technology, and might be reduced by 1 or 2 US cents where the sequestered carbon dioxide is used to enhance oil or coal-bed methane recovery. Enhanced oil and gas recovery using CO_2 is already in operation in several oil and gas fields.

Injection of carbon dioxide into the deep ocean in liquid form has been proposed. In principle, a large fraction of the carbon in known and recoverable reserves of fossil fuels could be stored in the oceans and calcareous ocean sediments. It would be pumped to a depth of 1000 metres or so, and there it would dissolve into the water. If sites were well chosen, this water would normally stay at depth for 1000 years or so, but it would change the chemistry of the deep ocean, including a slight reduction in pH, or increase in acidity. This could harm local sea life. Most deep-sea organisms are highly sensitive to small changes in water acidity, even as small as 0.2 to 0.5 units of pH.[151] Deposition at depths below 3000 m where CO_2 is denser than water, would allow it to form a 'lake' that would delay dissolution in the water.

However, although an amendment was added in 2006 to the London Convention on the prevention of marine pollution by dumping of wastes, allowing storage of carbon dioxide under the sea bed in geological formations, it does not allow injection into the oceans themselves.[152] Injection of carbon dioxide into the waters thus remains unlawful. In addition, verification of any emission reduction under the UNFCCC would depend on satisfying concerns about permanence, with respect to leakage and security. Moreover, these ocean 'dumping' techniques are likely to be opposed by the public, according to a survey conducted by the Tyndall

Centre for Climate Change Research in the UK in 2001, on the grounds of possible biological impacts and doubts about the permanence of carbon storage in the oceans.[153]

Another controversial technique is to fertilise the ocean surface with iron, since low iron concentrations are known to limit biological productivity in some parts of the ocean. Several experiments have tested this in a limited way, and some commercial groups are interested in fertilisation of the ocean to increase fisheries production. Adding iron in iron-poor regions of the oceans has caused algal blooms detectable from satellites, and this may indeed remove some carbon dioxide from the atmosphere. However, such algal blooms may cause undesirable changes in the ocean by reducing oxygen levels in the water, encouraging bacteria that may produce other greenhouse gases such as methane and nitrous oxide, possibly causing toxicity and altering the food chain. See later discussion in the section on geoengineering.

Experimental carbon geosequestration projects are under way in several countries including the UK, US, Australia, Canada and Japan. In most cases they are joint government and fossil fuel company projects subsidised by government funding. Key questions to be answered include their ability to handle large volumes, costs, safety, permanence and percentage of CO_2 actually captured.

Clearly governments and the fossil fuel industries are hopeful on all these points, as they are investing many millions of dollars in research and development.[154] However, some environmental groups and advocates of renewable energy argue that the cost of carbon capture and geosequestration will likely make the cost of fossil fuel energy greater than that of many renewables, and that in the meantime funding is being diverted from research, development and installation of renewable power. They argue that CCS is at best a temporary solution until renewables can take up the slack, and that investment in CCS research and development is in effect a delaying tactic allowing the continuation of the use of fossil fuels. The urgency of reducing emissions is also a growing issue, with CCS on a large scale unlikely within the next decade, as opposed to some proven renewables such as wind and solar that could be scaled up faster.[155]

Another possible contribution to CCS would be the use of a 'green' cement. Cement is usually made by heating limestone (calcium carbonate) until it breaks down into calcium oxide and CO_2 and then using the former to make cement. Cement manufacture at present contributes about 5% to global emissions of CO_2. One alternative is to use fly ash and slag from iron production. Another is to use captured CO_2 from power generation, passing it through seawater, in which carbonic acid is formed, which reacts with dissolved calcium or magnesium to make a calcium or magnesium carbonate, similar to marine coral material. The latter has the added advantage of removing calcium and magnesium from the seawater, making it easier to desalinate for water supplies. The seawater process is claimed to turn waste CO_2 into useful cement, which safely sequesters the CO_2 in buildings or roads.[156]

In summary, CCS is not yet proven at a commercial scale, and will not provide fully emissions-free power, due to less than 100% capture of CO_2. If and when it is developed it may provide a temporary bridge to a non-fossil-fuelled future when emission-free technologies are fully scaled up. Meanwhile, the most active policy question is whether new fossil-fuelled power stations should be permitted without CCS, or at least without a capacity for easy retro-fitting of CCS when it becomes available. Hopefully, if and when new power stations with CCS are built, they will be accompanied by the phasing out of old and less efficient power stations, thereby resulting in a net reduction in emissions.[157]

Land-based carbon sinks[158]

Agriculture and forestry have usually been seen as sources of carbon and other greenhouse gases due to the energy and fertilisers applied to their management and the large areas of land clearing that is destroying standing stock of carbon in vegetation and soils. Agriculture, agroforestry and bio-energy crops occupy some 40–50% of the Earth's land surface. In 2005 agriculture accounted for some 10–12% of global greenhouse gas emissions, including some 60% of nitrous oxide (from fertilisers) and 50% of methane (mainly from animals and anoxic decay of vegetable matter).

Increasing population and dietary changes (especially the greater consumption of milk and meat) mean that more land is being cleared, especially in developing countries where population growth is greatest. Forests are being cleared to make way for food and energy crops and harvested unsustainably for timber. Such societal trends seriously increase greenhouse gas emissions and mitigate against policies for sustainable development, especially if climate change and development lead to deterioration in soils and greater land clearing.

Biological sequestration on land is facilitated through better management of existing forests to safeguard and increase carbon stored in trees and soil, farm-scale or large-scale tree plantations, and farm management practices such as minimum tillage, which increase carbon stored in the soil. The IPCC 2007 report estimated that the global technical mitigation potential from agriculture by 2030, excluding offsets from biomass energy production, could be in the range of 5 or 6 Gt CO_2-equivalent per year, with about 90% being from sequestration of carbon in the soils. Only about 10% comes from reducing methane and nitrous oxide emissions. Actual future sequestration levels would be higher for larger carbon emission prices, as this makes sequestration more economic. Higher carbon prices lead to more land-use changes such as re-forestation and costly animal feed-based mitigation options.

Deforestation in the 1990s occurred mainly in the tropics and is estimated at about 6 Gt CO_2 per year. Expansion of forests and accumulation of woody biomass in temperate and high latitudes has offset some of the tropical deforestation, but estimates are uncertain, and there is some evidence that increasing drought and heat stress, with forest fires, may be reducing these gains.

IPCC 2007 gives estimates of economic potential for forestry mitigation for carbon costs up to US$100 per tonne of CO_2-equivalent, in the wide range of 1.3 to 13.8 Gt per year, with 'top-down' global estimates tending to be larger than more detailed regional estimates. Reducing deforestation is the largest short-term means to reduce emissions from the forestry sector, with loss of forest area between 2000 and 2005 estimated at 7.3 million ha per annum. This would significantly slow down the present increase in climate change forcing.

Biomass growth rates, and thus carbon storage, will rise with increasing atmospheric carbon dioxide due to fertilisation effects, but field studies with increased CO_2 concentrations suggest that this does not increase total storage in mature forests. Thus, even with a stop to deforestation and increased forestry plantations, the capacity to store more carbon will decrease as forests reach maturity and decay starts to match growth.

This decline may well be accentuated as global warming increases, and forests and soils change from sinks to sources of atmospheric carbon due to increased decay, forest die-back, changes in species competition and the danger of increased wildfires.[159] Fire protection, cessation of land clearing, and continuation of minimum tillage practices are essential to maintaining a biological carbon store. If plantations are to act effectively as permanent carbon stores, any harvesting of mature timber or other biomass generated must be used to replace fossil fuel emissions through biomass energy, to substitute for energy-intensive materials such as steel or aluminium, or for long-lasting timber such as in furniture or buildings. Verification of actual amounts of carbon permanently stored would be difficult and contentious.[160]

Other considerations regarding large forest plantations are their effect on the albedo or reflectivity of the Earth's surface to solar radiation. Forests in general absorb more sunlight than bare soil or grassland. Additional forests will therefore lead to additional warming, either locally or downwind due to the transport of latent heat from the increased evapotranspiration by the trees. This radiation absorption effect may go some way to cancelling out the effect of plantations in removing carbon dioxide from the atmosphere.[161] In addition, plantations tend to use more water than bare soil or grasslands, which will reduce runoff and thus water supplies. Especially in regions where water supply problems may be aggravated by climate change, this may be critical for dependent local communities.

The conventional view is thus that increased carbon stored in managed land ecosystems can only partly offset fossil fuel usage, and must be considered as a partial delaying mechanism until other mitigation measures take over. Moreover, consideration must be given to destruction of soil carbon content by any large-scale clearing for plantations, especially if accompanied by burning of trash, as is often done.

Plantations also tend to displace existing farming activities and people dependent on them. This is already the cause for opposition to plantations in some rural areas of Australia, and in some developing countries where large numbers of people may lose their livelihoods. Trees, however, may reduce dryland salinity, decrease soil erosion and in some cases increase local income. All in all, plantation forestry needs to be considered on a case-by-case basis, taking into account a complex web of factors.[162]

The UK Royal Society in a special report in 2001 summed up the conventional view of the role of land carbon sinks in mitigating global climate change in its final statement:

> ... our current knowledge indicates that the potential to enhance the land carbon sink through changes in land management practices is finite in size and duration. The amount of carbon that can be sequestered in these sinks is small in comparison to the ever-increasing global emissions of greenhouse gases. Projects designed to enhance carbon sinks must therefore not be allowed to divert financial and political resources away from the restructuring of energy generation and use (e.g. increased use of renewable energy), technological innovation (e.g. increased fuel efficiency, sequestration at source) and technology transfer to less developed countries. It is these that must provide the ultimate solution to the problem of reducing the concentration of greenhouse gases in the atmosphere.[163]

Contrary to this conventional view, recent publications argue for 'biosphere carbon stock management', with a large contribution from biomass energy production to substitute for fossil fuels, and the capture and sequestration of carbon from biomass. Estimates suggest that very large areas of land are potentially available and that these could be used to remove carbon from the atmosphere in large quantities, allowing carbon dioxide concentrations in the atmosphere to be not simply stabilised but reduced, thus enabling 'overshoot' scenarios for greenhouse gas emissions, discussed in the section above on targets, to be realised.[164]

Peter Read, in an editorial in *Climatic Change* in 2008, argues that, as part of the annual cycle of growth and decay, the terrestrial biosphere currently fixes six times as much carbon out of the atmosphere as is emitted into the atmosphere by human agency (although this amount is returned to the atmosphere by subsequent decay). He argues that we need to store this biospheric-fixed carbon in:

- growing forests,

- CO_2 capture and sequestration post-combustion,

- stable carbon biochar (charcoal produced in pyrolysis along with bio-oils) that can be stocked in the soil, and

- use of biomass in buildings and other long-lived structures.[164]

As discussed in the biomass energy section above, estimates of land available for such activities are large, but much of this land is occupied by people who practise hunting and gathering or slash-and-burn agriculture, and they will need to be convinced that it is beneficial. The essential gain in Read's argument is recognition of the need for and practicality of large-scale carbon capture and sequestration from biomass, allowing biomass to effectively pump CO_2 out of the atmosphere.

Christian Azar and colleagues have studied the costs and conversion efficiency of generating heat, electricity and hydrogen fuel from biomass energy with CO_2 capture and storage (BECS). They found that BECS would reduce overall costs of meeting low CO_2 stabilisation levels (350 or 450 ppm CO_2-equivalent) by tens of per cent.[165]

Long-lived or recalcitrant soil carbon stores exist naturally and can be enhanced by human management. Carbon in some soils (termed terra preta) have been found in the Amazon Basin to have remained stable for thousands of years. Such soils can be created by modified cultivation practices and provide additional benefits to farmers in terms of additional water-holding capacity and nutrient uptake efficiency. Leake in the same issue of *Climatic Change* estimates that wide uptake of bio-sequestration on arable lands could result in the uptake of some 190 Gt of carbon over 30 years. Lehmann and others estimate that biochar produced as a by-product of pyrolysis of biomass for biofuel production could improve soils and at the same time sequester as much carbon in 2100 as is currently emitted annually from fossil fuels.[166]

Another possibility is the use of, and preferential breeding of, crops that while being used for food, lock up large amounts of carbon in so-called plant stones or phytoliths. These are small balls of silica that form around a plant's cells as they take the mineral up from the soil. They trap some plant material and are very long-lasting so they sequester carbon. Some varieties of wheat, sorghum and sugar cane grow lots of phytoliths and so store lots of carbon in the soil.[167]

Geoengineering possibilities[168]

Geoengineering is loosely defined in the climate change context as ways of controlling or changing the climate so as to achieve a desired climatic state. This is in contrast to the uncontrolled experiment presently under way of changing the climate through the uncontrolled emission of greenhouse gases, principally carbon dioxide, over a few centuries, from fossil fuels laid down over millions of years. Here we will discuss two prominent proposals, one to reduce sunlight reaching the Earth's surface by reflecting it back into space via particles or mirrors placed in the upper atmosphere or space above the Earth, and the other to sequester large quantities of carbon dioxide in the oceans via fertilisation of the ocean to enhance biological capture of CO_2.[169] Control via planting forests or carbon capture and sequestration have already been covered under separate headings.

As stated in the IPCC 2007 report, these options tend to be speculative, many of their possible side effects have yet to be properly assessed, detailed cost estimates are not available, and they face problems of regulation, control and general acceptance. In short, they are controversial and may lead to serious international conflict, as they may be performed unilaterally with unknown effects on other countries that may have different preferences for climate or much higher aversion to the risk of uncertain outcomes.

The main attraction of geoengineering is that it may be cheap compared with the feared difficulties and large costs of reducing greenhouse gas emissions. This is largely denied by the IPCC and many enthusiasts for emission reductions through energy efficiency, renewables and nuclear or 'clean-coal' technology. Geoengineering may also, in the minds of some of its supporters, avoid deviation from 'business-as-usual' growth scenarios or changes in lifestyles. Most scientists who advocate consideration of geoengineering options do so with reluctance, because they have little faith that humans can in fact do the safer thing and act to reduce greenhouse emissions in time to avoid dangerous climate change and sea-level rise. They see geoengineering as a fall-back position in the face of imminent climatic disaster. However, the act of discussing and refining geoengineering schemes tends to provide an escape route for those who want to avoid the need to reduce greenhouse emissions, and may thus become a self-fulfilling prophecy.

Advocates of geoengineering schemes demonstrate a combination of pessimism when it comes to the technology of reducing emissions, and optimism when it comes to the technology of climate control. They are also pessimistic about the human ability to change lifestyles and technology of everyday living, but are optimistic about human readiness to accept unilateral global experiments with climate control without serious disagreement and conflict.

The US joint academies, in the report 'Greenhouse warming: mitigation, adaptation and the science base' in 1992 seriously considered geoengineering. The report commented:

> Our current inadvertent project in 'geoengineering' involves great uncertainty and great risk. Engineered countermeasures need to be evaluated but should not be implemented without broad understanding of the direct effects and potential side effects, the ethical issues, and the risks. Some do have the merit of being within the range of current short-term experience, and others could be 'turned off' if unintended effects occur.[170]

In 1996 a special section on geoengineering, edited by Gregg Marland of Oak Ridge National Laboratory was included in the journal *Climatic Change*. It was based on a special session of the 1994 annual meeting of the American Association for the Advancement of Science which heard ten papers on the subject. Several of these were published elsewhere. Marland pointed to the 'could we' and the 'should we' questions, and commented that:

> On the one hand, it [geoengineering] would allow more freedom to choose moderate response strategies when the consequences of climate change are uncertain, but, on the other hand, it might weaken the resolve needed for a substantive, preventative strategy in case the consequences of climate change turn out to be severe.[171]

Ten years further on, *Climatic Change* again published a group of papers on the subject, led by Paul Crutzen, the Nobel Prize winning atmospheric chemist. He put forward an assessment of the idea of increasing the Earth's albedo or reflectivity by injecting sunlight-reflecting aerosols into the upper atmosphere. He saw precedents both in pollution aerosols in the lower atmosphere from burning fossil fuels rich in sulfur, and in injections of sulfate aerosols into the upper atmosphere from major volcanic eruptions. He used both these precedents to scale up and estimate the amount that needed to be injected to counteract the enhanced greenhouse effect, and found it was not prohibitive. He also reckoned that if the experiment were to go wrong it could be stopped and the Earth would recover within a few years. He commented:

> If sizeable reductions in greenhouse gas emissions will not happen and temperatures rise rapidly, then climatic engineering, such as presented here, is the only option available to rapidly reduce temperature rises and counteract other climatic effects. Such a modification could also be stopped on short notice, if undesirable and unforeseen side effects become apparent, which would allow the atmosphere to return to its prior state within a few years. There is, therefore, a strong need to estimate negative, as well as positive, side effects of the proposed stratospheric modification schemes. If positive effects are greater than the negative effects, serious consideration should be given to the albedo modification scheme.[172]

Crutzen added: 'Importantly, [geoengineering schemes] should not be used to justify inadequate climate policies, but merely to create a possibility to combat potential drastic climate heating …'.

The problem with that argument in 2008 is that potential drastic heating and other climatic effects now look to be much more likely than they did even in 2006. Therefore drastic climate mitigation policies are needed, such as large reductions in greenhouse gas emissions. The crucial question then, is whether there are serious negative side effects of the geoengineering proposals.

The most obvious negative effect of the albedo modification schemes is that they do nothing to reduce acidification of the oceans, and indeed may add to it by producing acid rain from the added sulfate injected into the atmosphere, and by reducing the incentive to reduce carbon dioxide emissions. Ocean acidification will affect ocean ecosystems and therefore food supplies, lead to the death of coral reefs and thus expose coasts to greater storm surge and wave action, and may have other as yet poorly determined effects. However, Tom Wigley argues that a modest amount of geoengineering can buy time for reducing carbon dioxide emissions later, and that the latter would deal with the ocean acidification problem (if the delay is not too long).

Other negative effects will arise from changes in stratospheric temperatures and thus in atmospheric circulation, and other circulation changes such as changes to the monsoons and rainfall systems. Stratospheric ozone, which filters out dangerous ultraviolet radiation, may be destroyed and the reduction in direct solar radiation at the Earth's surface would cause a relatively large decrease in the efficiency of solar power stations, making reduction in emissions even harder.[173]

One recent paper by Kevin Trenberth and Aiguo Dai found that after the Mount Pinatubo volcanic eruption, used as an analogue of geoengineering, there was a substantial decrease in rainfall over land, and a record decrease in runoff and river discharge for 925 of the world's largest rivers.[174] Another paper modelled the effects of a sudden cessation of aerosol injections following continued emissions of CO_2. They found that with more CO_2 accumulated, the full effect of the now greatly enhanced greenhouse effect suddenly appeared. This suggests that once embarked on such a geoengineering fix, any interruption or failure would lead to drastic global consequences. There would be no danger-free way out and future generations would be obliged to maintain a continuous fail-safe geoengineering service.[175]

Such objections would also apply to other schemes to reduce sunlight striking the Earth, such as mirrors in space, which have been seriously suggested but which would be far more expensive.

A variation on the aerosol injection idea is to focus only on the Arctic, with aerosol injections

only at high northern latitudes, in order to enhance the sea-ice cover and stabilise the Greenland Ice Sheet. This would cool the whole Earth by increasing its albedo, thus reducing the total sunlight absorbed, although the Arctic would be most severely affected.[176] However, it is likely that this could be unacceptable to Russia and Canada, who in fact stand to gain initially from a slightly warmer world, especially from the opening up of the Arctic Ocean to shipping and resource exploitation. It would also cause impacts, good or bad, over a far wider area than the Arctic.

There is also a suggestion that specially built ships could spray seawater into the lower atmosphere to increase marine stratus cloud albedo in suitable regions.[177]

Another minor contender for albedo modification is making roofs of buildings or paved areas more reflective of sunlight. Hamwey has explored this possibility, but the surface area required to reflect enough sunlight back into space is very large, and many of the most sunny land areas are already deserts with low albedos. Nevertheless, reflective roofs would reduce solar heating of buildings in summer and thus reduce the energy needed for air conditioning, but using photovoltaic cells as roofing would be even better. Whitening road surfaces is possible at little cost, since many roads are already light coloured, and the focus would be on using such paving for new roads and for presently dark tarmac as it needs replacing.[178]

The other main contender for geoengineering is the idea that we can seed the oceans to increase biological activity and stimulate them to sequester more carbon dioxide. Two methods are being advocated: fertilisation with iron, or in different regions with urea/nitrogen, in areas where these are limiting to plankton growth. Both have been subject to limited field experiments, which tend to show some increase in plankton following fertilisation. However there is debate as to whether this has led to significant sequestration of carbon in the deep ocean, or mainly to stimulation of feeding and recycling of the carbon in shallower waters, with later re-release to the atmosphere. There are also worries as to its effect on natural ecosystems, and about the possible emission of greenhouse gases generated by the decay of dead plankton.[179]

One of the main worries with geoengineering is that unilateral action by the rich countries may well be affordable and very tempting in order to preserve their business-as-usual options and lifestyles. This could well be considered a hostile act by other countries that could be adversely affected by the side effects of climate control, or who disagree with the chosen climate settings.

This could lead directly to conflict, or it could come under the terms of the international *Convention on the Prohibition of Military or any other Hostile Use of Environmental Modifcation Techniques*, 1108 U.N.T.S. 151. Article II of this Convention states:

As used in Article I, the term 'environmental modification techniques' refers to any technique for changing – through the deliberate manipulation of natural processes the dynamics, composition or structure of the Earth, including its biota, lithosphere, hydrosphere and atmosphere, or of outer space.[180]

In an annex to the convention, a Consultative Committee of Experts decided that:

It is the understanding of the Committee that the following examples are illustrative of phenomena that could be caused by the use of environmental modification techniques as defined in Article II of the Convention: earthquakes, tsunamis; an upset in the ecological balance of a region; changes in weather patterns (clouds, precipitation, cyclones of various types and tornadic storms); changes in climate patterns; changes in ocean currents; changes in the state of the ozone layer; and changes in the state of the ionosphere.

So if other countries opposed unilateral actions to control climate, such action could be declared 'hostile' under the convention and would then clearly fall within its ambit and become unlawful. Michael MacCracken of The Climate Institute in Washington, in an editorial in 2006 concluded that: 'Given this situation and perspective, investing in

research, needed as it may be, might be seen as premature. Thus, at the very least, a treaty modification might be needed to get permission to move forward (and thus of how much change would be undertaken and who would decide optimal conditions, etc.)'.[181]

A number of papers on geoengineering are appearing as I write. These include a special issue of the *Philosophical Proceedings of the Royal Society* (UK). In a summary paper Stephen Schneider writes:

Rather than pin our hopes on the gamble that geoengineering will prove to be inexpensive, benign, and administratively sustainable over centuries – none of which can remotely be assured now – in my value system I – and most of the other authors of this volume as well – would prefer to start to lower human impact on the Earth through more conventional means.[182]

In summary, a pessimistic view of the likelihood of large emission reductions would lead to a decision that geoengineering to control climate might be justified as a fallback position. This, however, depends on a high level of confidence that the control would be real and without unforeseen or dangerous side effects, and that it would not lead to international conflict. Conflict is likely if the option is pursued unilaterally by a single country, or small group of countries, and in any case geoengineering would likely become a self-fulfilling prophecy by removing the incentive to reduce greenhouse gas emissions.

I believe it must mean negotiating a suitable amendment to the relevant international convention regarding environmental modification, and probably a mechanism for approval of any plan by a body such as the United Nations Security Council. Moreover, at present there is no guarantee that any such geoengineering scheme is without serious drawbacks. Most notably, none so far proposed avoids the ongoing acidification of the oceans. It might well be appropriate for all countries with an opinion on geoengineering to make that opinion known well in advance.

Technological innovation: attitude is vital

Technological change has been rapid and accelerating over the last century or so. The invention and refinement of the automobile, and later the aeroplane, radically changed society, urban structures, trade and warfare in the twentieth century. Communication technology has also increased rapidly, especially in the last few decades as computers and the World Wide Web have made the flow of information almost instantaneous for those with the wealth to afford it. Computer technology has leapt ahead so rapidly that many older but well-educated citizens have been left behind, while science has been able to achieve miracles in the area of computer modelling which now guide scientific developments and even manufacturing.

Nevertheless, people have an ambivalent attitude to technology. This is reflected in their policy preferences in relation to climate change. Many people (often associated with carbon-intensive industries) believe that, given climate change will happen, society has the ability to adapt, but that reducing carbon emissions would be too costly. This attitude displays technological optimism in the area of adaptation but pessimism regarding technology for mitigation. In effect, these people put the onus to innovate on those who will be affected by climate change (by saying it is easy), rather than on those whose activities may cause it (by saying it is too hard).

Other people, usually of an environmentalist bent, believe that carbon emissions can be reduced dramatically within a few years, but that adaptation will be unacceptably costly or impossible. These people have optimism about technology to reduce emissions (which in simplistic terms is not their responsibility), but pessimism about adaptation (which they would need to do).

This dichotomy is of course too simplistic. Most people stand somewhere between these extreme views. If we are to solve the problem of human-induced climate change we need to both adapt and mitigate. Therefore, we need to innovate in both areas, and have the optimism or faith to go ahead and try, then learn by doing. If technological change was increasingly rapid in the twentieth century, why can't it be even more rapid in the twenty-first, when we see the urgent need, and the direction in which we need to innovate? If, indeed, dangerous interference in the climate system is rapidly approaching, why can't we initiate urgent programs to innovate our way out of the problem, both by adaptation and mitigation? Private corporations and individuals set goals and programs for development and change every day, and in the area of defence governments do it all the time on the basis of perceived but uncertain threats, at great expense, and by setting very demanding research and development goals.

Technological optimism is perhaps well expressed by Wilson Tuckey, a conservative Australian politician. In a 2003 speech linking the hydrogen economy to a proposed tidal power project in Western Australia, he stated:

> So why are we panicking today? The basic technology exists at every level, refinement and financing is the challenge … We have got to develop our options. It does not matter that there will be other options for low emission energy production or hydrogen creation. But if we are going to maintain our standard of living … then we have got to have 'Greenhouse with Grunt'.[183]

A further exhortation to view climate change policy as an opportunity comes from the book *Natural Capitalism*, by Paul Hawken and others in 1999:

> … in the next half century, the climate problem could become as faded a memory as the energy crises of the seventies are now, because climate change is not an inevitable result of normal economic activity but an artefact of carrying out that activity in irrationally inefficient ways …

> If we vault the barrier, use energy in a way that saves money, and put enterprise where it belongs, in the vanguard of sound solutions, climate change will become a problem we can't afford,

don't need, and can avoid with huge financial savings to society.[184]

If some of us are indeed panicking today it is because too many governments, industries and entrepreneurs have not yet fully taken up the challenge of technological innovation to deal with climate change. Technological optimists say it can be done. We must find the will to produce solutions through ingenuity and innovation. Attitude is vital.[185]

The road to effective mitigation

It is sometimes said that if the enhanced greenhouse problem is real, someone will find a way to make money out of a solution, and so the market will take care of it. That is partly true. However, there are barriers or obstacles that can slow or prevent the spread of technologies and practices that could potentially reduce greenhouse gas emissions.[186]

The most obvious are so-called market failures, such as subsidies for fossil fuel industries, lack of competition or consumer choice, and inadequate information about alternatives. Others include initial capital costs, even though these costs may be exceeded by savings in a matter of a few years to a decade or so. An interesting example is rented housing, where the tenant pays the energy bills, but the landlord pays the upfront costs for energy-consuming equipment such as lighting, heaters and air-conditioners. This provides no incentive for the landlord to pay more for energy efficient equipment. Overcoming such barriers, for example by changing tax structures, giving innovative industries an initial tax break or subsidy, or extending capital loans at cheap rates, would lead to net savings over time and an economically viable alternative to some greenhouse gas intensive industries and technologies.

A second class of barrier is due to people's preferences and other social and cultural barriers to the spread of new technologies. Examples include preferences for private transport over public because of perceived convenience and safety, or for architectural styles that are not appropriate to energy-efficient living in a particular climate. These barriers can be overcome once they are recognised and addressed, for example by improving the timing, routing, staffing, security and reliability of public transport, or by information or guidelines on the savings to be made by energy-efficient housing design, such as having wide eaves or verandas on the sunny side of houses, adequate insulation, and so on. Subsidies and other incentives may also help. These can be removed once better practices have been widely adopted and become the norm. The idea that people's preferences are somehow fixed is nonsense, as any serious consideration of changing fashions in clothes or popular music will show. People react to many things that may change their preferences and habits, including new information, new technology, advertising campaigns, cheap introductory offers, examples and peer pressure.

This class of barriers includes the lack of provision of the necessary large-scale infrastructures necessary for the adoption of some technologies, for instance generation and distribution networks for hydrogen or other alternative fuels, user-friendly public transport, or energy-efficient urban planning and regulation. These can be achieved through local, regional or national government planning, preferably in collaboration with private industry, driven by consideration of long-term issues of sustainability and public good.

A third class of barrier is economic, for those technologies which would reduce greenhouse gas emissions, but which are presently too expensive for consumers. These economic barriers can be overcome by including in the price of competing technologies the environmental and social costs of pollution, thus making plain the benefits of switching to cleaner technologies. This can be achieved by imposing surcharges or taxes on polluting technologies, or by providing equivalent subsidies for non-polluting ones. If the most cost-effective non-polluting technologies are to be employed, such price penalties or incentives should be based on accurate estimates of the environmental and social costs and benefits. Such measures should be constructed so as to avoid bias towards one non-polluting technology over another that might be more efficient. This includes the concept of embedded energy emissions, discussed earlier.

The IPCC 2007 report summarises the conditions for induced technological change (ITC) that will lead to speedier and more economical emissions reductions. It says new technologies must overcome technical and market hurdles to enter into widespread commercial use. Factors include performance, cost, safety, consumer acceptance, financial risks, enabling infrastructure, incentive structures, regulatory compliance and environmental impacts. It states that: 'induced technological change is not a "free lunch", as it requires higher upfront investment and deployment of new technologies in order to achieve cost-reductions thereafter. This can lead to lower overall mitigation costs'.[186]

Regarding ITC, IPCC points out that new technology arises from a range of drivers, notably research and development (R&D), learning-by-doing and spillovers. R&D must of course have a purpose or vision, in this case to develop low-carbon technology that hopefully will succeed in the (global) market place. Learning-by-doing refers to the insights and technological benefits to be gained by early deployment in the market place. Spillover refers to the transfer of knowledge or economic benefits from one individual, firm, industry or country to another. New technology in one field can assist new technology in another and with the global challenge to reduce emissions, technological transfer between industries, and countries is essential.

Stabilising greenhouse gas concentrations is part of the objective of achieving sustainable development, since, without a stable climate sustainable development is impossible (see Chapter 9). In reviewing a book on energy and the challenge of sustainability, Walt Patterson from the Royal Institute of International Affairs in the UK said:

The authors ... realise that overcoming the economic, social, and political obstacles to sustainable development will take time. The long life cycles of some investments resist efforts to accelerate changes. Even after environmentally friendly technologies are developed, they must become affordable and available in the quantities and at the locations necessary for them to be effective. Inertia in human behaviour and consumer choices will have to be overcome. Today's purchasers are reluctant to pay for benefits that will not be delivered until some uncertain time in the future. The transition to an energy framework that will support sustainable development will require widespread public support along with informed political leadership and policy-making.[187]

In the book *Winning the Oil Endgame*, Amory Lovins of the Rocky Mountain Institute argues that: 'Firms that are quick to adopt innovative technologies and business models will be the winners of the 21st century; those that deny and resist change will join the dead from the last millennium'. He goes on to say:

What we can do, and have seen done repeatedly, is to transform markets by delivering greater utility at the same cost or the same utility at a lower cost, often by combining more advanced technologies with better business models. When this happens, the rate of change of markets normally exceeds our wildest forecasts and within a space of a few years a whole new technology has evolved.

Lovins seems to be suggesting that far-sighted entrepreneurs do not need much government intervention, but on the whole the market tends to react to short-term signals, measured in days to years, whereas the enhanced greenhouse and energy supply problems tend to exist on a longer time scale of decades to centuries. Also, the market normally takes into account only what has a market price, so issues like long-term sustainability, species extinctions, and even community health, are often neglected. For the market to work in relation to long-term problems, especially on issues that are not usually measured in dollars, mechanisms need to be built into the market to help it account for non-market values and to bring in the longer-term perspective. That is a role for governments and far-sighted businesses. Investments in initially unprofitable low-carbon technologies may well pay off, as Lovins argues, in the medium term as market niches, and eventually, as economies of scale are created.

With the prospect of more rapid climate change and of rapidly escalating oil supply problems, the time scale for change in markets is accelerating, with slow-to-change companies increasingly at risk. Governance of the market place via regulations, standards, flexible taxes, subsidies and incentives, needs to keep pace with the escalating climate change and energy supply problems.

Some governments have placed greatest emphasis on voluntary action by industry to reduce greenhouse gas emissions. This is achieved through education, technical advice, and in some cases subsidies. However, such programs lack a sense of urgency, and usually only succeed where emissions reductions can be achieved on a 'no regrets' basis within the existing price and taxation structures. They tend to focus on drawing industry attention to the energy savings that can be made in that small percentage of industry budgets devoted to energy costs, which has often been neglected by industry. However, many of the institutional obstacles mentioned above apply to voluntary and relatively uncoordinated actions.

Industry needs a level playing field where those who are far-sighted and innovative are not penalised by the market. This requires elimination of large subsidies presently paid to many fossil fuel or energy-intensive industries, such as:

- tax incentives for oil and gas exploration,

- energy subsidies for some energy-intensive industries such as aluminium manufacturers,

- regulatory systems favouring established industries,

- huge tax-derived expenditures on road networks favouring private energy-intensive transport over more efficient public transport,

- tax subsidies or flat rates for taxes on 'gas-guzzling' heavy vehicles often used for recreation, and

- preferential tariffs.[188]

Carbon taxes are often advocated as the best method to discourage the use of carbon intensive fuels. Just as often they are argued against. The argument against is that they add too much to industrial costs and thus slow the economy, create unemployment and reduce the surplus needed to devote to environmental benefits. There is some truth in both arguments.

However, carbon taxes should be part of an array of measures to foster a switch to a low-carbon economy. Such measures should include at least initial subsidies for non-carbon energy sources and the fostering of measures to create economies of scale for low-carbon alternatives. By itself, any tax that increases the overall tax burden on industry and investment is likely to have a negative effect on the economy through raising costs and prices. However, if the revenue from that tax is used to reduce other taxes, or fed back into the economy in the form of subsidies and incentives for low-carbon energy or improved energy efficiency, there may be an overall benefit to the economy. Such a package of measures can increase employment, increase efficiency, and reduce reliance on imported fuel.

Special attention should be paid to measures designed to encourage innovation in low-carbon emitting technology. Such measures include subsidies on research and development, low interest loans for initial capital investments by both suppliers and consumers, and public education. Other measures might include, where appropriate, regulated energy efficiency standards such as fuel economy in vehicles, and minimum proportions of renewable energy on electrical grids. Regulatory measures may be needed to require electricity suppliers to buy back excess electricity generated by home solar energy units, (that is, 'feed-in' tariffs) or to expedite siting for solar energy collectors and wind generators.

Local and district combined electricity, low- or zero-carbon automotive fuel and heat generation should be favoured over centralised generating stations where heat is wasted and automotive fuel delivery is a problem.

Building and planning regulations should be modified to encourage energy efficiency through insulation, proper siting with respect to the Sun, eaves and verandas on the sunny sides of houses, double glazing, solar hot water and other renewable energy devices. Urban planning is essential to provide denser population near to public transport facilities and to minimise daily travel requirements. Facilities for home offices and electronic commuting, such as planning permits and cabling, should be made.

The list of such measures will grow as new technologies are developed. Their urgency and stringency will need to be varied according to their effectiveness, acceptability and ongoing risk assessments of the reality of climate change and projections of its likely impacts. The faster climate changes the more urgent such measures will become.

Economic concerns require that the most economically efficient low-carbon technologies are developed, consistent with other environmental and social objectives. This requires care not to pick winners between alternative low-carbon technologies without good reason. It is better to use measures that maintain competition while fostering innovation. Thus tax concessions and subsidies should be based less on specific technologies and more on performance in terms of energy efficiency, low-carbon intensity, and ancillary social benefits. Various forms of carbon emissions trading, both within and between countries, may well provide incentives to reduce carbon emissions at least cost.

Carbon trading (sometimes called 'cap-and-trade') consists of issuing permits to emit certain amounts of greenhouse gases (or specifically carbon dioxide), which are then bought and sold. The amount of emissions permitted under each permit can be reduced with time, in order to meet more stringent overall reduction targets as required to mitigate climate change.

In rapidly developing countries the need for new infrastructure can be seized upon as an opportunity to invest in low-carbon emissions technology, leapfrogging over the more energy- and carbon-intensive technologies hitherto developed in the industrialised countries. Less emphasis on freeways and more on improving mass transit is essential in the mega-cities of the developing world. This will have many co-benefits in terms of minimising urban air pollution, and avoiding social costs such as road deaths and injuries. Similarly, emphasis on decentralised renewable energy supplies rather than centralised power grids is an opportunity rather than a burden. Access by developing countries to the latest low-carbon and energy-efficient technologies is vital, and should be a big part of any effort by the developed countries to minimise inequity and foster sustainable development. In addition, major developing countries such as China and India already have large R&D programs, which hopefully they will share with other lesser developed countries.

In the more developed countries, old carbon-intensive technologies will need to be phased out as quickly as possible, with a need to write off old infrastructure and invest in the new. Again, this is likely to have co-benefits in terms of increased efficiency and competitiveness, regional employment, reduced urban pollution, and a greater sense of community. New investments in old carbon-intensive technologies should be discouraged through insistence on low-carbon retro-fitting or closure.

Deep reductions in emissions of carbon dioxide are necessary to stabilise climate. Under most scenarios, according to the IPCC 2007 report, this will require the increasing introduction of natural gas and renewable energy in the first half of this century, and, for high energy use scenarios, either nuclear power or carbon capture and storage in the latter half of this century, as cost effective pathways. The cost-effectiveness of the last two options has yet to be demonstrated, and it may be that large-scale renewable energy coupled with rapid increases in energy efficiency are the only viable options.

However, as seen in the review above of mitigation options, none of these solutions by themselves will solve the problem. Certainly, continued large-scale use of coal and oil can only be considered in the short term, and then only with the urgent application of carbon removal and sequestration. But the stringent requirement of extremely low leakage of sequestered carbon back into the atmosphere, once amounts of sequestered carbon grow to hundreds of Gt of carbon, means that this cannot be seen as a long-term solution. Similarly, conventional terrestrial biomass sequestration (reforestation or minimum tillage) is only a short-term solution, useful only as a delaying mechanism, since the terrestrial biosphere is likely to change from a sink to a source within a matter of decades. More secure bio-sequestration via alternatives such as biochar will be necessary to take CO_2 out of the atmosphere.

Efficient use of natural gas through fuel cells may well increase energy efficiency and reduce carbon emissions substantially, but not totally eliminate carbon emissions. Continued growth in populations, economies and energy use will eventually require the almost complete phasing out of natural gas as well as coal and oil. Indeed, the continued growth of populations and per capita energy use, but not necessarily of a cleverer low-carbon economy, must eventually be questioned if emissions of greenhouse gases are to be stabilised.

The temptation to rely on geoengineering as a fall-back excuse not to rapidly reduce energy demand and greenhouse gas emissions is very dangerous. Resorting to planetary-scale geoengineering is in my view unacceptable for the twin reasons of unknown and largely unpredictable planetary-scale risks, and of the temptation to resort to unilateral action, which would likely lead to serious international conflict. The last thing the world needs is a major war spurred on by climate change, but that is a major risk of unilateral geoengineering. At the very least, geoengineering should be ruled out except when submitted to a proper international political and scientific approval process.

Further arguments regarding policy measures are discussed in Chapters 10 and 12.

Rapid development of renewable energy sources such as solar, wind, geothermal, biomass and tidal power, and perhaps safe nuclear power, along with a decline in growth of energy use through increasing energy efficiency and decreasing demand, are the only really long-term solutions. Each of these technologies, and maybe others not yet thought of, has its problems, but all will need to be pursued in the future, with a growing sense of urgency.

People with vision, energy and foresight are needed to lead the way. Companies and countries that adopt these new technologies are the wave of the future. Those who resist risk becoming history.

ENDNOTES

1. Quote from 'Energy supplies – the need for conservation', *Energy International* (September 1964).

2. See *Least-Cost Energy: Solving the CO_2 Problem*, Brick House, Andover, MA (1981).

3. See *Garnaut Climate Change Review*, Interim Report (February 2008), available at http://www.garnautreview.org.au.

4. A principal source for material on mitigation is the IPCC 2007 report WGIII (accessible at http://www.ipcc.ch). Other recommended sources for thinking on mitigation policy include International Energy Agency/OECD, *Beyond Kyoto: Energy Dynamics and Climate Stabilisation*, Paris, (2002), and Douglas Smith and others, *Designing a Climate-Friendly Energy Policy: Options for the Near Term*, Pew Center on Global Climate Change, Washington DC (2002), (see http://www.pewclimate.org/). See also numerous papers in journals such as *Environmental and Resource Economics*, *Climate Policy*, *Energy Policy* and *Mitigation and Adaptation Strategies for Global Change*. See also German Advisory

Council on Global Change (WBGU), *Climate Protection Strategies for the 21st Century: Kyoto and Beyond* (2003), (see http://www.wbgu.de).

5. Figure 26 is a simplified version of Figure 2.1 in the 2007 IPCC report, WGII, after Roger Jones, CMAR, Aspendale, Victoria.

6. The Stern Review is *Report on the Economics of Climate Change*, Cambridge University Press (2006). See references in Chapter 6, note 28.

7. From *Climate Code Red: The Case for a Sustainability Emergency*, David Spratt and Philip Sutton, Scribe Publications, Carlton North. See http://www.scribepublications.com.au.

8. James Hansen and others, 'Target atmospheric CO_2: where should humanity aim?', *Open Atmospheric Science Journal*, **2**, pp. 217–231 (2008).

9. See IPCC 2007 report, WGIII Summary for Policymakers, section 21.

10. See IPCC 2007 report, WGII, Figures TS1b and TS2b.

11. Palm oil is mostly from plantations on cleared forests in Malaysia, Sumatra and Borneo. See http://www.palmoilaction.org.au.

12. From James Hansen and others, 'Dangerous human-made interference with climate: a GISS model E study', *Atmospheric Chemistry and Physics*, **7**, pp. 2287–312 (2007), see http://www.atmos-chem-phys.net/7/2287/2007/, with permission. See also data in Appendix Table 1 of *Human Development Report 2007/2008, Fighting Climate Change: Human Solidarity in a Divided World*, UNDP (2008); Pew Center on Global Climate Change, *Facts and Figures Cumulative CO_2 Emissions (1850–2000)*; and the World Bank report 'Growth and CO_2 emissions: how do different countries fare?' (2007), available at http://www.wds.worldbank.org.

13. See Michael Raupach and others, 'Global and regional drivers of accelerating CO_2 emissions', in *Proceedings of the National Academy of Science*, **104**, pp. 10288–93 (12 June 2007); Josep Canadell and others, 'Contributions to accelerating atmospheric CO_2 growth from economic activity, carbon intensity, and efficiency of natural sinks', in *Proceedings of the National Academy of Science*, **104**, pp. 18866–70 (20 November 2007); Peter Sheehan 'The new growth path: implications for climate change analysis and policy' CSES Climate Change Working Paper no.14, Victoria University, Melbourne (2007) and related papers at http://www.cfses.com/publish/papers.htm.

14. See David King in *Science*, **303**, p. 176 (2004).

15. The CEO of Royal Dutch Shell is quoted by Reuters, 21 February 2008, as saying 'renewables are still too expensive … [they] may come to a solution but it will take decades before it is big'. For Shell's withdrawal from the wind farm see the *Guardian* (2 May 2008). Andrew Clark in the *Guardian* (2 April 2008) reports that at a Congressional committee hearing Exxon Mobil was attacked for not putting more funds into renewables. Instead it reportedly has funded groups denying that human-induced global warming is occurring.

16. See Socolow and Pacala in *Science*, **305**, pp. 968–972 (2004), and 'A Plan to Keep Carbon in Check', *Scientific American* (September 2006) pp. 28–35. The latter is part of a special issue of *Scientific American* entitled *Energy's Future: Beyond Carbon*. See also: 'Energy: a geoscience perspective', special issue of *Elements*, **3** (June 2007). For more on Sir David King's views see King and Walker, *The Hot Topic*, Bloomsbury, London (2008), and an article in the *Guardian* by Oliver Burkeman, (12 January 2008). Two excellent sources of material on renewable energy, in an Australian context but mostly relevant elsewhere, are: *Greenhouse Solutions with Sustainable Energy* by Mark Diesendorf, University of New South Wales Press (2007) and a special issue of *Environmental Studies*, **63** (6) (December 2006).

17. Arguments for individual action are put by Fred Pearce in *New Scientist* (17 November 2007) and Chris Goodall, *How to Live a Low-Carbon Life: The Individual's Guide to Stopping Climate Change*, Earthscan, London. See a reply by Chris Mooney in *New Scientist* (8 December 2007) that summarises arguments in Andrew Szasz's book *Shopping Our Way to Safety: How We Changed From Protecting the Environment to Protecting Ourselves*, University of Minnesota Press (2007).

18. See Ted Trainer of the University of New South Wales in Australia at http://ssis.arts.unsw.edu.au/tsw/. This is reminiscent of DH Meadows and others *The Limits to Growth*, Universe Books, NY (1972), EF Schumacher's *Small is Beautiful: A Study of Economics As If People Mattered*, Abacus, London (1974) and Herman Daly's *Steady-State Economics*, WH Freeman, San Francisco (1977).

19. Nanosolar claims to manufacture the world's lowest cost solar panels selling at about US$1 per watt. See http://www.nanosolar.com. Solana is building its first solar thermal power station near Gila, Arizona, for the Arizona Public Service Co., see http://www.aps.com/main/green/Solana/. Ausra has designed economical solar thermal power stations with steam heat storage for up to 20 hours operation each day. See http://ausra.com/technology/reports.html. See also the many links on http://www.unergy.org.

20. See *Least-Cost Energy: Solving the CO_2 Problem*, Brick House, Andover, MA (1981) and *Natural Capitalism: Creating the Next Industrial Revolution*, Little, Brown and Company, Boston (1999). See also http://www.natcap.org, where *Natural Capitalism* can be downloaded.

21. The economics is discussed in a book by Samuel Fankhauser *Valuing Climate Change: The Economics of the Greenhouse*, Earthscan, London (1995). He devotes a chapter to discounting. Costs are also addressed in JE Aldy, R Baronn and L Tunbiana 'The Political Economy of Climate Change', in *Beyond Kyoto: Advancing the International Effort Against Climate Change*, Pew Centre on Global Climate Change, (2003) (available from http://www.pewclimate.org.). See also the Stern Review and discussion of same in Chapter 6, endnote number 28, and WGIII of the IPCC 2007 report, Chapter 11 and Summary for Policymakers.

22. Estimated health costs from road transport pollution in Australia are given in *Fuel Tax Inquiry: The Air Pollution Costs of Transport in Australia*, by Paul Watkiss, AEA Technology, Abington, UK, (March 2002). See http://www.aeat.co.uk.

23. See Pielke, Wigley and Green in *Nature*, **452**, pp. 531–2 (3 April 2008) and comments by several others in *Nature*, **453**, pp. 154–5 (8 May 2008).

24. See Hansen's arguments in *Proceedings of the National Academy of Sciences*, **101**, 16109–14 (2004). The World Bank Global Gas Flaring Reduction Partnership is at http://web.worldbank.org/ggfr/.

25. See World Alliance for Decentralized Energy at http://www.localpower.org.

26. High Voltage DC cables for distance transmission are documented on Wikipedia at http://en.wikipedia.org/wiki/HVDC and are in operation in many countries. See also links on the various TREC websites ('Clean Power from the Deserts'), http://www.trecers.net, http://www.trec-uk.org.uk, and especially http://www.abbaustralia.com.au.

27. See *Clean Energy Trends 2008*, from Clean Edge Inc at http://www.cleanedge.com.

28. Apart from the IPCC report, progress with renewable energy technology is well documented in a number of newsletters and magazines. See for example: *Renewable Energy World* (http://www.renewable-energy-world.com); *Journal of Renewable and Sustainable Energy*, American Institute of Physics (http://jrse.aip.org); *Renewable Energy Focus* (http://www.renewableenergyfocus.com/); *International Journal of Alternative Propulsion* (https://www.inderscience.com/browse/index.php?journalID=68).

See also *A Clean Energy Future for Australia* a study by Energy Strategies for the Clean Energy Future Group (2004), available at http://www.wwf.org.au; 'Progress in renewable energy' in *Environment International*, **29**, 105–22 (2003); *Tackling Climate Change in the U.S.*, from the American Solar Energy Society (2007) at http://www.ases.org; and *The Case for an International Renewable Energy Agency (IRENA)*, German Federal Foreign Office (April 2008) at http://www.irena.org.

29. Books on peak oil include Kenneth S Deffeyes, *Hubbert's Peak: The Impending World Oil Shortage*, Princeton University Press (2001); Paul Roberts, *The End of Oil*, Bloomsbury, London (2004); and Jeremy Leggett, *Half Gone*, Portobello Books, London (2005). A more general book is *Crude: The Story of Oil*, by Sonia Shah, published by Allen and Unwin, Crows Nest, Australia, and Seven Stories Press, New York (2004). See also: Matt Simmons, *Twilight in the Desert: The Coming*

Saudi Oil Shock and the World Economy at http://www.twilightinthedesert.com/; *The Last Oil Shock* by David Strahan, at http://www.davidstrahan.com/blog/?p=100; and *The Coming Decline of Oil* by Gerald Leach in *Tiempo* (42), available at http://www.cru.uea.ac.uk/tiempo/. See also, Association for the Study of Peak Oil and Gas website at http://www.peakoil.net. This site has a newsletter and listing of relevant published articles. Other relevant sites: http://www.oilcrisis.com, http://www.peakoil.org, and Uppsala Hydrocarbon Depletion Study Group at http://www4.tsl.uu.se/isv/UHDSG. There is a copy of the *Uppsala Protocol* available at this site, which calls for an international accord to deal with the issue.

30. The Energy Watch Group is at http://www.energywatchgroup.org.

31. Two warnings originating with the IEA re oil shortages are reported in the *Financial Times* of London, 'World will face oil crunch "in five years"' by Javier Blas (9 July 2007) and 'The IEA warns; "the wheels might come off"' by Ed Crooks (8 November 2007). The latter provides a link to a full transcript of an interview with Fatih Birol, chief economist at the IEA. See also an article by George Monbiot in the *Guardian*, 15 December 2008.

32. The US National Petroleum Council report is available at http://www.npc.org/. Richard Kerr gives a concise summary in *Science*, **317**, p. 437 (27 July 2007). Another view is given by the Civil Society Institute and Ceres, *The Future of Oil: Energy Security, Climate Risks, and Market Opportunities* (June 2007) see http://www.civilsociety.org.

33. See 'Running out of and into oil: analyzing global oil depletion and transition through 2050' *Transportation Research Record* (no. 1880), pp.1–9 (2004), and for Canada see *Turning the Corner: Taking Action to Fight Climate Change* (2008), and *Canada's Fossil Energy Future: The Way Forward on Carbon Capture and Storage* (2008) at http://www.ecoaction.gc.ca. See also Alberta Provincial Government material at http://www.energy.gov.ab.ca, a comment on 20 June 2008, *Far From Turning the Corner*, by Matthew Bramley of the Pembina Institute at http://www.pembina.org, and the Oil Sands Watch website at http://www.oilsandswatch.org/.

34. See *Cities as Sustainable Ecosystems: Principles and Practice* by Peter Newman and Isabella Jennings, Island Press (2008), and http://www.arch.virginia.edu/event/1420.

35. The effects of the melting of Arctic sea-ice are discussed by Scott Borgerson in 'Arctic meltdown', *Foreign Affairs* (March/April 2008).

36. Mark Gilbert, in an article in the Melbourne *Age* (19 September 2005), (attributed to Bloomberg), suggests that in years to come, technology will replace oil in the same way it was used to replace salt, which was for centuries the most sought-after commodity. He cites *Salt: A World History* by Mark Kurlansky, Penguin Books (2003).

37. *Winning the Oil Endgame* is available at http://www.oilendgame.com/ReadTheBook.html.

38. See http://zeropollutionmotors.us/. See also http://www.mdi.lu and http://www.engineair.com.au. Regarding oil prices, the rapid fall in the latter part of 2008, due primarily to a fall in demand, is expected to be temporary. A cutting back in investments is predicted to exacerbate oil shortages once the economy recovers. See Jad Mouawad in the *New York Times*, 21 November 2008, and the International Energy Agency *World Energy Outlook 2008* at http://www.worldenergyoutlook.org.

39. Energy efficiency is discussed in the 2007 IPCC WGI report, Chapters 1.3.1.2, in Chapter 4 (energy), and Chapter 5 (transport). IPCC's Figure 1.5 shows trends in energy use and emission intensities.

40. The Australian Productivity Commission Inquiry report is *The Private Cost Effectiveness of Improving Energy Efficiency*, (36) (31 August 2005), available from http://www.pc.gov.au.

41. Energy efficient buildings are encouraged by the US Green Building Council through its *Leadership in Energy and Environmental Design (LEED) Green Building Rating System*, see http://www.usgbc.org. See also 'A new market paradigm for zero-energy homes' in *Environment* (US) **50** (1) (Jan/Feb 2008) pp. 19–32. See also an article on the effect of high albedo (reflective) roofs, 'Cool roofs cool the planet' in *Home Energy* (Sept/Oct 2006) pp. 38–41 at http://www.homeenergy.org. Energy rating systems have been developed for buildings in Australia, and a ratings calculator can be accessed on http://www.abgr.com.au. Similar systems operate in many other developed countries.

42. See Ian Lowe (*New Scientist*, Australia, 7 and 21 February 2004 and 7 August 2004) for the estimates of savings from energy efficient buildings and air conditioning. Thomas Casten's paper is 'Recycling energy to reduce costs and mitigate climate change', Chapter 20 in *Sudden and Disruptive Climate Change*, MC MacCracken, F Moore and JC Topping Jr (eds), Earthscan, London (2008).

43. See: 'Fueling up transportation future', *Scientific American* (September 2007) pp. 36–9; 'Less is more' in *New Scientist* (2 February 2008) pp. 33–6; 'Diesels come clean', *Scientific American* (March 2007) pp. 62–9; 'Gassing up with hydrogen', *Scientific American* (April 2007) pp. 62–9. See also 'Societal lifecycle costs of cars with alternative fuels/ engines', *Energy Policy*, **32**, pp. 7–27 (2004).

44. See *Proceedings of the (US) National Academy of Science*, **101**, 15827–9 (2004).

45. See *Winning the Oil Endgame*, at http://www.oilendgame.com/ReadTheBook.html.

46. See http://www.mdi.lu, http://zeropollutionmotors.us and http://www.tatamotors.com (press release 5 February 2007); and http://www.engineair.com.au for a rotary version of the motor. For possibilities for low-emission aeroplanes see 'Green sky thinking' in *New Scientist* (24 February 2007) pp. 32–38. Lifecycle costs of cars with various fuels or engines are discussed by John Ogden and others in *Energy Policy*, **32**, pp. 7–27 (2004).

47. The FAO report is 'Livestock's long shadow: environmental issues and options' by Henning Steinfeld and others (2006), available at http://www.fao.org. Arguments about this include 'A load of hot air?' by Simon Fairlie in the *Guardian* (30 January 2008) and 'How the myth of food miles hurts the planet' by Robin McKie in the *Observer* (23 March 2008). See also Meat and Livestock Australia, 'Addressing climate change' at http://www.mla.com.au. Books include *The Omnivore's Dilemma: A Natural History of Four Meals* by Michael Pollan, Penguin, (2008) , and *In Defense of Food* by the same author. See also *Food, Energy and Society*, by David Pimentel and Marcia Pimental (eds), CRC, 3rd edn (2007).

48. The Worldwatch Institute report *State of the World 2007: Our Urban Future* is available at http://www.worldwatch. org. See also: David Satterthwaite, *The Earthscan Reader in Sustainable Cities*, Earthscan, London (1999); Peter Newman and Jeffrey Kenworthy, *Sustainability and Cities: Overcoming Automobile Dependence*, Island Press, Washington (1999); Katie Williams and others, *Achieving Sustainable Urban Form*, Taylor and Francis (2000); and Phil McManus, *Vortex Cities to Sustainable Cities: Australia's Urban Challenge*, University of New South Wales (2005).

49. Peter Newman and Jeff Kenworthy, 'Costs of automobile dependence: Global survey of cities', *Transportation Research Record*, **1670** (1999).

50. A history and recent data on the Perth railway system can be found at http://www.pta.wa.gov.au. See also 'A bold blueprint', *ECOS* no. 118 (Jan–Mar 2004), pp. 13–16.

51. These include: United Cities and Local Governments at http://www.cities_localgovernments.org where a copy of their *Paris Declaration on Climate Change* is available; Cities Alliance at http://www.citiesalliance.org; and UN_ HABITAT at http://www.unhabitat.org; Local Governments for Sustainability (formerly International Council for Local Enviromental Initiatives) at http://www.iclei.org.

52. See also above in the 'Increased energy efficiency section'. Nissan Motors and Chrysler have announced their intention to jointly manufacture a small car in Japan for international markets in 2010. They expect the market for small, more fuel-efficient cars to grow and that for SUVs to drop, as has happened over the last decade. See story in the *Wall Street Journal* (22 October 2007) and update (15 April 2008).

53. See World Alliance for Decentralized Power at http://www.localpower.org, especially their report *Security via Decentralized Energy: Energy Security, Climate Change and Decentralized Power* (December 2007). For plug-in electric vehicles, including ones with recharge contracts, see http://dvice.com/archives/2008/04/top_10_worldcha.php.

54. Policies to provide incentives to reduce emissions are discussed in Chapters 10, 11 and 12. For better building design and standards in the US see the Green Building Council at http://www.usgbc.org. They have the Leadership in Energy and Environmental Design (LEED) Green Building Rating System, which provides certification and

benchmarks for buildings. Many other countries have federal, state or local government or NGO standards and certification programs. See also links in January/February 2008 issue of *Environment* magazine, and Architecture 2030 at http://www.architecture2030.org.

Other articles regarding green buildings include: 'A new market paradigm for zero-energy homes', *Environment* magazine (January/February 2008), pp. 19–32; 'How green is your house?', *New Scientist* (5 November 2005) pp. 24–25; 'Cool roofs cool the planet' *Home Energy* (September/October 2006) at http://www.homeenergy.org: and 'Wood – another low carbon footprint solution' in *ECOS* no. 129 (February/March 2006), pp. 12–13. Re plants on roofs see *New Scientist* (6 October 2007) p. 6, and websites http://www.greenroofs.com (US), http://www.greenroofs.org (Canada), and http://www.greenroofs.org.au (Australia).

55. You can easily search the web for these, but here are some starters: starting at the heavy end, the International Energy Agency has many publications some long and expensive, and others short and free at http://www.iea.org. See also http://www.climateark.org, http://www.climatechange.com.au, http://green.yahoo.com/, http://www.pewclimate.org, http://www.saveourenvironment.org, http://panda.org/, http://www.theclimategroup.org, and for some other heavy ones, http://www.chinadialogue.net and http://www.chathamhouse.org.uk/research/eedp/.

56. A good guide to carbon offsets can be found at http://www.theclimategroup.org. See also the Voluntary Carbon Offset Information Portal at http://www.tufts.edu/tie/tci/carbonoffsets/, *Carbon Reductions and Offsets* at http://www.globalcarbonproject.org, and article 'Look, no footprint' in *New Scientist* (10 March 2007) pp. 38–41. Also, International Energy Agency http://www.ieagreen.org.uk/glossies/Carbon%20Offsets%20(web).pdf.

57. George Monbiot, in the book *Heat*, Penguin/Allen Lane, London (2006) discusses various policy options for equitable personal emissions quotas.

58. See http://www.australianminesatlas.gov.au/education/fact_sheets/coal_bed_methane.jsp.

59. See http://www.hydro.com.au/home.

60. Information on methane hydrates comes from the websites of the Japan/US/Canada consortium currently producing methane from a research well at the Mallik Gas Hydrate field on Richard's Island, Mackenzie Delta, Canada, at http://ghff.nrcan.gc.ca/index_e.php, and various links. The US Federal Methane Hydrate Advisory Committee report to congress in June 2007 is available at http://www.fe.doe.gov/programs/oilgas/hydrates/MHAC-07-ReportToCongress-final.pdf. See also stories in *Nature*, **415**, 913–14 (2003) and *Science*, **303**, 946–7 (2004).

61. See for example M Sudiro and A Bertucco in *International Journal of Alternative Propulsion*, **2**, pp. 13–25 (2008).

62. The prospect of the GM electric car is reported in *Newsweek* (31 December 2007) and in the Melbourne *Age* (2 April 2008). See http://gm-volt.com and http://www.nicecarcompany.co.uk. Electric Nissans are reported on the way in the *Wall Street Journal* (2 May 2008). See also EV World at http://www.evworld.com and the Electric Car Owners Club at http://www.electriccarsociety.com for up-to-date information, and note 53 above. Compressed air cars are from http://www.zeropollutionmotors.com.

63. The 2007 IPCC report, WGIII, Chapter 4.3.2 provides a comprehensive discussion of aspects of nuclear power, with lots of references.

64. See *Nuclear Power* by Stefan Bakker, The Climate Group, Briefing Paper, 'Breaking the Climate Deadlock' at http://www.breakingtheclimatedeadlock.com.

65. European Commission, Memo/07/10 (10 January 2007) *A European approach to nuclear power, safety and security* at http://europa.eu/rapid/pressReleasesAction.do?reference=MEMO/07/10.

66. International Atomic Energy Agency reports and press releases can be found at http://www.iaea.org. The quoted statement in 2007 is: *Nuclear Power Worldwide: Status and Outlook* (23 October 2007).

67. The European Greens report is available at http://www.greens-efa.org/cms/topics/dok/95/95873.htm.

68. The quote from Sir David King is from the *Guardian* (12 January 2008). The IAEA report is *Global Public Opinion on Nuclear Issues and the IAEA* (October 2005) at http://www.iaea.org.

69. James Lovelock, *The Revenge of Gaia*, Penguin Books (2006).

70. See Pidgeon and others, *Global Environmental Change*, **18**, pp. 69–85 (2008).

71. The American Physical Society study is *Nuclear Power and Proliferation Resistance: Securing Benefits, Limiting Risks* (May 2005) available at http://www.aps.org/public_affairs/proliferation-resistance/.

72. Alisa Carrigan's article is 'Learning to build the bomb', *Physics Today* **60** (12) (December 2007) pp. 54–5.

73. The Generation IV International Forum was chartered in 2001 and signed the first agreement aimed at international collaboration on advanced nuclear systems in 2005. See http://www.gen-4.org. See also Phil McKenna, 'Nuke in a Box', *New Scientist* (2 August 2007).

74. The Massachusetts Institute of Technology report *The Future of Nuclear Power* (2002) is available at http://www.mit.edu/afs/athena/org/n/nuclearpower/. See also Declan Butler in *Nature*, **429**, 238–40 (2004), David Chandler in *New Scientist* (9 August 2003) pp. 10–13, and Jim Dawson in *Physics Today* (December 2003) p. 34. Various IAEA statements and reports are available at http://www.iaea.org, including the statement of 27 June 2004 cited in the text.

75. The nuclear fusion project is described on the ITER website http://www.iter.org. A major critique can be found in *Science*, **314** pp. 238–242 (13 October 2006).

76. A report arguing that nuclear power is relatively safe in the context of other risks is *What is Safe? The Risks of Living in a Nuclear Age*, by DR Williams, Royal Society of Chemistry, London (1998). Two strongly anti-nuclear books are: H Caldicott, *Nuclear power is not the answer*, New Press, New York (2006), and F Barnaby and J Kemp *Too Hot to Handle? The Future of Civil Nuclear Power*, Oxford Research Group (2007).

A good discussion of the pros and cons of nuclear power is in *Physics Today* (January 2007) pp. 13–14, and (September 2007) pp. 14–16. The *Harvard Review* ran a strong article against nuclear power 'Combating global climate change: the case against nuclear power' by M Boyd, see http://hir.harvard.edu/articles/print.php?article=1476. See also *New Scientist* (9 September 2006) p. 44 re nuclear waste storage and (10 June 2006) p. 8 re the human cost of uranium mining, *Scientific American* (September 2006) pp. 52–9 for a pro-nuclear article and *Guardian Unlimited* (10 July 2006) for a discussion of nuclear versus renewables in the UK. A debate between Amory Lovins, Steve Berry and Peter Bradford can be downloaded from the Rocky Mountain Institute website at http://www.rmi.org.

77. The IPCC 2007 report WGIII discusses hydropower on pp. 273–4. Additional references on hydropower include a special issue of *Energy Policy*, **30** (14) (November 2002), especially the introductory paper by Frans Koch, pp. 1207–13. See also a student paper *A Study of Hydroelectric Power: From a Global Perspective to a Local Application*, from CAUSE at the College of Earth and Mineral Sciences, Pennsylvania State University, 2003 http://www.ems.psu.edu/~elsworth/courses/cause2003/finalprojects/vikingpaper.pdf.

78. See *Dams and Development: A New Framework for Decision-Making*, World Commission on Dams at http://www.dams.org. See also *Dam Right: WWF's Dams Initiative*, report *To Dam or Not to Dam*, and *Rivers at Risk: Dams and the Future of Freshwater Ecosystems*, both at http://www.panda.org. See also the International Hydropower Association at http://www.hydropower.org; the International Commission on Large Dams at http://www.icold-cigb.net; and *The International Journal on Hydropower and Dams*, at http://www.hydropower-dams.com.

79. See World Alliance for Decentralized Energy at http://www.localpower.org.

80. I acknowledge the modelling groups, the Program for Climate Model Diagnosis and Intercomparison (PCMDI) and the WCRP's Working Group on Coupled Modelling (WGCM) for their roles in making available the WCRP CMIP3

multi-model dataset. Support of this dataset is provided by the Office of Science, US Department of Energy. Martin Dix of CSIRO Climate and Marine Research prepared the Figure.

81. See http://www.geni.org. See also ABB cables at http://www.abb.com.

82. *Clean Power from the Deserts* is sponsored by the Trans-Mediterranean Cooperation at http://www.trecers.net, with support groups in the UK at http://www.trec-uk.org.uk, and Australia at http://www.trec.net.au. A number of renewable energy sources already exist or are being built in the region, and in some cases will be linked to regional transmission networks soon. See the White Paper, presented to the European Parliament in 2007, at http://www.trecers.net/downloads/articles/trec_white_paper.pdf. Howes' proposal is at http://www.theoildrum.com/node/4508, and the Worley Parsons proposal appears in a presentation at http://www.worleyparsons.com/InvestorRelations/ASX/Pages/AdvancedSolar-ThermalPresentation.aspx. The Garnaut Draft Report (June 2008) is at http://www.garnautreview.org.au, see Chapter 17. See also http://business.smh.com.au/business/worleyparsons-billiondollar-solar-plan-20080812-3u3u.html. Details of HVDC cables can be found at http://www.abbaustralia.com.au.

83. The proposal to use CSP for water desalinisation is *AQUA-CSP: Concentrating Solar Power for Seawater Desalination*, Study by the German Aerospace Center (DLR) (2007) available at http://www.trecers.net/weblinks.html. The Sahara Forest Project is developing solar power plants and 'seawater greenhouses' to irrigate forest and food crops in North Africa and the Middle East. See Alok Jha in the *Guardian* (3 September 2006) http://www.guardian.co.uk.

84. See http://www.ren21.net/pdf/RE2007_global_Status_Report.pdf for 'Renewables 2007 global status report'. Other recent reviews include those in Diesendorf (2007) 'Greenhouse solutions with sustainable energy', University of New South Wales Press, and the *International Journal of Environmental Studies*, **63**, pp. 777–802 (2006). Other recent articles on solar power include: 'Sky power' in *Weatherwise* (November/December 2005) pp. 30–5; 'Every home should have one' in *New Scientist* (21 January 2006) pp. 36–9; 'A new day dawning' and 'Solar nation' in *Nature* (7 September 2006) pp. 19–24; and 'Our solar future' in *New Scientist* (8 December 2007) pp. 32–7. See also: *Concentrating Solar Power – From Research to Implementation*, Official Publication of the European Commission, 2007; *Tackling Climate Change in the U.S. – Potential Carbon Emissions Reductions from Energy Efficiency and Renewable Energy* by 2030, American Solar Energy Society, Charles F Kutscher (ed.) (January 2007) at http://www.ases.org; Clean Edge at http://www.cleanedge.com; *Scalable Electric Power from Solar Energy* by V Khosla, at http://www.breakingtheclimatedeadlock.com, and *Solar Energy Conversion*, by Crabtree and Lewis, *Physics Today* (March 2007) pp. 37–42.

85. The Nanosolar product is discussed at http://www.nanosolar.com, as do various linked media websites. See also 'Sunny days for silicon' by S Ashley in *Scientific American* (August 2008) pp. 19–20.

86. The SLIVER technology is described in E Franklin and others, *Advances in OptoElectronics*, **2007**, doi:10.1155/2007/3583, 'Sliver solar cells: high-efficiency, low-cost PV technology'. See also: http:/solar.anu.edu.au/research/sliver.php?=1, and http://www.originenergy.com.au/174/Solar-power. Solar thermal research at the ANU is documented at http://engnet.anu.edu.au/DEresearch/solarthermal/pages/pubs.php.

87. See http://www.solarsystems.com.au.

88. See http://www.ausra.com, along with links to a series of technical papers, and http://www.ecoworld.com/blog/2007/10/30/226/.

89. See http://www.aps.com/main/green/Solana/About.html.

90. Vanadium redox batteries were developed at the University of New South Wales (see *Journal of Power Sources*, **22**, pp. 59–67 (1988)) and are in operation in Australia, Japan, US and Ireland (see entry in Wikipedia). The technology is marketed internationally by VRB Powersystems at http://www.pinnaclevrb.com.au.

91. The US DOE workshop reports on Basic Energy Systems are at http://www.sc.doe.gov/bes/reports/list.html.

92. See also Leggett in *New Scientist* (6 September 2003) p. 23; *Science*, **309**, 548–51 (22 July 2005); and a report 'Basic research needs for solar energy utilization', Office of Science, US Department of Energy, from http://www.sc.doe.gov/bes/reports/list.html.

93. See http://www.enviromission.com.au for the solar tower proposal.

94. See, for example, the IEA website http://www.co2captureandstorage.info/networks/Biofixation.htm, and *Technology roadmap for biofixation of CO_2 and greenhouse gas abatement with microalgae* on the US DOE website at http://www.netl.doe.gov/publications/proceedings/03/carbon-seq/PDFs/017.pdf. See also papers in *Biomolecular Engineering*, **24**, pp. 405–13 (2007) by Skanes and others; *Energy Conversion and Management*, **46**, pp. 403–20 (2005) by Stewart and Hassami; and *Bioresource Technology*, **97**, pp. 322–9 (2006) by Chae and others.

95. IPCC 2007 discusses wind power in WGIII, pp. 274–5. Other statistics come from the American Wind Energy Association at http://www.awea.org. See also the Australian, British and Danish wind energy associations at http://www.auswea.com.au (now part of the Clean Energy Council at http://www.cleanenergycouncil.org.au), http://www.bwea.com, and http://www.windpower.dk, respectively. These organisations have many detailed reports and fact sheets. President Bush's statement is at http://www.state.gov/g/oes/rls/rm/2007/92938.htm. See also '*A Clean Energy Future for Australia*' by Hugh Saddler and others for Worldwide Fund for Nature at http://www.wwf.org.au (2004), and Null and Archer 'Blowing in the wind: clean and endless energy' in *Weatherwise*, July/August 2008, pp. 34–40. Pacific Hydro information is at http://www.pacifichydro.com.au.

96. See 'Global wind energy 2007 report' available at http://www.gwec.net. The executive summary of the IEA report is available at http://www.iea.org.

97. The quote from the BWEA Briefing Sheet 'Public attitudes to wind energy in the UK' and relevant survey data is available at http://www.bwea.com/ref/surveys.html.

98. The quote from Clive Hamilton comes from 'It's climate change, stupid' in *Australasian Science* (March 2002) p. 14. See also Jacobson and Masters 'Exploiting wind versus coal' *Science*, **293**, p. 1438 (24 August 2001).

99. A useful review by Martin Pasqualetti of wind power is in *Environment*, **46** (7), pp. 23–38 (September 2004). He also edited the book *Wind Power in View: Energy Landscapes in a Crowded World*, Academic Press (2002). Documentation on bird-kills from wind power versus other hazards is at http://www.currykerlinger.com/birds.htm and in the document 'Wind power myths vs. facts', available on the American Wind Energy Association website http://www.awea.oeg.

100. Optimum siting is discussed by Diesendorf in *International Journal of Environmental Studies*, **63**, pp. 765–76 (2006). See also the Danish website: http://www.windpower.org/en/tour/wres/siting.htm and CSIRO Australia's *Wind Resource Assessment in Australia: A Planners Guide*, at http://www.csiro.au/resources/pf16q.html.

101. Storing energy from wind farms for later use is similar to that for solar power, see endnotes 25 and 88–91. Another idea is to use compressed air in underground formations, see David Penlock, 'Squeeze the breeze', in *New Scientist* (29 September 2007) pp. 44–7.

102. Major reports may be found from the International Energy Agency at http://www.iea.org, including 'Biofuels for transport: an international perspective' (2004); the European Union at http://ec.europa.eu/energy/, notably 'Biofuels in the European Union: a vision for 2030 and beyond' (2006). Other reports include: 'Sustainable biofuels: prospects and challenges', from the British Royal Society, at http://www.royalsociety.org; 'Sustainable biofuels' by R Heap, The Climate Group (2008) at http://www.breakingthedeadlock.com; 'Are biofuels sustainable?' from the UK House of Commons Environmental Audit Committee (2008) at http://www.parliament.uk/parliamentary_committees/; and 'Getting biofuels right: eight steps for reaping real environmental benefits from biofuels', from the Natural Resources Defense Council at http://www.nrdc.org/policy.

103. See Gibbs and others, 'Carbon payback times for crop-based biofuel expansion: the effects of changing yield and technology' *Environmental Research Letters* **3**, doi:10.1088/1748-9326/3/3/034001 (2008); J Fargione, 'Land

clearing and the biofuel debt', *Science*, **319**, pp. 1235–8 (29 February 2008); T Searchinger and others, *Science*, **319**, pp. 1238–40 (29 February 2008); and discussion in *Science*, **320**, pp. 1419–22 (13 June 2008).

104. See *Renewable Energy for Development*, **17** (1), pp. 1–4, and **20** (2), p. 6 (Asia), p. 8 (Africa) and pp. 11–12 (Sweden) from the Stockholm Environment Institute at http://www.sei.se. See also: 'How green is ethanol as a renewable fuel?' in *Environmental Science and Technology* (8 February 2008) at http://www.pubs.acs.org; 'Top scientists warn against rush to biofuel' in the *Guardian* (25 March 2008); Farrell and others, 'Ethanol can contribute to energy and environmental goals', in *Science*, **311**, pp. 506–8 (27 January 2006); Hill and others 'Environmental, economic, and energetic costs and benefits of biodiesel and ethanol biofuels, *Proceedings National Academy of Sciences*, **103**, pp. 11 206–10 (2006); a discussion in *Science*, **312**, pp. 1743–8 (23 June 2006); and Adler and others, 'Life-cycle assessment of net greenhouse-gas flux for bioenergy cropping systems, *Ecological Applications*, **17**, pp. 675–91 (2007).

105. The Western Australian project proposal is at http://www.sustainability.dpc.wa.gov.au/docs/BGPapers/SarahBellDavidBennett.pdf, and a more recent report at http://www.verveenergy.com.au.

106. See: Berndes 'Bioenergy and water – the implications for large-scale bioenergy production for water use and supply', in *Global Environmental Change*, **12**, pp. 253–71 (2002); Jackson and others, 'Trading water for carbon with biological carbon sequestration', *Science*, **310**, pp. 1944–7 (2005). A general report on the global water problem is 'On the verge of new water scarcity' at http://www.siwi.org. See also Chapter 9 below.

107. See for example: Naylor and others, 'The ripple effect', *Environment* (November 2007) pp. 30–43; World Business Council for Sustainable Development (9 April 2008) 'Food shortages an emergency – FAO chief', at http://www.wbcsd.org; Food and Agriculture Organization (11 April 2008) 'Poorest countries' cereal bill continues to soar, governments try to limit impact' at http://www.fao.org; and Environmental and Energy Study Institute, 'Testimony before Commission on Security and Cooperation in Europe on biofuels, sustainability and food crisis concerns' (6 May 2008) at http://www.eesi.org. See also 'Food versus fuel' or the 'Salve for Africa?' from Khosla Ventures at http://www.khoslaventures.com, which also has other writings on biofuels; and the *Guardian* (17 April 2008) 'Brazil rejects criticism' by Anil Dawar.

108. See http://www.rabobank.com.au. Other factors including trade policies, the food futures market and the falling US dollar may have influenced the situation – see Raj Patel *Stuffed and Starved*, http://www.stuffedandstarved.com. See also Synthesis Report of the International Association for Agricultural Knowledge, Science and Technology (2008) at http://www.acfid.asn.au.

109. See 'Large-scale biomass for energy, with considerations and cautions: an editorial comment' in *Climatic Change*, **87**, pp. 335–42 (2008) by Marland and Obersteiner. This paper is one of the comments on a paper by Peter Read, 'Biosphere carbon stock management: addressing the threat of abrupt climate change in the next few decades: an editorial essay', *Climatic Change*, **87**, pp. 305–20 (April 2008).

110. The Brazilian experience with a large ethanol industry is described in Goldemberg and others, in *Energy Policy*, **32**, pp. 1141–6 (2004). See also International Energy Agency, 'Biofuels for transport: an international perspective' at http://www.iea.org, (2004).

111. National Resources Defense Council, 'Move over, gasoline: here comes biofuels' and 'Wind solar and biomass energy today' at http://www.nrdc.org.

112. The Australian study is 'The greenhouse and air quality emissions of biodiesel blends in Australia' by Tom Beer and others, CSIRO (2007) available via http://www.csiro.au. See also Foran and Crane on 'Testing the feasibility of biomass based transport fuels and electricity generation in Australia' in *Australian Journal of Environmental Management*, **9**, pp. 104–14 (2002); 'Wood for alcohol fuels'. Rural Industries Research and Development Corporation (November 2002) at http://www.rirdc.gov.au/reports/AFT/02-141sum.html; and a report on a particular ethanol proposal in Australia, 'Appropriateness of a 350 million litre biofuels target', Department of Industry Tourism and Resources, Australia (December 2003).

113. See for example: 'Plasma waste to energy technology' at http://www.magnegas.com; KJ Ptasinski, 'Energy analysis of hydrogen production methods from biomass' in *International Journal of Alternative Propulsion*, **2**, p. 39 (2008); Tiedje and Donohue 'Microbes in the energy grid', *Science*, **320**, p. 985 (23 May 2008); and the International Biochar Initiative at http://www.biochar-international.org. A report on the device for generating electricity from treatment of sewage is in *New Scientist* (13 March 2004) p. 21.

114. The quote from Richard Carew comes from Bob Acton, Landfall Walks Book no. 14: *Around Looe, Polperro and Liskeard*, Landfall Books, Truro, Cornwall (1999). Other old tidal mills exist at the Nendrum monastic site in Northern Ireland, Portu Errota in Spain, Moinhos de Mare in Portugal and numerous other locations (search the web for 'tidal mill').

115. Tidal current generators are reported in *Science*, **299**, (339) (2003). Companies involved include The Engineering Business Ltd (EB) at http://www.engb.com/, Marine Current Turbines Ltd. at http://www.marineturbines.com/home.htm, and Hammerfest Strom AS at http://www.e-tidevannsenergi.com/. Verdant Power is planning an installation in the East River, New York, *Nature*, news online (13 August 2004). See also Sustainable Development Commission UK at http://www.sd-commission.uk/pages/tidal.html.

116. The World Energy Council report is 'Survey of energy resources 2007', available at http://www.worldenergy.org/publications/survey_of_energy_resources_2007/tidal_energy/754.asp. Another recent report is 'Tidal power in the UK (2007)', available at http://www.sd-commission.org.uk/pages/tidal.html. See also the British Wind Energy Association, which also advocates wave and tidal power, at http://www.bwea.com/marine/index.html, and other links at the Wikipedia entry for 'Tidal power'.

117. The CETO technology is described at http://www.carnegiecorp.com.au.

118. Geothermal power is described briefly in the 2007 IPCC report, WGIII, pp. 277–8. See also: 'Renewables 2007: global status report', Renewable Energy Network at http://www.ren21.net; 'The great forgotten clean-energy source: Geothermal' in *Discover* (3 April 2008); 'Geothermal' at http://www.sustainable.energy.sa.gov.au; International Energy Agency Geothermal Homepage at http://www.iea-gia.org; the International Geothermal Association at http://www.iga.igg.cnr.it; the Geothermal Resources Council at http://www.geothermal.org; the Geothermal Energy Association at http://www.geo-energy.org; and the US Department of Energy Geothermal Technologies Program at http://www1.eere.energy.gov/geothermal/. See also the short article by Mark Fischetti in *Scientific American* (October 2007) pp. 80–1.

119. President Grimsson's testimony is 'A Clean Energy Future for the United States: The Case for Geothermal Power', US Senate (26 September 2007). See http://energy.senate.gov/public/_files/testimony.pdf.

120. Geodynamics Ltd is at http://www.geodynamics.com.au.

121. See Petratherm at http://www.petratherm.com.au, and also Torrens Energy at http://www.torrensenergy.com.

122. See http://www.geodynamics.com.au, *Industry Fact Sheet*, (as at September 2008) and ACIL Tasman report 'The impact of an ETS on the energy supply industry', at http://www.aciltasman.com.au/images/pdf/AT_Final_Report_ESAA_22July08.pdf.

123. See the 2007 IPCC report, WGIII, chapters 4.3.4.3 (energy) and 5.3.1.3 (transport), and the book *Hydrogen Energy: Challenges and Prospects*, by DAJ Rand and RM Dell, RSC Publishing, Cambridge, UK (2008). Two other useful websites are the International Partnership for the Hydrogen Economy at http://www.iphe.net, which has a long list of websites in 19 countries plus the EU, and the site of the American Hydrogen Association at http://www.clean-air.org, which also has many links. See also the European Fuel Cell Forum at http://www.efcf.com. Three working papers of the Tyndall Centre for Climate Change Research, UK, discuss hydrogen: WP#17 by Geoff Dunn is 'Hydrogen energy technology', #18 by Jim Watson is 'The development of large technical systems: implications for hydrogen', and #19 is by A Pridmore and AL Bristow, 'The role of hydrogen in powering road transport'. Available at http://www.tyndall.ac.uk/publications.

124. An anecdotal account of fuel cell development is *Powering the Future: The Ballard Fuel Cell and the Race to Change the World* by Tom Koppel, Wiley (1999) – see review in *Science*, **289**, pp. 457–8 (2000).

125. See 'Office of Fossil Energy – Hydrogen Program Plan', Hydrogen Coordination Group (June 2003) from http://www.fossil.energy.gov/programs/fuels/. A report *Basic Research Needs for the Hydrogen Economy* is available at http://www.sc.doe.gov/bes/reports/list.html. The FreedomCAR details are at http://www1.eere.energy.gov/vehiclesandfuels/about/partnerships/freedomcar/. See also http://www.hydrogen.gov.

126. See for example: http://www.gm.com/experience/technology/fuel_cells/; http://www.bmwgroup.com/; and http://www.chrysler.com/en/autoshow/concept_vehicles/ecovoyager/.

127. Details of the Australian program are at http://www.cmit.csiro.au. The International Energy Agency has a major report 'Prospects for hydrogen and fuel cells', available at http://www.iea.org/Textbase/publications/free_new_Desc.asp?PUBS_ID=1582.

128. Demirdoven and Deutch's article is in *Science*, **305**, pp. 974–6 (2004). The American Physical Society report is 'Hydrogen fuel cell vehicle study' (June 2003) see http://www.aps.org. Romm's *Hype About Hydrogen* is published by Island Press (2004). See also Ulf Bossel in *Proceedings of the IEEE*, **94**, pp. 1826–37 (2006).

129. Details of the European CUTE project and other hydrogen powered bus projects and fuel cell projects can be accessed via the Europa website http://www.europa.eu.

130. See http://www.shell.com/hydrogen.

131. Icelandic activities can be seen at http://www.ectos.is/newenergy/en/.

132. The Perth trial is outlined at http://www.dpi.wa.gov.au.

133. For biomass-derived hydrogen generation see *Nature*, **418**, pp. 964–7 (2002) by RD Cortright and others. For hydrogen from ethanol see *Science*, **303**, pp. 993–7 (2004) and *New Scientist* (21 February 2004) p. 23.

134. See for example http://cat.inist.fr/?aModele=afficheN&cpsidt=20067208, and http://cat.inist.fr/?aModele=afficheN&cpsidt=810791. The latter is a summary of J Benemann, 'Hydrogen production by microalgae' in *Journal of Applied Phycology*, **12**, pp. 291–300 (2007).

135. See Seth Dunn 'Routes to a Hydrogen Economy' in *Renewable Energy World* (July–August 2001). See also 'Hydrogen and the Hydrogen Economy' (2007) at the Murdoch University site http://www.rise.org.au/info/Res/hydrogen/index.html.

136. See Sunita Satyapal and others in 'Gassing with Hydrogen' in *Scientific American* (April 2007) pp. 62–7.

137. Legal liability for accidents with hydrogen is discussed by Russell Moy in *Science*, **301**, (47) (2003), and environmental problems of hydrogen leakage in *New Scientist* (15 November 2003) p. 6. The Rocky Mountain Institute publications are at http://www.rmi.org.

138. 'The hydrogen backlash' appeared in *Science*, **305**, pp. 958–61, and is part of a series of papers on 'Toward a hydrogen economy' in the issue (13 August 2004).

139. The quoted comments on the hydrogen economy come from a paper entitled 'The future of the hydrogen economy: bright or bleak?' by Eliasson and Bossel and Taylor, available at http://www.efcf.com/reports/. See also 'Hydrogen: Why its future in a sustainable energy economy will be bleak, not bright' by Bossel in *Renewable Energy World* (March–April 2004) pp. 155–9.

140. See correspondence regarding the use of ammonia as an energy carrier in *Physics Today* (June 2005) pp. 13–15 and references therein.

141. See 'Fuel cells for distributed power: benefits, barriers and perspectives' by Martin Pehnt and Stephan Ramesohl for WWF in cooperation with Fuel Cell Europe. See http://www.panda.org/downloads/europe/stationaryfuelcellsreport.pdf.

142. See the special report by the IPCC in 2005, 'Carbon dioxide capture and storage', available at http://www.ipcc.ch and the 2007 IPCC report, WGIII, section 4.3.6, pp. 284–6. See also: 'The future of coal: options for a carbon-constrained world', from the Massachusetts Institute of Technology (2007) at http://web.mit.edu/coal; US Department of Energy's Fossil Energy program at http://www.fossil.energy.gov, and related FutureGen program at http://www.futuregenalliance.org, including 'FutureGen: initial conceptual design report' (May 2007) an article on the US Regional Carbon Sequestration Partnerships program is in *Environment International*, **32**, pp. 128–44 (2006) by John Litynski and others.

143. See also the international Carbon Sequestration Leadership Forum at http://www.cslforum.org and its report *Geologic Storage of Carbon Dioxide: Staying Safely Underground*; *Carbon Capture and Storage*, by S Bakker and colleagues, The Climate Group at http://www.breakingtheclimatedeadlock.com; *Sustainable Fossil Fuels* by Mark Jaccard, Cambridge University Press, UK (2006) and a critical review of same by J Jowit and F Lowe in the *Guardian* (5 February 2006); and *Fundamentals of Carbon Capture and Storage Technology*, T Nicholls (ed.) The Petroleum Economist (2007).

144. See website at http://www.ieagreen.org.uk and http://www.co2captureandstorage.info, and the IEA periodical *Greenhouse Issues* at http://www.ieagreen.org.uk/newsletter/June90.pdf. Numerous other reports are available via these websites.

145. See report *Near Zero Emissions Technologies*, from the Australian Bureau of Agricultural and Resource Economics, Report 05.1 (January 2005) at http://www.abareconomics.com. See also: *Geophysical Research Abstracts*, **9** (05939) (2007) for a paper on 'Atmospheric monitoring of geological storage of CO_2 at the Otway Basin Pilot Project, Australia'; and the Australian Parliament Standing Committee on Science and Innovation, 'Between a rock and a hard place: the science of geosequestration' (August 2007) at http://www.aph.gov.au/house/committee/scin/geosequestration/index.htm.

146. There is a large literature on oil and gas leakages from submarine and other deposits, for instance: *Marine Geology*, **195** (1–4) (March 2003); *Marine Geology*, **198** (1–2) (June 2003); *Chemical Geology*, **205** (3–4) (May 2004); *Geo-Marine Letters*, **24** (3) 2004. A study of the economic implications of leakage from CO_2 storage by Minh Ha-Duong and David Keith is in *Clean Technologies and Environmental Policy*, **5**, pp. 181–9 (2003). See also Peter Haugan and Fortunat Joos in *Geophysical Research Letters*, **31**, L18202 (2004).

147. See 'Permanent carbon dioxide storage in deep-sea sediments' by KZ House and others, *Proceedings of the National Academy of Sciences*, **103**, pp. 12291–95 (15 August 2006).

148. See summary in *Greenhouse Issues* (June 2008) pp.10–11, or the full review at http://web.abo.fi/~rzevenho/.

149. Marburger is quoted in 'DOE, Congress to spur carbon sequestration' *Physics Today* (February 2008) p. 28.

150. See Deborah Adams in a review of *Fundamentals of Carbon Capture and Storage Technology* by T Nicholls (ed.), The Petroleum Economist (2007), in *Greenhouse Issues* (June 2008) pp. 12–13; and S Bakker and colleagues, *Carbon Capture and Storage*, The Climate Group, at http://www.breaktheclimatedeadlock,com. See also C Azar and colleagues in *Climatic Change*, **74**, pp. 47–79 (2006).

151. Effects of high CO_2 and ocean sequestration on the oceans is discussed in *Oceanography*, **17** (3), pp. 72–8 (2004) by the SCOR/IOC Symposium Planning Committee. Robert Socolow gives a critical overview in *Scientific American* (July 2005) with further references.

152. The amendment to the London Convention is documented at http://www.imo.org/Conventions/contents.asp?topic_id=258&doc_id=681.

153. See 'Burying Carbon under the Sea: An Initial Exploration of Public Opinions', in *Energy and Environment*, **13** (6) (November/December 2002) by C Gough and others.

154. Political commitment to CCS is discussed in a study by Andreas Tjernshaugen in *Mitigation and Adaptation Strategies*, **31**, pp. 1–21 (2006).

155. See a critical review by Curt White and colleagues for the US *Air and Waste Management Association*, in the Association's *Journal*, **53**, 643–715 (2003), and ensuing discussion in the same journal, **53**, pp. 1172–82 (2003). The environmentalist viewpoint is put in a WWF position paper, *Carbon Capture and Storage from Fossil Fuels*, at http://www.wwf.org; in 'False hope: why carbon capture and storage won't save the climate', by Greenpeace at http://www.greenpeace. org/raw/content/international/press/reports/false-hope.pdf; and in a paper 'Is "clean coal" an oxymoron?' by Mark Diesendorf at http://www.isosconference.org.au. See also an article in *Science*, **305**, pp. 962–3 (2004).

Other recent critiques include: several 'fact sheets' from the National Resources Defense Council at http://www. nrdc.org; 'Geosequestration: what is it and how can in contribute to a sustainable energy policy for Australia?' by Saddler and Riedy, The Australia Institute (2004) at http://www.tai.org.au; 'The war on coal: thinking outside the pits', White Paper at http://www.khoslaventures.com. See also: 'What to do about coal', *Scientific American* (September 2006) pp. 44–51; 'Putting the carbon back', *Nature*, **441**, pp. 620–3 (10 August 2006); and 'Cleaning up coal', *New Scientist* (29 March 2008).

156. See http://www.Zeobond.com, and 'Cement from CO_2: a cure for global warming?', *Scientific American*, August 7, 2008 at http://www.sciam.com/article.cfm?id=cement-from-carbon-dioxide&print=true. See also http://www. imperialinnovations.co.uk/?q=node/176.

157. David Hawkins and George Peridas argue in the Natural Defense Council Brief (March 2007) *No Time Like the Present* that there should be no new coal-fired powers stations without CCS. See http://www.nrdc.org.

158. Agriculture and forestry as sources and sinks of carbon and other greenhouse gases are discussed in IPCC 2007 report, WGIII, Chapters 8 and 9 respectively. Another useful source of information and links (as is the case for many subjects) is the Wikipedia entry http://en.wikipedia.org/wiki/Carbon_sequestration.

159. The potential saturation of terrestrial carbon sinks is discussed in Chapter 6 of *Terrestrial Ecosystems in a Changing World*, JG Canadell and others (eds), IGBP Series, Springer-Verlag, Berlin (2007).

160. Keuppers and others discuss a decision framework for deciding on land-use activities to mitigate climate change in *Climatic Change*, **63**, 247–57 (2004). Long-term changes are discussed by Harvey in *Climatic Change*, **63**, 259–90 (2004).

161. Bala and others 'Combined climate and carbon-cycle effects of large-scale deforestation' in *Proceedings of the National Academy of Science*, **104**, pp. 6550–5 (2007) discuss the albedo effects of forests.

162. An Australian study is 'Plantations, farm forestry and water: a discussion paper', by EO'Loughlin and EK Sadanandan Nambiar, in the series *Water and Salinity Issues in Agroforestry*, no. 8, RIRDC pub. no. 01/137. See http://www.rirdc.gov.au. Other accounts will be found in *New Scientist*, (15 April 2006) p. 24, 27; (October 2007) pp. 42–6; (22 March 2008) pp. 34–7; and *Science*, **316**, pp. 536–7 (27 April 2007). See also the Australian aid magazine *Partners*, 'Farm forests seen as commercial carbon sinks', (November 2007–February 2008) pp. 16–18.

163. See *The role of land carbon sinks in mitigating global climate change*, Public Document 10/01 (July 2001) The Royal Society (UK) at http://www.royalsoc.ac.uk. Forests as carbon sinks are advocated and documented at the Australian government website http://www.greenhouse.gov.au/nrm/forest-sinks.html.

164. 'Biospheric carbon stock management' is the subject of five editorial comments in *Climate Change*, **87** (3–4) pp. 305–46 (April 2008) by Peter Read and others, including JE Leake. See also J Lehmann and others, 'Bio-char sequestration in terrestrial ecosystems – a review', *Mitigation and Adaptation Strategies for Global Change*, **11**, pp. 395–419 (2006); and Wim Sombroek and others 'Amazonian dark earths as carbon stores and sinks' in *Amazonian Dark Earths: Origin Properties Management*, Johannes Lekmann and others (eds), Springer, Netherlands (2004). Biomass sequestration is also covered in 'Black is the new green' in *Nature*, **442**, pp. 624–6 (10 August 2006).

165. See C Azar and colleagues, 'Carbon capture and storage from fossil fuels and biomass – costs and potential role in stabilizing the atmosphere', *Climate Change*, **74**, pp. 47–9 (2006).

166. The International Biochar Initiative is coordinating research and advocacy on the use of biochar, see http://www.biochar-international.org. It is publishing a book *Biochar for Environmental Management: Science and Technology*, edited by J Lehmann and S Joseph.

167. The plant phytolith story is reported in *New Scientist* (5 January 2008) p. 9. See also JF Parr and LA Sullivan 'Soil carbon sequestration in phytoliths' in *Soil Biology and Biochemistry* **37**(1) pp. 117–24 (2005).

168. The IPCC 2007 discussion of geoengineering is in WGIII, Chapter 11, section 11.2.2, pp. 624–5. I am indebted to the Australian Broadcasting Corporation for material stimulated by their broadcast on 6 April 2008 'The Climate Engineers' on *Background Briefing*. This and related links can be found at http://www.abc.net.au/rn/backgroundbriefing/.

169. Papers on geoengineering include: JT Early, Space-based solar screen to offset the greenhouse effect, *Journal of the British Interplanetary Society* **42**, 567–9 (1989); BP Flannery and others, Chapter 8, 'Geoengineering Climate', pp. 379–427 in *The Engineering Response to Climate Change*, Robert G Watts (ed.), Lewis Publishers, Boca Raton (1997). A more recent paper is BK Govindasamy, K Caldeira and PB Duffy 'Geoengineering Earth's radiation balance to mitigate climate change from a quadrupling of CO_2', *Global and Planetary Change*, **37**, 157–68 (2003).

Semi-popular accounts include: Bob Henson, 'Big fixes for climate? *UCAR Quarterly* (Fall 2006) pp. 8–10; Thomas Schelling 'Climate change: the uncertainties, the certainties, and what they imply about action', *Economist's Voice* (July 2007) pp. 1–5 (available at http://www.bepress.com/ev); E Kintisch, (2007) 'Scientists say continued warming warrants closer look at drastic fixes', *Science*, **318**, 1054–5 (2007); McKie and Jowit, 'Can science really save the world?', in the *Guardian* (2 October 2007) (this foreshadows a special issue of *Philosophical Transactions of the Royal Society* on geoengineering, edited by Brian Launder of Manchester University); James Fleming 'The climate engineers' in *The Wilson Quarterly* (Spring 2007) at http://www.wilsoncenter.org; Jeff Goodell 'Can Dr. Evil save the world?', *Rolling Stone*, (November 2006) at http://www.rollingstone.com.

170. See report by US National Academy of Sciences (NAS), National Academy of Engineering (NAE), and Institute of Medicine (IOM), 1992: *Policy Implications of Greenhouse Warming: Mitigation, Adaptation, and the Science Base*, National Academy Press, Washington DC.

171. See 'Could we/should we engineer the Earth's climate?' in *Climatic Change*, **33**, pp. 275–8 (1996).

172. See 'Albedo enhancement by stratospheric sulfur injections: A contribution to resolve a policy dilemma?' in *Climatic Change*, **77**, pp. 211–19 (2006).

173. See *Science*, **314**, pp. 452–4 (20 October 2006).

174. See 'Effects of Mount Pinatubo volcanic eruption on the hydrological cycle as an analog of geoengineering' in *Geophysical Research Letters*, **34**, L15702 (2007). See also DJ Lunt and others, '"Sunshade World": A fully coupled GCM evaluation of the climatic impacts of geoengineering', *Geophysical Research Letters*, **35**, L 12710, doi:10.1029/2008GL033674 (2008).

175. See Matthews and Caldeira, 'Transient climate-carbon simulations of planetary geoengineering, in *Proceedings National Academy of Sciences*, **104**, pp. 9949–54 (12 June 2007).

176. This was suggested at a US DOE workshop in 2001(not published) by Michael MacCracken, and will be documented by K Caldeira, L Wood and M MacCracken (2008): 'Geoengineering Arctic climate' in preparation. See also S Tilmes and others, 'The sensitivity of polar ozone to proposed geoengineering schemes' *Science Express* (24 April 2008) doi:10.1126/science.1153966.

177. See S Salter and J Latham (2007), 'The reversal of global warming by the increase of the albedo of marine stratocumulus cloud', submitted to the *International Climate Change Conference*, Hong Kong, China.

178. See R Hamwey (2006) 'Active amplification of the terrestrial albedo to mitigate climate change: An exploratory study, mitigation and adaptation strategies for global change', *Mitigation and Adaptation Strategies for Global Change* **12**, 419–39.

179. See for example, Buesseler and others, 'The effects of iron fertilization on carbon sequestration in the Southern Ocean', *Science*, **303**, pp. 414–17 (16 April 2004); 'A drop in the ocean', *New Scientist* (15 September 2007) pp. 42–5; and S Basu 'Oceangoing iron', *Scientific American* (October 2007) pp. 11–12.

180. The Convention dealing with environmental modification is at http://www1.umn.edu/humanrts/peace/docs/conenvironmodification.html.

181. Mike MacCracken's editorial is in *Climatic Change*, **77**, pp. 235–43 (2006).

182. The special issue of *Philosphical Transactions of the Royal Society A*, **366**, no. 1882 (13 November 2008) has just appeared. Two other recent papers include: A Robock, 'Twenty reasons why geoengineering may be a bad idea', *Bulletin of the Atomic Scientists*, **64**, pp. 14–18 (2008); and A Robock, L Oman, and G Stenchikov (2008) 'Regional climate responses to geoengineering with tropical and Arctic SO_2 injections', *Journal of Geophysical Research*, **113**, D16101, doi:10.1029/2008JD010050 (2008).

183. The quote re 'greenhouse with grunt' is from Wilson Tuckey MP, in a speech *The Hydrogen Economy: and the Tidal Energy Link* (20 May 2003) Broome, Western Australia. This speech is no longer available on the web, but see his 2008 presentation on tidal power at http://www.wilsontuckey.com.au/.

184. *Natural Capitalism: Creating the Next Industrial Revolution*, is published by Little, Brown and Co., Boston (1999).

185. See also: Michael Grubb and Jonathan Koehler, 'Induced technical change in energy and environmental modelling: analytical approaches and policy implications', *Annual Review of Energy and Environment*, **27**, Annual Reviews, Palo Alto, USA, and other papers from http://www.econ.cam.ac.uk/faculty/grubb/publications. Also, Martin Hoffert and others, 'Advanced technology paths to global climate stability: energy for a greenhouse planet', *Science*, **298**, 981–7 (1 November 2002), and *Clean Energy*, by RM Dell and DAJ Rand, Royal Society of Chemistry, Cambridge, UK (2004). An Australian research and development effort is *Energy Transformed*, a National Research Flagship, at http://www.csiro.au. Another optimistic book on the value of technological innovation is *Winning the Oil Endgame* – see http://www.oilendgame.com/ReadTheBook.html.

186. Barriers to reaching full potential mitigation are discussed extensively in the 2007 IPCC report, WGIII, notably in Chapters 2.7.2 (re induced technological change), 3.4.3 (ditto), 6.7 (building technologies and practices), 7.6 (industry), 8.6.2 (agriculture), and Chapter 9 (forestry).

187. Walt Patterson is the author of *Keeping the Lights On*, Earthscan, London (2007) and many other books on energy issues. These are relevant reading. See endnote 185 for *Winning the Oil Endgame*.

188. Existing subsidies on fossil fuels are large in many countries. Briefing Note no. 2 of 2004 documents subsidies in the EU in 2001, see http://www.eea.eu.int.

9

Climate change in context

Non-climate stresses can increase vulnerability to climate change by reducing resilience and can also reduce adaptive capacity because of resource deployment to competing needs ... Vulnerable regions face multiple stresses that affect their exposure and sensitivity as well as their capacity to adapt. These stresses arise from, for example, current climate hazards, poverty and unequal access to resources, food insecurity, trends in globalisation, conflict, and incidence of diseases.

IPCC FOURTH ASSESSMENT REPORT, WORKING GROUP II, SUMMARY FOR POLICYMAKERS, 2007.[1]

... climate change is only part of a broader multi-stress setting of global through local changes. Privileging climate change policies over other concerns leads to tragic outcomes. Climate policies need to be designed for and integrated into this broader and challenging context.

HADI DOWLATABADI, 'ON INTEGRATION OF POLICIES FOR CLIMATE AND GLOBAL CHANGE', 2007.[2]

Today, the ongoing growth of the global population and – with economic development and rising consumer expectations – the increasingly great environmental impact of that population means that we may be less than one generation away from exhausting much of the biosphere's environmental buffering capacity.

PROFESSOR ANTHONY MCMICHAEL, *ENVIRONMENT* MAGAZINE, 2008.[3]

A common reaction to climatic change research by scientists in other disciplines, and by many decision-makers, is that there are other global change issues (such as land-use change, water supply or economic development) deserving of greater priority both for research funding and for policy concern and action. Up to a point this is undoubtedly true. Climate change must be seen in the context of these other problems and stresses. The climate change issue should be put in

context and given its due weight and not more. However, climate change is a truly global phenomenon, and over periods of several decades it will have appreciable impacts on many sectors and on the policy reactions required for these other problems. Climate change is one of a suite of problems and issues, and its true effects and appropriate policies cannot be understood without reference to the joint effect of other problems and stresses. There are multiple causes, multiple effects, possible synergies and other interactions between problems.

Donald Kennedy, editor of *Science* magazine in the US, put it this way:

> *... we have a great many pressing problems in the world. There's a population problem associated with economic development and pressure on resources. There is a continuing global security crisis augmented by the rise of terrorism. There is the chronically inequitable distribution in resources between the rich nations of the North and the poorer nations of the South. And, finally, there is the steadily growing body of evidence that we're about to undertake a major reorganization of the global climate regime.*
>
> *The proposition is simple. It is that the last issue is of great concern to us because it directly relates to the future of our children and grandchildren, but it's also important because it relates in an indirect way and a very powerful way to every single one of the other problems I've just listed.*[4]

In its 2007 report, the IPCC devoted a whole chapter in its Working Group II report to perspectives on climate change impacts and sustainability, while Working Group III, in dealing with mitigation, not only discusses each sector of the global economy, but the relationship of mitigation to sustainable development.

What is still needed, though, are more studies that attempt to include all the various causes and effects, and their interaction, on systems of interest. Such studies are termed 'integrated assessments'. This is already well under way with a number of global integrated models, referenced in the IPCC report. However, these are often too simple in their characterisations of complex processes. This is understandable, given limited computing and other resources, but more comprehensive impact assessments are needed.

Several of the interactions between issues merit separate discussion and are explored below, while others are touched on elsewhere in this book. A simple schematic diagram, shown in **Figure 32**, might help to visualise the connections.

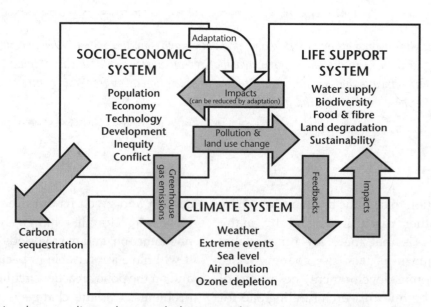

Figure 32: The connections between climate change and other issues. The socio-economic system and the life support system (for humans, animals and plants) interact independently of climate change. However, the climate system is affected by the socio-economic system and in turn affects the life support system. Feedbacks from the life support system also affect climate, while the socio-economic system has a limited capacity to adapt to changes in the life support system brought about by climate change.

Surface air pollution and climate change[5]

There are a number of connections and feedbacks between surface air pollution and climate change.

First, near-surface ozone air pollution and the emissions that drive it are important contributors to global climate change. Pollutants such as nitrogen oxides, carbon monoxide and volatile organic compounds lead to ozone pollution in urban environments and to a global increase in ozone concentrations in the lower atmosphere. Ozone in the lower atmosphere is the third largest human-induced contributor to global warming, after carbon dioxide and methane.

Second, the precursors of surface ozone pollution mainly come from the combustion of fossil fuels, so reducing fossil fuel emissions has co-benefits by limiting both global warming and urban air pollution.

Third, global warming tends to make urban air pollution and surface ozone concentrations worse (or at least different) by affecting the chemistry of the atmosphere, and changes in water vapour content and atmospheric circulation.[6]

Fourth, another major air pollutant in the lower atmosphere is sulfate particles and the resulting acid rain, formed from sulfur emissions from the burning of fossil fuels. Sulfate particles cause some regional cooling by reflecting sunlight back into space and are largely responsible for the so-called 'global dimming' effect discussed in Chapter 2. Sulfate particles presently mask some of the enhanced greenhouse effect, so reductions in sulfur emissions will in fact lead to greater warming.

Fifth, acid rain and tropospheric ozone have widespread adverse effects on land-based and aquatic ecosystems, human health and on many building materials. They add to the adverse effects of climate change on agriculture and food supplies and reduce the capacity of the biosphere to sequester carbon dioxide. Reducing tropospheric pollution may thus have desirable effects by reducing acid rain and ozone damage to crops and forests, thereby increasing carbon sequestration in the biosphere.[7]

Finally, soot particles or carbon black, produced by incomplete combustion, are strong absorbers of solar radiation and can lead to surface heating, thus adding to the global warming. Reductions in inefficient burning of fossil fuels or biomass will help reduce global warming.

Stratospheric ozone depletion[8]

There are also a number of links between climate change and stratospheric ozone depletion. Several of the chemicals causing ozone depletion in the stratosphere, notably the chlorofluorocarbons (CFCs), are important greenhouse gases and have been largely phased out of production because of their effects on ozone. However, other halocarbons that are less damaging to the ozone layer, namely hydrofluorocarbons, have been used as substitutes for the CFCs, but these are also greenhouse gases.

Another connection is that destruction of ozone in the stratosphere, or upper atmosphere, leads to less absorption of ultraviolet radiation from the Sun, so more ultraviolet radiation reaches the surface. This causes an increase in skin cancers and eye cataracts. It also adds synergistically to stresses on some food crops, and on coral reefs, which are adversely affected by both increased ultraviolet radiation and by climate change.

Ozone destruction in the stratosphere also leads to less absorption of solar energy in the upper atmosphere and therefore a cooling of the stratosphere. This impacts on the atmospheric circulation by increasing the equator to pole temperature difference, because most ozone destruction occurs at high latitudes. This increases the transport polewards of westerly angular momentum in the atmosphere, due to the rotation of the Earth, leading to stronger westerly winds that form the westerly low-pressure vortices around the Arctic and Antarctic regions. Like giant whirlpools, these strengthened vortices contract towards the poles. This in turn means that weather systems in the lower atmosphere move further polewards, with serious consequences for rainfall and storm patterns at the Earth's surface. These changes may also contribute to more rapid warming and melting of polar ice, at least along the Antarctic Peninsula.[9] Because the CFCs have a long lifetime in the atmosphere, the effect of ozone destruction, while now limited by cessation of production of CFCs in most countries, will continue for decades to come, so influencing climate well into the mid twenty-first century. This is a prime example of the importance of time lags in the atmospheric system.

Ozone destruction, and the way it is being dealt with under the Vienna Convention for the Protection of the Ozone Layer and the Montreal Protocol, sets an important precedent for dealing with the enhanced greenhouse effect. The time lag involved between remedial action under the Montreal Protocol and its effect, some 50 years or more, is also an object lesson that early action is needed on the greenhouse problem if we are to avoid dangerous impacts later this century and well into the twenty-second century.[10]

Land-use change, biodiversity, agriculture and forestry[11]

Changes in land-based and marine plant and animal systems occur for many reasons, including land-use change, pollution, climate change and increasing atmospheric concentrations of carbon dioxide.

In turn, changes in these biological systems affect climate by changing the exchange of greenhouse gases including carbon dioxide, methane and oxides of nitrogen between the land and ocean surfaces and the atmosphere. Land surface cover by vegetation also has an important effect on the reflection and absorption of sunlight at the Earth's surface, and thus on temperatures and evaporation. This should be taken into account in climate models, by including a variable biosphere that responds to climate change. Such combined models have now been run and show that an interactive biosphere can speed up the increase in greenhouse gases in the atmosphere.[12]

Massive land-clearing for agriculture or biomass production (for example from palm oil or other oil seed crops) can lead to a number of problems,

notably loss of stored biomass in existing forests and soils, changes in albedo or reflectivity of the surface, and the introduction of invasive species. The Asian giant reed (*Arundo donax*) is already invasive in parts of North and Central America, and the African oil palm (*Elaeis guineensis)* has become invasive in Brazil. Some of these problems have already been discussed in Chapter 8 regarding biomass energy and land-based carbon sinks. They can also lead to loss of biodiversity, with a strong implication that any biomass plantings should where possible be a mixture of native species.[13]

A recent report by Botanic Gardens Conservation International, 'Climate change and plants: which future?', states: 'It is clear that many species of wild plants are likely to become extinct within the next century, and, at least for some communities and ecosystems, climate change is already imposing huge costs. Uncertainty about how climate change will unfold or what the response of species and habitats will be must not prevent us from taking urgent action now. Conserving plant diversity will help in the maintenance of carbon sinks and will ensure options for future plant use under different climatic conditions'.[14]

Competition for land between agricultural production for food and for biomass energy is also a major consideration in relation to food shortages and prices, although, as discussed in Chapter 8, other factors such as increasing oil prices, population demand and market speculation may have played a larger role in recent food price escalation.

Natural climate variability, from year to year and decade to decade, demonstrates that the biosphere is sensitive to climate and thus to climate change. But the effects of other stresses such as erosion, fire, sea-level rise, salinisation and air pollution are also evident. These can amplify the effects of climate change, or at least add to stresses on humans reliant on the biosphere for food, fibre and shelter. Climate change effects on crop production are of course of vital importance, while changing patterns of crop growth and irrigation affect surface reflectivity, temperature and evaporation, and thus have an effect on climate, at least at a regional level.

Other stresses on the biosphere, many driven by the rapid growth in human population and consumption of resources, such as land-clearing, air and water pollution and over-exploitation also increase the vulnerability of the biosphere to climate change and sea-level rise. Coral reefs and estuarine ecosystems are notable examples, with pollution and over-fishing having deleterious effects on their survival. They may be pushed to the edge of extinction, at least locally, by climate change and sea-level rise. Similarly, loss and fragmentation of habitat due to land clearing renders many species and ecosystems more vulnerable to climate change by restricting opportunities to adapt by migration. Moreover, climate change can enhance the risk from the spread of pests and diseases and the risk from monocultures such as popular crop varieties or single species plantations, which can suffer widespread damage from a single pest or disease.

Land degradation and desertification

Desertification is the subject of the United Nations Convention to Combat Desertification, and many studies have linked it to climate change as one factor. The topic is not covered systematically in the 2007 IPCC report, although there are various passing references to soil erosion, effects on aridity, rainfall intensity and other aspects of the problem. Nevertheless, projected levels of climate change clearly would worsen the land degradation and desertification that has occurred over the last several centuries as the human population has expanded, water resources have been harnessed and diverted, monocultures established and forests cleared. The link was the subject of a statement by the UN Secretary-General on 17 June 2007, and of a Fact Sheet from the UN Convention office.[15]

Extreme climatic events historically are the main cause of land degradation, amplified by unwise land clearing in marginal areas where soil needs vegetation cover to remain fertile and to prevent erosion. Increased frequency and severity of droughts and floods, and increased fire frequency and intensity, will increase wind and water erosion of soil and loss of soil fertility in many regions.[16]

As populations grow and demand for food increases, more marginal land is likely to be exploited, increasing the synergetic interplay between climate change and loss of land cover, erosion and reduced soil fertility. Floods, landslides and related natural disasters will cause increased damage, loss of life and poverty. The pressing need to substitute biomass for fossil fuels will also place further pressure on land resources, with possible unfortunate consequences for sustainability, food production and human equity, although reforestation and biomass plantations may in some cases help protect or restore degraded land and provide jobs and income.

Any increase in fire and soil erosion will further decrease forest and soil carbon storage, adding to the rapidity of climate change and tending to defeat attempts at mitigation through sequestration of carbon on land. This is already a major issue in Kalimantan, Indonesia, where large areas of peat swamps were drained for agriculture, leading to large surface and underground fires during drought conditions, creating smoke haze and large greenhouse gas emissions.[17]

As discussed in Chapter 8, land clearing for biomass production of liquid fuels is a major threat, typified by palm oil plantations on cleared tropical forest land, releasing to the atmosphere carbon stored in peaty soil. However, properly managed biomass production for energy and/or carbon sequestration may well be needed to take carbon out of the atmosphere.

Freshwater supply

The 2007 IPCC report finds that all three classes of freshwater problems – too little, too much, and too dirty – may be made worse by climate change. Runoff will increase at high latitudes, decrease in many drier areas in mid-latitudes and the tropics, and become less potable due to increased storm runoff and eutrophication. Freshwater is essential for food supplies, sanitation and human health. It is also critical for natural ecosystems and for many industrial processes, including many existing water-cooled power stations.[18]

IPCC 2007 (WGII, p.175) states that:

Higher water temperatures, increased precipitation intensity, and longer periods of low flows exacerbate many forms of water pollution, with impacts on human health, water system reliability and operating costs.

When water withdrawals are greater than about 20% of the total renewable resources, water supply is often a limiting factor in development, while withdrawals of over 40% mean serious water stress. In many arid regions this is being overcome by withdrawals from underground reservoirs, which were laid down over thousands of years, leading to drops in water tables and diminishing resources. Others rely for irrigation and hydro-power on meltwater from glaciers, which increases temporarily with global warming until the glaciers are completely melted, when drastic reductions in summer river flow follow. Such unsustainable situations apply in wealthy countries like the United States, as well as in developing countries like Pakistan, Peru and Nepal. In 1950, groundwater accounted for 23% of total irrigation water in the United States, while in 2000 it accounted for 42% of the total. Seasonal glacier- and snow-fed supplies are also under threat in many regions due to rapid recession of glaciers and higher temperatures.[19]

One global study in 2000 reported that rising demand would greatly outweigh greenhouse warming in defining the state of global water systems by 2025. However, another study in 2004, for the international *Dialogue on Water and Climate*, concluded:

Our results suggest that water is going to be more plentiful in those regions of the world that are already 'water-rich'. However, water stresses will increase significantly in those regions and seasons that are already relatively dry. This could pose a very challenging problem for water resource management around the world. For soil moisture, *our results indicate reductions during much of the year in many semi-arid regions of the world, such as the southwestern regions of North America, the northeastern region of China, the Mediterranean coast of Europe, and the grasslands of Australia and Africa.[20]*

In 1990, about a third of the world's population lived in countries using more than 20% of their water resources. By the year 2025 it is estimated that some 60% of the then larger global population will be living in such water-stressed countries, simply due to population growth.

Climate change will add to these problems. The report for the *Dialogue on Water and Climate* in 2004 also states:

The hydrological cycle is speeding up. That means more frequent and extreme storms, floods and droughts in many parts of the world. ... The problems of climate variability are with us now. Every year, floods kill many thousands of people, make millions homeless and destroy the lives and hopes of millions more. ... annual losses from hydro-meteorological disasters increased tenfold between the 1950s and the 1990s ... including a rise from US$75 billion in the 1980s to more than $300 billion in the 1990s; successive droughts in Kenya in 1997–8 and 1999/2000 are estimated to have cost the country more than 40% of its GDP ... and Mozambique suffered a 23% reduction in its GDP after the 1999 floods ... It is the poor in the developing world who suffer most. Their fragile livelihoods and precarious homes are the first to go when disaster strikes, while poverty constrains their capacity to protect themselves in advance or to recover afterwards. Repeated disasters set back national economic progress and threaten the achievement of Millennium Development Goals.[21]

Strains on urban water systems are likely to increase due to global climate change. Typical strains are likely to include:

• increased water demand in hotter, drier seasons when water supply is at a minimum,

- floods exceeding the design capacity of protection works,

- more extreme rainfall events exceeding sewage design capacities, leading to overflows,

- less dilution of wastewater discharges into rivers with less dry-season flow,

- increased eutrophication and reduced water quality due to high nutrient loadings, low water flows and high temperatures,

- conflicts in the management of dams to simultaneously protect against greater floods, limit eutrophication, generate electricity and store water for dry seasons.

Other areas of concern include restoration of environmental flows to preserve riverine ecosystems and maintain freshwater fisheries, and the potential effects on runoff of reforestation (for various purposes, such as control of soil erosion and salinisation, and for carbon sequestration). A comparative study in Australia indicates that in one inland catchment, reforestation of 10% of the upper catchment would reduce runoff into the water storages by as much as the climate change by 2030. The combined effect would be far worse than either effect alone.[22]

Major technological fixes or adaptations being considered include water diversions between river systems in China, India, Australia and elsewhere. However, these are very costly and controversial, involving ecological problems and in some cases displacement of large numbers of people. Other costly solutions include desalinisation plants, which need large energy supplies. Rationalisations that these can be supplied from renewable sources such as wind power miss the fact that in most situations such renewable energy installations are urgently needed to replace fossil fuel energy for other uses. Alternative adaptations include demand management through water conservation and pricing and recycling of water. Reducing the extent and rapidity of climate change through mitigation actions appears necessary, as discussed in Chapter 8.[23]

Debate about measures to increase water supply in increasingly arid urban areas often misses a vital point. Runoff into dams is decreased not only by reduced rainfall, but by increased evaporation in catchments due to increasing temperatures. This leads to drier soil and thus reduced runoff when it does rain, leaving water storages seriously depleted. In contrast, runoff from roofs and paved areas is largely unaffected by higher evaporation, so that catching urban storm runoff in water tanks is more efficient.

Water stress, particularly on rivers that are shared resources for two or more countries, but also within countries, is, along with other pre-existing conditions and tensions, a potential or actual source of conflict. This will be exacerbated by climate change and raises serious issues regarding transboundary water management.[24]

Population growth

Ever since Thomas Malthus' *Essay on the Principle of Population* in 1798, global population growth has loomed as a major environmental issue. The Malthusian argument is that population growth would outstrip the capacity of the Earth to support the population.[25] Applied to the greenhouse effect, this relates to the Earth's capacity to accept additional greenhouse gas emissions without harm. In 1965, E Boserup offered the contrasting view that high population densities favour technological innovation that enables the environment to support more people.[26] Applied to the greenhouse effect this suggests that technological innovation may avoid harm by either increasing our capacity to adapt, or by providing less carbon-intensive means of supplying energy services.

Greenhouse gas emissions are a product of population, energy use per person, and carbon intensity of energy production. Population is thus a driver of greenhouse gas emissions, but it is usually downplayed relative to economic growth and a failure to decrease energy intensity since 2000. Empirical evidence from data from 1975 to 1996, analysed by Anquing Shi of the World Bank, indicates that greenhouse gas emissions increased more rapidly than population in developing countries, but less rapidly than population in developed countries.[27]

The 2007 IPCC report indicates that globally the contribution to growth in greenhouse gas emissions from 1970 to 2000 was about equally due to growth in population and growth in income per capita, with only small declines in carbon intensity (emissions per unit energy produced). Actual and projected emissions from 2000 to 2030, on the other hand, are twice as much due to growth in income per capita, than to population growth. The IPCC found decreases in energy intensity (energy per unit GDP) from 1970 until the present, and projects this trend to continue to 2030 (although energy intensity stopped decreasing around 2000 according to an analysis by Raupach and colleagues in 2007).[28]

As indicated in **Figure 30**, emissions per person are more than ten times as large in the United States and Australia than in the least developed countries such as India (and indeed most of Africa). Sustainable development in these developing countries clearly must include declining rates of population growth in order to safeguard many aspects of sustainability, including a stable climate. However, the real question is how this is to be done, given traditional attitudes, the development context in these countries, and questions of equity and human rights.

As we saw in Chapter 3, global population is expected by many experts to peak during this century. Population is already declining in most developed countries. This is thought to be a result of increased income, growing family security, and the education of women, which together provide both the incentive and the means to limit population growth. This is often referred to as the 'demographic transition' that comes with development. Population in the United States and Australia is still increasing, but in both cases this is largely due to immigration, much of it from poorer countries.

This suggests that until developing countries reach development levels at which a demographic transition begins, both their populations and emissions are likely to continue to increase rapidly unless there is a rapid transition to low-carbon technologies, or disease and malnutrition take a large toll. Moreover, as yet, most of the richer countries still have increases in emissions per person, starting from a much higher base rate: even with zero population growth developed countries need to greatly decrease their emissions.

It is notable that despite China's population control policy, its emissions are increasing rapidly due to its strong economic growth, which is still largely fuelled by coal and other fossil fuels. While emissions growth in China would probably have been much worse without a population policy, the rapid growth in emissions underlines the fact that population policy alone is not the answer.

Nevertheless, a study in 2008 by Michael Dalton and colleagues found that, with various projections of changes in population, age structure and urbanisation, for China and India, urbanisation led to a substantial increase in emissions, while ageing led to a decrease. They found that the net effect of demographic changes was to increase projected emissions from China by 45% by 2100, and from India by 25–55%.[29]

A US Congressional report in 2007 noted that the US population growth rate was 1.2% per annum in the 1990s, its income growth rate was 1.8% per annum, and therefore to stabilise emissions, emissions intensity (emissions per unit GDP) would have to decline by some 3.0% per annum compared to the actual rate of 1.6% per annum.[30]

The population issue boils down to one of sustainable development, with population growth declining when conditions are ripe for a demographic transition. Towards this end, a global population policy has in fact been devised through the United Nations International Conference on Population and Development in Cairo in 1994.

As suggested by Brian O'Neill and colleagues in their 2001 book *Population and Climate Change*, population and climate policy need to be linked.[31] They point out, however, that due to population age structure, family planning will take a generation or more to take effect, and thus will not substantially reduce emissions in the short term. Thus population measures, however necessary they may be in the long run, should not detract from the need for urgent reductions in emissions per person, especially where this is already high. Fostering energy conservation and low-carbon technology therefore remain critical, especially in the short term until a demographic transition occurs globally.[32]

Synergies and trade-offs

The numerous connections between climate change and other issues inevitably mean that there are ways in which action on any one issue may have an effect on another. In considering comprehensive greenhouse gas emission reduction measures, there will thus be co-benefits and synergies, but also possible trade-offs where action on climate change may aggravate some other issue or vice versa.[33]

Not all co-benefits are readily quantifiable in financial terms, for example, increased safety, employee satisfaction, quality of life, and enhanced environmental protection, but others lead to quantifiable financial gains such as reduced energy costs, increased employment, etc.

Environmental benefits from reducing greenhouse gas emissions include reduction of environmental problems such as urban air pollution and acid rain; and protection of forests, soils, watersheds and biodiversity. Socio-economic benefits would include reduced subsidies and taxes that presently distort the economy; greater energy efficiency; reduced road congestion and traffic accidents; decentralisation of energy supply and employment; and induced technological change and diffusion, with spin-offs into sustainable development and increased international equity.

Some mitigation measures may have both positive and negative impacts on other problems, depending in part on how mitigation is implemented.

Thus, reducing the carbon-intensity of energy supplies, with desirable effects on air pollution and acid rain, can be achieved through increasing the share of lower carbon emitting fuels, more energy efficient fossil fuel technologies, and renewable energy technologies. However, increased use of biomass as a substitute for fossil fuels could have positive or negative impacts on soils, salinisation, biodiversity and water availability. This will depend on how it is managed, what land-use patterns it displaces, and whether, for example, it increases water demand, displaces food production, or destroys wildlife habitat. Indeed, increased biomass production of ethanol is already being blamed for rises in food prices, although there are other factors such as population growth, increased demand for dairy products and meat, and rising oil prices that may be more important (see discussion in Chapter 8).

Similarly, carbon sequestration by plantation forestry can enhance carbon sinks and protect soils and biodiversity, but depending on how it is managed, could reduce biodiversity and water supplies. It may also lead to greater absorption of solar radiation due to reduced reflectivity of the Earth's surface, thereby reducing the benefits for climate (again see Chapter 8).

Some policies aimed at reducing other environmental problems may have major benefits for climate change reduction. This applies particularly to policies aimed at reducing urban air pollution, and at encouraging the use of public transport for economic and urban planning reasons. However, restricting sulfur emissions because of their impacts on human health and vegetation is already reducing sulfate particle concentrations in the atmosphere in some regions, which otherwise would help to reduce global warming. Moreover, some pollution control measures reduce the energy efficiency of power plants, thus increasing carbon dioxide emissions for the same amount of useable power.

Increasing energy efficiency has many benefits, including reduced pollution, reduced need for investment in power stations and electricity grids, improved export competitiveness, and reduced reliance on imported fossil fuels. Increased reliance on renewable energy, which generally comes from dispersed sources, increases decentralisation, and thus reduces urban sprawl. Both these measures, along with biomass fuels, may also reduce reliance on uncertain and increasingly costly imported oil and thus increase energy security.

Reducing vulnerability to climate change generally has many benefits in better managing climate variability, protecting threatened ecosystems from other stresses, reducing land degradation, and better managing freshwater resources. The converse is also true – better management for climate variability and extremes, and of threatened ecosystems and water resources provides better adaptability to climate change.

The 2007 IPCC report mentions many other co-benefits and trade-offs in the areas of residential and commercial buildings, industry, agriculture, forestry, waste management, air pollution, human health and natural ecosystems. The many co-benefits mean that many relevant actions may be taken primarily for purposes other than climate change mitigation, which is an additional benefit. Potential trade-offs provide an incentive to carefully consider the particular circumstances to maximise the utility of any action.

Integration, sustainable development and equity[34]

The above synergies, co-benefits and conflicts point to the need to integrate climate change policy decisions into the framework of decision-making on other issues. Climate change policy needs to be included in routine consideration of other social and environmental issues. Only then will the full benefits of consistent and well thought-out policies become achievable. Thus, for example, any decision-making procedure related to such issues as building design; urban planning; water supply; capital investments in agriculture, buildings, energy, transport or other infrastructure should consider impact on and resilience to climate change in any checklist of considerations. This is not a trivial matter, but in the long run it may save a lot of later changes and expenses. Retrofitting is in general less efficient and more costly than forward planning.

Climate change policy also needs to be linked to broader social and political issues such as equity. Equity, within countries, between countries, and between generations, is a major concern that must be considered. Overarching considerations include:

- Without equity within countries and between countries, policies to address climate change will not be widely supported by those who feel disadvantaged by such policies. This requires acceptance of responsibility on a user-pays principle, compensation or assistance to those harmed by climate change or policies to prevent it, and fairness in applying policies.

- Without wide acceptance of climate change mitigation and adaptation policies, those implemented will not be the most efficient. In particular, unless both developed and developing countries can agree that fair policies have been proposed they are unlikely to fully participate and act to achieve the necessary rapid reductions in overall greenhouse gas emissions.

- Growing inequity related to climate change impacts and measures will exacerbate existing problems of political tensions, instability and conflict, and may well create new tensions.

Equity issues will be considered further in the next chapter.

Integration of climate change policies into policies for sustainable development is the most likely way to ensure that the lesser- and more-developed countries can work together on this problem. The IPCC considers this very important, with extensive discussion of the links in both Working Group II relating to adaptation and in Working Group III in relation to mitigation.

It is important to note that, besides the UN Framework Convention on Climate Change

(New York, 1992) and the related Kyoto Protocol (Kyoto, 1997), many existing international agreements originally conceived for other concerns are relevant to the climate change issue. These include:

- The Antarctic Treaty (Washington, 1959)

- Convention on Wetlands of International Importance Especially as Waterfowl Habitat (the 'Ramsar Convention') (Ramsar, 1971)

- International Convention for the Prevention of Pollution from Ships (London, 1973)

- Convention on International Trade on Endangered Species of Wild Fauna and Flora (Washington, 1973)

- Convention on the Prevention of Marine Pollution from Land-based Sources (Paris, 1974)

- Convention on the Conservation of Migratory Species of Wild Animals (Bonn, 1979)

- UN/ECE Convention on Long-Range Transboundary Air Pollution (Geneva, 1979)

- United Nations Convention on the Law of the Sea (Montego Bay, 1982)

- Vienna Convention for the Protection of the Ozone Layer (Vienna, 1985), and the related Montreal Protocol (Montreal, 1987)

- Basel Convention on the Control of Transboundary Movements of Hazardous Wastes and Their Disposal (Basel, 1989)

- UN/ECE Convention on the Protection and Use of Transboundary Watercourses and International Lakes (Helsinki, 1992)

- Convention on Biological Diversity (Rio de Janeiro, 1992)

- UN Convention to Combat Desertification (Paris, 1994)

- Stockholm Convention on Persistent Organic Pollutants (Stockholm, 2001)

- United Nations Forum on Forests (New York, 2001).[35]

As discussed in Chapter 8, the Convention on the Prohibition of Military or other Hostile Use of Environmental Modification Techniques may also be relevant to climate geoengineering techniques, since these may have unforeseen or adverse effects on some countries by changing rainfall patterns or destroying stratospheric ozone.

Other agreements that arguably are relevant are the 1951 United Nations Convention and the 1967 Protocol Relating to the Status of Refugees, because climate change and sea-level rise may lead to the displacement of populations within and across national borders. Although these agreements do not include economic or environmental causes in their definition of refugees, it has been argued that the definition should be extended to do so.[36]

The Global Agreement on Tariffs and Trade (GATT) and the World Trade Organization (WTO), and associated agreements, should also be considered. These may affect the application of any subsidies and the enforcement of any trade restrictions or penalties under the UN Framework Convention on Climate Change, which are designed to encourage or ensure international compliance with mitigation and other measures. Issues are already arising about differing energy efficiency standards between countries for automobiles and other goods, and carbon trading schemes that put a price on carbon emissions that might have implications for trade with countries outside such schemes (see Chapter 10). The issue here is whether environmental values and sustainability should rate more highly than principles of free trade applied to environmentally damaging goods or services.[37]

As we have seen in this chapter, climate change should not be viewed in isolation. It is inevitably connected to many other issues in terms of multiple or common causation, effects which interact with other issues, and potential solutions which need to be examined for their co-benefits and trade-offs. Impact assessments and adaptation and mitigation strategies must consider these interactions; otherwise they run the multiple dangers of unexpectedly severe impacts due to synergies with other stresses, and unexpected side effects and conflicts that may render strategies unacceptable or ineffective.

Postscript: connections between economic and climate crises

As I finalise this book in December 2008 the world is facing a major economic crisis. There are a number of possible connections between economic crises and the climate change issue that deserve attention. Some have been clearly articulated by Laurence Gray, Regional Advocacy Director of World Vision Asia-Pacific, who compares the action taken by governments to help deal with the economic crisis of 2008 with that needed to deal with the developing climate crisis, which could be even more severe in its economic consequences.

Laurence writes:[38]

It is amazing the political will and financial resources that can be marshalled by rich nations when they are under threat. The result is hundreds of billions of dollars invested to prevent not just a meltdown of the US financial system but its tsunami impact on economies everywhere . . .

Just as in the debate over the financial crisis, climate change too has been marked by warnings, denials, anger, blame, grandstanding, a questioning of the forces at work and demands that the system – or the ecosystem – be left to correct itself. Unlike the financial crisis, what is lacking now from global leaders is a sense of foreboding, urgency and action . . .

Here are some lessons that should be applied from the financial crisis if we are to stand any chance of responding to climate change impacts.

Lesson one: Those at the bottom of the pyramid suffer most. In the US, low-income sub-prime mortgage defaulters have lost homes while many more are at risk. A worsening crisis means that those without savings and jobs will be extremely vulnerable.

Climate change likewise will disproportionately impact the poor. This is especially true in Asia with its massive coastal capitals, including Manila in the Philippines, Jakarta in Indonesia, and Dhaka in Bangladesh. A one-metre rise in sea level would inundate 800 000 sq km of land in Asia displacing more than 100 million people. In Vietnam alone 11% of the population would be displaced.

Lesson two: We are all inter-connected. Any collapse of Wall Street would domino across the globe resulting in devastating consequences for banks, bourses and economies. In turn this could lead to mass job losses and an increase in poverty and unknown economic, political and social consequences.

In a similar way our environment is 'globalised' – and therefore any nation's failure to significantly reduce greenhouse gases has severe implications for others. America's gas guzzling cars emit carbon dioxide that will lead to sea-level rises that will impact China, while Australian coal burnt in China's power stations will help fuel hurricanes that impact Florida. However, some wealthier nations have historically emitted more carbon dioxide and therefore have a larger obligation to act.

Lesson three: The money can be found. The US$700 billion dollar bailout package proves that wealthy nations can find the money when they have to and they can sell it to their electorates when the threat and cost of inaction is made clear.

In environmental terms, aside from a global commitment to reducing greenhouse gases, tens of billions of dollars must be spent to help the developing world prepare for climate change that is already locked into the system. This money is needed to help communities adapt, to build protective infrastructure, train children and adults how to prepare for and survive disasters. Every US$1 spent on building disaster resilience is a wise investment because it saves many more that would otherwise be spent on post disaster relief responses . . .

The challenge climate change presents has obvious parallels with how governments are responding to the current financial crisis. The danger signs are clear, the need for an urgent response is undeniable, and the money can be found.

All that is lacking is the decisive political will from wealthy nations to act quickly and comprehensively. If we fail to do so, we will all suffer, and the poor more than most. Time is running out.

I am reminded of the words on the back cover of the book *Climate Code Red: The Case for an Emergency Action* by David Spratt and Philip Sutton:

It is no longer a case of how much we can 'safely' emit, but whether we can stop emissions and produce a cooling before the Earth's climate system reaches a point beyond any hope of human restoration.

These imperatives are incompatible with 'politics as usual' and 'business as usual' – we face a sustainability emergency that urgently requires a clear break from the politics of failure-inducing compromise.[39]

The message is clear: we are at risk of a climatic disaster with economic consequences at least as dire as the present economic disaster. Comparable efforts are needed to avoid both outcomes.

Further connections between the present economic and the looming climatic disasters should be noted:

- The economic crisis has already slowed economic growth and industrial activity, thus decreasing energy use, especially fossil fuel use for steel, aluminium, cement, and automobiles. This has almost certainly slowed the increase in global greenhouse gas emissions, but is unlikely to greatly reduce them. The economic slowdown is also reducing the particulate pollution from fossil fuel burning which at present cancels some of the global warming. This latter process will have a more immediate effect, so the net result might be greater warming in regions such as India and China, where particulate pollution is greatest.

- Climate and sea-level rise are still playing catch-up with the increase in greenhouse gases since the Industrial Revolution. So even a temporary slowdown in emissions will not stop climate changes, ongoing sea-level rise, and the possible passing of thresholds to major and possibly irreversible changes in the climate system.

- Any temporary slowdown in emissions due to economic conditions might give us a little more time to get the global climate change issue under control, but it will not solve the climate change problem.

- The economic crisis makes it easier to state the obvious – that the free market needs regulation, especially to take account of external costs, risks, and of long-term human and environmental interests. As pointed out by the IPCC, markets have in-built barriers to innovation, hidden subsidies, and perverse effects. Markets must be regulated to avoid the consequences of short-term thinking, which include economic instability and environmental damage.

- Economic crises highlight the need for investment in infrastructure and innovation that will, through more sustainable development, help avoid further economic and environmental damage. We need to choose wisely between innovative low-carbon technologies and the old high carbon polluting technologies. We do not have to choose between the economy and the environment, but rather to tackle both together in a cohesive and synergetic manner. This is indeed an opportunity to do so.

ENDNOTES

1. Early IPCC discussions of the context and cross-cutting issues for climate change are in *Cross Cutting Issues Guidance Papers*, IPCC Supporting Material, Third Assessment Report, edited by R Pachauri, T Taniguchi and K Tanaka (July 2000). The Fourth Assessment Report (2007) discusses these issues, especially in WGI, Chapter 12, WGII, Chapter 20, and WGIII, Chapter 20. See http://www.ipcc.ch.

2. See Hadi Dowlatabadi in *Mitigation and Adaptation Strategies for Global Change*, **12**, pp. 651–63 (2007).

3. AJ McMichael, *Environment*, **50** (1) (January/February 2008) p. 58.

4. The quote from Donald Kennedy comes from the transcript of the conference *US Climate Policy: Toward a Sensible Center* held 24 June 2004, available at http://www.pewclimate.org.

5. The coupling between climate and air pollution is discussed extensively in the IPCC 2007 report, WGII, Chapter 7. Tropospheric ozone effects on crops are discussed in IPCC 2007 report, WGII, Box 5.2 (p. 278), and on human health in WGI, pp. 401–2 and 408–12.

6. The effect of changing precipitation and water vapour content on lower atmosphere pollution is discussed in a paper by Racherla and Adams in *Journal of Geophysical Research*, **111**, D24103 (2006).

7. See Sitch and others, *Nature*, **448**, pp. 791–94 (2007).

8. See WMO in *Scientific Assessment of Ozone Depletion: 2006* at http://www.wmo.int/pages/prog/arep/gawozone_2006 ozone_asst_report.html, and in a UNEP report, 'The 2006 assessment of the Scientific Assessment Panel' at http://ozone.unep.org/Assessment_Panels/SAP/Scientific_Assessment_2006/. Connections between safeguarding the ozone layer and climate change are covered in the IPCC/TEAC Special Report 'Safeguarding the ozone layer and the global climate system' (2005), Cambridge University Press.

9. See discussion and references in Chapter 5.

10. See *Protecting the Ozone Layer: The United Nations History* by Stephen Anderson and Madhava Sarma, Earthscan, London (2002). Two recent papers are 'The search for signs of recovery of the ozone layer' by Weatherhead and Andersen in *Nature*, **441**, pp. 39–45 (2006) and Eyring and others, 'Multimodel projections of stratospheric ozone in the 21st century' in *Journal of Geophysical Research*, **112**, D16303.

11. Extensive discussions of these issues are contained in the relevant sections of the 2007 IPCC report, WGs I, II (especially Chapters 4, 5, and 20) and WGIII (especially Chapters 8, 9 and 12). An older report that is still relevant is the IPCC Special Report 'Land use, land-use change, and forestry', Robert T Watson and others (eds) Cambridge University Press, UK (2000). See also the references in Chapter 8 above, re biomass energy and land-based carbon sinks, especially in regard to the biomass-food dilemma.

12. Land cover effects on climate are reported in a series of papers in *Geophysical Research Letters*, including ones by Gibbard and others **32**, L232705 (2005); Timbal and Arblaster **33**, L07717 (2006); McAlpine and others **34**, L22711 (2007); and Kueppers and others **34**, L03703 (2007).

13. Regarding invasive species and biomass energy, see The Nature Conservancy report at http://www.nature.org/initiatives/invasivespecies/strategies/art24885.html.

14. See Hawkins and others, 'Plants and climate change: which future?', Botanic Gardens Conservation International, Richmond, UK (2008), at http://www.bgci.org/climate/whichfuture.

15. See UN Convention to Combat Desertification at http://www.unccd.int/. Many reports and articles describe the links to climate change. For example, Eriksen in *Arid Lands Newsletter*, no. 49 (May/June 2001) at http://ag.arizona.edu/oals/ALN/aln49/eriksen-part1.html. See also the UNCCD Fact Sheet 10 at http://www.unccd.int/publicinfo/factsheets/showFS.php?number=10, and a paper by Alan Grainger and others 'Desertification and climate change: the case for greater convergence' in *Mitigation and Adaptation Strategies for Global Change*, **5**, pp. 361–77 (2000).

16. There is a discussion of the erosion issue in Australia in *Climate Change: An Australian Guide to the Science and Potential Impacts* by Barrie Pittock, Australian Greenhouse Office (2003) pp. 109–11, see http://greenhouse.gov.au/science/guide/index.html.

17. See *Nature*, **432**, pp. 144–6 (2004) and *New Scientist* (6 November 2004) p. 11.

18. The 2007 IPCC report deals with water issues in WGII, Chapter 3.

19. For the United States see water.usgs.gov/watuse/ (data for 2001–05 was in preparation, May 2008). See also report in *EOS* (23 March 2004) by Randy Showstack. A report on the effect of reduced snow pack on US water supplies is in *Science*, **303**, pp. 1124–7 (2004).

20. See Vorosmarty and colleagues in *Science*, **289**, pp. 284–8 (2000). The quote is from Manabe and colleagues, *Climatic Change*, **64**, 59–76 (2004).

21. The Dialogue on Water and Climate report '*Climate Changes the Water Rules*' is available via http://www.waterandclimate.org. The quote is from p. 94.

22. See Herron and others, *Journal of Environmental Management*, **65**, pp. 369–81 (2002).

23. Discussion of the hydrology and river linkage proposals in India are reported in *EOS* (11 May 2004). A review of the social and ecological problems associated with large dams is 'Neither temples nor tombs' by Sanjeev Khagram in *Environment*, **45**, pp. 28–37 (May 2003). See also World Commission on Dams at http://www.dams.org. A report 'On the verge of water scarcity', with policy recommendations, is available from the Stockholm International Water Institute (2007) at http://www.siwi.org. See also a large set of weblinks at the Global Water Partnership website, http://www.gwpforum.org.

24. Water as a potential or actual source of conflict is well documented. See: OECD Issues Brief, *Water and Violent Conflict* (2005), http://www.oecd.org/dataoecd/26/5/35785565.pdf; *Water Conflict Chronology* (update February 2008) at http://worldwater.org/conflictchronology.html. See also *Water in Conflict*, Global Policy Forum, which has an extensive reading list at http://www.globalpolicy.org/security/natres/waterindex.htm; *Sudan Post-Conflict Environmental Assessment*, UNEP (2007), at http://www.unep.org/sudan/. Climate change as a possible factor in conflict gets a brief mention in the 2007 IPCC report, WGII, pp. 442–3 in the chapter on Africa.

25. See TR Malthus (1798), *Essay on the Principle of Population*, 7th edn, Dent, London. The essay can be found at http://www.ac.wwu.edu/~stephan/malthus/malthus.0.html.

26. See E Boserup (1965), *The Conditions of Agricultural Growth*, Aldine, Chicago, Illinois, and E Boserup (1981), *Population and Technological Change: A Study of Long-Term Trends*, University of Chicago Press, Chicago, Illinois. See also the forum 'Is there a population implosion?' on the website of The Environmental Change and Security Project at http://ecsp.si.edu/listserv. Also see Joel E Cohen (2003), 'Human Population: The Next Half Century', *Science*, **302**, pp. 1172–5 (2003).

27. The study of the relation between population and emissions is by Anquing Shi (2003) in *Ecological Economics*, **44**, pp. 29–42.

28. The IPCC 2007 reference comes from WGII, Technical Summary Figure TS3. The Raupach and colleagues paper is 'Global and regional drivers of accelerating CO_2 emissions', in *Proceedings of the National Academy of Sciences*, **104**, pp. 10 288–93 (12 June 2007).

29. M Dalton and others, 'Demographic Change and Future Carbon Emissions in China and India', in *Proceedings Population Association of America 2007* Annual General Meeting, New York, at http://www.iiasa.ac.at/Research/PCC/pubs/dem-emiss/Daltonetal_PAA2007.pdf.

30. The US Congressional Research Service Report to Congress is 'Greenhouse gas emission drivers: population, economic development and growth, and energy use' (24 April 2007) John Blodgett and Larry Parker at http://ncseonline.org/NLE/CRSreports/07May/RL33970.pdf. See also a policy discussion in *Science*, **315**, pp. 1501–2 (16 March 2007) and the UK parliamentary report referred to therein.

31. Brian O'Neill, Landis MacKellar and Wolfgang Lutz (2001), *Population and Climate Policy*, Cambridge University Press, Cambridge, UK, and Programme of Action of the UN ICPD, at http://www.iisd.ca/Cairo/program/p01000.html.

32. Other relevant publications include: *The Crowded Greenhouse: Population, Climate Change, and Creating a sustainable World*, by John Firor and Judith Jacobson, Yale University Press (2002); *The End of World Population Growth: Human Capital and Sustainable Development in the 21st Century* W Lutz and W Sandersen (eds), Stylus Publishing (2005); and *Population Dynamics and Global Climate Change*, from Population Resource Center, at http://www.prcdc.org/globalpopulation/Population_and_Climate_Change/.

33. The IPCC 2007 report, WGIII discusses co-benefits and trade-offs in Chapters 6.6 (residential and commercial buildings), 7.10 (industry), 8.8 (agriculture), 9.7.2 (forestry), 10.5.7 (waste management), and 11.8 (air pollution, human health and natural ecosystems).

34. A major text on this subject is *Primer on Climate Change and Sustainable Development: Fact, Policy Analysis, and Applications*, by Mohan Munasinghe and Rob Swart, Cambridge University Press, Cambridge, UK (2005). The 2007 IPCC report discusses the relation between climate change and sustainability in WGII, Chapter 20 and in WGIII, Chapter 20. See also the UN Framework Convention on Climate Change report 'Climate change: impacts, vulnerabilities and adaptation in developing countries' (2007) at http://www.unfccc.int; reports from the International Institute for Environment and Development at http://www.iied.org, especially 'Climate change and development links', by Saleemul Huq and others (2006) Gatekeeper Series 123; the periodical *Tiempo* and its website http://www.tiempocyberclimate.org; the UNDP report 'Fighting climate change: human solidarity in a divided world', at http://hdr.undp.org/en/reports/global/hdr2007–2008/; 'Climate change and sustainable development: realizing the opportunity' by John Robinson and others, in *Ambio*, **35**, pp. 2–8 (2006); and 'Energy choices toward a sustainable future' by Jose Goldemberg in *Environment*, (December 2007) pp. 7–17. Climate change mitigation in the context of sustainable development is the subject of international dialogue in the Global Renewable Energy Forum, reported at http://www.iisd.ca/ymb/greb2008/.

35. The list of international agreements comes from the IPCC 2001 Synthesis Report, p. 134.

36. See 'Forced migration and the evolving humanitarian regime' by Susan Martin, Working Paper no. 20, UN High Commissioner for Refugees, Geneva (July 2000) at http://www.unhcr.org/research/RESEARCH/3ae6a0ce4.pdf. See also http://www.georgetown.edu/sfs/programs/isim/, and *The Uprooted: Improving Humanitarian Responses to Forced Migration*, by Susan Martin and others, Lexington Books, Lanham, MD (2005).

37. See for example: Joy Aeree Kim in *Global Environmental Change*, **11**, pp. 251–5 (2001); Thomas Brewer, in *Climate Policy*, **3**, pp. 329–41 (2003); and Jacob Werksman and colleagues, *International Environmental Agreements: Politics, Law and Economics*, **3**, pp. 59–86 (2003). See also Steve Charnovitz 'Trade and climate: potential conflicts and synergies' in *'Beyond Kyoto Series'*, Pew Center on global Climate Change, at http://www.pewclimate.org; the World Bank Report no. 41453 (1 January 2007), 'International trade and climate change: economic, legal, and institutional perspectives', available at http://www.worldbank.org/reference/; and the 'Climate Law Special Edition 2006' of *Sustainable Development Law and Policy*, Washington College of Law, at http://www.wcl.american.edu/org/sustainabledevelopment, especially the article by Daniel McNamee, pp. 41–4.

38. See Laurence Gray, 'Financial crisis may warm up politicians on climate change', at http://www.wvasiapacific.org, and the related report 'Planet prepare' at http://wvasiapacific.org/planet-prepare.html.

39. See *Climate Code Red: The Case for Emergency Action*, by David Spratt and Philip Sutton, Scribe Publishing, Melbourne (2008), and the related Climate Emergency Network at http://www.climatecodered.net.

10

The politics of greenhouse

Everyone has the right to a standard of living adequate for the health and well-being of himself and his family, including food, clothing, housing and medical care.
Everyone is entitled to a social and international order in which the rights and freedoms set forth in this Declaration can be fully realized.

UNIVERSAL DECLARATION OF HUMAN RIGHTS, ARTICLES 25 AND 28.

The Parties should protect the climate system for the benefit of present and future generations of humankind, on the basis of equity and in accordance with their common but differentiated responsibilities and respective capacities.

FROM ARTICLE 3, UNITED NATIONS FRAMEWORK CONVENTION ON CLIMATE CHANGE (UNFCCC)

Suppose today some dominant industry, built into the lives and fortunes of a great many people – to a degree of the whole nation – were found to be morally repugnant … When a "pecuniary interest" has that magnitude, it is a formidable opponent indeed. Rationalizations are supplied, positions are softened, conflicts are avoided, compromises are sought, careers are protected, life goes on. Don't try to change what can't be changed. Adapt to it.

FROM *ARGUING ABOUT SLAVERY: THE GREAT BATTLE IN THE UNITED STATES CONGRESS,* BY WL MILLER (1996)[1]

Whole volumes have been written on the politics of the enhanced greenhouse effect. Learned journals devoted to policy-related issues publish dozens of articles each year.[2] In this chapter I will confine myself to a brief, general discussion of key issues that divide decision-makers and which require agreement in order to ensure the most effective international action is taken. Previous chapters have dealt with a number of these issues, but a summary, placed in the context of the decision-making process, is useful.

Is the science credible?

As noted in Chapters 4 and 5, there are many uncertainties in relation to climate change. Nevertheless, the overwhelming body of evidence from relevant scientists is that there is a high probability that human-induced global warming, with associated changes in other climatic conditions, is happening. Moreover, the evidence is that warming will continue, at an accelerating pace, through the twenty-first century and beyond, unless urgent measures are taken to slow and eventually reverse the increase in greenhouse gases in the atmosphere.

These conclusions are hotly contested by a relatively small number of contrarians, discussed in Chapter 4, who for various reasons accuse so-called 'establishment scientists' of bias and poor science. Genuine sceptics exist and are welcomed, as they keep scientists on their toes and ensure that what is accepted is well based and relevant to the real world. However, contrarians often present misleading arguments, and frequently seize upon any discussion of uncertainty as an excuse for dismissing the whole topic, rather than arguing for a balanced policy of risk management. Too often contrarians repeat old arguments that have already been thoroughly discredited.

Where relevant, common arguments by the contrarians have been dealt with above. The truth is that in the reports by the Intergovernmental Panel on Climate Change (IPCC) we have the most thoroughly peer-reviewed and carefully written series of reports summarising the science of a major issue that have ever been published. Each report has gone through several sets of peer reviews by scientists. Moreover, the scientific authors have considered, but not necessarily accepted, comments from representatives of governments holding many different views and interests – including China, Russia, Saudi Arabia, the UK and the US – and the governments have signed off unanimously on the summaries for policy-makers. Such diversity does not allow for a single party line. Indeed, a guiding principle of the IPCC has been to present policy-relevant but not policy-prescriptive assessments. That is, it presents scientific assessments of the likely outcomes of various alternative policy choices, but does not advocate any one policy.

Examples of the discussion at plenary sessions of the IPCC, where government representatives are present, illustrate the detailed level of debate. In Chapter 7 on adaptation, I gave the example of suggested methods of adaptation to heat stress in dairy cattle (air conditioning), and to water shortages (desalinisation) where scientists rejected

unwarranted generalisation from the special Saudi Arabian experience to countries that could not afford such measures.

Another example concerns a draft that mentioned that many cereal crops would switch from gains to losses in productivity as global average warming increases beyond 2–3°C. Such an effect is shown in numerous crop simulations for different locations and scenarios of climate change, but with a range of numerical results. The effect is due to the changing balance between the beneficial effects of increasing carbon dioxide concentrations on crop growth and the effects of warming and rainfall changes. The latter turn negative due to increases in water stress and crop intolerance at too high temperatures. The argument from Russia was that regional warmings greater than 3°C would still be beneficial there, while some tropical countries argued that losses would start at less than 1°C. Some scientists suggested a compromise of replacing '2–3°C' by 'a few °C', since there are uncertainties and the number was not meant to be precise. However, China and other non-English speaking countries commented that a translation of 'a few' into their languages might convey a meaning of up to more than 3°C, while other countries wanted to stick to 2–3°C. In the end the scientists agreed on 'a few', and asked that any translators pay special attention to the English meaning. It being a scientific report, what the scientists agreed was accepted. The whole process took upwards of half an hour, on a fairly minor point, but the process was painstaking and true to the science. That is typical of IPCC deliberations.

This is not to say that the IPCC reports are perfect. As we saw in earlier chapters, climate changes are indeed happening near the upper end of the IPCC range of uncertainty, and it is the risk of such extreme outcomes that really matters. More emphasis thus should have been put on such extreme possibilities, as they affect policy. This is particularly the case now with projections of sea-level rise, which are very policy-relevant.

What about the uncertainty?

The role of uncertainty is of course central to the question of climate change. As discussed at length in Chapter 4, two main sources of uncertainty about the future nature and effects of climate change exist: one scientific, and the other due to future human and societal behaviour. Both are important and well recognised. Thus, any projection of the future will be uncertain and depend in part on human behaviour. There is nothing new in that. Every politician, business person and decision-maker lives with uncertainty every day, and has to make policy, investment and planning decisions despite uncertainty. It is done by assessing the risks of alternative courses of action and seeking to minimise risk and maximise gain. That is how it should be with climate change. We must get away from the idea that we should dismiss concerns or possibilities that lack certainty. Ordinary people make a risk assessment every day when they look at the weather forecast and decide whether or not to take a coat or an umbrella.

What is fairly new in the climate change issue is to recognise that the risks include much more than the relatively well understood ones due to gradual warming and slow changes in average rainfall. Possible changes in the frequency and intensity of extreme events like floods, droughts and severe storms also need to be taken into account, as well as the possibility of large-scale or sudden, and possibly irreversible changes to the climate system. This last category is particularly worrying because such events are very uncertain as to timing, likelihood and impacts. The likelihood of sudden large-scale changes in climate may be small, and they may not occur for decades or centuries. However, the possible magnitude of their effects may be so large that they cannot be considered as damaging only at the margins of society – they may cripple society as we know it. The risk posed by such possible disasters must be reduced, even at significant cost.

As mentioned previously, the common analogy used to justify some sort of investment in action to avoid climate change damages is taking out an insurance policy. It is not too bad an analogy, but it misses one important point. In the case of insurance we are spreading the risk to an insurance company that can compensate us if the worst comes to the worst. But in the case of global-scale climate change there is no outside insurer to pay compensation. If it happens, we lose. The point must be not how we can rebuild after a global disaster happens, but how to ensure that it never happens.

Another aspect of uncertainty is the role being played by natural climate change. We know that small and large climate changes, some of them sudden, have occurred before. They could occur again. Some argue that this means that we can survive climate change, and there is nothing we can do about it anyway. Both points are essentially wrong. First, no previous large climate change occurred when there were over 6000 million people living on Earth – we are in new territory here, and many of us would not survive. Second, past large-scale climate changes, especially abrupt ones, occurred when some natural change in external forcing was driving gradual climate change, and the climate system hit a threshold which triggered rapid change. Right now, humans are providing a driving force that is producing gradual, but nevertheless rapid climate change, compared with past natural changes. This is making it far more likely that the climate system will hit a threshold where abrupt change occurs. Third, the more seriously we take the possibilities of human-induced abrupt climate change the more we will learn about how to predict, avoid or cope with both human-induced and natural abrupt climate change.

Uncertainty has been used as a delaying tactic by those with a short-term interest in prolonging the use of fossil fuels. This is similar to the classic tactics adopted by the tobacco industry and asbestos manufacturers, which delayed action and cost many lives. Despite the contrarians, the weight of evidence that global warming is happening, and is in large part caused by human action, is now overwhelming, even if the details are still uncertain. Decisions must be taken, on the basis of minimising risk in accordance with prudent foresight. The real issue now is urgency, not whether it is really happening.

Uncertainty places us on a fast learning curve. We must learn how to minimise the risks posed now, given the uncertainties, and how to reduce the uncertainties as fast as possible so that we can better understand what must be done to avoid or adapt to climate change. This is not something we can put off while we get richer or while we deal instead with some other problems. Accumulating greenhouse gases and large time lags between cause and effect require that we address the climate change problem now, before we pass some poorly understood 'tipping point' at which it will be too late.

Here the words of Martin Luther King Jr come to mind:

> *Human progress is neither automatic nor inevitable. We are faced with the fact that tomorrow is today. We are confronted with the fierce urgency of now. In this unfolding conundrum of life and history there is such a thing as being too late ... We may cry out desperately for time to pause in her passage, but time is deaf to every plea and rushes on. Over the bleached bones and jumbled residues of numerous civilizations are written the pathetic words: Too late.*[3]

Not even the global financial crisis of 2008 can be allowed to delay urgent action.

How realistic are the scenarios?

This is an important question. Some economists have argued that for technical reasons the high emissions scenarios used by the IPCC 2001 and 2007 reports, such as the 'Special report on emissions scenarios' (SRES) A1F or A2 scenarios (see **Box 3** and **Figures 15** and **16**) are wrong, or at least highly unlikely. Thus they have argued that the high end of the range of estimates of global warming by 2100 shown in **Figures 15** and **16** is too high and unnecessarily scary. It gives total global emissions at 2100 of about 30 Gt of carbon per annum compared to the present figure of about 8 Gt. (The dubious validity of this argument is discussed more fully in Chapter 3).[4]

However, irrespective of the technical arguments of the sceptics on this point, simple arithmetic suggests that if 8 billion people in 2100 were each to emit nearly as much per head as the average US or Australian citizen does today (say 5 tonnes of carbon equivalent per annum), then global emissions would be about 40 GtC_e in 2100. This makes the A1FI and A2 scenario estimates look pretty moderate as an upper estimate for a fossil-fuel intensive global society. As we have seen in Chapter 3, actual observations show that to date emissions have in fact followed at or above the A1FI scenario due to far more rapid economic growth in China and India than was expected. Whether that will continue depends in part on whether the long-threatened peak in oil production has been, or will soon be, reached, and if so, whether that will result in an economic downturn, and more reliance on low-emissions renewable energy, or on the other hand, results in resort to shale oil and other higher emissions alternatives. (The economic problems of 2008 have at least temporarily reduced emissions, but also slowed investment in emissions reductions. It remains to be seen what long-term effects the 2008 troubles will have.)

Some contrarians also argue that the low SRES B1 scenario gives such low emissions (about 5 Gt or less by 2100) that no urgent emissions reduction actions, which they think would be damaging to the global economy, are needed. This is the thinking of those who believe that the so-called 'free market' will solve every problem, and in this case will automatically take the low emissions development path. This ignores the fact that the free market tends to operate on a short time scale while climate change operates on a longer time scale, with large lags built in. By the time the free market responds to an already-occurred impact it will likely be too late to prevent a far worse impact later on.

The IPCC 2001 report acknowledges, however, that the SRES scenarios are hypothetical futures, not predictions, and attaches no particular probability to them, just saying that they are 'plausible'. The SRES scenarios were in fact predicated on the idea that no policy actions determined by concern about climate change were included. This is why the contrarians have homed in on the low emissions scenarios, to argue that no policy actions are necessary.

The real point about the SRES scenarios is that they were never intended as predictions, but as a reasonable range over which to look at the sensitivity of climate change impacts to emissions. Any use of the IPCC results as unconditional predictions is wrong, although they do highlight possibilities, some of which we might well wish to avoid.

It must be conceded, however, that many climate scientists and even the IPCC, let alone journalists and others, have been careless in the use of language when discussing scenarios, projections, and predictions. It is a matter of semantics and nuances, but the fact remains that, whatever words have been used, the SRES scenarios are not, and were never intended to be, predictions, but rather projections based on story lines for plausible futures (see Chapter 3 for a discussion of these distinctions).

We may well ask, however, if the very low emissions in the B1 scenario are likely without policy action to limit climate change. We might well hope so. However, the IPCC description of the B1 scenario is of a future economy, 'with rapid change in economic structures toward a service and information economy, with reductions in material intensity and the introduction of clean and resource-efficient technologies' and 'with emphasis ... on global solutions to economic, social and environmental sustainability, including improved equity ...'. Is this really all that likely unless there are strong policies to ensure it happens? I doubt it, but that is what the advocates of business as usual would have us believe.

Choosing global and local emissions targets

The need for emissions reduction targets and their rough dimensions were discussed in Chapter 8, driven largely by the impacts as described in Chapter 6 and the uncertainties, which require that we take a risk reduction approach. As recognised in the UNFCCC, emissions reduction targets should be driven by estimates of the concentration of greenhouse gases in the atmosphere that would lead to dangerous impacts. As discussed earlier, what is dangerous is a value-laden subject, due to non-monetary values related to, for example, extinctions and loss of heritage, and uneven impacts on different countries and sectors of society. Moreover, we have to take account of possible large-scale or abrupt changes to the climate system, and the wide range of uncertainty in the climate's sensitivity, which determines the relationship between greenhouse gas concentrations and global warming.

The choice of a low warming target, and its achievement, is crucial to eventual outcomes. As Donald Brown of the Pennsylvania Consortium for Interdisciplinary Environmental Policy put it, in a paper on the ethical dimensions of climate policy:

> *Because this target will determine which people, plants, and animals will survive rising temperatures, increased disease, rising oceans, more intense storms, and increased floods and droughts, the greenhouse gas atmospheric target level issue raises profound ethical questions.*[5]

As we consider the policy implications of projected climate impacts, we should note that the various stabilisation scenarios, which are examined in the 2007 IPCC report, are far more policy-relevant than the SRES scenarios.[6] Summary results in terms of global warmings at equilibrium, are shown in **Table 4** (Chapter 5) and **Figure 28** (Chapter 8). When applied to regional impact assessments, comparisons of projected impacts for different levels of stabilisation demonstrate dramatically the value of achieving low greenhouse gas concentrations at stabilisation.

Figure 33 shows such an intercomparison of regional impacts at 2030 and 2070 for the full SRES range and for stabilisation at 450 and 550 ppm. The full range of uncertainties due to different possible climate sensitivities, and in the SRES case due to different plausible emissions scenarios, is shown. (Additional uncertainty may be appropriate to account for regional downscaling from the global climate models.)

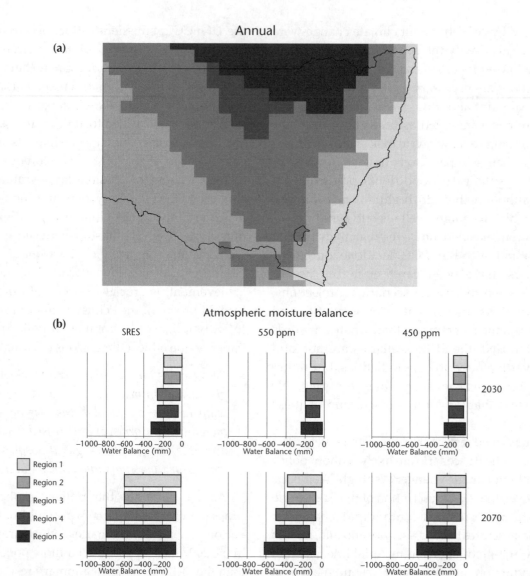

Figure 33: An example of the effect of stabilisation targets on regional climate change impacts. The shaded bars show the range of changes in the moisture balance (mm) in 2030 (top) and 2070 (bottom), relative to 1990, for areas on a map of the state of New South Wales (Australia) with the corresponding shading. Moisture balance is rainfall minus potential evaporation (the evaporation that would occur over a wet surface). The IPCC SRES scenarios do not include explicit actions to reduce greenhouse gas emissions. They include a wide range of 'plausible' futures. Impacts for the IPCC's 550 ppm and 450 ppm CO_2 stabilisation scenarios (or targets in a policy context) show marked reductions relative to the SRES range. (Results courtesy of CSIRO and the NSW Government.)[7]

It is apparent from these results, derived by CSIRO in Australia for the Government of New South Wales (NSW), that widespread reductions of the moisture balance, that is, drier conditions, are more likely than not in NSW under any of the scenarios. Severe drying appears likely without a greenhouse gas reductions policy, particularly in the north-central regions of the state. However, following the 550 ppm stabilisation scenario results in much less drying, and for 450 ppm stabilisation the effect is even less. It also shows that the benefits of emissions reductions, relative to the no-policy SRES scenarios, become greater with time. In this example, the range of reductions in moisture balance is halved in 2070 in the 450 ppm stabilisation scenario, relative to the no-policy range of scenarios. The relative reduction in impact would be even greater at later dates.

This is a policy-relevant result, as it demonstrates the advantages of a low stabilisation target. If some unacceptable level of drying can be determined from its potential impact on the state, this can lead to the adoption of a regionally appropriate target for emissions reductions to avoid such drying. This in turn may lead to the adoption by the Australian government of a target for reductions in emissions to be advocated internationally in order to serve Australia's national interest. Ideally, similar assessments should be made in other countries and for other potential impacts, some of which may be far more serious than regional drying in Australia. Assessments will also need to be updated as further improvements are made to climate and impact models.

Given the uncertainties, I suggested in Chapter 8 that equilibrium greenhouse concentrations equivalent to less than 400 ppm CO_2-equivalent might lead to a globally acceptable low level of risk of overall dangerous impacts, although the uncertainty about climate sensitivity and thresholds or 'tipping points' suggested that we should aim for concentrations as low as possible to be on the safe side.

Reference to **Table 4** suggests that such a target in the range below 445 ppm CO_2-equivalent (the lowest range considered in the IPCC modelling) requires a global reduction in emissions of more than 80% by 2050. Moreover, as the IPCC notes, such an equilibrium concentration target is only likely to be achieved by an overshoot scenario in which CO_2 is taken out of the atmosphere after reaching a peak above the long-term target. So this requires an eventual reduction of emissions beyond 100% to negative emissions. The less than 445 ppm figure is of course subjective. It is determined by a choice of an acceptable level of risk. Such choices are ultimately determined by politics.

Nevertheless, the choice of a target of an 80% reduction in global emissions by 2050 gains powerful and explicit support from Prof. Martin

Parry and others who were key leaders of the 2007 IPCC Working Group II Report on impacts, in a paper published on 29 May 2008. They state:

Limiting impacts to acceptable levels by mid-century and beyond would require an 80 per cent cut in global emissions by 2050. This cut would stabilize atmospheric greenhouse gas levels at 400–470 parts per million of carbon dioxide equivalents instead of the 450–550 parts per million that would be reached if we cut emissions by 50 per cent from 1990 levels … under this policy, there is almost no chance of exceeding 2°C in 2050 and only a small likelihood in 2100. Compared with 50 per cent, an 80 per cent target would substantially reduce the harm caused by climate change: for example, it would halve the population put at risk of water stress and flooding.

They went on to say:

We have lost ten years talking about climate change but not acting on it. Meanwhile, evidence from the IPCC indicates that the problem is bigger than we thought. A curious optimism – the belief that we can find a way to fully avoid all the serious threats illustrated above – pervades the political arenas of the G8 summit and UN climate meetings. This is false optimism, and it is obscuring reality. The sooner we recognise this delusion, confront the challenge and implement both stringent emissions cuts and major adaptation efforts, the less will be the damage that we and our children will have to live with.[8]

In taking such a public stand these scientists are going beyond their IPCC role as uncommitted scientists to exert their rights as citizens to make value judgements informed by their scientific knowledge. Exerting a similar right as responsible citizens in May 2008, more than 1700 US scientists and economists, including six Nobel Laureates and many members of the US Academies of Sciences and Engineering, and over 100 contributors to the IPCC reports, called for urgent US commitment to an emissions reduction target of 80% by 2050, with an interim goal of 15–20% below 2000 levels by 2030.[9]

But next consider that the developed countries historically have emitted the most greenhouse gases (see **Figure 30**), and have a great capacity to conserve energy and develop less carbon-intensive technologies. Developing countries, however, historically emitted little, are rapidly developing and need to increase their energy use, and most likely their emissions, in order to alleviate poverty. This brings in the equity issue, discussed further below, but let us make some small allowance for equity considerations here. International equity suggests that a round figure for developed countries might be well in excess of an 80% reduction in emissions by 2050, while developing countries should also try as hard as possible to limit their emissions even as they achieve stronger economies in the next few decades. Perhaps they should aim at rapidly reducing their emissions per unit GDP. This would allow for growth, but be a start towards an ultimate convergence of living standards and emissions per person between rich and poor. Help with the latest technology from the rich countries could accelerate this process. Even with this allowance for equity, people in developed countries would still be emitting more greenhouse gases per person in 2050 than those in most (if not all) developing nations.

It should be clear from this that two key policy issues are which target concentration provides an acceptable level of risk, and how the necessary emissions reductions should be split between the developed and developing countries. These are highly contentious issues. The above suggestion that the global target must be less than 445 ppm CO_2-equivalent is subject to revision as we learn more about the costs, achievability of the target, and the risks from climate change. Clearly, the choice of how to split the task of reaching this target concentration between developed and developing countries is another highly political one, with considerations of justice and achievability paramount. My hope, indeed the hope for the

world, is that large reductions in emissions may be easier than most of us think. We will only really know when we try, but the recent rise in the price of oil (for whatever reason) is making energy efficiency and renewable energy look more attractive, as does the need for energy security.

How urgently do we need to act?

One other key policy question, hotly contested politically, remains: how urgent is it to start reducing emissions? **Table 4** supplies the answer. That is, to have any hope of achieving stabilisation targets in the range at or below 445 ppm CO_2-equivalent, emissions need to peak between the years 2000 and 2015. The IPCC 2007 report already notes that to achieve these low stabilisation targets, modelling suggested that an overshoot scenario was needed, that is, that later this century emissions would need to become negative. Clearly early emission reductions would lessen the need for or magnitude of this overshoot later.

Some economic modelling has been done on the pros and cons of more or less drastic early emissions reductions. This suggests that less stringent reductions in the immediate future would require more stringent reductions later, but perhaps at a lower overall cost if some economic discounting is allowed, but that this leads to an ultimate penalty of some greater global warming and sea-level rise. If such delayed or slower mitigation action were to lead to the climate passing some tipping point leading to global climatic disaster, such as the disintegration of the Greenland and/or West Antarctic ice sheets, then the delay would have been extremely costly.

Early emissions reductions allow a slower rate of emissions reductions later, which may well have less severe effects on global economies and be more technologically feasible. Against this, those who prefer to gamble on the problem being exaggerated, possibly because early emissions reductions appear to be too costly, will push for delays in emissions reductions. While this wait-and-see argument had some appeal a few years ago, the recent accelerated rate of growth in emissions, global warming and most importantly loss of Arctic sea ice, suggests that we may have already passed an early tipping point towards dangerous climate impacts including rapid sea-level rise and further warming.[10]

Further, any delay in emissions reductions may lead to further investment in industries and infrastructure that may become obsolete and have to be written off in the event of a climate emergency in which the need for drastic emissions reductions becomes clearer. Thus, for example, new coal-fired power stations or shale oil production investments may prove to be bad investments, as they may soon have to be abandoned or at least retrofitted for carbon capture and sequestration at great expense. This issue becomes particularly acute if the primary response to rising oil prices is to build coal-to-oil or shale oil production facilities.

As noted earlier, global emissions have been increasing in the last decade at rates around 2–3% per annum. If we are to reduce emissions by more than 80% by 2050, we need to instead *reduce* emissions by 2–3% each year starting now. My view is that this should be our guide, with a learning-by-doing attitude, where we avoid new investments in high emitting infrastructure and encourage, with all the carrots and sticks we can, investments in low-carbon technologies. We can then see how easy or difficult it is. But we must be quite clear in our understanding that any delay in reducing emissions cuts off options for stabilisation at low concentrations, and is likely to raise the price for future generations. There can be no guarantees: we are in the risk management business, whether we like it or not.

How much will reducing emissions cost?

This question is often answered by considering only the cost of mitigation measures in isolation. In fact these costs must be weighed against the potential costs of damages due to climate change. Estimates of the latter have a strong ethical values-laden component that is often overlooked, namely non-market or uncertain costs such as damages to human health and the environment, extinctions, disproportionate effects on the world's poor, the potential for catastrophic damages or surprises, possible irreversible changes, and the increased danger resulting from delayed emissions reductions.

As discussed in Chapter 8, the IPCC 2007 report estimated the cost of emission reductions necessary to achieve a target stabilisation concentration of 445 ppm CO_2-equivalent at some 5.5% of the global average GDP by 2050. This amounts to a decrease in annual economic growth of about 0.12% per annum. Cost would be marginally higher for targets somewhat less than 445 ppm. The estimated costs depend on what is taken as the reference scenario, that is, the scenario with no reductions in greenhouse gas emissions due to concern about climate change (such as in the SRES scenarios). For high emissions reference scenarios in the SRES range (see **Box 3**, and **Figures 15** and **16**), for example the A1T and A1FI, costs are at the high end. For low SRES emissions scenarios as reference cases, such as the B1, the cost is nearer the 1% estimate. Thus it is evident that different development pathways, pursued for reasons other than greenhouse policy (for example an extremely high price for oil), would strongly influence the costs of emissions reductions. However, the likelihood of the world following either the extreme high or extreme low emissions scenarios in the absence of greenhouse policies is probably small.

The 'Stern review on the economics of climate change', published in the UK in 2006, prior to the IPCC 2007 Report, was very influential in demonstrating that the cost of emissions reductions may well be less than that of climate change impacts avoided.[11] While the Stern Review was roundly criticised at the time by some economists and others for its choice of low discount rates and high estimates of impacts, subsequent analyses, some included in the IPCC report and other later ones, have tended to come up with similar estimates. A lot depends on what allowance is made for damages from extreme events and irreversible changes in estimates of climate change damages. These were neglected in many earlier damage estimates.

Even some of the strongest critics of the Stern Review, Gary Yohe and Richard Tol, agree with the statement made by others that the Stern Review is 'right for the wrong reasons'. They say: '[Our] list of concerns, notwithstanding, we think there are sound economic arguments for greenhouse gas emission reduction that can inform both the long-term goals of climate policy and the short-term steps that should be taken immediately'.[12]

It bears repeating also, that if economic growth continues at rates of several per cent per year, GDP doubles in only a few decades. In that case, a 5 or 6% lower GDP by 2050 (the worst case) due to emissions reductions only delays the achievement of the same GDP by a year or two. Arguably, this is a small price to pay for greater safety in the face of the very significant risk of extremely costly climate change.

Another consideration is that research and development in carbon-efficient and low-carbon energy technologies and their implementation in the market place are open-ended and almost impossible to predict, beyond what is already in the pipeline. As we saw in Chapter 8, huge potential sources of renewable energy are available, as well as possibilities for carbon-removal and storage or sequestration. Cost study estimates so far have tended to confine themselves to existing technology, or modest innovations, with little allowance for dramatic reductions in cost likely to follow from human ingenuity and inventiveness. A ten-fold decrease in the cost of photovoltaic energy, as claimed by Nanosolar, or a cheaper and almost zero-emissions compressed air car, as claimed by Tata Motors in India and Zero Pollution Motors in the US, would put a different complexion on a low-carbon future. Energy and fuels from processing of urban waste, and biochar are other exciting developments. Revolutionary low-carbon technologies are waiting in the wings and could substantially reduce the cost of mitigation.

Moreover, the present trend in some developed countries towards personal fulfilment through ever larger and more energy-demanding automobiles, dwellings and lifestyles may be reversible through education, infrastructure planning and tax or other incentives. Examples of such behavioural changes in other areas include the rapid spread of recycling of waste in many developed countries, successful campaigns to reduce unprotected sunbathing because of ozone depletion and skin cancer, the wearing of seatbelts in cars and helmets on bicycles, decreases in smoking, and greater use of public transport where it is convenient and safe (as in many European cities and Perth in Australia). Profligate energy-wasting lifestyles are certainly not sustainable and impose many penalties on society such as pollution, urban sprawl (with loss of farm land) and ever-larger road systems, traffic congestion and accidents.

One interesting lifestyle suggestion that strikingly illustrates simultaneous benefits to the environment and other societal issues is that overweight people in developed countries, who are an increasing health problem, might be persuaded to walk or use bicycles instead of driving cars for short journeys. Such a change would lead to a healthier population, reduce medical expenses and at the same time save fossil fuel emissions. Paul and Millicent Higgins of Stanford and Michigan universities estimate that if the 39 million obese and 90 million overweight men and women in the US walked or biked instead of using cars for short journeys they would not only become healthier but might save up to 10% of US carbon dioxide emissions as at 1990 levels.[13]

Friedland and others argue that using public transport rather than private cars is far more environmentally important than recycling, which is widely adopted in many countries.[14]

Resource-intensive trends such as those followed historically in developed countries cannot be reproduced in the more populous countries of Asia, Africa and Latin America without unacceptable social costs. Increasing energy demand from China is already affecting the global oil price and adding to concerns about fossil energy supplies and the security of supply for developed countries. The economics and geopolitics of oil may already be playing a large part in motivating both developed and developing countries to reduce reliance on fossil fuel. The co-benefits of reduced fossil-energy use are becoming increasingly obvious.

Many opportunities are opened up by climate change mitigation, not only in specific low-carbon technologies, but also in the finance industry. This is perhaps epitomised in the paper 'Climate change and finance: new business opportunities', from the major international bank UBS, which points to a 'new market potential for a climate value investment product related to the implementation of the Kyoto Protocol mechanisms'.[15]

John Holdren of Harvard University and Director of the Woods Hole Research Center, has summarised the risks and opportunities for business firms and investors:

- Risks

  - climate-change damage to a firm's assets and operations,

  - climate-change damage to customers and markets,

  - financial and reputational liability for firm's contribution to climate-change risks,

  - competitive disadvantage from differential effects of government climate policies and failure to exploit opportunities presented.

- Opportunities

  - new/improved products and services in a climate-challenged world,

  - trading emissions permits and offsets,

  - 'green' portfolio development and management.[16]

It is also true that fossil fuel industries are at present heavily subsidised in many developed and developing countries. Economists Kym Anderson and Warwick McKibbin in 1997 calculated that reducing coal subsidies and trade barriers would lower emissions of carbon dioxide in OECD (developed) countries by 13% and global emissions by 5%. They also found that if low domestic prices for coal in major developing countries were raised to the level in international markets, their carbon dioxide emissions would be reduced by 4%. These market reforms are already under way in some European countries and to some extent in China, and are increasing economic efficiency rather than economic costs.[17]

The IPCC 2007 report estimates subsidies in the global energy sector as around 250–300 billion US$ per annum, of which only some 2–3% supports renewable energy. An OECD study in 2002 estimated that global CO_2 emissions could be reduced by more than 6% and real income increased by 0.1% by 2010 if support mechanisms on the fossil fuel and power-generation sectors were removed. Subsidies are presumably there for supposed socially desirable ends. What needs to be asked now is what are the relevant socially desirable ends, given the climate damages we are risking from continued greenhouse gas emissions.[18]

As pointed out in the book *Society, Behaviour and Climate Change Mitigation*, edited by E Jochem and colleagues, policy analysis is not a matter of a price comparison between different options, but of a choice between different interests, cultures and values. As one reviewer wrote:

Costs and benefits, as well as rights are all social constructs. What makes reduction of greenhouse gases, a cost? The same thing that made freeing slaves or giving women the vote, a cost? How would we feel if the same greenhouse mitigation activity was labelled an investment?[19]

It is what we value that counts, not what it costs in dollars and cents.

Meeting targets most efficiently

Two main issues are at stake regarding reducing greenhouse gas emissions to reduce the risk from climate change. One is whether changes to reduce fossil fuel emissions can be done without significantly slowing economic growth or lowering economic standards. Some economists, some others with vested interests in fossil fuel industries, and technological pessimists say it can only be done at great cost and with a lowering of living standards.

Others are more optimistic, believing that targeted research and development, together with economic incentives, can lead quickly to prosperous low-carbon-emissions futures through energy efficiency and technological change. As discussed by the IPCC in 2007 and others, induced technological change and learning by doing is critical to lower costs and increased efficiency.[20]

The other argument is whether emissions reductions are best achieved by a 'top-down' setting of mandatory emissions reduction targets, or best left to the so-called 'free market' on the basis that if there is a real problem, someone will find a way of making money out of solving it. A middle position, which I favour, is that this is an artificial dichotomy, since there is no such thing as a perfect free market, and the one we have is driven largely by short-term considerations of profit and has barriers to radical innovation.

Barriers include subsidies, incompatible infrastructure (sometimes known as the 'lock-in' effect) and economies of scale. Time lags in the operation of the market impede the rapid deployment of new and desirable technologies, so incentives are needed to speed up this process. Thus we need a combination of top-down goals and mechanisms and bottom-up market economics.[21]

The market is therefore best at deciding how to proceed most economically once long-term goals are set and appropriate mechanisms are in place. The market, properly regulated, should determine the most efficient way to meet our goals, but not the goals themselves, and in the case of an urgent need for change special mechanisms may be needed.

The relevant goal should be to minimise the risk of dangerous climate change, rather than setting immutable but debatable numerical targets. Interim targets need to be set, as discussed above, but these should be regularly revised in the light of experience and new knowledge.

A number of general principles seem to apply to efficiency in meeting such a broad policy aim as the reduction of greenhouse gas emissions, especially when no one technical measure seems likely to provide all the emissions savings needed. Such principles are listed in **Box 8**.

Several measures may be employed to foster these goals. They include the issuing of 'cap and trade' greenhouse gas emissions permits at provincial, national or global levels. Under this system, permits to emit greenhouse gases are issued according to some formula related to present emissions, and the amount that can be emitted is periodically reduced to meet progressively more stringent emission reduction targets, as needed. Permit holders can buy or sell their permits (termed 'carbon trading'), which logically means that those who can most easily and most economically reduce their emissions will do so and sell the excess permits to those who find it more difficult. This ensures that reductions in emissions are achieved at the least cost. Cap and trade permits were pioneered in the United States in relation to sulfur emissions, with great success, and came into operation for carbon dioxide in the EU in 2005, as well as being planned for Australia in 2010 and various other countries.[22]

Problems with carbon trading and carbon taxes include the impact on poor individuals and nations, and on workers in carbon-intensive industries. This will require special measures to guarantee their livelihoods by retraining and new job opportunities. Initial allocation of emissions permits should be at a uniform price so as not to reward high emitters or those with political influence. There are also considerable technical problems in the accurate assessment of emissions in the cases of emissions embedded in goods and services, especially those traded between countries or related to farming. However, all these problems, once recognised, can be overcome.

Special consideration must be given to the problem of 'leakage' of emissions to countries outside any carbon trading scheme. Leakage arises from the displacement of 'dirty' industries to countries that do not limit emissions. Preventing leakage is complicated by possible clashes with provisions under the World Trade Organization and is a strong reason for instituting a truly global carbon trading scheme.

The cap and trade system serves to encourage non-carbon emitting energy producers such as wind

BOX 8: EFFICIENT REDUCTION OF GREENHOUSE GAS EMISSIONS

Some principles applicable to efficient reduction of greenhouse gas emissions are:

- Include a wide range of contributions to the total solution, including both short-term (next two decades) and longer-term (next 20 to 100+ years) measures.

- Avoid favouring one technology over another without good reasons.

- Set broad standards and goals, thereby ensuring a stable and level playing field for public and private enterprise, encouraging long-term planning and investment.

- Provide incentives for research, development and market penetration that taper off with time and market share so as to ensure competitive and economical solutions.

- Ensure that any carrots (incentives) and sticks (penalties), such as subsidies or carbon taxes, apply equitably.

- Redistribute any tax revenue so as to stimulate rather than harm the economy, for example using revenue to reduce employment taxes.

- Facilitate the early retirement of energy- and carbon-intensive infrastructure through incentives, rapid depreciation allowances and provision of replacement infrastructure.

- Provide retraining and incentives for those otherwise adversely affected.

- Facilitate the transfer of energy- and carbon-efficient technology to developing countries through technological aid programs.

- Consider the wider context of climate change measures, such as energy and water security, food production, quality of life, sustainability and population policies.

- Be wary of unsubstantiated claims of low emissions, such as those that ignore embodied energy or claim difficult-to-quantify carbon sequestration.

- Objections to renewable energy technologies should be assessed on an equal footing with other technologies (for example the claimed adverse effects of wind farms on visual amenity or bird life compared to similar effects from overhead power lines, motorways or high-rise buildings).

and solar power generators by making their products more competitive with the carbon-emitting producers. This is because carbon emitters have to keep buying more permits to emit as the amount allowed under their existing permits shrinks with time, thus raising their prices. Moreover, as the market share of non-carbon emitting energy suppliers increases, their costs will decrease due to economies of scale and improved technology and infrastructure, and they will become more competitive.

Present large carbon emitters also can make money by increasing energy efficiency, changing their technology or diversifying into non-emitting activities. For example, companies with coal-fired power stations could phase out those stations, retrofit them with carbon capture and storage, or move to renewable energy sources. Each of these activities would enable them to recover the costs of emissions permits while continuing to supply the energy market. What they need is foresight and innovative skills.

Such foresight has been lamentably absent in many carbon-intensive industries over the last two decades as the case against carbon emissions has grown and the risk of making inappropriate investments in carbon-intensive processes has become greater. Many governments have encouraged, subsidised and even stood guarantors for such inappropriate investments, for example by guaranteeing low priced electricity for alumina smelters. This is now a matter for regret.

An alternative measure often proposed is a carbon tax that is introduced gradually but increases with time so as to eventually recover from energy users the full costs of energy production from whatever source, taking account of the environmental and health costs inflicted on the community. Such taxes are based on a 'user-pays' principle where users of polluting fuels pay for the costs inflicted on society by their use. For economic efficiency, these taxes must be varied from source to source according to the true external costs of their energy production. Based on the present cost of generation of electricity, wind and hydro-power (which are already competitive with coal and natural gas) would be more competitive if the external costs of generation from coal and natural gas were taken into account. With improved technologies, solar photovoltaic, solar thermal or other renewable technologies are becoming competitive also.

The principal argument against carbon taxes is that they will increase the price of energy, thus adversely affecting the economy. However, reducing taxes on production costs other than energy (for example payroll tax), and cheaper renewable energy as economies of scale and new technologies reduce

costs, would substantially negate this argument. Renewable energy is in general more labour intensive. This increases employment and thus reduces social welfare costs and increases income tax revenue.

Increased support for research and development for renewable energy and related infrastructure is being applied successfully in the EU and elsewhere. This includes mandatory targets for achieving market shares to bring these technologies into the market with economies of scale. Fossil fuel industries could also retain legitimacy by research and development of carbon sequestration methods, especially if retrofitted to existing generators. However, this would raise their costs, creating more of an opening for renewables, and is not likely to achieve substantial emission reductions in less than 10–20 years.

The process by which, decade by decade, the changing price structures for fossil fuel versus renewables might lead to a rapid increase in the market share of renewable energy is shown schematically in **Figure 34** with a corresponding reduction in greenhouse gas emissions.

In the first decade national or regional carbon taxes or carbon emission permits would marginally increase the price of fossil fuels, while renewable energy sources would be demonstrated and begin to penetrate the market. This is already happening in some countries, notably in the EU and in some states of the United States, such as California. Rapid increases in the price of oil (for reasons other than climate change policy) have already accelerated this process. By the next decade market penetration by renewables would have grown, with decreasing costs, and fossil fuel emissions would be reduced either by decreased use or carbon sequestration (which would gain credits under any carbon tax or permit system). In the third decade (or earlier with rapidly rising oil prices) proven renewable technologies would increase rapidly both in developed and developing countries. Decentralised renewables would often be preferred in developing countries due to lower infrastructure costs and more available sunshine in low latitude and arid

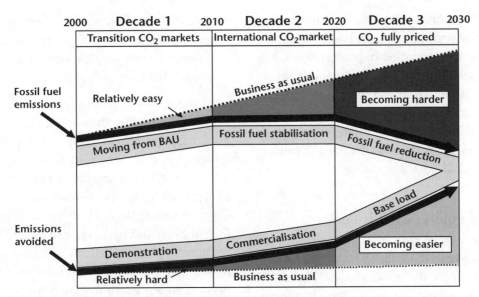

Figure 34: How renewables energy might increase their share of the total energy market. The upper black curve shows notional changes in fossil fuel emissions. The lower one shows the reduction in total emissions due to low-carbon energy. BAU is 'Business As Usual'. (Schematic courtesy of Dr Greg Bourne, WWF Australia.)

countries. Renewables are also becoming more practical for large baseline power supply as high voltage direct current power lines become available with low loss transmission.

Recent reports suggest that, in addition to wind energy, which is already comparable in price with fossil fuels, solar photovoltaic electricity in Germany should reach parity with grid prices within a few years, as it has done in California and Italy. China-based Suntech, one of the world's biggest makers of PV panels, with five factories and representation in China, Japan, Germany, Spain and Australia, plans to double its production from 540 MW in 2008 to 1 GW in 2009.[23]

The key to achieving a low-emissions technological scenario is a general realisation that it is essential in order to reduce risks from climate change. Energy businesses need to face up to the threat from competitors, customers, regulators and legislatures. Success in this new milieu will come from forward thinking, entrepreneurial activity, innovation, technological breakthroughs and start-ups. Progressive CEOs and entrepreneurs will win through at the expense of those who remain rooted in the past. The new industrial revolution is inevitable, but unpredictable in detail. It will

happen as people embrace it and learn by doing. Industries and companies that fail to adapt will become yesterday's industries.

In developing countries emissions reductions are also possible despite economic growth imperatives. As early as 2002, a study for the Pew Center on Global Climate Change, 'Climate Change Mitigation in Developing Countries' (see http://www.pewclimate.org) documented emissions reduction efforts in Brazil, China, India, Mexico, South Africa and Turkey, and suggested how further emissions savings could be made. The study concluded that:

- Many developing countries are already taking action reducing their greenhouse emissions growth.

- These efforts are driven not so much by climate policy as by imperatives for development and poverty alleviation, local environment protection, and energy security.

- Developing nations offer large opportunities for further emissions mitigation, but competing demands for resources may hamper progress.

Developing countries can use policies to leverage human capacity, investment, and technology to capture large-scale mitigation opportunities, while simultaneously fostering development, but equity will require that they have some special consideration as they grow their economies. China and India already have some of the largest renewable energy sectors in the world (see Chapter 11), putting many developed countries to shame.

International equity: what is fair?

Historically, developed countries have emitted the most greenhouse gases since the industrial revolution and become rich in the process (see **Figure 30** in Chapter 8). Advocates from less-developed countries argue that equity therefore requires that less-developed countries should be able to continue to use fossil fuels to develop, or else be compensated and assisted by richer countries if they are to reduce their reliance on fossil fuels. However, a simple extrapolation of recent growth rates in emissions in major developing countries such as India and China indicates that their emissions will dominate global emissions within the next several decades. Thus, if we are to limit climate change through global emissions reductions, the cooperation of developing countries is essential.

Any successful international effort to limit climate change and to cope with its impacts requires that both developed and developing countries play a significant role. Success will not be forthcoming if the key concerns of all major greenhouse gas emitting nations, including the United States, China, India and Brazil, are not adequately taken into account in the future development of the climate change regime under the UNFCCC. The support of lesser emitting nations, who will be adversely affected by climate change, is also essential. International equity is thus not only a matter of ethics and fairness, but also an essential means to persuading all relevant countries to adopt a joint action plan.

As Tom Athanasiou and Paul Baer put it in their book *Dead Heat: Global Justice and Global Warming*:

A climate treaty that indefinitely restricts a Chinese (or Indian) to lower emissions than an American (or European) will not be accepted as fair and, finally, will not be accepted at all. Climate equity, far from being a 'preference', is essential to ecological sustainability.[24]

Some developed country advocates argue that limiting global carbon emissions would slow economic growth in both developed and lesser-developed countries and that this would harm all countries. This argument is essentially a result of technological pessimism about economical emissions reductions. However, it merely postpones the problem and makes it more acute in the future, as more drastic reductions will be needed later on to stabilise the climate. If emission reductions are needed urgently now to reduce the risk from present and future climate change, postponing action is indeed dangerous. If time lags between cause and effect are important, it is urgent to act now.

Moreover, impacts of climate change will not be equitable. As the IPCC 2001 report authors concluded:

There is high confidence that developing countries will be more vulnerable to climate change than developed countries, and there is medium confidence that climate change would exacerbate income inequalities between and within countries.[25]

This means that progress on managing climate change risk requires that human impacts on climate, and historical responsibility for them, must be acknowledged and taken into account in the multilateral negotiations under the UNFCCC. Notwithstanding the necessity to negotiate extensions to the emissions reduction regime established under the Kyoto Protocol (see below) beyond the first commitment period (which expires in 2012), the issue of sharing climate impact burdens must be fully acknowledged, since many climate change and sea-level rise impacts have now become inevitable. How to do this is unclear, as it includes weighty questions such as what to do about 25 million Bangladeshis likely to be rendered homeless this century by sea-level rise.

Benito Muller of Oxford University has argued that a first step in this direction might be a call for a legally binding, mandatory Disaster Response Instrument under the UNFCCC. Other possible responses include an insurance fund, financed by the industrialised countries, to pay costs of climate change impacts, as was proposed by the Alliance of Small Island States, or a general increase in international aid for sustainable development. These measures would assist developing countries to cope with inevitable climate change, and predispose and enable them to work towards reducing greenhouse gas emissions.[26]

As stated by John Ashton (now UK Special Representative for Climate Change) and Xueman Wang in a valuable essay on equity and climate, 'equity', whether based in philosophy, morality or human nature, is an ideal that shapes our view of what is right or just. It is predicated on the notion of the common good, and at times may call on some to sacrifice for the sake of others. 'Interest', on the other hand, is what is best for the individual or nation. Interest, and especially national interest, may include equity as a consideration, but not necessarily the dominant one. Ashton and Wang note that the UNFCCC and the Kyoto Protocol both convey a palpable sense that the negotiators bent over backwards to find a package of outcomes that all could consider fair.[27]

Ashton and Wang identify five aspects of equity:

- *Responsibility*: when our interests are harmed, the question of who is to blame usually arises. This gives rise to the 'polluter pays' principle.

- *Equal entitlements*: all human beings have equal rights or entitlements, notably to liberty, security, impartial justice and opportunity. This is embodied in the United Nations Charter and in many national constitutions and laws. Such rights may include rights to land, water, food, housing and cultural identity, all of which may be threatened by climate change and sea-level rise.

- *Capacity*: the idea is that the most able should contribute most to the provision of a public good. This is the basis of progressive taxation and of philanthropy by the rich.

- *Basic needs*: this is the idea that the strong and well-endowed should help the weak and the poor in meeting their most basic needs, and is the basis of a 'safety net' in many countries for the poor and disadvantaged.

- *Comparable effort*: this compares the efforts of different parties to any overall effort, to ensure that they are 'fair' given the different circumstances of the parties. What people do about those in need may differ according to circumstances, but it should be fair.

Based on such considerations, Eileen Claussen and Lisa McNeilly of the Pew Center on Climate Change suggest a set of principles for climate change negotiations, shown in **Box 9**.[28] Many of these, and related principles such as the Precautionary Principle, are already included in the text of the UNFCCC and the Kyoto Protocol, but their consequences do not yet seem to have been adequately taken on board by all the countries which are parties to the UNFCCC.

The United States and Australia, although parties to the UNFCCC, objected to the provisions of the Kyoto Protocol, which attempt to define how the aims of the Convention might be implemented in the short-term (until 2012). Indeed the US withdrew from the 'Kyoto process' on the grounds that the mandated emissions reductions for developed countries would retard economic growth, and that in the first round of reductions in emissions no commitment is required of the lesser-developed countries. The latter is still characterised as 'unfair' by many US Congress members and some Australian politicians. However, after a change of government in late 2007, Australia has signed the Kyoto Protocol.

The charge of unfairness by the US and some Australian politicians is based on the idea that mandated emissions targets in developed countries but not in developing countries would lead to emissions intensive industries being transferred to developing countries. They suggest this would lead to loss of jobs in developed countries, and no real decrease in global emissions. However, a suitably

BOX 9: PRINCIPLES FOR CLIMATE NEGOTIATIONS

Eileen Claussen and Lisa McNeilly of the Pew Center on Global Climate Change suggest the following guiding principles for climate negotiations:

- All nations should be able to maintain or improve standards of living under a global climate change mitigation regime. Consequently, climate change mitigation should focus on alternative low-carbon development paths that don't reduce economic growth.

- More broadly, the outcome of UNFCCC negotiations should not undermine or hinder progress toward the goal of sustainable development.

- The countries most responsible for greenhouse gas concentrations in the atmosphere should be leaders in the effort to reduce emissions.

- All nations should work to the best of their abilities – or with help from other countries – to reduce emissions either absolutely or relative to business-as-usual trajectories.

- The world should take advantage of emission reduction opportunities where they exist.

framed system of emissions credits would largely obviate this problem, as would a revision of developing country obligations beyond 2012, the end of the first commitment period under the Kyoto Protocol. Many ideas are being put forward, from both developed and developing countries, regarding how this might be done and negotiations are continuing.

The arguments regarding unfairness of the Kyoto provisions tend to ignore many of the above considerations regarding equity, and confuse a short-term view of national self-interest with the question of equity. These arguments also ignore the fact that, for a variety of reasons, many developing countries, notably China, Brazil and India, have voluntarily reduced their emissions well below business-as-usual through various measures. These include removal of some energy subsidies, fostering of renewable energy, and in the case of China partial substitution of natural gas and renewables for coal. Indeed, China has a major solar energy program and one of its companies (Suntech) is a world leader in producing solar photovoltaics.[23, 29]

The American ethicist Thomas W Pogge of Columbia University argues that there are three basic reasons why increased inequity should concern us:

1. A duty to help people in distress.

2. A duty to oppose and reject systems and institutions which lead to or perpetuate poverty and from which we benefit.

3. Prudential considerations that others being poor may make us worse off (in the long run, for example, through loss of trade, instability, cross-border migration pressures, radical movements, and even terrorism).[30]

These reasons suggest a need for concern about inequity and poverty in general. Regrettably however, they have not been persuasive enough to make rich countries substantially eliminate inequity and poverty so far. Indeed, the percentage of rich nations' GDP being devoted to non-military aid has in recent decades significantly decreased. Nevertheless, it is worth looking closer at these reasons for concern in the narrower perspective of climate change.

The *first* reason is a positive duty to help people in distress. It is taught by all the world's great religions, but is usually followed only by some people in some cases. We quickly become overwhelmed by the needs of others and tend to close our eyes and ears except to those nearest to us or those whose plight is dramatised on television. It is easy to recognise when people are in distress, but also easy in many cases to rationalise not helping them.

Too often we find ways of blaming the poor for their poverty instead of seeking constructive ways to help. Moreover, reporting by the media of people in distress is highly selective, so that we are often unaware of the real extent of poverty and inequity. Not to put too fine a point on it, one rich person who dies in a traffic accident in London or New York is often more newsworthy than a hundred poor people who die of starvation in Africa. People in far off places, or from different religious or ethnic groups are often of less concern. That is why the Parable of the Good Samaritan is so powerful and challenging in the Christian tradition.[31]

The *second* duty is a more stringent negative one: not to uphold injustice, and not to contribute to or profit by the unjust impoverishment of others. Here the moral duty is plain, but recognising when we are indeed upholding unjust systems, and profiting by them, is more difficult and may be contentious.

Pogge develops a detailed set of criteria for determining when such unjust systems and institutions exist, including a shared institutional order that is shaped by the better-off and imposed on the worse-off, the possibility of an institutional alternative which would reduce the inequity, and the absence of other explanations for the inequity.

Applying these ideas to the question of climate change impacts, it is plain that continued and indeed increasing emissions of greenhouse gases are leading to increasing inequity, and that the developed nations are the main emitters historically, and on a per capita basis for the foreseeable future. This is historically the result of institutional arrangements that have allowed unrestricted emissions, with no strong incentive to reduce our reliance on carbon-intensive industry and development. Clearly, with the advent of the UNFCCC and the Kyoto Protocol there is an alternative institutional arrangement which seeks initially to limit emissions, and which foreshadows attempts to greatly reduce them. This would lead to a reduction in climate change and thus in the additional inequity increasing emissions would otherwise cause.[32]

On this analysis, the second reason clearly applies: developed countries actively contribute to a system that increases inequity, and they have historically profited by it through the provision of cheap energy and higher living standards. Again, the real problem for most people in rich countries is to realise the extent of their complicity in increasing inequity. This is a matter for analysis and education.

This concern for justice does motivate many people in developed countries, notably the churches and others of religious faith. Groups such as the *Evangelical Environmental Network* and *What Would Jesus Drive* campaign (which campaigns against the growing use of 'gas-guzzling' recreational vehicles) base their position squarely on a Biblical understanding of justice, concern for the poor and stewardship of God's creation. Indeed, a related 'Oxford Declaration on Global Warming' in 2002 argues on the basis of God's creation and of justice for the poor, that 'leaders in churches, business and government …[should]… take necessary action to maintain the climate system as a remarkable provision in creation for sustaining all life on Earth.'[33]

In similar vein, in 2003 Senators Joseph Lieberman and John McCain (the Republican presidential candidate in 2008) called their bill, placed before the US Senate to create a national carbon emissions cap-and-trade regime, the *Climate Stewardship Act*. Senator Lieberman stated:

The word stewardship in the title of the act was not chosen coincidentally, [but rather] because John McCain and I believe we have a stewardship responsibility over the earth and the people on it, who are, after all, God's creations.

Lieberman characterised the *Climate Stewardship Act*, which gained 43 votes out of 100 in the US Senate, as 'a faith-based initiative'.[34]

The *third* reason for concern about growing inequity is a more selfish one, justifying moral action (according to the first two reasons above), 'only' because reducing the hunger and poverty of others may increase our wellbeing or security. Nevertheless, in a world where profits and security are higher priorities for many in positions of power than altruistic moral conduct, prudential arguments may in the end be the more powerful for many decision-makers. Moreover, they need not exclude the moral arguments, but merely reinforce them.[35]

So what are the prudential reasons for seeking to avoid an increase in inequity due to climate change? Some possible reasons are shown in **Box 10**. These are each complex issues, and it is not possible to argue them fully here, but I skim lightly over them below.

Development has already been historically slowed in countries exposed to climatic disasters, such as Bangladesh (floods and typhoons), sub-Saharan Africa (drought), Mozambique (floods), several Pacific islands (tropical cyclones), and Honduras, Haiti and other Caribbean countries (hurricanes and floods). As this increases with climate change, more aid will be needed and more forced migration will occur for environmental and economic reasons.

Hamilton, Turton and Pollard argue that climate change will adversely affect developing country members of the British Commonwealth of Nations vis-à-vis developed members, so that developed members who do not reduce emissions are acting contrary to the principles of the Commonwealth which include a commitment to 'a more equitable international society'.[36]

Outbreaks of Severe Acute Respiratory Syndrome (SARS) and other diseases (for example malaria and

BOX 10: PRUDENTIAL REASONS FOR MINIMISING INEQUITY

Growing international inequity due to climate change might:

- Slow development in poor countries.

- Reduce trade between the developed and developing countries.

- Create more problems for aid programs.

- Add to trans-border health problems.

- Lead to millions of displaced people, either internally within countries, or across borders as environmental 'refugees'.

- Increase migration pressures on the borders of the rich countries.

- Foster political instability and radicalism in developing countries.

- Stimulate anger, hatred and hopelessness leading to potential terrorists, both among the poor and indeed among the idealistic or radical rich.

dengue fever), transmitted internationally by air transport, illustrate the threat from these and other possibly climatically-induced disease outbreaks. The uncontrolled transmission of diseases may well increase with increased climate change and sea-level rise induced cross-border migration, especially if it is not part of a regulated immigration or refugee program with health checks.

The problem of economically and environmentally forced migrations, both internal and across borders, is increasing. A paper presented at the International Association for the Study of Forced Migration in 2003 states:

> Addressing humanitarian crises involving mass migration is integral to maintaining international security and sustainable development. This is particularly the case post-September 11, when it has become apparent that such countries as Afghanistan that experience prolonged humanitarian emergencies can too easily become breeding grounds for terrorism.[37]

The paper points out that such forced migrants do not as yet share the same status in international law as refugees from political or other persecution, and urges a widening of the definition of 'refugees'. Many of these environmental refugees are unlikely to be able to return home.

In a study on the 'Environment and its relation to sustainable development' in 2003, the International Council for Science (ICSU) states:

> It could be forecasted with very high level of probability that the total number of environmental refugees will increase both in relative and absolute quantity ... Appearance of large numbers of environmental refugees could be one of the biggest problems for government in the 21st century.

Of the world's 19 megacities, 16 are situated on coastlines, and many will be vulnerable to sea-level rise, as will many other people living on low-lying islands and coastlines. A 1-metre rise in sea level would displace tens of millions of people in Bangladesh, Vietnam and elsewhere. Who will accept responsibility for them? Considering the possibilities, Molly Conisbee and Andrew Simms of the New Economics Foundation (UK) write:

> The spectre of wholesale relocation of populations raises fundamental questions about citizenship and nationality. Once land has been lost, will residual nationality be able to persist, or does there need to be a new category of 'world citizen'? Could such a status be created in acknowledgement of the fact that climate change is a collective problem and requires a collective solution?[38]

These are not going to be easy questions to address, but they will increasingly be consequences of climate change.

There will always be radical groups and individuals bent on extremism and anti-democratic behaviour, often wedded to some extreme ideology. However, poverty and a sense of inequity, injustice and hopelessness opens up grievances in the broader population and creates fertile ground for recruitment to radical groups. This occurs not only among the poor, but also among the richer and better educated elite, who for idealistic reasons identify with the poor and the oppressed. We have seen this in many places including Northern Ireland, Palestine and throughout the Islamic world, and in the UK. It may not lead to logical behaviour, is often accompanied by extremism and is often counter-productive, but it is fostered by perceived injustice and inequity.

It is not stretching things too much to see that such instability and extremism may be exacerbated by an increase in poverty and inequities associated with climate change and climatic disasters, especially if they can plausibly be blamed (at least in part) on the rich. This is hardly in the interests of the rich, although many in rich countries do not seem to see the connection.

A lot has been written about 'environmental security'. This means different things to different people. To some it is ensuring that each country secures its environment by military means if necessary, for example to protect water supplies or prevent mass movements across borders. To others it means demonstrating the inadequacy of a purely military approach to security in the face of environmental threats that cross borders, such as acid rain, oil spills or climate change.[39]

Environmental issues, and particularly climate have little respect for borders, although some countries will be more seriously affected than others. In some cases, climate change will provide added reasons for conflicts, whether over water, access to an ice-free Arctic, or to cross-border migration. In an increasingly globalised economic system, climate changes that adversely affect sections of the human race are likely to adversely affect the rest of us eventually, so we all have a stake in environmental security. The UNFCCC concept of 'dangerous' levels of climate change encapsulates the idea. Just because we may be rich does not mean we are immune from the effects of climate change.

The importance of equity within countries

Equity within countries is also an issue, as it is with many environmental and development issues. Different sectors and regions within countries will be differently affected by both climate change effects and emissions reduction measures.

Climate change will affect the most vulnerable, who are usually the poor and isolated, often living in low-lying, flood-prone areas or on hillsides vulnerable to erosion and landslides. Others live in communities where water is scarce and medical services inadequate. In developed countries this often includes indigenous communities and people in polluted urban slums.

Communities dependent on particular affected sectors such as farming or tourism may also be adversely affected by increased aridity, changing markets or loss of tourist attractions such as coral reefs or beaches. In the Australian irrigated agricultural region of Sunraysia, near Mildura, increasing aridity in the Murray-Darling Basin has led to severe cuts in irrigation supplies in recent years, with large areas of grapevines and orange groves having to be abandoned. Adaptation in these cases should include compensation, relief and special help in the form of improved health and emergency services, the fostering of alternative industries such as renewable power generation, relocation and retraining.

Alice Fothergill of the University of Vermont (US) and Lori Peek have documented the phenomenon in the United States where the poor are more vulnerable to natural disasters due to such factors as place and type of residence, building construction and social exclusion.[40] A recent report for the Congressional Black Caucus Foundation in the US concluded that:

- African Americans are already disproportionately burdened by the health effects of climate change. This includes deaths during heatwaves and from worsened air pollution.

- Economic hardship and unemployment associated with climate change will fall more heavily on African Americans.

- African Americans are less responsible for climate change than other Americans.

- Policies to reduce climate change can generate large health and economic benefits for African Americans.[41]

Emissions reduction programs will impact unevenly on sectors and communities, with those dependent on fossil fuel industries adversely affected and in need of retraining, relocation or other assistance. This should be made easier by the growth in employment in renewable energy sectors, although in some cases the same people may not be easily transferred from one job to another. In general, renewable energy is more labour intensive, so more jobs may be forthcoming, although often in other locations. Indeed DeCanio in *The Economics of Climate Change* points out that the annual rate of job growth in the US far exceeds the total jobs in the fossil fuels industry and that 'the role of policy is to minimize transition costs and to ensure that such costs do not fall disproportionately on narrow segments of the population such as coal industry employees'.[42]

Correctly managed, the move to less carbon-intensive industries should be an opportunity to lesson inequities within countries. For example, in remote Australia many Indigenous groups seek to maintain their ties to their traditional land, but others maintain that such communities are unsustainable due to lack of employment opportunities. With the support of local Aboriginal Land Councils, solar thermal, geothermal, tidal or wind power installations in these areas could provide meaningful employment and so sustain these communities.

Proper provision for people adversely affected by greenhouse gas emission reduction programs will be vital, not only as a matter of equity, but also in order to obtain community support for necessary changes. Indeed, the most influential opposition to mandatory greenhouse gas emissions programs, including the Kyoto Protocol, comes from people directly dependent on the fossil fuel extraction and energy-intensive industries, and who therefore see themselves disadvantaged by such programs. In some cases such as in Australia, however, miners' unions have seen the writing on the wall and are pressing for emissions reductions and other measures that will maintain jobs (although with possibly unrealistic expectations for the viability of carbon capture and sequestration).[43]

Provision must be made for orderly and non-threatening transitions from fossil fuels to renewables, with reinvestment of capital with accelerated investment cycles, and preferential redeployment of displaced labour. Carbon removal and sequestration programs in the fossil fuel industries may well play a major role in this transition, although, for reasons discussed earlier, it is unlikely to be economic or sustainable in the long run. Foresight and planning by fossil fuel companies for alternative technology investments and employment can play a big role in reducing the potential inequities of emission control measures. This has been shown already by several large corporations including BP and Shell, which have both established renewable energy businesses.

Equity between generations[44]

Climate change will alter and possibly restrict the choices and opportunities of generations to come, especially if sudden, large-scale and irreversible changes to the climate system are triggered, such as those discussed in Chapter 6. Losses of large areas of highly populated coastal land due to sea-level rise will be one such issue. Future generations will not be responsible for the climatic situation bequeathed by us, but they will be entitled to access to energy and also to an acceptable environment and livelihood. If we continue to emit large quantities of greenhouse gases, the effects of which may take many decades to work their way through the climate system, future generations are likely to suffer disastrous environmental effects and will be obliged to emit far less if they are to get the climate back within safe limits. They may even be obliged to remove greenhouse gases from the atmosphere, possibly at great cost.

We cannot know how easy it will be for future generations to cope with a climate that we have changed, nor what sort of extreme or rapid changes they may experience. Nor can we know how easily they will be able to make do with much reduced use of fossil fuels, which they may have to face if they are to stabilise or restore climate after we fail to act. Under these circumstances we have an obligation to adhere to the Precautionary Principle (see Chapter 4). The onus is on the present generation to make decisions regarding emissions of greenhouse gases that will not pose a significant risk of serious adverse consequences to future generations.

It is almost axiomatic that the faster we bring climate change under control, the less likely it is that we will damage the interests of future generations through climate change itself. However, some economists have argued that expenditure now on reducing greenhouse gas emissions reduces the opportunity to invest in other developments that could benefit future generations. As discussed earlier, this is usually allowed for by applying a discount rate, or rate of devaluation of future costs as against present costs. This rate is usually close to that of inflation, interest rates or rate of return on investments.

However, future costs from the impacts of climate change may not be merely marginal. They could be disastrous, leading to deflation and the collapse of economies. In that case normal discounting would not be sensible, the applicable rate is uncertain and could be zero (as in the UK Stern Report) or even negative. Uncertainty about future climate change impacts, with a risk of large adverse effects, makes early action to minimise climate change more desirable as a form of insurance or precaution. Moreover, uncertainty about the real costs of emissions reduction, given possible technological advances that might rapidly reduce costs, makes early action to stimulate appropriate new technology through research, development and market penetration highly advisable.

We now have an increasingly good appreciation of just how disastrous future uncontrolled climate change is likely to be, with massive sea-level rises possibly locked in, widespread water shortages in low and middle latitudes, acidification of the oceans, and widespread crop failures and loss of species. Food shortages, displaced populations, social instability and conflict are likely consequences. The worst effects will be delayed due to inertia in the natural and human systems, but this delay is looking less than we once thought. Our children and grandchildren, and possibly even us in our later years, will face horrendous problems if we do not act soon to curb greenhouse gas emissions. Future generations will not thank us for further delays in emissions reductions.

The role of governments and NGOs[45]

Modern democracies consist of representative governments usually elected for terms of three to six years. Moreover, global economic forces and the behaviour of markets often limit their freedom of action. Such market forces are often driven by short-term considerations, but in the case of major corporations longer time perspectives may apply. Governments also operate in a political climate where the voices and support or opposition from business groups, trade unions and community organisations play a vital role. Short-term thinking drives some of these organisations as well, but many have a longer time perspective and greater continuity than particular government administrations.

Issues such as climate change are highly complex, with imperfect information, highly technical and scientific connections, issues of human behaviour and values, and large uncertainties. In the case of climate change this is further complicated by large time lags between actions regarding greenhouse gas emissions, and their eventual consequences, which may be large but delayed by decades to centuries.

The electoral cycle for democratic governments is very short compared to the timescale on which climate change usually takes place. Moreover, politicians and the media too often focus on the short-term in terms of income, profits, taxes and jobs rather than on planning or investing for the following decades and generations. A key question is how longer-term thinking about cause and effect can be built in to the decision-making process, both of governments and of businesses. In part this must come from an informed and highly educated electorate. Institutions that have a longer time perspective than the next election are vital, because they can bring a greater level of foresight to government and the political process.

Examples include business companies and corporations, trade unions, trade and business associations, educational and research institutions, religious groups, environmental advocates, social justice advocates, professional bodies and many other associations, many with their own form of total or partial democracy. Collectively these groups are termed non-governmental organisations (NGOs). They, and their hopefully peaceful manner of operating, are often referred to as 'civil society'.

It is a legitimate and indeed necessary role of civil society to influence both governments and voters, especially regarding longer-term issues. In democracies, such influence is subject to the will of all citizens at government elections. Ideally, the role of governments vis-à-vis civil society is to take note of the concerns, and where necessary to mediate among often competing elements of society, before acting for the common good. In particular, governments have a role to encourage cooperation and competition across a level playing field, with a long-term perspective, in the long-term interests of the whole society.

The IPCC in its 2007 report says relatively little directly about what the national governments should do, partly because of its remit to be 'policy relevant but not policy-prescriptive'. Nevertheless, Working Group III does say that, while actions by regional and local governments, voluntary groups and NGOs to promote low-carbon programs and policies may limit GHG emissions, 'by themselves [these actions] generally have limited impact. To achieve significant emissions reductions, these actions must lead to changes in national policies'. Working Group III does, however, discuss extensively the various alternative actions that might be considered in national and international policy negotiations, and these are discussed later in this book.

Governments have a duty, therefore, to set standards, goals, and rules of behaviour on an equitable basis. Governments can facilitate the attainment of goals, although in most cases actually achieving change is up to individuals and groups, including businesses, consumers, investors and innovators. Policies and laws are only effective if civil society in the main wants them to work, otherwise they are empty rhetoric or worse.

Governments can in general offer a mixture of carrots and sticks. The pros and cons of specific policy options depend very much on perceived future impacts of climate change on the economies and national interests of each country, their likely success in limiting climate change, and the effects of emissions reductions on the various economies, both in the short and longer terms. Crucial to any judgement is to take account of the urgency of the measures and how successful they might be in avoiding damages and reducing risks from climate change both in the near future and for future generations.

Policies will also depend for their success on how well they stimulate changes in technology and behaviour to reduce the rate of climate change, and to adapt to whatever changes do occur. In an increasingly inter-dependent world, no one country's policies can succeed unless it is in concert with others. The global atmosphere and climate are both global 'commons' (that is, globally shared resources), so human influence on them can only be managed by global cooperation.

Until all governments accept their full role in combating climate change, one role of other affected governments and non-government organisations is to attempt to bring delinquent governments to account for the damage caused by climate change resulting from uncontrolled greenhouse gas emissions. In 2002 the Pacific nation of Tuvalu threatened to bring a lawsuit against the US, the UK and Australia in the International Court of Justice for their alleged failure to limit greenhouse gas emissions that could eventually render Tuvalu uninhabitable due to sea-level rise. This was consistent with a proposal by the Alliance of Small Island States (AOSIS) in 1991 for an insurance mechanism that would compensate small island states for loss of land due to sea-level rise.[46]

In 2005, representatives of the Inuit people of the United States and Canada submitted a petition to the Inter-American Commission on Human Rights (IACHR), with the backing of the Inuit Circumpolar Conference. IACHR, related to the Organization of American States (OAS), has a record of treating environmental degradation as a matter of human rights.[47]

Tol and Verheyen in a 2004 article argue that customary international law requires that countries may do each other no harm, and that this is violated if a country does damage to another country by any activity under its control, if it is done on purpose or due to carelessness. They argue that climate change falls into this category, especially due to its recognition in many declarations and treaties, notably the UNFCCC. The article then discusses the possible range of damages that might be paid, and that this depends particularly on rulings as to whether a country is liable for the results of all its greenhouse gas emissions, or only those in excess of some reasonable emissions abatement target.[48]

What role should business take?

Businesses are in existence to invest money and labour in producing and selling things, so producing income for themselves and their shareholders. Climate change will affect them directly via impacts on their activities, including raw material and production costs, insurance, prices and competitive position. They will also be affected by how greenhouse gas emission reduction measures may influence their costs and activities, and ultimately their competitive position. Whether or not business people believe that human-induced climate change is happening, they will be affected by how their competitors, governments and society perceive and act on the problem.

As with previous technological revolutions, such as the introduction of the steam engine, electricity, plastics, electronics and computers, industries will have to adapt to the push for a low-carbon emitting economy. Particular businesses will either change and adapt, or deny the need for change and eventually go under. Innovators and early movers will be at an advantage, as will businesses that live in a regulatory environment that facilitates change and fosters innovation. Moreover, renewable energy technology, especially on a large scale, may soon be cheaper than many fossil fuel technologies, especially if a price is put on carbon emissions. Fossil fuel industry investments will then become 'stranded assets' that have to be written off.

In a paper on the strategic implications of climate change policy for business, Andrew Hoffman, of the Boston University School of Management, states:

Many companies today are taking proactive steps on climate change by reducing or even sequestering their greenhouse gas emissions. But one cannot, as many now do, generalize from these examples the proposition that all companies can benefit from greenhouse gas reductions. Climate change controls represent a market shift; the formation of new markets in pollution, pollution credits, money and emission abatement technology. And in any such transition, there will be winners and losers, those that embrace the shift and those that resist it. The difference between these two postures lies in strategic factors such as capital asset management, market competencies, global competitiveness and managing institutional change.[49]

Similar sentiments are expressed in a cover story on global warming in *Business Weekly* (16 August 2004) that begins: '*Consensus is growing among scientists, governments, and business that they must act fast to combat climate change. This has already sparked efforts to limit CO_2 emissions. Many companies are now preparing for a carbon-constrained world*'. The article concludes: '*Companies have begun to respond, but there is a long way to go, and only two choices: Get serious about global warming – or be prepared for the consequences*'.

Businesses need to act now to limit greenhouse gas emissions and prepare for changes already happening. They can play a significant role in providing solutions that are both profitable and socially desirable. This is already being demonstrated by many businesses, including some in the fossil fuels sector, although others are holding out against change, based on a short-term view of their stockholders' interests. Robert Bradley of the Institute for Energy Research in Houston, Texas, expressed such a view when he argued for a narrow strategy that does not go beyond short-term 'no regrets' actions. This seems to be based in a sceptical view of the reality of climate change, and ignores the possibility of opening up new opportunities for growth.[50]

The experience of BP is salutary. Back in 1997 they decided to set a target of a 10% reduction in their in-house greenhouse gas emissions, and achieved this nine years ahead of schedule. This was done through a compulsory internal emissions trading scheme, which led to the identification of lots of business value. After three years they had generated an extra

US$650 million of shareholder value. This is only from their internal operations, which generate about 100 million tons of carbon dioxide each year. The emissions from their products are about 15 times as much. They publicly favour a global emissions reduction target aimed at keeping global warming below about 2°C. They estimate that this will require a new carbon-free primary energy industry equal in size to the present fossil-fuel based industry by 2050, and are setting about creating such an industry under the motto 'Beyond Petroleum'.[51]

Many governments are implementing domestic legislation and policies that are creating direct requirements to reduce greenhouse gas emissions and imposing liabilities on various sectors. This is happening at national levels in both developed and developing countries, and regionally in the European Union. Even in the US, despite the opposition of the Bush administration to the Kyoto Protocol, there has been considerable movement at state and local levels, including fuel efficiency measures, design criteria, and incipient carbon emissions permit trading. Under President Obama the US is expected to move forward, setting a new climate of regulations and incentives for business.

As Martijn Wilder of the international law firm Baker & McKenzie put it in a recent paper:

For corporations, and in particular multi-nationals, the emergence of a diversity of climate related laws, in both developed and developing countries, means that a clear understanding is required as to the nature of legal liabilities that now exist or are likely to exist in the future and how best to position themselves. Companies should be fully aware of the extent to which market based mechanisms within these regimes present opportunities to create carbon assets and offset liabilities or at the very least aware as to how to preserve ownership of such opportunities … and to be able to understand the carbon ramifications of key investment decisions and acquisitions.

It is also critical for corporations to be aware of the way in which global capital – especially within

the investment and insurance industries – is reassessing investments for carbon risk, and the growing reluctance of shareholders to tolerate corporate non-performance on greenhouse matters. When coupled with the recent commencement of climate litigation, companies and their directors need to be fully aware of the ramifications of such matters …[52]

Wilder goes on to detail various legal actions being pursued in the US and Australia by environmental groups and local governments, some acting on behalf of individuals. One action against a proposed coal-fired power station at Redbank in New South Wales was lost, but the state minister rejected an application for a second power plant due to high greenhouse gas emissions. This adds credibility to possible further legal actions in NSW against high local emitters of greenhouse gases. However, more recent planning permission in NSW for increased coal export infrastructure indicates that the state government is not yet serious about combating global climate change. Declining coal exports under a more rigorous global regime under which export partners reduce their reliance on coal may eventually make such infrastructure redundant.

In the US several legal actions were brought against the US EPA variously for failing to further limit emissions from motor vehicles, failure to regulate carbon dioxide emissions under the *US Clean Air Act*, and failure to update emission standards for power plants. In the case *Massachusetts v. Environmental Protection Agency*, the US Supreme Court in 2007 ruled that the twelve states and several cities that brought a case against the EPA to force it to regulate CO_2 and other greenhouse gases as pollutants had standing and that indeed the EPA was obliged to regulate these gases as pollutants.[53]

In July 2004 eight US states and New York City sued five large electric power companies that between them operate 170 power plants that are responsible for some 10% of the national total carbon dioxide emissions. The case, under federal common law of public nuisance, called for cuts of

3% a year in carbon dioxide emissions to 'curb air and water pollutants emanating from other states'. The Connecticut attorney general cited the states' successful suits against tobacco companies as evidence that such efforts can succeed. This case was lost on the basis that it presented a 'political question' unsuited for resolution by the judiciary, but the situation may change as evidence of harm becomes clearer.[54]

Wilder quotes an article in the *Financial Times* in 2003 in which it was said:

First it was tobacco and asbestos. Then it was the turn of the food sector. Now litigators have a new target in their sights: those responsible for climate change.

The main barrier to success in these litigations, according to Wilder, is in establishing causation – that is, showing the link between the action of the emitting party and the damage suffered by the plaintiff or damage to the environment. This is difficult to prove at present, but as with the case against the tobacco industry, as science progresses the links are becoming clearer. Attribution of an individual climate disaster to global warming may not be 100% certain, but if the change in probability of such disasters due to global warming can be established, then a percentage of the damages might be attributed to climate change. The argument for legal liability is enunciated in an editorial by William C. Clark in *Environment* magazine. He argues that under the terms of the UN Framework Convention on Climate Change, 'world leaders have in fact a duty to try to protect the world's citizens from [climate change] impacts'. This may well extend to major emitters of greenhouse gases, now that cause and effect is increasingly well established.[55]

The insurance industry has been one of the first to face up to the consequences of climate change. A report by the Association of British Insurers in 2004 states:

Climate change is no longer a marginal issue. We live with its effects every day. And we should prepare ourselves for its full impact in the years ahead. It is time to begin planning for climate change in the mainstream of business life.[56]

The Association went on to say that insurers are uniquely placed to contribute to the climate change debate because they understand risk and their customers. Insurance needs to manage its own risks and to engage with government and others who affect that risk. A 2007 report from the RAND corporation on wind insurance on the Gulf of Mexico coast following the 2005 hurricane season points to major impacts on insurance premiums and coverage, and thus on development.[57] Similar or worse effects will surely follow any rapid rise in sea level and ensuing coastal erosion in many coastal regions. Developers would therefore be wise to avoid vulnerable areas and planning authorities reluctant to permit development in such locations, as part of their 'duty of care'.

In 2002 the United Nations Environment Program Finance Initiatives presented a report that highlighted the need for financial institutions and professionals to become more familiar with the threats and opportunities posed by climate change issues, incorporate climate change considerations into all business processes, and work directly with policy-makers on effective strategies for mitigation and adaptation.[58]

The mining industry has also recognised that it needs to take climate change seriously. The Australian Minerals and Energy Foundation in a report in 2002 stated that:

Climate change is a major concern in relation to the minerals sector and sustainable development. It is, potentially, one of the greatest of all threats to the environment, to biodiversity and ultimately to our quality of life.

… [It] clearly raises important issues for the minerals industry's operations; relations with the broader community; and willingness to internalise important sustainable development principles, including the precautionary principle.[59]

Innovest Strategic Value Advisors, on behalf of 97 institutional investors with more than US$10 000 million worth of assets under management, wrote in 2003 to 500 of the world's largest companies, asking about their greenhouse gas emissions. In their report they pointed out the consequences of increased natural disasters amounting to US$70 billion in 2003 on key sectors and commodity markets, such that climate risk must now be considered. They also pointed out that carbon finance is now a reality, with the European Union's Emissions Trading Scheme in force as of January 2005, and that the future 'cost of carbon' is already of concern. They noted that FT500 companies are major participants in the global clean technology sector. Innovest reported that these trends have not been ignored, with more companies quantifying their carbon emissions, more 'carbon-neutral' products and companies being created, and more active climate risk management. It stated that the concepts of corporate leadership, transparency and brand value underpin approaches to climate change. Innovest has developed a 'Climate Leadership Index' to gauge company performance and has reported on the risks to shareholders in several US coal expansion projects, which will become uncompetitive with the onset of carbon pricing.[60]

In addition to the EU Emissions Trading Scheme, the Chicago Climate Exchange already exists. The EU scheme is largely decentralised in that it leaves room for some autonomy in individual member countries. This may be a forerunner of a flexible globally linked scheme. The Chicago Climate Exchange is a self-regulating exchange that administers a multi-national and multi-sector marketplace for reducing and trading greenhouse gas emissions. It is a 'voluntary, legally binding commitment by a cross-section of North American corporations, municipalities and other institutions to establish a rules-based market for reducing greenhouse gases'. It was started with 28 large companies including Ford, Dupont and BP America, and the cities of Chicago and Mexico City. It is partly driven by the expectation of some future, government-imposed emissions-reduction program in America.[61]

The Pew Center on Global Climate Change has set up the Business Environmental Leadership Council (BELC), a group of leading companies worldwide that are responding to the challenges posed by climate change. Its website lists 42 major companies, representing US$2.8 trillion in market capitalisation and over 3.8 million employees, and the targets they have set themselves to limit greenhouse gas emissions. The companies subscribe to the following belief statement:

1. We accept the views of most scientists that enough is known about the science and environmental impacts of climate change for us to take actions to address its consequences.

2. Businesses can and should take concrete steps now in the US and abroad to assess opportunities for emission reductions, establish and meet emission reduction objectives, and invest in new, more efficient products, practices and technologies.

3. The Kyoto agreement represents a first step in the international process, but more must be done both to implement the market-based mechanisms adopted in principle in Kyoto and to more fully involve the rest of the world in the solution.

4. We can make significant progress in addressing climate change and sustaining economic growth in the United States by adopting reasonable policies, programs and transition strategies.[62]

In April 2008 the Pew Center released a report 'Adapting to climate change: a business approach'. The report concludes that:

Those most at risk are companies facing decisions about long-term capital investments (infrastructure, equipment), those in sectors where weather and climate is an integral part of production (such as agriculture or construction), industries that rely heavily on transport and other infrastructure in their supply chains, or those facing reflected risks, such as the insurance industry. Risks will not be evenly spread geographically, and will depend on the incidence of extreme events – such as storms, drought, flooding, or wildfire – in the locations where core processes, supplies of inputs, customers, or other components of the value chain are located.[63]

The positive side of the business perspective on climate change is opportunity through new and growing markets for low-carbon technology. Many of these opportunities are discussed in Chapter 8 above and will not be repeated here, except to say that most renewable energy sectors have grown in recent decades, and especially in the last few years, at far more rapid rates than fossil-fuel based industries. Most of this growth in renewable energy is occurring in countries with favourable national or provincial/state policies, such as Denmark, Germany, Japan, Spain, China, India and parts of the United States. Countries which have set increased minimum levels for renewable energy in the electricity grid have seen large increases in investment in renewable energy, with increases in employment and taxes. Costs per unit energy for renewables have trended down steeply in the last decade. This trend is likely to continue with new technologies and larger scale production. There is therefore a great opportunity for innovative businesses.[64]

Most major business advisory groups and companies now have specialist teams advising on the risk and opportunities with climate change. These include the McKinsey Company, KPMG, Citigroup and many others. The McKinsey Global Institute report 'The carbon productivity challenge: curbing climate change and sustaining economic growth', sets out the needs to create market-based incentives to innovate and raise carbon productivity, to address market failures that prevent abatement opportunities from being captured, to resolve issues of allocation and fairness, and to accelerate progresss to avoid failure to meet critical emissions targets that would put climate at risk.[65]

The Investor Network on Climate Risk in the US developed a climate risk action plan which includes management of investments, engaging companies, investors and others, and supporting policy actions. These include:

- asset managers, consultants and advisors considering climate risks and opportunities,

- investing capital in companies developing and deploying clean technologies,

- improving the energy performance of real estate portfolios and investments,

- urging comprehensive corporate responses to climate risks,

- helping investors evaluate and address corporate climate risks across all financial activities,

- pushing for regulatory awareness of climate risks and sensitivity to shareholder concerns,

- encouraging companies and investors to support government action on climate policy,

- supporting policies at all levels to maximise energy efficiency.[66]

The role of state and local governments

In countries such as the US and Australia, where strong federal action on climate change was lacking until a change of federal governments in Australia in late 2007 and in the US in 2009, some state and local governments have led the way on emissions reduction programs. Local and state governments have authority over many areas affecting the environment, such as land-use planning, transportation, building standards, regulation of natural gas and electricity supply, air pollution standards and enforcement, and economic development. These regional and local authorities are thus able to exert pressure to minimise greenhouse gas emissions, encourage energy efficiency, and to foster renewable energy developments. They have also set standards and examples that others may follow.

Many states and cities are adopting polices that are reducing greenhouse gas emissions without threatening local economies, while achieving other benefits such as cleaner air and reduced traffic congestion. Some measures that are controversial at the federal level have been accepted at the state and local level, while others, including encouragement of wind power installations, are being debated and proven viable.

According to the Pew Center on Global Climate Change, in the US in 2008:

'States and regions across the country are adopting climate policies. These actions include the development of regional greenhouse gas reduction markets, the creation of state and local climate action and adaptation plans, and increasing renewable energy generation. In addition to addressing climate change, states and regions pursue these policies to reduce their vulnerability to energy price spikes, promote state economic development, and improve local air quality. State and regional climate policy will provide models for future national efforts, achieve greenhouse gas emissions reductions, and prepare for the impacts of climate change.'[67]

In 2008, 36 US states are involved in regional initiatives to cooperate on reducing greenhouse gas emissions, while 37 have climate action plans completed or in progress, 17 have emissions targets and 43 have emissions inventories. Most of the states have some form of energy sector incentives to encourage renewable energy, while two-thirds have residential and commercial building energy standards. Five states even have mandatory carbon emissions caps or offsets for coal-fired power stations.

With the advent of the Obama administration stronger federal initiatives and coordination are likely.

In Australia, despite the refusal of the conservative Howard federal government to ratify the Kyoto Protocol, the states (all with Australian Labor Party governments in 2007–2008) adopted greenhouse strategies, partly influenced by state-funded scientific advice. All six Australian states, plus the Northern Territory and the Australian Capital Territory, set up an Inter-Jurisdictional Emissions Trading Working Group, in January 2002, and the 'Garnaut climate change review' in April 2007, with the cooperation of the then federal opposition Labor Party. The states, with some support from the Howard government, encouraged renewable energy projects including wind power, tidal power in Western Australia, and geothermal and solar power.

Following the election of the Rudd Labor government federally, the Garnaut Review has recommended national action including the design of an Australian Emissions Trading Scheme. However, local action through state and local governments is already playing a major role, with 178 Australian cities and towns part of the international Cities for Climate Protection program. In 2006/07 they report actions that cut carbon emissions by about 3.7 million tonnes, and at the same time saved money, and reduced water use, air pollution and traffic congestion, and improved health and fitness.[68]

Globally, local governments have become actively involved, through the organisation Local Government for Sustainability, formerly the International Council for Local Environmental Initiatives (ICLEI). ICLEI has over 875 member towns, cities, counties and municipal associations in 70 countries and undertakes international campaigns, programs and regional projects on sustainable development, including the climate change issue. Its program Cities for Climate Protection (CCP) requires councils to make inventories of greenhouse gas emissions, estimate growth, establish reduction goals, draw up local action plans and monitor their progress.[69]

Mayors from many countries have urged a wide-ranging shift towards renewable energy in cities. They see their role especially in urban and environmental planning. This includes mandating or providing incentives for renewable energy sources and efficiencies, and investing in infrastructure and facilitating cooperation and financing strategies.

Carolyn Kouskey of Harvard University and Stephen Schneider of Stanford interviewed officials or staff from 23 municipalities in the US that had enacted climate policies. They found that most policies were based on what was considered to be 'good business' or rational policy choices, driven by cost savings and co-benefits rather than public pressure. They found that in many cases at least initial reductions in emissions can be made at cost savings.[70]

So what are the politics of greenhouse?

This chapter has only skimmed the surface of the politics of greenhouse. It is a huge and rapidly evolving subject with a huge literature. This is a brief summary.

The first key issue is whether we have something urgent to do about climate change, and if so, what. The answer hinges on how credible the science is, and what it means in terms of risk to us, and to our children and grandchildren. Despite all that the contrarians have thrown at it, the science is credible. If anything, the climate modellers and the IPCC have been conservative in the sense of not emphasising the worst possibilities. They have thus under-estimated the rate of change, as is clear from recent observed trends in emissions, CO_2 concentration, sea-level rise, and the melting of Arctic sea ice. There is a serious risk of highly damaging climate change impacts, which grows with every tonne of carbon dioxide we add to the atmosphere. The lag between cause and effect is long, so we must act on the basis of foresight rather than proven, has-been, observable fact. We are faced with a problem of risk management.

Next, we have looked at what is required, and found that it is a big ask. This raises questions about the potential cost and how to share that cost between the rich countries and the poor, and between the present and future generations. The message is that we need to reduce global emissions of greenhouse gases by 80% or more by 2050, and the sooner the better if we want to avoid some big risks. Whether this is possible has been debated, but there is a lot of

evidence that if we try we may well be able to do it, even at rather little cost. Estimates of what it will cost depend in part on subjective value judgements and guesses about the future – there cannot be completely objective cost estimates in dollars and cents, but they are likely to be less than a year or two of economic growth by 2050 and far less than world expenditure on the military.

The really key political question is how to do it. How do we ensure that large emissions reductions happen? Is it a matter for the free market, which will do it automatically if the problem is real, and make money out of it? Or does it need some far-sighted top-down direction and detailed targets to achieve such a goal? My tentative answer is that the free market has a big role, but left to its own devices it tends to take a short-term view, when we are talking about a long-term problem that requires urgent action now.

What we need are all elements of the civil society, including business people as well as environmentalists and others, pulling together towards shared goals. That is best accomplished through a genuine partnership between government and non-government agencies. Goals must be set together, and a level playing field established for innovation and competition to achieve emission reductions and the transition to a low-carbon economy with as little cost, and as much gain, as possible. For the sake of justice, and to ensure cooperation, we will need to help those who will be badly affected, either by climate change impacts that we cannot avoid, or by the impacts of emissions reductions. Creating the fairest and most effective possible means to achieve these goals is not going to be easy, but we have to do it.

The final question, then, which has been the biggest stumbling block so far in international negotiations, is what is a fair distribution of effort between the rich developed countries and the poorer developing ones. Historically, most of the problem has been due to emissions from the developed countries, generated while they got rich by burning fossil fuels and cutting down forests. The problem is that the poorer countries now want to catch up, but if they do so by imitating what the developed countries did, that is by burning lots of cheap coal and oil, we will all be in deeper trouble later this century and next. So we need both developed and developing countries to act, the first to reduce their emissions, and the second to seriously limit their increase in emissions. It is a matter of fairness, and of effectiveness. Unless we reach an equitable arrangement that gets both the rich and the poor pulling together we are all in trouble. How to do that is the nub of the problem.

In the next chapter we will look briefly at the history of attempts to deal with the problem to date, and at various national interests that may affect what countries do next. We will also look briefly at what people are thinking about as possible ways forward.

ENDNOTES

1. The extract from WL Miller was quoted by Marc D Davidson in 'Parallels in reactionary argumentation in the U.S. congressional debates on the abolition of slavery and the Kyoto Protocol', *Climatic Change*, **86**, pp. 67–82 (2008).

2. See for example the journals: *Energy Policy; Mitigation and Adaptation Strategies for Global Change; Climate Policy; Environmental and Resource Economics; International Environmental Agreements;* and *Journal of Environmental Management.*

3. The quote is from Martin Luther King Jr's book, *Where Do We Go from Here: Chaos or Community*, Beacon Press (1968). Cited in *Human Development Report 2007/2008*, UNDP.

4. See discussion in Chapter 3 and the relevant endnotes for that chapter. The argument is rather irrelevant to policy advice on the need to reduce greenhouse gas emissions, which relates more to the impacts of policy-driven emission scenarios.

5. See D Brown in *Global Environmental Change*, **13**, pp. 229–34, and the book *Dead Heat: Global Justice and Global Warming* by Tom Athanasiou and Paul Baer, Seven Stories Press, New York (2002).

6. See IPCC 2007 report, WGIII, Chapters 3.3.4 and 11.

7. Figure 33 is from Hennessy and others, 'Climate change in New South Wales part 1'. Consultancy report for the NSW Greenhouse Office, CSIRO Atmospheric Research, Aspendale (2004).

8. See Martin Parry, Jean Palutikof, Claire Hanson and Jason Lowe 'Climate policy: squaring up to reality', *Nature Reviews: Climate Change* (29 May 2008).

9. See 'US scientists and economists call for swift and deep cuts in greenhouse gas emissions', May (2008) available at http://www.ucsusa.org/assets/documents/global_warming/Scientist_Economists_Call_to_Action_fnl.pdf.

10. Recent modelling indicating urgency is by Matthews and Caldeira, 'Stabilizing climate requires near-zero emissions', *Geophysical Research Letters*, **35**, L04705 (2008).

11. The Stern Review on the Economics of Climate Change (2006) is available at http://www.hm-treasury.gov.uk/independent_reviews/independent_reviews_index.cfm.

12. The quote is from Yohe and Tol, *Climatic Change*, **89**, pp. 231–40 (2008), which is one of six related papers in that issue of *Climatic Change.*

13. See Higgins and Higgins, *Energy Policy*, **33**, pp. 1–4 (2005).

14. See A Friedland and others, 'Personal decisions and their impact on energy use and the environment', *Environmental Science and Policy*, **6**, pp. 175–9 (2003), and the book cited below in endnote 19.

15. 'Climate Change and Finance: new business opportunities' appears in *Corporate Environmental Strategy*, **7**, pp. 137–45 (2000).

16. See 'Sustainability and Risk: Climate Change and Fiduciary Duty for the Twenty-First Century Trustee', Workshop Report, Harvard University and CERES, 2004, at http://www.hks.harvard.edu/m-rcbg/CSRI/publications/report_3_Sustainability%20and%20Risk%20Report.pdf, or UN Chronicle Online, 'Investor Summit Assesses Climate Risks and Oppportunities' at http://www.un.org/Pubs/chronicle/2005/issue2/0205p75.html.

17. See 'Reducing coal subsidies and trade barriers: their contribution to greenhouse gas abatement', The Brookings Institute, available at http://www.brook.edu/. See also Riedy and Diesendorf in *Energy Policy*, **31**, pp. 125–37 (2003) re subsidies in Australia, and EEA Briefing Note No. 2, at http://www.eea.eu.int, re subsidies in the EU.

18. The IPCC 2007 discussion is in WGIII, p. 305. See also the OECD study Reforming Energy Subsidies, UN Environmental Programme and Organisation for Economic Cooperation and Development, OECD/IEA, Oxford, UK; Janet Sawin in *State of the World 2003*, Chapter 5 'Charting a new energy future', and the paper 'Mainstreaming Renewable Energy in the 21st Century', both from Worldwatch Institute, available at http://www.worldwatch.org. See also *Renewable Electricity Technology Cost Trends*, at Energy Analysis Office, http://www.nrel.gov/analysis/docs/cost-curves-2002.ppt.

19. The book *Society, Behaviour and Climate Change Mitigation* is edited by Eberhard Jochem and colleagues, Kluwer Academic Publishers, Hingham, MA (2002), and the review is by Hadi Dowlatabadi in *Climate Policy*, **3**, pp. 95–7 (2003).

20. Induced technological change and learning by doing are discussed in the 2007 IPCC report, WGII, Chapters 2.7.2, 3.4 and 11.5.

21. See 2007 IPCC report in WGIII, Chapters 2.7.2 and 3.4.3. The 'lock-in' effect is discussed by IPCC in WGIII Chapter 3.1.3. Equity issues in climate mitigation policy are discussed by the IPCC 2007 report in WGIII Chapter 2.6.

22. There is an immense literature on carbon trading and emissions taxes. See the 2007 IPCC report, WGIII, and the learned journals in endnote 2 above. The European Union policies on climate change can be found at http://ec.europa.eu/environment/climat/home_en.htm, and at other relevant websites by doing a web search for 'EU climate change policy' or similar.

23. The report on solar PV advances comes from Ashley Seager in the *Guardian*, UK (16 June 2008). See also: http://www.suntech-power.com/.

24. See endnote 5 above.

25. See IPCC 2001, WGII, p. 916.

26. Benito Muller, 'Equity in Climate Change: The Great Divide', Oxford Institute for Energy Studies (2002) (available at http://www.OxfordClimatePolicy.org.), and 'A New Delhi mandate', *Climate Policy*, **79**, pp. 1–3 (2002). For other papers by B Muller see http://www.wolfson.ox.ac.uk/~mueller/.

27. John Ashton and Xueman Wang 'Equity and Climate: In Principle and Practice' in *Beyond Kyoto: Advancing the International Effort Against Climate Change*, Pew Center on Global Climate Change, (2004) at http://www.pewclimate.org.

28. See Eileen Claussen and Lisa McNeilly *'Equity and Global Climate Change'*, Pew Center on Global Climate Change, October 1998 at http://www.pewclimate.org.

29. See 'Climate Change Mitigation in Developing Countries', Pew Center on Global Climate Change (October 2003), and reported in *Nature*, **419**, p. 869 (2002). See also 'Fatally Flawed Inequity' available on Muller website as above, and Chapter 11 below.

30. Thomas Pogge, 'Eradicating systemic poverty: brief for a global resources dividend' in *Ethics of Consumption: the Good Life, Justice, and Global Stewardship* (ed.) DA Crocker and T Linden, Rowman and Littlefield, Lanham, MD, pp. 501–36 (1998).

31. See Parable of the Good Samaritan in the *New Testament*, Luke 10, verses 30–37.

32. Ongoing climate change policy negotiations are continuing. See the International Institute for Sustainable Development website http://www.iisd.ca/process/climate_atm.htm.

33. The Evangelical Environmental Network (EEN) is at http://www.creationcare.org. The 'Oxford Declaration on Global Warming' can be found at http://www.climateforum2002.org. Sir John Houghton, a former Chair of IPCC and a committed Christian, testified before the US Senate Energy and Resources Committee on 21 July 2005, see EEN website above. See also the UK Stop Climate Chaos coalition at http://www.stopclimatechaos.org, and the US-based Environmental Justice and Climate Change Initiative at http://www.ejcc.org.

34. See the transcript of the conference *US Climate Policy: Toward a Sensible Center*, available at http://www.pewclimate.org. A number of more recent climate mitigation acts have been proposed in the US Congress, as discussed on the Pew Center website. See http://www.pewclimate.org/policy_center/analyses/s_139_summary.cfm

35. Other documents related to international equity issues include Brett Simpson, 'Participation of developing countries in a climate change convention protocol', *Asia Pacific Journal of Environmental Law*, **7**, pp. 39–74 (2002); and Yoshiro Matsui, 'Some aspects of the principle of "common but differentiated responsibilities"', *International Environmental Agreements: Politics, Law and Economics*, **2**, pp. 151–71 (2002).

36. See 'Climate change and Commonwealth nations', Discussion Paper 40, The Australia Institute (2001) (available at http://www.tai.org.au).

37. The cross-border migration issue is covered in 'Forced migration and the humanitarian regime', paper presented at meeting of the International Association for the Study of Forced Migration, Thailand, (January 2003) (see http://www.georgetown.edu/sfs/programs/isim). See also Susan Martin and others, *The Uprooted: Improving Humanitarian Responses to Forced Migration*, Lexington Books, Lanham, MD (2005).

38. See *Environmental Refugees: The Case for Recognition*, New Economics Foundation, London, http://www.neweconomics.org, and Hay and Beniston in *Tiempo*, issue 42 (2001).

39. The relation between environmental security and climate change is discussed by Barnett in *Global Environmental Change*, **13**, pp. 7–17 (2003). See also the discussion in Chapter 5 regarding security implications.

40. See Fothergill and Peek, *Natural Hazards*, **32**, pp. 89–110 (2004).

41. See *African Americans and Climate Change: An Unequal Burden*, Congressional Black Caucus Foundation (2004). See http://www.cbcfinc.org.

42. DeCanio's *The Economics of Climate Change* (1997), is at http://www.rprogress.org. See also Chapter 12 in the book *Natural Capitalism* by Paul Hawken and others, Little Brown and Co, Boston (1999).

43. The position of the Construction Forestry, Mining and Energy Union (CFMEU) in Australia is presented in detail at http://www.cfmeu.com.au.

44. There is a large and growing literature on intergenerational equity. An early but still useful survey is by Edith Brown Weiss, 'Climate change, intergenerational equity and international law: an introductory review', in *Climatic Change*, **15**, pp. 327–35 (1989). See also: FL Toth (1999), 'Integrated assessment of climate change policy: intergenerational equity and discounting', *International Atomic Energy Agency, FEEM Working Paper* No. 52.99; I Mintzer and D Michel, 'Climate change, rights of future generations and intergenerational equity: an inexpert exploration of a dark and cloudy path', *International Journal of Global Environmental Issues* (2001) **1**, pp. 203–22; M Ha-Duong and N Treich, 'Risk aversion, intergenerational equity and climate change' in *Environmental and Resource Economics* (2004) **28**, pp. 195–207; and a special issue of the *University of Chicago Law Review*, **74** (Winter 2007) on 'Intergenerational Equity and Discounting', see http://lawreview.uchicago.edu/issues/archive/v74/74_1/.

45. The IPCC discussion of the role of NGOs versus national governments is on p. 89 of Working Group III, and more extensively in Chapter 13.4. Chapter 13 deals more generally with policies, instruments and cooperative agreements.

46. The AOSIS proposal was submitted by Vanuatu on behalf of AOSIS. See UN Document A/AC.237/wg.II/CRP.8, in Report of the 4th INC session, UN Doc. A/AC.237/15, 126 ff.

47. The Inuit petition and other legal cases can be found on the Earth Justice website, http://www.earthjustice.org, and a brief report can be found in *Sustainable Law and Policy*, **5**, (2) pp. 66–7 (Spring 2005), see http://www.wcl.american.edu/org/sustainabledevelopment. Other legal issues are covered in the same issue of this journal, and at http://www.climatelaw.org.

48. See Tol and Verheyen 'State responsibility and compensation for climate change damages – a legal and economic assessment', *Energy Policy*, **32**, pp. 1109–30 (2004).

49. The quote from Andrew Hoffman comes from 'Examining the rhetoric: the strategic implications of climate change policy' in *Corporate Environmental Strategy*, **9** (4), pp. 329–37 (2002). See also the same publication, pp. 338–44, for a paper from the *Sustainable Enterprise Program* at World Resources Institute, Washington. WRI has a partnership program called Safe Climate, Sound business Initiative. Another useful publication is the Spring 2005 special issue of *Sustainable Development Law and Policy*, **V** (2), on 'Business responses to climate change', at http://www.wcl.american.edu/org/sustainabledevelopment.

50. See Robert Bradley in the *Electricity Journal*, August/September 2000, pp. 65–71.

51. The BP experience and views were presented by Chris Mottershead at the 2004 conference *US Climate Policy: Toward a Sensible Center*, available at http://www.pewclimate.org.

52. Martijn Wilder's paper 'In control of carbon climate law and policy: managing obligations, liabilities, commercial risks and opportunities' is available at http://www.bakernet.com.

53. Various legal cases are documented on the websites http://www.earthjustice.org and http://www.climatelaw.org, which also refer to several academic articles on the basis of climate change litigation. See also: the book *Global Climate Change and the U.S. Law* by MB Gerrard, American Bar Association (2007) and *Climate Change Litigation* by J Smith and D Shearman, Presidian Legal Publications (2006) from http://www.presidian.com.au. Details of some legal cases in the US can be found at http://www.endangeredlaws.org/.

54. The court case by the states and New York City against various emitters of CO_2 is reported in the *New York Times* (21 July 2004) by Andrew Revkin. See also http://www.freshfields.com/publications/pdfs/2007/may14/18641.pdf.

55. William Clark's editorial is in *Environment*, **47** (9) p. 3 (December 2005).

56. The Association of British Insurers report is *A Changing Climate for Insurance* (June 2004) available at http://www.abi.org.uk/climatechange. Further related reports include *Financial Costs of Climate Change*, available at the same website, and at http://www.climaterisk.co.uk. Munich Reinsurance produced a major report *Weather Catastrophes and Climate Change: Is There Still Hope For Us?* (2005) see http://www.munichre.com, report number 302-04591. See also 'Insurance in a climate of change' by Evan Mills in *Science*, **309**, pp. 1040–4 (12 August 2005).

57. See 'Commercial wind insurance in the Gulf states', available at http://www.rand.org/pubs/.

58. The UNEP report is 'UNEP finance initiatives, 2002, CEO briefing on climate change', available at http://www.unepfi.net/.

59. The report from the Australian Minerals and Energy Foundation is 'Facing the future' (May 2002) available at http://www.ameef.org.au.

60. See Innovest report 'Climate change and shareholder value in 2004' at the Carbon Disclosure Project http://www.cdproject.net. See also http://www.innovest.com.

61. The EU Emissions Trading Scheme is reviewed by Denny Ellerman and Paul Joskowi in 'The European Union's trading system in perspective' at http://www.pewclimate.org/eu-ets. Re its decentralised nature see Kruger and others in *Review of Environmental Economics and Policy*, **1**, pp. 112–33 (2007). See also 'EU Action against climate change. Leading global action to 2020 and beyond.' at http://bookshop.europa.eu, and AC Christiansen and J Wettestad, 'The EU as a forerunner on greenhouse gas emissions trading: how did it happen and will the EU succeed?' in *Climate Policy*, **3**, pp. 3–18 (2003). See also JA Kruger and WA Pizer, 'Greenhouse gas trading in Europe' in *Environment*, **46** (8), pp. 8–23 (October 2004).

62. For details of BELC see http://www.pewclimate.org/companies_leading_the_way_belc/. Data as at 2008.

63. Available at http://www.pewclimate.org. There is also the United States Climate Action Partnership, see http://www.pewclimate.org/uscap.cfm.

64. The growing investment in renewable energy is documented in Janet Sawin, *Mainstreaming Renewable Energy in the 21st Century*, Worldwatch Institute (2004) available at http://www.worldwatch.org. See also Janet Sawin, *National Policy Instruments: Policy Lessons for the Advancement and Diffusion of Renewable Energy technologies Around the World*, at http://www.renewables2004.de/pdf/tbp/TBP03-policies.pdf, and http://www.worldwatch.org/features/renewables/bonn/part1. See also Chapter 8.

65. Business consulting groups with active policies and groups working on climate change risks and opportunities include: McKinsey and Company at http://www.mckinsey.com; KPMG at http://www.kpmg.com: Ernst & Young at http://www.ey.com; PricewaterhouseCoopers at http://www.pwc.com; Deloitte Touche Tohmatsu at http://www.deloitte.com; Citigroup at http://www.citigroup.com; Synergy Management Consulting Group at http://www.synergymcg.com. The McKinsey Global Institute report 'The carbon productivity challenge: curbing climate change and sustaining economic growth', June 2008, is at http://www.mckinsey.com/mgi.

See also 'Corporations embrace bottom-line global warming plan' in *Physics Today* (December 2006) pp. 30–1; *The Natural Advantage of Nations: Business Opportunities, Innovation and Governance in the 21st Century*, K Hargroves and MH Smith (eds), from The Natural Edge Project, at http://www.naturaledgeproject.net/naon.aspx.; and for an Australian stand, 'The business case for early action' by the Australian Business Roundtable on climate change at http://www.businessroundtable.com.au.

66. See http://www.un.org/unop/Docs/Investor%20Network%20on%20Climate%20Risk%20Action%20Plan.pdf.

67. State activities on climate change in the US are documented at the Pew Center website http://www.pewclimate.org.

68. An Australian ICLEI report 'Local government action on climate change: CCP Australia measures evaluation report 2007' is available at http://www.iclei.org/index.php?id=7293.

69. Local government activities are documented via http://www.iclei.org. See especially the links to the *Local Governments' Renewables Declaration*.

70. The Kouskey and Schneider results are in *Climate Policy*, **3**, pp. 359–72 (2003). Action taken by Chicago is highlighted in an article in *Renewable Energy World* (March–April 2004) pp. 59–69.

11

International concern and national interests

Because the Romans did in these instances what all prudent princes ought to do, who have to regard not only present troubles, but also future ones, for which they must prepare with every energy, because, when foreseen, it is easy to remedy them; but if you wait until they approach, the medicine is no longer in time because the malady has become incurable ... Thus it happens in affairs of state, for when the evils that arise have been foreseen (which it is only given to a wise man to see), they can be quickly redressed, but when, through not having been foreseen, they have been permitted to grow in a way that every one can see them. There is no longer a remedy.

NICOLÒ MACHIAVELLI, *THE PRINCE*.[1]

Whether we wish it or not we are involved in the world's problems, and all the winds of heaven blow through our land.

WALTER LIPPMANN, *A PREFACE TO POLITICS*, 1913.

The Earth 's atmosphere is being changed at an unprecedented rate by pollutants resulting from human activities, inefficient and wasteful fossil fuel use and the effects of rapid population growth in many regions. These changes represent a major threat to international security and are already having harmful consequences over many parts of the globe.

STATEMENT FROM THE *INTERNATIONAL CONFERENCE ON THE CHANGING ATMOSPHERE: IMPLICATIONS FOR GLOBAL SECURITY*, TORONTO, JUNE 1988.

Climate change provides a potent reminder of the one thing that we share in common. It is called planet Earth. All nations and all peoples share the same atmosphere.

HUMAN DEVELOPMENT REPORT 2007/2008, UNDP.[2]

A brief history[3]

In 1827, the French mathematician-physicist Jean Baptiste Fourier was the first to suggest that the atmosphere keeps heat from escaping from the Earth, resulting in the Earth being warmer than if there were no atmosphere. John Tyndall then demonstrated in Britain in 1859 that methane and carbon dioxide control the Earth's surface air temperature by absorbing infra-red or heat radiation. This led the Swedish chemist Svante Arrhenius to suggest in 1896 that increasing atmospheric carbon dioxide could cause the planet to warm, amplified by increased atmospheric moisture in a warmer world. Arrhenius issued the first warning that human activities since the Industrial Revolution could lead to changes in the Earth's climate. With remarkable foresight, he estimated that a doubling of the concentration of carbon dioxide in the atmosphere could lead to the Earth's surface warming by around 4 to 6°C, which is only about twice the range estimated by the Intergovernmental Panel on Climate Change (IPCC) in 2007 of 1.5 to 4.5°C (and even closer to more recent estimates of climate sensitivity). GS Callendar in 1938 likewise warned of global warming from increasing carbon dioxide, and suggested that it may already be happening.[4]

Charles Keeling of the Scripps Institution of Oceanography in San Diego was instrumental in establishing the first carbon dioxide monitoring stations, at the South Pole and Mauna Loa in Hawaii. In 1957 he wrote:

Human beings are now carrying out a large scale geophysical experiment of a kind that could not have happened in the past nor be reproduced in the future. Within a few centuries we are returning to the atmosphere and oceans the concentrated organic carbon stored in sedimentary rocks over hundreds of millions of years.[5]

By the early 1970s, however, it was not warming but rather a global cooling trend of about 0.5°C observed in the 1950s and 1960s that was arousing concern, with some scientists fearing that it might be the beginning of a long lasting cooling or even of a new glaciation. A number of possible explanations were raised, particularly the cooling effect of increasing particulate matter (atmospheric aerosols) in the atmosphere. Moreover, it was feared that this effect might be amplified into a greater cooling by increased snow cover.[6]

Nevertheless, Wally Broecker of Columbia University commented in 1975 that:

… a strong case can be made that the present cooling will, within a decade or so, give way to

pronounced warming induced by carbon dioxide. Once this happens, the exponential rise in the atmospheric carbon dioxide content will tend to become a significant factor and by early next century will have driven the mean planetary temperature beyond the limits experienced during the last 1000 years.[7]

Doubting the reality of an ongoing global cooling, the World Meteorological Organization (WMO) in a special report in 1976 stressed the importance of shorter-term climate changes, which might be due to natural or man-made causes, which they said now required urgent attention and further study. Similar conclusions were reached by other scientific groups such as the Australian Academy of Science in 1976.[8]

By 1979, however, the WMO's First World Climate Conference in Geneva, stated that an increased amount of carbon dioxide in the atmosphere can contribute to a gradual warming of the lower atmosphere and that the world should try to 'foresee and prevent potential man-made changes in climate that might be adverse to the well-being of humanity'.[9]

By the 1980s it was clear that the cooling trend had ended, and many of the scientists who had been concerned about a cooling demonstrated their openness to new information by changing their minds. Continuing increases in greenhouse gas concentrations, and a realisation that the effective lifetime of CO_2 in the atmosphere was much longer than that of particulates, making for a greater cumulative warming effect, meant that by the early 1980s there was a growing scientific interest in assessing the likelihood and magnitude of global warming.

Indeed, a conference of scientists at Villach in Austria in October 1985, which was sponsored by the non-governmental International Council of Scientific Unions along with the WMO and the United Nations Environment Program (UNEP) agreed to a statement that raised the first collective scientific warning: '… it is now believed that in the first half of the next century a rise in global mean temperature could occur which is greater than any in human history'.[10]

Also in 1986, the Scientific Committee on Problems of the Environment (SCOPE), a committee of the International Council of Scientific Unions, issued a major report entitled 'The greenhouse effect, climate change and ecosystems', which reinforced the concern about global warming. The SCOPE report concluded that if the observed rate of increase of carbon dioxide continued, it would reach double pre-industrial values towards the end of the twenty-first century, and this would lead to global average warming in the range 1.5–5.5°C, with associated global average sea-level rise in the range 20–165 cm. The report went on to discuss possible impacts on agriculture, forests and ecosystems.[11]

By 1988 this concern had turned into a demand for action to reduce carbon dioxide emissions, adopted by over 300 scientists at the United Nations sponsored 'Conference on the Changing Atmosphere' in Toronto in 1988.[12] This called for an initial reduction in carbon dioxide emissions of 20% by 2005, stating that:

Humanity is conducting an unintended, uncontrolled, globally pervasive experiment whose ultimate consequences could be second only to a global nuclear war.

In response to these concerns, the WMO and the UNEP set up the Intergovernmental Panel on Climate Change (IPCC) in 1988.[13] The initial brief of the IPCC was to report to the Second World Climate Conference in November 1990, and the United Nations General Assembly, on 'the scientific information that is related to the various components of the climate change issue …' and 'formulating realistic response strategies for the management of the climate change issue'.

It was envisaged by some that this might lead to international negotiations directed towards an agreement to eventually limit greenhouse gas emissions and to adapt to unavoidable climate changes. IPCC established three Working Groups, one to assess available scientific information on climate change, a second to assess the environmental and socio-economic impacts, and a third to formulate response strategies.

To date, the IPCC has issued four major Assessment Reports, in 1990, 1995, 2001 and 2007, and a special report entitled 'The regional impacts of climate change', in 1998. There have been a number of other IPCC reports, including the 'Special report on emission scenarios' (SRES) in 2000, which produced a wide range of 'plausible scenarios' for future greenhouse gas emissions up to the year 2100.[13]

Under United Nations auspices, country representatives met in February 1991 to draw up a global Framework Convention on Climate Change (UNFCCC), to be signed at the Rio Earth Summit of 1992. This was a 'framework' convention, meaning that it set out broad principles and objectives, but left a lot of details to be negotiated subsequently. It aimed at stabilising greenhouse gas concentrations in order to avoid 'dangerous anthropogenic interference with the climate system'. The UNFCCC came into force on 21 March 1994, and as of 30 June 2008 has received instruments of ratification from 192 member countries that are 'parties' to the convention.[14]

Principles set out in the UNFCCC include:

- The need to limit climate change on a basis of equity, in accordance with each country's common but differentiated responsibilities and respective capacities. Accordingly, the developed countries were expected to take the lead.

- The need to recognise the specific needs and special circumstances of developing countries, especially the most vulnerable (such as low-lying island states and major fossil fuel exporters).

- The need for precautionary measures in the absence of full scientific certainty, qualified by the need to be cost-effective and comprehensive, by taking account of all sources and sinks, adaptation, and all economic sectors.

- The right to sustainable development, and the need to avoid unjustified discrimination or a disguised restriction on international trade.

How these principles can be worked out in practice is not easy, and involves a strong mixture of equity, overall purpose and national interests.

The first meeting of the Conference of Parties (COP-1) (the countries who signed the UNFCCC) in 1995 established a sub-group to negotiate an agreement, called the 'Berlin Mandate', aimed at strengthening efforts to combat climate change. Following intense negotiations up to and including the COP-3 meeting in Kyoto, Japan, in 1997, delegates agreed to what is now known as the Kyoto Protocol.

The Kyoto Protocol[15]

The Kyoto Protocol commits developed nations and countries in transition (former Soviet bloc countries) to achieve quantified reductions in greenhouse gas emissions. Representatives of these countries, termed Annex I Parties, agreed to reduce their combined emissions of six designated greenhouse gases to at least 5% below levels in 1990, between 2008 and 2012, with specific targets varying from country to country.

In 1997 the Parties to the Protocol arrived at assigned amounts, which are the total allowed emissions for a country over the first commitment period 2008–12. Three mechanisms to assist Annex I countries to meet their targets at the least cost were also agreed:

1. *Joint Implementation* (JI). JI refers to the generation and transfer of emission reductions by investment in a project in one Annex I country by another, thereby generating credit for the investing Party.

2. An *Emissions Trading Scheme*. Emissions trading allows for the buying or selling of emission allowances between Annex I countries. It is expected that domestic and international trading schemes will be set up to facilitate this, as in the EU in 2005 and is planned for Australia and several other countries by 2010.

3. A *Clean Development Mechanism* (CDM). The CDM is similar to JI, but generates credits for investing Annex I Parties from project investments in non-Annex I Parties (developing countries).

Further negotiations in Buenos Aires in 1998 and The Hague in 2000 led to a reconvening of the Parties to the Convention in Bonn in July 2001. However, in March 2001 prior to the meeting in Bonn, the United States withdrew from the process, stating that it considered the Kyoto Protocol to be 'fatally flawed', because it would damage the US economy and because it exempted key developing countries from emissions reduction targets. The United States withdrawal from the Kyoto negotiating process heightened political interest, and probably facilitated agreement reached in Bonn.

The remaining Parties in Bonn accepted a package of agreements, and referred drafts of others on mechanisms, compliance and land use, land-use change and forestry to a further meeting in Marrakesh, Morocco, in October–November 2001. Agreement was reached at Marrakesh on most points, although Australia, Canada, Japan, New Zealand and Russia had reservations on some points. In New Delhi in late 2002 further agreements were reached, including the 'Delhi Declaration on Climate Change and Sustainable Development'. This reaffirms development and poverty eradication as overriding principles in developing countries, and again recognises member countries' common but differentiated responsibilities and national development priorities and circumstances in implementing the commitments under the UNFCCC.

For the Protocol to come into force it had to be ratified by at least 55 countries, and also by enough Annex I countries to account for at least 55% of global carbon dioxide emissions in 1990. As of mid-2004, 122 countries had ratified the Protocol, but only 32 were Annex I countries and these accounted for only 44.2% of the global carbon dioxide emissions. Initially Russia was ambivalent about ratification, with deep divisions apparent among Russia's politicians and scientists, but it ratified the Protocol in November 2004 and so it came into force in early 2005. It should be noted, however, that only Parties who have ratified the Protocol (181 countries as of 13 May 2008, accounting for 63.7% of global emissions) are bound by it, hence there is ongoing controversy regarding countries that have not yet signed. The attitudes and interests of particular countries will be discussed later in this chapter.

The many rules and complications related to carbon sinks, accounting, verification, JI, CDM, funding mechanisms, and compliance procedures make the rules and procedures of the Kyoto Protocol hard to fully comprehend. I will not go into details here. Many books, learned papers and reports address these issues (see endnotes). I will give one example here to illustrate the complications that relate to land-based sinks.[16]

Land-based carbon sinks, that is, sequestering of carbon in plants and the soil (see Chapter 8), were not originally envisaged as part of the Kyoto Protocol for reducing greenhouse gas emissions – initially reductions were to be achieved simply by limiting the use of fossil fuels. However, some major emitters, including the US, pushed for their inclusion and this was made part of the Protocol in 1997, before the US withdrawal. What began as a simple low-cost alternative to reducing fossil fuel usage turned out to be controversial, with many complications in the detail of how the amounts are to be counted. Melvin Cannell of the UK Centre for Ecology and Hydrology has summarised some of these complications:

- *Definition of a forest.* Is it based on land-use or land-cover? Definitions and numerical criteria make a large difference to the areas that can be counted.

- *Unintended and unfair outcomes.* This relates to sequences of deforestation and reforestation in different commitment periods.

- *Sinks to be additional.* The proposed baseline of 1990 levels is poorly determined.

- *Sinks must be the direct result of human-induced actions.* This excludes natural processes or activities prior to 1990 such as recovery from earlier land-clearing, or fertilisation due to increasing carbon dioxide concentration.

- *Measurement and verification.* Sinks include biomass, soil carbon and litter, all of which are difficult to measure with accuracy across large areas.

- *Permanence and reversibility.* All land sinks are potentially reversible [for example by harvesting or fire], but temporary storage may be valuable in delaying impacts of climate change.

- *Leakage.* Actions to increase carbon storage in one place may create pressure to reduce it somewhere else, for instance by changing the market value of forest products.

- *Equity.* Many countries party to the UNFCCC wanted the developed countries to reduce their use of fossil fuels first, and not be able to offset this by increasing carbon storage. This was solved by placing limits on what could be claimed.

- *Collateral damages or benefits.* These include environmental impacts of changing land use, and socio-economic impacts such as on commodity prices, recreation and tourism, employment, and wealth or poverty.

The mandated reductions in emissions by developed countries under the first commitment period of the Kyoto Protocol (2008–12) would slow the growth in total world emissions, compared to 'business as usual'. However, unless strengthened beyond 2012, the Kyoto targets would nowhere near stop growth in world emissions, let alone reduce them, due to rapid growth in emissions, especially in the United States and developing countries.[17]

In 2002, the US Bush Administration proposed an alternative to setting a target of reducing total carbon emissions, namely, targeting a reduction in emissions *intensity*, that is, less emissions per unit growth in GDP. However, reducing emissions intensity would only reduce total emissions if the reduction in emissions intensity were enough to more than cancel out the effect of the growth in GDP. For example, if GDP were to double, halving emissions intensity would just leave total emissions unchanged. President Bush's stated target for the US was an 18 per cent *reduction* in US emissions intensity between 2002 and 2012. However, the US has an expected growth in GDP of about 30 per cent over the same period, so that total US emissions would in fact *increase* by about 12 per cent, and end up some 30% above 1990 levels.[18]

Thus both the first stage Kyoto Protocol measures and those proposed by the United States in 2002 postpone any absolute reduction in world emissions until after 2012.

This lack of immediate reductions in global emissions needs to be compared with the target reductions discussed in Chapters 8 and 10, which suggest the need for at least a 60–80% total reduction by 2050, relative to 1990 levels. The question of urgency hinges on the understanding of the role of inertia and time lags, and the possibility of greenhouse gas concentrations exceeding some critical level at which dangerous or irreversible changes occur. Delayed action will lead to greater long-term damages and the need for more drastic action later. It also hinges on how we value the right of future generations to inherit a world with more rather than less choices, and on how optimistic we are that our children and grandchildren will be able to find technological fixes for possibly catastrophic problems we have left them.

The work of the IPCC, with its wide range of plausible scenarios and its assessment of mitigation pathways, strongly asserts that a future world of low concentrations of greenhouse gases in the atmosphere is feasible. What is needed to achieve this is a development pathway that values sustainability and low-carbon technology over high-carbon technology, and that this is implemented with a real sense of urgency and deliberation. Development with foresight is needed.

The UNFCCC has provided an international framework within which cooperation towards these ends is possible. The challenge is to convince all countries that it is in their national interest to be part of this move towards a sustainable future, and to have the agreed targets and measures greatly strengthened. It is crucial to involve the developing countries, as well as the United States, in serious efforts to halt, and turn around, the present increase in emissions.

This can only happen when low-carbon technologies become a viable means to economic development. As Professor Ross Garnaut, the chief advisor to the Australian Government, said: 'The costs of mitigation will be lower the higher are the market prices of petroleum, coal and natural gas. This is because the "business as usual", to be compared with the costs of using the alternative, low-emissions technologies, will be higher. This is a matter of current interest, at this time of historically high fossil fuel prices'.[19]

Moreover, the costs of low-carbon technology are likely to drop rapidly once incentives are in place for research, development and deployment, as economies of scale will start to kick in.

National interests and climate change

Perceived national interests are central to the politics of climate change, and the ability of the global community to avoid dangerous levels of climate change. What should determine the bottom line of governments regarding their negotiating positions and national implementation programs? This will collectively determine the rate and extent of future climate change. Narrow self-interest is what may go down best in domestic politics, although this is tempered in most countries by some ethical standards, held by at least some of the population, relating to fairness or equity. Equity (see Chapter 10) will also play a role in determining what can be agreed internationally, and for this reason must temper narrow national interest. Negotiating positions must combine some mixture of national self-interest and international equity.

The questions of perceived versus real national interests, and of short-term versus long-term interests are of critical importance. These are both in part a matter of knowledge and education, but also of the time-horizons governing political discourse. Are people more concerned about short-term economic self-interest or about sustainability and the wellbeing of future generations? Here we home in, for various countries and regions, on those national interests that should convince decision-makers that limiting climate change is both necessary and urgent, and look briefly at some policy responses.

In considering individual country situations and national interests it may be useful to refer back to **Figure 30** in Chapter 8, where the absolute and per capita emissions of the 15 largest emitting nations are listed, along with their carbon intensities and changes in carbon intensity and GDP over the decade 1990–2000. Clearly no one country absolutely dominates global emissions, and many must collaborate if global emissions are to be reduced substantially, including eventually both developed and developing countries.

The discussion here is more pointed than was possible in the various IPCC reports. The IPCC reports were limited in what they could say by the need for diplomacy, for avoiding 'policy-prescriptive' language, and by the requirement for unanimous adoption of the summaries for policy-makers by member states at the IPCC Assemblies. Nevertheless, the uncertainties must still be acknowledged, especially when thinking about potential downstream effects of climate change, for instance on food security, population displacement and other socio-political issues. These may be sensitive and contentious issues. The points raised are not meant to be definitive, but rather provide my personal perspective and should be seen as discussion starters.

Readers are also advised that these national or regional descriptions are not just of local interest, but rather they carry lessons for other countries and for efforts to negotiate international cooperation. They are therefore highly policy-relevant.

Readers interested in similar analyses for other countries would do well to study the regional impacts chapters of the IPCC 2007 Working Group II report, which is accessible on the web at http://www.ipcc.ch, and the mitigation volume (Working Group III), which discusses development and equity in the context of possible mitigation actions.

African nations[20]

Africa is a huge and varied continent spanning the tropics, subtropics and warm temperate zones from 37°N to 35°S. Common elements across many countries include rapid population growth, low per capita income, and a relatively low capacity to adapt to climate change due to poverty and existing climate, which in many areas is hot and arid. This is exacerbated by a long history of regional floods, droughts and famines, chronic armed conflict in several regions over the last 30 years, and in many cases governments and other institutions that are under-funded, inefficient, or otherwise not able to deal well with emergencies and long-term planning.

While generalisations are risky and should not be taken as universal in application the IPCC in 2007 concluded that:

- Africa is one of the most vulnerable continents to climate change and variability, a situation aggravated by the interaction of 'multiple stresses' (such as poverty, ecosystem degradation and governance issues), occurring at various levels, and low adaptive capacity.

- African farmers have developed several adaptation options to cope with current climate variability, but such adaptations may not be sufficient for future changes of climate.

- Agricultural production and food security (including access to food) in many African countries and regions are likely to be severely compromised by climate change and climate variability.

- Climate change will aggravate the water stress currently faced by some countries, while some countries that currently do not experience water stress will become at risk of water stress.

- Changes in a variety of ecosystems are already being detected, particularly in southern African ecosystems, at a faster rate than anticipated.

- Sea-level rise, climate variability and change could result in low-lying lands being inundated, with resultant impacts on coastal cities and settlements, mangrove and coral ecosystems, tourism, and fisheries. Several highly-populated delta regions such as that of the Nile and Niger are at great risk of erosion, flooding and salinisation.

- Human health, already compromised by a range of factors, could be further negatively impacted by climate change and climate variability, for example, malaria in southern Africa and the East African highlands, but also Rift Valley Fever, dengue fever, cholera and others.

These conclusions are generally supported by many other recent reports, for example, *Africa: Up in Smoke?*, from the UK Working Group on Climate Change and Development, July 2005. This suggests that climate change impacts on Africa may retard economic growth and stifle efforts to alleviate poverty.[21] Several studies on climate change and security issues also point to climate change stresses as an additional cause of conflict on the African continent.

All these concerns, on top of other stresses such as AIDS and internal conflicts, add up to Africa being the region likely to be worst affected by enhanced climate change. This will add to the existing inequality between African nations and the richer developed countries. This cannot be good for Africa, nor for the developed nations, as it may limit world trade, increase political instability and tensions, and add to the problems of forced migration and necessary economic and emergency aid programs. It is clearly in the interest of African countries to see an urgent start on reducing total global greenhouse gas emissions, and it is important for the richer countries to see that this happens also.

At present African countries in general have the lowest standards of living and the lowest per capita emissions of greenhouse gases. African countries therefore need assistance in coping with the impacts of climate change and variability, and need development to raise standards of living and to make the populations more resilient to stresses including climate change. Both objectives might best be achieved through the large-scale dissemination of renewable energy technologies to the poor. These nations will therefore be pressing for aid in achieving sustainable development, including low-carbon energy sources, but are unlikely to agree to any arrangement that restricts their economic growth.

Equity considerations suggest that Africans have a strong moral claim to assistance and to the right to increase their very low per capita emissions. Hopefully it will not be necessary for them to increase their greenhouse gas emissions to anything like the per capita amounts in the developed countries. This can only happen through massive transfer of new low-carbon technologies. Lack of electricity grids and other centralised energy infrastructure means that wide dispersal of small-scale renewable energy generation systems (such as those based on solar and biomass energy) may be economically attractive in most of Africa. While many African countries have ratified the Kyoto Protocol, they have not committed to emissions reductions in the first commitment period, 2008–12, since none are Annex I countries.[22]

The Energy, Environment and Development Network for Africa (AFREPREN/FWD) coordinates energy research across much of Africa, including work on co-generation and renewable energy.[23] It reports on energy issues, and recent publications suggest there is a mixture of new coal-fired (Nigeria) and oil (Uganda) developments as well as hydro-electric (Cameroon), geothermal (Kenya), wind (South Africa) and biomass (Kenya, Mozambique, Nigeria, Zimbabwe) projects.

Australia and New Zealand[24]

Australia is one of the highest per capita emitters of greenhouse gases. But when it comes to the potential impacts of climate change, Australia is almost certainly the most vulnerable developed country. All developed countries, by virtue of their wealth, and technological and institutional capacities can be expected to have great advantages relative to less-developed countries in terms of capacity to adapt to climate change. But, as we have seen in Chapter 7, the ability to adapt is also affected by the severity of climate change-induced stresses experienced, and to bio-physical limits to adaptation.

In Australia several factors increase the severity of exposure to climate change relative to other developed countries, and limit the capacity to adapt. These include:

- *Vulnerability to warming*. Mainland Australia is in the lowest latitude band of any developed country. This exposes Australian plants and animals, and especially agricultural and forest cropping, to optimum or above-optimum temperatures for large parts of the year. Studies of potential crop production suggest that for key crops, such as wheat, warming will tend to increase yields only for the first two or three degrees Celsius, and only if local rainfall and soil moisture do not decrease. For greater warmings, yields will drop. Moreover, warming in inland parts of the country will not be moderated by the oceans and, relative to pre-industrial levels is likely to be 2–3°C by the mid-twenty-first century and as much as 5–7°C by 2100 unless large reductions in greenhouse gas emissions begin soon. Moreover, warming will tend to increase evaporation and thus reduce soil moisture. It is unlikely that plant breeding could provide suitable cultivars for summer temperatures, which could be well in excess of 45°C in some regions.

- *Regional reductions in rainfall*. Rainfall decreases are likely across much of southern and south-eastern Australia, which is the most populated region, with greatest agricultural production. This would seriously exacerbate the impact of warming by reducing soil moisture and runoff. Annual rainfall increases in the centre and north-west are likely, but in a region that is only sparsely populated. Rainfall and runoff decreased in the Perth catchment in the south-west of Western Australia starting in the 1970s (see **Box 7** in Chapter 7) and have not recovered, while similarly dramatic decreases have occurred in the south-eastern part of Australia since the mid-1990s.

- *Already stressed water resources*. Water resources are already suffering from increasing stresses, and are likely to be greatly reduced, especially

in southern and inland regions. Existing problems include dryland and riverine salinisation, eutrophication and toxic algal blooms, lack of environmental flows (those that sustain riverine ecosystems), and competition for limited supplies. According to climate models, climate changes would lead to reductions in runoff and water supply in the Murray-Darling Basin with central estimates of around 20% reduction as early as 2030. Indeed such changes have already occurred, since the mid-1990s, as illustrated in **Figure 35**.

Despite some increases in water use efficiency in the Murray-Darling river system, this decline in water supply is greatly reducing irrigation of both low and high value crops, and adversely affecting other water uses such as that for industry and town water supplies. Some grape and citrus plantations are being abandoned and irrigation areas such as the Riverland (SA) and Sunraysia (Victoria) districts are threatened with loss of livelihood.

The major cities of Perth, Adelaide, Melbourne, Sydney and Canberra have already been seriously affected by water shortages due to persistent droughts, consistent with the enhanced greenhouse effect, over the last decade. Perth has installed a water desalination plant and other cities are considering doing so. In Tasmania, hydro-electric generation has been cut due to lack of water, and coal-fired electricity has had to be brought in by undersea cable from Victoria. Water supply has become a major national and regional issue.

- *Vulnerable native plants and animals*. Many native Australian species of plants and animals, some already threatened by exotic predators and loss of habitat, have low tolerances to changes in climatic averages (although they are often well-adapted to short term climatic variability). This includes especially Alpine species, species in the biologically-rich south-west of Western Australia (which cannot migrate south due to

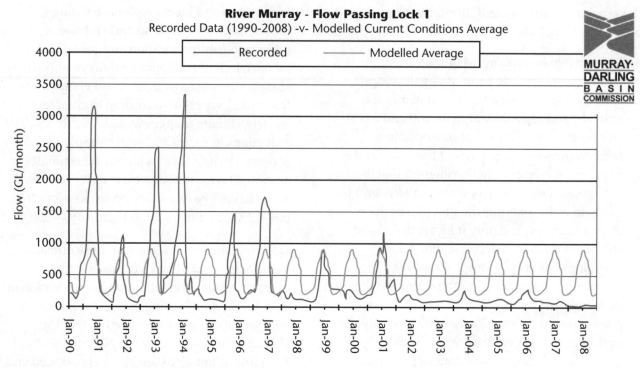

Murray-Darling Basin Commission March 2008

Figure 35: Recorded river flow (dark line) below Lock 1 on the lower Murray River at Blanchetown, South Australia, 1990–2008. Long-term average flow is indicated by the lighter grey line. Since 2002 river flow has been less than evaporation in the estuarine lakes, which are cutoff from the sea by an artificial barrier. Their level is now below sea-level, and this has exposed acid sulfate soil, which is leading to acidification of the lakes. (Graph courtesy of the Murray-Darling Basin Commission.)[25]

the coast), and Australia's very extensive coral reefs, where corals are already showing increasing damage due to more frequent and severe bleaching events. Death of corals would have a great adverse effect on the tourism industry and on fisheries.

- *Counter-adaptive trends.* Exposure to tropical cyclones and storm surges on the northern, western and eastern coasts of Australia is rapidly increasing due to population and investment growth in these areas, far greater than the national average. Projected increases in maximum intensities of tropical cyclones, their possible penetration further south, and mean sea-level rise would greatly increase the magnitude and frequency of storm surges. Conflicts in coastal areas between developers and local authorities concerned about potential sea-level rise are becoming more frequent.

- *More severe droughts.* Possible changes in the behaviour of the El Niño–Southern Oscillation

system (ENSO) towards a more El Niño-like average condition could greatly increase the frequency of major droughts in eastern Australia, and change the frequency of tropical cyclones, with increases in the west, but possible decreases in the east. The question of when episodic 'drought' becomes long-term climate change is a critical issue for rural policy, with traditional drought relief under 'exceptional circumstances' needing to be replaced by more fundamental structural adjustments.[26]

New Zealand is less vulnerable than Australia due to its location at higher latitudes and a climate more moderated by the oceans, which will slow warming over land. New Zealand also has ample water resources, although these differ greatly by region, with potential scarcity in the east. This could be exacerbated by a more El Niño-like mean oceanic state, and by a strengthening of the mid-latitude westerlies, which would increase rainfall on the already wet west coast, but reduce rainfall in the more populated east. New Zealand is sensitive to an increase in storm intensities and extreme rainfalls, due to its steep terrain and frequent landslides.

Australia and New Zealand will both be particularly vulnerable to increasing pressure to take immigrants from threatened low-lying island states in the South Pacific, where emigration will be one of the few means of adaptation. As rich neighbours, Australia and New Zealand will need to accept some responsibility for aid to neighbouring countries that are threatened by sea-level rise. Indeed both Australia and New Zealand have some special responsibility, as members of the (formerly British) 'Commonwealth of Nations', for its developing country members, some 27 of which are also members of the Alliance of Small Island States.[27]

New Zealand has constitutional and other arrangements in place to accept environmental and economically motivated migrants from some nations in the South Pacific. However, Australia under the previous conservative Howard government, strongly resisted any special consideration of such migration, and took a particularly hard line on so-called 'illegal' arrivals, which potentially would include environmental 'refugees' (see chapter 10 regarding equity issues).

Sea-level rise may also increase the pressure for migration to Australia, and to a lesser extent New Zealand, from low-lying parts of South-East Asia, including especially Bangladesh and low-lying coastal regions of Thailand, Indonesia, Indo-China, and even China. As the impacts of sea-level rise on these low-lying coastal regions increases, the threat of many tens of thousands of environmental refugees in the Australian–New Zealand region (and in other parts of the world) may become a reality. Issues of human rights and equity will be thrown into stark relief.

For all the above reasons, it is arguable that Australia has a particularly strong set of reasons for seeing effective global mitigation of climate change, as a matter of national interest. New Zealand also has good reasons, not the least being its close economic and political relationship with Australia, and the large number of New Zealanders who have traditionally resided in Australia.

In both Australia and New Zealand, some have argued that as these countries contribute little to total global emissions it is pointless for them to act to reduce their emissions before major polluters such as the United States, China and India do so. Besides the equity reasons of their large per capita emissions, this argument ignores the fact that most other rich countries (notably the EU countries) are moving to reduce their emissions, and that without action by the rich countries there is unlikely to be a next step by developing countries to limit their emissions. Indeed, before ratifying the Kyoto Protocol Australia provided the United States with the excuse that it was not alone amongst the rich countries in rejecting the Protocol. This may have already caused a costly delay for which the world, including Australia and New Zealand, will pay dearly in terms of increased climate change or more severe emissions reductions in the near future.

New Zealand ratified the Kyoto Protocol in 2002, and hopes to become carbon neutral (no net emissions), largely through more efficient farming, land management and transport, and an emissions trading scheme.[28] Australia, although a signatory to the UNFCCC, joined the United States in refusing to ratify the Protocol until 2007 when the new Rudd government signed the Protocol. The Australian government was on track to meet its Kyoto emissions target (which was an *increase* of 8% over 1990 levels) through voluntary energy conservation, restrictions on land clearing and other measures, but the new government is setting more stringent targets, and plans to have an emissions trading scheme in operation by 2010.[29]

Australia has a particularly large potential for renewable energy in the form of solar, wind, geothermal, and tidal power (see, for example, **Figure 31**). Over coming decades, growth in renewable energy resource industries (plus energy conservation) could provide ample power, a large potential for export of technology and hydrogen for fuel cells, and increased employment. It will require a national long-distance electric grid (possibly high voltage direct current cables – see Chapter 8) to get renewable energy from remote sources to the major cities, as is already being recognised by government and major geothermal power investors.

The setting of a global warming upper limit, or greenhouse gas concentration target, has been a vexed question in Australia, as elsewhere. As we have seen in earlier chapters, global warming, if we are to avoid 'dangerous' climate change, should probably stay below 2°C above pre-industrial levels, and if we are risk-averse this requires a CO_2-equivalent concentration target less than 400 ppm. The latter however is widely considered to be too difficult, at least initially. In the words of Professor Ross Garnaut, who has been the chief advisor on climate change to the Rudd government, in an interim report in February 2008:

> ... the prospects of achieving the global mitigation effort that would be necessary to achieve this outcome [400 ppm] appear to be remote in early 2008 ... To keep the possibility of eventual attainment of a 400 ppm objective (with overshooting) alive, the 450 ppm objective could be pursued with a view to tightening emissions targets if at some time the political and technological conditions for far-reaching mitigation has improved.[30]

Another contentious issue in Australian climate change policy is Australia's historic claim to be deserving of special treatment due to its large economic reliance on exports of direct energy commodities such as coal and natural gas as well as goods with large amounts of embodied energy (that is, goods requiring large amounts of energy to manufacture), especially aluminium and steel. This argument won Australia its generous target of a small increase of emissions under the Kyoto Protocol. With this export problem, Australia would benefit greatly, and perhaps equitably, from the addition of an international provision to make embodied energy in manufactured exports such as aluminium and steel a charge against the emissions quota of the consuming rather than the exporting country. But in any case, a truly global move to a lower carbon economy will mean that continued reliance on carbon-rich exports will lead to an eventual decrease in exports. Australia, like other countries, will have to move to a low-carbon economy.

The other oft-repeated claim in Australia, from industry and government, is that Australia's great reliance on coal-fired electricity means that carbon capture and sequestration (CCS) is an essential part of any emissions reduction strategy. Whether this will prove to be the case is highly doubtful, as carbon cap and trade measures, and rapid improvements in technology, will likely result in technological advances and cheaper large-scale renewable energy that may well come in at a lower cost than large-scale CCS. Moreover, carbon leakage in the CCS process is likely to be some 10–30% (see Chapter 8) after taking account of the energy needed for the CCS process. Thus any new coal-fired power station with CCS will still require large carbon offsets or to be accompanied by the decommissioning of older less-efficient power stations if a net increase in emissions is to be avoided.

Another fear in Australia is that emissions targets and a carbon trading scheme in Australia, if not part of a global system, will lead to 'leakage' of emissions and jobs to other countries where such regulations do not apply. This is unlikely as all countries, and most international corporations, are becoming increasingly concerned about their emissions. Moreover, Australia remains a large source of commodities that are best processed, at least in part, in Australia, where there is a highly trained workforce. Indeed a number of Chinese and other international companies are investing in the Australian resource and power industries. Moreover, a number of domestic and foreign companies are planning to develop large-scale renewable energy in Australia through investment in wind farms, and geothermal and solar power.[31]

Australian companies are becoming increasingly supportive of emissions reduction strategies. In July 2008 the president of the Business Council of Australia wrote:

> The Business Council of Australia supports the Government's plans to introduce an emissions trading scheme. The priority for the BCA and its members is to work with the Government on a scheme that is credible and effective, and achieves reductions at least cost ... The challenge we face

stems from the failure historically to price carbon to reflect the potential costs of accumulated greenhouse gas emissions. Much of the world's post-war prosperity has been built on energy that has, with hindsight, been too cheap. A significant part of Australia's comparative advantage has, of course, been built on cheap energy. We must recognise that shifting from this way of life presents a big transformation for the economy.[32]

The Rudd government announced its proposed Carbon Pollution Reduction Scheme in a White Paper on 15 December 2008. It proposes reductions in emissions in the range 5 to 15% by 2020, with many pollution permits given free to 'exposed' large carbon emitters. This target is considered inadequate by many scientists and green groups.[29]

China

China's rapidly increasing total greenhouse gas emissions exceeded that of the United States some time around 2007. However, China's population is four times greater than the United States, its historic emissions total far less (see **Figure 30**, Chapter 8), and its priorities are raising living standards (while limiting population growth) and promoting sustainable development. China is burning ever more coal, but it also has a thriving renewable energy industry and a national climate change program.

China has a long record of climatically related national disasters, including flood, drought, typhoons and famine. Major flood disasters occurred in 1852 (100 000 dead), 1887 (900 000 dead), 1931 (140 000 dead), 1954 (40 000 dead), and 1998 (3650 dead). Droughts, with associated famines, have been equally disastrous, while typhoons have frequently led to storm surge and riverine flooding in coastal regions. While major efforts have been made to control flooding and to store water for irrigation and hydro-electricity generation, increased population and encroachment on flood plains, as well as land clearing in catchment areas, have meant that the potential for disaster has not necessarily decreased.[33]

For example, in the early 1950s comprehensive flood control measures were taken in the Yangtze River valley. These included construction of dikes along the river to prevent overflowing, and the creation of flood diversion areas (polders) that could be inundated during floods to reduce the discharge in the river and lessen downstream flooding. The largest of these polders (Jingjiang), built in 1952, had an area of 920 km^2, and could store 6 billion cubic metres of water. During the great flood of 1954 this prevented the number of casualties from being much greater. However, some 50 years later, almost a million people have settled in this flood basin, and it can no longer be used for floodwater diversion. Thus cities and towns downstream, such as Wuhan (population around 5 million), are now more exposed than they were in 1954.

However, due to limited resources, assessments of the impact of climate change in China have so far focused mainly on changes in average temperature and rainfall rather than on changes in the frequency and intensity of extreme events. This has led to a somewhat optimistic view of China's vulnerability to climate change. Possibly a clearer understanding of China's vulnerability would help China to adopt forward commitments, which in turn would encourage the United States to make a commitment. Therefore, a critical assessment is required of risks to China from climate change, including especially extreme events.[34] These risks include:

- *Likely increases in flood magnitudes and frequencies.* Most global climate model simulations in the IPCC 2007 report show modest increases in average rainfall over most of China in summer, while a study by UK hydrologist Nigel Arnell shows increases in runoff especially in central and south-eastern China. Increases in rainfall intensity, and possibly in variability, are likely to lead to more frequent large floods, as found for China and elsewhere by US investigators Milly and colleagues in 2002.[35]

- *A tendency for more winter and spring runoff and less summer runoff* in snow-fed rivers, increasing the need to operate dams more for flood control rather than maximising storage for summer irrigation and hydro-electric power.[36]

- *Possible increases in drought intensity, frequency and duration,* due especially to increased year-to-year variability and greater evaporation rates. Already, there has been a tendency for reduced flow and sediment discharge by the Yellow River in northern China and a Chinese study predicts strong reductions in surface runoff by 2050. This may lead to increased erosion in the Gulf of Bohai and reduced water for irrigation. Depletion of deep aquifers in northern China due to unsustainable water withdrawals for irrigation is also a factor.[37]

- *Probable increases in typhoon intensity* and possibly in frequency and penetration to higher latitudes due to higher sea surface temperatures in the China Sea.

- *Rising sea level* adding to flooding of coastal regions, especially during storm surges or in association with river floods. This will reduce coastal wetland ecosystems as coasts retreat to areas protected by sea walls, thus reducing fish spawning grounds, and causing salt intrusion in river estuaries. It will also threaten the homes and livelihood of millions of people, especially in the heavily populated south-eastern region, including several large cities. The possibility of sea-level rise in excess of the IPCC 2007 estimates, possibly well over a metre by 2100 (see Chapters 5 and 6), would be devastating for many coastal cities and much agriculture on extensive deltaic coastal plains. Tens of millions of people could be displaced.[38]

- *Effects of any change in ENSO,* which would affect rainfall variability and frequency of typhoons in China.

- *Increased flushing of nutrients and chemicals into rivers, lakes and coastal waters* (due to pollution and more intense runoff events). With higher temperatures this would lead to more eutrophication and algal blooms in water supplies.

China has made great strides in energy efficiency, renewable energy and reforestation, mainly for reasons such as reducing local air pollution, economic efficiency, and controlling soil losses. Increased dam construction has boosted hydro-electric power resources, may smooth out seasonal variations in water supply and may reduce floods originating in the upper catchments. However, China's rapid economic growth has outstripped these mitigation measures by increasing greenhouse gas emissions, and this includes emissions in the production of goods for export.

Chinese official figures suggest a decline in China's energy intensity (energy per unit GDP) of a remarkable 60% between 1977 and 1997. However, this may be exaggerated, with other estimates suggesting a decline of 10% during the 1990s. More than 70% of China's energy use comes from coal, and with rapid economic growth carbon emissions per unit GDP have increased in recent years. This can only be turned around by increases in energy efficiency, huge increases in renewable energy, rapid expansion of nuclear power or lower-emissions coal via carbon capture and sequestration or other technologies.[39]

Discussion on appropriate domestic and international energy policies for China is ongoing and vigorous. This includes a new generation of nuclear reactors, fostering renewables, coal gasification with carbon removal and sequestration, and eventually hydrogen generation for transport. Princeton University's Eric Larson and colleagues modelled China's energy technology choices. They concluded that by using coal gasification, co-generation, liquid and gaseous energy carriers, carbon sequestration, expanded renewables and end-use efficiency, China could still develop over the next 50 years with secure energy supplies and improved environmental quality. This would include modest near-term reductions in greenhouse gas emissions, at a cost less than 'business as usual'. Robert Williams from Princeton University also discusses how China could achieve zero emissions from coal. Phasing out old and inefficient coal-based power stations is a key requirement, as is reducing other emissions such as sulfur, oxides of nitrogen and particulates for urban air quality purposes.[40]

China is looking to international assistance in leapfrogging over carbon intensive technology. This opens up a huge market for low-carbon technologies. In particular both the US and Australia are cooperating with China in developing carbon capture and sequestration technology, and China and the EU are developing a cooperative relationship on energy and climate security. One Chinese company, Suntech, is a leading world producer of solar photovoltaic systems, with major exports to Germany and Spain, and a number of Chinese cities have solar hot-water heaters on nearly every roof.[41]

China's 11th Five Year Plan (2005–10) embodied a number of policies aimed at energy efficiency and conservation. More recently, China has adopted a National Climate Change Programme under the auspices of the National Development and Reform Commission.[42] Under this program China has adopted the following principles:

- To address climate change within the framework of sustainable development.

- To follow the principle of 'common but differentiated responsibilities', that is, developed countries should take the lead in reducing emissions while developing countries give priority to development and poverty eradication.

- To place equal emphasis on both mitigation and adaptation.

- To integrate climate change policy with interrelated policies.

- To rely on the advancement of innovation and technology.

- To participate in international cooperation actively and extensively.

It is strongly in China's national interest to see an effective international regime to reduce greenhouse gas emissions as soon as possible, which will require limits to emissions both in developed and developing countries. China's interests would thus be well served by negotiating on the basis that progressively increasing commitments will be made by China and other developing countries once they are made by developed countries. Australia has a special role to play in this as a major supplier to China of coal, iron ore and natural gas.

Despite, and indeed because of potential economic rivalry between the two economic giants, China and the United States need to reach an agreement on how to bring an effective global emission reduction regime into being which allows for development in China and other developing countries while avoiding intolerable levels of climate change. In the words of John Ashton the UK special representative for climate change:

> … we need to build a global politics of interdependence. That's the biggest political challenge that we have and arguably the biggest political challenge that humanity has ever faced. China is enormously important to that jig-saw.[43]

European Union

The EU has a strong commitment to an effective mitigation regime, although the details of how it is being achieved is under debate. The reasons for the European commitment are outlined below.[44] They demonstrate the rationality of the EU position and the need for the EU to meet its commitments and to eventually bring both the US and the developing countries into the picture.

- *Increasing aridity in the Mediterranean region.* This is one of the clearest areas of agreement between different global climate models regarding rainfall changes, with reductions in rainfall as well as higher potential evaporation. In an area already experiencing water shortages, this could bite hard in the next few decades, especially affecting agriculture, increasing the frequency and severity of wildfires and adversely affecting tourism. This will tend to accentuate the difference between the more prosperous northern parts of Europe and the less prosperous south.[45]

- *More severe heatwaves.* Higher average temperatures and possibly increased variability are likely to increase the frequency and severity of heatwaves, causing thousands of additional deaths as in 2003 (see **Figure 5**). Air conditioning would reduce death rates, but would be expensive, increase energy demand – and hence emissions – and not reduce discomfort outdoors.[46]

- *Increased flash flood risks right across the EU.* This follows from increased rainfall intensities projected by climate models, in a region where flash flooding is already a recurring problem due to close settlement, steep topography and fast runoff.

- *Increased major flood risk in northern Europe.* This follows from the broad agreement of global climate models that total rainfall in northern Europe will increase, especially in the winter half year. In many catchments warming will shorten the snow season, pushing peak runoff more into winter. Severe and widespread flooding has become common in northern and central Europe in the last two decades. In combination with rising sea levels, flooding will be exacerbated in coastal lowlands, particularly where storm surges slow drainage.

- *Possible changes in storminess, including extreme winds and hail.* Many modelling studies suggest that mid-latitude storms may increase in intensity due to more intense convection, and possible changes in storm tracks. Severe wind storms in western and northern Europe in recent years have caused extensive damage to forests and buildings. This tendency may increase.

- *Thawing of permafrost.* This is already causing problems with buildings and infrastructure in far northern Europe and in the Alps. In the Alps this is increasing the danger of landslides affecting mountain slopes and valleys, and affecting buildings and infrastructure such as cable cars, ski lifts, roads, railways, mountain villages and towns.[47]

- *Loss of coastal wetlands due to sea-level rise.* This is of most concern in southern Europe. Local relative sea level will not be as severely affected in the north due to the continuing slow rebound (rising) of the land following the end of the last glaciation.

- *Pressures for population movement.* Pressure will come from both within Europe and from less-developed countries, from areas more adversely affected by climate change. This will increase pressure on migration policies and external aid programs. Growing aridity and possible food shortages in North Africa and the Middle East may be of particular concern.

- *Threats to peace and security.* There may be increased instability in less developed countries as they suffer adverse impacts and regional disputes over water in Europe, the Middle East and Central Asia.

- *Weakening or cessation of the North Atlantic thermo-haline circulation (THC).* The THC presently keeps Western Europe relatively warm (see Chapter 6). Regional cooling along the Atlantic and North Sea coasts by up to 6 to 8°C could occur if the THC breaks down during this century. The likelihood and impacts of such an event are poorly understood.

Several countries in the EU already have strong renewable energy sectors, notably wind power in Denmark, and solar power in Germany, largely due to government incentives. There is the potential to further develop such industries, for example, solar energy in Spain, and wind and tidal power in the UK. These are growth industries. Policies leading to early action, including research, development, and domestic market building, have already led to European exports such as wind turbines to Australia. A proposal backed by the Club of Rome aims to link Europe to large solar thermal power generators in North Africa and the Middle East via high voltage direct current cables. This is to be investigated under the proposed Union for the Mediterranean launched in Paris on 13 July 2008. Meanwhile, American and

Chinese solar energy photovoltaic companies are finding markets in Europe.[48]

The European Union has a comprehensive policy on climate change following its ratification of the Kyoto Protocol in 2002, and its adoption of emissions reduction targets of 30% below 1990 levels by 2020, with a view to achieving cuts of 60–80% by 2050. According to a 2007 EU document *EU action against climate change: Leading global action to 2020 and beyond*, the EU is aiming at limiting global warming to 2°C above pre-industrial temperatures. These targets are conditional on being 'part of a global and comprehensive post-2012 agreement, [with] other developed countries [committing] to comparable reductions and advanced developing countries also [contributing] adequately to the global effort according to their respective capabilities'.[49]

Meanwhile, the EU has made a firm commitment to cut its emissions to at least 20% below 1990 levels by 2020, via measures through the European Climate Change Programme, including the EU's pioneering Emissions Trading Scheme which became operational on 1 January 2005. This had some teething troubles but is now working fairly well. It allows individual countries a lot of autonomy in how they manage it, which makes it a good model for wider international action. It focuses initially on major companies and their emissions and is gradually being extended to take account of other sectors and activities, including airline emissions and possibly shipping.

Some critics claim that the EU is unlikely to meet its targets, and has to date looked good only because of the shift from coal to gas in the UK in the 1990s, the reform of the East German economy on reunification, and the relatively strong reliance on nuclear power.

On the other hand, an assessment by two researchers from the Massachusetts Institute of Technology for the Pew Center on Global Climate Change in May 2008 points out that the first three years from 2005 through 2007 constituted a trial period. Its primary goal was to develop the infrastructure and to provide the experience that would enable the successful use of the cap-and-trade system to limit European GHG emissions during a second trading period in 2008–12.[50]

The researchers conclude that: 'In the light of the speed with which the program was developed, the many sovereign countries involved, the need to develop the necessary data, information dissemination, compliance and market institutions, and the lack of experience with emissions trading in Europe, we think the system has performed surprisingly well'. The researchers go on to say: 'The initial challenge is simply to establish a system that will demonstrate the societal decision that the GHG emissions shall have a price and to provide a signal of what constitutes appropriate short-term and long-term measures to limit GHG emissions. In this, the EU has done more with the ETS, despite all its faults, than any other nation or set of nations'.

India, Pakistan and Bangladesh[51]

This section will focus mostly on India, which is the country with the second largest population in the world, the fourth largest economy, and a per capita income about half that of China. The neighbouring countries of Pakistan and Bangladesh share some of the same problems and climatic influences.

Global warming is expected to have profound effects on India, Pakistan and Bangladesh, although there are large uncertainties about the relative effects on the summer monsoon rains of global warming with or without taking account of aerosol (atmospheric particle) effects. Key potential impacts include:

- higher temperatures increasing potential evaporation and duration of heatwaves,

- significant decline in winter rainfall leading to severe water scarcity during early summer months,

- more intense droughts over larger areas adversely affecting crop production, especially wheat and rice,

- the per capita availability of freshwater in India is expected to drop from around 1900 cubic metres currently to 1000 cubic metres by 2025 due to a combination of population growth and climate change,

- more intense floods, especially in the flood plains of the eastern Himalayan rivers, their major tributaries and the delta regions,

- coastal flooding and salinity intrusion from sea-level rise in combination with the amplification of storm surges from more intense tropical cyclones in the Bay of Bengal,

- rapid melting of Himalayan glaciers, leading initially to greater river flows and hence sedimentation, and subsequent reduced flow, especially in the drier months,

- serious health impacts due to heat-related stress and vector-borne diseases,

- crop yields could decrease by up to 30% in South Asia by 2050,

- climate change will intensify other environmental pressures and impinge on sustainable development.

In summary, climatic changes would likely lead to more severe food shortages, increased loss of life and infrastructure from coastal inundation and riverine flooding, loss of life from heat stress and vector-borne diseases, and potential displacement of tens of millions of residents of low-lying coastal areas, especially in Bangladesh, causing problems of internal and cross-border migration.

Rapid industrialisation, urbanisation and population growth have already greatly increased water demand. Groundwater resources are under severe stress and expansion is limited. In response, the Indian government has initiated plans to link rivers across India. In the Himalayan rivers component water from the present water-surplus rivers of the north and east would be diverted to the drier central and western regions, while in Peninsula catchments various linkages would be made to supply Mumbai and to divert water to the south and east. This huge project is highly controversial, with concern from Bangladesh about its share of the waters, the possibility that climate change might decrease the water supply in the north making such a scheme less viable and other

concerns regarding ecosystems and displacement of people.[52]

India has one of the lowest per capita rates of greenhouse gas emissions, about roughly one-twentieth that of the US and Australia, has a high population growth rate (1.5% per year), and in recent years its economy grew at about 8–9% per year. Its energy use grew roughly 7% per year over the same period, and its carbon intensity (emissions per unit GDP) began to decline after 1995. India is heavily dependent on coal and traditional non-commercial biomass use. However, economic reforms and enforcement of clean air laws, combined with renewable energy incentives and developments have led to recent decreases in energy-related carbon emissions intensity. Nevertheless, approximately half of the Indian population lacks access to electricity.[53]

India has ratified the Kyoto Protocol, and while its priority is sustainable development, it is committed to a 'climate-friendly' approach. India's vehicle stock has been greatly modified in recent years, with public vehicles in Delhi converted to natural gas, and European-level emission standards applied to passenger vehicles in several major cities. With this background, the Indian government in June 2008 issued a National Action Plan on Climate Change, which identified harnessing renewable energy, including solar power, and energy efficiency as central to India's fight against global warming, and is setting up a climate change fund to research 'green' technologies. The Indian Prime Minister stated: 'Our vision is to make India's economic development energy efficient ... Our people have a right to economic and social development and to discard the ignominy of widespread poverty'. The Prime Minister went on: 'Despite our development imperatives, our per capita GHG emissions will not exceed the per capita emissions of the developed industrialised countries'. India would try to make a gradual shift from fossil fuels to renewable energy sources.[54]

The Indian National Action Plan identifies eight core 'national missions' running through 2017 and directs relevant ministries to submit detailed implementation plans to the Prime Minister's Council on Climate Change by December 2008. These national missions include: solar power, enhanced energy efficiency, sustainable habitat, a national water mission, sustaining the Himalayan ecosystem, achieving a 'green India', sustainable agriculture, and strategic knowledge for climate change.

Each of these missions has stated goals, but the critical test will be in the implementation plans and the priority that is given to them in relation to other development goals. These will be in addition to other existing programs such as the retirement of inefficient coal-fired power plants, renewable energy targets, and the *2001 Energy Conservation Act*.

Nevertheless, 'business as usual' projections suggest that India's GDP could be nearly five times the present by 2030, with a tripling of energy use and more than a doubling of carbon emissions. Additional emission reductions will require concerted measures aided by international carbon trading, the CDM and access to new technologies. In relation to international agreements on global emission reductions, equity on a per capita basis is a major issue for India and other developing countries. However, these countries may be more vulnerable to global warming than they fully appreciate, requiring major efforts to ensure that truly global emissions reductions do occur rapidly.[55]

Latin America[56]
Latin America covers a huge range of environments, from Central America and the Caribbean through the Amazon to the grasslands and ice sheets of Argentina and Chile, with diverse climates, ecosystems, human population distributions, living standards, and cultural traditions. Population growth and land-use changes are already exerting major pressures on the environment, so that climate change and sea-level rise are just adding to the stresses. Some considerations related to climate change include:

- *Warming patterns.* Indications are that Central and South America generally will warm at about the global average rate, although probably faster in inland South America.

- *Rainfall patterns.* Sub-regional detail is limited. However, indications are that Central America will tend to have less rainfall, with patterns in South America varying greatly from location to location, with major drying indicated in some model projections. Rainfall changes in parts of South America may be dominated by changes in the El Niño–Southern Oscillation (ENSO) pattern, which has great influence. A southward movement of the mid-latitude westerlies and the high-pressure belt is now considered likely due to both the enhanced greenhouse effect and stratospheric ozone depletion, affecting rainfall in southern Argentina and Chile.

- *ENSO.* Under enhanced greenhouse warming, El Niño-like conditions may become more frequent and intense. This would lead to drier conditions in Mexico, the Amazon region and Central America. Higher temperatures would exacerbate such droughts by increasing rates of evaporation of existing soil moisture.

- *The Amazon region.* Some, but not all, global climate models show a reduction in rainfall in the Amazon basin. Deforestation, currently occurring due to land clearing, leads to reduced evapotranspiration (atmospheric moisture input from trees), which provides about half of the moisture in the region recycled as rainfall. Forest fragmentation and drying leads to greatly increased danger of widespread fires. This would be greatly exacerbated by more El Niño-associated droughts. The danger is that death of forests due to land clearing and fire may lead to an irreversible decline in regional rainfall, to large increases in carbon dioxide input to the atmosphere, and amplification of the greenhouse effect.

- *Agriculture.* Under climate change conditions, subsistence farming would be severely threatened in some parts of Latin America, such as north-east Brazil and Mexico. Increased temperatures may also reduce yields in other parts of Latin America, even allowing for the physiological benefits of increased carbon dioxide concentrations.

- *Health.* Higher temperatures will make urban air pollution worse in major cities. More intense rainfalls from storms generally and tropical cyclones (hurricanes) in Central America will increase the risk of flash flooding and landslides endangering lives and property. Vector-borne diseases are also likely to increase especially in poorer populations where medical services are limited, and food shortages (especially of rice, cattle and dairy products) are likely to be exacerbated in some regions.

- *Glaciers.* Those in the high Andes and the ice sheets in southern South America are already retreating, and will retreat much more. This will lead to changes in the total and annual cycle of river flow in some rivers, threatening some urban water supplies (notably in Peru), irrigation and loss of tourism.

- *Tropical cyclones.* These are expected to become more intense. They have major impacts on the Caribbean and Central American States, causing great economic and human losses, for instance Hurricane Mitch in 1998 caused losses of about 40% and 70% of the GDP in Nicaragua and Honduras, respectively. The possibility that tropical cyclones may form in the South Atlantic must now be treated seriously following the unprecedented Hurricane Catarina that struck Brazil in March 2004.[57]

Overall, climate change may bring some benefits to some regions of Latin America, but increasing environmental deterioration, and changes in water supply and agricultural lands may make any gains negligible. Adaptability of Latin American socio-economic systems to extreme climate events is very low and vulnerability is high, especially for the many urban and rural poor.

With the exception of Venezuela and Mexico, Latin America is poorly supplied with fossil fuels, and energy imports are a large drain on the economies of the region. Brazil has been in the forefront of developing renewable energy sources, notably hydropower for electricity (90% of total power generation in 1999) and ethanol for transport. Brazil has also been very active in climate policy negotiations, with proposals to provide for equitable participation of developing countries. However, rapid economic growth and an electric power shortage has led to a growth over the last couple of decades in coal-, oil- and gas-based power generation, which can be built faster and closer to centres of high power demand. This trend is expected to continue.[58]

Despite this recent trend to increased use of fossil fuels, Brazilian experience in initially subsidising the use of ethanol from sugarcane is instructive. Not only have costs gone down and ethanol become economically competitive with petroleum, but ethanol production has supplied far more employment per unit energy than coal, oil or hydropower. The federal government of Brazil has recently mandated a minimum share of new renewable sources in electricity generation in Brazil, and proposed similar global targets and time frames internationally. Possible competition between biofuel production and food is a critical issue but solvable through appropriate policies including use of cellulosic material rather than grain starch and sugars. It is essential that Brazil, as one of the largest developing countries, be engaged in the post-Kyoto global mitigation regime.

The Russian Federation[59]

The Russian Federation covers a vast territory from the Baltic Sea in the west to the Bering Sea in the east, and from south of 45°N to the high Arctic beyond 70°N. Much of northern Russia is tundra overlaying permafrost, with vast boreal forests further south, and arid areas in Central Asia. Obviously, people who are heavily snow-bound in winter with sub-zero temperatures would welcome a little more warmth. However, it is a complex business, since vegetation, ecosystems and human society have adapted to the existing climate over hundreds and thousands of years. Some key issues include:

- The melting of Arctic sea ice would facilitate shipping over a longer season, and Russia has already laid claim to parts of the Arctic sea bed with a view to exploiting oil and gas deposits. (The geo-political implications are discussed in Chapter 6 and references therein.) On the other hand, melting of permafrost may restrict access to inland sites. The exposure of coasts to storm and wave action would increase erosion along the Arctic shores, made worse by sea-level rise.[60]

- Indigenous communities dependent on hunting of reindeer, polar bear, walrus and some species of seal, for example in Chukotka in the far east, will be threatened.

- Many human settlements and developments, including buildings, roads, rail, airfields and oil and gas pipelines have been built on permanently frozen ground. As is the case in Alaska, costs from damage to these structures as foundations shift, could be large. The southern limit of permafrost is projected to move northward by several hundred kilometres by 2100.

- Winter heating costs could be reduced, but cooling may become increasingly necessary in summer.

- Some crops in more temperate regions would have longer growing seasons and could increase their yield at least for warmings of up to about 5°C, especially where accompanied by increased winter snow and summer rain, as is likely in many mid- to high-latitude regions. However, warming in inland regions is expected to be more than twice the global average, so it could well be 5 to 10°C warmer by 2100. The continental interior may also experience summer drought, exacerbated by the high temperatures, leading to heat and water stress on crops. In regions where rainfall increases, waterlogging of crops may become a problem.

- Warming, and melting of snow cover would increase the range and length of season for insect pests, allowing more generations over a growing season, affecting crop yields and human health.

- Boreal forests would be exposed to higher temperatures, and increasingly frequent and severe summer droughts. Coupled with increased exposure to insect pests, this would lead to dieback and increased danger of wildfires. Eventually boreal forests may extend further north, but losses at their southern boundaries are likely to occur sooner and to be greater. According to the Canadian Forest Service such effects are already occurring in Canada. Growth of boreal bogs has caused death of trees in some areas.[61]

- The episodic impacts of increasingly severe floods, droughts, severe storms and insect infestations may prove to be a major concern.

Whatever the balance between the gains and losses listed above, which will become increasingly negative with increased warming beyond a few degrees, other considerations will impact on the Russian national interest. These include likely deleterious effects on Russia's southern neighbours, most of which are in the drier continental interior that will become much warmer and may not have increases in rainfall. Growing poverty, food shortages and other factors may lead to increasing unrest and instability, requiring Russian aid or leading to adverse impacts from insurgencies and environmental refugees.

These and other considerations led to heated discussion within the Russian Federation as to whether it should ratify the Kyoto Protocol. Russia ratified the Protocol in November 2005, despite the opposition of some influential advisers. Argument hinged in part on what economic benefits might accrue to Russia in the short term from possible sale of surplus greenhouse gas emission rights, and from Joint Implementation projects. While these were initially thought to be large due to the collapse of the Russian economy after the break-up of the USSR, recent signs of economic recovery suggest that Russia may have less surplus emissions for sale.

The politics of Russia's relationship to the Kyoto Protocol were reviewed by Jacqueline Karas of the Royal Institute of International Affairs in March 2004. Among the Russian scientists and economists opposed to ratification of the Protocol were Professor Yuri Israel, who has long maintained that Russia will benefit from moderate global warming, and Andrei Illarionov, then President Putin's economic advisor. Russia's role as a major exporter of oil and gas may have been critical to the decision to ratify the Protocol. This may have been influenced by the prospect of carbon removal and sequestration becoming a major mitigation strategy. Anna Korppoo of Imperial College, London, wrote that improving Russian energy efficiency would have been unlikely without investment made possible by the Protocol, which is likely to lead to Joint Implementation projects in Russia, particularly by members of the EU.[62]

Small Island States[63]

Small Island States include a mixture of islands in many different locations and having different physical characteristics. These include:

- *Atolls.* These are rings of coral reefs enclosing a lagoon. Around the rim of the reef are small islands, usually with average heights above sea level of only a few metres. Obviously, these will be severely affected by sea-level rise, storm surges and wave action. Atoll nations and their estimated populations in 2005 include Kiribati (population 99 000), the Maldives (population 329 000), the Marshall Islands (population 63 000), Tokelau (population 1500, plus another 6000 in New Zealand) and Tuvalu (population 11 000).

- *Islands with higher elevations.* These islands are usually of volcanic origin and often have low-lying fringes that contain much of the arable and populated land. Depending on their size and distribution of land, some

islands such as the main islands of Fiji, Tonga and Samoa may be severely affected by sea-level rise, although they will not become completely uninhabitable.

- *Multi-Island States.* These consist of a mixture of atolls and higher elevation islands. They will suffer various degrees of stress, especially associated with loss of resources and forced internal migration or emigration. Examples include Tonga (population 115 000 in 2005), and Fiji (population 850 000 in 2005).

- *Low-latitude islands.* Most Small Island States lie in tropical or subtropical waters such as the Pacific and Indian oceans and the Caribbean Sea. Those within about six degrees of latitude of the Equator are not directly subject to tropical cyclone (typhoon or hurricane) impacts (although they may still experience storm surges from weather disturbances at a distance). Those further from the Equator may suffer direct hits from such storms.

- *Mid-latitude Small Island States.* Examples are Cyprus and Malta. These are less low-lying and less exposed to storm surge events.

There are also many other small low-lying islands, often populated, which have many of the same potential problems from sea-level rise and climate change, but which are part of metropolitan countries or are in political association with them. These include American Samoa, Guam, and the Federated States of Micronesia (all associated with the US), many low-lying islands in the Philippines and Indonesia, and the islands of the Torres Strait in Australia. We will focus here on those islands that form independent states, and thus have national interests as such, although we note that the interests of the associated metropolitan states should include those of their associated islands.

Small Island States are not major contributors to the total emission of greenhouse gases, although they may be severely affected by consequent sea-level rise and climate change. In most cases they also have very limited resources and standards of living, and thus are less able to adapt to climate change than other states, unless they receive foreign aid to do so.

Major impacts affecting national interests include:

- Mean sea-level rise, which will increase the salinity of groundwater, especially on atolls where groundwater is often the only source of freshwater for human consumption and agriculture.[64]

- Extreme sea level, storm surges and high wave energy events, which will increasingly lead to wave overtopping and flooding of atolls and low-lying coastal fringes, threatening lives, infrastructure and property. Probable increases in the average and peak intensity of tropical cyclones (typhoons or hurricanes), and possibly of mid-latitude storms also, will exacerbate these problems. **Figure 36** vividly illustrates the existing highly vulnerable state of many inhabited low-lying coral atolls.

- Damage to coral reefs from more frequent and intense coral bleaching and wave damage, leading to loss of wave protection, loss of fisheries, and loss of attraction for the tourist industry. Acidification of the oceans will also reduce calcification of corals and endanger other marine biota and ecosystems.

- Many atolls, and some atoll states, could become uninhabitable during the twenty-first century or beyond with consequent loss of nationhood and cultural heritage. In order of vulnerability, Small Island States that could become uninhabitable in the next 50 years include Tokelau, the Maldives, Tuvalu, the Marshall Islands and Kiribati, with a total population at present of more than 500 000. Recent trends in sea level are rises of about 3 to 8 centimetres per decade across the South Pacific region, with acceleration probably occurring.

- In higher elevation islands, increased rainfall intensity associated with storms will increase erosion and riverine flooding.

- Changes in weather patterns, ocean currents and sea levels associated with regional climatic phenomena such as ENSO, the Intertropical Convergence Zone (ITCZ) and the South Pacific Convergence Zone (SPCZ) could lead to major changes in average rainfall and cloud cover and inter-annual variability, including the frequency and intensity of floods and droughts. These will be highly location-specific.

Figure 36: Graphic illustration of the vulnerability of coral atolls. Left: The normal view from the Meteorological Service office across the airport runway from the main town of Funafuti Atoll, Tuvalu, in the South Pacific. Right: Inundation caused by the spring tides in 2002. (Photos courtesy of Kathy Mcinnes, CSIRO, Australia (left) and Chalapan Kaluwin, AMSAT, Fiji, (right).)

- Threats to crop production due to higher temperatures and water demand, more saline groundwater, changed annual and inter-annual rainfall patterns, and storm damages.

- Increased costs of fossil fuels and freight, due to mitigation measures will put a premium on locally produced renewable energy and self-sufficiency.

Adaptation to climate change and sea-level rise is not easy for the Small Island States due to their limited resources, isolation and fundamental threats to their environmental support systems (land, fresh water, food supplies and so on).[65] Disaster preparedness and relief is one option, but options are limited, and if sea-level rise continues, ultimately the low-lying Small Island States are faced with the prospect of emigration as the last resort. This would have deep personal and cultural consequences, and demands a willingness by other nations to accept responsibility.

These and other considerations mean that it will be in the interests of the Small Island States, and especially of the low-lying ones, to:

- Increase use of local renewable energy supplies and foster increased self-sufficiency.

- Reduce reliance on groundwater on atolls and in coastal zones.

- Develop a population policy, including consideration of large-scale emigration to metropolitan states. This will entail negotiated migration agreements where these do not yet exist (as they do for former New Zealand dependencies). This provides a potential bargaining point in relation to the greenhouse mitigation policies and aid policies of the metropolitan states.

- Foster pro-active mitigation policies in both developed and developing countries. This includes a mediating role between those developed states that resist large emission reduction commitments until the lesser-developed states accept commitments, and those lesser-developed states that are unwilling to make forward commitments until the developed states act.

- Place emphasis on the global significance of the issues of equity, sovereignty and cultural assets raised by the possibility of populated atolls becoming uninhabitable.

Various UN and other treaties and agreements bear on these issues, as do the commitments to them already made in principle by many states. For example, the Commonwealth Heads of Government declared in their Langkawi Declaration in 1989 that they were deeply concerned at the serious deterioration in the environment, noting especially that some islands and low-lying areas are threatened by the prospect of rising sea level. It is interesting to note that 27 of the 54 members of the Commonwealth are also members of the Alliance of Small Island States. The Commonwealth is also committed in principle to 'a more equitable society', a principle that is seriously negated by continuing large per capita greenhouse gas emissions in developed countries.[66]

In the words of an editorial in the *Business Island Monthly*, Suva, January 2004:

> *Along with other countries alarmed by what climate change and sea level rise predictions imply for them, the Pacific Islands have been asking the big ask for a decade. Except for the European Union countries, the response to the protest clamour from the world's great climate polluters has generally been to sidestep, prevaricate, dodge, sabotage, obstruct, make excuses or to display open hostility to the notion that they have a duty to clean up their acts.*

This situation may be changing with changes of governments in some key developed countries. The process would be assisted by the Small Island States continuing to press for appropriate action by all countries.

United States of America

In an announcement by President Bush on 14 February 2002, the United States reaffirmed its commitment to the UNFCCC and its central goal of stabilisation of greenhouse gas concentrations at a level that will prevent dangerous interference with the climate system. However, the US withdrew from the Kyoto Protocol process, and Bush's commitment in 2002 was only to reduce US greenhouse gas *intensity* (that is, emissions per unit GDP) by 18% over the next 10 years. This is very close to the reduction in greenhouse gas *intensity* that the US achieved over the previous 10 years, when *total* US emissions (not per unit GDP) increased by 12%. This increase in actual emissions was due to a much larger (32%) increase in GDP over the same period. Assuming continued US economic growth, the Bush commitment for the next decade amounted, in terms of actual emissions, to about a 30% increase above 1990 emissions levels by 2012, compared to the 7% reduction originally agreed to by the United States at the Kyoto conference.[67]

As stabilisation of carbon dioxide levels will only occur after a massive decrease in global emissions (much more than agreed under the Kyoto Protocol), the US stance demonstrated no real commitment to stabilisation of carbon dioxide concentrations in the foreseeable future. As the United States emits about a third of total global emissions, and its participation in global trading of carbon emissions is vital to a strong market in emissions, US policy is important to the future success of global initiatives to deal with climate change. Moreover, action in the major developing countries is in part conditional on real US action.

The stated reason for this lack of commitment to real emissions reductions was concern about what was alleged to be a large cost to the US economy of real reductions. Leaving aside the question of whether this large cost is realistic (but see Chapter 10 for a discussion of evidence that it has probably been greatly exaggerated), it is pertinent to examine what is most at risk for the United States if climate change proceeds as projected in the absence of large emission reductions.

The United States is particularly vulnerable[68] to:

- Sea-level rise and storm surges on the Pacific, Atlantic and Gulf of Mexico coasts, including

areas in the south-east such as Louisiana, Florida, North Carolina and the eastern shore of Chesapeake Bay. James Titus and Charlie Richman of the US Environment Protection Agency estimate that some 58 000 square km along the Atlantic and Gulf coasts is less than 1.5 m above sea level.[69] These areas are highly vulnerable to the likely combination of sea-level rises of 50 cm or more by the year 2100, high tides and storm surges.

More than half of the US population now live in the 17% of the land area that comprises the coastal zone, and the largest population growth during the next several decades is projected to be in this area. As in New Orleans in 2005, numerous US cities, including Boston, New York and Miami lie close to sea level and major sections could be inundated by a combination of river flooding, storm surge and sea-level rise, with heavy loss of life and infrastructure damages. As with New Orleans, many US cities are not adequately protected from such impacts.

- The extent of the US Coastal Barriers Resources System is almost certainly inadequate and is being eroded. This consists largely of undeveloped lands along the US Atlantic, Gulf of Mexico and Great Lakes coasts, protecting development further inland. One suggestion is that all vulnerable shorelines, regardless of their stage of development, should be included. These would be removed from federal assistance, so that they would need to rely on private insurance, which if not forthcoming would make building impractical. A RAND Corporation study in 2007 found that following Hurricane Katrina, such insurance is now much more expensive or unavailable.[70]

- Decreases in winter snow pack in the Pacific North-west, the Sierras and the Rocky Mountains leading to increased river flow and flooding in winter and spring, and less water storage for summer irrigation. Dams will need to be operated for flood protection, by keeping water levels low, and will thus not maximise their storage for irrigation. An analysis by Tim Barnett of the Scripps Institution of Oceanography and colleagues in 2008 showed that up to 60% of climate-related trends of river flow, winter air temperature and snow pack between 1950 and 1999 are human-induced. The authors state that in conjunction with previous work, they portend 'a coming crisis in water supply for the western United States'.[71]

- Increasing aridity in the South-west and Great Plains regions and possibly elsewhere due to higher evaporation and likely decreases in rainfall. The strong view coming out of the 2007 IPCC assessment and other more recent studies is that rainfall is likely to decrease across most of the southern half of the United States, and that this will be exacerbated by higher temperatures and thus evaporation (see **Figure 17** in Chapter 5). Extended drought conditions in these regions are already occurring and have been at least partially ascribed to human-induced climate change.[72] Lake levels in the Great Lakes are expected to fall.[73] The South-west is among the most rapidly growing areas of the country and has had lowering water tables for many years due to extensive use of aquifers for irrigation and urban water supplies. Increasing aridity will likely force rises in water prices and restrict urban and industrial growth. Crop yields will be adversely affected by increasing aridity, which may well counter any advantages from longer growing seasons and increased concentrations of carbon dioxide.

- Increased frequency of major floods in the large river basins of the US. Researchers from the US Geological Survey and the National Oceanographic and Atmospheric Administration report that great floods in 29 large river basins worldwide have increased in frequency since 1953, and are projected to further increase in frequency during the twenty-first century by a factor of 2 to 8 times. This includes the Mississippi Basin.[74]

- Increased risk of wildfires and damages, especially in the western US. There seems to be an increase in recent decades, and a further increase is projected.[75]

- Effects of any changes in ENSO and the North Atlantic Oscillation (NAO). Both these global weather systems have large impacts on extreme events in the US. A more El Niño-like mean state is projected under global warming, and the behaviour of the NAO may also change. El Niño conditions are associated with more Pacific and less Atlantic hurricanes along the US coast.

- Increased health risks from weather-related disasters, heatwaves, and air pollution in cities. This will impact particularly on the urban poor, and is a focus of concern by the Congressional Black Caucus.[76] A study by Katherine Hayhoe of ATMOS Research and others using high and low emissions pathways looked at impacts in California. They found that a high emissions pathway led to major impacts on heat-related mortality, snow pack and water supplies.[77]

- Risk of possibly severe impacts from a decrease or cessation in the North Atlantic thermo-haline circulation, especially for the north-east states. This effect is unlikely (but not impossible) during the twenty-first century, but it may be irreversibly set in train by continuing high emissions of greenhouse gases this century (see Chapter 6).

- Major increases in aridity in Central America, including Mexico,[78] which would almost certainly lead to increasing pressure for economic migration to the United States across its long land border with Mexico, and to a need for economic aid.

- A 2007 study on regional impacts of climate change in the US elaborates on four regional issues including heatwaves in the Midwest, wildfire scenarios in the West, impacts on coastal wetlands on the Gulf Coast, and hypoxia (lack of oxygen) in Chesapeake Bay.[79]

The US will also need to address the following issues:

- The need for greater energy efficiency and less reliance on imported oil for national security and economic competitiveness. This provides a major co-benefit of reducing greenhouse gas emissions.

- Its vested interest in political stability and international cooperation, which will be undermined by environmental stresses imposed by climate change, especially in many lesser-developed countries.

President Bush's reflex action regarding the oil and national security was to push for greater exploration for oil, first in nature reserves in Alaska, and then in offshore areas protected from oil drilling. He also mandated a subsidy for ethanol biofuel production which has been very successful in diverting much corn production from food to ethanol. As discussed in Chapter 8, this has been first generation biofuel technology using the sugars and starches in the crops, rather than cellulosic material as in second generation biofuels. The first has been widely blamed for rising world oil prices, but the US Department of Energy has argued against this using some of the arguments discussed in Chapter 8 above. However, the criticism has some force as long as first generation technology is used.[80]

The vulnerability of the US to climate change suggests it has a strong, if under-acknowledged, national interest in effective global mitigation of climate change, and the science suggests that this is urgent. The economic case for urgent action is heightened by the fact that other countries, and notably the EU, are acting to foster energy efficiency, the use of renewable energy, and to reduce the carbon intensity of their economies. Subject to interpretation of agreements under the World Trade Organization (WTO), new standards adopted in other countries may limit US exports to markets where US products do not comply, and where new and alternative technologies, stimulated by carbon trading, are gaining market share.

A 2004 study of world car manufacturers by the World Resources Institute in Washington and Sustainable Asset Management in Zurich found that potential increases in manufacturing costs to meet carbon constraints (policy measures to limit greenhouse gas emissions), and possible loss of market share to manufacturers of less carbon-intensive vehicles, posed risks for US manufacturers.[81] Opportunities lie in the potential to develop low-carbon technologies ahead of economic competitors. This would reap the benefits of technological leadership, brand differentiation and enhanced profits. The study, based on then corporate behaviour, rated Toyota as most favourably placed, and GM and Ford the least, with an estimated relative difference due to carbon constraints of 20% of earnings before interest and tax.

More recent news has vindicated this study. Both GM and Ford have suffered losses relative to Japanese and other manufacturers, through the former's focus on larger and higher fuel consumption vehicles including SUVs. There is now growing competition to produce smaller and more fuel efficient vehicles. This trend has been accentuated by the rapid rise in oil prices. The Tesla all-electric car, the General Motors Chevrolet Volt and the compressed air-powered Zero Pollution Motors car may improve the competitive US position when they come on sale around 2010. Stricter fuel efficiency standards, pioneered in the US by California, but resisted by car manufacturers, will also help keep US manufacturers up to international standards.[82]

Government assistance for struggling car manufacturers both in the US and Australia is increasingly being linked to manufacturing 'greener' cars.

Apart from the Bush Administration's withdrawal from the Kyoto process, and its stated goal of a decrease in US energy intensity (but not in total emissions), the US adopted a voluntary program of emissions reporting and energy conservation and a seemingly comprehensive low-carbon energy research program. The US Secretary of the Department of Energy, Spencer

Abraham, in June 2004, described 'six pillars of collaborative research'. These were hydrogen, clean coal, safe nuclear power, fusion, energy efficiency and renewable energy. Underlying this policy, Secretary Abraham stated:

> ... we've operated from a very simple point of view. Across the planet, countries including the United States have very substantial reserves of coal at their disposal, and ultimately this coal will be used.[83]

Secretary Abraham described the six pillars as:

1. The *Hydrogen Initiative.* This includes the *Freedom Car,* which is to be powered by hydrogen-based fuel cells, which leaves open the source of the hydrogen: from electricity generated either from nuclear power stations or fossil fuel with carbon capture and sequestration, or perhaps from renewable energy sources. This is a multi-decadal program that will do nothing to reduce carbon emissions in the near future, although it may be valuable in the later decades of the twenty-first century.[84]

2. The *Clean Coal Research Initiative,* dubbed *FutureGen.* This is a 'cost-shared program between government and industry to quickly demonstrate emerging technologies in coal-based power generation and to accelerate their commercialisation'. The aim is to use gasification to break coal down, with carbon capture, efficient generation of electricity and production of hydrogen. Carbon sequestration is one of the highest priorities, with the formation of the Carbon Sequestration Leadership Forum, involving 15 countries and the European Commission. However, progress has been slow, with funding cuts, and commercialisation looks like being decades away.[85]

3. *New generation nuclear energy.* This is to avoid undue dependence on other fuels, and because 'nuclear power simply has such great capacity to provide clean energy to the world'. Again, the US has developed a multi-national program,

Generation IV, to develop new reactor designs which will be safer, more economical and secure, and able to produce hydrogen. The hope was to have candidate reactor designs by 2020, but again, actual large-scale deployment of such reactors would be several more decades away.[86]

4. *Nuclear fusion,* aimed at production of hydrogen as well as electricity. This too is via an international collaborative project, ITER (ITER means 'the way'). Funding has been limited, and first operational experiments will not take place until next decade at the earliest. There is no certainty that fusion's potential can be realised.[87]

5 and 6. *Energy efficiency and renewable energy.* These are being developed through the Federal Energy Management Program, and the Department of Energy with the aim to reduce the cost of renewables. Again, some international collaborative efforts are under way, as well as a domestic Climate Vision Program aimed at reducing the growth of emissions by energy-intensive industry.[88] Funding, however, has been minimal and local opposition and other restrictions have been put in place that have greatly troubled renewable energy entrepreneurs.[89]

A prime example is a moratorium placed on new solar power plants on millions of acres of public land in the six western states of Arizona, California, Colorado, Nevada, New Mexico and Utah, which have the highest solar energy potentials in the US. Galvanised by the demand for clean energy, solar companies have filed more than 130 proposals with the Bureau of Land Management since 2005. The delay, put in place in June 2008, is until the Bureau of Land Management completes an environmental study to determine how solar plants might affect the land, and reportedly might take two years. Proponents of solar power say that rules to protect native ecosystems are justified but in the meanwhile planned projects should be allowed to proceed.[89]

As discussed in Chapter 8, solar power has great potential in the US. Indeed it is thought to become competitive with coal-fired power stations possibly as soon as 2010. Indeed, the American Solar Energy Society in a report 'Tackling climate change in the US', argues that 'energy efficiency and renewable energy technologies have the potential to provide most, if not all, of the US carbon emissions reductions that will be needed to help limit the atmospheric concentration of carbon dioxide to 450 to 500 ppm'. This general view is supported by analyses by Shinnar and Citro in 2006, and by McKinsey and Company in 2008. McKinsey and Company conclude that the US could reduce greenhouse gas emissions in 2030 by 3.0 to 4.5 gigatons of carbon dioxide-equivalent using tested and high-potential emerging technologies, with marginal costs less than US$50 per ton. They add that: 'Achieving these reductions at the lowest cost to the economy, however, will require strong, coordinated, economy-wide action that begins in the near future'.[90]

Despite a lack of regulatory action or financial incentives from the US Federal Administration up to late 2008, many or even most States and many cities in the US have acted on climate change with emission targets and incentives. As discussed in Chapter 10 above, many state and regional initiatives have been taken. While Governor Schwarzenegger has had the highest profile, many other leaders have been involved. This has been comprehensively documented by the Pew Center on Global Climate Change in many reports and news items (see http://www.pewclimate.org).

In a 2008 report 'Toward a constructive dialogue on federal and state roles in U.S. climate change policy', Franz Litz of the World Resources Institute states:

In the United States to date, states have taken most of the significant actions to address climate change. Yet enactment of a nationwide program requiring reductions across the entire United States is both necessary and increasingly likely ... The key question is not whether responsibility for climate change action should rest exclusively with the federal government or the states, but rather how and to what degree the federal government and the states should share responsibility for tackling the problem ... States have historically played a role as effective first-movers on important environmental issues ... [they] also bring an understanding of the unique circumstances within their boundaries and a familiarity with their stakeholders ... A federal program would bring every state into the climate change effort and tend to level the playing field for businesses in all 50 states. Federal action offers a platform for engaging with other nations in forging an international emissions reduction agreement. A national GHG cap-and-trade program would keep costs manageable and drive climate-friendly technological innovation, and could link with other markets around the world.

As documented by the Pew Center, since the 2006 congressional elections a number of congressional resolutions and bills on climate change policy were discussed in Congress, with increasing support.[91] It now appears that the Obama administration is likely to support strong federal action on climate change. This may not include signing the Kyoto Protocol, but is likely to include acceptance of global emissions reduction targets primarily in rich countries, with agreements to guarantee continuing economic development in developing countries along with targets for reductions in their emission intensities and strong support for renewable energy in the United States.

According to a Yale University interactive website, which has combined 25 leading economic models, reducing carbon emissions could help, not harm, the US economy. According to the originator, economics professor Robert Repetto, a national policy to cut carbon emissions by as much as 40 per cent over the next 20 years could still result in economic growth.[92]

This will not be easy. However, growing evidence of damaging climate change has fuelled a realisation that action is necessary. Indeed, a poll of Americans taken in 2007 by Yale University found that 68% of Americans supported an international treaty requiring the United States to cut its emissions by 90% by the year 2050. The director of the survey stated: 'Nearly half of Americans now believe that global warming is either already having dangerous impacts on people around the world or will in the next 10 years – a 20-percentage-point increase since 2004. These results indicate a sea change in public opinion'.[93]

The common interest in global solutions

This brief and incomplete survey of national interests suggests some common themes. One is that every nation will be directly and indirectly affected by climate change. There will be gains, especially in higher latitudes in the short-term, but also losses, which will increase with time. Among the indirect effects, which will reverberate around the world, is a potential increase in inequity, as the poor countries and poor people everywhere are most adversely affected. This will have unfortunate effects in an increasingly globalised society.

Even those countries that might expect to gain in the short-term from global warming, of which the Russian Federation is the prime example, are likely to suffer adverse effects in the longer term, especially from indirect effects such as increased instability on their borders. Full participation in global mitigation opportunities through Joint Implementation and emissions trading is also a decisive issue. These create economic growth opportunities.

Countries such as the United States and Australia, and also China, India and Russia, rely heavily on fossil fuels for domestic consumption, economic development or exports. These countries have an interest in continuing the use of fossil fuels as long as possible. It is significant that the US, and Australia until its change of government in 2007, are the two developed countries which refused to sign the Kyoto Protocol, evidently because these governments felt that mandatory emission reduction strategies were against their national interests. Yet both countries have embarked on government-funded programs to develop 'clean coal' technologies including carbon removal and sequestration, and subsidise some other voluntary programs. Australia signed the Kyoto Protocol in late 2007 and is about to implement a cap-and-trade carbon emissions scheme.

Even in the United States and Australia the dubious arguments against the reality of human-induced climate change are increasingly irrelevant to the policy debate, which has moved on to look at the most appropriate means to reduce emissions, and the urgency of doing so. Both governments now concede that there is a real problem from human-induced climate change. However, both have argued that continued reliance on fossil fuels is economically essential, and appeal to carbon removal and sequestration as one of the great hopes for the future, with the United States adding safe and secure nuclear energy as the second technological saviour.

What is lacking in many countries is a clear recognition of the urgency of the problem. This urgency is due to the large delays or lags in the climate system, which mean that action taken (or not taken) today will affect the climate and sea level decades, and indeed centuries, into the future. Unless urgent action is taken in the next decade or two to substantially reduce greenhouse gas emissions, it will be impossible to stabilise the climate at what may be considered safe levels of change. A target of at least an 80% reduction in emissions in developed countries by 2050 is entirely reasonable if we are to avoid high risks of climate change induced disasters. Every delay in reducing greenhouse gas emissions increases the risk of dangerous climate change impacts and makes necessary future action ever more drastic.

Carbon removal and sequestration, and indeed safe and secure nuclear energy may well be essential as part of a package of solutions, but neither is as yet proven safe and economically viable, nor is it possible to install these technologies fast enough to avert a high risk of dangerous climate change. Other urgent measures must be taken such as demand management, increasing energy efficiency, and rapid development and deployment of renewable energy technologies that are already available. The Obama administration seems likely to move in this direction, and Australia will likely follow.

It is ironic, however, that it is the poorer developing countries such as China and India that may pioneer many of these developments. They have to build new energy infrastructure in the twenty-first century, and have the opportunity to do so using low-carbon technologies. They could leapfrog over the pollution and health problems brought on by the Industrial Revolution of the eighteenth, nineteenth and twentieth centuries. By contrast, the developed countries are mired in the past due to large investments in outdated technology. They require more innovative, forward-looking and entrepreneurial citizens who will bring the developed world into a new age of low-carbon technology. Public opinion has already changed substantially in favour of urgent action. The problem is to persuade vested interests and the political elites to accept this necessary change and its urgency.[94] It is to be hoped that we do not have to wait for further climatic disasters to get urgent action.

ENDNOTES

1. Machiavelli (1515) *The Prince*, Chapter 3, regarding the foreign policy of the Roman Empire, written c. 1505AD.

2. From the *Human Development Report* 2007/2008, the United Nations Development Programme, summary, p. 8.

3. A history of the discovery of the enhanced greenhouse effect is *The Discovery of Global Warming* (2003) by Spencer Weart, Harvard University Press, Cambridge, Massachusetts. See reviews in *Science*, **304**, p. 685 (2004) and *EOS* (13 July 2004). There is also a website with lots of other material at http://www.aip.org/history/climate.

4. Fourier's paper was published in *Memoires Academie des Sciences Institut de France*, **6**, p. 568 (1828) and Arrhenius in *Philosophical Magazine*, **41**, p. 266 (1896). Callendar's work was published in *Quarterly Journal of the Royal Meteorological Society* **64**, pp. 223–40 (1938).

5. See Charles Keeling, *Tellus* **12**, pp. 200–03 (1960).

6. A statement re cooling was made by the Board of Trustees of the International Federation of Institutes for Advanced Studies, Stockholm (3 October 1974). See also Federal Council for Science and Technology (1974) 'Report of the ad hoc panel on the present interglacial', Interdepartmental Committee for Atmospheric Science, ICAS 18B-FY75, Federal Council for Science and Technology, National Science Foundation, Washington DC.

7. Broecker's 1975 comment is in *Science* **189**, pp. 460–4, and a similar comment in *Nature*, **328**, p. 123 (1987).

8. See 'Statement on climate change' (June 1976) World Meteorological Organization, Geneva and Australian Academy of Sciences report 'Report of a committee on climate change', Report no. 21, (1976) AAS, Canberra.

9. The 1979 WMO statement is in *First World Climate Conference*, Proceedings, Geneva, (1979) p. 125. See also *Environmental Law and Policy*, no. 5 (1979), p. 65 and no. 6 (1980), p. 103, and *Climate Change Fact Sheet* 213, UNEP Information Unit on Climate Change.

10. Villach Conference statement, available at http://www.icsu-scope.org/downloadpubs/scope29/statement.html.

11. *The Greenhouse Effect, Climatic Change, and Ecosystems*, SCOPE 29 (1986), B Bolin, BR Doos, J Jaeger and RA Warrick (eds), John Wiley and Sons, Chichester.

12. The Toronto Conference report is briefly summarised in the UNFCCC *Climate Change Fact Sheet 15*. See also Zaelke and Cameron in *American Journal of International Law and Policy*, **5** (2) pp. 276–78 (1990).

13. See http://www.ipcc.ch for a brief history and mandate of the IPCC, and access to all its reports. Each IPCC report is in three volumes, all published by Cambridge University Press. The Fourth Assessment Report consists of:

   • *Climate Change 2007: The Physical Science Basis.*

   • *Climate Change 2007: Impacts, Adaptation and Vulnerability.*

   • *Climate Change 2007: Mitigation.*

There is also a regional assessment report: RT Watson, MC Zinyowera, RH Moss and DJ Dokken 'Regional impacts of climate change: an assessment of vulnerability' (1998), A Special Report of the IPCC Working Group II, Cambridge University Press.

The SRES report is 'Special report on emission scenarios' (2000), A special report of Working Group III of the Intergovernmental Panel on Climate Change, Cambridge University Press.

14. The UNFCCC history, mandate and progress are all available at http://www.unfccc.int.

    The UNFCCC negotiations are documented in some detail in the *Earth Negotiations Bulletin*, published by the International Institute for Environment and Development (IISD), available online at http://www.iisd.ca/process/climate_atm.htm.

15. Two key books recounting the history of the Kyoto Protocol and issues up to 1999 are: *The Kyoto Protocol: A Guide and Assessment* (1999) by Michael Grubb with Christiaan Vrolijk and Duncan Brack, Royal Institute of International Affairs and Earthscan, London and *The Kyoto Protocol: International Climate Policy for the 21st Century* (1999) by Sebastian Oberthur and Hermann Ott, Springer-Verlag, Berlin. See also the more recent book, *Climate Change Policy: A Survey* (2002) Schneider, Rosencranz and Niles (eds), Island Press, Washington, especially the chapter by Jonathan Wiener, pp. 151–87; and the websites http://www.iisd.ca/process/climate_atm.htm and http://unfccc.int/kyoto_protocol/items/2830.php. See also: RB Stewart and JB Wiener, *Reconstructing Climate Policy* (2003), American Enterprise Institute, Washington DC, and a number of books and papers available through http://www.questia.com/library/kyoto-prototcol.jsp.

16. See Cannell in Chapter 13, 'Land sinks: the Kyoto Process and scientific implications' in *Forests at the Land–Atmosphere Interface* (2004), M Mencuccini and others (eds), CAB International, Wallingford, UK, pp. 189–202.

17. The effect on CO_2 concentrations of the Kyoto Protocol, if implemented as is, is evaluated by Wigley in *Geophysical Research Letters*, **25**, pp. 2285–88 (1998).

18. President Bush's policy statement is at http://www.whitehouse.gov/news/releases/2002/02/20020214-5.html. The impact of the Bush proposal on US emissions is discussed by Detlef van Vuuren and others in *Climate Policy*, **2**, pp. 293–301 (2002). See also media advisory of Environmental Defense Council (14 February 2002) at http://www.environmentaldefense.org, the Natural Resources Defense Council and the World Resources Institute (14 February 2002) and a report in the *New York Times* (15 February 2002) by Paul Krugman.

19. Ross Garnaut's statement is in a speech *Measuring the Immeasurable: The Costs and Benefits of Climate Mitigation* (5 June 2008) available at http://www.garnautreview.org.au. The subsequent fall in oil prices is slowing this process, but it is expected to be temporary.

20. The discussion of African national interests follows fairly closely the conclusions of the IPCC 2007 report, especially WGII, Chapter 9.

21. *Africa: Up in Smoke?* from the UK Working Group on Climate Change and Development (July 2005) is available from http://www.iied.org/pubs.

22. Renewable energy policy in South Africa is discussed by Winkler in *Energy Policy*, **33**, pp. 27–38 (2005), and Stephen Karakezi evaluates the potential of renewables in meeting the energy needs of Africa's poor in *Energy Policy*, **30**, pp. 1059–69 (2002). African attitudes to mitigation versus development are discussed in Sokona and Denton, *Climate Policy*, **1**, pp. 117–23 (2001). North African countries will likely benefit greatly from schemes linking their large solar energy resources to European power grids, as advocated, for example, by DESERTEC at http://www.trecers.net. See Chapter 8 section on solar energy.

23. For the AFREPREN work, see http://www.afrepren.org/, where many publications are listed, including a regular newsletter. The World Bank, Washington DC, has a climate change research program with a focus on Africa, see http://econ.worldbank.org/ and follow the prompts. See also the book *Climate Change and*

Agriculture in Africa: Impact Assessment and Adaptation Strategies (2008) Ariel Dinar and others, Earthscan, London. There are numerous African Studies Centres in various countries that can be found by a web search. Many have relevant publications. There is also a special issue of the journal *Climatic Change* dealing with Africa and climate change, **83** (3) (1 August 2007).

24. The discussion on Australia and New Zealand is largely based on Chapter 11 of the IPCC 2007 report WGII, and in the case of Australia on a book by Barrie Pittock, *Climate Change: An Australian Guide to the Science and Potential Impacts*, Australian Greenhouse Office, available at http://www.greenhouse.gov.au/. See also KB Pearce, PN Holper, M Hopkins, WJ Bouma, PH Whetton, KJ Hennessy and SB Power (eds), 'Climate change in Australia: technical report 2007' (2007), CSIRO Marine and Atmospheric Research, Aspendale at http://www.cmar.csiro.au/cgi-bin/pubsearch.pl.

25. Figure 35 comes from the report 'Lakes Alexandrina and Albert ecological condition progress report', by the South Australian Murray-Darling Basin Natural Resource Management Board (April 2008). See also http://www.samdbnrm.sa.gov.au/TheDrought.aspx and http://www.clw.csiro.au/acidsulfatesoils/murray.html.

26. The question of policy responses to episodic drought versus climate change is discussed more fully in section 4.3.6 of the book by Barrie Pittock referred to in endnote 24.

27. The responsibility of developed country members of the (British) Commonwealth, especially Australia, towards developing country members is argued in Hamilton and others, *Climate Change and Commonwealth Nations*, Discussion Paper no.40, The Australia Institute (2001) see http://www.tai.org.au.

28. New Zealand climate change policy is documented at http://www.climatechange.govt.nz.

29. Documentation of Australia's climate change policy is ongoing at http://www.climatechange.gov.au/. See also the Garnaut Review website at http://www.garnautreview.org.au.

30. See 'Garnaut climate change review: interim report' (February 2008) p. 25. The Garnaut Review Draft Report of June 2008 also discusses a national electrical grid to better access renewable energy.

31. WorleyParsons, BHP Billiton and Rio Tinto are all mentioned in a *Business Age* article (12 August 2008) related to billions of dollars in investments. See http://www.business.theage.com.au, and the WorleyParsons *Annual Report 2008* at http://www.worleyparsons.com. See also the discussion in Chapter 8.

32. The Business Council of Australia article cited is *Growth Key to Emission Plan* by Greg Gailey, *Business Age* (3 July 2008) Melbourne.

33. The account of the flood problem in China is based in part on the Munich Re Group, *Topics 2000, Natural Catastrophes – The Current Position*, pp. 82 and 122–23 at http://www.munichre.com.

34. Conclusions re impacts on China come largely from the IPCC 2007, WGII, Chapter 10, although that covers all of Asia and is necessarily brief re China per se. Agreement between global climate model simulations of rainfall changes, including over China, are summarised in the IPCC 2007 report, WGII, Figure TS5. Observed and projected climate changes in China are also summarised in *China's National Climate Change Programme*, National Development and Reform Commission, PRC (June 2007) see http://en.ndrc.gov.cn/.

35. The Arnell results are in *Global Environmental Change*, **9**, S11–S49 (1999). More frequent large floods are projected by Milly and others, *Nature*, **415**, pp. 514–17 (2002).

36. WWF reported on glacier retreat in Nepal, India and China in 'An overview of glaciers, glacier retreat, and subsequent impacts in Nepal, India and China' (March 2005), see: http://assets.panda.org/downloads/himalayaglaciersreport2005.pdf. See also: 'Variations of snow cover in the source regions of the Yangtze and Yellow Rivers in China between 1960 and 1999' by Jianping Yang and others, *Journal of Glaciology*, **53** (182), p. 420 (2007); and 'The third pole' by Jane Qiu in *Nature*, **454**, pp. 393–96 (24 July 2008) regarding changes to the Tibetan Plateau.

37. The drying of the Yellow River is reported in Yang and others, *EOS* (1 December 1998) pp. 589 and 592. This is partly due to greater withdrawals, but also increased evaporative losses due to recent warming. Manabe and others, in *Climatic Change*, **64**, pp. 59–76 (2004) project reduced soil moisture in north-eastern China, and Quin Dahe, in *WMO Bulletin*, **53**, pp. 50–4 (2004), discussed the situation in western China. The Chinese study of runoff into the Yellow River is from the Lanzhou Yellow River Hydrology and Water Resources Research Institute in 2005, see: http://www.china.org.cn/english/environment/160531.htm. See also: X Gou, F Chen, E Cook, G Jacoby, M Yang, and J Li (2007) 'Streamflow variations of the Yellow River over the past 593 years in western China reconstructed from tree rings', *Water Resources Research*, **43**, W06434, doi:10.1029/2006WR005705.

38. Possible effects of sea-level rise on the Pearl River Delta region were discussed in two articles in *China Daily* (30 March 2007) and (30 August 2007) see archives at http://www.chinadaily.com.cn.

39. China's greenhouse gas emissions, and progress towards mitigation, are discussed in the well-documented Pew Center paper *Climate Change Mitigation in Developing Countries*, available at http://www.pewclimate.org. The growing importance of China in world energy markets is documented in *Petro-dragon's Rise: What It Means for China and the World*, Xiaojie Xu (ed.), European Press Academic Publishers, Fucecchio, Italy (see http://www.e-p-a-p.com) and review in *Energy Policy*, **33** (127) (2005). See also Ni Weidou and Thomas Johansson, in *Energy Policy*, **32**, pp. 1225–29 (2004) and references therein; Victoria University, Climate Change Working Paper no. 13 (2007), *Energy Use In China: Interpreting Changing Trends and Future Directions*, by Peter Sheehan and Fiona Sun, at http://www.vu.edu.au: and *Stoking the Fire* by Jeff Tollefson in *Nature*, **454**, pp. 388–92 (24 July 2008). The role of exports is discussed in the Tyndall Centre Briefing Note no. 23 (October 2007) at http://www.tyndall.ac.uk.

40. The Pew Center summarises China's mitigation measures up to 2007 (including its 11th Five Year Plan) in its International Brief 1 (April 2007) at http://www.pewclimate.org. The Larson and colleagues study is reported in *Energy Policy*, **31**, pp. 1189–204 (2003) and contains a useful set of detailed conclusions and recommendations. RH Williams' paper on zero emissions from coal in China is in *Energy and Sustainable Development*, **V**, pp. 39–65 (November 2001). See also: *China's Clean Revolution*, from The Climate Group (July 2008) at http://www.theclimategroup.org.

41. See *New Scientist* (10 November 2007) pp. 40–2 (which also talks about solar hot water), and http://www.suntech-power.com. See also a report by WWF China, 'China solar PV report' (2007) at http://www.wwfchina.org/english/loca.php?loca=103; and 'Visions of China', in *Nature*, **454**, pp. 384–87 (24 July 2008). The China–EU cooperation is being strengthened by the UK Chatham House project on *Interdependencies on Energy and Climate Security for China and Europe* at http://www.eu-china-energy-climate.net, which lists a number of relevant reports and studies. See also the McKinsey and Company report (July 2007) 'Leapfrogging to higher energy productivity in China' at http://www.mckinsey.com; 'China's green journey' in *New Scientist*, 9 August 2008, p.18; and 'China to be world's top manufacturer of green energy (update1)' by J Efstathiou Jr., at http://www.bloomberg.com, 1 August 2008. 42. See *China's National Climate Change Programme* (June 2007) at http://en.ndrc.gov.cn/.

42. See http://www.gov.cn/english/special/115y_index.htm for the 11th Five Year Plan, and http://www.ccchina.gov.cn/website/ccchina/Upfile/File188.pdf for China's National Climate Change Programme.

43. See John Ashton (27 November 2006) 'Building a politics of interdependence' at http://www.chinadialogue.net.

44. Potential impacts on Europe are taken mainly from the IPCC 2007 report, WGII, Chapter 12, with some updating as in Chapter 6 above. Numerous more recent studies can be found in the relevant journals, especially *Geophysical Research Letters*. Two special issues of the journal *Climatic Change* deal with European studies: **81** (Supplement 1) (May 2007) report high spatial resolution studies, while **87** (1–2) (March 2008) reports on modelling results for northern Europe.

45. See for example: Tapiador and others in *Geophysical Research Letters* **34**, L06701 (2007), and the article 'Desert is claiming southeast Spain' in the *International Herald Tribune* (2 June 2008).

46. The major European heatwave of 2003 is discussed in Schar and others, *Nature*, **427**, pp. 332–36 (2004); Beniston and Diaz in *Global and Planetary Change*, **44**, pp. 73–81 (2004); *ECMWF Newsletter*, no. 99 (2003) pp. 2–8; and *Weatherwise* (March/April 2004) pp. 24 and 27. Projections into the late 21st century are in *Science*, **305**, pp. 994–7 (2004).

47. A brief discussion of impacts of melting of permafrost on mountain hazard zones is in Watson and Haeberli, *Ambio Special Report 13* (November 2004) pp. 2–10.

48. Renewable energy activities in Europe are covered in Chapter 8. The EU directive for a target of 20% share for renewables in energy consumption by 2020 is at http://ec.europa.eu/energy/climate_actions/doc/2008_res_directive_en.pdf. The possibility that this could come via a 'super-grid' is reported at http://www.euractiv.com/en/energy/eu-eyes-supergrid-harness-saharan-sun/article-174508. There are numerous web links there. See also http://www.trecers.net.

49. The 2007 EU document, and other relevant documents, can be found at http://ec.europa.eu/climateaction/index_en.htm.

50. The Pew Center document is *The European Union's Emissions Trading System in Perspective* (2008) by Denny Ellerman and Paul Joskow at http://www.pewclimate.org/eu-ets. The value of the EU ETS as an example for international emissions trading schemes is also discussed by Joeph Kruger and others in *Review of Environmental Economics and Policy*, **1** (1), pp. 112–3 (2007), 'Decentralization in the EU emissions trading scheme and lessons for global policy'.

51. Climate change impacts on India, Pakistan and Bangladesh are discussed in the IPCC 2007 report, WGII, Chapter 10.

52. See 'Interdisciplinary discussions of hydrology and river linking take place in India', *EOS* (11 May 2004). Details of India's water plans can be found at the National Water Development Agency website, http://www.nwda.gov.in.

53. See climate and energy related materials at http://www.teriin.org, including *Environmental Threats, Vulnerability, and Adaptation: Case Studies from India* (2004). For Bangladesh, see *Science*, **294**, p. 1617 (2004), *Tiempo*, no. 47, pp. 13–16 (2003), see http://www.cru.uea.ac.uk/tiempo, and the Bangladesh Centre for Advanced Studies, Dhaka, at http://bcas.net/. See also 'Facing up to climate change in South Asia', IIED Gatekeeper Series no. 118, available at http://www.iied.org/pubs/.

54. The quotations from the Indian Prime Minister come from the *Economic Times* (30 June 2008). A summary of the Indian National Action Plan on Climate Change is given by the Pew Center at http://www.pewclimate.org. This also has a link to the Indian document.

55. Emissions and mitigation prospects in India are documented in 'Climate change mitigation in developing countries', Pew Center for Global Climate Change (October 2002) at http://www.pewclimate.org. See also: 'India: climate friendly development', Ministry of Environment and Forests, Government of India (2002) at http://www.envfor.nic.in/cc/cop8/moefbk.htm, and a special section on climate change and India in *Current Science*, **90**, (3) (10 February 2006) and *Environmental Threats, Vulnerability and Adaptation: Case Studies from India*, from TERI, 2nd edn (2004) at http://www.teriin.org.

56. Climate impacts on Latin America are largely summarised in the IPCC 2007 report, WGII, Chapter 13. See also: *Up in smoke? Latin America and the Caribbean; The threat from climate change to the environment and human development*, WWF at http://www.panda.org (2006), and *The Vital Climate Graphics for Latin America and the Caribbean*, from the United Nations Environment Programme at http://grida.no/publications/vg/lac/.

57. Hurricane Catarina that hit Brazil is discussed by Pezza and Simmonds in *Geophysical Research Letters*, **32**, L15712, doi: 10.1029/2005GL023390 (2005).

58. The growth of fossil fuel-based power generation in Brazil is documented in Xavier and co-authors, *Energy Policy*, **32**, pp. 914–27 (2004). Policies for advancing energy efficiency and renewable energy in Brazil are described in Geller and others, *Energy Policy*, **32**, pp. 1437–50 (2004). Goldemberg and others in *Energy Policy*, **32**, pp. 1141–6 (2004) describe how policies can push renewables, using the Brazilian ethanol program as an example.

59. Impacts on the Russian Federation are largely based on material in the IPCC 2007 report, WGII, Chapters 12 (Europe), 10 (Asia) and also 15 (Polar regions).

60. Projected changes in the Arctic region, including Russia, are documented in the multi-national Arctic Climate Impact Assessment (ACIA), *Impacts of a Warming Arctic* (2004) see http://www.acia.uaf.edu. See also *Indigenous Peoples and Climate Change* (2007), Jan Salick and Andja Byg (eds), from the Tyndall Centre for Climate Change Research, at http://www.tyndall.ac.uk.

61. Evidence for increased forest fire potential in boreal forests in Canada and Russia comes from Stocks and colleagues, *Climatic Change*, **38**, pp. 1–13 (1998); Flannigan and others, *The Science of the Total Environment*, **262**, pp. 221–9 (2000); and Gillett and others, *Geophysical Research Letters*, **31**, L18211 (2004). See also in IPCC 2007 report, WGII, section 5.4.5.2, p. 290.

62. President Putin's indication that Russia may ratify the Kyoto Protocol was reported in *Science* on 28 May 2004, and widely in the popular media. Jacqueline Karas's briefing note *Russia and the Kyoto Protocol: Political Challenges* (March 2004) is available at http://www.riia.org. Russian energy efficiency projects are reviewed by Anna Korppoo in *Energy Policy*, **33**, pp. 113–26 (2005), and the report of a meeting in April 2003, *Implementing Kyoto in Russia and the CIS: Moving from Theory to Practice* can be found at http://www.climate-strategies.org/russiaworkshop. See also *Climate Policy*, **2**, pp. 387–93 (2002), and *What the Kyoto Protocol Means for the Russians*, at http://www.wwf.ru. An interesting account of the Moscow World Conference on Climate change in 2003 gives insights into the debate in Russia, see *Climate Policy*, **3**, pp. 475–77 (2003).

63. Small Island State impacts are described in IPCC 2007 report, WGII, Chapter 16. See also John Connell in *Tiempo*, no. 42 (2001) at http://www.cru.uea.ac.uk/tiempo. The vulnerability of various islands is documented in Barnett and Adger, Tyndall Centre WP, no. 9 (2001) at http://www.tyndall.ac.uk, and *Surviving Climate Change in Small Islands: A Guidebook* (2003) Tyndall Centre. Popular accounts of the situation on Tuvalu appears in the *Smithsonian* (August 2004) pp. 44–52, and in *Nature*, **440**, pp. 734–36 (6 April 2006). The UNFCCC has a publication *Small Island Developing States and Climate Change* (2005) available at http://unfccc.int/resource/docs/publications/cc_sids. pdf.

64. Sea-level rise data for the South Pacific is available from the Australian Bureau of Meteorology South Pacific Sea Level and Climate Monitoring Project, at http://www.bom.gov.au/pacificsealevel/. See especially a presentation by Phillip Hall in November 2006 available at this website.

65. A summary of one attempt to review resilience and adaptation options for the Pacific Islands is recorded in *Proceedings of the APN Workshop on Ethnographic Perspectives on Resilience to Climate Variability in Pacific Island Countries* (December 2001) Macmillan Brown Centre for Pacific Studies, University of Canterbury, Christchurch, New Zealand. See also the Tyndall Centre Guide, mentioned in endnote 62. The migration issue is discussed by Hay and Beniston in *Tiempo*, no. 42 (2001), along with many other relevant articles in other issues at http://www. tiempocyberclimate.org. The United Nations Environment Programme has a report 'In the front line: shoreline protection and other ecosystem services from mangroves and coral reefs' (2006) at http://www.unep-wcmc.org. Also see *Not If But When: Adapting to Natural Hazards in the Pacific Islands Region: A Policy Note* (2006) from the World Bank at http://web.worldbank.org/.

66. See *Climate Change and Commonwealth Nations* by Clive Hamilton and others, The Australia Institute, Discussion Paper no. 40 (available at http://www.tai.org). See also the discussion in *Indigenous Peoples and Climate Change* (2007), Jan Salick and Andja Byg (eds), Tyndall Centre for Climate Change Research, at http://www.tyndall.ac.uk.

67. The commitment by US President Bush is at http://www.whitehouse.gov/news/releases/2002/02/20020214-5. html. An evaluation of the Bush initiative is provided by van Vuuren and colleagues in *Climate Policy*, **2**, pp. 293–301 (2002). See also Blanchard and Perkaus, *Energy Policy*, **32**, pp. 1993–8 (2004) and the media advisory: '"Bold new" proposal on climate is neither "bold" nor "new"', Environmental Defense, Washington, DC (14 February 2002).

68. Impacts on the US are described briefly in the IPCC 2007 report, WGII, Chapter 14, and more extensively in the 2002 US National Assessment, *Climate Change Impacts on the United States: Potential Consequences of Climate Variability and Change, US Global Change Research Program*, Cambridge University Press. A more up-to-date assessment was in draft

stage (but not for quotation) in July–August 2008, as *Global Climate Change in the United States* and was available for comment at hrrp://www.usgcrp.gov/usgcrp/default.php. My summary in this chapter is broadly consistent with the US draft report. See also *A Synthesis of Potential Climate Change Impacts on the U.S.*, by Joel Smith, and *Coping with Climate Change: The Role of Adaptation in the United States*, by Easterling and others, both from the Pew Center on Global Climate Change (April 2004) at http://www.pewclimate.org and the Pew Center's *Regional Impacts of Climate Change: Four Case Studies in the United States* (December 2007). *Climatic Change* has a special issue on climate change and California, **87** (Supplement 1) (March 2008).

69. The Titus and Richman paper is in *Climate Research*, **18**, pp. 205–28 (2001), and the New Orleans situation prior to Katrina was described by Fischetti in *Scientific American* (October 2001) pp. 69–77. See also *Science* (23 September 2004) p. 388. According to a Federal Emergency Management Agency report in 2000, at http://www.fema.gov/nwz00/erosion.shtm, 25% of homes within 500 feet of the US coastline will be affected by erosion within the next 60 years, apparently without taking into account global sea-level rise. For references related to possible increases in hurricane intensities, and Hurricanes Katrina and Rita, see notes in Chapters 5 and 6.

70. The question of the adequacy of the US Coastal Barriers System was discussed in a US Congressional Hearing on 8 November 2005 (see report in *EOS*, **86** (46) 15 November 2005). See also 'Commercial wind insurance in the Gulf states: developments since Hurricane Katrina and challenges moving forward', available at http://www.rand.org.

71. The paper by Tim Barnett and others is 'Human-induced changes in the hydrology of the western United States', *Science*, **319**, pp. 1080–83 (22 February 2008). See also Stewart and colleagues in *Climatic Change*, **62**, pp. 217–32 (2004), and Messerli and others in *Ambio Special Report* **13** (November 2004) pp. 29–34, especially p. 33.

72. Other reports regarding growing aridity in the US include: MacDonald and others, 'Climate warming and 21st century drought in southwestern North America', *EOS*, **89** (9) p. 82 (26 February 2008); Richard Kerr in *Science*, **318**, p. 1859 (21 December 2007); Richard Seager and colleagues, 'Model projections of an imminent transition to a more arid climate in southwestern North America', *Science*, **316**, pp. 1181–4 (25 May 2007), and Barbara Levi in *Physics Today* (April 2008) pp. 16–18. Water shortages in Los Angeles are reported on the Los Angeles Department of Water and Power website at http://www.ladwp.com/ladwps/cms/ under the heading *Water Past and Present*. Extended drought in Georgia and Atlanta is documented at the University of Georgia website http://www.caes.uga.edu/topics/disasters/drought/. See also two articles on US water supplies: 'America's water war' by Tom Engelhardt, at http://www.salon.com/new/features, and 'The future is drying up', by Jon Gertner, in the *New York Times* (21 October 2007) at http://www.nytimes.com/2007/10/21/magazine/. National US drought information is at the website of the National Integrated Information System, at http://www.drought.gov/portal/. Conflict over access to water is already a major issue in the South-west, for example between farmers in the Imperial Valley and San Diego County (see *New Scientist* (5 July 2003) p. 48–49, and http://www.saltonsea.ca.gov/press/testimony/7-25-02.htm.).

73. For effects of high temperature on runoff into the Great Lakes and resultant record drops in water levels, see Assel and others in *Bulletin of the American Meteorological Society*, **85**, pp. 1143–5 (2004), and *Confronting Climate Change in the Great Lakes Region*, from the Union of Concerned Scientists, available at http://ucsusa.org/greatlakes/glchallengereport.html.

74. The major flood study is by Milly and colleagues in *Nature*, **415**, pp. 514–17 (2002).

75. A special issue of *Climatic Change*, **62**, nos. 1–3 (2004), covers the effects of climate change on wildfires as well as water resources, and oceanic biology in the western US. Increased risk of wildfires is demonstrated especially for the northern Rockies, Great Basin and the South-west by Brown and others, in *Climatic Change*, **62**, pp. 365–88 (2004), supporting many earlier studies such as Flannigan and others, *The Science of the Total Environment*, **262**, pp. 221–9 (2000).

76. The best summary of impacts on the poor in the US is *African Americans and Climate: An Unequal Burden*, Congressional Black Caucus Foundation (July 2004) see http://www.cbcfinc.org. See also Tara Bahrampour, 'The staggering toll of US heat waves' in the *International Herald Tribune* (15 August 2002), see http://www.iht.com. That the poor are most vulnerable to disasters is documented in Fothergill and Peek, *Natural Hazards*, **32**, pp. 89–110 (2004).

77. See Hayhoe and others in *Proceedings of the National Academy of Sciences* USA, doi:10.1073/pnas.0404500101 (2004). A 60% increase in the number of unhealthy summer days is projected for 15 cities in the eastern US by the 2050s, in *Heat Advisory: How Global Warming Causes More Bad Air Days*, Natural Resources Defense Council (July 2004) at http://www.nrdc.org. Meehl and Tebaldi in *Science*, **305**, pp. 994–7 (2004) also project increases in the frequency and severity of heatwaves in the US. Two papers explain warming in the US in part by human induced climate change: Meehl and others, in *Geophysical Research Letters*, **34**, L19709, doi:10.1029/2007GL030948 (2007), and Hoerling and others, *Explaining the record US warmth of 2006*, also in *Geophysical Research Letters*, doi:10.1029/2007GL030643; while effects of increased heatwaves in the US were calculated by Kalkstein and Greene, *Environmental Health Perspectives*, **105**, pp. 84–93 (1997).

78. Increased aridity in Mexico is likely due to both warming and decreased rainfall (IPCC 2001 report, WGI Technical Summary, Figure 23).

79. The regional studies for the Pew Center are in *Regional Impacts of Climate Change*, (December 2007) at http://www.pewclimate.org.

80. The Bush Administration's defence of its biofuels program can be found at http://www.energy.gov, as a DOE press release (11 June 2008).

81. The 2004 study of car manufacturers is *Changing Drivers: The Impact of Climate Change on Competitiveness and Value Creation in the Automotive Industry*, available at http://www.wri.org. See story by Danny Hakim in the *New York Times* (25 July 2004).

82. Two articles in the UK *Guardian* newspaper give a flavour of the US car makers' progress, with a story on 8 January 2007, 'US car giants launch green drive' and on 23 July 2008, 'GM looks to an electric vehicle'. The General Motors Chevrolet Volt car can be seen at http://www.chevrolet.com and the Tesla Motors car at http://www.teslamotors.com. Both will be powered with lithium-ion batteries, but will be far more expensive than the claimed price for the Zero Pollution Motors compressed-air car, which can be seen at http://zeropollutionmotors.us/.

83. Secretary Abraham's remarks are taken from the transcript of a meeting *U.S. Climate Policy: Toward a Sensible Center*, sponsored by the Brookings Institution and the Pew Center on Global Climate Change, held in Washington DC (24 June 2004), see http://www.pewclimate.org. Secretary Abraham also had an article in *Science*, **305**, pp. 616–7 (30 July 2004).

84. The US hydrogen research program can be accessed via http://www.fe.doe.gov/programs/fuels/, and the International Partnership for the Hydrogen Economy via http://www.state.gov/g/oes/rls/fs/2003/25983.htm. See discussion in Chapter 8.

85. The US Clean Coal Power Initiative is at http://www.fe.doe.gov/programs/powersystems/cleancoal/ and the Carbon Sequestration Leadership Forum at http://www.fe.doe.gov/programs/sequestration/cslf/. Again, see Chapter 8.

86. The US Generation IV Program is at http://gen-iv.ne.doe.gov.

87. The US fusion program ITER is at http://www.iter.org/.

88. The Office of Energy Efficiency and Renewable Energy is located at http://www.eere.energy.gov/. See also http://www.climatevision.gov, and http://www.epa.gov/climateleaders, http://www.epa.gov/smartway. Another over-arching website is http://www.energy.gov.

89. Reports of funding cuts for low-carbon energy programs can be found in *Nature*, **440**, p. 12 (2 March 2006); *Science*, **312**, p. 675 (5 May 2006); and *Physics Today* (February 2008) pp. 20–1. The moratorium on solar energy development is reported in 'Citing need for assessments, US freezes solar energy projects', by Dan Frosch, *New York Times* (27 June 2008).

90. The American Solar Energy Society report (January 2007) is available at http://www.ases.org. The Shinnar and Citro report, 'A road map to US decarbonization', is in *Science* (1 September 2006) **313**, pp. 1243–4. The 2008 McKinsey and Company report is available at http://www.mckinsey.com/clientservice/ccsi/greenhousegas.asp.

91. Congressional actions in 2006–08 include discussion of the Lugar-Biden Senate Resolution 312 and of the *Lieberman-Warner Climate Security Act* of 2008 (S3036). These are documented on the Pew Center website. See also, for example, discussion in *Nature* **450** (2007) and *Science*, **320**, pp. 1410–11 (13 June 2008). A comment on these bills is in *Nature*, **450**, pp. 342–41 (2007).

92. See http://www.climate.yale.edu/seeforyourself.

93. The Yale opinion survey is *American Opinions on Global Warming*, with principal investigator Anthony Leiserowitz. See http://environment.yale.edu/news/Research/5310/american-opinions-on-global-warming/. Similar results from another opinion survey are reported in the *New Scientist* (1 March 2008) p. 5, and (23 June 2007) p. 16.

94. It is interesting that Pulitzer Prize-winning author Thomas L. Friedman has just published a book on how green technology can save the world economy. See: Thomas Friedman, *Hot, Flat and Crowded: Why We Need a Green Revolution – and How it Can Renew America*, Farrar, Straus and Giroux (2008). See article by Steve Mirsky, 'The US needs to lead in green tech' at http://www.sciam.com (10 December 2008).

12

Accepting the challenge

We are now faced with the fact that tomorrow is today. We are confronted with the fierce urgency of now. In this unfolding conundrum of life and history there is such a thing as being too late. Procrastination is still the thief of time. Life often leaves us standing bare, naked and dejected with a lost opportunity. The 'tide in the affairs of men' does not remain at the flood; it ebbs. We may cry out desperately for time to pause in her passage, but time is deaf to every plea and rushes on. Over the bleached bones and jumbled residue of numerous civilizations are written the pathetic words: 'Too late. . . .'

REVEREND DR MARTIN LUTHER KING, JR.

The whole history of international environmental action has been of arriving at destinations which looked impossibly distant at the moment of departure.

TONY BRENTON, *THE GREENING OF MACHIAVELLI.*

Taking small steps never feels entirely satisfactory. Nor does taking action without scientific knowledge. But certainty and perfection have never figured prominently in the story of human progress. Business, in particular, is accustomed to making decisions in conditions of considerable uncertainty, applying its experience and skills to areas of activity where much is unknown. That is why it will have a vital role in meeting the challenge of climate change – and why the contribution it is already making is so encouraging.

JOHN BROWNE, GROUP CHIEF EXECUTIVE OF BP IN *FOREIGN AFFAIRS*, JULY–AUGUST 2004.

When President John F Kennedy called the United States to action in the space race, he uttered words that might apply even more convincingly to the cause of securing our civilisation from the risk of human-induced dangerous climate change. He said:

We choose to do these things not because they are easy, but because they are hard, because the goal will serve to organize and measure the best of our energies and skills, because the challenge is one we are willing to accept, one we are unwilling to postpone, and one which we intend to win.[1]

Coping with the climate change issue is in many ways a greater challenge than the space race. It is more multi-faceted, more fundamental to our civilisation, and likely to be an ongoing challenge for this and future generations. It is a question of foresight, because it involves seeing into the future to see what is required of us today. It is a matter of risk management, because we cannot predict the future, but merely look at the possibilities, attach tentative probabilities conditional on human behaviour, and use that to decide policy today.

It is also a matter of faith – faith in science, faith in people to meet the challenge, and faith that human ingenuity and adaptability can cope with the challenge. Faith and hope, like despair, can be self-fulfilling prophecies. If people believe they can make a difference, they will act and, in so doing, *will* make a difference. If, however, they despair and choose to do nothing, they will be overtaken by events: they will have abdicated their choice. People either choose and act for a sustainable future, or they contribute to a growing environmental disaster. Climate change is serious and urgent stuff, but you can make a difference.

People hate doom and gloom – it turns people off. That is not what this is about. It is about new and exciting technologies, creating new markets, making new investments and taking advantage of new opportunities. It is about solving several problems at once, co-benefits and complementary strategies. It is about enjoying our relationship with nature and creating a sustainable future. It is about making life better.

History tells us that humans are adaptable and ingenious in devising new technologies. Thus the twentieth century saw the birth and spread of many amazing new technologies such as the internal combustion engine, flight, telecommunications, medicines that have eliminated ancient scourges, and the World Wide Web. These inventions have transformed human existence.

It is therefore strange that some think we are so ingenious that we can adapt to anything, yet not be able to reduce greenhouse gas emissions at an affordable cost. And others argue the opposite – that we are so clever that we can almost instantly cut greenhouse gas emissions at acceptable cost, yet cannot adapt to even minor climate changes. We can and must do both. We can simultaneously devise new technologies to reduce greenhouse emissions thus building a low-carbon economy over the next half-century, while at the same time adapt to the changes we have not been able to prevent.

On both the mitigation and adaptation fronts there are great opportunities ahead. If we seize these opportunities we can achieve wonders, and even do so while developing our economies and simultaneously reducing poverty and inequity.

An interesting developing country perspective is provided by Jose Goldemberg, former Minister for Science and Technology, Brazil:

> *Renewable energy is inexhaustible and abundant. It is clear therefore that in due time renewable energies will dominate the world's energy system, due to their inherent advantages such as mitigation of climate change, generation of employment and reduction of poverty, as well as increased energy security and supply.*[2]

In *Natural Capitalism* (1999), after reviewing numerous real case studies, Paul Hawken, Amory Lovins and L Hunter Lovins of the Rocky Mountain Institute in Colorado go further:

> *In the past fifty years, the world's annual carbon emissions have quadrupled. But in the next half century, the climate problem could become as faded a memory as the energy crises of the seventies are now, because climate change is not an inevitable result of normal economic activity but an artefact of carrying out that activity in irrationally inefficient ways. Climate protection can save us all money – even coal miners, who deserve the just transition that the nation's energy savings could finance a hundred times over.*[3]

Besides *Natural Capitalism*, there are many other sources of information, including case studies, on how to reduce greenhouse gas emissions. I will mention two here, but there are more in the endnotes. One good site is that of The Climate Group.[4] This is a group of companies, NGOs and local, regional and national governments 'committed to adopting a leadership agenda on climate protection and to reducing greenhouse gas emissions'. Another is the International Council for Local Environmental Initiatives (ICLEI), which has over 875 local government members, runs meetings and has specialist advisory groups.[5]

It is worth reminding ourselves that in the range of IPCC SRES scenarios for future emissions to 2100 (see Chapter 3) one scenario (B1) resulted in emissions that would lead to less than 550 ppm of CO_2-equivalent by 2100. This equilibrium concentration remains higher than the low level of greenhouse gas concentrations that may be needed, around 450 ppm as suggested in Chapter 8. Nevertheless, the B1 SRES scenario was based on a hypothetical world with an emphasis on local solutions to economic, social and environmental sustainability, but with no overt climate change policies. Thus the authors of the SRES report agree with the authors of *Natural Capitalism* that it is plausible, and maybe even desirable, to follow a relatively safe emissions pathway in the twenty-first century for reasons other than climate change. Of course, SRES also had some alternative very high emissions scenarios which SRES considered to be plausible without climate change policies.

The message is clear – we have a choice about the future, and the choice has serious consequences for future climate and for human societies. Risks associated with climate change should influence that choice. It is important here to remember that the IPCC deliberately did not attach probabilities to its SRES scenarios. However, if we examine the assumptions underlying the B1 scenario, we see that it requires reductions in material intensity (raw materials per unit quality of life) and the introduction of clean and resource-efficient technologies, with an emphasis on global solutions, sustainability and improved equity. How probable are these developments without some deliberate policy choices, and indeed without community/government decisions, goals and incentives? The SRES scenarios say this is possible, but not that it is likely without deliberate efforts to make it happen.

Business Weekly, in a cover story on global warming on 16 August 2004, reports G Michael Purdy, Director of the Lamont-Doherty Laboratory as saying that the reasons for the present lack of urgency in reducing greenhouse gas emissions is 'not the science and not the economics', but rather 'it is the lack of public knowledge, the lack of

leadership, and the lack of political will'. All that is necessary is for us to create the will to make it happen.

The situation is urgent, with both adaptation and mitigation needed. Moreover, no potential contributions to emissions reduction should be ruled out on the basis of prejudice against particular technologies or socio-economic biases. Whether it is wind power, geosequestration or nuclear power, mitigation options should be examined for timeliness, safety, acceptability and economic potential, rather than ruled out on the basis of some pre-existing ideological position. Infighting on an either/or basis is counter-productive, although the pros and cons of particular solutions may vary from place to place or be determined ultimately by costs and timeliness. The outcome may well be determined by a process of learning by doing. Such a process can lower costs and determine what is most appropriate in the local context.

Faced with the challenge of achieving rapid sustainable development, countries like China, India and Brazil are starting to build new low-carbon technologies (see Chapter 11), and will gain competitive advantages from doing so. They will reduce local air pollution problems, increase employment, and avoid excessive reliance on foreign sources of fossil fuels. According to The Climate Group, in the report 'China's clean revolution' (2008), 'China is already the world's leading renewable energy producer and is over-taking more developed economies in exploiting valuable economic opportunities, creating green-collar jobs and leading development of critical low-carbon technologies'.[4]

Developing countries are not necessarily consistent in this, as the increasing use of private automobiles in China, rather than bicycles and public transport, testifies. Yet the challenge is being faced, and these developing countries have the opportunity to adopt strategies and to design and build infrastructures that will achieve sustainability, including a stable climate.

The danger is that developing countries are being seduced by the example of highly carbon-intensive developed country lifestyles and technologies that will exacerbate the global climate problem and lead to worse impacts of climate change on themselves. Putting development before limiting greenhouse gas emissions may have the perverse effect of stifling development through climatic disasters. Development has to be clean development if it is to succeed in the long run.

The poorer lesser-developed countries, such as much of sub-Saharan Africa and parts of Asia, are in many cases not yet on a rapid development pathway. Instead they are struggling to cope with poverty, natural and man-made disasters such as floods, drought and civil wars, unrest and instability. For them energy policy is a matter of survival, and climate change considerations rate low on their list of priorities. Yet, as the IPCC has pointed out, they are likely to be worst affected by climate change, with reduced crop yields, more climatic disasters and flooding due to sea-level rise. For these countries sustainable development needs to come first in the form of disaster preparedness, aid in developing dispersed forms of renewable energy, and efforts by the rest of the world not to make matters worse through climate change.

A special issue of *Climatic Change* in 2007 deals with the issue of climate change mitigation and its relationship to development.[6] The authors argue that rapid increases in emissions in developing countries comes mainly with increases in middle class consumption, which needs to be targeted by appliance energy standards, public transport friendly urban development and similar measures. They go on to discuss the relevance of, and problems with, the Kyoto Protocol's Clean Development Mechanism in this task.

The challenge in developed countries is in some ways greater because they have so much more already invested in inappropriate and unsustainable infrastructures. These include inefficient coal-fired power stations; hundreds of millions of polluting motor vehicles; vast road systems designed for private transport; under-utilised, run-down or even abandoned public transport systems; and highly energy-inefficient building stock. Much of this existing stock needs to be transformed and upgraded, or written off and replaced, in order to meet more sustainable standards.

Central to all these situations is how to foster rapid growth in renewable energy and energy efficiency, and how to minimise greenhouse gas emissions now. Urgent results can only be achieved through existing technologies such as greater energy efficiency (insulation, hybrid cars and so on) and proven renewable technology such as biomass ethanol, and solar and wind power. This must be backed up with new and emerging technology, including appropriate carbon removal and sequestration, and even safe and secure nuclear power. But these latter capital-expensive technologies will only achieve massive reductions in greenhouse gas emissions over the course of many decades, due to the need for research and development, large embedded energy costs and slow uptake. They are as yet largely unproven and require large long-term research, development and investment.

It is government policies that can engender a sense of urgency. This might come from mandatory targets for energy efficiency, renewable energy and reductions in emissions. And it is carbon emissions trading, tax incentives and other measures that would accelerate the development and commercialisation of low-carbon technology by internalising environmental costs. As we saw in Chapter 10, many state and local government initiatives in both the United States and Australia have been developed to fill the gaps in federal government programs in these two countries. The change in government in Australia in late 2007 is generating federal initiatives also. Initiatives to reduce emissions will have maximum effectiveness only when they are implemented federally, and indeed internationally, thereby achieving economies of scale and greater planning certainty for industry.

In some developed countries, notably the European Union countries, and since 2007 in Australia, federal governments or groupings of governments, and indeed business, are accepting the challenge of developing low-carbon technology to meet necessary targets. However, there is debate about how realistic the measures being implemented are in achieving these goals, and about transitional arrangements to encourage a smooth but ongoing transition to a low-carbon economy. It is in part a process of learning by doing.[7]

As Sean Lucy, Director of Climate Change Services at PricewaterhouseCoopers stated in 2007:

Clarity on early abatement opportunities will be eagerly awaited by business. Early adopters of a robust carbon management strategy are likely to receive real material benefit and see a positive impact on shareholder value. The effectiveness of a company's carbon strategy is already a key metric in investor decision-making.

Later he added:

Everyone is still learning and this is a relatively immature regulatory environment. Governments are working hard to develop models that work best and there will be, inevitably, a process of seeing what works and fine tuning it. There will be some push back from business when government oversteps, and hopefully we'll get a common sense position in the middle.[8]

Recognition and ownership of the climate change problem, measured in terms of real, substantial and effective action is urgent. It requires understanding, education of the population, and action by governments to set standards and create the business climate in which innovators and entrepreneurs can flourish. Markets may be efficient in achieving least-cost solutions when they recognise a problem or opportunity, but too often they are focused on the short-term and fail to recognise long-term challenges. As Sir Nicholas Stern said in his 2006 report to the UK government:

The science tells us that GHG emissions are an externality; in other words, our emissions affect the lives of others. When people do not pay for the consequences of their actions we have market failure. This is the greatest market failure the world has seen. It is an externality that goes beyond those of ordinary congestion or pollution, although many of the same economic principles apply for its analysis.

This externality is different in 4 key ways that shape the whole policy of a rational response. It is: global; long term; involves risks and uncertainties; and potentially involves major and irreversible change.[9]

Climate change requires urgent global action in the short-term, to fulfil long-term goals. Mandatory targets, subject to revision as new information emerges, and other government carrots and sticks can and indeed must be used to stimulate this sense of urgency.

Looking beyond the Kyoto Protocol

Most of the world has accepted that the Kyoto Protocol is a good starting point in getting greenhouse gas emissions under control. Together with its parent Framework Convention on Climate Change, the Kyoto Protocol has set initial emissions targets for the developed countries, to be achieved by 2008–12, along with several principles and mechanisms. Central to the thinking in the Kyoto Protocol is the idea of differentiated responsibilities, with developed countries, who are the largest per capita emitters, taking the lead in the first commitment period, and the idea of sustainable development for all countries, especially the less developed ones.

It is important to remember that the Kyoto Protocol emissions targets, and exclusion of developing countries from them, apply only until 2012, after which a new formula must be put in place. Ongoing negotiations on such a formula necessarily include at least the major developing countries in one form or another. More explicit mechanisms are needed for aid to developing countries in the form of the transfer of low-carbon technologies to assist in economic development, and for aid in adapting to unavoidable climate change, including climatic disasters.

International agreements are necessary as they are more likely to create a level playing field where countries and businesses have equitable access to markets and standards and know what to expect, foster international equity and sustainable development, and discourage or penalise free-loaders. By creating truly international markets such agreements can also achieve greatest efficiency in emissions reductions, and in so doing foster a real sense of urgency.

How effective such a post-Kyoto agreement would be, and whether in fact agreement can be reached, is of course dependent on the outcome of the negotiations. Arguments over possible post-Kyoto arrangements are complex, voluminous and often highly specialised. A 2004 document from the Pew Center on Global Climate Change lists some 40 proposals and provides a succinct summary.[10] This is not the place to go into the proposals in any depth. However, I will mention some ideas and point, in the endnotes, to where you can follow up on them.

Negotiations and academic studies of them are ongoing, and the negotiations can be followed via reports on the websites of the Institute for Sustainable Development and the UN Framework Convention on Climate Change, as well as many other websites cited in this book.[11] The IPCC 2007 Working Group III report has a whole chapter on Policies, Instruments and Co-operative Arrangements (Chapter 13).

Considerations in arriving at any new international agreement to reduce greenhouse gas emissions include:

- building on what has already been agreed,

- encouraging least-cost effectiveness in mitigation actions,

- promoting cooperative arrangements to cope with or adapt to unavoidable climate change via capacity building and emergency relief,

- achieving co-benefits, especially sustainable development,

- allowing for equity, relating to the agreed ideas of differentiated responsibilities and capacities,

- avoiding unwanted outcomes,

- minimising risk of failure,

- ensuring effectiveness in achieving rapid reductions in emissions,

- leaving room for adaptability as new information comes to hand regarding risks and effectiveness (including revised targets in the light of developments), and

- monitoring progress and enforcing agreements.

Whatever we may want – and the UN Framework Convention on Climate Change goal of avoiding dangerous levels of greenhouse gases seems like a reasonable objective (despite difficulties in quantifying it) – the strategy must be related to a realistic assessment of the success likely to be achieved. As Sir Winston Churchill once said:

However beautiful the strategy, you should occasionally look at the results.

A lot of thought has gone into what might follow the Kyoto Protocol. Niklas Hohne of ECOFYS, a European research and consulting company, outlined a number of possible approaches to a future mitigation agreement in work done for the German Federal Environmental Agency.[12] The Climate Group in a 'Breaking the Climate Deadlock' initiative, and the Pew Center on Global Climate Change have each developed proposals.[13] Some key proposals include:

- *Continuing Kyoto.* This might include ad hoc negotiated emissions reduction targets increasing every ten years for developed countries, and increasing participation of other countries as their GDP per capita rises closer to the global average.

- *Intensity targets.* This approach would define emissions targets in terms of emissions per unit GDP (carbon intensity), and was favoured by the US Bush Administration. It allows for economic growth, but would not lead to reductions in actual emissions unless the decrease in carbon intensity is more rapid than economic growth. This is presently not the case in most countries including the US, and is, in a sense, the key problem. Expressing mitigation targets in such terms makes it difficult to define what actual reductions in emissions would be achieved, as these would depend on economic growth rates.

- *Contraction and convergence.* This proposal, originally from the Global Commons Institute in the UK, defines as the goal a target stabilised greenhouse gas concentration, assesses a global emissions pathway (variation in emissions with time) that would lead to this goal, and allocates emissions pathways to individual countries aimed at converging on the same emissions per capita at some future date such as 2050 or 2100. This would allow for some initial increase in emissions for some countries with present low emissions per capita, but greater reductions for countries with high emissions per capita.

- *Sectoral agreements.* This approach would assign different emissions reduction criteria to different sectors such as domestic, industry, electricity, agriculture and forestry. It was one basis of the formula used in the EU to share the burden between different member countries under the Kyoto Protocol. The domestic sector would require convergence of per-capita emissions, industry would require growth in energy efficiency, electricity would require a proportion of renewables, agriculture would require stabilisation at 1990 levels, and forestry would aim at zero net emissions.

One interesting variation, which potentially accommodates large differences between countries, involves negotiating a package of multi-component commitments by each country based on national circumstances, negotiated from the bottom up, as in multilateral trade agreements. How far this proposal differs from what was attempted in the Kyoto Protocol is not clear. The author, Robert Reinstein, former chief US negotiator for the UNFCCC, argues that a commitment to a target for emissions reduction must be accompanied by an illustrative package of policies and measures that might be expected to result in the target. Conversely, he argues that commitment to a package of polices and measures should be

accompanied by a projection of the emissions reduction expected to result. Such estimates are a key to seeing whether the targets or policies and measures are working. He adds that government actions alone will not be sufficient to achieve results, since most investment decisions and technology dissemination are carried out by the private sector. But governments can help to create an enabling environment to encourage such private sector participation.[14]

Reinstein goes on to state that in negotiating a balanced package of commitments by all countries, it is important to distinguish between short-term and longer-term commitments. The former begin the process and send a political signal. Actions in response to short-term commitments begin to change the psychology and reinforce expectations of change, which influence market behaviour. Longer-term commitments to promote low-carbon technology and subsequent changes in capital stock and transformation of infrastructure are supported by short-term changes. Major reductions in greenhouse gas emissions will in general occur over the longer term as a result of both short-term and longer-term processes. Where I would go beyond Reinstein is to place greater emphasis on the urgency of the short-term commitments, since early reductions in emissions are crucial to reducing the risk of dangerous climate change.

To accomplish this difficult challenge, Mike MacCracken of the US Climate Institute proposes a reciprocal arrangement under which:

> *(1) developed nations move rapidly to demonstrate that a modern society can function without reliance on technologies that release carbon dioxide (CO_2) and other non-CO_2 greenhouse gases to the atmosphere; and (2) ... developing nations act in the near-term to sharply limit their non-CO_2 emissions while minimizing growth in CO_2 emissions, and then in the long-term join with the developed nations to reduce all emissions as cost effective technologies are developed.[15]*

Under this approach developing nations at the outset would focus on low hanging fruit–emissions reductions with significant ability to limit radiative forcing and that are achievable at low relative cost. These include greatly reducing emissions of methane, air pollutants that contribute to tropospheric ozone, and black soot, which blackens glaciers, in turn causing greater absorption of solar radiation and melting of glaciers that are crucial to the water supply of a large portion of humanity. Initially, the primary efforts to limit CO_2 emissions in developing nations would focus on ending deforestation and on implementing energy efficiency measures, for example, reducing power consumption for lighting, reducing conversion loss and transmission loss, and encouraging energy recycling including combined heat and power.

A 2007 paper by Lewis and Diringer of the Pew Center argues for policy-based commitments as an avenue for developing countries to reduce emissions growth, without fixing a firm target. They suggest this could evolve from voluntary to binding commitments that other parties to any agreement would consider adequate and reliable.[16] Warwick McKibben and Peter Wilcoxen in 2002 provided another alternative that would provide a fixed number of tradable long-term emissions permits with an elastic supply of short-term permits, which they argued would better control costs.[17]

These and many other approaches are open for discussion and have been modelled using various economic and energy sector models to see how they might work out.[18] Critical to their acceptance and usefulness is how they fit in with each country's national interests and their overall effectiveness in achieving urgent and continuing emission reductions. Substantial reductions of emissions in developed countries are necessary in all approaches, and these reductions clearly must be much larger for a 450 ppm concentration target than the emissions reductions required under the Kyoto Protocol. Early involvement of developing countries is necessary, but many approaches and variations on future actions are possible, with none being ideal. A mixture of approaches may be a good compromise, but one that ensures that tight controls or disincentives on emissions in developed countries do not lead to a transfer of polluting activities to developing countries.[19]

Addressing the key issues

In this book we have seen that, despite the uncertainties, there is a real and present danger that our continuing large-scale burning of fossil fuels is pushing the climate system into a situation where there is a risk of serious damage to us and our children. This danger increases with every year that we fail to take appropriate action, yet there are potential solutions out there, which we could apply.

Recent modelling of carbon budgets illustrates this point.[20] For example, Mignone and colleagues found that if the rate at which future emissions of greenhouse gases can be reduced is limited to no greater than say 1% each year, then any delay in starting to reduce emissions leads to a larger peak concentration. They found that with a decline in emissions of 1% per year starting in 2008, concentrations would peak near 475 ppm, but that for each year that reductions are postponed the eventual peak increases by 9 ppm. This greatly increases the danger of reaching some uncertain but likely 'dangerous' level. Each year of delay in emissions reductions increases the risk of dangerous climate change.

Here are some key findings that should guide us:

- There is a need to achieve a *target of a stabilised concentration of about 450 ppm carbon dioxide equivalent*, or even lower if some recent results are borne out. These suggest a high risk, with concentrations around 450 ppm, of reaching a 'tipping point' at which some key part of the climate system becomes unstable (such as disintegration of the Greenland Ice Sheet). Higher concentrations would lead to too great a risk of unacceptable consequences (see Chapter 6). This takes account of large uncertainties and factors them into a risk assessment.

- To achieve this, *global emissions must peak before 2050*, and then decline rapidly. This requires sizeable reductions *starting as soon as possible*.

- *If concentrations of greenhouse gases peak above about 450 ppm CO_2-equivalent they may have to be brought down later* in the twenty-first century, by removing greenhouse gases from the atmosphere. This may best be done by growing biomass and sequestering carbon from it as biochar or by other means.

- Effective international action requires *agreement between developed and developing countries* on emissions reduction schedules consistent with sustainable development for all. This is in everyone's interests (see Chapter 10), and probably requires eventual convergence on equal emissions per person across all countries.

- This requires that *emissions in developed countries must decrease by some 60–80% by 2050*, (see Chapter 8) and that increases in emissions in developing countries be kept as low as possible. This requires a rapid transfer to, or development of, low-carbon technology in developing countries.

- *Proven methods for reducing emissions should be applied urgently* in the next decade or two, because early emissions reductions are essential to avoid dangerous climate change.

- *Research and development should be encouraged for other potential low-carbon technologies*, at least while they seem feasible and acceptable on other grounds. They will be needed in the latter part of the twenty-first century.

- *Government intervention is necessary* to remove direct and hidden subsidies for fossil fuels and inefficient carbon-intensive activities, and to provide incentives for low-carbon technologies via the polluter pays principle. Start-up subsidies may be needed to develop new technologies, especially to achieve economies of scale.

- *Market mechanisms* should be used to achieve maximum efficiency through real competition on a level playing field.

- *National and international carbon emissions trading* looks like the best overall mechanism to internalise the environmental costs of emissions. This mechanism has proven efficient and acceptable in the US through the trading of sulfur emissions and is already being implemented for greenhouse gases in the EU and elsewhere. It is complex but difficulties can be worked through.

- *Some potential damages due to climate changes are inevitable* due to climate changes that cannot be avoided because of inertia in the economic and climate systems and where adaptation proves too expensive.

- *Adaptation measures will be necessary to minimise damages*. Adaptation has limits, will not avoid all damages, will have side effects and may be costly (see Chapter 7).

- *Mitigation and adaptation measures need to be integrated into normal decision-making* on all matters of development, planning, innovation and investment.

- *Aid will be necessary* for communities and countries with low adaptive capacities, and for those suffering damages. Resettlement aid will be necessary for people displaced by sea-level rise and loss of livelihoods.

This list provides many pointers to what must be done. With a level playing field, and proper incentives, many proven low-carbon energy sources and energy saving strategies can be implemented quickly. According to the experience of many businesses, entrepreneurs and innovators, this can be done at little cost, and may even be profitable. How easy this really is will become clear only as we learn by doing. If it turns out to be easy, then targets below 450 ppm become feasible. Otherwise we may have to resort to more drastic measures.

Possibilities for mitigation were discussed in Chapter 8. Pacala and Socolow of Princeton University, among others, provide an excellent summary list.[21] Such a list (slightly expanded) might include:

- Improving energy efficiency and conservation by:

  – increasing fuel economy in cars, including hybrid, fully electric and compressed air cars,

– reducing reliance on cars, with better public transport, bike paths and urban design,

– building or retrofitting more efficient buildings with better use of insulation, shade, cogeneration plants, and automatic controls,

– increasing power plant efficiency.

• Decreasing carbon emissions from electricity and fuels by using alternatives such as:

– substitution of natural gas for coal and oil,

– wind-generated electricity,

– solar photovoltaics and solar thermal power,

– geothermal power,

– wave and tidal power,

– energy storage from renewables by various means including pumped hydro, hydrogen generation, efficient batteries, electrolyte generation, fuel cells and compressed air,

– second-generation (cellulosic) biofuels, avoiding land clearing and competition with food production,

– carbon capture and sequestration from power plants,

– carbon capture and sequestration from synthetic fuel plants,

– nuclear power with all safeguards.

• Increasing the effectiveness of natural sinks by:

– improving forest management, including plantations and on-farm forestry,

– improving management of agricultural soils,

– biochar and other means of taking greenhouse gases out of the atmosphere.

Nearly all of these options are already operating at a pilot or industrial scale, and could be massively scaled up over the next five to 40 years to provide large reductions in global emissions. With priority given to implementing the short-term solutions such as energy efficiency and conservation and rapid deployment of proven renewable power technologies, these options provide an excellent agenda for action.

It is absolutely crucial that options for reducing greenhouse gas emissions be pursued with a real sense of urgency. Every extra tonne of carbon dioxide placed into the atmosphere increases the very real risk of dangerous climate change, and nobody will escape the direct or indirect consequences.

We are in danger of inadvertently tripping the 'on' switch to disaster, with an inevitably long delay before it can be turned off again. What is done now that enhances climate change cannot be easily undone, so we should err on the side of caution.

But it is not all doom and gloom: we can save the day. As we have seen earlier in this book, the technology already exists to rapidly reduce emissions via large investments in energy efficiency (which saves money) and renewable base-load power (which will rapidly come down in price as it is scaled up). Supplemented later this century by large-scale carbon capture and sequestration and (if necessary) by safe nuclear power, the peak in greenhouse gas concentrations can be minimised and then brought down.

We need to reduce carbon emissions, and we need to do it fast. Although we are facing an emergency, with an appropriate allocation of ingenuity and resources, together we can do it. We owe that, at least, to our children.

ENDNOTES

1. Speech at Rice University, Houston, Texas (12 September 1962). See http://www.jfklibrary.org.

2. From his speech at the 2004 Bonn Conference on Renewable Energy, quoted in 'The price of power: poverty, climate change, the coming energy crisis and the renewable revolution' (2004), New Economics Foundation at http://www.neweconomics.org.

3. Paul Hawken, Amory Lovins and L Hunter Lovins, *Natural Capitalism*, Little, Brown and Co., Boston (1999).

4. The Climate Group website is at http://www.theclimategroup.org.

5. ICLEI's website is at http://www.iclei.org.

6. The special issue of *Climatic Change* on climate and development is **84**, (1) (September 2007), A and K Michaelowa (eds).

7. Learning by doing is discussed in a special issue of *Climatic Change*, **89**, (1–2) (July 2008), '*Learning and Climate Change*'. Climate change mitigation and development issues, including the operation of the Clean Development Mechanism, are discussed in *Climatic Change* special issue, **84** (1) (September 2007) 'Climate or Development?'

8. The first quote from Sean Lucy is from a press release by PriceWaterhouseCoopers (17 July 2007) available at http://www.pwc.com/extweb/ncpressrelease.nsf/. The second is from a Melbourne *Age* newspaper article, 'Seeing the light' (21 September 2007).

9. The quote from the Stern Review is highlighted in an article in *The New Economist* (30 June 2006) available at http://neweconomist.blogs.com/new_economist/2006/10/stern_review_2.html.

10. See *International Climate Efforts Beyond 2012: A Survey of Approaches* (November 2004), at: http://www.pewclimate.org/global-warming-in-depth/all_reports/international_climate_efforts.

11. See http://www.iisd.ca/process/climate_atm.htm and http://www.unfccc.int, respectively.

12. See *Evolution of commitments under the UNFCCC: Involving newly industrialized economies and developing countries*, and *Protecting the climate after 2012*, available at http://www.umweltbundesamt.de. See also: http://www.ecofys.com/com/publications/reports_books.asp, and http://assets.panda.org/downloads/ecofyspost2012targets20sept05.pdf.

13. The Climate Group studies are available at http://www.theclimategroup.org, under the 'Breaking the Climate Deadlock' prompt. The Pew Center reports are at http://www.pewclimate.org under the 'Publications and Reports' and 'Climate Dialogue at Pocantico' prompts.

14. The paper by Robert Reinstein is 'A possible way forward on climate change' in *Mitigation and Adaptation Strategies for Global Change*, **9**, pp. 295–309 (2004).

15. See http://www.climate.org/topics/climate-change/maccracken-proposal-north-south-framework.html and a longer account is in *Journal of the Air and Water Waste Management Association*, **58**, pp. 735–86 (2008).

16. See 'Policy-based commitments in a post-2012 climate framework', at http://www.pewclimate.org.

17. See *Climate Change Policy After Kyoto: Blueprint for a Realistic Approach* (2002) from The Brookings Institute in Washington DC, at http://www.brookings.edu.

18. Links to many other proposals and policy discussions can be found at the website of the *Future International Action on Climate Change Network*, http://www.fiacc.net. See also ongoing policy discussions in a number of journals, notably: *Climate Policy* (http://www.climatepolicy.com); *Energy Policy* (http://www.elsevier.com/locate/enpol); *Environmental Modelling and Assessment* (http://www.springerlink.com); *Environmental Science and Policy* (http://www.elsevier.com/locate/envsci); *International Environmental Agreements: Politics, Law and Economics* (http://www.springerlink.com); *Mitigation and Adaptation Strategies for Global Change* (http://www.springerlink.com).

19. Other publications and websites relating to climate change policy include: *Beyond Kyoto: Advancing the International Effort Against Climate Change*, Pew Center on Global Climate Change (December 2003) at http://www.pewclimate.org; W McKibben and P Wilcoxen, *Climate Change Policy After Kyoto: A Blueprint for a Realistic Approach*, Brookings Institution, see http://www.sensiblepolicy.com; 'Climate policy beyond 2012: a survey of long-term targets and future frameworks', CICERO Center for International Climate and Environmental Research, Oslo, at http://www.cicero.uio.no; 'Climate protection strategies for the 21st century: Kyoto and beyond', German Advisory Council on Climate Change (WBGU), Special Report, see http://www.wbgu.de; *Contraction and Convergence – The Global*

CLIMATE CHANGE: THE SCIENCE, IMPACTS AND SOLUTIONS

Solution to Climate Change, Global Commons Institute, at http://www.gci.org.uk; *Dealing with Climate Change: Policies and Measures in IEA Member Countries*, International Energy Agency (October 2002) at http://www.iea.org; *Economy-Energy-Environment Simulation: Beyond the Kyoto Protocol*, Kimio Uno (ed.) Kluwer Academic Publishers, Boston (2002); Benito Muller, *Framing Future Commitments*, Oxford Institute for Energy Studies at http://www.OxfordEnergy.org; Bernd Brouns, *Overview of Ongoing Activities on the Future Design of the Climate Regime*, Wuppertal Institute for Climate, Environment and Energy, http://www.wupperinst.org; *Tiempo*, for latest news and information on climate and development, at http://www.tiempocyberclimate.org. These are all excellent sources of information, but even a brief summary is beyond the scope of this book. Use them as resources for your further thinking and action.

For a useful summary of policy lessons for advancing renewable energy technologies at the national level see the thematic background paper, 'National policy instruments' (2004) by Janet Sawin for the Conference for Renewable Energies, Bonn, at http://www.renewables2004.de. See also many other studies for particular countries, such as the series by The Climate Group at http://www.breakingtheclimatedeadlock.com, and those from various environmental and industry groups. For example, 'American energy: the renewable path to energy security', by the Worldwatch Institute and Center for American Progress (September 2006), at http://www.worldwatch.org; and 'How emissions trading can work for the environment and the economy', Business Council of Australia, at http://www.bca.com.au; and relevant publications from the Centre to Energy and Environmental Markets, University of New South Wales, http://www.ceem.unsw.edu.au. See also *RMI Solutions Journal*, from the Rocky Mountain Institute at http://www.rmi.org and endnotes in Chapter 8.

20. Discussion of the carbon cycle, and in particular of delays in reducing emissions, is contained in a special issue of *Climatic Change*, **88**, (3–4) (June 2008). See especially the paper by Bryan Mignone and others, 'Atmospheric stabilization and the timing of carbon mitigation', pp. 251–65.

21. See *Science*, **305**, pp. 968–72 (2004) with supporting material at http://www.sciencemag.org/cgi/content/full/305/5686/968/DC1.

GLOSSARY (with acronyms)

Note: This is a short glossary merged with acronyms. Some items are more fully explained in the text. These and many other relevant items can be found in many other glossaries, notably those to be found at the back of each of the three main reports of the IPCC Fourth Assessment at http://www.ipcc.ch. There is also a short table of acronyms for powers of ten as used in units.

ACIA or **Arctic Climate Impact Assessment** An international project of the intergovernmental forum, the *Arctic Council* and the *International Arctic Science Committee*, consisting of relevant NGOs, to evaluate and synthesise knowledge on climate variability, climate change, and increased ultraviolet radiation and their consequences. The results of the assessment were released at the ACIA International Scientific Symposium held in Reykjavik, Iceland, in November 2004. See http://www.acia.uaf.edu/.

Adaptation Initiatives and measures to reduce the vulnerability of natural and human systems against actual or expected climate change effects. Various types of adaptation exist, e.g. anticipatory and reactive, private and public, autonomous and planned.

Aerosols Small particulates suspended in the atmosphere. These may be dust or carbon black (soot), or particles formed in situ from polluting gases such as sulfur dioxide or hydrogen sulfide.

Airborne fraction That fraction of CO_2 emissions that remains in the atmosphere.

Albedo The fraction of solar radiation reflected from a surface or object. Ice and snow have high albedo and vegetation or open ocean low albedo.

Annex I Parties The group of countries included in Annex I (as amended in 1998) to the *UNFCCC* (q.v.), including all the OECD countries and economies in transition. By default, the other countries (developing countries) are referred to as Non-Annex I countries.

Annular mode Preferred patterns of change and variability in atmospheric circulation with changes in the zonally averaged mid-latitude westerly winds. Northern and Southern Annular Modes (NAM and SAM, respectively) refer to those in the northern and southern hemispheres respectively.

Antarctic Oscillation or **AAO** A low-frequency mode of atmospheric variability of the southern hemisphere, also known as the Southern Annular Mode (SAM). In this mode atmospheric pressure over the polar region varies in opposition to that over middle latitudes (about 45°S).

Anthropogenic Caused by or of human origin.

Aphelion Point of farthest distance from the Sun of the Earth in its elliptical orbit around the Sun.

AR4 Fourth Assessment Report of the IPCC, published in 2007.

Arctic Oscillation (AO) An atmospheric circulation pattern in which the atmospheric pressure over the polar regions varies in opposition with that over middle latitudes (about 45°N) on time scales ranging from weeks to decades. It is closely related to the *North Atlantic Oscillation* (NAO) (q.v.) and the Northern Annular Mode.

Atmosphere The gaseous envelope surrounding the Earth. The dry atmosphere has about 78% nitrogen, 21% oxygen, and 1% other trace gases including greenhouse gases such as carbon dioxide (currently about 0.038%) and water vapour (which has highly variable concentrations by location and season).

Bayesian statistics A statistical method that bases statistical inferences and decisions on a combination of information derived from observation or experiment and from prior knowledge or expert judgment. This contrasts with classical statistics, which is based entirely on data from observations or experiments.

Berlin Mandate A ruling in 1995 from the first Conference of the Parties (COP 1) to the UN Framework Convention on Climate Change. The Berlin Mandate establishes a process that would enable the Parties to take stronger action beyond the commitment period of the Kyoto Protocol, which expires in 2012.

Biochar Charcoal formed from biomass by *pyrolysis* (q.v.) or heating without oxygen. Biochar is highly stable and can be sequestered in soil, with desirable effects on the soil including storage of water and nutrients.

Biofuel Any liquid, gaseous, or solid fuel produced from plant or animal organic matter, for example, soybean oil, alcohol from fermented sugar, black liquor from the paper manufacturing process, wood as fuel, etc. **First-generation biofuels** are produced from starches and thus tend to compete with food production. **Second-generation biofuels** are products such as ethanol and biodiesel derived from ligno-cellulosic biomass or other biological waste by chemical or biological processes.

Biomass The total mass of living organisms including plants, animals and soil microbes in a given area or volume. Dead material of biological origin may also be included.

Biome A major or regional element of the biosphere, typically consisting of several ecosystems, in their environmental context. They are characterised by typical communities of plants and animals.

Biosphere That part of the Earth system comprising all plants, animals and soil biota and dead organic matter such as litter and detritus.

Brunn Rule A commonly applied rule to explain and quantify erosion of sandy shores in response to sea-level rise. It describes the cross-shore response of a long sandy beach to sea-level rise. It states that the beach will adjust to maintain its equilibrium profile relative to the still water level. Thus eroded sediments at the landward end of the profile are deposited in the lower portion of the profile, thereby raising the bed and causing a retreat inland of the shoreline by 50 to 100 times the sea-level rise. It can be a poor approximation in more complex coastal settings.

Cap Mandated restraint set as an upper limit on carbon dioxide (or other) emissions, globally, regionally or for individual emitters, usually as part of an *emissions trading scheme* (q.v.).

Carbon Capture and Storage (CCS) A process consisting of separation of carbon dioxide from industrial and energy-related sources, transport to a storage location, and long-term isolation from the atmosphere.

Carbon cycle The set of processes such as photosynthesis, respiration, decomposition, and air-sea exchange, by which carbon continuously cycles through various reservoirs, such as the atmosphere, living organisms, soils, and oceans.

Carbon dioxide-equivalent The amount of carbon dioxide that would have the same radiative effect as all the greenhouse gases in the atmosphere.

Carbon dioxide fertilisation The enhancement of the growth of plants because of increased atmospheric carbon dioxide concentration.

Carbon intensity The amount of emissions of carbon dioxide per unit of gross domestic product GDP.

Cascade of uncertainty The compounding effect of a series of uncertainties of individual factors or stages, which in complex situations contribute to the uncertainty of the final result.

CDM or **Clean Development Mechanism** Defined in the *Kyoto Protocol* (q.v.), the CDM is intended to enable *Annex I Parties* (q.v.) to obtain carbon credits for projects that limit or reduce GHG emissions in non-Annex I countries (developing countries) A share of the proceeds from such activities is used to assist developing countries that are particularly vulnerable to the adverse effects of climate change to meet the costs of adaptation.

Climate change forcing Climate change forcing is the physical cause of climate change, usually measured as the net downward minus upward energy radiation at the *tropopause* (q.v.). It can be due to a number of physical causes such as variations in solar radiation, changes in the Earth's orbit around the Sun, volcanic dust, or changes in greenhouse gas concentrations in the atmosphere.

Conference of Parties or **COP** Meetings of countries that signed the *UNFCCC* (q.v.).

Counter-adaptive trends Societal or other trends that make adaptation to climate change and sea-level rise more difficult or expensive, for example rapid growth in population or investment in low-lying coastal regions potentially subject to flooding as sea-level rises.

Countries in transition Former Soviet Union countries, whose economic systems are changing from centrally planned to market economies.

Cryosphere The part of the Earth system that consists of all the snow, ice and frozen ground (*permafrost*) (q.v.) on and beneath the surface of the Earth and oceans.

Dansgaard/Oeschger events Abrupt warming events followed by gradual cooling, found in the palaeoclimatic record, seen primarily in the Greenland and North Atlantic regions at intervals of 1.5 to 7 thousand years during glacial periods.

El Niño See *ENSO* (q.v.).

Emissions Trading Scheme or ETS A market-based approach to achieving environmental objectives. It allows those reducing GHG emissions below their allocated emission cap to use or trade the excess reductions to offset emissions at another source inside or outside the country. In general, trading can occur at the intra-company, domestic, and international levels. Emissions trading under Article 17 of the Kyoto Protocol is a tradable quota system based on the assigned amounts calculated from the emission reduction and limitation commitments listed in Annex B of the Protocol. Various voluntary or compulsory ETS systems are already in place, notably that in the European Union, and various other regional or national schemes are being set up. Emission caps are generally reduced over time to achieve overall emissions reduction targets. Emissions trading was pioneered in the US to reduce sulfur emissions and thus acid rain.

Energy efficiency The ratio of useful energy or other output (e.g. services) of a system, conversion process or activity to its energy input.

Energy intensity The ratio of energy use to economic output. At the national level, energy intensity is the ratio of total domestic primary energy use or final energy use to Gross Domestic Product.

Energy security The security of a nation's energy supply, and the measures that a given nation, or the global community as a whole, must carry out to maintain an adequate energy supply.

ENSO or El Niño–La Niña cycle The El Niño–Southern Oscillation system. This is an irregular quasi-periodic oscillation, usually over two to seven years, between conditions in the Equatorial Pacific Ocean. During an El Niño, the trade winds weaken, reducing upwelling in the eastern Equatorial Pacific, leading to regional surface warming. The surface pressure pattern changes across the Pacific, with changes in rainfall leading to drought in the Indonesian and Australian region but heavy rains on the South American west coast. During a La Niña more or less opposite conditions prevail. Influences extend much further afield to Africa, India, North America and even to parts of Europe.

Eutrophication The process where a body of water becomes excessively rich in nutrients, leading to algal blooms or other biomass growth that remove oxygen from the water, adversely affecting fish, and sometimes making it poisonous to animals and humans.

Evapotranspiration The combined process of evaporation from the Earth's surface and transpiration from plants.

Extreme weather events A weather event that is rare at a particular place and time of year. These occur naturally with a low frequency, but this frequency may change with climatic change, either natural or *anthropogenic* (q.v.). They often cause damage because systems are not well adjusted to cope with them. The frequency of extreme events changes rapidly with changes in average conditions.

Geo-engineering Technological efforts to stabilise the climate system by direct intervention in the energy balance of the Earth for reducing global warming.

Glaciations or glacial periods Globally, these are cold periods with widespread ice cover and glaciers. In the last two million years they have occurred roughly every 100 thousand years, with ice caps or sheets covering much land at mid- to high latitudes in both hemispheres. They lead to large decreases (around 160 m) in global average sea level as water is stored in ice sheets on land, and thus to large changes in coastlines.

Glacier A mass of ice that flows downhill under gravity, through internal deformation and sliding at its lower boundary. Summer melt-water at the surface can penetrate via crevasses to the base, helping to lubricate the flow.

Global dimming This refers to observed widespread decreases in solar radiation at the Earth's surface from about the 1960s to around 1990. It was at least partly due to high levels of particulate pollution which reflected some sunlight back into space. Decreases in particulate pollution in the 1990s may have reversed the trend.

Greenhouse gases These are natural and anthropogenic gases that absorb and emit heat radiation from the Sun and the Earth's surface, leading to a relative warming at the Earth's surface and a cooling in the upper atmosphere. Main greenhouse gases are water and carbon dioxide, but also nitrous oxide, methane and ozone, and solely human-made gases such as the halocarbons and other chlorine and bromine containing substances. Total concentrations are often expressed as the amount of carbon dioxide-equivalent concentration, that is, the amount of carbon dioxide that would have the same radiative effect.

Grounding line The line where a glacier or ice sheet with its base below sea level starts to float. Such a grounding line can retreat inland with rising sea level or melting from below by warm water, thus accelerating ice outflow and sea-level rise.

Hydrosphere The part of the Earth's system that comprises all liquid surface and subterranean water, such as oceans, seas, rivers, lakes and underground water.

Ice cap A small *ice sheet* (q.v.).

Ice sheet A mass of land ice that covers most of the underlying bedrock topography, with a shape largely determined by its ice dynamics or flow. These are broadly dome-shaped with outlet glaciers at the coast, often filling valleys that are below sea level and often floating at their coastal ends.

Ice shelf A floating slab of ice of considerable thickness extending from and attached to the coast, often filling embayments and originating from outflow of ice from the continental glaciers.

ICLEI The International Council for Local Environmental Initiatives, founded in 1990, is now called Local Governments for Sustainability. It is an international association of local governments, as well as national and regional local government organisations, that have made a commitment to sustainable development. It consists of over 996 cities, towns, counties, and their associations worldwide.

IIASA, or the International Institute of Applied Systems Analysis An international research organisation conducting inter-disciplinary scientific studies on environmental, economic, technological, and social issues in the context of human dimensions of global change. IIASA is located in Laxenburg, Austria.

IPCC or **Intergovernmental Panel on Climate Change** An intergovernmental scientific body set up by the World Meteorological Organization (WMO) and the United Nations Environment Programme (UNEP). It is made up of the governments of all member countries of WMO and UNEP. Government representatives participate in plenary sessions of the IPCC where the main decisions about the IPCC work programme are taken and reports are reviewed, accepted, adopted and approved. Hundreds of scientists all over the world contribute to the work of the IPCC as authors, contributors and reviewers.

Isostatic rebound The vertical movement of continental surfaces which 'float' on the molten interior of the Earth, as they recover from the reduced weight (or gravitational force) following the removal of ice sheets after the last glaciation. Rebound is slow and continues for many thousands of years. There is also flexing of the continental plates with formerly ice-laden surfaces rising, while areas of the same continental plate that were not ice-covered tend to fall.

ITCZ or **Intertropical Convergence Zone** An equatorial belt of low atmospheric pressure where the north-east and south-east trade winds meet. Moist air is forced upwards resulting in a heavy band of cloud and rain. The ITCZ moves seasonally.

ITER The International Thermonuclear Experimental Reactor project. The reactor is being constructed in France to see whether nuclear fusion can fulfil its promise as a power source.

Joint Implementation or **JI** A market-based implementation mechanism defined in Article 6 of the Kyoto Protocol, allowing *Annex I Parties* (q.v.) or companies from these countries to implement projects jointly that limit or reduce emissions or enhance sinks. JI activity is also permitted in Article 4.2(a) of the UNFCCC.

Kyoto Protocol The Kyoto Protocol to the UNFCCC was adopted at the Third Session of the Conference of the Parties (COP) in 1997 and came into force in 2005. It contains legally binding commitments, in addition to those included in the UNFCCC. Annex B countries (mostly developed countries) agreed to reduce their anthropogenic GHG emissions (carbon dioxide, methane, nitrous oxide, hydrofluorocarbons, perfluorocarbons and sulfur hexafluoride) on average by at least 5% below 1990 levels in the period 2008–2012.

Little Ice Age A period between about AD 1400 and 1900 when temperatures in the northern hemisphere were generally colder than in the 20th century, especially in Europe.

Maunder Minimum The period roughly from 1645 to 1715, when sunspots were relatively rare. It is named after the solar astronomer Edward W Maunder (1851–1928) who documented the dearth of sunspots during that period.

Medieval Warm Period A period about 1000 to 1300 AD when in some regions of the northern hemisphere, particularly the North Atlantic region, it was warmer than in the Little Ice Age that followed.

MER or **market exchange rates** The rate at which foreign currencies are exchanged.

Meridional Overturning Circulation or **MOC** A meridional (north–south) ocean circulation in which warmer and/or less saline (and thus less dense) water moves poleward and is cooled by evaporation, becomes more saline and eventually sinks to deeper levels. It is particularly important in the North Atlantic where the northward flowing Gulf Stream becomes denser and the water sinks, with return flow at greater depths. It can be modified by changes in freshwater inflow into the North Atlantic from rivers and melting ice.

Mitigation In the usage of the IPCC this is human intervention to reduce the sources or enhance the sinks of greenhouse gases and thus to reduce the extent of climate change. An alternative usage would apply this to reductions in the adverse impacts of climate change, but the latter is called *'adaptation'* (q.v.) in IPCC usage.

Negative feedback A process whereby a change in one part of the climate system causes a change in another part of the system that reduces the first change, thereby tending to stabilise the system.

NGOs Non-governmental organisations.

NOAA The United States National Oceanic and Atmospheric Administration

Normal distribution A theoretical distribution of the frequency of numbers in a set of variable data, usually represented by a bell-shaped curve symmetrical about the average or mean. It is sometimes called a *Gaussian distribution*. Many observed variables are normally distributed, but not all (e.g. rainfall, which cannot be negative). See also *'probability distribution'*, q.v.

North Atlantic Oscillation or **NAO** Fluctuations in the surface pressure difference between the Icelandic and Azores regions. Corresponds to fluctuations in the strength of the westerly winds across the North Atlantic and associated storms.

OECD or **Organisation for Economic Cooperation and Development** The OECD brings together the governments of 'countries committed to democracy and the market economy from around the world'.

Overshoot scenario A scenario, or possible future trajectory of change, of greenhouse gas emissions and concentrations, in which concentrations peak at some level and then decrease towards some defined stabilisation concentration. In general this will require the active removal of greenhouse gases from the atmosphere by such means as sequestering carbon from biomass harvesting.

Ozone/ozone hole Ozone (O_3) is a greenhouse gas present in the atmosphere near the surface, formed in photochemical smog, and in the stratosphere (q.v.). An 'ozone hole' is a region with reduced ozone concentrations, due to the effects of ozone-destroying chemical pollution.

Peer review (or **refereeing**) The process of subjecting an author's publications, research or ideas to the scrutiny of others who are experts in the same field. This process, while not requiring agreement, encourages authors to meet the accepted standards of their discipline and prevents the dissemination of irrelevant findings, unwarranted claims, unacceptable interpretations, and personal views. Publications that have not undergone peer review are often regarded with suspicion by scholars and professionals. The IPCC has a strict peer review process.

Perihelion Point of closest distance from the Sun of the Earth in its elliptical orbit around the Sun.

Permafrost Ground (soil or rock and included organic material and ice) in high latitudes or mountainous regions, which remains below freezing point for at least two consecutive years. Melting of permafrost can reduce the ground's structural strength, threatening infrastructure built on it, and release carbon dioxide and methane from decaying organic matter or from gases trapped in the ice.

Pew Center on Global Climate Change A non-profit, non-partisan and independent organisation established in the United States in 1998 to provide 'credible information, straight answers, and innovative solutions in the effort to address global climate change'.

Positive feedback A process where a change in one part of the climate system causes a change in another part of the system that increases the change in the first part, thereby amplifying the change and tending to destabilise the system.

PPP or purchasing power parity The purchasing power of a currency expressed using a basket of goods and services that can be bought with a given amount in the home country. International comparison of, e.g. Gross Domestic Products of countries, can be based on the purchasing power of currencies rather than on current exchange rates. PPP estimates tend to lower per capita GDPs in industrialised countries and raise per capita GDPs in developing countries.

Precautionary Principle A provision under Article 3 of the UNFCCC, stipulating that the parties should take precautionary measures to anticipate, prevent or minimise the causes of climate change and mitigate its adverse effects. Where there are threats of serious or irreversible damage, lack of full scientific certainty should not be used as a reason to postpone such measures, taking into account that policies and measures to deal with climate change should be cost-effective in order to ensure global benefits at the lowest possible cost. It is an expression of the proper degree of risk management in the face of uncertainty.

Predictions A best estimate of future behaviour of the climate system. As there are uncertainties in initial conditions, representation of all processes, and in various assumptions such as future emissions, climatologists prefer to use the term *projections* (q.v.) to emphasise that there are recognised uncertainties.

Probability distribution Strictly called a *probability density function*, it is a function or graph that indicates the relative chances of occurrence of different outcomes or values of a variable. It integrates to unity (i.e. a 100% chance) over its domain and has the property that the area under a portion of the graph equals the probability of outcomes within the sub-domain. A '*normal distribution*' (q.v.) is a special case of a probability distribution.

Projections Potential future evolution of a quantity or set of quantities, often based on model calculations with various assumptions and simplifications. Projections are often repeated with varying plausible assumptions and representations to provide a range of plausible outcomes.

Proxy data Indicators of past climatic conditions based on known relationships between such indicators, that are preserved in the geological or archaeological record, and local climatic conditions. Examples include tree ring widths, pollen types, isotopic records from air or dust trapped in ice cores, and characteristics of ancient corals.

Pyrolysis Heating of organic matter without oxygen to the point where it decomposes into gases such as hydrogen and methane, leaving charcoal. The gases can be used to do the heating, and the excess used for other purposes such as generation of electricity. The charcoal, called *biochar* (q.v.), can be sequestered in soil, where it enriches the soil by absorbing water and nutrients but remains stable there for thousands of years.

Radiative forcing Radiative forcing is the change in the net vertical irradiance (expressed in Watts per square metre: W/m^2) at the *tropopause* (q.v.) due to an internal change or a change in the external forcing of the climate system, such as, for example, a change in the concentration of CO_2 or in the output of the sun.

RAPID or Rapid Climate Change Programme Based in the UK Natural Environment Research Council, RAPID explores what causes rapid switches in climate, with a main (but not exclusive) focus on the Atlantic Ocean's *thermo-haline circulation* (q.v.).

Salinisation Increase in saltiness in soils or water. Often caused by rising water tables following irrigation, bringing dissolved salt from lower levels to the surface where it concentrates as water evaporates. Sea water intrusion as sea-level rises can cause salinisation in coastal areas.

Scenario A plausible and often simplified description of how the future might develop, based on assumptions about driving forces and key relationships. While they may be plausible, it is usually difficult or impossible to attach probabilities to their occurrence.

SCOPE or Scientific Committee on Problems of the Environment A committee under the International Council of Scientific Unions (ICSU), and an interdisciplinary body including physical and social scientists focused on global environmental issues.

Sequestration Carbon storage in terrestrial or marine reservoirs. Carbon dioxide can be liquefied and pumped underground into porous layers, but cost and permanence remain issues. Biological sequestration includes direct removal of carbon dioxide from the atmosphere through land-use change, afforestation, reforestation, carbon storage in landfills and practices that enhance soil carbon in agriculture such as minimum tillage and generation of *biochar* (q.v.).

Sink A process, activity or mechanism that removes a greenhouse gas or its precursor from the atmosphere, including plant growth on land, plankton growth in the oceans, and dissolving of carbon dioxide in the oceans.

Source Source mostly refers to any process, activity or mechanism that releases a greenhouse gas, or its precursor into the atmosphere. The main sources of carbon dioxide are the burning of fossil fuels, cement making, and land-use change. Warming of the oceans and melting of permafrost can also release carbon dioxide and methane into the atmosphere.

SPCZ or South Pacific Convergence Zone A persistent and greatly elongated zone of low-level convergence of air (i.e. flowing together, leading to an updraft) extending from approximately 140°E near the equator to approximately 120°W at 30°S. The zone is orientated more west to east near the equator and has a more diagonal orientation (north-west to south-east) at higher latitudes. The low-level convergence of moisture leads to a persistent cloud band along the SPCZ.

SRES or Special Report on Emission Scenarios A report prepared by the *Intergovernmental Panel on Climate Change (IPCC)* (q.v.) for its Third Assessment Report (TAR) in 2001, on plausible scenarios of future emissions to be used for driving global climate models to develop a range of scenarios of future climate change. The SRES Scenarios were also used for the Fourth Assessment Report (AR4) in 2007.

Stratosphere The highly stratified region of the atmosphere above the *tropopause* (q.v.), extending from about 10 or 20 km to about 50 km altitude.

TAR The Third Assessment Report of the IPCC (q.v.), published in 2001.

Thermo-Haline Circulation or THC See *Meridional Overturning Circulation*.

Tidewater glacier A glacier, the lower end of which lies in a valley the bottom of which is below sea level. Warm sea water can melt the underside of such a glacier causing the *grounding line* (q.v.) to retreat, reducing the resistance to outflow.

Tropopause The tropopause (region of minimum temperature in the atmosphere) varies in altitude from about 9 km in high latitudes to about 20 km near the Equator. Atmospheric temperatures decrease upwards to the tropopause and increase above it.

Troposphere The part of the atmosphere from the Earth's surface to the *tropopause* (q.v.) or region of minimum temperature. It is relatively unstable due to decreasing temperature with altitude.

UNDP or United Nations Development Programme The UN's global development network, an organisation 'advocating for change and connecting countries to knowledge, experience and resources to help people build a better life'. See http://www.undp.org.

UNEP or United Nations Environment Programme UNEP was set up by the United Nations 'to provide leadership and encourage partnership in caring for the environment by inspiring, informing, and enabling nations and peoples to improve their quality of life without compromising that of future generations'.

UNFCCC or United Nations Framework Convention on Climate Change An international treaty signed at the Rio Earth Summit in 1992 to consider what can be done to reduce global warming and to cope with whatever temperature increases are inevitable. It is a 'framework convention' meaning that it set broad objectives but left the details for implementation to be worked out later. The UNFCCC secretariat supports all institutions involved in the climate change process, particularly the Conference of Parties (COP), the subsidiary bodies and their Bureau. See http://unfccc.int/2860.php.

Urban heat island The relative warmth of a city compared to the surrounding rural areas, due to the city's heat output, ability to absorb heat during the day and retain it at night, and differences in runoff (affecting cooling by evaporation), reflectivity, pollution and aerosols.

WAIS or West Antarctic Ice Sheet The ice sheet covering the western portion of the Antarctic continent. It has large areas grounded on rock which lies below sea level and thus is less stable than the East Antarctic Ice Sheet, since any sea-level rise will cause more of the ice to float, thus reducing resistance to outflow. It has an ice volume which if melted would produce at least a 5 or 6 m rise in global sea level.

WMO or **World Meteorological Organization** A specialised agency of the United Nations. It is the UN system's authoritative voice on the state and behaviour of the Earth's atmosphere, its interaction with the oceans, the climate it produces and the resulting distribution of water resources.

WTO or **World Trade Organization** The only global international organisation dealing with the rules of trade between countries. WTO agreements are negotiated and signed by the bulk of the world's trading nations and ratified in their parliaments. The goal is to help producers of goods and services, exporters, and importers conduct their business.

Younger Dryas A paleoclimatic period, some 12.9 to 11.6 thousand years ago, during the transition from the last glacial period to the present inter-glacial. There was a temporary return to colder conditions in many locations, especially around the North Atlantic region. The transition from a warm to a cold period occurred very rapidly, as did the subsequent rapid warming some 1200 years later.

Prefixes for basic physical units

Name	Symbol	Factor
kilo	k	10^3
mega	M	10^6
giga	G	10^9
tera	T	10^{12}
peta	P	10^{15}
exa	E	10^{18}

INDEX